Complete
Speaker's
Almanac

Leonard Spinrad and Thelma Spinrad

Prentice-Hall, Inc.
Englewood Cliffs, N.J.

Prentice-Hall International, Inc., *London*
Prentice-Hall of Australia, Pty. Ltd., *Sydney*
Prentice-Hall Canada, Inc., *Toronto*
Prentice-Hall of India Private Ltd., *New Delhi*
Prentice-Hall of Japan, Inc., *Tokyo*
Prentice-Hall of Southeast Asia Pte. Ltd., *Singapore*
Whitehall Books, Ltd., Wellington, *New Zealand*
Editora Prentice-Hall do Brasil Ltda., *Rio de Janeiro*

© 1984 by

Leonard Spinrad and Thelma Spinrad

Library of Congress Cataloging in Publication Data

Spinrad, Leonard.
    Complete speaker's almanac.

    Includes index.
    1. Public speaking—Handbooks, manuals, etc.
2. Calendars. I. Spinrad, Thelma. II. Title.
PN4193.I5S63 1984   081   83-24472
ISBN 0-13-163379-1

Printed in the United States of America

DEDICATED

to the Spinrad family dinner table,
where we all learned to talk to one another.

BY THE SAME AUTHORS

Speaker's Lifetime Library
Instant Almanac
Treasury of Great American Sayings

HOW TO USE THIS ALMANAC

Whatever the day of the year, whatever the speaking occasion, *Complete Speaker's Almanac* offers subjects and actual speech materials to answer these questions: What should I say? How can I begin? How can I best illustrate my points? How can I build human interest into my talk?

On the basis of four separate ideas for each day of the year, there are 1,464 ideas for speeches, Leap Year Day included. But in point of fact, you will find many more ideas than that in these pages if you use the Almanac properly.

When you are preparing a speech for a particular date, you can use two general approaches. First and foremost, look at the speech angles for the appropriate date and for nearby dates. Second, if you have a specific topic about which you want to talk, use the Index to look up lead-ins related to that topic.

Every single paragraph contains not merely the approach to a particular speech but also several subsidiary angles. For example, on January 13 the first topic is the Soviet Union's walkout from the United Nations Security Council in 1950. We talk about how the walkout backfired when the Soviet Union wasn't around later to block a UN vote of condemnation for communist aggression in Korea, and we use that idea to introduce a discussion of U.S. international relations. But early on in the course of the entry, we state that "these boycotts sometimes have a way" of backfiring. You can move from that point, if you wish, to a discussion of such events as the United States' brief pipeline supply boycott of Russia, or the effects of OPEC's use of oil as a political weapon, or a half a dozen other topics. We have given you a flexible topical lead-in for the day.

The most important thing to remember in using this book is that you are not pinned down to an individual date. If you are speaking on, say, August 14, there is no reason why you can't use a speech angle from another nearby date. For example, you might refer back to August 8 and use one of that day's topics. On August 14 you could say, "Six days ago there was the anniversary of the date in 1925 when the Ku Klux Klan staged a public march in the nation's capital"; and proceed with the August 8 speech idea headed "Klan March in Washington."

There is no law that says a reference to an historical event must be on the exact anniversary of its occurrence. You need not hesitate to say on December 31, utilizing a speech angle for December 7, that "One of the great watchwords of America was born this month, amid the havoc of the Japanese surprise attack on Pearl Harbor on December 7, 1941 . . .," picking up the "Praise the Lord" text under the December 7 date.

Another extremely helpful expansion of the use of this book lies in full utilization of the index. The index contains references to various topics and people throughout the text. For example, if you choose to take as your topic the December 14 anniversary of the death of George Washington, but you want additional quotations of his, you will find every quotation, no matter what the date, listed in the index under Washington, George with an identifying *q* to indicate that the particular reference is indeed a quotation.

If you are making a speech on Vietnam pegged to our paragraph on the subject on December 19, you can amplify that or go off on different angles by consulting the index for references to Vietnam.

The important point in speechmaking is to use your opening remarks as a means both to get into your subject and to catch the attention of your audience. Most of our paragraphs try to do that early on.

While the purpose of the book is not to give you the total text for *full* addresses you are going to deliver, it provides you with a choice of apt topics and of graceful and interesting ways to get into them. Of course, if you want to make a brief address, you will find sufficient material in one or more of our paragraphs to fill the bill—it is always better to be brief than to be too longwinded.

In selecting the basis for your speech, try to keep in mind that traditional anniversaries carry more interest. If you are speaking on the hundredth anniversary of an event, that will be more effective than the seventy-eighth anniversary of another occurrence, even though both happenings are the subject of speech entries for the same day.

Try not to reach too far for your speaking angle. If you are speaking at the commemoration of a local tragedy, it would not be wise to use a lighthearted paragraph you might find under that date. Remember that the purpose of this Almanac is to provide as great a variety of approaches as possible. Not every approach is suitable for every occasion.

Be guided by the nature of your audience. If you are speaking to a group of adolescents, avoid material referring to people they may not recognize. It comes as a great surprise to some middle-aged folks, for example, that many teenagers do not know who Adlai Stevenson was. So when you are selecting your approach, make sure you consider the frame of reference for the particular audience you will be addressing.

The most important requirement of all is that you make up your mind beforehand about the point of your remarks. You cannot simply select a speech angle and let it take you where it will. You have to know exactly where you are going.

There is no reason why you cannot use several different speech angles in your remarks. You may start with one and end up with another. A speech on December 15 might begin with the paragraph headed "Matter of Principle" and conclude with the material from the "Bill of Rights Day" entry for the same date. Or you can use material from two different days, maybe starting with the "Human Rights Day" paragraph of December 10, followed by the "Forefathers' Day" item of December 21.

We live in an interesting and challenging world, and the events of the past provide so many different lessons for the present that no one book can contain them all. But we believe that in *Complete Speaker's Almanac* you will find suitable content for virtually any speaking occasion that may arise.

Leonard Spinrad

Thelma Spinrad

CONTENTS

11

dle 23) National Handwriting Day • Bathysphere Record • Charles
Wilson's Quote • Brainwashing Anniversary 24) U.S.S. *Maine* to
Havana • Death of Churchill • First Boy Scout Troop • Russians Crossed
the Oder 25) Robert Burns Day • Shays' Rebellion • Return of Hostages
from Iran • Henry VIII and Anne Boleyn 26) Franklin on the Bald
Eagle • Jefferson's Library • MacArthur's Birthday • January Is Different
Now 27) Vietnam War's End • Outer Space Treaty • Samuel Gompers'
Birthday • National Geographic Society 28) Beverly Hills Incor-
porated • Peace Corps • Claes Oldenburg's Birthday • Burma
Road 29) Baseball Hall of Fame Begins • Learned Hand on Dissent • Founding of Singapore • American League's Birthday 30) Purchase
of Jefferson's Books • FDR's Birthday • Winter Carnival Season • Launch-
ing of U.S.S. *Monitor* 31) John Marshall on Supreme Court • H-Bomb
Work Ordered • *Explorer I* Launched • Nauru Free

FEBRUARY   60–97

1) Khomeini's Return • American History Month • Shortest Month •
National Freedom Day 2) Abscam Revealed • Nazis Surrender at
Stalingrad • National League Birthday • American Music Month
3) Gertrude Stein's Birthday • James Michener's Birthday • First U.S.
Woman Doctor • Norman Rockwell's Birthday 4) Election of First President of U.S. • Betty Friedan's Birthday • USO Anniversary • McCarthy's
"20 Years of Treason" 5) Pay Your Bills Week • FDR's Court Packing
Plan • Huey Long's Share-the-Wealth Plan • Birthday of James Otis
6) Ronald Reagan's Birthday • Emerson's Way to Prevent the Civil War •
Voltaire and God's Side • Aaron Burr's Birthday 7) The Beatles • Sir
Thomas More's Birthday • Washington's Warning • Babe Ruth's Birthday
8) William T. Sherman's Birthday • Boy Scout Anniversary • Vice President Richard M. Johnson • Whatever Happened to *The Clansman*?
9) President John Quincy Adams • Confederate States of America • Globa-
loney • Future Homemakers Week 10) Justice Sutherland on Free Press •
"I'll Never Tell a Lie" • *Death of a Salesman* • Twenty-fifth Amendment
11) Inventors Day • National Crime Prevention Week • Clifford Irving's
Hoax • Madison Square Garden 12) NAACP Birthday • Washington's
Accounts • Lincoln's Birthday • Februare 13) John Adams on
Revolution • Solzhenitsyn's Deportation • ASCAP • Mrs. Lincoln and the
Thumbs 14) Valentine's Day • Henry Grattan's Wisdom • Sir Henry Irv-
ing on Deserved Obscurity • Jack Benny's Birthday 15) Brotherhood
Week • Susan B. Anthony Day • Shooting at FDR • Cyrus McCormick
16) Cleveland's Dictum • Decatur in Tripoli • Lithuanian Independence

Day   18) Gideon v. Wainwright • First Walk in Space • The Lion and the
Lamb • Caruso's Records   19) U.S.S. *Franklin* • William Jennings
Bryan • Who's Got the Ball? • House on TV   20) National Wildlife
Week • The Harvard Classics • Ibsen • Nutrition Time   21) Civil Rights
March • Pennsylvania Turnpike • UN Verbosity • Benito Juarez   22) Anti-
Gambling Law • Russian Democracy • Birthday of Fifth Avenue • Equal
Rights   23) Dr. King's Warning • Danish Courage • Nisei • Non-
cooperation with Evil   24) The First Bomb • Applicant Grant • Goodbye
SST • Philippine Independence   25) Maryland Day • Treaty of
Rome • The Last New Year's Day • Coxey's Army   26) Mount St.
Helens • Israel-Egypt Peace Treaty • Miami Beach • Frost and Whit-
man   27) Cherry Tree Anniversary • Ponce de Leon • Libel • Walkouts
28) Three Mile Island • Censure of a President • Rewards of
Evil • Washing Machine   29) Honor Vietnam Veterans Day •
Rehabilitating Juvenile Delinquents • Exit Truman • Wage Protection for
Women   30) Shooting of Reagan • Van Gogh • Cuffless, Pleat-
less • Voting   31) Virgin Islands Transfer Day • LBJ's Exit • CCC • Eiffel
Tower

APRIL   142-179

1) Savarin • Air Force Academy • Weather Satellite • National Mime
Week   2) Bartholdi • Emile Zola • International Children's Book
Day • Casanova   3) Edward Everett Hale • Pony Express • United
America • Freedom Shrine Month   4) *The Perils of Pauline* • Killing of
Dr. King • World Trade Center • Home Decorating Month   5) Howard
Hughes • Joseph Lister • Churchill Resigns • Hot Line   6) "Over
There" • Later Retirement • Satellite Communication • Historic
Quorum   7) St. Francis Xavier • Baseball Season • World Health
Day • Wordsworth   8) WPA • Domino Theory • King Aaron • Jefferson
on Fear   9) First U.S. Astronauts • Who Sits Where • Vanzetti
Speaks • Taking the Fifth   10) The Safety Pin • The First Charter of
Virginia • Joseph Pulitzer • ORT   11) Barber Shop Quartet Day • Dust
Storms • Spanish American War • Shostakovich Defection   12) Kennedy
on Falling Barriers • Halifax Day • Catcher's Mask • Double Space Anniversary   13) John Hanson • Social Pioneering • $2 Bill • Samuel
Beckett   14) Webster's Dictionary • Lincoln's Assassination • FDR's View
of Fate • Peep Show   15) Garfield's Reassurance • Churchill Wedding • Carman's April • What Came of a Payroll Robbery   16) Book of
the Month Club • Charlie Chaplin • Nepotism • Philanthropic Anniversary   17) Bay of Pigs • Truman's Wrong Pew • Walter Camp • Adams

MAY   180-220

change • Heyerdahl Adrift   18) Mt. St. Helens • First Election • Halley's
Comet • Going to School   19) Spanish Armada • Hoover on
Privacy • Nellie Melba • United in America   20) Weights and Measures
Day • Homestead Act • John Stuart Mill • Timetable   21) Speed
Limit • Conventions • Lincoln Center • No Price Fixing   22) End of the
Third International • Lincoln's Patent • Violence in Congress • First Per-
sonally Delivered Veto   23) Bonnie and Clyde • Savonarola • Mesmer-
ized • Bifocals   24) Night Baseball • Good Day • John Brown of Kan-
sas • Benjamin Cardozo   25) African Freedom Day • Washington's
Rebellion • End of the Model T • Constitutional Convention   26) Chips
Away in Atlantic City • Justice Holmes on Free Tonight • Freeing *The
Miracle* • The Imperfect Lesson   27) Wind Tunnel • Rachel Carson • Julia
Ward Howe • Vision of the Postal Service   28) Armenian Independence
Day • Louis Agassiz • Neville Chamberlain • Nature as
Mediator   29) Oswald Spengler • Fall of Constantinople • John F. Ken-
nedy • Everest   30) Memorial Day • International Terror • Lincoln
Memorial • Unknown Soldiers   31) Walt Whitman • Copyright •
Taxi • Sally Rand

JUNE   221-260

1) Marilyn Monroe • Brigham Young • June Weddings • John
Masefield   2) Commencement Speeches • Italian Day • Battle of the War-
saw Ghetto • Government Salaries   3) Pope John XXIII • School Vaca-
tions • Battle of Midway • New Deal   4) Spelling Bee • Brandeis on Liber-
ty • Roquefort Cheese • Jefferson's Narrow Escape   5) World Environment
Day • Socrates • First Hot Air Balloon • Bananas   6) Snow in New
England • Drive-Ins • British Peace Commission • SEC   7) Beau Brum-
mell • Freedom of the Press Day • Independence Resolution • Lincoln and
Johnson   8) Solzhenitsyn on the Right Not to Know • Robert
Schumann • Frank Lloyd Wright • Crassus and Nero   9) Little League
Baseball Week • Truman vs. Congress • John Howard Payne • "O Prom-
ise Me"   10) Alcoholics Anonymous • Vigilantes • FDR on
Youth • Coincidences and History   11) Kamehameha Day • A Very
Special Committee • John Wayne • Alf Landon   12) Anne Frank • Baseball
Strike • Interracial Marriage • Doubleday's Baseball   13) Pentagon
Papers • Miranda • Yeats • No More Worlds to Conquer   14) California
Republic Day • Flag Day • Jefferson's Theory • Peace Corps   15) Income
Tax Payment • Magna Carta • Representing People, Not
Acres • Rubber   16) Madison on Encroachments • Woman in
Space • Adams' Oration • Gold in Alaska   17) Bunker Hill • Water-

JULY   261–302

Skies Proposal • *Lady Chatterley's Lover* • Reuter   22) Gregor
Mendel • Bretton Woods • Alexander Calder • Stephen Vincent
Benet   23) Liberty Island • Olympics • Robert Emmet's Revolt • Spanish
Armada   24) Coubertin's View • Nixon-Khrushchev Debate • Simeon the
Stylite • Amelia Earhart   25) Test-Tube Baby • Nuclear Test
Ban • Lundy's Lane • Balfour   26) George Bernard Shaw • Post Of-
fice • Churchill Resigns • Prison Problems   27) Leo Durocher • Shah
Dies • State Department • Hot Dog   28) Bonus Army Dispersed • United
Nations • Jacques Piccard • Robespierre   29) Rain Day in Waynesburg,
Penna • Dr. Rush's Advice • Alexis de Tocqueville • International Atomic
Energy Agency   30) Parkinson • Casey Stengel • Medicare • Henry
Moore   31) Patent • Lincoln-Douglas • Lafayette Commissioned • John
Ericsson

AUGUST   303–345

1) National Clown Week • Francis Scott Key • Herman Melville • Watch
That Tolstoy   2) Coolidge Does Not Choose • Hatch Act • Letter
Boxes • Wild Bill Hickok   3) Black Sox • Cheating • *Nautilus* • Hello Col-
umbus   4) National Smile Week • Chicago • Anne Frank • Hamilton and
Zenger   5) Damn the Torpedoes • Marilyn Monroe • Neil Armstrong • State Fair Season   6) Ban the *World Almanac* • Sir Alexander
Fleming • Atom Bomb • Voting Rights Act   7) Ralph Bunche • Order of
the Purple Heart • Whiskey Rebellion • Revolving Door   8) International
Character Day • Davis Cup • Klan March in Washington • Mimeograph
9) John Dryden • Sleepy Time • *Walden* • Jesse Owens   10) *E Pluribus
Unum* • Herbert Hoover • FDR's Polio • Greenwich Time
11) SOS • Mr. Justice Holmes • Andrew Carnegie • Gifford Pin-
chot   12) First Police • Soviet H-Bomb • Julius Rosenwald • Christy
Mathewson   13) Lefthanders Day • Annie Oakley • Man o'War • Lucy
Stone   14) Krafft-Ebing • Social Security • William Randolph
Hearst • Land Offering   15) Sir Walter Scott • T. E. Lawrence • In-
dia • Napoleon's Birthday   16) Bennington Battle Day • Death of Elvis
Presley • Surrender of Detroit • Siamese Twins   17) Balloon Cross-
ing • Self-Starter • Chicken-Cooking Contest • Hiss and
Chambers   18) Soap Box Derby • Meriwether Lewis • Woman's Suf-
frage • Merchandising Candidates   19) Midget at the Bat • Bennett's
Blues • Daguerre • National Aviation Day   20) Exit Trotsky • *The
Mikado* • Owed to So Few • Red Takeover   21) Nat Turner's
Rebellion • American Bar Association • Casey at the Bat • Lincoln-Douglas
Debates   22) Arnold's Trick • Taft's Law • America's Cup • Mona

SEPTEMBER   346–389

gerald • Babe Ruth   25) Easy Solutions • William Faulkner • Hunting and
Fishing Day • *Publick Occurrences*   26) George Gershwin • Gold Star
Mothers Day • T.S. Eliot • Kennedy-Nixon Debate   27) Samuel
Adams • Alfred Thayer Mahan • Radar • Warsaw Surrenders
28) Confucius • Black Sox • Galloway • Dogpatch   29) Scotland
Yard • Babi Yar • Caesar's Air • National Foundation on Arts and
Humanities   30) Ether • Goodbye September • Rayon • Taxicabs

OCTOBER   390–430

1) International Music Day • World Vegetarian Day • Pennsylvania Turn-
pike • Babe Ruth's Feat   2) Mahatma Gandi • Damned Public • American
Enterprise • Thurgood Marshall   3) Hitler's Announcement • National 4-H
Club Week • St. Francis of Assisi • The Lesson of Standish   4) "Dick
Tracy" • Rembrandt • Damon Runyon • Sulzberger's Idea of Responsibili-
ty   5) The Right to Vote • Real Miracles • International Country Music
Month • Diderot   6) Sadat Assassinated • George Westinghouse • First
Turkish Bath • American Library Association   7) Christian's
Gesture • Stamp Act Congress • Hidden Photography • 222 to 0   8) Mrs.
O'Leary's Cow • Alvin York • Fall Leaves • John Clarke   9) The Speech
That Lost an Election • Chance, Not Choice • Peshtigo Fire • Leif Eric-
son Day   10) Spiro Agnew • Naval Academy • The Mingling of the
Waters • Fridtjof Nansen   11) Battle of Tours • Edison Re-
jected • D.A.R. • Political Television   12) Rediscovering
America • Khrushchev's Shoe • Robert E. Lee • First State Universi-
ty   13) Molly Pitcher • Cornerstones • Baby Bonus • Makeshift
Science   14) Speed • Space Broadcast • Declaration and
Resolves • Eisenhower   15) World Poetry Day • P.G. Wodehouse • War
Crimes Finale • Nietzsche   16) World Food Day • Eugene O'Neill • John
Paul II • Enter Lincoln   17) Einstein Arrives • Capone
Caught • Burgoyne's Surrender • Bessemer   18) Cyclamates • Lucy
Stone • First Guilds • Alaska Day   19) Sir Thomas Browne • Napoleon
Leaves Moscow • Stamp Act Congress • Round-the-World
Race   20) Religion • Sir Christopher Wren • John Dewey • Mau
Mau   21) Guggenheim Museum • Pledge of Allegiance • U.S.S. *Constitu-
tion* • R.O.T.C.   22) Metropolitan Opera • Sarah Bernhardt • The Shah in
New York • Bank Run   23) Johnny Carson • El Alamein • Hungarian
Freedom Day • The Swallows of Capistrano   24) Cold War • Risk for
Risk • 40-Hour Week • Alarm Clock   25) Battle of Balaclava • Pablo
Picasso • Forgotten Plea • St. Crispin's Day   26) Gunfight at the OK Cor-
ral • Smallpox • Transportation Anniversaries • Mule History   27) Boss

DECEMBER   470-514

1) Civil Rights Start • Antarctica • Mutiny • Christmas Club   2)
EPA • Pan American Health Day • John Brown's Body • Model
A   3) Housing • Co-ed • Pumpkin Papers • St. Francis Xavier   4) Wash-
ington's Farewell • The Peace Ship • Carlyle • Wilson's Voyage   5) Van
Buren • Mozart's Death • Phi Beta Kappa • Repeal   6) Finnish In-
dependence Day • Lincoln in Washington • Naval Observatory • St.
Nicholas Day   7) Instant Replay • Praise the Lord • New York Philhar-
monic • Two Anniversaries   8) Eli Whitney • John Lennon • Thurber's
War • American Federation of Labor   9) Christmas Seals • John Birch
Society • The Charge of the Light Brigade • Christmas Cards   10) Equal
Taxation • Emily Dickinson • Human Rights Day • William Lloyd Gar-
rison   11) Abdication • Rockefeller's Gift • UNICEF • Robert
Koch   12) John Jay • *Panay* • Ford Gift • Lincoln's Wait   13) End of the
Honeymoon • Nostradamus • Johnson's View • Sullivan's
War   14) Washington's Death • World Trade Center • Margaret Chase
Smith • Desegregation   15) Bill of Rights Day • Matter of Princi-
ple • Sitting Bull • Hartford Convention   16) Khrushchev's
Harangue • Santayana • Noel Coward • Catastrophes   17) Truman's Ad-
vice • Whittier • Charlie McCarthy • *A Christmas Carol*   18) 13th Amend-
ment • Prohibition • Saki • Investigating Pearl Harbor   19) Vietnam • *Poor
Richard's Almanac* • Valley Forge • Ty Cobb   20) Branch
Rickey • History's Biggest Bargain • Edison's Light • Pneumatic
Tire   21) Crossword • Radium • Winter • Forefathers
Day   22) International Arbor Day • The Questionable Laurel • Lodge's
Complaint • Dreyfus Convicted   23) First Loan • Federal Reserve Act •
Transistor • Metric Conversion   24) "The Night before Christmas" •
Invasion of Afghanistan • Benjamin Rush • *Aida*   25) Clara Barton • Jeffer-
son's Cynicism • Newton's World • Christmas Gifts   26) Victory Day •
Day after Christmas • Thomas Gray • Mao Tse-tung   27) Carry Nation •
The Voyage of the *Beagle* • *Show Boat* • Louis Pasteur   28) Woodrow
Wilson • Soccer Pool • *Cyrano de Bergerac* • Westminster Abbey
29) Taming the Tiger • How Good Is America? • Andrew Johnson • Billy
Mitchell   30) USSR • Rudyard Kipling • Stephen Leacock • Shooting at
Santa Claus   31) Lincoln on Action • Bowl Football • George C. Mit-
chell • Getting Away from It All

JANUARY 1

The Name of the Month

Here we are in the month named after the Roman god Janus, an appropriate personification of the start of the new year. This particular Roman god had two faces so that he could look ahead toward the future and back at the past at the same time. As we get rid of an old year and look toward a new one, we all try to be a little like Janus. We know through experience what we did wrong and what we did right, and we hope to do better this year. Some people make ambitious New Year's resolutions; others just take a deep breath and hope for the best. As we look to the future, we may not all share exactly the same vision. Nevertheless, there are some broad hopes that I think we all share.

The Lost City

New Year's Day is an anniversary of many things. My favorite is that on this day back in 1898 this great country of ours lost a whole city—a city of more than a million people, as a matter of fact. It didn't disappear; it simply ceased to exist as a city because it became part of a neighboring metropolis. The city was a little place called Brooklyn. In 1898 the city of Brooklyn was merged into what was thereafter known as greater New York. What happened to Brooklyn was an extreme example of the fact that cities are not static institutions. Very few have the courage that Brooklyn showed when it gave up its separate identity. Actually, of course, its identity is what it didn't give up. Brooklyn is more famous today than it was in 1898. And, incidentally, it is bigger, too. Some of our other cities, which are wrestling with the problems that arise from being artificial entities in today's metropolitan areas, might profit by the example. It is time to look at our cities, old and new, in terms of how they can best be governed. It is time to look at the bedroom suburbs and some of the weird boundary lines and figure out a way, if we can't make more cities disappear, to make at least some of their problems disappear.

Homestead Act

One of the most significant and inspiring pieces of legislation in the history of this nation went into effect on this day a long time ago, back in 1863. It was the Homestead Act. The Homestead Act enabled people to settle on land, work on it, live there for five years, and then claim it as their own. It opened up and democratized the great American Midwest and much of the West. It was one of the great examples of how America has been a land of opportunity for millions of people. The Homestead Act was typical of our nation in another way: it didn't give you something for nothing. You had to work for it. That is the real meaning of opportunity—a chance to show what you can do. Today it takes more than a Homestead Act to provide opportunities for all of the Americans who need this chance. It takes cooperation and good citizenship on the part of the more fortunate, and honest pride and energy on the part of those for whom the opportunities are needed. What can you and I do about it?

Recalling Some Rose Bowls

This is a day with all kinds of thrills and all kinds of memories for football fans. Some like to remember the courageous upsets, like Columbia's amazing Rose Bowl victory in 1934. But I prefer to think of two games in which people's ability to foul things up came to the fore. Let us today mark the anniversary of Roy Riegels' historic 69-yard run in the Rose Bowl game of 1929, when this fine football player got a little mixed up and ran the wrong way. Let us mark also the anniversary of the 1954 Cotton Bowl, when a fine runner for Rice Institute was on his way to a touchdown until a "twelfth man," unable to restrain himself, jumped off the Alabama bench to tackle him. The officials gave Rice the touchdown anyway, but that twelfth man also gained a place in the record book. So, as this New Year's Day moves toward becoming history, let us be mindful that anything can happen—and probably will. Let us, indeed, talk about a few other timely miracles or mishaps.

JANUARY 2

Betsy Ross Day

This is known to some people as Betsy Ross Day, marking the raising of the first U.S. flag by the Continental Army in 1776. We had a flag before we were a nation. It was six months later that the Declaration of Independence was signed. Flag waving is not always in style, but what the flag stands for is and always will be the heart and soul of America. We are a nation driven by the desire to do right. I stress both words. First, we are filled with the need and the determination to do—to accomplish, to achieve. Secondly, we try to judge whatever we do by one simple standard—is it right? We don't always measure up to our own standard, but I have never known us not to try. Never give up trying. Never retire just to playing safe. The world is full of challenges, and we must face those challenges with our flag waving.

Cuban Reminder

In Cuba this day is celebrated as the Day of Revolution and the Feast of Martyrs, a reminder to Cubans of pages of their history from which they seek to draw inspiration. Cuba has celebrated the Day of Revolution by seeking more revolution, the Feast of Martyrs by a continuing willingness to create new martyrs. By contrast, an interesting aspect of the American Revolution was that it was a domestic revolution, neither intended nor destined for export. It is part of our democratic heritage to believe that every people is entitled to choose its own way, without dictators and without the imposition of foreign philosophies. When we forget that heritage, when we try to export our way of life, we get into foreign adventures. At the same time, we should recognize and support those in other nations who are our friends. Who are our friends today?

The Washington News Correspondent

Today we mark the anniversary of a great American institution, the Washington news correspondent. James Gordon Bennett was the first real such luminary, and he began with a dispatch in the January 2, 1828, edition of *The New York Enquirer*. Since then, news correspondents in our nation's capital have covered it to a fare-thee-well. I wonder sometimes whether they merely report the news or help make it. I am sure that there are things done by Washington officials that wouldn't be done if they weren't reported and publicized. Some of our officials like to operate behind a cloudy veil of secrecy, but far more operate in a climate of press releases, headlines, and spotlights. If the news media would give less coverage to the clowns and find out more about the blacked-out operations of government they would do us all a service. For example, here are some news questions to which I would like answers.

Dismissal of Esek Hopkins

On this day in 1778, the first commodore of the American Navy, Esek Hopkins, was dismissed. His officers brought charges against him and, though several of these officers were themselves court-martialed, they brought him down in the end. I mention this because if command was a difficult obligation in the times of the American Revolution, it is far more difficult and far more complicated today. The temptation is always strong to go into ad hominem arguments against those officials with whom we disagree. It is much easier to criticize someone else's performance than to perform yourself.

JANUARY 3

Edwin Booth's Return

When John Wilkes Booth assassinated Abraham Lincoln in the spring of 1865, there was another casualty, one you won't find in most of the history books. John Wilkes Booth was the younger brother of America's greatest actor, Edwin Booth. And after John Wilkes had become a symbol of American madness his brother was ashamed to appear on the stage. Edwin Booth retired. January 3, 1866, almost a year later, he finally returned to the stage as Hamlet and went on to even greater acclaim. In this country, thank goodness, we judge people on their own merits rather than by their relatives. We must judge individuals on their own performance and their own records. To aid in that judgment, let me focus on these performances in particular.

Father Damien

Today is the birthday of Joseph de Veuster, a name I doubt will be recognized by many in this audience. He was better known by his religious name, Father Damien. He was the Belgian missionary to Hawaii who became the leader and benefactor of the lepers' colony at Molokai, dying himself of leprosy in 1889. The name of Father Damien is synonymous with courage, compassion, and self-sacrifice—qualities that all of us have great need of. In the spirit of Father Damien, I ask you to join me in considering and caring about the condition of those less fortunate than ourselves.

The March of Dimes

Back in 1938 this country was led by one of our most inspiring presidents, and a president who was undoubtedly the most physically handicapped. His name was Franklin D. Roosevelt, and on this day in 1938 his former law partner and a group of other public-spirited citizens organized the March of Dimes to fight the disease that had crippled him, polio or infantile paralysis. That fight was crowned with success when anti-polio vaccines were developed, and the March of Dimes has gone on to fight against birth defects. Success can't be as complete or even as speedy here, but the fight is certainly worth the effort. And it is worth remembering that no matter how total the victory or how extinct one particular disease, the organization and the dollars that produced that victory can always find other equally noble objectives. As quickly as we meet today's challenges, new challenges are waiting for us. The important thing is never to rest upon our laurels. In that spirit I ask you to join me in trying to do something about this challenging situation.

Brooklyn Bridge

Just about this time in 1870 a group of engineers began construction of what in its time was the eighth wonder of the world—a tremendous suspension bridge carried by steel cable between towers in Manhattan and Brooklyn, the fabulous device still known as the Brooklyn Bridge. It represented the vision of the Roebling family. America was built by visionaries like the Roeblings, who were not content to do things simply as they had been done before, and who refused to be limited by what had been done in the past. We still need and have opportunities for such visionaries—people who figure out better ways to do more than has been done before. We can always find people to tell us why we can't do something. Let's listen instead to those who tell how to do what we couldn't do before. Let us dream—and then let us work together to make those dreams come true

JANUARY 4

Louis Braille

Today is the birthday of a Frenchman named Louis Braille, who was born in 1809. Many of you will recognize his name, because it is also the name of a system of writing and reading for the blind. Louis Braille developed a way for blind people to read, write, and enjoy the literature of the world. This was a remarkable achievement. It was even more remarkable because Louis Braille himself was blind. Far from being handicapped, he gave the world much more than many a person with full vision has been able to accomplish. I think the story of Louis Braille has a lesson for all of us here today. It is wrong for us to feel sorry for ourselves or to find convenient excuses for not doing things that need to be done. Whatever the handicap, we should and must try to overcome it. It is much more important to try to figure out how something can be done than why it shouldn't be done. In these times, when we are concerned about what government does for us, maybe we should be more concerned about what we can do for ourselves.

Carnegie's Decision

This is the day when, in 1901, a very rich man named Andrew Carnegie decided he had devoted enough of his life to making money. He had done very well at it, and when he sold out to U.S. Steel he had a very tidy nest egg. What is interesting is that he somehow escaped the virus that affects so many of us—no matter how much we have done and how much we have won, we want more. Andrew Carnegie was a happier man for knowing when to quit, and even happier for knowing what he wanted to do with his money. His philanthropies live on, and he is better known today because, in addition to doing well, he did good. One need not be possessed of the Carnegie millions to follow his example, giving of one's substance and of oneself to the things one believes in. Have you given yourself to the causes in which you believe? Now is a very good time for that kind of commitment.

Emile Coué

Back on the fourth of January in 1923, a French psychologist arrived in the United States and proceeded to turn the country on its ear. His name was Emile Coué, and his formula for dealing with worry and nervous ills was highlighted by having the patient repeat to himself or herself as often as needed, "Every day in every way I am getting better and better." "Every day in every way I am getting better and better." Today we live in times when thriving therapists seem to be devoting more and more time to helping us find new things to worry or be mad about. Under the broad rubric of consciousness raising, we are telling ourselves we were fools to think we were happy; we are cataloguing and group agonizing about problems somebody else had to come and tell us we had. Maybe it is time for a new Emile Coué to tell us how much better we are getting every day in every way. Because we are better. I ask this gathering to consider just a few ways in which we, our community, and our nation are better today than we used to be.

Social Security

This is the anniversary of the beginning of one of the great changes in American life. On January 4, 1935, President Franklin D. Roosevelt proposed what became the Social Security Act, a nationwide system of old-age pensions, unemployment benefits, and other forms of social insurance. The idea of providing security for people as they grow older is a great one; the challenge of paying for it is also great. The good things in life, we keep finding out, are not always free; and when they are not free the price tags keep going up and up. What we face more and more as time goes on is a new tax—a tax on our ingenuity.

JANUARY 5

Stephen Decatur

This is the birthday of Stephen Decatur, the great naval hero and author of that immortal toast: "Our country! In her intercourse with foreign nations may she always be in the right; but our country, right or wrong!" Stephen Decatur was fortunate to have lived spectacularly in times when there was no doubt about his country being right. What is more right than ever about this great country of ours is the compassion and the concern of its citizens. When our country is wrong, it is up to us to assert our rights as citizens to set things straight; but above all, like Stephen Decatur, we should remember that this, and no other place on earth, is our country, to have, to hold, to defend, to improve, to protect.

Capture of Captain John Smith

Captain John Smith, it is said, had very good reason to remember this day. It was on this date in 1608, according to the story, that he was captured by the Indians and ultimately saved by the intercession of an Indian princess named Pocahontas. However, when he returned to Jamestown the settlers were so angry at Captain Smith for having messed up his mission of exploration that *they* wanted to execute him. Fortunately, the arrival of new supplies from England eased the pressure, and John Smith survived to go down in legend. History—not just American history but history in general—is full of anonymous John Smiths, who got into trouble and were saved by forces beyond their control. What this suggests is that good things have a way of happening when the skies seem darkest, and we should never give up expecting a better tomorrow. If things look dark to you today, I ask you to remember these indicators of better times to come.

One Baseball

Baseball has been with us since the first half of the nineteenth century, so I find it rather surprising that not until this day in 1934 did the National and American Leagues come around to the idea of both using the same baseball. Even with that valiant step toward one standard for the national pastime, the two leagues seem never to have agreed on exactly where the strike zone begins and ends, and for years they couldn't agree on whether or not there should be a designated hitter. Now, if we can't agree about how we play baseball, how in the world can we agree about more weighty matters, such as taxes and the defense budget? I would like to suggest that disagreement is the American way, that part of the strength of the nation is the robustness and strength with which we argue. Indeed, I believe there are some additional areas where this kind of vigorous public discussion is called for.

Babe Ruth Traded

Back in 1920 the Boston Red Sox had a pitcher-outfielder named George Herman Ruth. On this day they sold him to the New York Yankees for $125,000 plus a mortgage on Fenway Park. That was a lot of money then, but it is safe to say that George Herman, or Babe Ruth, proved to be worth it and a lot more. Somehow, expenses that look huge today have a way of seeming wise tomorrow, as long as you are buying something worthwhile. I think we might apply that yardstick to our current national debt and judge it by what we are buying rather than today's cost. What will it cost us tomorrow if we don't spend the money today?

JANUARY 6

Haym Solomon

The men who signed the Declaration of Independence noted that they pledged their lives, their fortunes, and their sacred honor. A man who was probably born on this day in about 1740 is far less known, but he too pledged his fortune and his honor to the cause of the American Revolution. His name was Haym Solomon; he was a broker, money lender, and merchant who helped finance the Revolution. Maybe the Revolution would have succeeded without him, but he certainly helped, and his name is a reminder today that behind every well-known hero there are less well-known people who helped do the job. Today I want to salute some of the less well-known for the jobs they are doing right now.

Sherlock Holmes

Those who like the great detective best claim that today is the birthday of that legendary sleuth, Sherlock Holmes. Sherlock Holmes was created by the British author, Arthur Conan Doyle, and he has become the virtually living symbol of deductive reasoning in crime detection. His birthday is a particularly appropriate time to take a look at the condition of crime, crime detection, and crime prevention in our lives today.

Crop Limitation

We like to think that the idea of limiting crops is a modern brainstorm, but on this day back in 1639 the General Assembly of Virginia ordered that half the tobacco crop be destroyed in order to maintain the market price. The idea of artificially limiting commodity supplies obviously goes way back in our history. I find it interesting that after more than three centuries we still haven't found a better way to protect the growers without hurting the consumers. This remains the great—I could even say the consuming—challenge of our times.

Football Season Fade-Out

We are at last coming close to the end of what used to be an autumn-only sport—football. Most of the bowl games are behind us, but the big one, the Superbowl, is yet to come, and the postseason festivities are still under way in various parts of the nation. When Americans find a good thing, they certainly hate to let go, and football has been a very good thing. As the curtain begins to come down on the late football season, except for the newer off-season ventures, I would like to salute those other red-blooded Americans, the non-football fans who have had to put up with this annual madness. The end is coming, and now we can talk about other things.

JANUARY 7

Millard Fillmore

The birthday of a president is often the occasion for civic functions and celebrations. That is how we commemorate the arrival of George Washington and Thomas Jefferson and Abraham Lincoln. Today I rise in celebration of a less widely observed occasion, the birthday of the thirteenth president of the United States, Millard Fillmore. Maybe it was because he was the thirteenth, maybe it was because he only served from 1850 to 1853, after the death of Zachary Taylor, but the fact remains that Millard Fillmore is not a household name.

He didn't help himself by running for the presidency in 1856 on the Know-Nothing ticket, but nevertheless I believe that on his birthday he deserves to be remembered. And maybe Millard Fillmore's birthday is a good time to remind ourselves of several other things that need remembering.

First National Election

We don't think of January as an election month, but back in 1789 on this day the first voting under the new Constitution took place, and it resulted in a gentleman named George Washington being elected President. It's nice to know that in this country presidential elections have been held regularly and peacefully ever since, even in the middle of wars. Let's face it. We are a nation with a proven talent for self-government. It is a talent we need very badly today. Nowadays self-government isn't merely the choosing of representatives and presidents; it is also conducting ourselves as good citizens, facing up to and voluntarily carrying out those responsibilities each of us has as obligations to our community. Some of these may sound trivial, but when you put them together they can make a very real difference in our way of life.

Truman's H-Bomb Announcement

In his State of the Union message on this date in 1953, President Harry S. Truman made a momentous announcement. He reported that the United States had developed a hydrogen bomb. It is fair to say that the world hasn't been the same ever since. We live today upon a nuclear brink, with our H-bombs versus the H-bombs of other nations. Nobody yet has found a way to achieve mutual trust among nations that know the other guy can wipe them off the face of the earth. But as long as nobody pulls the nuclear trigger, mutual distrust is better than chaos. Nuclear scientists long ago ran their doomsday clock down to about a minute before the end. As long as we keep that clock from winding down, we still have a chance to do things better.

Nothing Ventured

This is the anniversary of perhaps the most productive subsidy in history. On this day in 1839 the French government agreed to pay Louis Daguerre to describe publicly his newly developed process for taking and reproducing photographs. The payment was a modest one, but when a fire destroyed Daguerre's laboratory two months later he was able to continue his work, and in August the world heard how Daguerre worked his magic. From this modest beginning came billion-dollar industries and priceless historical archives. And if you think a minute about what photography has given us, just imagine what it might have given us if it had been around earlier. Start with the scene when Moses came down the mountain with the Ten Commandments and pick your own snapshots from that point on.

JANUARY 8

Elvis Presley

This is the birthday of the late Elvis Presley, of whom it is fair to say that in some ways he killed himself trying to live up to the legend he had created. The world into which he was born in 1935 was a lot different from the world he helped create with his music. Like most popular idols he turned out to have feet of clay, but to his admirers, and they were legion, this made very little difference. We have a tendency to see in people what we want to see in them and to overlook what we don't want to see. And we have this same tendency with events and issues. When we don't want to confront them we tell ourselves they aren't there. But there are issues today that, no matter how much we want to avoid them, we simply have to face.

Galileo

On this day in 1642, one of the greatest and certainly one of the most persecuted of scientists died. His name was Galileo Galilei. He was the astronomer who discovered the regularity of the swing of a pendulum and charted the path of a projectile. He didn't invent the telescope, but he greatly improved it and he started observing the planets of what later generations came to know as the solar system. He didn't invent that concept either. That honor belonged to Copernicus, but Galileo charted and explained the positions of the planets. When his views came into conflict with accepted interpretations of the Scriptures, Galileo was told to stick to astronomy, but though he abided by the advice for a while, he shortly published his greatest book, reasserting his views and flying in the face of papal injunctions. He was summoned to Rome by the Inquisition. Though publicly silenced, he continued his work until he went blind. The world is better off today for the courage and stubbornness of this lone holdout against the established orthodoxy of his time. Who knows where the Galileos of our own time may be? Conformism is easily corrupted to tyranny. We don't have to look very far to find examples.

Watergate Trials

On this day in 1973 the nation began a painful spectacle—the Watergate trials. It was a nasty little scandal that grew and grew and grew. Some countries would have hushed it up. To our credit, we did the reverse. America makes no bones about seeing itself, warts and all. Today I continue that healthy process.

Washington's First Annual Address

George Washington made his first annual address to Congress on this day in 1790. "To be prepared for war," said our first president and Revolutionary

War commander-in-chief, "is one of the most effectual means of preserving peace." That is as true today as it was in 1790. To keep the peace, we must be prepared for war.

JANUARY 9

MacArthur's Pledge

On this day in 1945 that flamboyant warrior Douglas MacArthur kept a pledge. When he had fled from the Philippines at FDR's orders in 1942, he vowed he would return. And on January 9, 1945, at the head of an American invasion force, he kept his word. He returned. Now General MacArthur knew drama when he made it, but war needs drama in its leadership. That's what brings out the vital little bit extra in the fighting men. My friends, I am here today to say that peace also needs its drama, its flamboyant leaders. Ask yourselves, who upon the current scene provides that dramatic spark, that sense of spiritual mission?

Execution in Saudi Arabia

In 1980 on this day the rulers of Saudi Arabia closed the last chapter in the story of the terrorists who had seized their Grand Mosque. Those terrorists were beheaded. This is an ancient and very direct form of punishment. It is in extreme contrast to our American system of justice, both in the speed with which it was done and in the fact that it was not a sentence subject to later amelioration by a parole board. Somewhere between the way the Saudi system works and the way our own operates there must be a sensible middle ground. We seem to have managed to turn due process of law into undue process. It is time we did something about it.

Carrie Chapman Catt

This is the birthday of Carrie Chapman Catt, who was born in 1859. From 1900 on she was the preeminent leader of the women's suffrage movement. She led the campaign that gave women the vote in the United States, and when that was done she went on to fight against child labor, to help refugees, and to work tirelessly for world peace. She died at 88, still working, still fighting. If Carrie Chapman Catt were alive today, I can think of a few causes she'd probably be working for, and I'd like to talk here about some of them.

Seeing Eye

Today is the anniversary of the beginning of a doggone good idea. On this date in 1929, "The Seeing Eye" was incorporated in Tennessee to train guide dogs for the blind. The remarkable work of Seeing Eye dogs is only one example of the many ways we are finding good work for man's oldest friend. Dogs sniff for bombs and for drugs; they trace the scent of missing persons; they guard the peace in the subways of New York—and, of course, they still perform their ancient agricultural functions of protecting the sheep and the chickens. Give a dog a chance to help you, and he or she will. I like to hope that human beings will do the same. The spirit of friendliness and community is not dead. As witness these examples.

JANUARY 10

Paine's "Common Sense"

Thomas Paine came from England to America less than a year before the outbreak of the American Revolution. On this very day in 1776, he published a little pamphlet entitled *Common Sense*. He wrote: "We have it in our power to begin the world all over again." I would like to suggest to you here today that this spirit can and should motivate us today—for we do have it in our power to begin the world all over again. But we must not do it by simply destroying the world as it is.

Bonhomme Richard

John Paul Jones was a veteran American ship captain when he was given command of a wreck of a ship acquired from France and named the *Duc de Duras* on this day in 1779. Captain Jones and his crew loaded the vessel with more guns than it had a right to, patched it up, and renamed it after Benjamin Franklin's popular American character, Poor Richard. They translated that into French, and the ship became the *Bonhomme Richard*. When they went to sea later that year, Jones got into battle with the better-equipped British fighting vessel *Serapis*. You know the story. Jones captured the *Serapis*, even though the *Bonhomme Richard* was sunk. There is a moral here for us today. The fact that you're on a sinking ship doesn't mean you should give up the fight. If one vehicle doesn't work, don't give up the trip; just find yourself another vehicle.

Penny Post

It is with some bitterness, or at the least some nostalgia, that I rise to point out an anniversary today—the anniversary of the introduction of the penny post. It started in 1840 in England, where they got the brilliant idea of charging a uniform rate for the mail and noting the payment of the charge by affixing a stamp on the envelope. That was the beginning of the modern postal system, but penny post, even in terms of a British penny that was worth more than ours until fairly recently, is no longer penny anything. Postage is probably the average person's most immediate measurement of inflation. Today I would like to talk to you about some other types of inflation—the revolution of higher standards and higher expectations, and the counterrevolution that seems to have declared war on any standard at all.

Lewis and Clark Report

President Thomas Jefferson on this day in 1807 received the report of the Lewis and Clark expedition. That expedition for some reason has never had the glamor associated with Stanley finding Livingstone or people exploring the moon, but for sustained, gut-wrenching physical hardship and accomplishment, Meriwether Lewis and William Clark were really the champions. If they never really achieved the recognition or the honor they deserved, they are not alone. History is replete with unsung or inadequately honored heroes—and our times are no exceptions. Today I'd like to salute just a few of them.

JANUARY 11

Designated Hitter

On this day in 1973, one of baseball's revolutions took place. The American League was allowed to establish a designated hitter, who would go to bat whenever it was the pitcher's turn to step to the plate. We seem to have adopted the designated hitter syndrome in our public life. If an office holder proves inadequate to one of his or her tasks, appoint somebody else in addition to deal with that particular task. Government is full of pitchers who can't hit and designated hitters who don't pitch. Let me cite some examples.

Surgeon General's Cigarette Report

On this date in 1964, the surgeon general of the United States issued a report linking cigarette smoking and health problems. After years of sound and fury and challenge, the basic conclusions of that report remain those of the government today; yet, for many years afterward, the selfsame government continued to provide agricultural subsidies for the tobacco crop. This kind of contradiction in government policies is not unique to smoking. For years we worried about how to lower the price of milk and cheese, and meanwhile dairy products were being bought at artificially maintained prices and stored by the government. One government bureau tries to take people off the benefit rolls, and other government bureaus labor to put them on. The contradictory activities of government are a challenge to all of us.

First Life Insurance

On this day in 1759, in the city of Philadelphia, there was incorporated the "Corporation for the Relief of Poor and Distressed Presbyterian Ministers and of the Poor and Distressed Widows and Children of Presbyterian Ministers." The idea was a simple one. It was life insurance. Whether or not you believe in life after death, you've got to admit that we have built a mighty financial edifice around the idea that you can find a way to leave something to those who live after you. I wonder, though, whether in the age of Social Security, pensions, and the like, young people today pay as much attention as they should to planning for their survivors.

A Child Miseducated

"A child miseducated," said President John F. Kennedy on this day in 1962, "is a child lost." How many children are we losing today? How can we save them? Where are we going wrong, and what are we going to do about it?

JANUARY 12

NCAA

On this day in 1906, a group of college people responded to the urgent appeal of the president of the United States. Theodore Roosevelt, a devotee of the strenuous life, thought that college athletics were getting a little out of hand and needed some kind of governing body. Out of that feeling came the formation of the National Collegiate Athletic Association, and the NCAA has been a major force in American amateur athletics ever since. I think this anniversary is worth noting for one reason above all others. Here was a president, a chief of government, who saw the need for a form of regulation but made sure it wasn't left to government to do the regulating. I have a feeling that this kind of catalytic action by government, rather than having Uncle Sam step in to be the Great White Father, can serve as a model today.

Edmund Burke

Today is the birthday of Edmund Burke, whom the world remembers as a great orator. If his own country, Great Britain, had listened to him and followed his advice rather than simply admiring his oratory, we would have a vastly different world today. For example, Burke strongly favored recognizing the demands of the American colonists for a greater degree of self-government. If he had been listened to, the United States and England might still be one nation today. But most people seem to prefer being entertained by great speakers to being led by them. The greatest orators in the history of this country, with the exception of Franklin D. Roosevelt, never made it to the top. This, of course, is a very discouraging thing for a speaker to realize as he stands before you. But you are such a special audience that you give me new confidence.

Charles Perrault

On this day back in 1628, a man was born in France whose influence on the world ever since cannot be overstated. His name was Charles Perrault. He was a writer who collected folk tales and put them into a book. But these were no ordinary folk tales. Among them were "Sleeping Beauty," "Little Red Riding Hood," "Puss in Boots," "Tom Thumb," and many others. Generation after generation has grown up dreaming of the prince who awakens the beauty, the wolf that lurks in the forest and gobbles up Red Riding Hood's grandmother, and many other familiar characters. Perrault kept trying to write poems and serious books of history, little dreaming that it was his fairy tales that would gain him immortality. Many of us, like Charles Perrault, keep trying to do other things instead of what we do best. We might be better off if we knew better where our strengths lie.

Samuel Johnson on Prejudices

A very wise man named Samuel Johnson, on this day in 1751, commented that—and I quote—"there are, in every age, new errors to be rectified, and new prejudices to be opposed." I don't think I have to take time here to catalog the errors of our age, of which we are all painfully aware. But I would like to call to your attention some current prejudices.

JANUARY 13

Soviet Walkout

What was viewed at the time as a great challenge to the United Nations took place on this day in 1950 when the Soviet Union walked out of the Security Council in a boycott prompted by the council's refusal to remove Nationalist China from the UN. As these boycotts sometimes have a way of doing, this one backfired. When North Korea invaded South Korea a few months later, Soviet Russia wasn't around to block a UN vote of condemnation, as a result of which troops of many nations joined in aiding the South Koreans. When we cut off the rest of the world, the first people we cut off are ourselves. Applying that reasoning to our current foreign affairs, it seems to me that our immediate course is clear.

Jaycees' Honors

About this time of the year the U.S. Jaycees meet to honor those they have chosen as the ten outstanding young men of the year. I don't know if anybody has come back twenty-five years later and checked out the Jaycees' outstanding young men to see how they turned out. I suspect they would find the batting average was pretty good. Bright young people usually go on to bright careers. The time to worry is when they are young, and the worry must be that they get their chance.

Thirteen

Today is the first occurrence of the number thirteen in this year's calendar. Thirteen is not the world's favorite number. In many buildings, we go from the twelfth to the fourteenth floor with nary a number in between, but we've never found a way to get around the fact that there is a thirteenth day of the month. Somehow a date like January 12½ doesn't seem likely to gain wide acceptance. It is interesting that some numbers have very definite attributes—Sweet Sixteen, a Perfect Thirty-Six, the Terrible Teens, the Roaring Forties. But nothing has the peculiar significance of thirteen. And so I am happy to give you good news today. On this particular thirteenth day, I will make my remarks short and sweet.

Horatio Alger

Although there has been some uncertainty about it over the years, today is now generally accepted as the birthday of a clergyman named Horatio Alger, who was born back in 1834 and proceeded to encourage the dreams of success of several generations of young people with his books. Their titles tell what they are about: *Strive and Succeed, Struggling Upward,* and more than a hundred other stories of people who rose from rags to riches. It is nice to know that Horatio Alger stories still happen in real life. Today I would like to salute some successes that seem to be in his tradition.

JANUARY 14

$35 Bills

At least one source tells us that on this date in 1779 the Continental Congress issued $35, $45, and $55 bills. These are interesting denominations. We have been wedded to the decimal system of currency for so long that something like a $35 bill seems strange. In currency, this country, as a matter of fact, has proved to be very hard-ribbed indeed. The $2 bill has never really made a comeback, and Susan Anthony's dollar coin proved that people could be as stubborn as—or more stubborn than—the U.S. Mint. This country has always known not only the value of a dollar but also exactly how it wants its dollars denominated. Now, if we could only have the same broad agreement on where to get them and how to spend them.

Ford's Assembly Line

When Henry Ford began the idea, back in 1914 on this date, of having a continuous assembly line for cars, he probably never dreamed that one day the assembly line would be manned, if that is the proper word, by robots. The problem of our times, increasingly, is not the invention of new machines but rather what to do with the human workers machines are replacing. Finding ways for humans to live in peace is a great challenge, but the greater challenge is to find ways for all human beings to be constructive parts of the new machine age.

Meeting at the White House

In 1948 on this day, a group of business and union leaders met with President Harry S. Truman at the White House to tell him that the public was very restive, and that something had to be done about prices, interest, and taxation to restore public confidence. I wish I had a nickel for every time this same message has been delivered to the White House since then. Too often we have fallen into the trap of thinking that our chief executive can somehow push a few buttons to right the economy. It takes all of us, plus a few acts of God connected with crops, lack of disasters, lack of wars, and so forth. Years ago, what we asked of the White House in the main was to leave us alone to take care of ourselves. It turned out we needed help. Then the national pendulum swung the other way. Isn't it time to realize that, whatever our political persuasion, we are all active members of the team, and the president is only its captain?

Hamilton on the National Debt

On this day in 1790, the secretary of the treasury, Alexander Hamilton, recommended that the national government assume the debts incurred by the individual states during the Revolution. If that sounds okay to you, it didn't sound very okay to such states as Virginia. Virginia and other southern states were comparatively solvent and able to take care of their state debts. It was the New England states that had the largest debts and the toughest prospects. What is interesting is the way Hamilton and James Madison of Virginia worked it out. Madison agreed to work for the Hamilton plan if Hamilton would see that the national capital, which was expected to remain in Philadelphia, went instead to somewhere in the area of Virginia. The District of Columbia was established on the banks of the Potomac, and Hamilton's plans for national assumption of the debt were approved. So the next time you begin to wonder why so many deals are made in Washington, D.C., you might reflect that the very existence of Washington is the result of a deal. It goes with the territory. Viewing things in that light, here are a few deals I'd like to propose.

JANUARY 15

The Pentagon

Today is the birthday of the Pentagon, that incredible office building that houses the Department of Defense on the banks of the Potomac. It was back in 1943 that this huge complex, the largest office building of its time, was completed. We may not have the biggest defense force in the world, but we have as big a headquarters building as anybody. Maybe in one sense that is as pertinent a commentary on our defense situation as need be made.

Ford Foundation

We should be grateful for those who arranged with Henry Ford on this day in 1936 to incorporate a nonprofit organization called the Ford Foundation. Some twenty years later, this foundation was responsible for one of the most extensive programs of philanthropy in the history of our nation. There aren't too many countries on earth where they have found as good a way to achieve good works. As a nation we have been brought up not merely to respect philanthropy but to regard it as the obligation of the fortunate, and that brings me to the point.

Church and Economic Life

This week is usually observed by many Protestant churches as Church and Economic Life Week. There was a time when churches tried to hold themselves aloof from economic life. That becomes more difficult all the time, not only because churches have budgets to meet but also because churches are part of a social community that reflects and responds to economic conditions. Churches face the same problems of remaining solvent and avoiding bankruptcy that plague businesses. They aren't businesses, although some of the newer sects have made the line of demarcation hard to find. Indeed, one of the great problems of our time is first to define when a church becomes a business, and second what to do about it.

Birth of Vermont

In the middle of the American Revolution there was another revolution, and in a sense it began on this day in 1777, when delegates from the area known then as the New Hampshire Grants but better known now as Vermont met in a convention and within the next twenty-four hours adopted their own declaration of independence, calling themselves New Connecticut. The state of Vermont began functioning under the name by which it is known today, but not until 1790 did it get recognition, with New York leading the way. It was admitted to the United States on its own in 1791 as the fourteenth state. If you think Vermonters are stubborn and independent, this history may tell you why. And I bring up this story on the anniversary day because it is such a good illustration that if you believe in something, persist in fighting for it, and can be patient long enough, you will usually win in the end.

JANUARY 16

Dizzy Dean's Birthday

Today is the birthday of a unique American athlete, Dizzy Dean, who was born in 1911. Dizzy's performance as a pitcher with the St. Louis Cardinals

Gas House Gang is a matter for the record books. His use of the English language when he was a broadcaster later was even more memorable. On one occasion, he said of a baserunner, "He slud into third." Contemplating a difficult situation, he remarked, "I shoulda stood in bed." I hope that my remarks today will not tempt anyone to feel that you—or I—"shoulda stood in bed."

Amending the Constitution

It took this country 131 years to get the Eighteenth Amendment to the Constitution. On this day in 1920 that amendment, better known as Prohibition, went into effect. It lasted only until 1933, when it was repealed by another amendment. After the Bill of Rights, consisting of the first ten amendments to the Constitution, was added in 1791, it took 129 years to make eight other changes in the basic law of the land. But then eight later amendments were enacted in less than half that time. Clearly, we are a lot quicker to amend the Constitution now than we used to be. Nothing these days is written in stone. If human beings cannot agree in their interpretation of the Ten Commandments, how can the Constitution not be susceptible to competing interpretations, amendments, and tinkering? Let me give you the story of one pending amendment proposal.

National Nothing Day

We are exactly halfway through the month of January, which has also been observed through years as March of Dimes Month, Blood Donor Month, Polka Month, and Cerebral Palsy Month. It has also been observed on occasion as Burglar and Fire Alarm Protection Month. All this may be why one sardonic sponsor some years ago chose today in the middle of the month, January 16, to be designated—and this is true—as National Nothing Day. There aren't enough days, weeks, and months to go around; not enough to deal adequately with the needs of our earthly community. There are so many worthy causes that the Advertising Council, contributing the services of major agencies, advertisers, and media, has to ration public service time and space among them. We are still a society that believes in voluntary services and contributions. We give of ourselves on an unprecedented scale. I am here today in furtherance of a voluntary cause that deserves your gifts and your support.

The Shah Flees

Today in 1979, a faraway event occurred which was to leave far more of an imprint on us than we could have known. The Shah of Iran was forced to flee from his country. Still to come was the fullness—or the awfulness—of the revolution there. Still to come was the seizure of the American embassy, the ordeal of the hostages, and the subsequent rediscovery of unabashed patriotism in the U.S.A. Today I want to talk to you about another seemingly remote event—remote, that is, for many of us—and what I see as its future consequences.

JANUARY 17

Purchase of Virgin Islands

This is the anniversary of the U.S. purchase of the Virgin Islands from Denmark in 1917. It is particularly nice to recall this anniversary today, because while it is winter elsewhere in the United States it is tropical sunshine and sunlit beaches in the Virgins. So let us put aside the mundane humors of the season and think of some of the other wonderful things that are part of the good old U.S.A.

Brink's Robbery

It was on this date in 1950 that a robbery of Brink's Express in Boston set what was then a new record for loot—$1,200,000 in cash and $1,500,000 in money orders. J. Edgar Hoover of the FBI called the robbery part of a communist conspiracy, and most of the money was never recovered. If the Communists got it, they certainly didn't prosper with it. Somehow the nation survived. I raise the point simply to emphasize that calling something a plot is no way of stopping it or solving it. We have lots of problems today that we can blame on others, but the fact remains that to solve them we've got to do something ourselves.

Eisenhower on the Military-Industrial Complex

President Dwight D. Eisenhower gave his farewell message to the American people on this day in 1961, as his term was coming to a close, and I believe his remarks bear repetition. This wise man, who was himself the product of the U.S. Military Academy and one of the most distinguished military careers in the nation's history, told his fellow Americans, "In the councils of government, we must guard against the acquisition of unwarranted influence, whether sought or unsought, by the military–industrial complex. The potential for the disastrous rise of misplaced power exists and will persist." He was referring to the strange relationship between some military suppliers and the government which awards their contracts. The military–industrial complex, as far as I am concerned, has to be watched as long as big money is to be made in supplying defense needs. There are some points we should be especially wary of right now.

Wake Island

In 1899 on this day, the United States took possession of a small island in the Pacific. The acquisition was called Wake Island, and in World War II its defenders against the Japanese wrote one of the epics of courage and ingenuity. I am all for reminding ourselves of this kind of history. So join me today in remembering Wake Island and recalling that America always seems to rise to the challenge once the battle is joined.

JANUARY 18

Today's Birthdays

This is the birthday of a number of people who have had a way with words—Muhammad Ali, Daniel Webster, and a physician named Peter Mark Roget, an Englishman born in 1779. Dr. Roget helped to create the University of London, but his crowning achievement was the writing of his dictionary of synonyms. *Roget's Thesaurus* is one of the most widely consulted books of all time, and on Dr. Roget's birthday it is important to choose one's words wisely, well, judiciously, in good order, with proper emphasis and clarity. The least we can do in his honor is to try to use the words correctly, and, with your kind indulgence, I will proceed with that effort.

First Plane Landing on a Ship

It was in 1911 on this day, we are told, that a pilot named Eugene Ely flew an airplane to the first landing on a ship. The ship was the *U.S.S. Pennsylvania* in San Francisco Harbor. After landing, it is chronicled, Ely took off from the ship and landed in San Francisco. Out of this small beginning there grew the mighty aircraft carriers and seaborne aviation of the present day. It is that way with ideas. Good ones have a way of generating other, bigger, and better ones. Perhaps some of the seeds we plant here today can be responsible for exciting things in years to come.

Muhammad Ali's Birthday

In their time many people have been regarded as the greatest. A man was born on this day in 1942 who referred to himself that way so convincingly that a great many people believed him. Muhammad Ali, born Cassius Clay, had a great career as heavyweight champion of the world, but in the annals of sport he is also one of the not too many who gave up all the glory to maintain his faith. He resisted the draft in the Vietnam War because of his Muslim faith. He lost his title as a result, but in the end his moral stand was respected and he went on to take his title back. He will always be remembered for his boxing skill and mighty punch, but I suspect that in the long view of history he will be remembered as a man who stood up for his beliefs. He stood up to be counted. Let us, in our own arena, now do the same.

A. A. Milne's Birthday

On the birthday of A. A. Milne, the creator of the immortal Winnie the Pooh, I rise to salute his immortal lines, "I am a Bear of very little brain, and long words bother me." I don't know about long words, but long speeches definitely bother me, and I don't intend to make one. I always recall that the great-

est applause for a speaker usually comes when he or she sits down—and, frankly, that's what I'm bucking for.

JANUARY 19

First Televised Presidential Press Conference

On this day in 1955, President Dwight D. Eisenhower held the first press
conference that was televised. Many people have debated whether televised press
conferences serve any real and constructive purpose, since the person at the
rostrum in general answers only those questions he or she wishes to answer
and usually manages to evade or parry the rest. One might just as easily compare a formal speech with a question-and-answer session. I don't know what
questions you might throw at me in such a session here today, but I know what
I want to talk to *you* about, and I thank you for this forum.

Webster-Hayne Debate

The Senate of the United States has seen some historic tub-thumbing but
little to compare to the debate between Senator Daniel Webster and Senator
Robert Y. Hayne, which began on this day in 1830. It started as an argument
over states' rights and ended as the great historical discussion of the Constitution. Nothing I have to say is of quite that historical significance, nor do I expect my eloquence to pose any challenge to the reputation of Daniel Webster,
but I remind you the art of debate flourished in an age when people paid close
attention to speechmakers, and I hope that my words will somehow encourage
you to do the same.

Wilkes' Discovery of Antarctica

The name and the accomplishments of Charles Wilkes are largely forgotten
today, although a portion of the continent of Antarctica bears his name. On
or about this date in 1840, Wilkes discovered that Antarctica was actually a
continent. That discovery was challenged bitterly, but it is now generally con-
ceded that Wilkes recognized Antarctica for what it was while others were still
poking around the edges. Today I do not expect to poke around the edges of
my topic. Instead, I will proceed to the solid base of my subject without delay.

Virginia's Bill for Religious Freedom

On this day in 1786, the hard work of James Madison and Thomas Jefferson resulted in the state of Virginia adopting a bill for religious freedom. "No
man," said this new step in American law, "shall be compelled to frequent or
support any religious worship, place, or ministry whatsoever . . . nor
shall . . . suffer on account of his religious opinions or belief; . . . All men shall

be free to profess, and by argument to maintain, their opinion in matters of religion, and . . . the same shall in no wise diminish, enlarge, or affect their civil capacities." It took Madison and Jefferson many years to get this historic legislation adopted in Virginia, and their work became the model for a key section of the Bill of Rights when the first ten amendments were added later to the Constitution of the United States. This, therefore, is a very meaningful and wonderful anniversary in the history of our country. It is a shame we do not commemorate it, but we can at least justify it by continuing to voice our ideas freely and without prejudice. That is what I will try to do here today.

JANUARY 20

End of the Lame Duck

This is the anniversary of the death of a familiar old bird, the lame duck. In 1937, Franklin D. Roosevelt became the first president to be sworn in on this day, January 20, rather than on March 4, as a result of the adoption of the Twentieth Amendment. The terms of the president, vice-president, and Congress were moved to start on January 20 rather than in March. In tribute to the passing of the lame duck, I will try not to overstay my welcome here today.

The Wickersham Report

On this day in 1931, a presidential commission came up with a report that surprised no one but gave a sort of official imprimatur to a judgment the public had already reached. President Herbert Hoover had appointed the Wickersham Commission to take a look at how Prohibition was working, and on this day the president submitted their report to Congress. The commission said Prohibition wasn't working, but instead of urging repeal they urged revision of the enforcement policy. Presidential commissions very rarely recommend the outright abolition of a governmental function but one of the privileges of a private citizen is to be able to do so without a presidential commission. Here are some governmental operations that I think belong among the discards, right there alongside Prohibition.

President Kennedy's Exhortation

This was the day in 1961 when John F. Kennedy told the nation, "Ask not what your country can do for you; ask what you can do for your country." There have been periods since then when it might be better to say, "Don't ask." Patriotism has not always been in fashion and at times has been denigrated as cornball or naively sentimental. It is neither of these. What you do for your country has a very direct connection with what your country can do for you. And it is never the wrong time to ask ourselves what we can do for our country.

Beginning of Parliament

Along about this time in the year 1265, Lord Simon de Montfort, who was busy trying to be a kingmaker in England, convened a legislative assembly with representatives of various areas as well as hereditary lords. This was in some respects the beginning of Parliament and one of the early steps in the Anglo-Saxon–Norman world toward the development of representative government. After more than seven centuries, we're still working on it. And we still have a ways to go.

JANUARY 21

Exit Tyrants

This is not too good a day for absolute rulers. Two of them, King Louis XVI of France and Nikolai Lenin of Soviet Russia, died on this day. Louis was executed in the French Revolution, and Lenin, who led the Bolshevik Revolution in Russia, died of natural causes. One succumbed in defeat, one at the peak of his victory. What this suggests is that while a certain amount of our destiny is of our own making, the final decision is usually somebody else's. What we all try to do during our lifetimes is to pile up credits so that when the final decision is out of our hands, the powers that be will dispose of us kindly. For some of us that means accumulating and then distributing meaningful worldly goods, but for all of us what we really want, or should want, is to leave the world a better place than when we found it. We don't always agree on what to do to make that better world, but there are a few fundamentals we might consider.

After Super Bowl, What?

One of the notable aspects of January is that this is the month when the annual football madness finally climaxes. The Super Bowl may be followed by some other gridiron attractions, but once the NFL championship is decided the footballs can go back into the locker for the season. We go on to another enthusiasm, possibly bordering on seasonal frenzy. Our capacity to get involved in new competitions and old rivalries is without limits. Indeed, I sometimes wonder whether we don't carry the Super Bowl spirit over into too many other aspects of life. We seem to be engaging in meaningless contests to outdo the other folks—more needless luxuries for our children, more conspicuous consumption. Grantland Rice wrote that "when the One Great Scorer comes to write against your name He marks—not that you won or lost—but how you played that game." I hope we haven't forgotten that.

Kiwanis Birthday

This is the birthday of Kiwanis. The first Kiwanis Club was chartered in Detroit in 1915, and Kiwanians—businessmen and professionals, for the most part—have been joining together in good works ever since. Sometimes cynics scoff at the so-called civic booster organizations, but we would have a tremendous need for them if they didn't exist. Above all, they provide a good way for the average citizen, who may be hesitant to do things on his or her own, to join with others in the comfortable anonymity of group good works. If there is a single word that I can leave with you here today, that word is *join*. Join with your fellow citizens and make your efforts go further.

President Carter's Amnesty

On this day in 1977, President Jimmy Carter wrote finis to one of the great periods of bitterness when he proclaimed a pardon for those who violated the Selective Service Act from 1964 to 1973, the era of the Vietnam War. It takes great courage for a president to proclaim a pardon that may not be very popular with a lot of people. The fact that our presidents have not hesitated to do this is less of a tribute to them than it is to you, the people. Right now, there are some ideas many people will not forgive, but over the long haul if the past is any model old foes will find it in their hearts, if not to agree with each other, at least to forgive. I suggest that it is not too early for us to do this with some of the issues that are dividing us today. Is any single issue more important than our democratic process?

JANUARY 22

Ukrainian Day

A few people with long memories or lasting attachments to their native land still observe today as Ukrainian Day. On this day in 1918, there was proclaimed the Free Ukrainian Republic, but all too soon the Ukraine was absorbed by the Soviet Union; its brief freedom from Russia turned out to be just an interlude. Americans, I suspect, continue to cherish the idea that some day every nation will be able to assert its identity and enjoy its own destiny. Have you stopped meanwhile to think how many captive nations there are in the world today?

Byron's Birthday

A poet named George Noel Gordon, Lord Byron, was born on this day in 1788. In a strange way his greatest monument was born 150 years later. When Franklin D. Roosevelt and Winston Churchill wanted a name to describe the allied countries of the free world in World War II, they considered the term Associated Powers, until Churchill quoted some lines from Lord Byron's great poem, "Childe Harold's Pilgrimage." What he quoted was this: "Millions of tongues record thee, and anew/Their children's lips shall echo them, and say—/'Here, where the sword united nations drew,/Our countrymen were warring on that day!'" And thus was born the name of the United Nations. We don't usually think of poets as influencing any portion of world affairs, but perhaps the fine arts, including poetry, are more pertinent than we thought.

First American Novel

The first American novel was published on this day in 1789. Even though it was issued in the upright city of Boston, it dealt with the possibility of incest, secret loves, and suicide. It was called *The Power of Sympathy,* and its author called herself Philenia. Judging by the current novels on the newsstand, Philenia would be right at home today. We sometimes think that our tastes are more scandalous than those of our forebears, but that isn't true. In some respects, we are just more easily shocked.

Cleopatra's Needle

This is the anniversary of the installation of the obelisk known as Cleopatra's Needle in Central Park in New York City in 1881. That it is known as Cleopatra's Needle is intriguing; the obelisk was originally put up in Egypt several thousand years before Cleopatra was around. Obviously, Cleopatra's Needle is something of a misnomer. But then we do go in for this sort of thing. A dark horse can sometimes be a white hope; we forget that Frankenstein was the scientist, not the monster. It is time to look beyond labels and concentrate on substance.

JANUARY 23

National Handwriting Day

It is probably very fitting that today should have been designated as National Handwriting Day, since it is the birthday of the bearer of the most famous signature in our nation's history. The signature, and the birthday, are those of John Hancock, born in 1737. It was his name which led all the rest that were appended to the Declaration of Independence. National Handwriting Day is a good time to speak on the subject of standing up to be counted. The saddest words a citizen can speak are, "I don't want to be involved." I urge you all to put your own John Hancock on the line, stand up for what you believe in, make your position known, and fight for it.

Bathysphere Record

In 1960, on this twenty-third day of January, the U.S. Navy bathysphere *Trieste* explored the bottom of the Pacific Ocean, 35,820 feet down in the Marianas Trench. So this is a very good day for a speaker to get into deep water, and I shall be mindful of that as I proceed with my remarks.

Charles Wilson's Quote

Charles E. Wilson was the head of General Motors when he was called to Washington to serve as a member of President Dwight D. Eisenhower's cabinet. Testifying before a Senate committee, he was asked to tell the committee how he would feel about doing something as a public official that was against the interest of General Motors. He answered, "For many years I thought what was good for the country was good for General Motors and vice versa." When that quotation appeared in the newspapers on this day in 1953, a storm broke, and "Engine Charlie" Wilson spent valuable time afterward trying to justify what he meant. In the long perspective of history, I think what he meant is clear and important to remember. What is good for the country, in the long run, has to be good for the country's business and the country's labor, too. If one goes down, the others won't be far behind.

Brainwashing Anniversary

A modern phenomenon that recalls the cruel days of the past is that type of psychological pressure called brainwashing. On this day in 1937, one of the first and most dramatic instances hit the headlines from Moscow, when seventeen communist leaders "confessed" that they had conspired against the Bolshevik dictatorship of Josef Stalin. Since then, the world has seen all too many examples of how ruthless jailers can bend the minds of some of their victims.

JANUARY 24

U.S.S. Maine to Havana

On this day in 1898, a mighty battleship called the *U.S.S. Maine* was ordered to Havana, where a rebellion against Spain was moving into high gear. Nobody knew that what happened to the *Maine* some time later was going to start the Spanish–American War, but in the long view of history we find ourselves wondering whether there isn't a lesson here for current diplomats. It seems to me that if you poke a loaded gun into an explosive situation you are making that situation more likely to explode. Current application? Look at the world map and take your pick.

Death of Churchill

One of the giants of world history, Winston Churchill, died on this day in 1965. More than any man of his time, he proved that words can be weapons as strong and as effective as guns, when he rallied the free world with speeches and phrases that will live forever. Democracies have had a great knack for coming up with Winston Churchills when they are needed. I think it only fair to note that when Churchill became prime minister of England in World War II, when he finally began to show the greatness his country needed, he was already past 65.

First Boy Scout Troop

The first Boy Scout troop was founded on this day in 1908 by a British general, Lord Robert Baden-Powell. A couple of years later the idea came to our shores. Remembering the birthday of the Boy Scouts is a timely way to remind ourselves that our young people are always eager to learn, willing to work together, and responsive to good leaderships. Now, as always, I suspect that the problem is getting parents to do their share.

Russians Crossed the Oder

At the Oder River that runs into Germany from Mittel Europe, this was a very big day in 1945, and it greatly influenced the postwar world. The Russians crossed the Oder and raced into the heart of Germany while the Allies were still hundreds of miles away. The Russians were out to put as much of German territory in the arms of communism as they could embrace with their occupying forces. The Russian bear is fierce indeed when he smells territorial opportunities.

JANUARY 25

Robert Burns Day

Today is Robert Burns Day, marking the birth of the great Scottish poet in 1759. It was Burns who wrote, "Oh wad some power the giftie gie us/To see oursels as others see us!" Americans always feel hurt and misunderstood when we see ourselves as others see us, but it is necessary experience in the world today. We are, if anything, usually too sensitive to the rest of the world's view of us; we don't want to be the ugly Americans. But if we truly see ourselves as the others see us, we might be a lot more hardboiled about our international friendships.

Shays' Rebellion

On this day in 1787, an unhappy captain in the Revolutionary Army led some 2,000 men in a march on the Federal Arsenal in Springfield, Massachusetts.

His name was Daniel Shays, and his rebellion was quickly broken up. Shays received no lasting punishment, and some relief measures were passed to help him and his group. In this country you can fight city hall and you can go a lot higher. Daniel Shays was the first in a long line of Americans who have thought that the way to get government to listen to you is, so to speak, to punch government in the nose. One wonders what would have happened with Shays' Rebellion if there had been the kind of press and television coverage given demonstrators today. In the long run, maybe the modern method is better; nobody has to shoot guns or get hurt.

Return of Hostages from Iran

One of the most searing episodes of American history came officially to its close on this day in 1981, when the American hostages who had just been freed from their long captivity in Iran finally came back to American soil, arriving at West Point in New York. The long futility of American efforts to get them out had depressed the nation but also, for the first time since the long agony of the Vietnam War, had united all of us. What the Iranian hostages' captivity brought home to all of us was and is that we Americans don't like others to push any of us around. Let us hope that in the aftermath of the hostage experience we will continue to feel that whoever hurts any group of us hurts us all.

Henry VIII and Anne Boleyn

A marriage that changed the world took place on this day in England in 1533. The participants were Henry VIII and Anne Boleyn, she already heavy with child, he recently divorced from Catherine of Aragon. It was that divorce which triggered Henry's being excommunicated by the Catholic Church and created the Protestant state in England. And Anne Boleyn's baby turned out to be Elizabeth I, the great queen who built the British Empire. History is often particularly interesting because the whims, amours, and problems of individuals sometimes change the course of the world. We are fortunate in our country to have a system of checks and balances that saves us from our own Henry VIIIs.

JANUARY 26

Franklin on the Bald Eagle

On this day in 1784, Ben Franklin was rather upset, and he wrote his daughter to tell her why. "I wish," said Franklin, "the Bald Eagle had not been chosen as the Representative of our Country; he is a bird of bad moral character. . . . The Turkey is a much more respectable Bird, and withal a true original Native of America." Well, the bald eagle seems to have survived Ben Franklin's vote of no confidence, but generation after generation of American speakers has found it wise to talk turkey to the American people, and I do not propose to do otherwise today.

Jefferson's Library

It was just about this time of year, back in 1815, that Thomas Jefferson offered to convey to the Library of Congress, which had been destroyed by the British in the War of 1812, more than 6,000 books which he had assembled as his personal library at his home in Monticello over the course of fifty years. This collection provided the foundation for the modern Library of Congress. But you may be surprised to know that there were plenty of voices raised in Congress to urge that Jefferson's offer be turned down. "We don't need the books," they said. "The price tag was too high," they said. "Let's just pick the books we agree with." Fortunately, these voices didn't prevail. But there are still voices in the land trying to limit our sources of information and seeking to turn away new knowledge and different points of view. Like Jefferson, we must do everything in our power to make knowledge more available, to give people a chance to think for themselves. Let us talk together today about one area where not enough is known by enough people.

MacArthur's Birthday

Today is the birthday of a man who was loved and who was hated with an ardor few arouse. He was Douglas MacArthur, born on an Army post in Arkansas on January 26, 1880. It would have taken a legion of lesser men to accomplish what he accomplished, not only as a battle commander but as the virtual viceroy of prostrate, defeated Japan. And yet, not once but several times, this amazing man overreached himself. He miscalculated his power and popularity in a clash with an ex-haberdasher named Harry Truman, who happened to be president at the time. He flirted with political candidacy and then decided, probably wisely, that the war of the ballot box was not his kind of battle. Douglas MacArthur discovered, as lesser men and women are forever amazed to discover in their time, that while the public wants to be led it gives its ultimate loyalty to ideas rather than individuals. And so today I want to talk about an idea—an idea whose time has come.

January Is Different Now

We are living in topsy-turvy times. Here it is the end of January, and what has happened to the traditional January White Sales, for example? They have turned all colors. It gets harder to find a white sheet or a white towel all the time. And what about the January vacationer? It used to be that the only people who took January vacations were the rich and the retired, who went south to keep warm. Now people by the thousands head north; instead of trying to escape the snow they are trying to find where the snow is the best. Yes, these are topsy-turvy times. Professional athletes make more money—much more money—than the president of the United States. Kids explain kinky sex to their parents. Tiny island republics have an equal vote with the United States in the General Assembly of the United Nations. I wish I could stand here today and announce the return of sanity to the world. But the best I can do is to light one small candle in the gathering darkness. So here goes.

JANUARY 27

Vietnam War's End

On this day in 1973, for the first time in its history, the United States ended a war without being victorious. That was when the ceasefire took effect in Vietnam. Americans are a proud people, and it was not easy for us to accept a military failure, but out of the depths of the generation gap and the malaise that the Vietnam War had plunged us into, we emerged surprisingly whole. I think there is a lesson here for us and our nation today. As one oppressed group of citizens used to sing, "We shall overcome." We look upward and onward, confident of a better tomorrow.

Outer Space Treaty

In 1967 on this day, the United States, the Soviet Union, and sixty other nations signed a treaty limiting military activity in outer space. Since nobody at that time was terribly active militarily in outer space, it was easier to negotiate that treaty than to get together about more conventional armaments. Perhaps there is a lesson here for us. Why don't we and all the other nations of the world sign agreements about the armaments none of us yet have? We could, for example, agree that none of us would turn off the other's sunlight. Then, when we have mutually given up these as yet imaginary weapons, we can move carefully into dealing with more practical ones.

Samuel Gompers' Birthday

Samuel Gompers, the pioneer of the organized labor movement in the United States, was born in London on this day in 1850. Under Gompers, the American Federation of Labor maintained its independence from both political parties, and while from time to time the loyalties of most union members were considered the assets of one of the parties, it has never been an organized political monolith—never as politically doctrinaire as British labor, for example. One of the lessons I think American labor, like other American groups, learned early is that you can get more in American politics by shopping around than by blind continuous loyalty to one party or one label.

National Geographic Society

Today is the birthday of the National Geographic Society, which was founded in Washington, D.C., in 1888. I don't know whether geography will ever be a truly popular branch of human knowledge, but the National Geographic Society has made geography fascinating for countless generations. Yet even today, we don't know each other. In the age of instantaneous communication, easterners still have odd ideas about Texas, and Texans have odd ideas about other places. Most of us go our own insular way. We have simply got to know more about each other and get rid of regional myths and prejudices.

JANUARY 28

Beverly Hills Incorporated

It is recorded in history that on this date in 1914 in Southern California, the town that became the richest enclave in the nation was incorporated. That was the start of Beverly Hills, some five square miles totally surrounded by the vast city of Los Angeles but very definitely with a personality of its own. Beverly Hills is the home of Rodeo Drive, the most ridiculously expensive shopping street in the world. It has also, in the past, been the fountainhead for the somewhat unreal view of the world that marked the Hollywood movie colony, for while the movies were made in and around Hollywood, the moviemakers went home to their own little Camelot in Beverly Hills. Unfortunately, we have a tendency in this country to create our own little Camelot, our own little Beverly Hills, no matter what our economic level or cultural pretensions. We may not have a Rodeo Drive in our neighborhood, but we darned well want to keep the neighborhood to ourselves. The trouble is, it is hard to run a world that way.

Peace Corps

It was on this day in 1961, just eight days after John F. Kennedy had been inaugurated as president of the United States, that the State Department announced plans for setting up a Peace Corps of Young Americans to do volunteer work overseas. The Peace Corps succeeded in making some far corners of the world just a little bit better, and it helped greatly to maintain the image of America as the hope of a better world. The woods, unfortunately, are full of worthy causes these days. We can only hope that the woods are full enough of Americans ready to give of themselves.

Claes Oldenburg's Birthday

Art is as old as time, but every now and then an artist comes along who gives us something different. One such creative talent was born on this day in 1929. His name is Claes Oldenburg, and his specialty is so-called soft sculpture. Using cloth and rubber and other soft materials, he sculpted a soft automobile, a six-foot tube of toothpaste, and a giant hamburger. Long before Oldenburg's sculptures were accepted as fine art, they were accepted as great fun. When you can combine those two types of acceptance—aesthetic and popular—you have arrived. Art is a lot more fun when artists are free to let their imaginations run wild. It is not by accident that the modern free world has produced the greatest output of quality art. The moment you restrict and censor the artists, life begins to lose its special flavor.

Burma Road

For centuries, the search for convenient land routes to China occupied the attention of adventurers, explorers, and conquerors. On this day in 1945, one such major road finally became a reality when an American truck cavalcade drove onto what was called the Burma Road. The Burma Road was envisioned as a vital artery that would bring strength to China's fight against the Empire of Japan, but it was too late. The atom bombs a few months later forced Japan's surrender, and Chiang Kai Shek's Chinese—Burma Road or no Burma Road—grew steadily weaker thereafter against the upsurging Chinese Communists of Mao Tse-tung. Perhaps if the Burma Road had existed ten years earlier, things might have been different. But this anniversary reminds us that getting something done is only half the battle. The other half is getting it done in time. We have a tendency to build new schools after the peak of pupil enrollment has been reached, to build two-lane highways just in time for four lanes of traffic. The real job is to anticipate the needs, not to scurry after them.

JANUARY 29

Baseball Hall of Fame Begins

On this day in 1936, the first members of the Baseball Hall of Fame were elected. They were Ty Cobb, Walter Johnson, Christy Mathewson, Babe Ruth, and Honus Wagner. Of these five baseball immortals, two played for teams that don't exist any more. Walter Johnson's Washington Senators took their players elsewhere and emerged in a new city with a new name, and Christy Mathewson's immortal New York Giants ended up as a San Francisco ball club. Even a monument, my friends, can lose its pedestal. Occupying a place of honor in American history is no guarantee of permanence. We are very demanding people. An institution has to fight to maintain its life; it can't just stand there and expect to be appreciated and nurtured.

Learned Hand on Dissent

There are some great judges who, although they don't get named to the Supreme Court, nevertheless leave an imprint upon American jurisprudence as great as any of the learned brethren. One such was the late Learned Hand—what a wonderful name for a legal scholar. On this day in 1955, Judge Hand said something that is as concise and clear an explanation as I have ever heard of what American freedom is all about. "All discussion," said Judge Hand, "all debate, all dissidence tends to question, and in consequence to upset convictions; that is precisely its purpose and its justification." I hope the time will never come in this great land of ours when we will all speak with the same tongue or voice the same ideas. And because of that hope, I am not here today to get you to agree with me about what I have to say. Rather, I rise to speak in the hope that what I have to say will encourage each of you, in your own way, to take a stand.

Founding of Singapore

We think of the Far East as mysterious, glamorous, exotic, and, above all, ancient. It comes as a surprise, therefore, to realize that Singapore, whose very name breathes the tradition of the Orient, is younger than Los Angeles. Singapore was founded by Sir Stamford Raffles on this day in 1819. Its amazing growth into a commercial and industrial center, with perhaps the most polyglot population of any Asian city, is a testimonial to the vitality of that part of the world, the brilliance of the British, and, above all, the continuing opportunities a growing world presents. Singapore is in some ways the Holland of the East. It is a very small nation and a very smart one. In our constant search for greater size, we keep forgetting that good things also come in smaller packages. Let us not always try to be the biggest if, instead, we can be the best.

American League's Birthday

Today is the birthday of baseball's American League, without which there would be nobody for the National League to play against in the World Series. When the American League began, the National League refused to recognize it, operating on the age-old principle that if you don't recognize someone or something they will go away. But the American League refused to go away, just as nations that the United States refused to recognize have somehow managed to survive. We have simply got to find some form of disapproval that is more effective than refusing to recognize a nation or a situation we want to see changed.

JANUARY 30

Purchase of Jefferson's Books

On this day in 1815, after some heated debate, Congress finally agreed to purchase Thomas Jefferson's library as the nucleus for the Library of Congress, which was to be rebuilt after being burned by the British in the War of 1812. It was a noble gesture by Jefferson, who loved his books dearly, but historians now tell us it wasn't pure nobility. Jefferson, it seems, needed the money. I hate to spoil a beautiful legend by citing this fact, but life is like that. Jefferson was smart enough not to let foolish pride stand in the way of an honest buck. We as a nation might bear that in mind when we consider our role in the world. How much of our overseas military expenditure, for example, is for defense and how much is for national pride?

FDR's Birthday

Today is the birthday of Franklin D. Roosevelt, born in 1882 in Hyde Park, N.Y. The birthday of Franklin Roosevelt is observed with particular warmth by those who remember that he was the first president to make the government provide for the welfare of the elderly and the unemployed. The system he brought about created many problems of its own, but it helped to save the nation. And his golden oratory led the nation and the world in the dark days of World War II. In some ways, every president since FDR has been measured against him. Even though later revelations surprised his admirers—revelations of his unwilling-ness to admit more refugees, for example, or revelations of his treatment of his wife—he remains among the great. The answer, I think, is that if you do enough good it is the good, not the bad, that will be remembered. And so I have some areas to suggest where I hope you will each be able to do some good.

Winter Carnival Season

This is the season of the winter carnivals, which merchants, inn-keepers, and college communities have found to be an excellent way of getting some excitement going during the snowy months. But even though it is winter carni-val season, I am not here to take you for a sleigh ride. In deference to the sea-son I plan to give you cold facts, in the hope that they will light enough fires to make things a little warmer.

Launching of *U.S.S. Monitor*

A strange-looking vessel indeed was launched on this day in 1862 in Green-point, Long Island. Except for a turret in the middle, the whole boat seemed to be just under water, and the whole structure was covered with steel armor. It was named the *Monitor,* and it had been designed by John Ericsson for the U.S. Navy to combat a Confederate ship that had also been covered with ar-mor. The Confederate ship, of course, was the *Merrimac.* The *Monitor* and the *Merrimac* were destined to meet in combat in a naval engagement that changed the navies of the world—the first battle between ironclad ships. The interest-ing thing is that neither ship won this first ironclad battle, and both ships sank before the end of the year. A Cassandra could have said at the time, "See what a ridiculous idea this is. You can't go with ironclads. They'll sink." It's very easy to take potshots at new ideas when they seem to falter. But wiser heads saw the brilliance of the basic idea of the ironclad warship. And wiser heads are always prepared to see the longer-term applications of things. That is why long-range planning is so important today for major corporations—and for the government, too. Instead of looking simply to tomorrow, let us try to look a little to the day after, and the day after that.

JANUARY 31

John Marshall on the Supreme Court

When John Marshall took his seat on the Supreme Court on this day in 1801, neither he nor anyone else knew that he would serve an incredible 34 years as chief justice, or that by the force of his vision and personality he would make the Constitution undeniably the supreme law of the land. Without good judges you cannot have good government. The crises of our own times, in government and in law enforcement in particular, call for the best judges we can find and encourage to stay on the bench. We have only begun to realize that fact. Too many judgeships are still political rewards. It is time we took a long, hard look at the men and women who are supposed to take a long, hard look at crime and the law.

H-Bomb Work Ordered

In 1950, President Harry Truman chose this day to order work begun on a fearsome new weapon, the hydrogen bomb. Soviet Russia was trying to develop the same weapon. How do you stop this evil balance of forces, which bleeds us all dry and gives no one lasting security? That is a question it is not only proper for our leaders to address, but vital that they meet and deal with.

Explorer I Launched

The first U.S. satellite, *Explorer I*, was launched on this day in 1958. Eleven years later, an American walked on the moon. Americans look for the impossible, and then do it. So let's not give any credence to the people who say we have run out of worlds to conquer, that there are no new ideas left to work on, that we should just sit tight and adjust our sights to lower horizons. I do not believe in a shrinking America. I do not believe our glory is exclusively in the past. I do not believe that the land of promise has run out of promise, any more than it has run out of land. Let us remember *Explorer I* and keep on sending our arrows into the air, to fall on earth we know not where.

Nauru Free

This is the day when the Pacific island of Nauru became an independent nation in 1968. It has an area of eight square miles and a population of some 8,000. Nauru does not have to sustain itself with imperialist ambitions or dreams of getting bigger. Making small things bigger is not always wise, any more than

it is wise to try to make children adults before their time. We have a tendency
to try to speed up time—to make sophisticates out of adolescents, to introduce
children to sex before they are ready, to demand immediate success from something that needs time to develop. Let us not be impatient with results that take
a little longer than we would like. Patience and fortitude!

FEBRUARY 1

Khomeini's Return

Little did we know on this day in 1979 that an event we were inclined to applaud was going to lead to a long spasm of national agony. On this day a hitherto obscure Iranian clergyman, the Ayatollah Khomeini, returned to his native land from exile in Paris. He was a symbol at that time of the loosening of the Shah's control over the ancient kingdom. We learned in short order that the cure was worse than the disease. Led by the fanaticism of the Ayatollah, the revolutionaries ran riot, captured the American Embassy, and held our people as hostages for 14 long months. It wasn't the first time a foreign leader had fooled us. We hailed Castro as a liberator, too, when he burst upon the world scene. Perhaps we should be a little slower in coming to conclusions about people we don't really know.

American History Month

This is American History Month. There is a tendency on the part of some Americans to emphasize the nation's faults—and certainly we have our faults. But we have our triumphs, too, and I think it is time we devoted some attention to the glories of Old Glory. We have provided a haven for the homeless and the helpless—not as much as we might have, but more than any other country. We have sent food and dollars to the needy in every corner of the world. For eleven months of the year those who want to can look at America and see only the warts—but in February, American History Month, I suggest we look at the larger picture and see our nation as the hope of the world.

Shortest Month

We are at the beginning of the shortest month of the year, and one of the busiest. February may not have as many days as the other months, but it has more holidays than most of them. It has the birthdays of our greatest presidents, Mardi Gras, Valentine's Day, the beginning of the Five and Dime and of the Republican Party, and a host of other historic commemorations. February is a time when we get a lot done in a minimum of days. This might not be a bad model for my remarks here today, so let me try to make my points, like February itself, in short order.

National Freedom Day

Today is National Freedom Day. It commemorates President Lincoln's approval of the proposal in 1865 to adopt the Thirteenth Amendment to the

U.S. Constitution, forbidding slavery. Our definition of freedom has expanded considerably since then. Franklin Roosevelt, for example, spoke of freedom from want and freedom from fear. In those terms, the emancipation of America still has more ground to cover. But I like to think that our nation is united in its determination to do something about this, even though we may differ regarding the methods to be employed.

FEBRUARY 2

Abscam Revealed

Today is the anniversary of the government's announcement of the great Abscam scandal back in 1980. That, as you may recall, was the Justice Department's investigation of governmental corruption involving G-men masquerading as Arab sheiks and trying to corrupt congressmen and others. Unfortunately, all too many office holders proved to be available to the phony Arab dollars. Despite cries of entrapment, a succession of members of Congress, including a senator, were caught in the net and convicted. Abscam, if it did nothing else, made office holders a little more cautious, at least for a while, about how and where they use their influence and their favors. But we have only to look around to realize that there is still plenty of room for improvement.

Nazis Surrender at Stalingrad

One of the Nazis' proudest boasts in World War II was that they were going to destroy the Russian armed forces at Stalingrad. They encircled that Soviet city and waited for its surrender. But on this day in 1943, things worked out somewhat differently. After months of agonizing uncertainty, the tide turned. It was the Nazi forces that were in trouble until, in the first such disaster to befall the Germans in World War II, Field Marshall von Paulus and his whole Army were forced to surrender. It was not only a great victory against Nazism; it was a stirring proof that the Nazis were indeed vulnerable—a reminder that no evil force is so strong that it can't be beaten. We should never give up the fight against bullies and terror-mongers.

National League Birthday

A new idea in sports was born on this day in 1876, when a hardy group of pioneer baseball people organized what they called the National League. Of the eight original cities in the league, five still had National League teams more than a hundred years later. Baseball has been a major American sport for all those years, and I believe the reason is that it is the quintessential team sport. Americans enjoy themselves the most and achieve the most when they work together. Maybe that is the lesson of baseball. Maybe the true genius of America is the fact that we try to give everybody a turn at the plate.

American Music Month

February for many years has been American Music Month. Our indigenous melodies, from jazz to country to blues, have captured the feeling of our people and, apparently, of the other peoples of the world as well. Music, they say, is an international language. Maybe if the world could learn to sing together the wars of words could be turned into a chorus of lasting peace. Meanwhile, of course, the band plays on and we have to face the music. We have to face the dissonance of an uneasy world. But if we listen, we can also hear the promise of harmony as well.

FEBRUARY 3

Gertrude Stein's Birthday

Gertrude Stein was born on this day in 1874. As perhaps the most famous American expatriate in the Paris of her time, Gertrude Stein's unique writing puzzled people but also made some very clear points. For example, she wrote this: "In the United States there is more space where nobody is than where anybody is." Think about that for a minute. Gertrude Stein wrote it in 1936, but it is still true. This is a big, big country, and even when we add millions of new people to our cities and towns, there still is more "space where nobody is than where anybody is." That is why I remain a long-range optimist about America and its place in the world. We have resources, we have scope, we have room. Now let's make sure we have the imagination and the human energy to do something about it.

James Michener's Birthday

When James Michener was born on this day in 1907, most of the places he was to write about had their most spectacular history ahead of them. Certainly that was the case with the South Pacific and with the Holy Land. Part of the genius of Michener, as represented in his books, is that he has been able to show the continuum of history, whether in Chesapeake Bay, South Africa, or Spain, from early days right up to modern times. An understanding of history is one of the things that differentiates humanity from the animals. An understanding of history also helps greatly in understanding our own times. You cannot look at America's problems today, for example, without knowing how America solved its problems in the past. If we know what we did right—and what we did wrong—in our history, we can write better history for tomorrow.

First U.S. Woman Doctor

Not too many people today know the name of Elizabeth Blackwell, who was born on this day in 1821 in England. If I describe her as Elizabeth Blackwell M.D., that may provide a clue. Dr. Blackwell, who came to this country at the age of eleven, graduated in 1848 as the first woman doctor in modern history. She founded the New York Infirmary, a hospital whose entire staff was female, and she founded the first woman's medical college. It is hard to imagine the odds she had to overcome in her medical studies and practice. And don't think that kind of fight is a thing of the past. Today we are confronted with prejudices just as strong and just as evil as the idea that women couldn't be doctors.

Norman Rockwell's Birthday

Probably no artist in the history of our country captured the sentimental spirit of America like Norman Rockwell, who was born on this day in 1894. Long after his death, his paintings continue to be national favorites. We are a sentimental people. We like to think of an America that matches the Norman Rockwell pictures; whether it was ever that kind of land may be open to question. We all cherish a yearning for the kind of world that Norman Rockwell painted, and maybe, as we go on collecting his pictures, they will help us reassert the timeless, heartwarming human values he portrayed. It may not be the real world, but it's a good world to shoot for.

FEBRUARY 4

Election of First President of United States

On this day in 1789, the electoral college chose the first president of the United States under the Constitution, George Washington. Washington was his country's ranking general before he became president. He probably could have been elected king, or certainly president for life, but he chose to limit his period in office, and he carefully avoided overpowering the Congress. He set an example for the various generals who, in later years, also came to the presidency. Our generals-turned-presidents have been good citizens first and foremost, not would-be dictators. They are the best argument for the American system of civilian-controlled military service. Is that civilian control as strong today as in the past?

Betty Friedan's Birthday

Much of the history of social reform in this country has been sparked by popular books. That was the case, for example, with *Uncle Tom's Cabin* and *The History of Standard Oil*. In more recent times, it was accomplished by Betty Friedan, who was born on this day in 1921. She wrote *The Feminine Mystique*, which preceded and helped so much to trigger the rise of modern feminism. It is interesting that when the feminist movement began Betty Friedan was considered one of its radical bellwethers, but as the movement progressed her views—which were largely unchanged—began to be perceived by more militant feminists as conservative and perhaps even retrogressive. Every generation discovers for itself; every generation distrusts what its elders tell it. Given that fact, we have to expect that every generation will come up with Betty Friedans of its own, and we can expect to be surprised by what bugs them.

USO Anniversary

In 1941, to provide soldiers with off-duty relaxation that was wholesome and reassuring, the United Service Organizations, better known as the USO, came into being. It would be hard to estimate how many millions of service people since that day in 1941 have been entertained and cared for by the USO. Before there was a USO, soldiers and sailors had good reason to feel that they were second-class citizens, and that is a bad thing for all concerned. We owe it to our armed forces to keep them closely and warmly in touch with the communities in which they serve.

McCarthy's "Twenty Years of Treason"

On this day in 1954, Senator Joseph R. McCarthy of Wisconsin began a speaking tour to denounce "20 years of treason" of Democratic administrations in Washington. Senator McCarthy had been charging communist conspiracies in high places in Washington in his speeches beginning in 1950, but with the "20 years of treason" charge he really became all-encompassing, including in his attacks before he was finished General George C. Marshall and President Dwight D. Eisenhower. His decline was as rapid and spectacular as his rise in the headlines, sparked by a televised Senate hearing that the entire country witnessed. What probably ensured his ultimate descent was the extremism with which he attacked purported extremists. America has never been happy for long with extremism, and the pendulum keeps swinging back more or less to the center. If we do not see that happening today, we can be reasonably sure it will happen tomorrow.

FEBRUARY 5

Pay Your Bills Week

The first week of the month of February was designated a number of years ago by the professional bill collectors association as Pay Your Bills Week. One might reasonably expect this observance a little closer to Christmas, when we all run up those bills, but apparently the collectors have hearts; they are willing to give us a little time. In any case, it is fitting that Pay Your Bills Week should come smack in the middle of the winter. Everybody knows it will be a cold day when we get out of debt. Meanwhile, I suppose the best we can do is to see that we are getting our money's worth. That is enough of a challenge in these uncertain times.

FDR's Court-Packing Plan

Franklin D. Roosevelt did not suffer many lasting defeats in his presidency, but on this day in 1937 he left himself open to a major setback. He proposed to Congress a plan to enlarge the Supreme Court, and, despite his claim that he was just trying to improve its performance by bringing in some younger judges, most everybody agreed with the plan's opponents that it was an attempt to "pack" the Court with Roosevelt allies. This was probably the only time that FDR's sense of politics and timing led him wrong, but if it can happen to such a master politician, why should we be surprised when it happens to lesser leaders? At any moment in history, the time is right for some reforms and wrong for others. As, for example, right now.

Huey Long's Share-the-Wealth Plan

Huey P. Long, senator from Louisiana in the early days of the New Deal, was the darling of a new populist movement in the South, and on this day in 1934 he gave the Senate his program for ending the depression. He called it "Share the Wealth" and used as his motto "Every man a king." He proposed to achieve this goal by guaranteeing a minimum annual income of $5,000 to every family. In 1934, incidentally, $5,000 was a sizable amount of money. Huey Long, who was known as the Kingfish, was regarded by most of the country as a feckless demagogue, and when he was assassinated some years later the mourning was not universal, particularly after vicious hate-mongers took over his Share-the-Wealth movement. But it is interesting to consider the number of very respectable and well-regarded people who, in later years, have advocated a guaranteed annual income. What seems radical and demagogic in one era has a way of becoming at least acceptable for debate before too long.

Birthday of James Otis

On this day in 1725, in the Cape Cod town of West Barnstable, a man named James Otis was born. If he is remembered at all today, it is probably for something he didn't say: "Taxation without representation is tyranny." He was the first great leader of the movement for self-government in Massachusetts, and the principle that taxation without representation is tyranny was part of that movement. He was a lawyer, a brilliant pamphleteer, and the leader of the Stamp Act Congress, which was one of the first joint meetings of the colonies. In 1769, in an altercation with a British officer, he was hit on the head and lost his sanity. Others took over the leadership of the liberty movement in Massachusetts, and in the course of time the contribution of James Otis was largely forgotten. There are many unsung heroes in the defense of freedom. In our own time, there are people who are doing great things without getting headlines. They deserve our recognition and our applause.

FEBRUARY 6

Ronald Reagan's Birthday

Ronald Reagan, the fortieth President of the United States, was born on this day in 1911. He was the oldest man to take the oath as our Chief Executive, just a few weeks short of his seventieth birthday when he began his term in office. He was also the first actor to attain the White House, and it was interesting to observe that the old prejudice against actors was not completely dead. Some of his opponents suggested that his profession rendered him unequipped to lead the nation. Being different is every citizen's right. I don't advocate putting the eccentrics of punk rock in positions of authority, but we simply have to stop judging people in general terms and view them as individuals. Just look at the way so many of us inaccurately characterize blacks or hard-hats or Hispanics in group terms, and you'll see what I mean.

Emerson's Way to Prevent the Civil War

Ralph Waldo Emerson was one of the most respected leaders of the American intellectual community. On this day in 1855, he proposed in a message to the Anti-Slavery Society of New York that slavery be ended by paying off the slaveholders. He estimated that it would cost about $200 million, a tremendous sum in those days. The proposal went nowhere. And in the Civil War that began six years later more than 280,000 people died. That was the cost in human terms. Somehow, it seems to me that we measure costs too much in dollar terms and not enough in terms of human lives. We never try to estimate how much it costs *not* to feed the hungry, for example.

Voltaire and God's Side

One of the more familiar quotations comes from Voltaire, who is supposed to have said on this day in 1770, "It is said that God is always for the big battalions." Sometimes it is translated simply as "God is on the side of the big battalions." We all claim God for our side. We all deny God to the other side. We see the world in black and white, when in fact there is a whole rainbow of colors—and of rightness and wrongness—in between. That is the case today to a frightening degree, particularly with the single-issue political groups who see only evil except for their own specialized cause, and who carry on their guerrilla warfare under self-proclaimed holy banners. Nobody has a patent on morality—or on God's will.

Aaron Burr's Birthday

Today is the birthday of the most controversial political figure in America's history. Within a single decade he ran a dead heat for the presidency with a man named Thomas Jefferson—the House of Representatives broke the tie by choosing Jefferson—killed Alexander Hamilton in a duel, and was tried and acquitted on a charge of treason for an attempt to create a new nation in the West. His name, as you may have guessed, was Aaron Burr. If one vote in the electoral college—one single vote—had gone the other way, Aaron Burr would have been President and Thomas Jefferson might simply have been a glorious footnote in history. There is no such thing, in the electoral college or at your neighborhood polling place, as an unimportant vote. We can never know how the ballot each of us casts may change the course of history.

FEBRUARY 7

The Beatles

On this day in 1964, four young men from Liverpool came to the United States. Their fame had preceded them, so America gave a rousing reception to the Beatles and their music. It is hard to look at photographs of their first performances here and recall the storm that arose over their long hair. By later standards their hair wasn't long at all, but in 1964 it seemed like a deliberate flouting of accepted manners and conventions—and so did some of the Beatles' music. Times changed. When John Lennon was killed many years later in New York, he was mourned not only as a musical pioneer but also as a good man, a man of peace and good will. Whoever speaks of believing in first impressions is talking nonsense. Many ideas, many personalities, many things have to grow on us; we resist what is different, unless we are adolescents, when we may be inclined to embrace it uncritically simply because it is different. We are all creatures of our prejudices, whether the prejudice deals with the length of a man's hair, the cut of a jib, the color of a skin, or the details of a faith. The way to avoid wrapping ourselves in unchangeable first impressions is simple: get to know one another better.

Sir Thomas More's Birthday

On Milk Street in the city of London on this day in the year 1478, there was born a man who defied a king. His name was Sir Thomas More, and he was the chancellor of England when King Henry VIII, in order to divorce one wife and take another, broke with the church of Rome. When Henry declared himself the head of the church in England, Sir Thomas More refused to change his faith. In 1535, at the age of 57, he was beheaded in the Tower of London. In the hundreds of years since then, the name of Sir Thomas More, sanctified as Saint Thomas More, has come to symbolize the courage of conscience, an item which is never in oversupply. Conscience must be exercised if men and women are to remain free. No force of government or society should be used to force people to change their thoughts. No penalties should be attached to opinions.

Washington's Warning

On February 7, 1788, when the new Constitution of the United States was not yet in effect, George Washington wrote a letter to the Marquis de Lafayette. He described the agreement on the Constitution among the thirteen founding states as "little short of a miracle," and then spoke of how it was written to endure for the ages, unless there were—and I quote—"corruption of morals, profligacy of manners, and listlessness for the preservation of the natural and unalienable rights of mankind. . . ." The nation was in its infancy, and its founding father already perceived the danger of "listlessness for the preservation" of rights. I suggest that today, as in Washington's time, we must be ever on our guard against the things he feared then: corruption of morals, profligacy of manners, and listlessness for the preservation of natural rights.

Babe Ruth's Birthday

George Herman Ruth was born in Baltimore on this day back in 1895. Not too many people ever knew him as George Herman Ruth, but to millions he was the Babe—Babe Ruth, probably more responsible than any other single American for making baseball America's national pastime. It was Babe Ruth who filled the ballparks and drew enough crowds so that they built bigger ballparks. Isn't it a great country that can draw so much enthusiasm for a ballplayer? In America we applaud people who do things better than they have been done before. We think big, and we like big accomplishments.

FEBRUARY 8

William T. Sherman's Birthday

William Tecumseh Sherman, born on this day in 1820 in Lancaster, Ohio, was the general who sent this famous message when his name was being considered for nomination for the presidency: "If nominated, I will not accept. If elected, I will not serve." I will try here today to be clear and terse, but I doubt that I can possibly be as clear, as terse, or as level-headed as William Tecumseh Sherman.

Boy Scout Anniversary

The Boy Scouts of America won a charter in Washington, D.C., on this day in 1910. I hesitate to estimate how many good deeds have been done since then in pursuit of a merit badge. Some people used to laugh at the Boy Scouts, but generation after generation has come to realize that scouting has proved you don't have to be an athlete to be a member of the team; you don't have to march with guns to wear a uniform with pride; you don't have to go through the growing years of life alone. The BSA has taught countless youngsters how to work together and help each other—and that is knowledge we can all use today in our adult life. Life, after all, is a mixture of competition and cooperation. Knowing when to cooperate and when to compete is the key to successful living. Keeping up with the Joneses isn't as important as keeping the Joneses up.

Vice-President Richard M. Johnson

Nobody in U.S. history is more obscure than a former Vice-President, but on this day in 1837, a Vice-President made history. The man who became President that year was outgoing President Andrew Jackson's Vice-President, Martin Van Buren. But the electoral college couldn't choose a Vice-President. None of the four candidates received sufficient electoral votes. So, for the first time in American history, the Vice-President was actually elected by the Senate of the United States. On this day in 1837, they chose Van Buren's running mate, Richard M. Johnson of Kentucky. Unlike a Vice-President elected by Congress more than a century later—Gerald Ford—Vice-President Johnson was never called to higher office, but his election was a reassuring proof that, faced with a never-before-seen situation, the Constitution and government of the United States are able to handle things. We have proven that on many occasions. The government works, if we let it. We all talk about the times when it strips a gear or misses a beat, but let's remember all the things it does so well.

Whatever Happened to *The Clansman?*

Once upon a time a young filmmaker named David Wark Griffith decided to make a feature motion picture much longer and more ambitious than anything that had ever been filmed in the United States. It opened in Cline's Auditorium in Los Angeles on this day in 1915, under the title *The Clansman,* drawn from a book of the same title by Thomas Dixon. But when it had its official world premiere in New York on March 3, it had a new title. It was called *The Birth of a Nation.* The film, full of prejudice against blacks, was criticized by many intellectual leaders as false, shallow, and evil. But it was the greatest use of the motion picture medium that anyone had seen up to that time. Its camera angles, editing, use of close-ups all pioneered new scope for film. It was a masterpiece flawed beyond measure by its social and political bias, but nevertheless an epic milestone in film history. Over the years we have become more concerned with content and less with technique, more interested in the message than in the medium. This is as it should be. I like to think that if *The Birth of a Nation* were to debut today, the audience would say to hell with the technique, the message is wrong, and let it go at that. It is time we stopped worrying about the wrapping and started judging what's inside.

FEBRUARY 9

President John Quincy Adams

When the presidential election of 1824 went to the electoral college Andrew Jackson was the leading candidate, but he couldn't achieve a majority, so the choosing of the sixth President of the United States was up to the House of Representatives. On this day in 1825, thanks to the support of an unsuccessful presidential candidate named Henry Clay, John Quincy Adams was elected President. He was the first Chief Executive who was the son of a previous President. He came to the White House with a distinguished record, and he had a distinguished record after he left the White House, but thanks to the bitter opposition he encountered during his administration, he was generally powerless during his term of office. John Quincy Adams had no political organization worthy of the name behind him. During his presidency the Democratic Party as we know it today began to gain strength behind Andrew Jackson. A good man by himself proved no match for a grassroots party. For the most part the United States has had party government ever since. In politics we seem to have learned that a knight in shining armor may be fine, but if you want him to get things done he needs the organization, the discipline, the from-the-ground-up intelligence of a cohesive political party. We like to think of ourselves as individualists, but we work best when we are a team.

Confederate States of America

This is the anniversary of the selection of Jefferson Davis as provisional President of the Confederate States of America in 1861. Almost inevitably the gathering clouds of the coming Civil War became more real. There would be no turning back. Neither side at this juncture seemed inclined to compromise. North and South marched to different drummers, and the blood of both sides was spilled in torrents for more than four years thereafter. Could it have been avoided? Can we today be wiser and luckier than the Jefferson Davises of 1861? Can we somehow achieve compromise with honor, settle world differences without force of arms? What are the chances?

Globaloney

In a speech in the House of Representatives on this day in 1943, Representative Clare Booth Luce, commenting on the views of Henry Wallace, said, "Much of what Mr. Wallace calls his global thinking is, no matter how you slice it, still globaloney." I regret to say that globaloney is still with us. I am tired of having our nation called cruel when we stay out of other nations' affairs, selfish when we get involved, incompetent when foreign affairs get messed up, cowardly when we refuse to clean up other folks' messes, and so forth. Globaloney! Here are some specifics.

Future Homemakers Week

For many years, around this time in February, the nation observed Future Homemakers Week. What will the future home be like? Will the children be sent to day-care centers at six months so Mom and Pop can hold full-time jobs? Will families live as separate units, or are they going to be collectivized? Whatever will become of grandparents? We are told—indeed, we have been told for generations—that the so-called nuclear family is changing. Where do we go from here? Who, indeed, *are* the future homemakers of America?

FEBRUARY 10

Justice Sutherland on Free Press

In the annals of the Supreme Court, Justice George Sutherland does not stand out as a notable champion of enlightened liberalism. Nevertheless, in a Court decision he delivered on this day in 1936, he wrote one of the clearest defenses of freedom of the press this nation had heard. "A free press," said Justice Sutherland, "stands as one of the great interpreters between the government and the people. To allow it to be fettered is to fetter ourselves." That comment is well worth remembering the next time a government official tries to keep the press quiet.

"I'll Never Tell a Lie"

History records that on this day in 1976, as possibly on other occasions on the campaign trail, a presidential candidate named Jimmy Carter told the American voters, "I'll never tell a lie." That may have been the riskiest statement ever made by any presidential candidate since the dawn of time. Jimmy Carter was elected, but throughout his single term of office that promise kept coming back to haunt him. The American public simply cannot believe that an American politician can go through life never telling a lie. We are not surprised when candidates fail to keep campaign promises—we are surprised when they *do* keep them. Let us take the current political scene as a case in point.

Death of a Salesman

It was on this day in 1949 that Broadway saw the premiere of Arthur Miller's play *Death of a Salesman*. It was more than a great play. It was the obituary of the great age of the American traveling salesman, that ambassador of commercial good will who depended on being liked. We desperately wanted to be liked. And when we discovered that as a political entity, as a nation, we were envied more than liked, it came as a rude shock. Have we learned that being liked is not enough? Have we stopped entering popularity contests and let Willy Loman retire to his golden age?

Twenty-fifth Amendment

On this day in 1967, the twenty-fifth amendment to the Constitution of the United States was adopted. It dealt with the succession to the presidency if the President is deemed disabled and with the filling of a vacancy in the Vice-Presidency. Nobody could have foreseen when the Amendment was adopted that in less than seven years it would be needed to replace a Vice-President who resigned in disgrace. Thanks to the process provided for in the Amendment, Gerald Ford was nominated by President Richard Nixon to replace Spiro Agnew as Vice-President and was confirmed by vote of both houses of Congress. A year later Nixon himself resigned under fire, and the Vice-President who was in office as a result of the Twenty-fifth Amendment became the President of the United States. Now, we can't claim that every amendment or every provision of the Constitution is as foresighted as this one turned out to be, but we have ample proof in our history that the Constitution is the most remarkable fundamental law of government that has ever been devised. It's a pity more Americans don't know about it. They have failed in survey after survey even to recognize the principles stated in the Bill of Rights, the first ten Amendments. So I'd like to talk about these fundamental rights and how they apply to our world today.

FEBRUARY 11

Inventors Day

Today is often observed as National Inventors Day on the anniversary of the birth in 1847 of our most productive inventor, Thomas Alva Edison. Our inventors have made our country great, from the cotton gin to the transistor and the silicon chip. Yankee ingenuity is still our most potent weapon. Its wonders seem never to cease. As we move deeper into what has been called the age of artificial intelligence the world will continue to look to American imagination and Yankee ingenuity to develop the miracles of tomorrow—whether for activities in outer space or for greater comfort at home on Earth. Looking into my crystal ball I see these advances on the more or less immediate horizon.

National Crime Prevention Week

For reasons best known to the National Exchange Club, they observe the week that comes around now as National Crime Prevention Week. The problem with crime prevention is that there are so many different approaches—more severe penalties, more peace officers to enforce the law, more services for disadvantaged juveniles and addicts to keep them from becoming hardened criminals, better correctional facilities, less poverty, and so forth. But there is one method of crime prevention that deserves to be singled out and recommended. It is called good citizenship. Too often a witness to a crime doesn't want to be bothered going to court and testifying or fears the consequences of testifying against a professional criminal. An aroused citizenry has to be the first line of defense against crime. There are really no bystanders in the fight against crime. We all have to do our parts. Are you doing yours?

Clifford Irving's Hoax

In 1972, Howard Hughes was the most famous and puzzling mystery man in the world. He was fabulously rich, fabulously eccentric, and fabulously invisible. A writer named Clifford Irving claimed that he had obtained the authentic story of Howard Hughes, a biography verified by the mystery man himself. On this eleventh day of February in 1972, after Hughes's denial and their own investigations, McGraw-Hill and *Life* magazine announced that they were canceling plans for the publication because they believed it to be a hoax. Irving subsequently went to jail after admitting the fraud. This was probably the most spectacular con game of its time, but eleven years later an even more feckless phony, the so-called Hitler diaries, made an even bigger splash before they were exposed. I suspect that every year there are similar, purportedly authentic revelations that are equally spurious. When one deals with scandal and mystery, who is to know the true facts? We unfortunately have publications and writers who profit by nibbling at the reputations of famous people. And the main reason for this is that people are nosy. We have an apparently insatiable appetite for dirty details about our household gods. Why do we encourage scandal-mongers and "now it can be told" dirty linen?

Madison Square Garden

On this day in 1968, Madison Square Garden moved into its newest home, in the Pennsylvania Station complex in New York City. Like so many other American institutions, it isn't what its name implies. It hasn't been located on Madison Square for more than half a century, and it certainly isn't a garden. But say "Madison Square Garden" and people know exactly what you mean; in a broader sense, do people know the difference between a recession and a depression, or a cold war and a cold peace? We label things with words that can be euphemisms or battle cries, and we rally around banners we don't always understand. Some time ago an organization named itself Morality in Media, but whose morality was it proposing? Obviously, its own.

FEBRUARY 12

NAACP Birthday

The National Association for the Advancement of Colored People has a name that seems slightly anachronistic today, but when it was launched on this day in 1909—although the name came a little later—"colored people" was considered the genteel way to refer to our black fellow citizens. In 1909, and for almost half a century thereafter, we had the government's active approval for Jim Crow laws, total discrimination in many parts of the land, and few if any voting rights for the folks who had to go to the back of the bus. The price of the progress we have made has not been an easy one; men and women have died in this cause, and even today hard-won freedoms can only be maintained by eternal vigilance. Freedom is like the air we breathe; if we aren't careful, we can pollute it and poison ourselves. Even when we may not agree with organizations like the NAACP, they serve a healthy and fundamental purpose in our great American democracy, for we can never have too many embattled voices raised in vigilant protection of liberty and equality. The time to be most on our guard is the time when we sit back and say smugly that we have it made. Certainly, we cannot sit back today.

Washington's Accounts

George Washington was in Newburgh, New York, concerned with the closing stages of his victory in the American Revolutionary War, when on this day in 1783 he wrote to the relative who was managing his estate at Mount Vernon. Washington complained that he had not received an accounting, and he added, "I want to know before I come home (as I shall come home with empty pockets, whenever Peace shall take place) how affairs stand with me, and what my dependence is." This, bear in mind, was the complaint of a general who stood in command of a surprisingly victorious army. None of us is immune to concern about what we have put away or what we have on tap for tomorrow. None of us is in total command of our future fortunes. All of us are or should be concerned about the security of our coming years. It is to that concern that I address my remarks today.

Lincoln's Birthday

The observance of Abraham Lincoln's birthday, marking his birth on this day in 1809, is one of special appeal for many Americans. When Lincoln came to the presidency he was not a national hero. He grew with the demands of the job, as other presidents have done after him. And I think that is the real message of Lincoln's birthday, that we never really know how much there is in us until we are asked to do more than we have ever done before. The challenges that face us are perhaps greater than they have been in some time, but I think we will meet them. I think the signs are there, right now.

Februare

This is the month of February, whose name is thought by most scholars to be drawn from the Latin word *februare*, which means "to purify." In February every year the ancient Romans had a purification ceremony. They also gave the month less days than any other month of the year, which may indicate that purification is fine but it has its limits. In modern times, the purification aspects of February have been set aside in favor of everything from winter carnivals to the St. Valentine's Day massacre, but some remnants of the old Roman tradition remain. Certainly, in this month we renew the purity of our dedication to American ideals, with the observance of Lincoln's and Washington's birthdays, Brotherhood Week, and other reminders of the good aspects of human life. So, in the middle of purification month, I rise to salute the renewal of American ideals, the resurgence of conscience, and the hope of better things.

FEBRUARY 13

John Adams on Revolution

More than 40 years after the American Revolution one of the leaders of that great uprising, John Adams, wrote a letter to an editor on this day in 1818. "The Revolution," Adams said, "was effected before the War commenced. The Revolution was in the Minds and Hearts of the People." But that does not happen overnight. It is the product of failures to make wrongs right, the product of repeated injustice. The way to avoid revolution is to see that justice does not lag and need does not go unmet. That is a challenge to us as it was to the United States of 1932 and 1865 and every era of our history.

Solzhenitsyn's Deportation

In the dismal climate of the Russian communist dictatorship, one of the heroes was Aleksandr Solzhenitsyn, who survived prison camps to give the world a series of magnificent literary works about conditions in the USSR. The Soviets tried to silence him, and when that failed they came up with a typical dictator's solution. On this day in 1974, after he had committed the unforgivable crime of winning the Nobel Prize in addition to his other glories, they deported Solzhenitsyn to West Germany. The one thing that dictatorship cannot stand is a free voice; the one thing that freedom must have is a chorus of free voices.

What you say is not as important as having the right to say it. I hope what I have to say here will meet with your approval. But how comforting it is to know that I don't have to toe any official party line, and nobody is going to throw me out of my country for opening my mouth.

ASCAP

On this day in 1914, Victor Herbert and other writers of the songs America was singing organized ASCAP, the American Society of Composers, Authors, and Publishers. Their purpose was to make sure that songwriters and publishers were compensated for public performances of their music. Back in 1914, nobody could have foreseen the way radio, television, sound motion pictures, and various types of recording would expand the value of property rights in music. But they did know one thing that is always true: everyone is entitled to the fruits of his or her labor. We will always have some people trying to take advantage of other people, and we will always have some people who are natural targets. But if we refuse to benefit from this kind of injustice—if, for example, we don't buy goods from countries where forced labor is the rule—we will be doing for everyday people what Victor Herbert and his friends started doing for songwriters on this day in 1914. None of us can do this kind of thing alone, but we can do an awful lot if we do it together.

Mrs. Lincoln and the Thumbs

One of today's more unusual anniversaries caught my attention as I was reviewing things that happened on this day in the past. On February 13, 1863, we are told, the First Lady, Mrs. Lincoln, entertained a couple of famous Americans at the White House. She served tea to General and Mrs. Tom Thumb just a few days after their marriage. Now, Tom and Lavinia Thumb were not the only members of show business to be welcomed in their time to the White House, but they certainly were the smallest of the entertainment world's big names. There is something that defies the imagination about Mrs. Lincoln welcoming General Tom Thumb to the White House, particularly in the middle of the Civil War. I suppose it was reassuring to know that even then there was satisfaction to be gained from paying attention to little things. There is no indication that Abe Lincoln, our tallest president, stopped by to say hello to the Thumbs; if he had, that would have been one of the great photographic opportunities. But we do know that General Tom Thumb and his miniature lady, billed as the smallest people in the world, had a very large place in the affections of the American people. They represented no threat to anybody, and so everybody liked them. Our trouble today is that we are big enough and strong enough to represent a threat to some of the world's bullies. They are trying very hard to cut us down to size.

FEBRUARY 14

Valentine's Day

Today is Valentine's Day, which somehow seems to have developed into a great day for the greeting card companies. Even the spirit of love, it seems, finds expression in mass-produced printed materials. Have we become more bashful, or lazier, over the course of the years? Is that why we go to the greeting card store to find ways to say "I love you"? Valentine's Day is more than a printed card sent through the mail. It suggests that if we care about one another we should tell each other, and in person. We should try to get to know one another, instead of erecting barriers.

Henry Grattan's Wisdom

Henry Grattan was called the Irish Demosthenes, and on this day in 1800 he rose in the Irish Parliament, in the midst of a heated debate, to make a remark well worth remembering. "There are times," he said, "when the insignificance of the accuser is lost in the magnitude of the accusation." That is as sad a fact today as it was in Henry Grattan's time. It seems as though anybody can attract considerable attention if the accusation is horrendous enough and the accused is prominent enough. We all have our pet sweeping generalizations—all people on welfare are lazy, all politicians are crooked, all used car dealers are cheats, and so forth. In too many situations we seem to start off with a mind-set that colors our approach.

Sir Henry Irving on Deserved Obscurity

Sir Henry Irving was a great British actor who didn't hesitate to speak his mind. He remarked on this day in 1898 that "some persons who were intended by nature to adorn an inviolable privacy are thrust upon us by paragraphers and interviewers, whose existence is a dubious blessing." One has only to scan any of the gossip columns today or view any of the innumerable interview shows on television to agree with Sir Henry. This may be the age of information, but it is a time when we are being overrun with what I call nuisance information. I trust my remarks here today will not prove to be part of that bombardment.

Jack Benny's Birthday

Today is the birthday of one of America's greatest comedians, now sadly gone but still fondly remembered. His name was Benny Kubelsky, but he appeared on stage, screen, and television for some 60 years as Jack Benny, born on this day in 1894 in Waukegan, Illinois. Jack Benny made thriftiness and age 39 his comedy trademarks. He never admitted to being more than 39, and his comedy routines portrayed him as the most parsimonious miser in the history of money. In real life, of course, he was the total opposite, but in performance he was the perfect caricature of the insecure American. He made a joke of America's two major worries—money and age. Even when you know that you'll have enough money to live on in your old age, you can be made old before your time if you are deprived of the opportunity to be an active, participating citizen. I am here to proselyte for the active life, wherever you are and whatever your age.

FEBRUARY 15

Brotherhood Week

At this time of the year we observe Brotherhood Week. I get the impression sometimes that by setting aside one week for brotherhood we are somehow implying that the other 51 weeks are okay for feuding with one another—but that of course is an unduly cynical view. We have indeed come a long way, 52 weeks of the year, from the hatred of the past. We have, I believe, come a long way from thinking that all Italians are this and all Poles are that. We have come a long way, but we certainly still have a long way to go. As long as we have one group claiming superior morality over another in our own country, we have a long way to go.

Susan B. Anthony Day

In recent times Susan B. Anthony has been famous as the face on the most unpopular coin the nation ever had—the Susan B. Anthony dollar. But unpopularity with a large segment of the nation's population would not have dismayed Susan B. Anthony, because she encountered that reaction during her lifetime. She was born on this day in 1820 and spent her lifetime fighting for women's rights and women's suffrage. She died in 1906, long before either of those battles was won, but when they were won it was largely because Susan B. Anthony had carried on the good fight for so long. She was not discouraged, and those of us who have worthy causes of our own to fight for these days might bear her example in mind. This is not the time to give up the fight.

Shooting at FDR

Franklin D. Roosevelt was within a month of becoming president of the United States when he visited Miami on this day in 1933. It was very nearly his last day on earth. A deranged assassin tried to shoot him dead. FDR escaped, but the mayor of Chicago, Anton Cermak, who was accompanying him, was killed. The United States, which had gone for more than 30 years without a presidential assassination, was reminded once again that any president—or president-elect—can be the target of a twisted mind. Just a bit more than 30 years after the attempt on Roosevelt's life, another assassin succeeded in killing President John F. Kennedy. One aspect that most presidential assassination attempts have in common is their sheer illogic. They have been the products of disturbed minds, as was the attempt in 1981 on President Ronald Reagan. Not just in the case of presidential assassinations, but in everyday life, mental disturbance seems to be our most unconquerable problem. We cannot shove it under the table.

Cyrus McCormick

In America's galaxy of great inventors, Cyrus Hall McCormick is probably not as famous as he deserves to be, for it was this man, born on this day in 1809 in Virginia, who invented and perfected the mechanical reaper. Thanks to the reaper the harvest of American grain has been the most plentiful the world has ever seen. One of the modern miracles is the way we keep getting more from less—more crops from less acreage, more electronic miracles from smaller and smaller chips, more channels for communication through fiber optics, and so forth. Whenever I hear people selling the message that smaller is better, I think of pioneers like Cyrus McCormick, who operated on another principle—more is better—and I salute those ingenious men and women who today are giving us more than any prior generation ever had to work with.

FEBRUARY 16

Cleveland's Dictum

On this day in 1887, in the course of vetoing a bill, President Grover Cleveland commented that "while the people should patriotically and cheerfully support their government, its functions do not include the support of the people." We seem to have come a long way round since then. One fact that bears remembering is that when the government helps support a needy person, the government is also helping the rest of us who might otherwise have the burden of aiding that needy person or protecting ourselves from that person's desperation. The question is not whether we should help the unfortunate but rather how we can best do that to help ourselves as well.

Decatur in Tripoli

When our nation was fairly new in the early 1800s, we were plagued, as were the peoples of Europe, by the Barbary pirates. On this day in 1804, a U.S. Navy lieutenant named Stephen Decatur led a Navy crew into the pirate harbor of Tripoli in North Africa and destroyed the U.S. warship *Philadelphia*, which the pirates had captured. That was the first of a series of Decatur's victories over the pirates. Even as a very young nation, the United States was determined to show that it couldn't be pushed around. For all the international rules, one of the most persuasive tools today is still your opponent's knowledge that you have a few Stephen Decaturs around. You don't have to throw punches as long as your opponents know you have the punching power and can, if need be, use it.

Lithuanian Independence Day

Today is Lithuanian Independence Day, a reminder of one of the small free nations that was gobbled up by the Soviet Union. Lithuania declared itself an independent country in 1918, after having been an unwilling part of tsarist Russia. But independence didn't last very long. Russia, whether communist or tsarist, had no intention of letting its subject peoples go free. This anniversary of Lithuania's short-lived declaration of freedom is a reminder that imperialism and communism go hand in hand.

Future Farmers Week

In mid-February lovers of agriculture have observed Future Farmers of America Week, designed, I assume, to strengthen the interest of our young people in raising the crops and the livestock that feed the nation and a good part of the world. We can't be sure what future farmers will find facing them when they grow up, say, ten or twenty years from now. The challenge is to make farm life more attractive and maybe more secure.

FEBRUARY 17

Burke on Piety

The orator Edmund Burke, on this day in 1788, said that "religious persecution may shield itself under the guise of a mistaken and overzealous piety." How true today, when single-cause pleaders wrap themselves in the cloak of religious piety and claim a monopoly on the truth in some particular area.

PTA

The National Congress of Mothers was established in 1897 on this day in Washington, D.C. You would know it better as the National Congress of Parents and Teachers. Back in 1897, parents were not about to turn over any of their responsibility to teachers. Today, however, we seem to expect the schools to do many of the things that the home used to be responsible for. We can only hope that the home and the school still teach the same values rather than contradicting each other. We can only hope that taxpayers don't vent their understandable resentment at the cost of government by unduly squeezing the schools. And one good test of parenting is this: if you have a child in school, are you active in your PTA?

Legislative Representation

It was not until 1964—or this day in 1964, to be precise—that the Supreme Court made it the law of the land that the population of each congressional district and each district in a state legislature had to be the same. That is, in a state legislature all the senate districts had to represent the same number of people; all the assembly districts had to be equal in population. If you stop and think about it, this means that it took 175 years to achieve this kind of equal treatment. Next time you become impatient about what seems to be an obvious deficiency in the way our government is run, keep this in mind. The job of interested citizens is always to find ways to make government move faster on the causes in which we believe.

The Fighting Submarine

On this day in 1864—or, to be more precise, on this night—the first submarine to sink an enemy warship did so in the Civil War. It was the Confederate submersible *Hunley*, which sank the U.S. Navy's *Housatonic*. There was only one problem. The *Hunley* was swamped by the explosion of its torpedo against the *Housatonic*, and its crew was wiped out. It was not until World War I, half a century later, that the submarine became a workable weapon. The first American submersible for fighting purposes was David Bushnell's *American Turtle*, which failed in 1776 to sink Admiral Howe's flagship in New York Harbor. We are very impatient these days about miraculous new weapons; if they don't work in the course of just a few years we try something else. But we might consider how long it took to make the fighting submarine practical. We might also consider the need not to freeze our defense equipment into already existent modes. Remember what happened to France's supposedly impregnable Maginot Line in World War II.

FEBRUARY 18

First Emmy Awards

On this day in 1952, the Academy of Television Arts and Sciences presented its first awards, the Emmies. And they surprised the skeptics. First of all, they endured, which few thought they would at the outset. Secondly, they proved in many instances to be an encouragement to quality in the medium— not always, by a darned sight, but often enough so that on occasion an Emmy, in the face of mediocre ratings, persuaded a network or station to continue a program and give it another chance. Since the Emmies began we have had all kinds of annual awards—Grammies and Edgars and many others. And though sometimes the number of them seems to vitiate the honors, they have to be a good idea. And so, here and now, I would like to announce my own awards.

Sam Ervin on Sunlight

Shortly after Sam Ervin, rich in his years, retired from the U.S. Senate, he made a speech at Mountain View College in Dallas. It was on this day in 1976, and among the things Sam Ervin said was this: "Sunlight is the best disinfectant for all things. The more sunlight shed on a thing, the less harmful it's going to be." Every time I hear some function of government trying to cover up what it is doing under the heading of national security, I think of Sam Ervin's remark.

Planet Pluto

On this day in 1930, Clyde W. Tombaugh at the Lowell Observatory in Flagstaff, Arizona, proved what Professor Percival Lowell had predicted. He discovered the planet Pluto, the smallest and farthest away in the solar system. At the time there didn't seem to be any great significance in the discovery, but that, of course, was before we really entered into the space exploration age. That's why it is important to encourage scientific research that seems to have no immediate practical application. You never can tell where it is going to lead or what progress it will spark. The miracles of tomorrow, after all, are being born in the pure science laboratories of today.

Pointing Japan East

The imperialism of Japan, which America fought so effectively in World War II, may well have had some of its roots in an event that happened on this day in 1908. At the insistence of President Theodore Roosevelt, Japan sent the United States a note agreeing to U.S. restriction on the immigration of Japanese to our shores. And on this same day a few years later in 1932, a Japanese puppet empire was established in Manchuria. Although diplomatic eyebrows were raised, nobody marched in to stop the Japanese. The world was exercised at aggression in the Orient, but as long as it could keep Orientals out of the West there was not going to be a war about it. When the Japanese started to look westward, it became a different story. Maybe we are beginning to understand that injustice in a far corner of the world has a way of creeping closer if you don't try to contain it.

FEBRUARY 19

Phonograph

It was in 1878, on this day, that Thomas Edison received his patent on the phonograph. The ability to record sound really revolutionized the world, by bringing a new realism to history, for example. Generations yet to come can hear the voices of Franklin D. Roosevelt and Winston Churchill and Dwight D. Eisenhower and John F. Kennedy. The music of the Beatles doesn't have to be described—it can be heard. We use recording devices to unlock the secrets of airplane crashes and to detect crime and capture moments in the family circle. And, let us face it—any speaker who, like myself, rises to address a group faces the possibility that somebody is recording the remarks. I suppose that has given new meaning to speaking for the record. I can only hope that my remarks here today will prove worthy of your attention.

National Cherry Month

A number of years ago February was first designated as National Cherry Month, and I am sure that the birthday of George Washington had something to do with it. The phony story made up by Parson Weems about young George and the cherry tree connects the father of our country firmly and irrevocably with cherries. National Cherry Month, therefore, celebrates not only a great American fruit but also a great American tradition. Like so many great American traditions, it happens to have a commercial sponsor, the organization of people who deal with the growing and marketing of red cherries. So, as we sit here in the middle of National Cherry Month, we should recognize the fact that some people have a greater degree of self-interest in noble sentiments than other people. The people who are the most patriotic are those who recognize the value their country has for them. They enjoy the fruit of the tree, while the skeptics just notice the pits. Today I urge you to stop contemplating the pits and join me in considering the blessed fruitfulness of our land.

Iwo Jima

Some place names stir a graphic picture in the minds of Americans. The battle green in Lexington, Massachusetts; Bunker Hill; Gettysburg; Pearl Harbor; Iwo Jima. Today is the anniversary of the landing of the fighting men of the Fourth and Fifth U.S. Marine divisions on a mountainous South Pacific island called Iwo Jima in 1945. It took days to reach the mountaintop and plant the American flag, in that scene we all know so well, which is memorialized in the Iwo Jima monument at Arlington National Cemetery. Iwo Jima was not by any means the first Japanese-held island to be invaded by U.S. troops, nor was it unique in the fierceness of the fighting. What makes Iwo Jima memorable is the scene cameraman Joe Rosenthal captured for all time of the Stars and Stripes on the mountaintop. Abstract ideas can be wonderful, but an idea that can be expressed in a visual image is even greater. The raising of an embattled American flag is that kind of image. We laugh at the corny invocation of Mom and apple pie, but let's face it—in our mind's eye each of us has a picture of America as we want it to be, or perhaps as we remember it. America is indeed all things to all people. That is the essence of its greatness.

A Month for Heroes

February is our shortest month, but it is a month full of memories of the people who made and continue to make America great. The four chaplains who gave their lives in the sinking of a transport in World War II so that their comrades might live did that noble deed in February. Lincoln and Washington were born in this month of heroes. Stephen Decatur's first victory in Tripoli came in February. In American history we must regard this month as a breeding ground for greatness. And, for all the cynicism with which many of us view the world around us today, this February finds many occasions for us to remember—and perhaps restore—our glorious history.

FEBRUARY 20

American Heart Month

We are three-quarters of the way through American Heart Month, the annual campaign to remind us to take care of our hearts. Since the first observance of Heart Month, remarkable progress has been made in heart health—not merely in the treatment of people with heart ailments but in understanding how to eat and how to live so as to avoid coronary illnesses. The lessons we have learned medically about protecting our hearts go beyond individual health, however. For example, we have learned that too rich a diet is a medical risk. High living isn't just drinking too much or eating too much. It is eating the wrong things. For the nation, high living carries the risk of wasting our national resources, burning up our national strengths, sapping our national energies. Anything that strains the national arteries is a threat to the national heart. Sometimes we have to strain, but sometimes we do it through sheer cussedness or sheer foolishness. Let me give you some examples.

Postal Service Act

On this day in 1792, President George Washington signed the first Postal Service Act to be written into law under the Constitution. It provided for a rate system quite different from what we have known in our own time. The rate for a letter depended on the distance it was being sent, from six cents for trips of less than thirty miles to 12½ cents for mail going between 100 and 150 miles. The mind positively boggles at what the Postal Service could do today with that kind of rate system for ordinary mail. For the fact is that while a common postal rate, regardless of the domestic distance, is a lot simpler to understand, it ends up with the bigger cities subsidizing rural and remote deliveries. Postal service is the one public utility that has been a government operation from the beginning. The rise of organizations like the express agencies and United Parcel Service raises a very real question, it seems to me, about whether ordinary first class mail should return to George Washington's 1792 mileage system.

Metropolitan Museum of Art

On the east side of Central Park in New York City stands one of the great and majestic buildings of the world, and what is inside is even greater and more majestic. The building is the Metropolitan Museum of Art. On this day in 1872, the Museum began in a rented house on Fifth Avenue. Today it stands as a symbol of the degree to which America has become the great patron of the arts. And what is important to remember is that this is a popularly supported patronage. Great gifts have been made by rich people, but the people who crowd daily through the doors of the Metropolitan and other museums throughout the country are everyday people—students, senior citizens, art lovers of every shape, size, and age. Art is more available to the common people today than ever before. It adds something very real and very important to life.

Generation Gap

On this day in 1852, Henry David Thoreau wrote in his journal, "The slope from the last generation to this seems steeper than any part of history." In 1852, before movies, radio, television, punk rock, birth control pills, widespread drug abuse, consciousness raising, and psychoanalysis, before all those things we blame for much of our own generation gap, calm Thoreau thought the generation gap was already as broad and unbridgeable as it had ever been. Every generation, I suppose, comes to the point where it despairs of the one it follows and the one it precedes.

FEBRUARY 21

Exit Adams

Most presidents, when they leave the White House, are content to become elder statesmen—perhaps write their memoirs, remain available for counsel, and generally enjoy honorable retirement. But when John Quincy Adams was defeated for a second term as president, he ran for and was elected to the House of Representatives. He was a member of Congress for some 17 years, serving with distinction and eloquence. He was one of the House's voices of conscience. He fought against slavery, and he opposed the Mexican War because he felt it would extend slavery. In the course of this fight, on this day in 1848, Adams collapsed of a stroke on the floor of the House. He died two days later. The voices of true conscience in the halls of government are rare enough so that we should remember and honor those whose sense of duty and patriotism keeps them in public service at tremendous personal cost.

Washington Monument

On this day in 1885, the great Washington Monument was dedicated. Like the man himself, the Washington Monument is big, far from subtle, and, above all, clearly dominating the landscape around it. The great good fortune of our country is that towering leaders like Washington have come forth when they were needed. Maybe that in itself says something about our nation. Maybe that in itself should strengthen the faith of Americans that they and their leaders will handle any challenge that comes along.

Telephone Directory

On this day in 1878, a brand new type of publication was presented to the public. It was issued in New Haven, Connecticut, and it was called a telephone directory. We are told that about fifty names were listed. From that small beginning has grown what may well be the single greatest source and most used repository of information in history. But any U.S. telephone directory is more than that. It is a wonderful symbol of our free and open society. With some few exceptions the vast majority of us see no reason to fear or avoid having our names, addresses, phone numbers, and sometimes our businesses identified for the information of all. We are not afraid to call or to answer the telephone. If that sounds like nothing extraordinary, reflect the situation in many foreign countries where telephone numbers are state secrets or privileges reserved for the select few. When folks sing the praises of other ways of life, show them a big fat U.S. telephone book and challenge them to match it.

W. H. Auden

Since today is the birthday of that great English—American poet W. H. Auden, who was born in Britain in 1907, it seems appropriate to recall one of the statements he made. In "The Shield of Achilles," he wrote, "They lost their pride/And died as men before their bodies died." We have a tendency to confuse pride and vanity, or pride and vainglory, and so there are those who scoff at taking pride in country, or showing pride in your children, or evidencing pride in your own accomplishments. I stand here today to urge the return of old-fashioned pride. Instead of dwelling on all the things that are wrong, let us be proud of what is right and of our ability to correct what is wrong. Instead of shrugging our shoulders and saying that in this regard or that we must now accept second-class status, let us buckle down so that we can take pride in being number one again.

FEBRUARY 22

First Woolworth's

This is the anniversary of a great idea in marketing, which was born when Frank W. Woolworth opened his first 5- and 10-cent store in Utica, New York. The idea of fixed-price merchandise easily available on well-stocked shelves has been one of the pillars of American commercial growth. There was a song many years ago entitled, "I Found a Million-Dollar Baby in a Five- and Ten-Cent Store." Frank Woolworth's million-dollar baby created a whole new concept of easy shopping—not the only one in the nation that also created the mail-order concept and the supermarket, but, since it started in 1879, the first of the business inspirations of America's golden age! Firmly believe that America's golden age of business is not yet over.

Eisenhower's Highway Message

In 1955 on this day President Dwight D. Eisenhower submitted to Congress a proposal for a $100-billion highway construction program over a period of ten years. This was the beginning of the great interstate road construction program that, although it ultimately proved inadequate, did so much to bring American vehicular transportation into a new age. The whole history of the development of this nation has been tied to roads, from the early wilderness road to the Lincoln Highway and the modern interstates. Mobility is one of the keys to American progress. When we cease to be a nation on the move we will lose something very precious from American life. We cannot sit and vegetate. Cities grow; other cities decline; but what is maintained is the dynamic, overall growth of the nation as a whole. We haven't run out of frontiers yet.

Schopenhauer

Today is the birthday of the patron saint of pessimism, the philosopher Arthur Schopenhauer, who was born in Danzig in 1788. His personal life may have contributed to his philosophical outlook. We are told he had no friends, never married, and didn't speak to his mother for about the last twenty years of her life. So let us say he had a lot to be pessimistic about. But if you want to look on the dark side of things you can always find it. If there weren't bad things we wouldn't know how good the good things are. If you persuade yourself that things won't get better, things will probably get worse. Even the iron laws of economics are bent by the state of popular morale. When people are confident, they buy more, invest more, exert more effort. So it isn't just ego gratification when the leaders of a nation try to make the people accept the vision of a brighter future. We need hopes and dreams and great expectations around which to rally.

James Russell Lowell

If this were not George Washington's birthday it might be known, at least in New England, as the birthday of James Russell Lowell. Born in 1819, Lowell was part of the golden age that saw the flowering of New England and America's cultural coming of age. He was one of the great poets of his time, whose most-quoted line is undoubtedly, "What is so rare as a day in June?" though another that we have all heard is this: "No man is born into the world whose work/Is not born with him. . . ." Lowell had more than talent. He had the burning desire to leave his mark in the world. "No man is born into the world whose work/Is not born with him." That is no less true today than in the time of James Russell Lowell. Each of us has a function, a role, a contribution to make to the world. We were not put on this earth to be spectators.

FEBRUARY 23

The Moral Issue

Jane Addams was a great lady who pioneered in organized community service in Chicago. She was invited to speak to the Union League Club in that city on this day in 1903, and she said, "What is a great man who has made his mark upon history? Every time, if we think far enough, he is a man who has looked through the confusion of the moment and has seen the moral issue involved. . . ." No nation ever achieved lasting greatness by practicing immorality in its public policies, at least in the modern era. We cannot solve our problems by victimizing one class of our citizenry or another. And so I ask you here today to look at what we as a nation are doing and judge by a simple standard: is it moral?

The Salk Vaccine

It was on this day in 1954 in the city of Pittsburgh that one of the great achievements of modern science began to take shape. The experimental Salk vaccine against polio was administered by inoculation to children in that city. This was the breakthrough that led to the control of what had been one of the most terrible killers and cripplers of children—and not only of children. Franklin D. Roosevelt was a mature man when polio struck him down. The development of antipolio vaccines was only one in a long parade of miracles of preventive medicine—so many that we are entitled to hope for even more miracles to come. Alas, we have all too many diseases that so far have defied prevention. And even where we know how to prevent them—sometimes by simply providing enough of the proper food—we haven't yet done as good a job as we should. Sometimes it seems that humanity is determined to kill itself—if not by war, then by drugs or improper diets or reckless disregard of elementary facts of public health such as waste disposal. It is interesting that we somehow can get more worked up about a penny arcade in the wrong part of town than about careless dumping of hazardous wastes or adulteration of food. It is time, I suggest, not merely to worry about public health but to do something about it.

Federal Radio Commission

Radio was the hot new medium, busting out all over the place, back on this day in 1927, when Congress passed a bill to set up a Federal Radio Commission. This was the forerunner of the later Federal Communications Commission. It was also the dawn of a new day in government regulation. For the first time, government was licensing and regulating a news medium. What is unthinkable for the printed press was regarded then as perfectly respectable when applied to the airwaves. And we still are inclined to try to tell broadcasters what to report.

Samuel Pepys

On this day in 1633 in the city of London, a son was born to a local tailor. His name was Samuel Pepys. He kept a diary conscientiously for years, and it has become one of the most important sources for the history of the beginning of the British Restoration. I wonder what kind of diary Pepys would keep if he were living today. I am inclined to think that the essential elements—relationships between people, for example—remain the same. In Pepys's time there were power struggles and gossip and all the rest. They still exist. All that has changed is the number of people and the pace. If I were Samuel Pepys writing in my diary today, I would have an entry like this.

FEBRUARY 24

Estonia

On this day in 1919, the defenders of an independent little nation named Estonia, located on the Gulf of Finland, happily reported that the invading Bolshevik army had been cleared from the country. Estonia had been part of tsarist Russia, but had opted through its parliament for independence in November 1917 and finally proclaimed its free status on this date in 1918. It took exactly a year to get first the Germans and then the Bolsheviks out of the country. Unfortunately, this anniversary does not have a happy ending. After twenty years, when Nazi Germany and Soviet Russia signed a nonaggression treaty, Estonia was put into the Soviet sphere of influence. In 1940, Soviet forces occupied the nation, and on August 6 of that year Estonia was brought back into Russia. There is a lesson for all of us in this story. The Soviets do not change their objectives. They merely bide their time, waiting to act at the appropriate moment. This is not necessarily a Bolshevik peculiarity. It is, if history can be trusted, a Russian characteristic. And we should always be aware of it, even when the regime in Moscow changes.

February Face

In William Shakespeare's *Much Ado about Nothing*, there is a description of what the playwright calls "a February face." A February face, it seems, is "full of frost, of storm and cloudiness." I am looking out at this moment into a sea of February faces, and I am happy to report that I see no frost, no storm, and very little cloudiness. I can only hope that as I proceed with my remarks today those gloomy February faces that Shakespeare wrote about will continue to be simply figments of his imagination.

Intermission

Although the practice has changed in many educational institutions because the school calendar is different, February remains for many students the time of the welcome break between semesters. It is also the month that encourages speakers. February speakers in most parts of the country know that unless they are hopeless bores they provide a palatable alternative to going out into the cold.

O'Connell's Maxim

The great Irish leader Daniel O'Connell was a fiery champion of Irish freedom but an implacable foe of violence. On this day in 1824, he stated his basic view. "Whatever little we have gained," he said, "we have gained by agitation, while we have uniformly lost by moderation." That remark bears some attention today. Daniel O'Connell knew, as some leaders of purported independence movements today do not seem to realize, that demonstrations can be more effective than bombs, campaign speeches more productive than whisperings. Terrorism fails when terrorists learn that they cannot intimidate whole nations; it succeeds when nations, understandably to save lives, give in to terrorist demands. Yet the virus remains. We live in times when violence is too much with us. The challenge to us is not just to do something about it but to do the right thing.

FEBRUARY 25

Income Tax

Something that happened on this day in 1913 has left its mark on all of us. The event was the ratification of the Sixteenth Amendment to the U.S.

Constitution. The Sixteenth Amendment, to refresh your memory, authorizes Uncle Sam to impose an income tax. Uncle Sam has not been bashful about using that authority. Once the government gets the power to do something, that power is generally used more and more. The income tax began with a very modest rate and grew and grew. In recent years there has been growing pressure for all kinds of constitutional amendments. That makes it more important than ever to learn the lesson of the Sixteenth Amendment: give the government an inch of new power and it will grow to a mile. We should ask ourselves every time an amendment is proposed what sort of doors it opens to new areas of government power.

José de San Martín

Today is the birthday of one of the great heroes of independence in Latin America. On this day in 1778 in a town on the Uruguay River, José de San Martín was born. San Martín was the general whose military brilliance was responsible for freeing Argentina, Chile, and Peru from Spanish rule, but he appears to have collided with Simón Bolívar. After a meeting of the two South American independence leaders, San Martín withdrew to private life, ultimately as an exile in Europe. Sadly, he lived and died in poverty; not even the nations he had led to freedom availed themselves of his services. History is full of generals who went on to become leaders of nations. San Martín's story is a reminder that such success is not automatic, and even a great commander may find he is not the indispensable man. That is a lesson we can almost always apply to our own bailiwick.

Sir Christopher Wren

Some men and women are great in their own time but leave no lasting mark on history. A few gifted people leave a heritage for the ages. When Sir Christopher Wren died at the age of 90 on this day in 1723, he was among his masterpieces, and he was buried in one of them, St. Paul's Cathedral. Christopher Wren was fortunate not only to have been born with a God-given talent for architecture but also to have been given an opportunity few people can duplicate. When he was in his thirties the Great Fire of London destroyed much of that city. Wren was called upon to design no less than 52 churches, as well as to reconstruct the great St. Paul's Cathedral. He also designed buildings in other parts of England, but the city of London contained his showpieces, and some, like St. Paul's, survive gloriously today. Others of his triumphs include Kensington Palace and Hampton Court. It is worth nothing that Wren's distinguished career began in a moment of great trauma for his city, and therefore for his country. Somehow, difficult times seem to produce men and women capable of meeting the challenge. Can we expect less in our own day?

First Gasoline Tax

The federal income tax was born on this day, but this is the anniversary as well of another ingenious way for government to get money from the public. On this day in 1919, we are told, the state of Oregon pioneered a brand new government charge—the first tax on gasoline. From that humble beginning we have developed a laundry list of excise and sales taxes that has one notable characteristic. It seems never to shrink. The Founding Fathers fought a revolution in protest against taxation without representation. The question is what we can do about taxation *with* representation.

FEBRUARY 26

Victor Hugo

Today is the birthday of Victor Hugo, the author of *The Hunchback of Notre Dame.* Hugo, one of the giants of French literature, was born in 1802 and lived through a stormy period. He went into exile when Louis Napoleon took over as a dictator, then returned to the Third Republic for high honors and membership in the senate. He was idolized and treated as a demigod in his native land, not only for *Notre Dame de Paris, Les Miserables,* and his many other great works but also for his public positions. Few literary giants have achieved the public acclaim that was Hugo's in his lifetime. We have a tendency to be blasé about authors today. If Hugo were an American writer of today we might expect to see him on the television talk shows, but if he sought public office the chances are that people would scoff and say, "After all, he's only a writer." And—oh, yes—if Hugo were writing today in America I am sure there would be those who would want his books kept out of libraries.

Grand Canyon National Park

On this day in 1919, Congress voted to give the Grand Canyon status as a national park. Looking back with the perspective of subsequent years, we should be profoundly grateful that this magnificent work of nature has been saved from being decorated with refreshment stands, souvenir shops, and commercial developments. Without some kind of government action, such as designating an area as a national park, we can be relied upon to move in on nature, commercialize, and, yes, even destroy. There has to be a middle ground between extreme conservationism, which makes every piece of nature untouchable, and extreme commercialism, which makes every piece of nature exploitable. I think it is time for those of us who are at neither end of that spectrum to speak up in behalf of the sensible compromise.

Round the World

On this day in 1949, a B-50 superfortress airplane named *Lucky Lady II* took off from Carswell Air Force Base in Texas to try to fly nonstop around the world. Thanks to four midair refuelings it succeeded, flying the more than 23,000 miles in 94 hours, at an average speed of some 294 miles an hour. Today, the average commercial plane flies at twice that speed. We get wherever we are going faster. Life today is more impatient than it was in 1949. Everything is speeded up. We pass a law and look for its effects the next day. We search for instant cures, quick profits, fast tracks. I am here today to call for a more deliberate outlook, more patience. As in the case I have chosen to make my point.

From Here to Eternity

On this day an unusual novel by a former soldier was published in 1951. The author was James Jones and the book was *From Here to Eternity,* an enlisted man's view of the U.S. Army in peace and war. The novel was published half a dozen years after the war it talked about had ended. It probably could not have appeared much sooner, because when we are in a war we tend to romanticize it and to reject hardboiled, realistic fiction about it. In bad times it is often difficult to get people to pay enough attention to realistic novels about those times. *The Grapes of Wrath,* John Steinbeck's masterpiece about the Dust Bowl and the plight of the Okies, appeared in 1939 when that story was already history. And so it is today. There are issues that deserve more attention than they are getting, conditions some future novelist will capture to great applause.

FEBRUARY 27

Lincoln at Cooper Union

In 1860 on this day, a lanky man came to New York from Illinois. He delivered a speech at Cooper Union. When it was over Abraham Lincoln was a national figure to be reckoned with, and nine months later he was elected president. Probably the most quoted statement from Lincoln's Cooper Union address is this: "Let us have faith that right makes might, and in that faith let us to the end dare to do our duty as we understand it." Not a bad theme for our time as well as Lincoln's. We have the altogether human tendency sometimes to prefer what is expedient to what is right. Generally speaking, what is expedient is rarely right and is often dead wrong. Applying palliatives to social problems when vigorous changes are needed is just such an expedient. We should not be expedient today. We should be right.

Ralph Nader

The consumerist movement in the United States has many champions, but if one name stood out in the formative years it would probably be that of Ralph Nader, who was born on this day in 1934 in Winsted, Connecticut. In looking at the rise of Ralph Nader, I am struck by the part played by his first major target, General Motors. Although Nader had already written a best-selling book entitled *Unsafe at Any Speed*, what really put him in the headlines and made him an outstandingly newsworthy figure was the revelation, first denied and then admitted by General Motors, that the company had conducted an investigation of him with "some harassment." Sometimes it is not our friends but our enemies who give us stature. How often have you taken a position on a public issue because of the nature of the opposition? In looking at the problems that confront us today, it is often worthwhile to look at the identity and the tactics of the antagonists.

Nixon in China

President Richard M. Nixon is probably principally remembered as the central figure in the Watergate case, but on this day in 1972 he may well have had his finest hour. That was when he completed his historic visit to the People's Republic of China, ending the long years of hostility and silence between that country and the United States. It was commonly thought at the time that Nixon was able to persuade the American people to support his visit to China because there wasn't the slightest suspicion that he shared any of the political philosophy of his hosts. We accept actions from some people that we don't accept from others. While on occasion we judge an action dispassionately, we are more likely to look at the motives of the people involved. And that isn't a bad idea. In looking at our national policies, the first question we should ask about any element of policy is "Why?" That is what I will be asking and endeavoring to answer here today.

Fifteenth Amendment

On this day in 1869, Congress passed what became the Fifteenth Amendment to the Constitution, designed to guarantee that—and I quote—"the right of citizens of the United States to vote shall not be denied or abridged by the United States or by any State on account of race, color, or previous condition of servitude." We had just fought a civil war that freed the slaves, and the winning side was determined to see that as freed people the new citizens could make their voices heard at the polls. But it didn't work out that way for almost another hundred years, because Congress and its supporters underestimated the ingenuity with which local officials in the erstwhile slave states managed to disqualify black voters. The Fifteenth was not the only amendment to be made a mockery by lack of public support. It happened to the Eighteenth Amendment, Prohibition, as well. It simply isn't enough to pass a law to deal with a problem. With or without a law the most important ingredient is public support. That is why an informed public is always our best defense. I don't know whether the information I am about to give you will be new to you, but I do know that it concerns issues on which it is important that each of you take a stand.

FEBRUARY 28

Republican Party

Today is the anniversary of an historic meeting that was held in Ripon, Wisconsin, in 1854. Members of the crumbling Whig party and antislavery leaders met to suggest that it was time for this country to have a new political party, for which they proposed the name *Republican*. It was only seven years later that the first Republican president, Abraham Lincoln, moved into the White House. We like to think of our times as moving much faster than earlier centuries, but the story of the rise of the Republican Party reminds us not to underestimate new political movements. If we look around, we can see party stirrings that are incubating the issues and loyalties of tomorrow and the day after. Some things that may seem far-out today will be the burning questions of the future.

Montaigne

The great French essayist Michel de Montaigne was born on this day in 1533, which makes it appropriate for me to quote him. He wrote, "The value of life lies not in its time span but in the way we use it; a man may live long yet get little from life. It depends on your own will, rather than on the length of your years, whether your life has been sufficient." Ladies and gentlemen, that is the question we must ask ourselves. Am I using my life so as to get the most out of it? This is not a question of dollars and cents or of creature comforts. It involves doing your part to make the world a better place. There are so many worthy causes that need your help—as contributors, as volunteers, or as champions—that there is ample opportunity for everyone. Today I want to speak to you about one particular cause.

France vs. Soda Pop

At about this time in 1950, the sovereign republic of France declared war on soda pop, ordering a limit on the availability of soft drinks. I assume, of course, that Perrier water and Vichy were exempted from the onslaught. France, of course, is the leading wine producer and wants to see people drink that product rather than anything else. A French Premier named Pierre Mendes France once suggested that milk was a better drink, and all hell broke loose among his constituents. You can't change habits or nip the popularity of something people want to consume simply by passing a law or issuing a manifesto. It takes a long educational campaign, as for example the assault on smoking, before you can begin to see results. We've been trying to educate people about the dangers of many over-the-counter pills, and we still have a long way to go. The question for each of us is a simple one: Am I doing my part to deal with this or some other clear and present danger? If not, it is never too late to start.

Hot Stove League

We are approaching the end of the hot stove league season in baseball as the players head south to training camp, but before the hot stove league time comes to an end I would like to say a few words about how things have changed. Years ago the subjects of discussion about baseball in the winter were player trades and the physical condition of this star or that. In recent seasons, however, most of the talk has been about money. This seems to be happening in many other fields of endeavor. The dollar sign is taking over. We are judging things by their market value rather than by their intrinsic merit. Some of this is inevitable; a great deal of the essentials of life, from food to housing, must be bought over the counter, and price is one of the considerations. But we are too tolerant of landlords who gouge, storekeepers who raise prices of what is already on their shelves when a future shortage looms because of weather conditions, free-loaders in government positions, and the like. These are just a few of the things that I'd like to discuss in my own hot stove league.

FEBRUARY 29

Seal Hunting Crisis

On this day in 1892, the United States and Great Britain, after a bitter war of words, concluded a treaty agreeing to international arbitration of a controversy over the right to hunt seals in the Bering Sea. The United States had ordered British ships to stop hunting seals there beyond the three-mile coastal limit because the United States had awarded exclusive rights to a private contractor. The British claimed the United States could not exercise such exclusivity, and the international tribunal of Italian, French, and Swedish representatives found the United States was wrong and went on to prohibit sealing in a large zone around the Pribilof Islands of Alaska for part of the year. That particular limitation on seal hunting didn't last beyond 1908, but it was a beginning. More importantly, what could have been a sore point for years was settled peacefully and in a civilized fashion, proving that it can be done if nations are sensible. Can the United Nations become that kind of arbitrator? Is there any other method—other than the toothless World Court—of peaceful settlement of bitter international disputes?

Neutrality Act of 1936

After Italy's invasion of Ethiopia in 1935, Congress authorized the president under certain conditions to prohibit arms shipments to belligerents, with a six-month time limit on this authorization. The Neutrality Act of 1936, effective on this date, extended the provisions of the 1935 act and added a prohibition against granting loans or credits to nations at war. The following year further neutrality provisions were added. These laws were still in effect when World War II began. Before America entered the war, its neutrality was something less than total, thanks to the lend-lease program for aid to Britain. We had learned that neutrality ends when our own way of life is threatened. But the dilemma remains. When is neutrality in our own interest, and when is it giving aid and comfort to an enemy? What are our choices today?

Leap Year Day

This used to be the one day every four years when the girls could propose to the boys. Leap Year Day was a very special opportunity, but the whole idea can't help seeming a little archaic today. Happily, there are very few restrictions on today's woman as compared to the man. Today, I would like to speak on some of the discriminations that remain, and Leap Year Day seems to be a good time for that subject.

John P. Holland

There is an interesting aspect to the career of the father of the U.S. navy submarine, John P. Holland, who was born on this day in 1840 in Ireland. Holland came to this country when he was 33 years old and was already involved in designing submarines. In 1875, the U.S. Navy rejected his ideas, but he got financing to continue his work from a surprising source. He was backed by the Fenian Society, Irishmen who were working for independence from Great Britain while living in the United States. It is supposed that they thought they might use submarines in that fight. After a number of failures Holland built a new kind of submarine and in 1900 the Navy bought the vessel to start its submarine branch. So we can thank a group of Irish expatriates who were interested in things other than the defense of the United States for helping to bring this country—and the world—into the age of the submarine. I guess this proves a couple of things. The first is that if your bright ideas get turned down the first time it doesn't mean they'll be turned down again when you polish them. The second thing that John Holland's story suggests is that if you're turned down by your primary angel, there's always a chance that another angel will turn up. Today I'd like to speak about some ideas which, like John Holland's early submarine, deserve a second chance.

MARCH 1

New Year's Day

I want to wish each of you a very happy new year. If you think this is a strange time to be taking note of a new year, let me assure you that I have historical precedent. Long ago, in the times before the year 154 B.C., today was the start of the new year. And nowadays, even though the calendar recognizes January 1 as the starting point, the fact is that March is still the month when a lot of annual things begin and the winter comes to an end. So, in speaking to you today, I suggest that we are at the beginning of new times. Times for new ideas and new starts. We need to discard some of the ingrained notions that have weighed us down.

Red Cross Month

Today we start the annual observance of Red Cross Month. We have Red Cross Month because throughout the year the Red Cross works without the benefit of too much publicity, and every year we have to be reminded that it is out there doing its job and looking to us for support. The Red Cross—and most service organizations—look to the public not only for cash but for volunteers. If you can't give money you can still give of yourself. Volunteerism is one of America's great strengths. There are literally dozens, maybe even hundreds, of ways you can serve your community, not with money but by *doing* something.

Articles of Confederation

Today is a sort of birthday for the United States, even though we pay very little attention to it. It was on this day in 1781 that the Articles of Confederation, the first attempt to provide an overall governmental pattern for the union of the various colonies, were ratified. The next day the Continental Congress assumed a new title, calling itself the United States in Congress Assembled. The Articles of Confederation didn't work out very satisfactorily, and after less than a decade a stronger system of government, under a brand new Constitution, went into effect. But today marked a formal beginning in 1781 of a new nation that was still learning how to pull itself together. We can't sit back these many years later and say we're pulling together all the way. Sectional rivalries still exist; regional blocs still swing weight in the Congress. There probably isn't a single part of the country where the people, if you asked them, would say they are getting their fair share of federal expenditures and that other sections are also getting fair shares. Everybody always wants a bigger piece of the pie. But have you looked at that pie lately?

Gunfire in the House

One does not normally regard service in the House of Representatives as combat duty, but on this day in 1954 five congressmen were wounded in the Capitol when Puerto Rican terrorists opened fire. Since then, terrorism, which we used to think of as purely a foreign problem, has become all too commonplace even in our own country. Most terrorist groups use violence because they don't have popular support. They try to impose their will on others through force and threats of force. I, on the other hand, come to you unarmed—except, I hope, with some information and comments that you will find persuasive.

MARCH 2

Time

This was the day back in 1923 when the news magazine *Time* was first published. It brought a new dimension to the reporting of news, not merely summarizing what had already appeared in the daily newspapers but adding further information and background. It was accused time and time again of adding editorial coloration, but the seeming thoroughness of *Time*'s reporting won millions of readers and became the foundation of a great publishing empire. What this tells me is that in most news there is more than first meets the eye. Dig a little deeper, and you may be surprised. Accordingly, I have dug a little deeper into one particular matter, which I think is worth reporting to you.

Elastic Rules

In the early years of his presidency, Franklin D. Roosevelt had his troubles with a Supreme Court that he felt was interpreting the Constitution too narrowly. When he was governor of New York he had expounded quite a different view of our basic law. On this day in 1930, Roosevelt said, "The United States Constitution has proved itself the most marvelously elastic compilation of rules of government ever written." Another governor of the state of New York, Charles Evans Hughes, who was later to become Chief Justice of the United States, said, "We are under a Constitution, but the Constitution is what the judges say it is." We see things, whether in the Constitution's words or in everyday life, from a perspective—either our own perspective or that of the person who is reporting to us. What I am going to speak about here today is the product of my own perspective.

Dr. Seuss

Today is the birthday of an artist–writer who truly stands alone in his field. His name is Theodore S. Geisel, and when I tell you what the S stands for you will recognize him immediately. It stands for Seuss, and he is better known as Dr. Seuss. He was born on this day in 1904. Dr. Seuss created a whole fascinating world of strange creatures whose stories he told in simple poetry that a child could understand and an adult could enjoy as well. The grinch who stole Christmas, Horton the elephant who hatched an egg, and all the rest of Dr. Seuss's wonderful characters have brightened the lives of millions. Dr. Seuss's characters are not your usual idealized creatures for children, but they have one thing in common. They all work out all right. That's a nice message for growing children, and not a bad one for adults either. And in that spirit I'd like to talk to you today about some of the hopeful signs in our troubled world.

President Hayes

On this day in 1877, a split and allegedly partisan special electoral commission declared Rutherford B. Hayes the winner over Samuel Tilden in the presidential election that had been held the previous November. The commission's decision came barely forty-eight hours before the new president was due to be inaugurated. To date, that is the most delayed and complicated presidential election we have known. It points up some of the potential complications in our still cumbersome presidential election process. We are still using a horse-and-buggy procedure for picking our presidents, beginning with the convention horse trading and winding up with an electoral college that makes it possible for the candidate with the largest popular vote to lose. How can we bring this process into the twentieth century?

MARCH 3

The Limits of Free Speech

Associate Justice Oliver Wendell Holmes Jr. was one of the outstanding liberal justices of his time, but on this day in 1919, in a decision that remains a landmark, he put a common-sense limitation on the right of free speech. "The most stringent protection of free speech," he wrote, "would not protect a man in falsely shouting fire in a theater and causing a panic." Today, hopeful of not giving you cries of fire falsely uttered in a crowded theater, I intend simply to give you some food for thought.

First Veto Override

In 1845 this was a landmark day. For the first time in our history a presidential veto was overridden by Congress. Up to then, whenever a president objected to a bill placed on his desk, he was able to make his veto stick. Now, I happen to think that what Congress did on this day in 1845, without regard for the particular bill involved, was good. It is part of our governmental system of checks and balances that each branch of government has power to deal with the actions of the other branches—not unlimited power, by any means, but enough to keep any branch from having a free hand. This system of checks and balances is good for our country not only in government but in everyday life for the individual citizen as well. It is important for each of us not only to have the opportunity to speak up but to be protected against government on occasion as well as against other individuals. What is the state of that kind of protection today?

Peanut Month

For many years March has been observed as Peanut Month, in honor of one of our U.S. crops that, however popular, has never achieved the status of wheat or cattle. When Jimmy Carter ran for president he was described as a peanut farmer, and some of his opponents used that as a term of reproach. Nobody ever suggested that a wheat farmer was small potatoes, but somehow the peanut just hasn't rated the same prestige. When we speak of a peanut brain, we are not being complimentary; when we say that someone's earnings are peanuts, we aren't speaking well of either the earnings or the peanuts. We have a lot of very worthy products and ideas that, like the peanut, deserve a better public image than they seem to have. Today I'd like to talk about one of them.

Department of the Interior

I find it interesting that when the U.S. Department of the Interior was created on this day in 1849 it had another name. It was called the Home Department. Of course, what they meant was home as compared to foreign, not home where the family lives, but the old name reminds us how much the job of the Department of the Interior has changed. Back in 1849 they didn't have any national parks or offshore oil rights to worry about. As is the case with most things, life today is a lot more complicated than it was more than a hundred years ago. Some of the modern complications have come from growth and technological change and expanded public conscience. Yet many others have arisen simply because of somebody's eloquent salesmanship. I plan to do my best here today to be eloquent, but I hope that what I have to say produces no complications.

MARCH 4

Save Your Vision Week

Early every March one of the special observances, dating back quite a while, is National Save Your Vision Week. It's sponsored by the optometrists, not the spiritualists, but the kind of vision I'd like to talk about today is not what enables you to see things as they are. I'd like to discuss some visions of things as they ought to be, and how we can make them real.

Pulaski

Today is the birthday of a fighter for Polish independence. How ironic that hundreds of years later that fight is still being fought. The Polish independence fighter came to this country in 1777 to join George Washington's Continental Army. He was Casimir Pulaski, born in 1747 and killed in October 1779, in the Battle of Savannah. The American Revolution in its time was the hope of lovers of freedom all over the world. Some, like Casimir Pulaski, didn't merely root for our side; they fought with us, side by side. I believe that America is still the hope of lovers of freedom all over the world. They may jeer at "Uncle Shylock" or at the U.S. nuclear arsenal, but this is the country they want to come to and live in. Today I'd like to talk about some of the reasons this is so.

Vermont

If you think Vermonters are stubborn, something that happened on this day in 1791 is worth noting. That was the day when Vermont, which had fought gallantly in the American Revolution, notably represented by Ethan Allen and his Green Mountain Boys, finally settled its other dispute. Back in 1749, the royal governor of New Hampshire had claimed title to Vermont. It was then called the New Hampshire Grants, and a lot of people from Connecticut and Massachusetts purchased land there and built their homes. Then, in 1770, the New York courts ruled that New Hampshire's claim to Vermont, at least the eastern portion bordering New York State, was invalid, which meant that New York was claiming the land the New Hampshire Grants had sold to the farmers. That was when Ethan Allen organized the Green Mountain Boys, long before the American Revolution, to defend the New Hampshire Grants. During the Revolution, Vermont issued its own declaration of independence in 1777 and adopted a constitution that was, incidentally, the first to prohibit slavery. But although Vermonters continued prominently as Revolutionary War soldiers, their state was not recognized by the others. It was not until 1790 that New York accepted Vermont's independence, after extracting a payment of $30,000. On this day in 1791, the Green Mountain State finally was admitted to the United States. It was the fourteenth state, the first after the original thirteen. Now, as far as I'm concerned, that is a good testimonial to the stubbornness of Vermonters. It is an equally good testimonial to the fact that, in this country, if you fight hard enough and long enough for what you believe in, you are likely to win in the end. The question is, what do we really believe in today?

Presidential Eloquence

This is one day of the year when there is so much eloquence to recall that it can make a speaker self-conscious. Until after Franklin D. Roosevelt's first term, this was Presidential Inauguration Day, before it was pushed up to January 20. It was on this day in 1801 that Thomas Jefferson looked at America's relations with other countries and urged "entangling alliances with none." Abraham Lincoln spoke "with malice toward none; with charity for all; with firmness in the right, as God gives us to see the right." And FDR told us back in 1933 that "the only thing we have to fear is fear itself." I do not propose to try to equal any of these examples of March 4 eloquence, even though I speak with malice toward none and with firmness in the right as God gives me to see the right. I stand at this podium to speak plainly, and I thank you for your attention.

MARCH 5

Banks Closed

This is the day when, in 1933, just 24 hours after he became president, Franklin D. Roosevelt ordered the banks closed and banned the export of gold to stop a growing panic as the Depression intensified. What FDR did was unprecedented. He also called Congress into special session beginning March 9. Roosevelt's prompt action worked. The depression didn't end, but the panic did. And I suspect it wasn't because of what Roosevelt did but rather because he didn't just stand there—he did something. If you think something needs doing, do it. Do it now, and don't do it halfway. I think those standards also apply to speakers. If you have something to say, say it, say it without wasting time, and say it frankly and unhesitatingly. Having noted those standards, I leave myself no way out but to try to live up to them here today.

Nuclear Nonproliferation

On this day in 1970, a nuclear nonproliferation treaty signed by the United States, the Soviet Union, and 41 other nations went into effect. How much it may have slowed or deterred the nuclear arms race is hard to determine, because we don't know what would have happened without it. That is one of the problems that arise when you try to achieve a total judgment about a national or international policy. Unless it proves to be a total disaster or a total success, you can't be sure whether or not it was the best course. Not even in hindsight can you deliver an absolutely total judgment, and I won't do so today.

Steinway in America

On this day in 1853, a German immigrant whose name was anglicized to Henry Steinway opened a factory in New York to manufacture pianos. The quality of his long-lasting product is legendary. Sometimes I wish that instead of a speaker's rostrum I had a piano and the ability to play it in front of you. Few people get angrily upset over good music, whereas if a speaker takes a controversial position some of the audience may take strong exception. But I am here to talk, not to concertize, so I might as well face the music.

Hancock's Words

John Hancock, the President of the Continental Congress, was a speaker at the memorial meeting in Boston on this day in 1774, in tribute to the victims of the Boston Massacre, when British troops had killed demonstrating Americans. Describing the unwelcome presence of the British forces, Hancock said, "Our streets nightly resounded with the noise of riot and debauchery; our peaceful citizens were hourly exposed to shameful insults. . . ." I find it interesting that there are some places in America where what Hancock said in 1774 applies today, not because of armies of occupation but because of some of our own unruly people. Walt Kelly, the cartoonist, had his character Pogo say in one panel, "We have met the enemy and he is us." It is true, and I am here today to ask what we are going to do about it.

MARCH 6

National Procrastination Week

There is a familiar saying: "Never put off till tomorrow what you can put off any longer." In that spirit the month of March brings National Procrastination Week, an observance dedicated to the idea that if you don't do anything about it, whatever it is, it may go away. When a speaker is introduced to an audience, however, he or she can't really procrastinate. A speaker may take time to get to the point, but silence is not one of our privileges. I don't want you to think that I am being forced to make my remarks here today. Indeed, I think the time is ripe, if not overdue, for somebody to say what I am about to say to you.

World Day of Prayer

The first Friday in March is currently observed as World Day of Prayer, and I must confess that this year, as in most years, we have plenty to pray about in this season. So it seems an appropriate time for me to talk to you about some of the hopes and dreams that are important to all of us.

Lincoln's Attempt to Buy Peace

Abraham Lincoln is justifiably remembered for such great acts as the Emancipation Proclamation, but not too long before he issued that historic document he tried a different approach to the problem of slavery, an approach he hoped might end the Civil War. Today is the anniversary of Lincoln's 1862 message to Congress proposing that the United States give financial compensation to the states, which in turn would compensate slaveowners for freeing their slaves. "Any member of Congress," said President Lincoln, "with the census tables and treasury reports before him, can readily see for himself how very soon the current expenditures of the war would purchase, at fair valuation, all the slaves in any named State." Lincoln found out in short order that this entirely sensible scheme satisfied nobody. Wars, once started, are hard to stop. Perhaps if Lincoln had made his proposal before the shooting began, it might have had more of a chance. The important thing is not just to have a good idea but to have it at the right time. I can only hope that the ideas I am about to present to you meet that standard.

Frozen Food

Birdseye frozen foods were introduced on this day in 1930 in Springfield, Massachusetts, and we have been accumulating frozen assets on the grocery shelves ever since. This was one of the high points in people's unceasing efforts to make things last longer. But one thing that shouldn't last any longer than necessary is a speech. Frozen foods go on and on, but speakers, in addition to knowing how to start, have to make sure they know when to stop. Let's see whether I pass the test.

MARCH 7

Levittown

It was on this day in 1949 that a revolution in housing developments began, as the mass-produced, single-family dwellings of a new community, named Levittown after its developer, opened on Long Island. It wasn't too long before Levittown became not only the name of several communities all built from scratch on a mass-production basis, but also the symbol of a particular kind of living. Using a single word to describe a whole way of life is convenient verbal shorthand, but unfortunately we do too much of it. We pin labels on people and things that apply only to some, not all, aspects of them. We concern ourselves too much with whether a person is on the left or in the middle, rather than informing ourselves about where that person stands on particular issues. We speak of organized labor, or the establishment, or Wall Street, as if each of these were a complete monolith rather than a cauldron of conflicting views. I do not intend to do that here today. We have enough easily recognized proponents of most current issues on all sides so that we can be specific, and that is my goal now.

Holmes at 90

When the great Justice Oliver Wendell Holmes previewed his 90th birthday on this day in 1931, in his brief remarks in a radio program he said, "The work is never done while the power to work remains." We have so much we could do, so much that retired people could be doing for and with us. Today I'd like to talk about some of these needs and the opportunities they present.

Women Drivers

One of the sidelight items of history for this day is that in 1908 the Mayor of Cincinnati is supposed to have told his city council that women just weren't able to drive cars. The Mayor was obviously operating with very foggy headlights, but he wasn't unique. Long before and after him millions of men have been positive that women couldn't do the things that men do. This doesn't prove that millions of men are villains. What it indicates is that the bulk of support of prejudice in this country doesn't come from haters. It comes from people, men and women, who give aid and comfort to it simply by doing nothing about it. For example, because you think some job is too much for women doesn't give you the right to deny them a crack at it. But if you go along with denials of equal opportunity simply by not acting against them you are encouraging the denial of equal opportunity. And that brings us to the question of the day. What can we do in practical terms, as individuals, about prejudice in this country?

Anthony Comstock

Today is the birthday of the most persistent self-appointed guardian of public morality this country has known. His name was Anthony Comstock, and he was born in 1844. Comstock made a career of ferreting out and prosecuting what he regarded as public immorality. He had plenty of legitimate targets, but, like so many crusaders, he let his zeal overpower his common sense. He wanted Victoria Woodhull, a woman's rights crusader, criminally prosecuted for exposing an affair between the Reverend Henry Ward Beecher and one of the Reverend's parishioners, and he went to court to try to suppress George Bernard Shaw's play *Mrs. Warren's Profession.* Shaw retaliated by inventing the word *comstockery* to describe the kind of narrowmindedness that Anthony Comstock represented. Anthony Comstock is long dead, but both pornography and comstockery still live. It seems to me that what is involved is basically a challenge to raise the level of public taste. How do we do that?

MARCH 8

International Women's Day

This day, the eighth of March, has been observed for years as International Women's Day, not to indicate that women are any more international than men but to emphasize the continuing struggle to obtain and protect rights for women around the world. Although the struggle is worldwide, some parts of the earth, like the United States, are way ahead of the others. There may still be some distant places where the women can't talk until the men let them. In this country some men contend that their problem is getting a word in edgewise. For a public speaker, however, the problem is not getting a word in edgewise but rather getting the right words out. With your indulgence I will proceed to that assignment.

Stamp Act

Britain's House of Lords has little or no power today, but back in 1765 on this day it possessed a good deal more authority, which it did not use wisely. This was the day when the House of Lords passed the Stamp Act. As many of you know, the Stamp Act imposed all kinds of taxes on the American colonies, supposedly to pay for their defense. It was this ill-considered piece of legislation that led to the outcry in America against "taxation without representation" and ultimately to the American Revolution. Today one of the most intolerable impositions on the public is of a different kind—not just a government that loots your pocketbook but a public speaker who taxes your patience. Instead, I shall try today to catch your fancy.

Troops in Vietnam

This was the day when the die was cast. In 1965 on this day, the first U.S. land fighting force of 3,500 Marines landed at Danang in Vietnam, and all too soon we were knee deep in the most frustrating war in our history. This was not the pure beginning of our involvement; advisers and small units had been dispatched to Vietnam long before. But this was the beginning of real fighting commitment. It is, I think, a day to remember—not a happy memory, but a significant one. One of the things it tells us is that nations, like individual human beings, can find themselves getting deeper and deeper into something, with the best of motives, that ends up being far more of an impossible situation than we ever anticipated. That has turned out to be true not just of military actions but of things like government entitlement programs, installment purchases, and many other things. Today I would like to put up some caution signs to prevent us from getting deeper and deeper into some future traps.

Fingerprints

On this day in 1911, in New York City, a man named Caesar Cella committed a burglary. We know this because his fingerprints were introduced as evidence at his trial, and he was convicted. This was the first use of fingerprints for criminal identification in the United States. I wonder where crime fighting would be today without the use of fingerprints. I know, as I stand here, I face the fact that my words, inevitably, can't be half as distinctive as my fingerprints. But my fingerprints can't tell you what I think or how I feel about things that concern us all. For that, this platform is a welcome opportunity, and I thank you for your attention.

MARCH 9

FDR's 100 Days

Today is the anniversary of the commencement of the so-called "100 days" of 1933. On this day the 73rd Congress met in a special session convened by the brand new President, Franklin D. Roosevelt. In the period of 100 days, that Congress produced some of the most important legislation this country had seen. Designed to reverse the growing crisis of a raging economic depression, the new laws included the establishment of a Civilian Conservation Corps with up to 250,000 jobs for young males in conservation work, the establishment of parity prices and subsidies for farm products, the Tennessee Valley Authority, the first meaningful regulation of newly issued securities on the stock exchanges, and homeowners' refinancing, as well as a new farm credit act. Congress has very rarely, if ever, produced a higher ratio of action to talk. With all the legislation, there wasn't much time for talk. The situation here today, at least in this room, is very different. We have no legislative power, but I have not merely an opportunity but indeed an invitation to talk. And I accept, with thanks.

Lincoln Takes the Plunge

On this day in 1832, an announcement was distributed in New Salem, Illinois, and the surrounding area. A young man newly arrived in New Salem, 23 years old, declared his candidacy for the Illinois State Assembly. His name, as you may have guessed, was Abraham Lincoln, and he was doomed to momentary disappointment. He lost the election. In later years, of course, he was more successful. Lincoln had set his sights on public office. How wonderful for the nation that he did not let a defeat the first time out destroy his long-range ambition! And how important it is today for each and every one of us to stick to our hopes and dreams for the future in the face of momentary discouragement.

We always think that our problems are worse than those our parents faced. They thought the same thing about themselves and their parents. They didn't give up, and neither must we. Instead, we should be devoting our attention to doing something about it. Here are some suggestions.

FDR's Court-Packing Speech

Franklin D. Roosevelt was probably the most effective public speaker this country has had. He invented the broadcast fireside chat. He demolished political opponents and charmed the rest of the nation. But this is an anniversary of one of the few times his oratory got him nowhere. On this day in 1937, just after beginning his second term in a tremendous election victory, he went directly to the people in a fireside chat to try to save his plan for reorganizing the Supreme Court to a maximum of 15 justices instead of nine. Congress and the press had been less than cordial to the proposal, so FDR went to the audience that always supported him, the people. But it didn't work. Even the greatest political speaker of his time couldn't turn the tide. The plan for the Supreme Court was rejected. Now, if so great an orator couldn't make his message stick, anyone who gets up to present another message should remember that words can only accomplish just so much. My subject today, of course, is not quite as profound as the organization of the Supreme Court. Nevertheless, I hope that what I have to say will give you something to think about.

Amerigo Vespucci Day

This is the day when the man who gave his name to America was born. He was Amerigo Vespucci, and he was born in Florence, Italy, in 1451. Vespucci's purported explorations of the New World were proudly written up by him in works referring to the "lands of Amerigo Vespucci," which soon became known as the lands of America. We are fortunate, I suppose. If he hadn't used his first name in the title of his works, we might be living now in the United States of Vespucci. We are not, of course, living in anything like the world that Vespucci knew, but some things remain constant. It still takes imagination and daring and often a great deal of money to explore new frontiers, and sometimes we hesitate to make that kind of commitment. But I wonder. Is this a time to hesitate? Can we afford to lay back on our efforts to make a better world?

MARCH 10

Lillian D. Wald

One of the glories of our nation is that through the years its people have steadily found new ways to do good. This is the birthday of a great American benefactor, Lillian D. Wald, who was born in Cincinnati in 1867, and it is an occasion that deserves to be noted. Lillian Wald was the founder of the Henry

Street Settlement, one of the great landmarks of social work, and she established a new type of medical care, the Visiting Nurse Service, which brought trained nurses into the homes of the sick. If that seems commonplace today, it is only because it was such a good idea when Lillian Wald started it. Some people say it was a lot easier to make that kind of contribution in Lillian Wald's time because we needed so many other things. But as long as there are people in need and people fighting for their health, as long as there are people who are struggling against poverty, the opportunities for doing something are right in front of us.

Harriet Tubman

When Harriet Tubman died on this day in 1913 in Auburn, New York, where she had lived for many years, she was in her nineties and sixty years away from the adventures of her youth. Those adventures were an American epic. After Harriet Tubman escaped from slavery in the South in 1849, she was not content to let it go at that. She became the outstanding heroine of the Underground Railroad that brought other slaves clandestinely to freedom in the North. After the Civil War she fought for schools for the newly freed blacks in the South. There have been many great women in America but few who rose to such heights from such depths. I like to think that today the depths are not as deep—for slavery is now barred by law, and racial prejudice no longer has social sanction—and I hope that the opportunities for service are less risky than the Underground Railroad. Some people ask, "What can I, as one person, do?" I'd like to try to supply some answers here today.

Sullivan vs. Mitchell

In a woodland setting in France on this day in 1888, the bare-knuckle heavyweight champion of the world, John L. Sullivan, fought the English challenger, Charlie Mitchell. The fight went 44 rounds, and although Mitchell was on the canvas 15 times the decision was a draw. Looking back at this slugfest, what impresses me is not the decision but the fact that these two pugilists fought for three hours. Can you imagine modern fighters, padded gloves and all, fighting that long?

In many sports today—and probably in other walks of life—it seems to me that we are demanding much less of people in terms of physical or mental effort. We pay football players to be defensive or offensive specialists, whereas the early gridiron professional went all the way both ways. We platoon right-handed and left-handed batters in baseball. We limit fighters to 15 rounds. Go into a retail store, and you are apt to find the clerk using a calculator for addition that used to be done with a pencil on the back of a bag. In some fast-food places the prices are preset on a register, and the machine also figures out what the change should be. I don't deplore any of this. But I feel it is all increasing the pressure on us to take the easy way out in whatever we do, and I don't believe that is a very good idea. Calculators are great, but they are no substitute for knowing how to do arithmetic. Isn't it time to put new emphasis on some fundamentals?

Salvation Army

An army landed on the shore of the United States on this day in 1880, and not a shot was fired. That was because this was the Salvation Army, whose first mission to the United States arrived in New York from England, where the organization had been founded. We think of people looking for streets paved of gold or virgin land waiting to be tilled when we think of immigration to this country. We sometimes forget the number of people who came here for spiritual reasons—not just the Salvation Army but people like the New England colonists seeking religious freedom. Faith and idealism are powerful motivations; they moved the Salvation Army to come here and serve the needy. I think faith and idealism motivate more people than we realize today. And I believe that all of us could do well to have our batteries of faith recharged. I speak not so much of religious faith as of faith in the goodness and the potential of America.

MARCH 11

First Daily Newspaper

It was on this day in 1702 that the first daily newspaper in English began publication in London. It has long ceased to exist, but it created a new form for journalism that increased the flow of information to the public tremendously. We take daily newspapers and our other sources of current information for granted, as if they were always there, but each of the media had to be thought up—invented, if you will—by someone at some time. It is important that creative thinkers, at any period in our history, pursue their ideas without first deciding whether they are practical. Pure research, without an eye to the marketplace, has produced many techniques and many products that later created new markets and new industries. And I believe the same is true of seemingly abstract ideas. I believe that a great deal of progress begins with asking questions. Ask the questions and someone, some time, will find the answers. With that premise, here are some questions I would like to put before you.

Kissinger on Our History

Something Henry Kissinger said on this day in 1976 furnishes me with the basis of my remarks here today. He said, "Americans have always made history rather than let history chart our course." Not all of that American history, as we look back, was made so gloriously by us. We have had our share of bad moments. But we have somehow always felt that we were the masters of our ship, the shapers of our own triumphs. This is not to say that we thumbed our noses at divine Providence. Instead, we prided ourselves on not letting other people or foreign alliances tell us what to do or when to do it. In recent years, it seems to me, we have been fudging it. We have been blaming other nations' trade policies for our own problems. We have been trimming our sails on public issues because of criticism from or sensitivities of other nations. I am not standing up here to argue that we should go back to sending in the Marines. I am, however, taking this occasion to suggest that we try once again to make our own history instead of letting others make it for us. One way to do this, it seems to me, is to avoid making ourselves so responsive to outside currents. Why, for example, should our government subsidize loans to communist nations? Sure, they buy our grain, let us say, but it usually turns out that they are doing it with our money. Why should we accept so many college students from countries that are enemies of ours, at the cost of places for some of our own students? Some may say I am calling for a new isolationism. Not so. What I am calling for is a reassessment of some of the things we don't have to do for other people but are doing at a cost to our own people. I am sure each of you can draw up your own laundry list.

Employ the Older Worker Week

Around this time in March the nation some years ago began to observe National Employ the Older Worker Week. Of course, if older Americans work they pay Social Security taxes instead of collecting Social Security. But I would not want to accuse the government, which proclaimed National Employ the Older Worker Week, of being devious or sneaky. I do not recall, in the annual proclamations of the week that I have seen, any definition of who or what age constitutes an older worker. If it is 50-year-olds, then my comment about Social Security does not apply. If it is 70-year-olds, that is another matter. There is no doubt in my mind that there is a prejudice against older people in this country. And it certainly includes the employer who just wants young people on the payroll or the university that keeps a middle-aged teacher without tenure on the hot seat at job renewal time each year. I would like to suggest that we stop thinking of people by their chronological age and judge them each as individuals. And I would like to ask you whether, if you search your souls, you are not, like me, guilty of prejudice against other age groups.

Johnny Appleseed Day

It isn't very widely observed, but for some people today is Johnny Appleseed Day, marking the death of that real but legendary gentleman on this day in 1845. Other people have marked Johnny Appleseed Day on the anniversary of his birth rather than his death, but there is no disagreement about how Johnny

Appleseed, born John Chapman, got his nickname or how much he meant to the nation. He roamed the frontier of his time for many years, planting apple trees and distributing seeds to farmers. He was a card-carrying eccentric, who reputedly wore a tin plate for a hat. He was definitely not your run-of-the-mill do-gooder, but he did more good than most. The American Library Association in one of its publications described him as the patron saint of American orchards. I am happy to use the occasion of Johnny Appleseed Day to make the point that it isn't what you wear but what you do that really counts. What kind of seeds, if any, are you or I planting?

MARCH 12

Truman Doctrine

On this day in 1946, President Harry Truman set forth a foreign policy, later endorsed by the Congress, that probably changed the complexion of the world. This was the day he enunciated the Truman Doctrine, which said that U.S. resources, including military forces, would be used to stop Soviet expansion, particularly in Europe. That was the basis for our aid to Greece and Turkey in the face of attempted Red takeovers of those countries. We could probably argue long into the night about where and when the Truman Doctrine took us and the world, but we cannot argue that there was any doubt about U.S. foreign policy when Harry Truman said what he planned for this country to do. It seems to me that the biggest danger is often not this plan or that but simply uncertainty. If we don't know ourselves what we are going to do, we are, to say the least, at a disadvantage. And that applies as much to domestic policy as to international affairs. It may be fine for me to ad lib up here on the speaker's platform, but not if I haven't got a pretty good idea of what I am going to say. Let me reassure you—and proceed to speak my mind.

Shadow in New Hampshire

This was the day of the first presidential primary vote in the campaign of 1968, and the leadoff state was New Hampshire. What happened in New Hampshire may have been unusually influential that year. In the Democratic primary, a candidate opposed to our Vietnam efforts, Senator Eugene McCarthy of Minnesota, running against the President of the United States, Lyndon B. Johnson, and running with no organization other than a group of enthusiastic young supporters, did not win but came much too close for LBJ's comfort. Less than two weeks later the President announced that he would not be a candidate for reelection. The history of this country is full of cases of individuals who challenged seemingly entrenched people or entrenched positions and managed to change the course of events. You have long heard the admonition that you *can* make a difference. Given the right idea, you or I can make a difference. As I present some ideas to you here today, I ask you to remember this great fact about our way of life. It is a way of life in which you can fight city hall, you can turn the rascals out, you can make waves. Above all, you can make up your own mind and speak your mind. I thank you for the opportunity you give me to do just that here today.

March Winds

We are in the middle of March, traditionally the month of big winds. I want you to know that I recognize my obligation not to contribute more wind to a month that already has so much of it. I am also mindful of the fact that the weather in March does not normally have too much hot air. I trust that my remarks here today will contribute neither wind nor hot air, but you'll have to be the judges of that.

Adolph S. Ochs

Today is the birthday of Adolph S. Ochs, who came out of Tennessee to take over the stumbling *New York Times* and made it into the nation's, if not the world's, leading newspaper. Ochs, of course, did not do it alone. He built a remarkable staff. But however great their ability, it was he who set the basic journalistic standard for them. We have only to look around us to see the great enterprises that began with the ideas and the energies of one person. The challenge to us is to maintain a way of life in which this kind of individual success is still possible. Government policy plays an important role, but not *the* most important role. Our own attitudes, our training, our basic beliefs are also involved, and they are the things I want to discuss with you here today.

MARCH 13

Anti-evolution

On this day in 1925, a bill became law in the state of Tennessee banning the teaching of the theory of evolution. This was the statute that led to the famous Scopes trial, in which teacher John T. Scopes was prosecuted with the aid of William Jennings Bryan and defended by Clarence Darrow. That trial ended with Darrow's complete destruction of Bryan on the witness stand and Bryan's death a short time later. At the time people thought it marked the end of antievolutionist pressure on school curriculums. But years later, the creationists, as they now called themselves, were still carrying on their efforts against the teaching of evolution. I am glad to see that they still feel free to espouse their ideas, and I am equally glad that the teaching of evolution has been defended in the available channels of our democratic republic. The freedom of anyone to use those channels to argue for his or her ideas is an integral part of our nation, and so is the freedom of opponents to use those channels for their own cause. That is what America is all about. In that tradition, I will speak my mind here today. I hope you will agree with what I have to say; in any case, I thank you for the opportunity to say it.

Brinkley on News

David Brinkley was one of the great pioneers of television news reporting, to which he brought a wry quality that was all his own. When the clamor arose to do more news broadcasts, he was moved to voice his dissent. In remarks at the University of Southern California on this day in 1978, Brinkley commented, "People have the illusion that all over the world all kinds of sensational events are happening all the time. The fact is that over most of the world, most of the time, nothing is happening." I don't know whether that is literally true, but I do know that the press sometimes comes upon something that has been happening routinely for years and treats it as breaking news. Part of that is the competitive nature of the press—and I include broadcasters as part of the press. But the main reason, it seems to me, is the public's insatiable appetite for excitement, sensationalism, and discovery. There is more news in violence, for example, than in good deeds. As a result we assign priorities to problems that aren't always the correct ones. We get impressions of rampant crime that aren't always the correct ones. We forget about poverty because we don't always see it in our neck of the woods. Today I want to talk about some important things that, I fear, do not come under the heading of hot news.

Alliance for Progress

Back in 1961, on this day, President John F. Kennedy announced the formation of the Alliance for Progress to promote the economies and social progress of Latin American countries friendly to the United States. Six months later we committed ourselves, in furtherance of the Alliance, to providing $10 billion to 19 countries over a decade. This was by no means the first or the last of our country's attempts to buy friendship or protection—take your choice of objectives—by sending money overseas. Now, I am well aware that much and sometimes all of this money comes back in the form of trade, or perhaps the saving of other defense expenditures, but there is something about the whole idea that bothers me. Why, after all these years, should some countries be so hard up, perennially, that they keep looking to us for more? Why is the most generous country in the world almost universally attacked as "Uncle Shylock"? Why, over the years, have rioting groups in foreign lands, in the course of protesting local conditions, attacked the U.S. Embassy and inevitably blamed the CIA for their country's problems?

Pluto

On this day in 1930, the existence of a new planet, which had actually been discovered a month before, was announced to a world that took the news rather calmly. They called the newly discovered planet Pluto, and for at least 50 years after its discovery nobody, particularly the general public, got too excited about it. That provides a salutary thought for me as I appear before you today. If the news of the discovery of a new planet could cause so few ripples, the views of a public speaker should be susceptible to being spoken frankly without turning the earth upside down.

MARCH 14

Paul Ehrlich

Today is the birthday of Dr. Paul Ehrlich, who in the course of developing the so-called magic bullet for the treatment of venereal disease became one of the pioneers of chemotherapy. The use of chemicals in the treatment of all kinds of diseases has expanded almost beyond belief since the time of Ehrlich, who was born in 1854 and made his key discovery in the field of chemotherapy in 1910. But I don't think Dr. Ehrlich envisioned an age in which the knowledge of chemotherapy would be applied to devising pep pills, weight reduction, and artificial highs and lows. We seem to be very consistent in taking every newly discovered boon and developing new excesses with it—pill-popping, reckless driving, sexual promiscuity. We haven't yet found a miracle cure for moral weakness, but we certainly have developed increased tolerance of it.

Poison Prevention Week

Quite a few years ago they began observing Poison Prevention Week at about this time in March. Unfortunately, we go on eating poison and smoking poison even when we should know better. I am, of course, using the word *poison* loosely. The substances to which I refer are everyday commodities that poison only when they are overused, like salt or some other preservatives. If we didn't have them in so many canned and frozen foods those foods might have a shorter shelf life and consequently be more expensive. But fewer of us would come down with circulatory ailments. I believe we have sacrificed some of our health in our zeal for easy ways to do things—convenience foods, quick action insect sprays, and who knows how many other products. I am here today to speak against some parts of our easy way of life.

Geneva Anniversary

On this day in 1962, a 17-nation disarmament conference opened in Geneva, Switzerland. There was, of course, a great deal of talk. I can only hope that my remarks here today will prove to be a little more productive.

First Town Meeting

Some historians advise us that the first town meeting was held on this day in 1743 in Boston. I am somewhat dubious about the truth of this item, because New England had been settled for 100 years by then, and I cannot conceive of New Englanders going 100 years before they held a town meeting. Town meetings are too good an idea, as long as the community is not so large as to make them unwieldy. Getting people to listen to one another's ideas is always a good idea itself. Unfortunately, I have the advantage over you here today, because this is not a town meeting and I can speak without any immediate rebuttal. Even with that situation, I hope that what I have to say will meet not with your desire for rebuttal but rather with your approval. Let's see about that right now.

MARCH 15

Exit Julius Caesar

This is supposedly the day when his best friend killed Julius Caesar in ancient Rome in the year 44 B.C. For the Romans this date was the Ides of March, and when Shakespeare wrote his great play about Caesar he expressed the admonishment "Beware the Ides of March." I do not hold with that advice. I am here today to suggest that it is never a good idea to look to the future with foreboding. It is hard enough to contend with the problems we already have without trying to anticipate future ones. What I suggest is that when we look to the future we think not of how gloomy it promises to be but rather how we can make it better than today. And I have some ideas to present to you in that field.

Rostropovich De-Sovietized

It was on this day in 1978 that the Soviet Union provided one of its recurrent examples of the implacable rigidity with which it treats people. Mstislav Rostropovich, the greatest cellist and a leading conductor of his time, and his wife, Galina Vishnavskaya, a distinguished singer, who had left their native Russia in continuance of their musical careers, were deprived of their citizenship in their native land. It certainly did not put much of a crimp in

Rostropovich's career and was, more than anything else, a petty venting of spleen by a mighty power. We should never underestimate the pettiness of great powers or of powerful individuals. In dictatorships like Soviet Russia, there isn't much appeal. When it happens in our own country, there are, thank goodness, strong possibilities for self-defense and appeal through the democratic and judicial processes of government. Today I would like to talk about those processes and how we can improve them.

Andrew Jackson

Today is the birthday of Andrew Jackson, who was born in South Carolina in 1767. When he was only a child he was an eyewitness to some of the fighting of the American Revolutionary War. He helped found the state of Tennessee. In the War of 1812 he led the campaign against the Creek Indians, who were allied with the British, and he took over tremendous territory for the Stars and Stripes. After he defeated the Creeks, he captured Pensacola, Florida, on his way to New Orleans. It was there that he won his greatest victory in the Battle of New Orleans, where, with the help of Jean LaFitte's erstwhile pirates, he soundly defeated the invading British. The Battle of New Orleans was actually fought after the war had ended with the signing of a peace treaty, but the news of the signing of the treaty in Europe had not yet reached this country. After the war Jackson went on to take over Florida for Uncle Sam, and he was elected president in 1828. He served in that office for two terms, retiring in 1837. I have gone into detail about Jackson's career because it illustrates something marvelous about America, something that is still true. This one man, Andrew Jackson, in his own lifetime saw the infant colonies begin their struggle for independence, saw us win another important war, saw the nation expand its frontiers, and, finally, fifty years after the Revolution, became president of a thriving, dynamic country. That dynamism, ladies and gentlemen, still exists. In our own lifetimes we have seen the nation grow and change as dramatically as it did in Jackson's day. We have seen a tremendous expansion of our population, a revolution in the handling of information, an incredible shift of people and work to the sun country, a burst of household conveniences that Jackson's contemporaries never knew, a familiarity with and communications closeness to the rest of the world that makes the delayed news of the 1815 peace treaty seem almost incredible today. So much has been done. How can we stop now?

First Blood Bank

The first modern blood bank in this country was established on this day in 1937, and I think it is something well worth remembering. Blood transfusions made possible by blood banks have saved more lives and helped more people continue to lead useful lives than we could have dreamed of back in 1937. And yet, consistently, blood banks have a great deal of trouble getting enough donors. Contributing blood is painless and virtually risk free, yet most people either shy away from it or never even contemplate it. There are a lot of good things that we can do as individuals but somehow never get around to doing. If today I can persuade anybody in this audience to give a little more of himself or herself, I will be doing you all—and myself—a service.

MARCH 16

Freedom of Information Day

Back in 1980, several journalistic organizations proposed that this day, March 16, be observed as Freedom of Information Day. They chose the date because it is the birthday of one of the fathers of our freedom of the press, James Madison. Shooting off your mouth, whether by voice or in print, is a most cherished right. I guess that is one reason you are stuck with me here on the podium.

Docking in Space

Back in 1966 on this day, astronaut Neil Armstrong, who was later to become the first man to walk on the moon, and David Scott conducted the first docking of two space vehicles out in space. It was a spectacular achievement that was soon outshone by even more spectacular accomplishments in that period of almost frantic progress in space travel. When we Americans get started on something new, we tackle it with tremendous energy, imagination, and enthusiasm, until something newer comes along. The watchword of our lives seems to be "What's new?" I would like to rise to suggest another watchword, namely, "What's needed?"

Geneva Convention

Today is the anniversary of the United States Senate's approval in 1882 of the Geneva Convention for the care of wartime wounded. It is one international agreement which, while often honored in the breach, has nevertheless provided an often effective set of guidelines in the midst of man's inhumanity to man. So when we look at the world today, we might bear in mind that cynicism does not always prevail and that not every international agreement is doomed to turn to dust. It is with that fact in mind that I speak to you here today about some things on which I believe we and rival nations can find a common ground.

Henny Youngman

Today is the birthday of an old-time comedian who was by all accounts the patron saint of the one-liner. It was Henny Youngman, born in England in 1906, who gave us such quips as "Take my wife, please," and the quote from the dissatisfied restaurant patron, "This food isn't fit to eat—and such small portions." Although I will not venture into Henny Youngman's territory today, I do find one quote of his that provides me with an apt beginning. "By the time you learn to make the most of life," he remarked, "most of it is gone." I am here to suggest some things that can help us make the most of life while we still have most of our lives to enjoy.

MARCH 17

Camp Fire Girls Founders Day

This is Camp Fire Girls Founders Day, marking the start of that organization in 1912. I don't know how many thousands of women have been Camp Fire Girls in their youth, but I do know groups like this add a significant dimension to the growing-up years. Being part of a voluntary group of your contemporaries, doing things you might not otherwise be able to do, is another kind of schooling. It shouldn't be reserved for children only. In the midst of all the social life of adults in the United States, there are all too many orphans of the storm, people who lead lonely, neglected lives. One of the challenges we face is to bring lonely, neglected people into the mainstream of society. I'd like to talk today about some of the things we can do to help.

Murder, Inc.

It was on this day in 1940 that a coldblooded kill-for-hire gang in Brooklyn came to light. The group was dubbed Murder, Inc., by the press, and the chronicle of its destruction by law enforcement agencies was a real-life thriller. But the homicides attributed to Murder, Inc., cannot hold a candle to the number of Americans who unwittingly kill *themselves* every year. I am not talking about suicides or the victims of accidents. Rather, I refer to those who ignore medical problems until it is too late. There are lots of problems with medical care in this country—cost, availability, inconvenience to the patient. But the biggest problem, it seems to me, is persuading people to take care of themselves. What can we do about it?

UN Veto

It is interesting to note that the United Nations was just a quarter of a century old before the United States ever used this country's right to veto in the Security Council. On this day in 1970, we vetoed a UN censure of Great Britain over the question of Rhodesia. The veto power in the UN Security Council, reserved for the permanent members of the council, has been exercised many times before and since that first U.S. action. It is a comfort to Americans, I am sure, that our country has that veto power in a council whose actions have not always been either prudent or just. But I find myself wondering how it would work if, for example, the Senate delegations of the thirteen founding states could each exercise a veto in the U.S. Senate. Maybe that's not a fair example, because the members of the Senate have a lot more in common, including a common national allegiance, than the assorted nations of the UN Security Council. Indeed, the very fact that a UN veto is needed—and I believe that it is fundamental to U.S. membership in the world organization—tells us something about the monumental job confronting the United Nations. I said monumental. Some people would say impossible. But I happen not only to regard the United Nations as worthwhile, despite everything, but I also believe that if it didn't exist we would have to invent it. Let me tell you why.

St. Patrick's Day

This great day for the Irish has many reasons to be interesting for all of us. Not the least interesting aspect of the day is that we have more celebrations of it in the United States than they do in Ireland, but that is understandable because we have more Irish. We have so many people of so many different ethnic origins that we sometimes outnumber the population of the mother country. Israel Zangwill dubbed America's population mix "the melting pot." It may be an appropriate term because melting pots can have a low boiling point, and relations between various groups in this country have also sometimes had low boiling points. But I believe we have all learned to live together and build a common heritage in our nation. I am supported in this belief by the fact that good St. Patrick himself was an immigrant to Ireland. Immigrants have been bringing new vigor to their new homes ever since—as you have only to look at your backgrounds to confirm.

MARCH 18

Gideon v. *Wainwright*

It comes as a surprise to many people that the right of an accused to have a lawyer was only finally guaranteed by the Supreme Court in 1963; we think of this as such an intrinsic right. But it was on this day in 1963, in the case of *Gideon* v. *Wainwright*, that the Supreme Court of the United States ruled that denial of counsel was a violation of due process of law. There had been an earlier decision, back in 1942, which the Gideon case reversed. The law in this country is a living thing. It moves with the times, and it has the strength that comes from the broad principles laid down in the Constitution. That is why I—and I hope you as well—find myself increasingly impatient with people who try to circumvent orderly processes and prefer agitprop, sit-ins, and other forms of such blackmail-like pressure. It is very dramatic to block traffic, or to force a school or set of offices to close, but it is also a way of giving our courts and our democratic processes the runaround. I stand here to condemn those so-called voices of the people who try to subvert the people's proper avenues, as the preamble to the Constitution puts it, "to establish justice."

First Walk in Space

A Russian cosmonaut named Aleksei Lenov took the first gravity-free stroll outside a spaceship on this day in 1965. He was outside for ten minutes. The greatness of the achievement was not how long he did it but rather that he proved it could be done. That is something worth keeping in mind today. When the government—or an individual, for that matter—tries something new, we expect it to be a success right away, or forget it; but sometimes success comes after a series of halting and sometimes discouraging results. So I would like to take a look with you today at some things that are not yet successes but hold wonderful promise for the future.

The Lion and the Lamb

This month of March is the time of the lion who goes out like a lamb or, if you prefer, the lamb who comes in like a lion. I will try on the podium this mid-March day to find a halfway point, neither roaring at you like a lion nor getting as woolly as a lamb. Instead, if I may pursue the animal analogy, I will simply try to talk turkey.

Caruso's Records

On this day in 1902, in a makeshift studio in Milan, Italy, Enrico Caruso, perhaps the greatest operatic tenor the world has ever heard, recorded ten arias for that newfangled contraption, the phonograph. For these ten recordings he received a payment of—are you ready?—$500. I am not overly humble, but if Caruso received $500 for ten recordings, most speakers, including me, should be grateful we don't have to pay you in the audience to listen to us. It is with that chastened and humbling realization that I speak to you now.

MARCH 19

U.S.S. Franklin

Today is the anniversary of an epic of heroism that awakened the pride of people throughout the United States in World War II but has somehow faded into the dusty pages of history. On this day in 1945, the U.S. aircraft carrier *Franklin*, heavily damaged by Japanese planes in the Pacific with a loss of 832 lives, was saved by the magnificent efforts of the surviving crew. It is an anniversary well worth remembering. But there are no special anniversary dates for much of the quiet heroism that helps make America as great as it is. Every day, law enforcement and firefighting men and women risk their lives in the causes of safety and protection of the public. Dedicated volunteers and poorly paid professionals give of themselves to help the less fortunate. Yes, we have many heroes and heroines, and I would like to salute some of them here today.

William Jennings Bryan

Today is the birthday of the "Great Commoner," William Jennings Bryan, who was born in Salem, Illinois, in 1860. Bryan was virtually a prodigy as a young man. He was elected to the House of Representatives from Nebraska when he was 30, and six years later came out of political nowhere to electrify the Democratic Convention with his eloquent "Cross of Gold" speech. It made such an impression that at age 36 he won the Democratic nomination for president. And that was the high point of his career. He didn't win in 1896, he didn't win when he was the Democratic candidate four years later in 1900, and he didn't win in 1908 when he was again the candidate of the Democrats. He was briefly Woodrow Wilson's Secretary of State, until he resigned because he thought Wilson wasn't neutral enough. When Tennessee put a teacher named John T. Scopes on trial in 1925 for teaching the Darwin theory of evolution, Bryan volunteered to lead the prosecution. He did, and was demolished by the defense attorney, Clarence Darrow. Even worse, he became a laughingstock for many. Not long after the Scopes trial ended, William Jennings Bryan died. One cannot describe a man who ran three times for the Presidency as simply a flash in the pan. But a look at the career of William Jennings Bryan tells us that one generation's wonder may become the next generation's anachronism. If we do not learn, if we do not stretch ourselves, we lose our effectiveness. How do we stretch ourselves? I have some suggestions.

Who's Got the Ball?

This is the anniversary of one of the funniest football stories of all time. Reporting on the first big West Coast football game, which had taken place the day before in 1892 in San Francisco, the San Francisco Chronicle said there had been an unexpected delay when Stanford University and California at Berkeley had lined up. Nobody had brought a football. They had to send someone out to get a ball. Bringing together two football teams and forgetting to bring a ball is like some aspects of life today. For example, we perfect more and more complicated instruments of industry only to find them used by other nations so often to invade our markets. That is why I think it is so important to take a good long look at ourselves and at our ideas.

House on TV

This is the anniversary of an event some people assured us would obstruct the course of government and other people thought might provide an exciting new area of information service. It did neither. I am referring to the beginning of television coverage of the sessions of the House of Representatives. It started on this day in 1979, amid forecasts that it would bring out so much ham in members of Congress that the House's business would be disrupted. Not only did that not happen but the sessions also disappointed those who hoped for television drama like the McCarthy or crime investigation hearings. Instead, the House went on as it always had done. We have a tendency to blame the media for the way people act, but it seems to me that people have been acting that way ever since there were people. We say television has given opportunities for tiny groups to get news coverage of their staged picketing, sit-ins, and so forth. I think we're blaming the messenger instead of seeing the message for what it is. And I don't think phony demonstrations fool anybody anymore. The point is, who judges what is phony, and how?

MARCH 20

National Wildlife Week

One of the strange contradictions of modern life is that the beasts and birds and other creatures we call wild have to be protected from civilized humans. That, when you get down to it, is the basic reason for the observance in March of National Wildlife Week. Today, in tribute to National Wildlife Week and to illustrate that the birds and beasts are not the problem, I'd like to talk about some of the human wildlife that confronts us.

The Harvard Classics

Charles William Eliot, who was born in Boston on this day in 1834, was the President of Harvard University for an incredible forty years. He edited the Harvard Classics, the famous five-foot shelf of books that brought learning and culture through great literature to masses of people. We think of Harvard when we think of education. We think of other fine schools. Yet we rarely think of libraries as the great educational instruments they are. And, strangely enough, many people who don't hesitate to buy books for their children never think of helping to support their local libraries. That is true as well of other extracurricular groups with great educational impact—Boy Scouts, Girl Scouts, Y's and such. You don't have to buy a five-foot shelf of classics to help educate a lot of people.

Ibsen

This is the birthday of the great Norwegian poet and playwright, Henrik Ibsen, who was born in 1828. His greatness came not only from the brilliance of the realism with which he created the characters in his dramas but also from the fact that he consistently tackled social issues. Some observers call him the father of modern stage drama. *Hedda Gabler, The Master Builder,* and *An Enemy of the People* are only a few of his plays which are still performed on the stages of the world. On Ibsen's birthday it is only fitting that we, here and now, confront a few realities of our own.

Nutrition Time

In the 1980s they began celebrating March as Nutrition Month, or Nutrition Time. Whatever the name, it suggests that my appearance before you today is an appropriate time to present some nutritious food for thought, and that is what I am about to attempt.

MARCH 21

Civil Rights March

On this day back in 1965, Dr. Martin Luther King Jr. led a civil rights march out of Selma, Alabama, headed for Montgomery. The marchers had been blocked by Alabama state police on a previous attempt, but this time they made it to Montgomery, though at shocking cost. A white civil rights worker, Viola Liuzzo, was killed by Ku Klux Klansmen outside the city. The march did more than make news. It was one of the catalysts for the passage of the Civil Rights Act, because it captured the conscience of much of the nation. One of the wonderful things about America is that there is a public conscience and a form of government that gives public conscience access to the government, even when, as in the case of the civil rights movement, it took mass demonstrations and the spilling of blood to arouse enough attention. Arousing the conscience of the public is the dream of everyone with a cause to plead. I am not immune to that temptation, as you will soon see.

Pennsylvania Turnpike

Nobody had ever done it before when, on this day in 1937, the Pennsylvania legislature authorized the building of a superhighway between Harrisburg and Pittsburgh. It was to be a high-speed road with fairly widely spaced exits and entrances. What it was, of course, was the Pennsylvania Turnpike, the first such express highway in the nation and the model for what is now a nationwide system. The modern, limited-access interstate highways have made every part of the nation closer to the rest, but somehow the system is never adequate in peak travel periods. In road construction, as in housing or other aspects of modern American life, we never seem to stay caught up for very long. To me, that does not mean bad planning. It means explosive growth, and that growth continues in this country in good times and bad. We have more people going more places and doing more things all the time. And, as happens in any such growth, you have the displaced, the disadvantaged, the people who fall by the wayside or somehow never quite get into the mainstream. They are people our planning forgets or pushes under the rug. They are people I want to talk about here today.

UN Verbosity

Some years ago the United Nations picked the month of March for the observance of UN Week of Solidarity with Peoples Struggling against Racism and Racial Discrimination. Then, as the decade of the 1980s began, they raised their sights; they declared the UN Decade for Action to Combat Racism and Racial Discrimination. The objectives are noble and praiseworthy, but did you ever hear such longwindedness? One of the problems of the United Nations, or any gathering of diplomats, is that they have such a tendency to complicate the language. This is not a UN meeting, and I therefore have no obligation to complicate my language. So let me get right to the point.

Benito Juárez

If we were in Mexico there would be no need for me to tell you what day this is, because in Mexico it is a great historic day. The holiday commemorates the birth of Benito Juárez, the great Mexican leader, in 1806. Juárez, the humble Indian who became President of Mexico, was the leader of the country's defense against the French attempt to install the Emperor Maximilian as Mexico's ruler. For a time it looked as though the French armies would succeed in conquering Mexico, but Juárez finally drove them out. Like our own George Washington, he rallied his forces and led them to victory. One of the characteristics of great men like Juárez is that, even when all seems lost, they don't give up. Unlike Washington, however, Juárez did not retire at the height of his prestige. He stayed on, and when he died he was facing a strong rebellion. So the moral, I suppose, is to take your stand, but when you've made your point take your seat. I will try to follow that advice here today.

MARCH 22

Antigambling Law

The first antigambling law in this country was passed on this day in 1630, when Bostonians were told to get rid of any dice or cards they had in their homes. At this late juncture, it is hard to know how much crap shooting and card playing went on in Boston in the ensuing years, but we do know that a number of states have decided, as regards gambling, if you can't lick them join them. In addition to betting on horse racing, we have legally licensed casinos and many state lotteries. We still persist, however, in raiding those floating crap games while we sanction church bingo. If ever there was an area of double standards in this country, gambling is it. Clearly, we do not always practice what we preach. My function here today—which, I hasten to add, has nothing to do with gambling—is not to practice what I preach but rather to preach what I think we ought to practice.

Russian Democracy

This is the anniversary of the recognition of a moderate provisional government in Russia by the United States in 1917. It was this provisional government that conducted a free national election in Russia later in the year, only to have the Bolsheviks take over by force of arms. We have a tendency to forget, with the passage of time, that it was not the autocratic tsarist regime that was overthrown in Russia; it was a democratically elected parliament that the Communists never permitted to function. Communism is dedicated to defeating democracy. Bearing that in mind, we can understand why it is important to defeat communism.

Birthday of Fifth Avenue

New York City's fancy Fifth Avenue did not even exist when its name first appeared on a map on this day in 1811. They started building the Avenue in 1824, but after it was finished the world came to know it well. It became synonymous with the height of luxury and fashion, the home of the fanciest of Easter parades. Now, there is no indication that the little old mapmaker back in 1811 had any such future in mind when, with a thoroughgoing lack of inspiration, he named and laid out the new road. The other great streets of the world have names, not numbers—Champs Elysees, Regent Street, Broadway, Unter den Linden, and so forth—but good old Fifth Avenue has done pretty well with just a number. There is a lesson for a public speaker here. It isn't the title, it's the substance that counts. So let's get down to substance.

Equal Rights

It was on this day in 1972 that Congress passed and sent to the states a proposed constitutional amendment covering equal rights for women. The proposed amendment was faced with a seven-year deadline, but as the seven years came to an end the requisite number of states still had not ratified it, and several states that had ratified were seeking to withdraw their ratifications. Congress extended the ratification period for another two years. This was a perhaps extreme example of the fact that states do indeed have some power and that state legislatures play a significant role not only in governing their own bailiwicks but in amending the national Constitution. We are a democratic society, but there are some respects in which a single voter in, say, Rhode Island, is more important than a single voter in California. That is because a lot fewer people elect the Rhode Island legislature than the millions who vote for the California legislature. And yet the legislatures of the two states have an equal voice in adopting or rejecting a constitutional amendment. The concern of the Founding Fathers was essentially that all voices be heard, for out of this multiplicity of voices comes a multiplicity of ideas in the marketplace, and out of the multiplicity of ideas comes informed decision making. I will not pretend that the ideas I present to you here today are all brand new contributions to the marketplace, but I hope that what I have to say will add to and stimulate your own thinking on the subjects involved.

MARCH 23

Dr. King's Warning

When Dr. Martin Luther King Jr. spoke in St. Louis on this day in 1964, he told his audience, "We must learn to live together as brothers or perish together as fools." He was speaking of race relations in this country, but he could have been speaking of international affairs as well. The hardest job we have as human beings is to learn to live together. If I can contribute in any way here today to that learning process, even if it is just by getting you to relax a little, my talk will not have been in vain.

Danish Courage

In World War II a number of nations shocked the rest of the world by their lack of effective moral resistance to the Nazi tide. One nation that stood out for a brave and different course was Denmark. The Nazis occupied their country, but nevertheless on this day in 1943 the Danes went into their election booths and voted 99 to 1 against the Nazis. It was the Danes, incidentally, who smuggled all of the Danish Jews out of the country, most to neutral Sweden, to save them from the Nazis. This kind of courage deserves to be remembered. This kind of human decency deserves to be remembered. In one of the darkest hours of western civilization, the Danes lit a beacon. Surely we can do likewise today. Let me tell you how.

Nisei

It took a long time for the truth to sink in, but when it did most Americans were properly ashamed of what happened at about this time in 1942. That was when, as we confronted Japan in World War II, the whole Japanese American population on the West Coast was relocated—homes uprooted, land taken away— as they were interned in the more inland areas. Even after Nisei soldiers distinguished themselves in the fighting in Italy, the conscience of the nation was not truly responsive to the injustice that had been done by the relocation. It took forty years for the government to get around to modest reparations. We who are so quick to see the mote in an overseas neighbor's eye don't pay quite as much attention to what we have done here at home. All too often, we actively resent having such matters called to our immediate attention. So the temptation is great for a speaker to talk only about what is good, to tell us how wonderful we are. There is, of course, another temptation for the speaker, which is to tell you how wonderful *he* or *she* is. Ladies and gentlemen, I am up here to resist temptation.

Noncooperation with Evil

Mahatma Gandhi was still better known as Mohandas K. Gandhi on this day in 1922, when he appeared before a judge in British India to defend himself against charges of sedition for some articles he had written. In the course of an eloquent address to the court, Gandhi said, "Noncooperation with evil is as much a duty as is cooperation with good." It was in line with that principle that he organized the nonviolence campaign of civil disobedience that brought India together and did so much to earn independence. Noncooperation with evil is as much a duty as is cooperation with good. Perhaps we should ask ourselves how our policies and our conduct measure up to that principle. Let me ask it more specifically here today.

MARCH 24

The First Bomb

Knowing that I was going to be talking to you on this date, I browsed through some books to see what interesting events might have taken place on earlier March 24s. I found two entries that were particularly interesting. One said that this day, according to the ancient Romans, was to be a day of mourning and of abstinence. The other notation was that in 1580 the first bombs were thrown, in Holland. I cannot tell you anything more about either of these March 24 highlights, but I can assure you that my remarks here today will not be in the tradition of either bomb throwing or mourning and abstinence. I will not abstain from candor, I will offer no bewailing or lamentation, and I certainly have no intention of hurling any verbal bombs.

Applicant Grant

On this day in 1861, a former Army captain who had been clerking in a store in Galena, Illinois, wrote to the Army asking to be recalled to service as an officer in the impending Civil War. He got no answer. Fortunately, the state of Illinois was more interested, and he finally won appointment as a colonel in their militia. The man's name, as you may have guessed, was Ulysses S.

Grant. He ultimately led the Union armies to victory in the war and went on to become president of the United States. I don't know who it was in the office of the adjutant general of the Army who put Grant's letter of application in the file-and-forget area, and I daresay the culprit was not about to confess in the light of later history. What this story tells me is that major historical events can sometimes depend on the strangest petty bureaucracy, and that you can never tell who will inadvertently throw a monkey wrench into the wheels of progress. You also can never tell whether one single person, in the midst of a larger group, may not turn out to be the one who makes a positive difference, and every public speaker, when he or she gets up to talk, is hoping that his or her remarks will find that kind of let's-do-something-about-it response from at least part of the audience. That certainly is my hope here today.

Goodbye SST

This is the anniversary of the day in 1971 when the U.S. Senate voted to stop developing a supersonic civilian transport plane. There had been a bitter dispute about the SST, and the gamble we took was that other countries might develop a practical supersonic transport plane while we were, so to speak, out to lunch. What happened, of course, was that the British–French consortium and the Russians introduced such planes, but they were never able to make them earn enough money to sell any more than the original models. We know that, but we don't know whether American ingenuity, backed by enough government subsidies, might have produced a more cost-effective SST. Unfortunately, that is one of those what-if questions of which we have so many. When you make decisions, you have to ask yourself, "What if?" But I don't think that is the primary question. The primary question is "Why?" Why do we need this or that new project? And the second question is "How much?" How much will it cost, and how much of that cost can we ever expect to get back? Today those are the questions that are uppermost in my mind. The suggestions I make here today will, I hope, make a lot more sense if I can tell you why I recommend them, as well as how much it will cost to do them versus how much it will cost to leave them undone.

Philippine Independence

This is the anniversary of our government's adoption in 1934 of the Philippine Independence Act, which laid out an orderly timetable for giving the Philippines total freedom from the United States. Even though the long period of World War II intervened, and even though the Philippines for some of that time were occupied by Japan, independence came on schedule on July 4, 1946. I don't think there is any other nation in the world that can match the U.S. record of permitting nations it won in battle to choose their own future course. We are often regaled by our critics with stories of U.S. imperialism and dollar

diplomacy, but I challenge any other nation to match our record of putting conquered territory back into self-government. This is only one aspect of the slander
against the United States. Today I'd like to talk about some of the other fine
accomplishments and characteristics that too often go unsung in the profile of
the greatest country on earth.

MARCH 25

Maryland Day

It was on this day in the year 1634 that settlers first began the colonization
of what we know as Maryland. Maryland was settled by a minority group, the
English Catholics headed by the Calvert family. Within the first half-century
of settlement in English and Dutch America, Protestantism, Catholicism, and
Judaism were all represented among the settlers, and America has been giving
lessons to the world in freedom of religion ever since, even though there were
some difficult times along the way. We have learned to live with our different
faiths, but there is a growing chasm between, for example, the mainstream and
a developing and seemingly permanent underclass. It is this kind of growing
apart that I want to address here today.

Treaty of Rome

This is the anniversary of the signing of the Treaty of Rome, which created
the European Common Market in 1957. It marked a new departure in international economic cooperation, and it didn't develop real difficulties for almost
a quarter of a century, although every now and then this or that member nation became restive as new countries were added to the Common Market and
new problems arose. That is only to be expected. If you find a system working
perfectly, or rather if nobody has any complaints about it, you'd better look
into the matter a little further. And that has its blessings. For one thing, it means
that a public speaker always has something to talk about—either what is wrong
or how to make a good thing better. I thank you for the opportunity to do so
here today.

The Last New Year's Day

Under certain circumstances, I would start by wishing you all a happy new
year today. Yes, that's right, but we would have to have been in England prior
to 1752. Before that time, the English were stubbornly resisting what most of
the rest of the western world had long adopted, an improved method of dating
called the Gregorian calendar. For the English, the New Year began on March
25—until 1752. The Gregorian calendar is now the standard of the western
world, except for some religious observances. But I am not at all sure that, for

all the convenience this kind of unanimity gives us, it wouldn't be a more interesting world if the English had gone right on observing today as New Year's Day. Incidentally, if they had, we might also be doing the same, because in 1752 America was part of Great Britain. Conformism is efficient, but nonconformism can be a lot more interesting. In that spirit, I would like to look at and challenge some current conformities.

Coxey's Army

It was on this day in 1894 that a strange army went on the march in America's heartland. It was the so-called Coxey's Army, led by Jacob S. Coxey, and it marched to Washington, D.C., to get a program of public works employment for the unemployed. Coxey started out from Massillon, Ohio, and his followers began to gather en route from many parts of the country. But it was a month's march, and by the time Coxey's Army reached Washington it wasn't even a battalion, only some 400 marchers. The leaders of the march were arrested for trespassing at the Capitol, and the rest of the troops disbanded. What I think is worth remembering about this march is that it was one of the earliest such peaceful demonstrations, the antecedent in some ways of the civil rights and anti-Vietnam War marches of later years. We have no stomach here for violence and insurrection, but the right to demonstrate peacefully for redress of grievances is one that Americans of many different persuasions cherish. It is, after all, a logical extension of the right I am utilizing here today—the right to shoot one's mouth off. Unlike General Coxey, I have no ragtag army to urge to charge; all I have to present to you are some thoughts I hope you will find of interest.

MARCH 26

Mount St. Helens

On this day in 1980, the first glimmerings of trouble at Mount St. Helens were noted, but few people envisioned the tremendous power and havoc that occurred when the Pacific volcano blew its top that May. We find it difficult to accept the imminence of Mother Nature's temper tantrums. People live unconcerned on top of the San Andreas Fault in California and in towns that are flooded as regularly as clockwork. We eat tons of things that we know are bad for us, and through all this we maintain either an incredible optimism or an incredible fatalism. *Que será será;* what will be will be. We operate on the theory that some things are immutable, inevitable, or beyond our control. But, ladies and gentlemen, that is often a copout. We can make ourselves healthier by eating more wisely. We can escape some of the ravages of nature if we don't underestimate them and if we don't, so to speak, defy nature to do her worst to us.

Nature, like the economy and the society in which we live, has a rather extensive early warning system. Today I'd like to discuss some of the early warnings—natural or economic or sociological—of which we should be aware.

Israel–Egypt Peace Treaty

This is the anniversary of the signing of the peace treaty between Israel and Egypt in Washington, D.C., in 1979. It was a surprising turn of events for two nations that had been fighting on and off for more than a quarter of a century, and for Egypt's Anwar Sadat and Israel's Menachem Begin, whose friendship, once they decided to stop fighting each other, became amazingly warm and demonstrative. Leaders, it seems, can change far more quickly than their constituencies. That, of course, is one reason why they are leaders. So-called leaders who merely reflect the view of their constituents are not leading; at best they are representing, which is something else again. True leaders are those who dare to move in a different direction and try to bring their constituencies along with them—or sometimes to move in defiance of their constituencies. There is no doubt that a democracy needs people in leadership positions who are willing if need be to swim against the tide or to explore new territory. We of the electorate may slap them down, but we also find sometimes that their ideas are worth pursuing. I will not be troubled, and I hope you won't be troubled either, if you find what I say to you here today flying in the face of established dogma or sanctified positions—as long as what I have to say moves you to think about it.

Miami Beach

This day marks the anniversary of the founding of Miami Beach in 1915. Miami Beach was one of the first communities to try to reshape the beaches the sea had created, only to find that the sea is a pretty mighty adversary. But the sea was less of an adversary than the progress of the times. When the airplane replaced slower means of transportation, newer resorts challenged Miami Beach, and it became not wholly a vacation resort but also to a large extent a retirement home. Young people follow the sun; elderly people settle in the sun. From Miami Beach the tide of retirees spread in Florida, before the southwestern sunbelt challenged our southernmost state. The retirees were good for Florida. Permanent residents help support business. The rest of the country was inclined to sneer and call Florida an old folks' home, but if that had any validity it was as a symptom of the prejudice with which Americans, more than any other people on earth, deplore and deride age and worship youth. Today I would like to raise my aging voice in praise of the oldest generation.

Frost and Whitman

This day was a twin milestone for American eloquence, a special time for two of our greatest poets. Robert Frost was born in 1874, and Walt Whitman died in 1892 on this day. If our nation had poet laureates, both of these men would have been so honored. For their poetry was not merely beautiful words strung together; it was a collection of challenging thoughts as well. I could quote some examples, but I have put myself at too much of a handicap already by citing their illustrious ways with words as a prelude to my own efforts here today. On this anniversary of poetic greatness I can only hope that, if my words do not sing, they will at least make sense.

MARCH 27

Cherry Tree Anniversary

On this day in 1912, the first Japanese cherry trees were planted in Washington, D.C. It was a gracious gesture of friendship, but some cynics in the years since then have suggested that we should have been on our guard for all of the other Japanese products that came to our shores to compete with American industry. The old motto was, "If you can't lick 'em, join 'em." Japan and Germany added a new element to that advice when, after their defeat in World War II, they became our friends. "If you can't lick 'em, join 'em, and try economic invasion." There is a lesson for us here. National defense is, of course, a must, but I believe that the age of military victory for major powers is gone. Military victory, it turns out, is not as lasting or as good as economic victory. Peaceful wars of trade produce more booty than shooting wars of bombs and guns. That is why it seems to me that our major challenges are and always will be economic in the long haul, and it is economic talk I plan to give you here today.

Ponce de Leon

It was about this time in the year 1513 that a Spanish explorer named Ponce de Leon first saw his great discovery, a land he called Florida. It had no condominiums, no golf courses, and, to his subsequent disappointment, no fountain of youth. Most of the Florida we know was developed later, on the basis of nature's breathtaking original creation. And for as long as I can remember we Americans have been arguing over how much of nature's work, all over the planet, we should leave alone and what so-called improvements are the right things to do. We ourselves, after all, are Mother Nature's children, too, and we need an ever-increasing territory for our own growth, sustenance, and relaxation. How much of our life is properly a competition with nature and how much is, or should be, a benefiting from and accommodation to nature?

Libel

It was on this day in 1981 that most of the nation heard, and applauded, the news that Carol Burnett had won her libel suit against a weekly tabloid the previous day. The tabloid had printed a story about her that was a report of a supposed incident of misconduct by the performer. Even though the newspaper later published a retraction, she sued—and won, to the approval not only of the mass of the public but also of the many other Hollywood personalities who had suffered similar slings and arrows over the years. Some other suits were filed in the wake of the Burnett victory. Only a few small voices on the editorial pages of the nation's newspapers raised a question about the more than a million-dollar dimensions of the original Burnett award—an award that was later reduced considerably. Their point was that this kind of verdict could put a newspaper out of business, and even if this particular tabloid was as objectionable as so many people deemed it, using a damage award for that purpose was a dangerous precedent. So we had a classic collision between two basic American rights. We have any number of these collisions. We have a tendency in this country to think of rights in individual terms, but there are also the rights of institutions and, more important, the rights of society as a whole. Let me cite some examples of how, today, this conflict in rights ties us up in knots.

Walkouts

On this day in 1946, the Soviet delegate to the United Nations introduced a new note to that organization's deliberations. He walked out of the Security Council when the Council decided to investigate the continued presence of Soviet troops in Iran. Insisting on talking is one way of disrupting an effective conversation, but the Russians went further. They just walked away from the whole subject. Characteristically, they weren't very subtle about it. All too often, people or even nations can appear to be listening and to have their ears closed, and their minds as well. That's one of the problems for a public speaker. Some speakers don't worry in private. They punctuate their speeches with such questions as, "Am I getting through to you?" The audience, of course, sometimes has a similar question for the speaker, though a bit shorter. They may wonder *when* the speaker's getting through. I hope neither you nor I will be prompted to ask those questions here today.

MARCH 28

Three Mile Island

We Americans can be very brave and very blasé about threatening situations, but not always. On this day in 1979, when an accident at the Three Mile Island nuclear power plant in Pennsylvania raised fears of an explosion and/or a serious radiation leak, the whole nation held its breath, and the opponents of nuclear energy brought out their doomsday prophecies. Not too long before and after the Three Mile Island leak, there were fatal explosions of gas and chemical tanks in various parts of the country, some of them with danger-ous leakage of poisonous materials, but somehow these events didn't trigger any overall anxiety on the part of the nation. There are those who say the comparative dangers are not the same, but my point is more a matter of the way we think and react than of measurable peril. We are so transfixed, and have been for years, by nuclear dangers that we are much more easily alarmed when a reactor leaks than when a tank of totally deadly poison leaks. Somehow, nuclear death seems much more horrible for us to contemplate than death from nonnuclear poison or simple, if I can use that word, explosions. We are full of this kind of discriminatory thinking in our lives. We prosecute prostitutes, particularly female prostitutes, and let their customers go scot free most of the time. We, at least as a society, have condoned what used to be called "living in sin" but deplore bigamy. Today I'd like to focus on some of the other con-tradictions in American life.

Censure of a President

This is the anniversary of the day in 1834 when the Senate of the United States adopted a resolution censuring the President, Andrew Jackson, for his actions with regard to the Bank of the United States. The House of Representa-tives did not go along with the censure, but the Senate's action was the first such censure of a sitting President. It was later rescinded, but it was in some ways a partial precedent for the later attempt to impeach President Andrew Johnson. In our twentieth century, of course, we saw Congress help to force the unprecedented resignation of another President, Richard M. Nixon. I men-tion these incidents as perhaps the best illustration that even the highest office in the land is not an unassailable fortress. One of the strengths of our way of life is that we can fight city hall, and we can fight a lot higher up than city hall as well. The important question is not whether we can fight but what we should be fighting about. In that connection I have a few issues to discuss with you.

Rewards of Evil

When Griffin Bell was Attorney General of the United States and a mem-ber of Jimmy Carter's cabinet, he made a speech on this day in 1978 in which he noted that "we have a strange bent of mind in America: you get into some kind of trouble and you can write a book. You do very well indeed. You can also become a campus lecturer." Years later that same deplorable situation is still true. Maybe we should look not only at our laws but also at our attitudes. If we talk about this, it may motivate some of us to do something about it.

Washing Machine

The first washing machine patent in the United States was granted on this day in 1797, but it took almost 150 years for home laundry to succumb to the machine. That wasn't because the American public kept rejecting the idea; it was because the good idea of 1797 took that long to achieve practical results. This is something we seem to forget. We hail a new invention with predictions that it will revolutionize our way of life, and then we are dismayed when somebody comes up with an almost equally revolutionary improvement or revision of the original device. We enthusiastically applaud the infusion of humanitarianism into our laws, and then we quickly become impatient when the laws turn out to be still imperfect. Of course, we have much with which to be impatient. Realizing that fact, I would nevertheless like to seize the opportunity to get some of my impatience off my chest here today.

MARCH 29

Honor Vietnam Veterans Day

Some half-dozen years after the last American forces left Vietnam on this day in 1973, there were efforts to have this day observed annually as Honor Vietnam Veterans Day. It was an indication of the uneasy public attitude toward our Vietnam veterans that Honor Vietnam Veterans Day ran into so much difficulty and original nonsupport, and that the Vietnam memorial in Washington took so long to become a reality. Some felt this was because of the fact that we did not win the Vietnam War; some felt it was caused by resentment of those veterans who came out of service with drug or other behavioral problems. Whatever the reason, the popular reaction was totally different from the way veterans of previous wars had been received at home. What this seems to suggest is that in America our primary standard is not what you have done or what you have gone through but rather whether or not, in terms of public opinion, you made America look good. *Looking* good is more of an obsession in this country, I fear, than *doing* good. And doing good seems to take second place to doing well. I don't happen to think this is as it should be, and I have some ideas to present that I hope will do well with you but, more important, will do some good.

Rehabilitating Juvenile Delinquents

The hope of better things inspires men and women of every generation, and I salute the good people of New York City of 1824. On this day in that long ago year, they founded the Society for the Rehabilitation of Juvenile Delinquents, which opened one of the very first reformatories for children in the western world. I wonder what the founders of that group would say if they saw the condition of juvenile delinquency in the United States today. In the course of growing and making everyday life more convenient, we have most assuredly not done away with the problems of antisocial actions by children. Indeed, if only because there are so many more of us these days, juvenile delinquency is that much more with us. And not only the delinquent children represent a challenge. All of today's children, the citizens of tomorrow, challenge our building of a better America. How are we responding to that challenge?

Exit Truman

History has come to regard Harry Truman as one of the more notable presidents, but when he announced on this day in 1952 that he would not run for reelection there was no overwhelming public lamentation. The Korean War was still going on, with no end in sight; the communist witch-hunt mood was continuing; there were labor troubles in the steel industry and the railroads; and Congress and the President didn't seem to be operating on the same wavelength. But when we think of Harry Truman today—those of us who remember him—we don't think of these things as much as we remember the president who said, "The buck stops here," and, "If you don't like the heat stay out of the kitchen." It seems that the lasting impact of an individual on the conscience of the nation comes not so much from what he or she does as from the kind of person he or she is or appears to be. That is often the case with a speaker, and much as I would like to be remembered by you for my personal attributes here today, I would be far more gratified if it is what I have to say, rather than what I seem to be, that you choose to remember.

Wage Protection for Women

This is the anniversary of the 1937 Supreme Court decision in the case of *West Coast Hotel Company* v. *Parrish,* a decision that illustrates how public concepts change. What this decision said was that it was acceptable to have a state law establishing minimum standards of wages and conditions of labor for women and children. In 1937, it was felt that special legislation to apply to women was a means of protecting them, particularly against exploitation by avaricious employers. But thirty years later and thereafter, what militant women were fighting for was not special protection. Equal protection was the goal. A lot of ideas about the peculiar vulnerability and frailty of females had gone by the boards. This is a particularly good illustration of the fact that one generation's truths are not necessarily the truths of following generations. One is not flying in the face of progress to challenge the shibboleths and tabus he or she inherited. Indeed, the best thing a speaker can do is to stimulate the thinking of the audience. With your kind indulgence, that is what I hope to do here today.

MARCH 30

Shooting of Reagan

On this day in 1981, the president of the United States, Ronald Reagan, was shot in full view of television cameras by John W. Hinckley. A year later, thanks to a variety of legal processes and maneuvers, Hinckley still had not been brought to trial or adjudged insane and unable to stand trial. Meanwhile, the would-be assassin who had shot the Pope a bit later had been tried, convicted, sentenced, and imprisoned long since in Italy. That was an extreme example of one of the continuing problems of our country, the slowness, uncertainty, and tentativeness with which the wheels of justice sometimes turn here. Why does this happen, and what can we do about it?

Van Gogh

This is the birthday of Vincent van Gogh, who was born on this day in 1853 in Brabant, Holland. Van Gogh, one of the towering geniuses of art, is probably better known to some people because in a fit of madness he cut off his own ear. I hope all of you have more constructive uses for your ears today, and I appreciate the opportunity you give me to be heard from this dais.

Cuffless, Pleatless

On this day in 1942, as a wartime measure to conserve cloth, tailors in this country and clothing manufacturers in general were barred from making trousers with cuffs or pleats. It was one of the hardships of war that was more easily withstood. I look back on it as a prime example of the wastefulness of our society. I grant that pleats, rather more than cuffs, can be flattering to some male figures, but men have survived and prospered through periods in peaceful times when cuffs or pleats were out of fashion without notable effect on the economy or on public morale. We go in for conspicuous waste, to adapt Thorstein Veblen's terminology, with very little excuse other than forced obsolescence, an economic tactic that is not exactly the road to lasting prosperity. Wide ties and narrow ties, wide trousers and narrow trousers, wide lapels and narrow lapels, straight-line pants and flare pants, and so on far, far into the night. You see, one can work oneself into a state of virtuous excitement over some things besides national or international policy crises and public morals. Let me offer some other samples.

Voting

On this day in 1963, President John F. Kennedy appointed the Commission on Registration and Voting Participation to find out why so small a proportion of Americans bothered to vote. The Commission recommended many reforms that were subsequently adopted—abolition of poll taxes and literacy tests and lowering the voting age to 18, for example. And I guess you know the rest. The percentage of voters going to the polls went down. You can't solve a problem of apathy by passing a law. You solve a problem by first getting people to care enough. So I am here today as a problem solver, because I am going to be talking about things I want you to care about.

MARCH 31

Virgin Islands Transfer Day

This is Virgin Islands Transfer Day, commemorating the U.S. acquisition of what had been the Danish West Indies in 1917. We bought the islands for $25 million, which was considerably more than the $7 million we paid for Alaska fifty years earlier. Alaska, of course, turned out to be one of the great bargains of history, and the Virgin Islands were a bargain, too, if you consider the extent of today's tourist trade and other economic activity in the islands. Investments in real estate, if you hold on to them long enough, have a way of producing dividends you may not have expected at the outset. The same, I believe, is true of human beings. The investment in human beings you make when they need it, by providing jobs and schools and such, is almost guaranteed to produce more than it cost over the long haul. The trouble is that some of the return is not as easily measurable as the flow of oil or gold from Alaska or the tourists in St. Croix. Some of the return is in terms of human fulfillment, which we are apt to recognize most when it isn't there. One of the questions that intrigues me is what particular sort of investment in human beings would be most productive these days.

LBJ's Exit

Probably the most popular thing that Lyndon B. Johnson did in the last year of his presidency was to announce, as he did on this day in 1968, that he would not run for reelection. He did not want to outstay his welcome. That is something every public speaker should keep in mind, as I will try not to outstay my welcome here today.

CCC

It had a lengthy name, but its central idea was a simple one. I am referring to a law passed by Congress on this date in 1933 as part of President Franklin D. Roosevelt's plans to get America out of the Depression. It was entitled the Civilian Conservation Corps Reforestation Relief Act. It authorized the enrollment of 250,000 young men in national reforestation, flood control, and other conservation projects. By the time America found another assignment for a lot of young men when we went to war in 1941, more than two million youths had been part of the CCC, and they had saved and improved many natural areas throughout the United States. The CCC was unique in that it also contributed to the health of these young people by giving them sensible diets and the opportunity to breathe clean air and to do the kind of work that helps build strong bodies. It is interesting that while the WPA and other so-called make-work projects aroused a great deal of criticism, the CCC, both at the time and in the backward glances of history, gets generally excellent grades as a good idea well executed. Surely there is room today for more such good ideas that serve both the public and the needs of the jobless. It is a subject that deserves our close attention.

Eiffel Tower

This is the day when the Eiffel Tower was completed in Paris in 1889. We have been building higher and higher ever since. No matter how much we deny it, we seem to be reaching for the stars while somehow keeping our feet on something connected solidly to the ground. The number of places that have been able to impose height restrictions on buildings within their jurisdictions keeps on shrinking. Paris succumbed; London succumbed. We are still slaves to the idea that bigger, or maybe just taller, is better. Today I want to dispute that concept; I want to help you all to think small.

APRIL 1

Savarin

In the eighteenth century, when revolution was in the air and politics was the very essence of life, some people stood aloof from the battles to savor the joys of life. One such was Anthelme Brillat-Savarin, born in France on this day in 1755, who wrote the classic book on the art of eating, *The Physiology of Taste.* For Savarin, food was the most important thing of all, and eating it wisely was truly an art. On his birthday today, therefore, I shall try to give you food for thought and hope that it is suitably tasty.

Air Force Academy

The bill creating the Air Force Academy was signed into law by President Dwight D. Eisenhower on this day in 1954. It meant that the Air Force would train its own corps of officers, instead of drawing them from West Point and Annapolis, as it had done up until then. Setting up the Air Force Academy was an important step in maintaining the esprit de corps of that branch of the armed forces. We all like to be recognized as specialists, and having your own institution of higher education reinforces your pride in your chosen field. But in the end, it is not really the individual specialist who calls the long-range tune but rather the people we vote into power, so if the buck stops anywhere it stops, ladies and gentlemen, with us. In speaking to you here today I feel I am given the opportunity to talk to the owners of the establishment—some of the more than 200 million owners. Thank you for that opportunity.

Weather Satellite

This is the anniversary of the launching of the pioneering weather satellite *Tiros I* in 1960. Utilizing these eyes in orbit above the earth, forecasters have been able to be far more accurate in their long-range weather predictions, but Mother Nature still has ways of confounding and double-crossing the forecasters. What nature does in its confrontations with science is, essentially, to show us that no matter how much we know there are still more mysteries yet unsolved, more secrets of the universe yet unknown to us. Every time someone speaks to you as the custodian of absolute truth and knowledge, you are entitled to wonder whether there isn't a little more to the subject. Mindful of that fact, I want to assure you that what I say here today is my own view, not Holy Writ.

National Mime Week

Some years ago they began celebrating the week that begins today as National Mime Week, which I probably shouldn't even mention. I shouldn't mention it because as its title came out of my mouth I realize that mime is the art of conveying a message without words, wholly in pantomime. That, ladies and gentlemen, is asking too much of an ordinary speaker like me. So, National Mime Week notwithstanding, I shall use precious little pantomime and a full quota of spoken words to convey my message to you here today.

APRIL 2

Bartholdi

This is the birthday of Frédéric Auguste Bartholdi, whose name you may not immediately recognize but whose work you all know well. It was Bartholdi, born in France in 1834, who created the Statue of Liberty that stands in New York Harbor as a gift to the United States from France. There are many great symbols in the world today but none more meaningful than the Lady with the Torch. All over the world, the Statue of Liberty means the United States of America. That is a fact we ought to remember, because in our own territory we sometimes take liberty so much for granted that we don't notice when it is being challenged. It is awfully easy to overlook violations of the principles of liberty when you aren't the victim. It is easy, but dangerous. And so I am here to sound some alarms.

Émile Zola

Today is the birthday of Émile Zola, born in 1840 and destined to be the French author who led in the development of the realistic novel. But I like to remember the Zola who looked at the frame-up conspiracy that led to the imprisonment of Alfred Dreyfus and raised his voice to cry out, "*J'accuse.*" His protests fired up the people of France to look into the Dreyfus case further. When the evidence of frame-up was unmistakable, Zola's position—and Dreyfus's—was ultimately vindicated. Ladies and gentlemen, it was Zola who wrote, "The truth is on the march and nothing can stop it." I hope that today we can make some small contribution to keep truth on the march.

International Children's Book Day

It has been customary to observe International Children's Book Day today, which happens to be the birthday of the great author of children's stories, Hans Christian Andersen. I am delighted to note that in the age of television children not only read books but also devour magazines especially designed for their age levels. But illiteracy, like poor nutrition, is so widespread that it cries out for cure. And don't think that illiteracy just means an inability to read. If you don't know how to read there are also a lot of spoken words you don't understand. If I were speaking to an audience of illiterates here today I would have a hard time getting through to them. Thank you for making my job easier.

Casanova

Today is the birthday of a man who spent the last thirteen years of his life as a librarian, which doesn't sound terribly interesting until I tell you that the man was Giovanni Jacopo Casanova, whose name has become synonymous with romantic adventure. Casanova arrived on this earth in romantic Venice in 1725. While still in his teens he was expelled from a seminary for scandalous conduct, and thereafter in the course of his pursuit of love he also pursued careers as a musician, a preacher, an alchemist, a gambler, and a sedate businessman. He was imprisoned as a spy when he came back to his native Venice. When he escaped he went to Paris and turned up as director of the state lottery. He roamed through much of western Europe, was expelled from Florence, and was decorated by the Pope in Rome. He even went to Russia and got involved in a duel in Poland which, naturally, caused him to take to the road again. I cannot begin to name all of the other places that invited him to leave, but he finally found sanctuary as a librarian in Bohemia. I mention Casanova's spectacular and scandalous career because it illustrates so well that people who profess to be motivated by love are not necessarily lovable. When we vote for candidates on the basis of their good looks, when we buy products because the package is attractive, or when we let outer appearances rather than real substance guide our judgment, we are playing Casanova's game. All the world, it is said, loves a lover. But true love and the gigolo kind are rather different. Smooth words are no substitute for real meaning. So I ask you to pay less attention to my words here today than to the thoughts they express.

APRIL 3

Edward Everett Hale

Today is the birthday of Edward Everett Hale, who was born in Boston in 1822 and is best remembered as the author of that famous story "The Man without a Country." He wrote many books, was one of the most sought-after lecturers of his time, and served as chaplain of the U.S. Senate, but it is as the author of one story that he is best remembered. It is usually not the whole body of a man's or woman's work that is remembered but rather a single high or low point. Bearing that in mind, I can only hope that if you find anything worth remembering in my remarks, it will be the high points rather than the low ones.

Pony Express

This is the anniversary of the commencement of the Pony Express in 1860, and I am fighting the temptation to suggest that the mail got through faster on horseback than it does today. I guess virtually every American has heard about or seen a depiction of the Pony Express, but the surprising fact is that it only operated for a year and a half. Obviously, it doesn't take long to make a lasting impression—a fact I will keep in mind to hold my remarks here today to a manageable length.

United America

On this day in 1981, just a short time after an assassination attempt that wounded President Ronald Reagan, Vernon Jordan Jr., who was then president of the National Urban League, asked a very pertinent question. "Why is it," he inquired, "that Americans seem able to be united only in times of tragedy or crisis?" It is a good question. We can always find occasions to kindle or renew the fires of controversy. Today I expect and hope to resist that temptation. My aim is harmony, and my voice, I hope, is the voice of moderation.

Freedom Shrine Month

A long time ago the National Exchange Club began sponsoring the observance of Freedom Shrine Month in April. One of the aspects of freedom is the right of an individual to make his or her views known, and any place where he or she can do that, as far as I am concerned, is a Freedom Shrine. I want to thank you for inviting me to this particular Freedom Shrine, whose acoustics I will be testing for a little while.

APRIL 4

The Perils of Pauline

This is the anniversary of the premiere of the most famous cliffhanger movie of them all, the serial called *The Perils of Pauline,* which opened in New York in 1914 and left the heroine facing an incredible danger at the end of every episode, keeping the audience in suspense till the next adventure next week. *The Perils of Pauline* helped introduce the cliffhanger as a movie form. After all, we have so many cliffhangers in workaday life, why not in entertainment as well? Even in public speaking, the cliffhanger risk is present. How long will this speaker talk? How long will it take him or her to get to the point, and how long will it take him or her to stop beating us over the head with it? Ladies and gentlemen, I will try to make this cliffhanger short and to the point.

Killing of Dr. King

On this day in 1968, the Reverend Dr. Martin Luther King Jr. was assassinated in a motel in Memphis, a murder for which James Earl Ray was convicted and for which hatred was the only remotely sane motive. The question of whether a murderer is sane or insane has sometimes tied the legal proceedings in knots, but it seems to me that the very act of murder, particularly when it is not part of a profit-seeking crime like robbery, is a form of madness. There are nations today ruled by unstable leaders capable of doing the same things as a James Earl Ray. There are terrorist groups literally mad for power who will stop at nothing to get it. What can we do to prevent or defang this kind of madness? What do other countries do?

World Trade Center

On this day in 1973, the World Trade Center in New York was dedicated. It was also known at the time as Rockefeller's Folly, a giant complex that took years to rent fully. The World Trade Center has become a landmark, a meeting-place, and a showplace for New York City and the world. Sometimes thinking big can produce a gigantic white elephant. Sometimes the big thinkers are just a little ahead of their times, but the times have a way of catching up. I am here today to suggest what I can only describe as some big thinking about some very big current issues.

Home Decorating Month

For reasons best known to the sponsors, April was chosen some time back as the annual time for National Home Decorating Month. I suppose it derives from the fact that when spring comes the first task is spring cleaning, which leaves the home ripe and ready for new decorations. In honor of the occasion I will make every effort to enable you to get back to your homes today without having had your mental living rooms cluttered up by a stem-winding, torch-waving oration.

APRIL 5

Howard Hughes

On this day in 1976, the greatest mystery man of his time died on his way to a hospital in Texas. His name was Howard Hughes, and although we know the bare biographical facts about him, he is in some respects as great a mystery now as when he was alive. The settlement of his huge estate only added to the confusion, with so many competing claims and questions about purported wills. I think it is fortunate that not too many of us are as mad for privacy as Howard

Hughes. I admit I have a selfish motive in saying this, because if we were all like Howard Hughes we would certainly not meet together like this, and none of us, myself included, would have the nerve to stand up in front of the rest and deliver a speech.

Joseph Lister

On this day in 1827, Joseph Lister was born. There can't be more than a handful of people in all the history of world who have made greater contributions to medicine and surgery than Joseph Lister, but I expect that his name became most famous when, long after his death, it was used as part of the title of a mouthwash. In our own century people like Jonas Salk won worldwide and lasting fame for their medical genius, but Lister lived in an earlier age. He transformed that age by discovering and developing the place of antisepsis in surgery. He took surgery into the germ-free operating room and out of the middle ages. We accept as everyday routine things that were positively revolutionary when first suggested by men like Lister. We are far more progressive with regard to medical advances than we are with things like the structure of government or the basic rules of baseball. We are essentially—even the young among us—comforted by things that are familiar. The young, of course, are more venturesome if less experienced. But for all of us it is sometimes a very healthy experience to contemplate something that has been there or has been going on for years and simply ask ourselves, "Why?" Today I wish to do just that, to present you with a brief summary of an existing situation and ask you, and myself, "Why?"

Churchill Resigns

On this day in 1955, Great Britain's great man of the century, Winston Churchill, resigned as Prime Minister. He was eighty-one and aging fast, and except for regret at the mortality of this magnificent wartime tower of strength, there was generally relief in his own country and overseas that the reins of his nation had been put in younger hands. It is a sad fact that great men, popular heroes though they may be, are the last to realize for themselves the inadequacies of great age. And when you are at the very top it is extremely difficult to remain active but settle for a lesser role. We are all subject to the human frailty of delighting in the spotlight as we stand center stage. The temptation to go on an ego trip unfortunately seems to go with a rostrum and an audience. I will try to resist that temptation here today and let my words speak for themselves.

Hot Line

On this day in 1963, the United States and the Soviet Union agreed to maintain a 24-hour-a-day hot-line telephone connection between their respective heads of government. The hot line had one great advantage. When somebody called, the other end certainly listened. Every public speaker hopes for that same kind of alert attention on the part of the audience, and this particular speaker hopes with equal fervor that you will find what I have to say worthy of that kind of attention.

APRIL 6

"Over There"

In 1917 on this historic day, when the United States declared war on Germany and joined in World War I, the legendary George M. Cohan introduced a war song he had written called "Over There." It became the rallying song for our war effort, and all America thrilled to its sentiment—"Johnny, get your gun." We have had war songs in later conflicts, but the only one that came close to the rootin', shootin' spirit of "Over There" was "Praise the Lord and Pass the Ammunition," and even that one somehow lacks the sheer belligerency of George M. Cohan's rousing work. The inspiring songs of our own time have been somewhat differently oriented, like "We Shall Overcome." The spirit of belligerency has been replaced by the spirit of determined resistance. Songs change because times change, and times change people. The unquestioned truths of yesterday are challenged and sometimes disproved today. The wisdom of the past, unless it too changes with the times, can become outmoded. It seems to me that one of the opportunities for a speaker is to help focus the audience's attention on that which has changed or that which needs changing, even perhaps surprising you with some of the resultant observations.

Later Retirement

On this day in 1978, President Jimmy Carter signed into law a statute barring compulsory retirement before age 70. The basis for the law was the belief that making people retire at age 65 deprived both the nation and the older workers of working years in which they could be healthily productive. Forced retirement, it was said, can even bore some people to death. We deny to many older people the figurative food and drink, the life-giving nourishment that comes from keeping them in a meaningful relationship with their children and grandchildren, their neighbors of all ages. We didn't plan it that way. Things just happened to work out like that. When children marry these days, they often move to distant cities. The cost of keeping someone in the house with an elderly father or mother while all the children and in-laws are busy with daytime jobs is often prohibitive. If people have changed it is because our environment and our way of life have changed. But some things do not change. Among the eternal verities is the fact that listening to boring speeches can make you old before your time. I will do my best, ladies and gentlemen, not to age you too much with my remarks here today.

Satellite Communication

On this day in 1965, the first commercial communications satellite was launched by Comsat, the Communications Satellite Corporation. Talk between Europe and the U.S. mainland became easier to arrange, and, in the long view, that kind of talk became cheap. Cheapness in rates, ladies and gentlemen, is the only kind of cheap talk worth your attention. I hope that my remarks today will merit your kind indulgence and not be cheap talk at all.

Historic Quorum

The Senate of the United States came into being on March 4, 1789. But when it convened on that day not enough of the 26 senators were present to constitute a quorum, so they had to adjourn without conducting any business. For over a month they kept calling sessions and adjourning them because of the lack of a quorum. But finally, on this day in 1789, enough senators showed up so that the Senate could finally have a meeting. I am glad to note, ladies and gentlemen, that this gathering seems to have no quorum problems, and so I will proceed immediately to the business at hand.

APRIL 7

St. Francis Xavier

This is the anniversary of the birth of St. Francis Xavier in 1506, and there is a story about something he did which I'd like to tell you today. When St. Francis began his missionary career in the Portuguese settlement of Goa on the coast of India, he wanted to talk to the people, so he went out into the street and rang a bell until he had collected an audience. I am happy to note that even if I had a bell like St. Francis Xavier you have saved me the trouble of ringing it to collect an audience. From this point on, of course, unlike that sainted prophet, I am on my own.

Baseball Season

The major league baseball season is once again upon us, and millions of otherwise peaceful Americans will be going out to the ballparks to cheer and boo the players and to give the umpires a piece of their mind. If baseball were played in silence it would be a different game indeed. We Americans like to communicate, even if the communication is all one-way, like fans yelling at the umpire. I stand here in another kind of one-way communication, because I have been asked to deliver a speech, not to conduct a dialogue with you. I can assure you, however, that I will be somewhat less abusive than a fan giving his compliments to an umpire, and I thank you for giving me this time at bat.

World Health Day

This is World Health Day, a United Nations observance of the birthday of the World Health Organization. The exchange of lifesaving medical information and techniques is an international success story, which has helped to stamp out some dreaded diseases and to prolong lives. It shows that when nations, like people, are willing to communicate they can do more together than any of them can do separately. In that spirit I come before you today hopeful that my remarks may spark some of you who are more gifted than I to explore a new idea or two.

Wordsworth

On this birthday of William Wordsworth, the great English poet, I am reminded of a line he wrote in his "Ecclesiastical Sonnet." "Habit," he said, "rules the unreflecting herd." Habit also rules us, to the point where sometimes we too become an unreflecting herd. Today I want to challenge some of the habits of our time—and hope that you will reflect upon them.

APRIL 8

WPA

On this day in 1935, with the country confronted by mass unemployment and the continuing Depression, the Emergency Relief Appropriation Act was passed. The major arm of relief under the Act was the Works Progress Administration, better known as the WPA. There were a lot of jokes about the WPA and its so-called "made work," which gave jobs to millions of people. Only years later, from the perspective of time, did we realize how much good the WPA had managed to accomplish. Obviously, many people did not need the perspective of time to see and seize the opportunity the WPA presented. Today I would like to anticipate the future perspective on some current matters and suggest some marvelous opportunities we have to make tomorrow better.

Domino Theory

President Dwight D. Eisenhower held a press conference on this day in 1954. The conference has long since faded into history, but something that Eisenhower said has become familiar to all of us. It was at that 1954 session that we first heard of the "domino theory" of communist aggression. President Eisenhower declared that if you permitted one free country to fall under communist domination, other countries would follow in a domino effect. Domino theory, cold war, iron curtain—interestingly, we seem to use these convenient phrases to describe threatening and unpleasant situations, rather than friendly ones. We have developed many intermediate stages between all-out war and all-out peace, and we need language that describes them in convenient terms. I do not propose to invent any new phrases in my remarks to you here today but I will try to state my thesis without resorting to fancy language or murky meanings.

King Aaron

This was the day in 1974 when one of those records we had thought might stand forever was broken. Hank Aaron hit the home run that brought his lifetime accumulation of major league four-baggers ahead of the immortal Babe Ruth. He did it almost twenty years after Ruth's final game, and he went on to hit quite a few more home runs before he was done. Records, however great, are made to be broken. Improvement is an eternal target for mankind. Even those things which we think can never be done better turn out eventually to be subject to improvement. I wish I could approach this rostrum with confidence that my remarks would also represent an improvement over previous speeches on previous occasions. If I cannot make that promise, I can at least be encouraged by the fact that audiences today are better informed and with a broader perspective, thanks to the information explosion, than they used to be; and with that reinforcement I step confidently up to bat.

Jefferson on Fear

This is the anniversary of an 1816 letter from Thomas Jefferson to John Adams that I think bears quotation here. Noting that he would be glad to live his seventy or so years over again, Jefferson said, "I think with you, that it is a good world on the whole; that it has been framed on a principle of benevolence, and more pleasure than pain dealt out to us. . . . How much pain have cost us the evils which have never happened!" Close quote. I will not talk today about the potential evils which have never happened. Instead, I will ask you to look with me at the good things that we can make even better.

APRIL 9

First U.S. Astronauts

It seems hard to believe that it was back in 1959, on this day, that the United States chose seven members of the armed forces to be the first Americans in space. Astronauts were a new kind of hero for us then, preparing to go where nobody had gone before, facing dangers we could only imagine. We made them great national heroes, even before they rode to glory. But after the passage of years ventures into space became, if not routine, a great deal more commonplace. We held our breath and were glued to the television set for their takeoffs and landings, but we began to take the astronauts themselves pretty much for granted. Isn't it odd that bad things, like street crime, never lose their morbid fascination, but heroism of a particular kind becomes routine? A speaker can get more attention by talking about evil than by talking about good. But I will resist that temptation, first because there is so much good that is not sufficiently talked about, and second because bad news seems to travel on its own. So, let us turn for a few moments at least to the bright side.

Who Sits Where

On this day in 1929, while the United States was enjoying the last moments of a wave of prosperity in what some people later called "the era of wonderful nonsense," a bitter dispute enlivened life in Washington, D.C. It was the question of which of two ladies took precedence at diplomatic functions, the wife of the Speaker of the House of Representatives, Alice Roosevelt Longworth, or the sister and official hostess of the vice-president, Dolly Gann. You cannot begin to imagine the amount of attention this question aroused, until it was settled on this day in 1929 by the diplomatic corps' decision that Mrs. Gann should be given the privileges of a vice-president's wife. Storms in teacups are sometimes far more interesting than simmering underground volcanoes in policy matters. Gossip often finds a larger audience than grave governmental matters. The speaker who offers a routine of jokes and fancy patter can win more applause than one who deals with serious issues. So you see, I stand before you with a choice of my own to make.

Vanzetti Speaks

The trial of Sacco and Vanzetti was the center of a public controversy that lasted for generations after their execution. On this day in 1927, Bartolomeo Vanzetti made his last statement in court. Denying that he and Nicola Sacco had committed the murder of which they had been found guilty, he said, "But my conviction is that I have suffered for things that I am guilty of. I am suffering because I am a radical and indeed I am a radical. . . ." The verdict of history leans toward the belief that Vanzetti was right, that he was found guilty not by the weight of evidence but because he was an alien in thought and background, a radical in a time of conservatism, an Italian immigrant in a time of jingoism. All too often we reject ideas not because of the ideas themselves but because we object to the champions of those ideas as too young or too old, too foreign or too old-fashioned, or too radical in lifestyle. We look at the issuers instead of the issues. Let's change that. Let's use this occasion to consider some recent proposals on their own.

Taking the Fifth

The Fifth Amendment to the Constitution protects citizens against being forced to be witnesses against themselves. On this day in 1956, the Supreme

Court of the United States, applying that protection, held that a public employee could not be discharged for invoking the Fifth Amendment and condemned the practice of "impugning a sinister meaning to the exercise of a person's constitutional right under the Fifth Amendment." It is nevertheless a hard fact of human nature that we are inclined to judge people not only by what they say but also by what they refuse to say. I am happy to know that your judgment today will be based on my words, and I will give you very little silence in the meantime.

APRIL 10

The Safety Pin

This is the anniversary of the issuance of a patent for the invention of the safety pin in 1849. When I think of the number of babies whose diapers were held in place by the safety pin before the age of disposables, or the other garments that were held together in emergencies by Walter Hunt's invention, it is hard to imagine a more popular device. The ideas that succeed in this world don't have to be ideas that reshape the world. Sometimes modest contributions can succeed where earth-shaking changes fail. There is a parallel in public speaking. One need not deliver a stem-winding, tub-thumping, drum-beating oration to make a modest point or two, so I have not brought my stem winder, my tub, or my drum. Instead, I have brought simply some thoughts that I welcome the opportunity to share with you.

The First Charter of Virginia

On this day in 1606, King James granted the first charter for the settlement of that part of the New World which was called Virginia. This charter first laid the basis for British colonization of our country. The charter was interesting because it didn't just grant land rights to the two colonization companies that had been organized. It also took pains to specify the type of government Virginia should have. Before you start governing, map out how your government is going to be constructed. Years and years later, when we began our independence as a nation, we soon discovered that we had to create a detailed, written Constitution as the structure for our federal government. Sometimes there can be too many rules, or too complicated rules, or too stupid rules, but to operate without any rules would be to invite anarchy. Even the protection of freedom requires rules. And rules are not made to be changed lightly and casually. It is much easier for a speaker to criticize existing rules than to prove that suggested substitutions are better. But let me give that difficult assignment my best effort, here and how.

Joseph Pulitzer

In the town of Mako in Hungary, Joseph Pulitzer was born on this day in 1847. He was 17 when he came to this country, just in time to serve in the Union Army in the Civil War. He became a reporter for a German-language newspaper in St. Louis, had a brief career in politics, and finally bought the *St. Louis Dispatch,* which was the beginning of his publishing triumphs. But his most lasting contributions to his adopted country are not newspapers at all, though they are closely related. His will provided for the creation of the Pulitzer School of Journalism at Columbia University and for the establishment of the Pulitzer Prizes. The School of Journalism, which became a graduate school in 1936, and the Pulitzer Prizes, which recognize achievements in the writing of newspaper material, photography, drama, books, and music, have been important factors in raising the standards of reporting and writing. We have so many annual awards these days in so many different fields that the process has been greatly overdone. Nevertheless, I warn you that I am going to succumb to temptation here today and make my own award nominations. It is a very convenient way to spotlight outstanding examples of the points I wish to make.

ORT

On this day in 1880, the Organization for Rehabilitation through Training was founded by Jews in Imperial Russia to train their coreligionists for industrial work. On its hundredth anniversary in 1980, ORT, as it is known, was described by President Jimmy Carter as "the largest voluntary, nongovernmental job training program in the world." I hasten to add that its headquarters and heart moved long ago out of Europe and onto the cordial soil of America. This is only one example of the way good ideas have become bigger and better when they were brought here. Americans of every faith are the most generous people in the world. No country has ever shared its knowledge, its resources, and its expertise as broadly around the world as this nation of ours. No country has given more encouragement and growth to good causes and worthwhile organizations having their roots in other parts of the world. And I have a feeling that no country has ever been subjected to more appeals, more charitable solicitations, more high-pressure selling. So today, in recognition of that fact, the only selling I will try is to persuade you of the validity of some views of mine, and I thank you for permitting me to get my foot in the door.

APRIL 11

Barber Shop Quartet Day

We are meeting here on Barber Shop Quartet Day, the anniversary of the 1938 launching of the Society for the Preservation and Encouragement of Barber

Shop Quartet Singing in America. In light of the anniversary I must apologize to you for occupying this rostrum alone, and I hope you will find something of value in this one person's opinion, even if it doesn't come from a quartet.

Dust Storms

It was about this time in 1935 that the great midwestern dust storms ravaged the countryside, giving soil conservation a new significance and disrupting the lives of thousands of people. Since then we've had a different kind of dust storm, manmade, created by the clouds of dust that we generate around so many basic issues. Today, with your kind permission, I will endeavor to clear some of that dust.

Spanish American War

This is the anniversary of two key dates in the war we fought against Spain at the close of the nineteenth century. On this day in 1898, President William McKinley asked Congress to declare war as the basis for forcible U.S. intervention against Spanish rule of Cuba; exactly one year later, the treaty of peace was declared in effect. The Spanish American War was the last, so to speak, "cheap" war in which the United States was involved. The fighting all took place on foreign soil, and our casualties on the battlefield were few. Just as the "cheap" war is a thing of the past, cheap talk these days has a way of sometimes turning out to be expensive. I can only hope my remarks today will find a middle course, which, for want of a better term, I will call responsibility.

Shostakovich Defection

Every now and then something happens to remind us how lucky we are. This is the anniversary of one such event. On this day in 1981, two bearers of one of the most famous names in Soviet Russia, the son and grandson of composer Dmitri Shostakovich, defected to the sanctuary in the West. They said they did it because they wanted to live as free individuals. How fortunate we are to live in freedom! We don't have to escape from behind an Iron Curtain to find liberty, because liberty is our birthright here. But it isn't enough to enjoy liberty. We have to be vigilant in defense of liberty. Where should our vigilance be directed these days?

APRIL 12

Kennedy on Falling Barriers

John F. Kennedy was still a U.S. Senator from Massachusetts when he spoke in Indianapolis on this day in 1959. It was a time when civil rights were still being denied to many blacks, discrimination against such others as women and Hispanics was widespread, and the unpleasant echoes of earlier Red-baiting were not forgotten. Against this background, Senator Kennedy was moved to make a comment. "Irrational barriers," he said, "and ancient prejudices fall quickly when the question of survival itself is at stake." Are we at that point? Is the question of survival at stake? And if so, what are we doing to make sure that we stand—or fall—together?

Halifax Day

On this day in 1776, the Provincial Congress of North Carolina, meeting in the town of Halifax, passed a resolution calling for all of the colonies to declare their independence of Great Britain. This was the first such action by a colonial legislature—although Mecklenburg County in North Carolina had proclaimed its own independence of Great Britain the year before. It is interesting that when we think of those who opted for independence we think of Adams of Massachusetts, Jefferson of Virginia, Hancock of Massachusetts, Franklin of Pennsylvania, before the North Carolinians who had actually led the way. Great movements are not always led by the people who start them. The greatest leaders are those who see the value of somebody else's idea and are willing to run with it. The leaders to fear are those who reject a good idea simply because they didn't think of it first. I am here to talk about and advocate some ideas that other people thought of first, and I only wish I had been smart enough to think of them myself.

Catcher's Mask

Enshrined in the records of this day in history is the fact that in 1877, on this very same April 12, the catcher's mask was first used in a baseball game. Baseball players in the years since then have acquired a whole wardrobe of other protective devices, businesses have developed new kinds of protective fences and surveillance units, and the police have gone in for bulletproof vests. But one group remains as vulnerable and unprotected as ever. I refer, ladies and gentlemen, to you, the audience. Sometimes you are even called a captive audience, because you are at the mercy of a longwinded or fuzzy speaker. You have my promise that I shall try to be neither of the above.

Double Space Anniversary

This is a double anniversary for space exploration. In 1961 on this day, Yuri Gagarin, the Russian cosmonaut, became the first man to orbit the earth in a space vehicle. On this same day exactly twenty years later in 1981, two American astronauts, John Young and Robert L. Crippen, became the first to take off from earth in a reusable spaceship, the *Columbia,* the first to make multiple voyages in space. There is no question that the exploration of space benefited from the rivalry between Soviet Russia and the United States. There is much to be said for peaceful rivalries; they seem to stimulate greater effort on the part of the contestants. Similarly, the competition of different ideas in the marketplace often speeds up progress. I thank you for giving me this opportunity to present my ideas as part of this process.

APRIL 13

John Hanson

This is the birthday of the first President of the United States, which may come as a surprise to those of you who know it isn't February. But the fact is that the first President of the United States was not George Washington. *He* was the first President under the Constitution. While the United States was a collection of virtually independent governments doing business together under the Articles of Confederation, the President was the man who presided over its Congress, John Hanson of Maryland. He was elected President of the United States in Congress Assembled in 1781 for a one-year term. The fact that John Hanson, not George Washington, was the first President of the United States is not important in the overview of history. It is only the most dramatic of the misconceptions prevalent in our view of ourselves and our history. And it gives me the occasion to discuss some of those other misconceptions today.

Social Pioneering

On this day in 1936, President Franklin D. Roosevelt made a speech in Baltimore in which he said, "The period of social pioneering is only at its beginning." That was a long time ago, and it raises an obvious question for our own time. Is that period of social pioneering at its end?

$2 Bill

On this date in 1976, the bicentennial year of Thomas Jefferson's immortal Declaration of Independence and the day of Jefferson's 233rd birthday, the United States reissued the $2 bill. By no coincidence whatsoever, the President pictured on the $2 bill was also Thomas Jefferson. But the centers of population, particularly in the East, would have none of it. You can issue $2 bills, but you can't force the public to embrace them. And you can give a speaker the rostrum, but you can't make the audience listen; that is the speaker's job, which I shall now proceed to try to do.

Samuel Beckett

This is the birthday of Samuel Beckett, the Irish novelist and playwright who was born in Dublin in 1906. It was Beckett, a Nobel laureate, who examined life's theater of the absurd in such works as *Waiting for Godot*. The artistry of Samuel Beckett is such that what you seé in his plays is often different from what others in the audience see; you draw your own meanings from his bare stages and isolated characters. What Beckett does in his writing is not easy; that is why so few playwrights who try it ultimately succeed. And that is true of excellence in many fields. It may look easy to duplicate, but it isn't. The answer, of course, is to try to be original, not someone else's carbon copy. I don't know whether many of the thoughts I am going to present to you here today are really my own originals, but I can assure you that they represent some strongly held opinions that I am delighted to have the opportunity to share with you.

APRIL 14

Webster's Dictionary

This is the anniversary of the first publication of Noah Webster's *American Dictionary of the English Language* in 1828. Words fail me in attempting to describe the impact of that classic work. However, I shall try to use some of Noah Webster's best vocabulary here today to convey my message, beginning with an expression of my appreciation for the welcome you have given me.

Lincoln's Assassination

For the first three-quarters of a century of the American republic, we never had to face the shock and grief of the assassination of a president. That fine record ended on this day in 1865, when John Wilkes Booth shot Abraham Lincoln, and in the years since then other presidents' names have been added to the list of martyrs, victims of mad assassins. It seems strange that in the years up to 1865, with passions running so high on issues like slavery and state rights, even when duels to the death between rival politicians and other public figures were taking place, the presidency was less risky than it became closer to our own time. In the course of making life easier we seem to have also made the violent ending of life easier as well. This is only one of the contradictions that confront us these days. Today I would like to talk about some of the other contradictions, not simply in a mood of hand wringing, but rather in hope that you and I can do something about it.

FDR's View of Fate

When President Franklin D. Roosevelt delivered his Pan-American Day address on this day in 1939, he said, "Men are not prisoners of fate, but only prisoners of their own minds." Getting people to change their minds, especially when this means accepting something they have tried to reject, is not easy. But it is important. Otherwise we let preconceived attitudes and emotions, rather than common sense, govern us and guide our actions. So today I want to take dead aim at some of our persistent preconceived notions and wonder out loud whether it isn't time to change them.

Peep Show

The direct ancestor of the modern movie made its debut on this day in 1894, when a machine invented by Thomas Edison went into public use in New York City. It was a peep show that displayed moving pictures to one person at a time. Peep shows did not seem any more respectable in those days than later on, but Edison's device was used to display pictures of famous people like Annie Oakley and Buffalo Bill and thereby encouraged other impresarios to explore the possibility of using movies not simply for an audience of one person at a time but for groups of people. It was less than a year later that the first showing of real movies on a screen took place. This is the way a lot of good ideas come to fruition. They seem small and impractical in their original versions, but then the improvements come along. And sometimes the improvements can make a seemingly bad idea into a good one. Someone I know guides his life by this rule: "I never did anything I couldn't find a way to improve." In that spirit I will venture here today to look at some of our modern ideas and how I think they can be improved.

APRIL 15

Garfield's Reassurance

When the news of President Abraham Lincoln's death from an assassin's bullet reached Wall Street on this day in 1865, Representative James A. Garfield of Ohio was in the financial district. He said to a grieving crowd, "God reigns and the government at Washington still lives!" It was an odd twist of fate that the next president to be assassinated was James A. Garfield himself, sixteen years later. But it is important to remember what he said on this day in 1865: "The government at Washington still lives." Not even the assassination of so dominating and great a figure as Abraham Lincoln brought the government down. Our system has survived assassinations, resignations, and debilitating illnesses. And I think it will be rewarding for us here today—rewarding and encouraging—to see why and how this government of ours endures.

Churchill Wedding

Today is the anniversary of the wedding of a vivacious American named Jenny Jerome to Britain's Lord Randolph Churchill in 1874. Their first child was Winston Churchill. This distinguished offspring of a British—American union was destined to be one of the prime figures in saving a far larger British—American union seventy years later in World War II. If any man's words were ever truly weapons on their own, Churchill was that man, rallying his people to withstand blitzes and invasions and persuading them that they could do it. I have much more modest ambitions for my words here today—and, as a wit like Churchill might well say—I bring much more modest talents to the task.

Carman's April

The poet Bliss Carman wrote, "Make me over, Mother April,/When the sap begins to stir!" I would like to hope that neither Carman nor Mother Nature was referring to April speakers. There is enough sap stirring elsewhere, without your being subjected to more sap here. Mindful of that fact, I take this opportunity to plant some seeds of thought in the hope that they will blossom.

What Came of a Payroll Robbery

On this day in 1920, two men were murdered in a payroll robbery at South Braintree, Massachusetts. It was not, as crimes of violence go, the most sensational crime of its time by any means, but it led to one of the most debated stories in the history of American justice. The men arrested for the Braintree crime were named Nicola Sacco and Bartolomeo Vanzetti; they were immigrants and radicals. For years thereafter, the debate over their guilt or innocence and over the way the trial was handled raged not merely in the United States but around the world. Epochal events have a way of developing out of seemingly isolated incidents. A bungled break-in led to the great Watergate scandal; the assassination of the playboy heir to the throne of Austria–Hungary ended with the whole world at war; a small British detachment confronted a group of colonials on the green at Lexington and triggered the American Revolutionary War. So it is wise to keep on the lookout for the kinds of things that seem to carry the seeds of future crises. If I may, I should like today to tell you of some of the signs and portents I detect on the current scene.

APRIL 16

Book of the Month Club

This month marks the birthday of the Book of the Month Club, which originated the idea of a monthly membership sales service back in 1926. In this country we have developed many great merchandising ideas—books clubs, supermarkets, shopping centers, and many others. We like to remember all of the great technical inventions that the United States gave to the world, but when you get right down to the nitty gritty, the great merchandising ideas are probably even more universal in their appeal. That, I think, is because they involve people rather than machines. We speak the language of people—every sort of people around the world. That is why they listen to our songs and watch our movies. It is this people orientation that I believe we must preserve against the encroachments of the age of automation and pushbuttons. Now more than ever we must encourage those things which bring people together—whether they are social organizations or shopping plazas. We are in danger, it seems to me, of becoming an information-terminal society rather than a person-to-person one. And so I welcome the opportunity to present to you today some thoughts about maintaining the dignity of the individual in the age of the robot.

Charlie Chaplin

This is the birthday of the man who may have been the world's greatest screen comedian, Charlie Chaplin, born in England in 1889. Like those of so many comedians, his is a bittersweet story—self-made success after a poverty-stricken childhood, acclaim in his adopted land turning ultimately to ashes when he chose to stick to some unpopular opinions, and, finally, in a calmer time, an old age laden with the honors earlier denied him. What is interesting is that Charlie Chaplin, the man, didn't really change; public opinion about him changed. Public opinion is volatile and never bothered with consistency. It is easy for a public speaker to detect the way public opinion is moving and to please the crowd by voicing what are clearly its current sentiments. That is not something to be deplored; a speaker who takes that road can help to define and focus and clarify the opinions he or she is echoing. I would like to hope, however, that I can offer more than an echo for you here today. If you do not agree with what I am about to say, perhaps nevertheless it will clarify some aspects of the world in which we live.

Nepotism

I don't know what occasioned the remark, but when Senator Margaret Chase Smith of Maine addressed a National Women's Republican Conference on this day in 1962, she said, "I do not condemn nepotism, provided the relatives really work." It seems to me that the important thing is not how Junior got the job. The important thing is how well Junior does what he is being paid to do. I believe we must always put our primary emphasis on the quality of the job performance, and I believe that holding a job should be dependent on the adequacy of the way the job is done. What happens when you apply that standard to the current scene?

Philanthropic Anniversary

On this date in 1905, $10 million from Andrew Carnegie created the Carnegie Foundation for the Advancement of Teaching. It was this foundation that underwrote the establishment of pension systems for college professors and other teachers, a truly immeasurable contribution to the health of the educational system of the United States. On the anniversary of that forward step it seems appropriate to spend a little time contemplating the opportunities that still remain for private philanthropy to contribute to the public good, and I welcome the opportunity to talk along those lines here today.

APRIL 17

Bay of Pigs

Today is the anniversary of the ill-fated invasion of Fidel Castro's Cuba by a group of exiles at the Bay of Pigs in 1961. Its tragic failure became a haunting memory and a symbol of the danger of underestimating a military task. Why don't we have as long a memory or as strong an impression from our victories, not only on the field of battle but in the more constructive areas of life? Why don't we pay more attention to the good things we do? Today, it is some of those good things that I want to talk about.

Truman's Wrong Pew

Harry Truman was preparing his election campaign when he remarked, on this day in 1948, "Whenever the press quits abusing me, I know I'm in the wrong pew." Every president, including the Franklin D. Roosevelt whom so many press people idolized, had the same complaint. I am happy to say that on an occasion like this a public speaker is not subject to either of these worries. You would not have invited me to share this occasion with you if you disagreed with what you thought I might say. It is therefore with a very comfortable and appreciative feeling that I stand before you, encouraged to present my thoughts to you and grateful for your kind invitation.

Walter Camp

Today, April 17, is the birthday of Walter Camp, the great football figure who was responsible for creating that effective national concept, the All-American. He was born in 1859 in Connecticut, went to Yale, and ultimately became one of the first football coaches, at that university. A year after he began coaching he conceived the idea of selecting an All-American football team from among all of the football players at the various colleges around the country. He also led the way in bringing the rules of football up to date. He wrote many books about football and physical fitness and was the father of the idea of regular daily fitness exercises. Among other things, Walter Camp was the living proof that if something is worth doing it is worth talking about. Today I approach this rostrum with the other side of that particular coin. I believe that the things I find worth talking about are worth doing, and that is precisely what I am going to be talking about today.

Adams on Politics

In one of his last letters to his old friend Thomas Jefferson, John Adams on this day in 1826 commented that "public affairs go on pretty much as usual: perpetual chicanery and rather more personal abuse than there used to be."

That, of course, is a constant complaint. I don't think we will ever reach the point where all differences of political opinion will be kept on a high level of either intelligence or etiquette. Nevertheless, I will try to make my own uplifting contribution by confining my discussion of some hot issues today to their merits and demerits without suggesting that my opponents are either stupid or wicked. I do not contend that they are either of the above. Mistaken, yes. Now let me tell you why.

APRIL 18

Ernie Pyle

This is the day Ernie Pyle was killed, reporting the fighting front in the Pacific phase of World War II in 1945. For those of you who do not know his name, let me say he was the most famous battlefield correspondent of that war—particularly because he reported the war from the point of view of the enlisted man in the heart of the fighting. All too often we get our news from the commanding officers, not the folks on the front line, and sometimes the front-line workers and the commanders don't see things quite the same way. It is important to get both perspectives. So, even if you find you disagree with what I am about to say, I hope that it will nevertheless add to your overall perspective on some matters of interest.

The Doolittle Raid

On this day in 1942, America's attitude toward the war against Japan was tremendously bolstered by the first U.S. bombing raid against the Japanese mainland. Colonel James H. Doolittle led a contingent of B-52 bombing planes that took off from carriers far out in the Pacific. It was a tremendous flying achievement, but it was something more than that. The Japanese had successfully invaded U.S. territory all over the Pacific. Now we had demonstrated that we could bring the war home to them. America has never relished being on the defensive, and the Doolittle raid came as a sign that the defensive phase of the war could and would end. It is important to realize how much the American public feeds on encouraging news. We are a nation of emotional people, and we like to feel we are on the right path. Indeed, probably no question is before the American public more than this one: Are we on the right path? That question, and my own version of the answer, furnishes the subject matter for my remarks here today.

Secretaries

This is the time in April when, long ago, the custom began of observing Secretaries Week and its focal point, Secretaries Day, in tribute to the people who, in some ways, really keep America going. In the 1980s, they changed it to Professional Secretaries Week and Day. When the women's equality movement was most aggressive some years ago, there was a strong tendency to downgrade secretarial work. It was a tendency encouraged by feminists, because most secretaries were women and secretarial work was thought by the feminists to be a sort of women's ghetto on the business scene. Times, I am happy to note, have changed. No longer does a secretary see the promotion parade pass her, or him, by. Professional secretarial work is as good as any means known for entering the business world and gaining a foothold. The situation that used to apply was an ideal example of how prejudice can foul things up. Employers who were prejudiced against promoting woman secretaries and extremists who sold the theory that secretarial work was demeaning both made secretarial work unattractive and less productive. Prejudice always has this kind of weakening effect. Today I want to take aim publicly against some more recent prejudices, which I think it is important first to recognize and then to combat.

Eire

On this day in 1949, Eire—the Republic of Ireland—was formally established. It was the first time in hundreds of years that the major portion of the island enjoyed full freedom from British rule. The peace that prevailed in the Irish Republic was in glaring contrast with the decades of fighting and tension that were to be the lot of still British Northern Ireland. We are not immune to these dangers here in our own blessed land. There are those who would import foreign fights to our shores, and there are those who would fight against anything they regard as foreign. The important thing to remember, I believe, is that we have effective peaceful means to resort to and that we must maintain everyone's right to resort to those means. So today I am going to talk about how we can best protect that right.

APRIL 19

Came the Revolution

President Dwight D. Eisenhower made a speech on this day in 1956 from which I want to quote one sentence. "One hundred and eight-one years ago," he said, "our forefathers started a revolution that still goes on." He was referring to the Battle of Lexington and Concord, which triggered the American Revolutionary War. But he was also referring to a great American tradition—the tradition of constant change. Ours is a continuing revolution, a continuing refusal to keep things always exactly as they are. We have become a great nation by tinkering, so to speak, with success; we have always felt that whatever we had still offered room for improvement. That is the note I wish to sound today—room for improvement.

Battle Memories

For some reason this is a day that recalls many battles in many wars. The first shots of the American Revolutionary War in 1775 were fired on this day; the first bloodshed of the Civil War came on this day in 1861 when a force of Union soldiers was attacked by a mob in Baltimore; there were casualties on both sides. And on this day in 1917, the U.S. Navy fired its first shots of World War I in a warning to a German boat in the Pacific. I don't know what makes April 19 so pugnacious, but I can assure you that I have no guns to fire across your bow here today. Nor will I bombard you with threats of doom and disaster. Instead, I invite you to join with me in contemplation of some happier things.

Victims' Rights Week

In 1981, President Ronald Reagan proclaimed the observance at this time of year of national Victims' Rights Week. The observance recognized the sad and longstanding fact that we often do more to try to rehabilitate criminals than we do to aid the victims of their crimes. What can we do to balance this equation?

Theater Guild

On this day in 1919, a new idea in theatergoing was born with the founding of the Theater Guild. The idea was to sell a subscription for a series of dramatic presentations rather than sell tickets for each on its own. In the years since the founding of the Theater Guild, all kinds of cultural organizations—theater groups, concert programs, lecture groupings—have marketed their offerings on a season subscription basis and helped spark the greatest explosion of such types of entertainment in our nation's history. The lesson, I suppose, is that good things are more attractive in bunches, or that all of us like to think we are buying wholesale, at wholesale prices. What it comes down to is another version of a great American technique—mass marketing. Why sell one attraction when with the same effort you can sell a whole series? I would like to apply that principle today to a discussion of some phases of American life where things might be improved by the same technique.

APRIL 20

Interest Note

Today is the anniversary of an act of Congress in 1957 that raised the interest on E and H bonds to—are you ready?—3¼ percent. If that doesn't tell you how long we have been in the age of rising expectations, I don't know what will. If you stop to think about it, one of the few things that hasn't inflated, like interest rates, is oratory. If speeches had grown like interest rates you could anticipate a five- or six-hour address from me here today. Don't be alarmed; I couldn't talk that long if I wanted to. I know what I want to say, and I will make it brief.

School Busing

On this day in 1971, the Supreme Court of the United States ruled that busing of children to achieve school desegregation was legal and permissible. I don't think we realized then how long the problem of segregation would persist. We are a hopeful people, and we often think that complex problems can be solved quickly with simplistic solutions. Life, however, has a way of complicating things for us. We underestimate the stubbornness of old ways and the sticktoitiveness of early enthusiasts. And we fear so much the onus of being corny that we hesitate to raise our public voices time after time in the same cause. Ladies and gentlemen, I do not hesitate to defy that fear here today. I am going to say some things you may have heard before, and I am going to say them here and now because I believe they need saying; they demand your attention.

Jefferson on Longwindedness

This is the anniversary of a comment by Thomas Jefferson that should be called to the attention of every speaker. He said on this day in 1824, "Amplification is the vice of modern oratory. . . . Speeches measured by the hours die with the hour." Bearing that in mind, I shall try to be brief and to the point today, for if terseness was good enough for Thomas Jefferson, it had certainly better be good enough for me.

Citizenship Achievement

Some of the bright moments of American history seem so commonplace today that we don't give them the recognition they deserve. One such occurred on April 20, 1657, in the Dutch settlement of New Amsterdam, when the first Jews in the city won the right to full citizenship. That was one of the landmarks of religious freedom in America—not the only one, by any means, but one of the more important. Yet it seems routine today because it refers to a liberty that has been ours for so many generations. I suppose that is why we are so casual about so many of the blessings of life in this free nation. But if you look at the rest of the world you get a new feeling of pride in the way our concept of liberty tops them all. Let me cite some examples.

APRIL 21

John Muir

Today is the birthday of the great American naturalist John Muir, who was born in Scotland in 1838 and grew up in Wisconsin. Muir is the father of the conservation movement in the United States, and it was because of his efforts that the Yosemite National Park was created and the idea of national forest preserves was adopted. So much of our energy is devoted to change that it is important to have among us people who fight against changing the landscape. Nature, of course, is far from defenseless, but sometimes she moves slowly in taking her revenge. If we divert too much water from the land, it doesn't become a desert overnight; it changes slowly and inexorably. So we need the alarm-sounders and the nay-sayers, and today I am about to join their ranks.

The $64 Question

On a radio quiz program that had its premiere on this day in 1940, we first heard the phrase "the $64 question." At that time, $64 constituted a truly princely sum, and the nation was thrilled to hear the contestant try for this kind of big money. It wasn't too long, after an intervening world war, before the ante was upped to $64,000, and greed truly had its day. The only thing we haven't inflated, it seems to me, is oratory. Daniel Webster was a lot more verbose and grandiloquent than today's leading orators. We speak more plainly and less lengthily in public today—a point which I hope I am about to illustrate to you.

Maryland Toleration Act

The colony of Maryland was dominated by Catholics in 1649, and its founder, Lord Baltimore, was upset over charges that his fellow Catholics were intolerant toward Protestants. On this day he succeeded in having Maryland pass the so-called Toleration Act to protect the practice of Protestantism. Five years later the Puritans came to power in Maryland and instituted measures against the Catholics. Tolerance, it appears, does not always breed tolerance in return. The victims of intolerance, given the chance, can be as intolerant as anybody else. There are some people who pride themselves on being different, and there are some who insist on seeing differences where none really exist. Both views reinforce the kind of cultural apartheid that classifies people by their complexions or whether their last names end in a vowel or whether they worship God on Saturday or Sunday. This apartheid isn't always enforced by a majority against a minority; it is also practiced on a considerable scale by minorities as a form of protection. If you live with others of your kind—and there is a hateful phrase if there ever was one—you may feel safer and less exposed. I hope this cultural apartheid is on the way out. And to that end I have some suggestions.

Svetlana Alliluyeva

So many people have fled to freedom in the West from behind the iron curtain of Soviet Russia that the news that a lady named Svetlana Alliluyeva had done so on this day in 1967 might not seem to be particularly sensational.

But this particular lady, arriving in the United States, as she put it, to "seek the self-expression denied me in Russia," happened to be the daughter of Josef Stalin, the longtime dictator of the USSR. Her father was dead when she fled, and things were supposedly a little less restrictive after his passing, but his daughter still knew where liberty lived, and it wasn't in Russia. Now, if even Stalin's daughter found her beacon of hope shining here in America, how much must the presence of this blessed land mean to the oppressed masses in so many parts of the world—and what can we do to keep the beacon of hope lit for them?

APRIL 22

One to Watch

Thomas B. Reed of the state of Maine was the brilliant if at times autocratic speaker of the U.S. House of Representatives, but even before he reached that office he was known for his political wisdom. On this day in 1880, Representative Reed offered as succinct a definition of party politics in our nation as has yet been given. "The best system," he said, "is to have one party govern and the other party watch." Having somebody watch the way you do your job is a very salutary experience. Nobody knows that better than a speaker getting ready to address an audience. This isn't the kind of job you do in private. You do it in full view and full hearing of a group of thinking people who are there to consider what you have to say and how you say it. I can only hope my remarks will meet your standards.

London Naval Treaty

On April 22, this day in 1930, the London Naval Treaty was signed by the United States, Great Britain, and Japan. The treaty expired in 1936, and its disarmament provisions were so temporary as to prove altogether futile in the long view of history. But it was a try. The likelihood that an international agreement won't last is not a good reason to abandon the effort. Even if all it buys is a little time, it is worth trying. In the same sense, talking of how we can maintain peace is never futile, because talking peace is usually less dangerous than talking war. Somebody once said that talk is cheap; the history of humanity suggests that all too often not talking is expensive indeed. If my remarks here today can produce even a scintilla of peaceful progress, then my time—and yours—has not been wasted.

Bertillon

Today is the birthday of the man who killed anonymity. His name was Alphonse Bertillon, and he was born in France in 1853. He introduced the system of identifying people by skull and skeletal measurements. Although it was later superseded by fingerprinting, it was the first identification system to be based on the idea that every person's physical attributes provide a unique and identifying pattern. Fingerprinting is a lot simpler and more reliable, of course. What Bertillon did is something that science has been doing for centuries--proving the truth of the fact that every human being is an individual; we are not totally identical products of a mass-production assembly line. Perhaps if we remembered that, instead of speaking of that faceless mass called "the unemployed" or "teenagers" or "welfare families" or "big business" or "organized labor," we would be able to focus better on the problems of people. And so today I want to talk to you about some people whose situations are not unique, but whose identities are totally their own.

In God We Trust

On this day in 1864, Congress approved placing on all U.S. coins the motto "In God We Trust." Cynics may say that by so doing we rendered unto Caesar that which was God's—or that we drove the moneychangers back into the temple. But the facts belie the cynicism. Some infinite power has blessed our land and has been good to us. It is always fashionable to talk about what is wrong with the United States. It seems to come with our Puritan heritage. But today I would like to consider how the God in whom we trust has indeed rewarded that trust. I would like to highlight some of our good things.

APRIL 23

William Shakespeare

Today is both the birthday and the anniversary of the death of William Shakespeare, born 1564, died 1516. Anybody who is asked to make a speech on this historic day faces the fact that it saw the beginning and the end of the greatest fashioner of speeches the English language ever knew. As Shakespeare wrote, however, "an honest tale speeds best being plainly told," and so I shall, if not waxing oratorical, try instead to speak plainly.

Global Weather Watch

History notes that on this day in 1962, the United States and the Soviet Union agreed to work together in a global weather watch. I don't know that this rare example of cooperation produced any significant improvement either in the weather or in the forecasting, but at least, as has been said of the assessment of the medicinal value of chicken soup, "it don't hurt." Cooperation with countries whose way of life is so diametrically opposed to our own is often hard to swallow, even when the purposes are clearly in the best interests of both; but we have to make up our minds to deal with the world as it is before we can make it what we would like it to be. I can't remember a time when we could say with a clear conscience that all of our international friends had the same concept of human rights that we do, yet one authoritarian regime may be an ally while another is a foe. What should our priorities be in international friendships?

A Note from Hitler

Not too many of the remarks of Adolf Hitler are worth quoting, but one that he made on this day in 1933 bears repeating. "It is not the neutrals or the lukewarms," he said, "who make history." There are evils in the world about which we cannot afford to be neutral or lukewarm. We don't have to look overseas for them. We have evils enough in this country about which to be exercised. To avoid the do-nothingness of neutrality on these domestic evils, we have to act—and I propose today to suggest some courses of action.

The End of the World

In the annals of history there are many occasions when some self-endowed prophet has announced a specific date for the end of the world. This day in 1843 was one of those days. A man named William Miller had predicted the second coming, and the folks who believed him gathered with their spiritual bags packed to await the magic moment. It didn't happen, but Miller, unabashed, revised his calculations and picked a new date, October 22, 1844. When that date came and passed uneventfully, the Miller movement fell apart. Most prophets don't make the mistake of being as specific as William Miller. It's one thing to talk about a discernible trend and quite another to predict in terms of an exact day or date. Mindful of the sad story of William Miller, I will talk today only in trend terms, which is the only way to be realistic.

APRIL 24

Hostage Rescue Fiasco

One of the things we don't particularly like to remember about this day happened in 1980, when a U.S. armed forces attempt to rescue the hostages being held in Iran ended in total failure, not because of Iranian opposition but because of accidents, bad weather, and a combination of circumstances that resulted in tragic casualties and an embarrassing fiasco. When we finally negotiated the release of the hostages we put the failed rescue attempt out of our minds, but I suggest that it is worth remembering on several counts. First and foremost, brave men gave their lives because mistakes were made. Second, military might and success don't always go hand in hand. Third, we try to forget failures when we might do better by remembering and gaining lessons from them.

Sir Winston

In 1953, in the twilight of his epic career, Winston Churchill finally agreed to accept knighthood from his Queen. Sir Winston needed no title of nobility, and when it came it was still a modest capping for a life that was anything but modest. Some people concern themselves so much with the trappings and perquisites of power that they lose sight of more fundamental roles. When I see democratic leaders surround themselves with the trappings of royalty, I think of Winston Churchill; his most regal weapon was the English language, which he mobilized as few people have done. I thank you for the opportunity to use that same tool, the English language, before you today; but I must confess that compared to Churchill I come unarmed.

The Trojan Horse

According to some calculations, this was the day back in about 1184 B.C. when the Greeks used their Trojan horse to get inside besieged Troy and win their war. The Trojan horse, you will recall, was a huge wooden replica with soldiers hidden inside. The Trojans, consumed by curiosity about this strange thing the Greeks had parked outside the wall, brought it into the city to study it, and once the hidden soldiers were inside the city they came out of the horse with a sneak attack. That was a long, long time ago, but life has been full of Trojan horses ever since. We continue to be fascinated by things we haven't seen before, and we continue to play with these things before we realize the dangers. We go in for diet fads and offbeat economic theories simply because they seem so different. I would like to suggest that we balance our love of the new with a little more respect for the proven, that we do a bit less tinkering with success and a lot more examination of possible consequences. Let me apply those precepts to our current situation.

Burning of Washington

Today marks the anniversary of the burning of Washington, D.C., by the British in the War of 1812, in 1814. Only the British didn't do all of the burning. The Navy Yard was destroyed by our own people to prevent it from falling into British hands. This was undoubtedly the most ignominious page in American history. I think of that time when I contemplate the public wails of anguish of those who now despair of America's future and wallow in predictions of doom. We survived the burning of our capital; we will survive and triumph over the assorted other adversities that, from time to time, may befall us. All too often we overlook the basic strengths of this land of ours. Today, I want to talk about those strengths—because they are worth talking about.

APRIL 25

Oliver Cromwell

This is the birthday of Oliver Cromwell, born in England in 1599. He was the strange, driven man who ousted a king, ruled as Lord Protector but turned down the crown of England. He was dictatorial and combative, full of Puritan intolerance—in short, like so many leaders, a man who ultimately fell prey to the belief in his own divine mandate. All too many people have the same belief in their divine mandates. They refuse to concede that on this or that issue the other side might have a case. They clothe themselves in the garments of virtue, whether the garments fit or not. It is difficult to hold a rational discussion with folks like this, because they start with the assumption that if you oppose them you are, wittingly or unwittingly, an instrument of the devil. It is this devil theory in American public life that I want to discuss here today.

Suez Canal

On this day in 1859, construction of the Suez Canal got under way. It proved to be a major engineering achievement, but not even the men who conceived it could have foretold how important it would become. After all, in 1859 nobody knew how much oil the world would need, and the fact that there was oil in the Middle East, which would have to be transported to the West by ocean ships, was totally unknown. When we try to predict the good or the bad that will come of some great human effort, we are in fact dealing with the unknown. The people who object to new undertakings are also dealing with the unknown. They merchandise fear of the unknown rather than trying to figure out how to build in the protections we may need. We are told repeatedly not to try new scientific approaches until we realize the consequences, but, as with the Suez Canal, we can't know the consequences until later. I am concerned both with those who would needlessly and recklessly experiment at the risk of countless lives and those who would block anything new just to be safe. Above all, I deplore unproven charges of impending horrors. Let me cite some recent examples of this kind of scare tactic.

The Wisdom of Age

When psychoanalyst Erik Erikson was 69 years old he was attending a professional conference on this day in 1971. Invited to comment to the press, he said, "If I don't open my mouth they may take it for the wisdom of age." You have been kind enough to invite me to address you here today, and I am flattered that you have done so, but I keep worrying that your good opinion of me may not last when I open my mouth. So I can only hope that in the next few minutes you will not be disappointed.

Revolution in Portugal

After half a century of authoritarian rule the dictatorship was overthrown in Portugal by a military junta that, within 48 hours of taking over on this day in 1974, promised to restore democracy and free elections. And they kept their promise. I like to think of this when I hear people say that after generations of dictatorship people can't handle liberty. As long as people know how to think for themselves—even if for years they've had to do that thinking in private—they can govern themselves, too. I mention that because, with all our concern about nations that backslide from democracy into dictatorship, we often forget to pay enough attention to the nations that have done the reverse. Today I would like to call your attention to the signs of hope I see in so many different parts of the world.

APRIL 26

Confederate Memorial Day

A day of memorial for Confederate casualties of the Civil War is observed around this time in some southern states. Unlike the rest of the nation, the South has consistently honored the memory of its heroes who fell in a losing cause. This is in contrast to the casualness with which most of us treat the memory of the Korean War stalemate and the Vietnam War morass, although the men who died in those conflicts deserve no less regard than their World War counterparts. The South has always had more respect for the past than the rest of us; that, as well as climate, may be why in our own time the South seems to have found the key to the future. For a knowledge of the past is the best way to ensure that we don't repeat it. And, as I look around at our world these days, I see many things that give me a sense of déjà vu or of history repeating itself.

Artemus Ward

Today is the birthday of Charles Farrar Browne, who wrote and lectured under the pen name of Artemus Ward. He was one of the favorite comic commentators of several generations of Americans and quite a few English people as well. He was born on this day in 1834 in Maine. It was Artemus Ward who said, "Let us all be happy and live within our means, even if we have to borrow the money to do it with." He also wrote, describing a physical encounter, "By a sudden and adroit movement I placed my left eye against the Secesher's fist." These are funny words, but, alas, they seem to be a sadly accurate account of the way our government does business. We tell ourselves we are governing within our means, but we keep borrowing to do it. We tell ourselves we are always the most peaceful of nations, but somehow our national eye every now and then collides with another nation's fist. I am here today to wonder aloud, with you, how come?

The Power to Tax

I suppose every student of American history is familiar with Chief Justice John Marshall's famous dictum that the power to tax is the power to destroy. On this day in 1971, the man who was then mayor of New York City updated Justice Marshall. Speaking at a New York state commission hearing, Mayor John Lindsay said, "The power to tax is the power to live, at least as far as local government is concerned." That, ladies and gentlemen, brings us to the nub of the problem. How much do we want our governments to live at our expense? How much of the taxes we pay are for our protection and our good, and how much are for the preservation of the power and perquisites of those who do the governing? As the people who pay the bills, I believe we are entitled to examine closely and constantly the way that amorphous thing called the government spends our money. Let me report to you what I have found in the course of that examination.

Guérnica

On this day in 1937, in the Spanish Civil War, the old Basque city of Guérnica was bombed by German planes of the Luftwaffe. It was estimated that 10,000 people died in the bombing. The outrage of much of the world was expressed most lastingly by Pablo Picasso in one of his greatest paintings, which has made the name Guérnica immortal. But the military lesson of the bombing was somehow lost on the free world. When the Nazis brought their dive bombers into play in the blitzkrieg days of World War II, the Allied forces were taken almost completely by surprise. The world did not want to see the Spanish Civil War for what it really was, a rehearsal of fascist fighting techniques using the handy battlegrounds of a nation torn apart by its own internal differences. Leaders of nations, like ordinary mortals, sometimes see only what they want to see. Right now, as at almost any time in our history, I can cite situations that you and I encounter every day but which the higher-ups of government somehow do not see. I have some examples.

APRIL 27

Babe Ruth Day

George Herman Ruth never pretended to be anything other than what he was, a fun-loving man who could hit a baseball farther and more often than anybody else. Babe Ruth was no intellectual; he caroused, he played his way through life, and he was the greatest national hero of his time. When the news broke that Babe Ruth was mortally ill the nation was shocked, and on this day in 1947 Babe Ruth Day was observed wherever baseball was played. At Yankee Stadium, informally known as "the house that Ruth built," more than 58,000 people gathered to hail the Babe, to show him how much they cared, and, as it turned out, to bid him goodbye. He died a year later. America cheers its heroes when they are up, but every now and then an even nicer American trait comes through, when we have an outpouring of affection and cheer for a falling hero. I don't think there are any other people in the world who, under the right circumstances, can match us for compassion and for caring. That is the spirit which I am trying to enlist here today, as I tell you about an area of concern where compassion and caring are unfortunately in insufficient supply.

Marines at Tripoli

All of us are familiar with the words of the U.S. Marines hymn that recalls exploits "from the halls of Montezuma to the shores of Tripoli." Today, it so happens, is the anniversary of what happened on the shores of Tripoli in 1805, when the Marines captured the fort at Derna in combat against the Barbary pirates. The Marines know what their job is, and they prepare to do it; their job is the basic fighting, not the grand strategy or the science-fiction devices. They are usually not diverted from their single-minded pursuit of hand-fighting excellence, so to speak. And I think there is a lesson here for the rest of us, including, if I must admit, public speakers. The first assignment is to reduce what you have to do to the simplest, most basic terms. The second assignment is to avoid complicating the task with side issues or with extra baggage. So let me get right to the point of my remarks here today.

April Showers

This is the season of the April showers that are supposed to bring the May flowers. It is not, however, the season for a shower of words. Rather than overwhelm you with an outpouring of oratory, I prefer simply to try to plant a few seeds of thought, and I want to thank you for providing so fertile a garden and so warm a reception.

Social Security

This is the anniversary of the day in 1937 when the first Social Security checks were distributed in the United States. It was a brand new experience for many Americans. Today, so many years later, it is hard for us to figure out how we got along as a nation without Social Security—or how long we can get along with it. Like everything else, it costs more and more, and the burden for our children grows greater. What one generation has to fight for becomes the accustomed lot of the next generation. And when I consider that fact I stop to wonder what improvements in the social structure of American life we are creating to pass on to the generations that follow us. It is a question that I believe may teach us something about ourselves, and it is the subject of my remarks here today.

APRIL 28

James Monroe

James Monroe, who was born on this day in 1758, was the President of the United States in 1823, when he enunciated what has become the basic principle of our Latin American policy, the Monroe Doctrine. But history tells us that the guiding spirit behind the Monroe Doctrine was actually Monroe's Secretary of State, a gentleman by the name of John Quincy Adams. Even the things in history that seem like the inspiration of one person come to fruition only because other men and women are persuaded of their rightness. When we look at the successes or failures of our leaders, we should also, in many cases, be looking at ourselves. Indeed, looking at ourselves is a rewarding exercise and an education, even when we are not trying to assign the blame for a failure or the credit for a success. For example, if we look at ourselves as a nation or a society today, what do we—or should we—see?

Dim-out

On this day in 1942, during World War II, places within fifteen miles of the Atlantic Ocean were told to dim out their lights at night to avoid helping enemy submarines. It seems hard to believe that at that late date, even after aircraft carriers had launched the planes that sneak-attacked Pearl Harbor, we were more concerned on the East Coast about submarines bombarding the shore. I think this is another illustration of the way, at the outset of every war, we approach the fight with the outmoded concepts of the previous war. I believe we also do the same thing in peacetime. We try methods to cope with an economic problem that we tried the last time we had that problem, regardless of whether they had worked or not. We build our social and economic Maginot lines, only to have them overrun by newer developments. Ladies and gentlemen, I believe we need up-to-date ideas to deal with up-to-date problems, and I hope that here today I can contribute some thoughts along those lines.

Days of Remembrance

In 1978, pursuant to a resolution passed unanimously by both houses of Congress, this day and the next were designated as Days of Remembrance of Victims of the Holocaust. Even while these observances were being conducted, some Americans, including some claiming to be scholars, were contending that the holocaust never took place, that the millions of murders and the concentration camps corpses seen by so many witnesses were figments of the imagination. More important, purveyors of religious and racial hatred, the Nazis' stock in trade, were still active, defacing places of worship, wearing swastika-bedecked uniforms, and exploiting the basic permissiveness of our free society. So on this year's days of remembrance I rise to remind us all of how important it is to see that no holocaust takes place again and to explore what we can do to help attain that simple goal.

Canada–U.S. Good Will Week

This is the time of year when we commemorate the Rush–Bagot Agreement of 1817, which called for an unfortified border between the United States and Canada. We have had our peaceful disagreements with our northern neighbors, but peaceful collaboration has been the order of the day ever since that pact in 1817. Friendship grows slowly and gains strength with time. It also grows when both parties have the same concept of freedom—and that is asking a lot in this divided world. But as we observe Canada–U.S. Good Will Week now, we might spare a thought or two for how and when we can observe a similar *World*–U.S. Good Will Week.

APRIL 29

Vassar

This is the birthday of Matthew Vassar, best known as the founder of Vassar College. He was born in England in 1792 but grew up near Poughkeepsie, New York, and it was there that he endowed Vassar Female College in 1861. Higher education for women was not a very popular idea in those days, but Matthew Vassar insisted that his college had to be just as demanding and just as educationally advanced as any male institution, and he built a school that lived up to his hopes. Many generations later, when equal education opportunities for women were no longer arguable, Vassar College began admitting men as well, and I suppose that the spirit of Matthew Vassar felt he had proven his point. When I listen to some of the firebrands of feminism—or for that matter of most any other movement—I am reminded that it is the Matthew Vassars, not the professional causists, who get things done, who make the reforms into realities. We cannot look to single-issue pleaders to win the battles. If justice is to be done, if wrongs are to be righted, the groundswell must come from us, the people. It is among us that the new Matthew Vassars will be found. As I make my own special plea to you here today, I ask you particularly to remember that the decisions—the actions—are up to you.

Apple Blossom Festivals

This is the time of the apple blossom festivals, when we celebrate the annual blooming of the oldest of the fruit trees. Apple blossom time is the heart of the springtime season, when hope springs eternal. And it is a very appropriate season for a public speaker to look at the future hopefully. I looked at the future before I came here today, and I'd like to tell you what I think I saw.

Duke Ellington

This is the birthday of Duke Ellington, the great jazz composer. But Edward Kennedy Ellington, born on this day in 1899, was more than a great jazz composer, pianist, and orchestra leader. He was recognized in his own time as a creator of outstanding music regardless of whether it was jazz or classical, and as a black man he brought to the world a new awareness of the potential of his people. He moved with grace and distinction in the highest circles of his own country and the whole world. Duke Ellington let his music talk for him, and it spoke a universal language. Those of us whose language is mere words rarely capture the mood of a people or a time as the Duke did. He *wrote* the music; we can only *face* the music. He sounded the notes of sophistication and melody; today I stand before you, I must confess, to sound a far different note.

Street Light

The first electrically illuminated street in the world turned on the lights on this day in 1879. The city was Cleveland, and the source of the light was a newfangled invention called electricity. I don't know what wonders the city of Cleveland or the rest of the world expected from being able to light the way back in 1879. I suspect that in some degree their expectations were higher than what actually developed. Hope, said the poet, springs eternal, and in this season of budding flowers and normally pleasant sunshine it can also be said that spring hopes eternal. We know we have problems, but we renew the hunt for solutions. It is in that mood that I come before you today, not to view with alarm but rather to tell why and to what I look forward with such anticipation.

APRIL 30

Walpurgis Night

This is the day of Walpurgis Night, when northern Europe holds festivals to ward off the witches and the demons. It seems to be an appropriate time for us to consider some of the witches and demons that bedevil us, so I will use this occasion to discuss some of the forces of evil that confront us.

Louisiana Purchase

This day in the year of 1803 was the date of record for the transaction whereby, at a cost of some $15 million, the United States acquired from France the Louisiana territory. But at the time there were strong voices raised against the purchase, and it was suggested that Thomas Jefferson was abusing his office as president under the Constitution in acquiring the territory We, of course, have the advantage of several centuries of perspective, and so we know better now. But I wonder what that kind of perspective will tell future generations about our own actions—if they are around to judge us. Now, it s very difficult for any of us to project ourselves 200 years ahead and then try to look back at what we are doing today. But there are some contrasts that we can see even without the passage of that much time. For example, Jefferson was criticized for acquiring land; in recent years we have criticized government for trying to dispose of land. Let me cite some of the other interesting comparisons.

Daylight Savings Time

One of the more pleasant aspects of spring for most of us is that it brings daylight savings time, more of our waking hours in the light of day and less in the black of night. Americans have a built-in fondness for daylight, including more light on the operations of their government. We all know that bureaucrats who have about as much to do with national defense as the corner supermarket tend to wrap themselves in the security cocoon whenever their actions are questioned. The trouble is that we don't really know whether national security is involved if we don't know what they are hiding. In this kind of dilemma, you end up taking on faith or distrusting on inst nct the assurances of either the bureaucrat or of someone else who knows what the bureaucrat is hiding. That seems a terrible way to do business, but on the other hand it isn't that different from what we do every day. We believe this person totally and discount what that person is saying, not necessarily because we know the subject but because we have arrived at a judgment about the person. I operate on the theory that you don't invite speakers you don't have confidence or trust in, and on that premise I thank you for the compliment implied n your invitation to me to address you. Now it is up to me to bring my own kind of daylight in.

War Month

I was struck as I contemplated the various historical entries for April by one interesting fact about this normally pleasant spring month. We seem to have made a habit of getting into wars in April. The shooting phase of the American Revolution began in April at Lexington and Concord. The Civil War began with the firing on Fort Sumter in April. The Spanish-American War was formally declared by both sides in April. And we declared that a state of war existed with Germany in World War I also in April. So I suppose, now that we have reached the last day of the month in a condition of peace, we should be very grateful. And I shall not roil the waters by using this rostrum even to declare war on crime or any other domestic condition. Instead, I should like to consider with you the peaceful things this country does so well, and wonder aloud whether in some cases we might do even better.

MAY 1

Empire State Building

This is the day when the Empire State Building was dedicated in 1931 as what was then the world's tallest structure. In May of 1931, the Depression was a worldwide disaster. The predictions were that the Empire State Building would never succeed in renting all of its office space. It was a marvelous technical achievement, *but.* . . . This, of course, is a familiar refrain. Every time someone tries something taller or bigger or more ambitious, the nay-sayers are there to tell you it will never work. But when you aim high, even though it may take a while to succeed, success often comes. And the higher you aim, the more the success will mean. With that in mind, I propose today to look at some areas where I don't think we are aiming high enough.

Better Speech and Hearing Month

The observance of May as Better Speach and Hearing Month began quite a few years ago. I would like to hope that since it began more and more Americans are hearing better and better. As for the speech, I will present my remarks here today and let you judge for yourselves.

"Pious Fraud"

It was James Russell Lowell who wrote, in his *Under the Willows,* that "May is a pious fraud of the almanac." With all due respect to Mr. Lowell, I beg to differ. Far from being a pious fraud, May is the time when the creations of nature come out in their true colors, the college students also come out, and the rest of us come up for air. The first of May is traditionally a day for merry-making or political demonstrations, and not for stem-winding oratory, so I shall wind no stems here today and instead will try to get May off to a pleasant start for all of us.

North Korean Republic

This is the anniversary of the establishment in 1948 of the Democratic People's Republic of North Korea. What we did not know at the time was that two years later this communist nation would launch an invasion of South Korea—not a guerrilla people's war but a full-fledged old-fashioned imperialist invasion. No communist nation has been as barefaced in its aggression and in its hostility as the republic that was born in North Korea on this day in 1948. It is something to remember, however unpleasant, and it serves as a reminder today that not everybody in this world is our friend. That isn't surprising, since even here at home not everybody is our friend. Competing ideas in the marketplace of ideas provide a healthy climate, but not when the competition is a form of warfare. Yet right here at home we have people and organizations that, as surely as the Democratic People's Republic of North Korea, mean no good for our way of life. Today I would like to examine some of these.

MAY 2

Stonewall Jackson

On this day in 1863, one of the great men of American history suffered a mortal wound from which he died ten days later. Sad though his death was, it was made even sadder first by the fact that he died in a doomed cause and second by the fact that this great general, Stonewall Jackson, was accidentally shot by his own troops at the Battle of Chancellorsville. His talents were of no avail in the circumstances of his death. And that should teach us a lesson. Whatever our talents or great personal traits, we are all the prisoners of circumstances and the beneficiaries of opportunity. When we talk of our current situation, it seems to me that it is more important to look at the opportunities than at the personalities, so it is the examination of opportunities that provides my subject for today.

H. M. Robert

The name of Henry Martyn Robert may not be familiar to you, so the fact that Henry Martyn Robert was born on this day in 1837 may not seem to be of any great interest. Let me explain the gentleman's identity a bit further. He was the man who wrote Robert's Rules of Order, and I can't imagine having meetings without those rules. Not everybody who influences our lives is himself or herself a household name. And not every influence is a spectacular or exciting one. We are surrounded and often guided by unspectacular, unexciting things like Robert's Rules of Order, which help make possible the efficient working of a civilized society. Occasionally, as is the case with meetings run under Robert's Rules, some changes are called for. Today I would like to rise on a point of personal privilege to suggest a few rule changes for our way of life.

Theodore Herzl

Theodore Herzl, who was born on this day in 1860 in Hungary, did not live to see the fruition of the movement he inspired. The movement was Zionism, which was a vague dream before Herzl and an active movement after he made it the target of his life. Single-minded people, given the boon of appropriate times, can indeed change the world. Unfortunately, not all single-minded people have the right idea on their mind, and not all of their changes are for the better—as witness Adolf Hitler or Nikolai Lenin. It is not enough to be single-minded and dedicated; it is even more important not to be mistaken. I will, therefore, in my remarks here today, be single-minded in my dedication to trying to be right. Only you—and time—will tell whether I have succeeded.

Hudson's Bay Company

This is the birthday of the issuance of a royal charter in 1670 to an organization that was given the name "The Governor and Company of Adventurers of England into Hudson's Bay." What is most interesting about the organization, which came to be known as the Hudson's Bay Company, is that this private-venture capital business not only financed and managed much of the exploration of Canada but also continued as a trading company into our own time, with stores from coast to coast throughout Canada. Entrepreneurs played tremendous roles in making the world bigger and better. But the first part of the task of any entrepreneur has to be self-preservation in the competition of the marketplace, and that means knowing how to knit the various parts of a business into a team that works efficiently and smoothly. In that, the challenge is not much different from what confronts a government. Just as a business must have the confidence and support of its customers, a government—in our concept of government—must have the will of the people behind it. Something similar exists in the case of a speaker. It is not enough simply to have a spot on the dais or to be the one closest to the microphone. The essential ingredient for the speaker is an interested audience, and in giving me that you give me a head start.

MAY 3

Balloon Duel

On this day in 1808, the archives of well-forgotten lore tell us that the first incident of aerial warfare took place when two Frenchmen got into their balloons, soared above Paris, and then shot at each other while they were both in the air. I am sorry I cannot report to you what weighty problem resulted in this odd confrontation; considering the way the balloons were sent aloft, I would have to confine myself to saying it was a triumph of hot air. On that basis, it is an anniversary I will try to keep in mind as I address you here today, because while I want to win you over to my point of view I most assuredly do not want it to be another triumph of hot air.

Toll Bridge Anniversary

This is the anniversary of the beginning in America of a great moneymaking idea. It was called a toll bridge. The first opened in 1654 across the river at Rowley, Massachusetts, and on this day it was permitted to charge a toll for animals. Human beings crossed for free. As you know, modern toll bridges and tunnels have made some improvements. Human beings pay, but animals usually go free (if they are permitted at all), and just to keep consistent with history, at rush hour the toll-takers sometimes treat the human beings like animals. Today I am here to illustrate one of the important differences between human beings and other animals. It is to the credit of the dogs, cats, horses, and creatures of the field that not one of them has stood up in front of a gathering like this one and tried to make a speech. Only we human beings impose our views upon each other that way. I will try here today to make that imposition as painless as possible.

Jacob A. Riis

This is the birthday of Jacob A. Riis, born in Denmark in 1849. A long time ago Riis turned his journalistic talent and his camera upon life in the tenements of the teeming city. His reports helped awaken the conscience of the nation and began the process of reform. Perhaps it helped that he came to this country from abroad, so that conditions native Americans had seen since birth came as a shock to him—and ultimately, thanks to him, as a shock to many of the rest of us. That is a great argument for trying to see things through someone else's eyes, and it encourages me to ask you to see some things through my eyes here today.

First State Sales Tax

Today is the anniversary of a less than auspicious invention. On this day in 1921, West Virginia approved the first state sales tax. Government had found a new way into our pocketbooks. And you know the rest of that story. Today I shall try very hard not to get into the government's act. I shall try not to tax your patience.

MAY 4

Rhode Island Independence Day

Rhode Island is our smallest state, but on this day in 1776 it stood tall indeed when it proclaimed itself independent of Great Britain, two months before the Continental Congress adopted the Declaration of Independence. The governments of the colonies of 1776 did not equivocate. They did not count up their muskets before they proclaimed liberty and announced their willingness to defend it. They did not issue a tentative statement as a trial balloon and wait to see how it went over. They did not call in the public opinion pollsters. They listened to their consciences, and that was that. Today every special pleader seeks to appeal to the conscience of government and the conscience of the public.

The issues are infinitely more complex than the simple rallying cry against taxation without representation. But we have one thing in common with the Founding Fathers. We, too, can meet and talk things over. And that is the opportunity I welcome here today.

The Right to Communicate

In 1970 the Supreme Court of the United States was asked to decide the constitutionality of a law aimed at preventing the sending of erotic mail to people who didn't want to receive it. On this day in that year, the Court decided unanimously that the law was proper, and Chief Justice Burger put the issue in very clear terms. "The right of every person 'to be let alone,' " he said, "must be placed in the scales with the right of others to communicate." Unfortunately, ladies and gentlemen, you temporarily gave up that right when you joined this audience, because it is very difficult for a speaker to address remarks to you and, at the same time, let you alone. I can only express the hope that you will find what I have to say worthy of the sacrifice.

Horace Mann

Today is the birthday of Horace Mann, the great educator. Born in Massachusetts in 1796, he was a lawyer and state legislator before he became secretary of the state board of education in Massachusetts, and then he really got going. He founded the first normal schools in the nation to train teachers, he established professional standards for free public education, and he crusaded to have the public know more and care more about the quality of the teaching of children. He didn't do all of this alone, but he was the heart and soul of the great leap forward made by public education in his lifetime. Horace Mann was an eloquent illustration of what one person, caring enough, can do. If one person, caring enough, can do that much, then what can a group of us, caring deeply, hope to accomplish? That is what I am going to talk about here today.

Peter Minuit

The history books note the fact that this was the day in 1626 when Peter Minuit landed on Manhattan Island to take charge of the new Dutch settlement there called New Amsterdam. Minuit was destined to eternal fame as the man who bought Manhattan for $24, perhaps the biggest bargain in history. But the bargain wasn't quite what it seemed. The Indians who sold the island, it turns out, didn't own it. They crossed over from Brooklyn when they wanted new ground to hunt or play in, but Manhattan was definitely not their island. That, I am afraid, is the story with a lot of bargains. You've got to look into them before you decide who's cheating whom, or who's gotten the better end of it. The same, my friends, is true of individuals dealing with the government. From where we sit, it may look as though a lot of people are feeding themselves at the government trough, and not too graciously. From where *they* sit, the government is not that good a provider, and they never have any leeway to move around in. It's very hard, even under the best of circumstances, to be able to see a question from both sides, but that is what I hope to be able to help you do here today.

MAY 5

Three Nations Free

This is an auspicious day for a free and open discussion, because it is a notable anniversary day for freedom. In Mexico it is Cinco de Mayo, commemorating the great Mexican victory over the forces of French-backed, would-be Emperor Maximilian. In West Germany it marks the day in 1955 when the Federal Republic became a free and independent nation. And in Denmark it is Liberation Day, the anniversary of the end of the Nazi occupation of that country in 1945. So it is a day when we know, looking back in history, that democratic self-government has the kind of staying power that enables it to survive. It is in that mood of justified optimism that I propose to take a look with you today at some of the problems of freedom in our own wonderful land.

The End of Napoleon

On this day in 1821, on the remote island of St. Helena off the coast of Africa, the most ambitious man of his time died in exile. His name, of course, was Napoleon Bonaparte. Various little Napoleons, including one named Hitler, have followed in his footsteps. So when we Americans detect what seems to be an excess of ambition in a public figure, we are understandably wary—except, it seems to me, when that excess of ambition is expressed in monetary terms. We have not been sufficiently wary of election campaigns where the money flows like water, of millionaires who almost literally buy their elections by outspending all opponents a hundred to one. Why are they able to do that? Is there something wrong with the system, or is there something wrong with us, the voters? Today I would like to discuss the peculiar habits of the individual with whom the buck stops, the great American voter.

John T. Scopes

On this day in 1925, a Tennessee biology teacher named John T. Scopes was arrested for teaching the theory of evolution in a Dayton, Tennessee, school. Tennessee had adopted a law banning such teaching. Before the Scopes trial was over, great national figures had become involved—Clarence Darrow as a defense attorney and William Jennings Bryan as an expert for the prosecution. In an epic confrontation, Darrow made Bryan a national laughingstock. Bryan's literal view of the Bible had made the confrontation inevitable, but even the millions of Americans who favored the teaching of evolution had to be upset by the utter destruction of a man whose faith was clear and whose record of public service was so distinguished. One of the unhappy consequences of differences of opinion is that they can lead people into total confrontations and the kinds of battles in which no prisoners are taken. I rise here today not so much to take sides in a bitter discussion of issues as to plead for keeping such discussion on a decent, democratic level. Appeals to reason are always worthy arguments. Appeals to hatred and fear are something else again, and today I want to draw a bead on these unfortunately all too prevalent tactics.

Hambletonian

Today is a birthday that I think deserves to be mentioned. It is the birthday of a horse—a very special horse. His name was Hambletonian, born in New York in 1849. Many of you may recognize the name, which has not only been given to great trotters but also to the national trotting classic race, the Hambletonian. The original Hambletonian led a busy life; among other things, he sired 1,331 offspring. In horse racing, as opposed to human existence, we encourage the reproduction of the best of the breed. What makes the story of Hambletonian particularly interesting to me is that this paragon of equine perfection was born to a crippled mare. Nature has a way of righting wrongs over the course of generations. Beasts can't talk, but they can strive for perfection in other ways, such as speeding on the track or producing outstanding offspring. Human beings, on the other hand, while they can do these same things, also can talk, and sometimes we talk instead of doing. I hope my words today will not prove to be a substitute for action but will, instead, be a help in lighting the path.

MAY 6

Be Kind to Animals Week

This is the time of May when we have become accustomed to observing Be Kind to Animals Week. I believe it is a time when we should be considerate of all living things, and in observance of the occasion I will try to be kind to you here today by not taxing your patience unduly with my remarks. And I thank you for your kindness to me in asking me to be with you.

Wilson on Eloquence

Woodrow Wilson remarked on this day in 1911 that—and I quote—"the man with power but without conscience, could, with an eloquent tongue, if he cared for nothing but his own power, put this whole country into a flame. . . ."

Close quote. When Wilson made that observation, we had no radios and no television networks; for the most part, except for the crowd in a speaker's immediate audience, his or her remarks were read later on in the newspapers. Now, if Wilson felt that eloquence could be that dangerous even when distilled into print, how much more extreme would he find the situation today, when miraculous means of communication can provide instant contact with millions upon millions of people? Not every speech is transmitted that way, thank goodness—not every speech is worthy of that kind of attention. But I'll tell you a secret. No public speaker hopes to be ignored. We enjoy the opportunity to communicate with a sympathetic audience, even if we are not planning any earth-shaking revelations. We appreciate the opportunity to sound off, and I thank you for giving me that opportunity here today.

Manhattan Anniversary

This day, or one reasonably close to it, in the year of 1626 saw a wise Dutchman named Peter Minuit trade $24 worth of trinkets for the island of Manhattan. We are commonly given to understand that Minuit got far the better of that deal than the Indians. Manhattan Island, of course, has appreciated considerably in value, but a lot of the added value is because of what generations of hardworking people put into building a great city. The trinkets, on the other hand, would have increased in value simply by surviving in identifiable form. What this seems to illustrate is that there are two kinds of wealth—first, the riches that exist simply because they are there, priced in terms of how scarce and how wanted they are, and second, the riches that are almost literally created by human work, like buildings and improved land. All too many of us keep looking for that one big moment that will set us up for the rest of our lives. I am not here to knock that one big moment, but I know, as surely as I am standing here talking to you, that most of us have a far better chance for happy lives filled with a series of not quite so big moments of accomplishment and success. There is an old saying about keeping your eyes on the stars, which is fine, but you had better also keep your eyes every now and then on the path you are walking. Even on the stairway to the stars there may be a batch of potholes. And it is some of those potholes that I want to talk about here today.

WPA

On this day in 1935, Harry Hopkins was appointed head of the New Deal's Works Progress Administration, better known as the WPA. The relatively unknown Hopkins, who had worked with President Franklin D. Roosevelt since 1931, became known as the world's biggest spender because of the billions of dollars he dispensed in providing work relief for the unemployed. He became FDR's trusted right-hand man, and as such shared much of the abuse that was heaped upon Roosevelt by his opponents. But Hopkins quietly ran his relief programs and, despite all the jokes about men leaning upon their rakes while the leaves blew away, he ran it well. He had never before come even close to dealing with the amount of money that was at his disposal in the WPA, but he rose to the challenge. Today I would like to talk about some hardworking people of our own time who are also faced with bigger jobs than they may ever have dreamed of handling, and who are doing those jobs well.

MAY 7

Edwin Land

Today is the birthday of a man who changed the way we look at things. Edwin Land, the founder of the Polaroid Company and the father of polarized light devices, was born on this day in 1909 in Connecticut. In addition to developing light polarization devices like sunglasses, he was also the father of the modern instant camera. Dr. Land and his company achieved their greatest success in the very years when many people were complaining that the entrepreneur didn't stand a chance anymore. Land proved that the pessimists were wrong, and other creative entrepreneurs have been proving the same thing ever since. My purpose in mentioning Edwin Land here today is to point up the essential strength of this country, which is the strength of good ideas ardently pursued. And there is no lack of good ideas today. I would like to use this opportunity to talk about some of them.

Asian/Pacific American Heritage Week

Some years ago we began observing this time of May as Asian/Pacific American Heritage Week. In proclaiming the week in 1980, President Jimmy Carter commented that America's strength is "in the richness of its cultural diversity." Asian and Pacific peoples continue to add new vigor to the strength of that diversity, not only by the different cultures they bring to our shores but also by the energy and dedication with which they devote themselves to becoming worthy citizens of the land that has adopted them. They are not unique in this regard. Every wave of immigration has brought to our shores a new influx of energetic people anxious to make good use of their new freedom. Ladies and gentlemen, we are still a melting pot, not from intermarriage but from intercultural living. We have much to learn from one another, and today I would like to tell you some of the things I have learned.

The Same Boat

Whitney Young Jr. was the great black leader of the Urban League who died entirely too young. He made a speech on this day in 1970, which deserves to be remembered for this pointed remark: "We may have come over on different ships, but we're all in the same boat now." Given that inescapable fact, I stand here to sound a call for the spirit of cooperation. We can accomplish more by helping one another than by competing with one another. Let me be specific.

A Notable Set of Birthdays

Today is the birthday of a truly notable group of experts at composing words or music. Johannes Brahms was born on this day in 1833, Peter Ilyitch Tschaikowsky in 1840, the great Indian writer–philosopher Rabindranath Tagore in 1861, and the poet Robert Browning in 1812. On such an auspicious day I guess there is no alternative but for me to face the music with the best words I can muster, so here I go.

MAY 8

Triple Play

Not all the historic milestones are immortalized in our memory. One of the less celebrated occurred on this day in 1878, when we are told that in a game between two New England baseball teams a player for Providence named Paul Hines pulled off the first unassisted triple play. I could not find too many details of this historic feat, but it is a puzzler since the one thing I do know is that Paul Hines was the Providence center fielder, and center field is hardly the focal point for your average, garden variety of unassisted triple play. History, I regret to say, is full of gaps and mysteries like this one. We fill in the unknown parts with surmises, logical deductions, and just plain guesswork, and over the course of time the guesswork becomes part of the gospel of the overall legend. We have this kind of mythology in our everyday lives as well—the myth that crime does not pay, the myth that only loafers get welfare, the myth that the basis of the American economy is private enterprise, and so forth. Today I will examine life under the myths and, perhaps, in the course of that presentation, come up with a few surprises for you.

V-E Day

This is V-E Day, commemorating the Allied victory in Europe over Nazi Germany, which climaxed with Germany's surrender on this day in 1945. It was a hard-won and historic victory, and we did not realize then how many more battles would have to be fought and how many more people would die in the quest for a lasting and just peace. V-E Day seems to me to be a very appropriate time to look at the state of the world and the state of peace. Those are my topics for today.

Target Nixon

When Richard M. Nixon was Dwight D. Eisenhower's Vice-President, he paid an official visit to South America. In 1958 on this day in Peru, the second highest officer of the United States of America was spat at and stoned. It was neither the first nor the last time representatives of the United States have been subjected to abuse overseas, but, perhaps because Nixon was not exactly the most popular man in his own country, the nation's sense of outrage was well restrained. Indeed, we showed then as we have shown since that the United States can be insulted with far more impunity than a prickly power like the Soviet Union. I am not suggesting that we keep a chip on our shoulder, but I think we might well be a bit more prickly. Anti-American rallies are whipped up on the flimsiest of excuses in foreign capitals, and we ignore them. I wonder what would happen if we reacted, not with an answering rally but, for example, with a cut in some of the items we supply to those countries. Or are we as defenseless against this kind of propaganda as it sometimes seems? I keep wondering why, somehow, the Russians are so rarely targeted for this kind of demonstration in those same overseas cities. Could it be because they react quickly and strongly? I am not here to suggest that we start fixing our bayonets, but I do want to propose that we be a little more sensitive, so that troublemakers overseas may think twice before impugning us in the future.

World Red Cross Day

This is World Red Cross Day, marking the birth in 1828 of the man who founded the International Red Cross, Henri Dunant. Bearing in mind that on World Red Cross Day even a speaker should show a little compassion, I will spare you any extra oratorical flourishes and try to use my time on this rostrum as painlessly as possible.

MAY 9

Italy Annexes Ethiopia

In our own time the free democratic republic of Italy has been such a good international citizen that it comes as a shock to realize that today is the anniversary of the most barefaced international aggression of its time, and the Italy of Benito Mussolini was the aggressor. This was the day in 1936 when the founder of fascism, Mussolini, having successfully invaded Ethiopia, declared that ancient nation part of his new fascist empire. Mussolini's success at flouting international law encouraged his partner, Adolf Hitler, to expand Nazi Germany's European domain. Ethiopia was by no means the last Third World nation to find itself subjugated by an imperialistic power. After the second World

War was over and the fascist Axis powers had been defeated, Soviet Russian imperialism took over. We will never have a world composed entirely of good guys in white hats. Under such circumstances it is important to have reliable sources of information about what is happening in the world of which we are a part. That is why having American correspondents overseas is so important—and why it is equally important for us here to be able to analyze what is happening overseas. Today, I would like to give you my view of the current international situation.

Vast Wasteland

When the chairman of the Federal Communications Commission came to address the National Association of Broadcasters on this day in 1961, he gave them both barrels. The chairman, Newton Minow, told the assembled broadcasters that the television airwaves were a "vast wasteland" of bad programming. At that time, observers referred to the decade of the 1950s as television's golden age. Interestingly, as we look back to television in 1961 and for some years thereafter, we are inclined to regard what we saw then as part of the golden age, but at the time Minow's criticism found plenty of popular support. I suppose that from one point of view mass taste was already on a downward cycle, which Minow and those who agreed with him had already discerned, but the medium was then and is now the victim of generalizations. In television's worst years there have been fine programs, and in television's best years there have been plenty of bad programs. The same can be said of popular taste—some of it is good; some is disgraceful. Unfortunately we are altogether too tolerant of bad taste—not just on television but everywhere. Let me cite some examples.

Book Burning

On this day and into the next in 1933, the Nazis had a bonfire in Berlin. It wasn't just a bonfire. It was the deliberate burning of 25,000 books that the Nazis did not like, including, we are told, a copy of the Bible. We don't burn books in this country very much, but we are constantly beset by demands to ban if not to burn. We didn't learn the lesson of Prohibition. There are still among us decent, honorable people who think you can keep dirty ideas away by banning books. Of course, there is the added difficulty that what one citizen thinks is a dirty idea another citizen may regard as idealistic and noble. On this anniversary of the Nazi book burning, I think it is fitting and appropriate to talk about the importance of protecting the freedom to read.

First Newspaper Cartoon

The first cartoon ever to appear in an American newspaper was published on this day in 1754 by Benjamin Franklin in his *Pennsylvania Gazette*. It was a political cartoon, showing the colonies as separated sections of a snake under the caption "Join or Die." Cartoons have been among the most powerful propaganda weapons ever since. Unfortunately, as your speaker here today, my tool is words, not a sketch pad. Word pictures take a little more time than cartoons, but I hope you will find the time well spent.

MAY 10

Woodhull for President

On this day in 1872, the most unlikely presidential candidacy of all time was formalized. A group called the National Radical Reform Party nominated one of its stalwarts for president of the United States and a great lecturer and abolitionist leader for vice-president. There were only a couple of problems. The nominee for president, Victoria Woodhull, was a woman, and as such she wasn't entitled to vote. The nominee for vice-president, black orator Frederick Douglass, was realistic enough to want no part of the action. Woodhull used her candidacy as a platform to argue for women's rights and gained further attention by trying vainly to be admitted to cast a vote herself. I doubt that too many of the people who laughed at Victoria Woodhull in 1872 would have believed that less than fifty years later women would have the vote and 100 years later black leaders would run for high office and get elected. Goals that seem totally out of reach for one generation have a way of becoming entirely possible for the next or for the generation after that. Change is often very slow in coming, but in a modern western society change is inevitable. That is always a comfort to speakers, because it gives us, automatically, our choice of two general approaches: first, why things must change and how, and alternatively, why we should try to stop things from changing. Today I have chosen the approach of column A—the inevitability of some changes and how best we can shape them to the right ends.

Mother's Day

The first officially proclaimed Mother's Day was observed on this day in 1908 in Philadelphia. Miss Anna Jarvis, who had initiated the campaign for Mother's Day, was a Philadelphian, so the City of Brotherly Love also became the first city of motherly recognition. Since then, of course, Mother's Day has become a national observance that the telephone companies, florists, and greeting card manufacturers cherish dearly. America has never been averse to making sentiment pay, and nothing demands the filial loyalty that Mother's Day does. Find me a politician who fails to pay proper obeisance to the institution of motherhood, and I will point out a politician with a dubious future. So it is a surprise, I suppose, that given our great American devotion to Mom, we don't do too well by our mothers. Let me, if you please, count the ways we don't do too well, beginning while Mother is still expecting and going through the day camp years and beyond.

Second Continental Congress

On this day in 1775, with the colonies at war against England, the second Continental Congress convened in Philadelphia. There were a number of delegates who hadn't been at the first Continental Congress the year before, and I think it is safe to say they were an improvement. Among the newcomers were Benjamin Franklin, John Hancock, and, a bit later on, a gangly redhead from Virginia named Thomas Jefferson. Within two months, two of these men—Jefferson and Franklin—would be members of the committee that drew up the Declaration of Independence. One cannot tell when a group of concerned people gathers what notable developments will come from their meeting, and while this is certainly not another Continental Congress, it too is a gathering whose concerns may well be reflected in the shape of later events. I bear that much in mind as I address you here today.

Kefauver on Crime

I doubt that either Vice-President Barkley or Senator Estes Kefauver knew the show they were starting when on this day in 1950 Barkley appointed the senator to head a Senate subcommittee to investigate crime. The Kefauver Committee's hearings were televised, and the sight of well-known figures of menace taking the fifth amendment became one of the most widely viewed broadcast attractions of its time. I don't think history records any significant advances in crime prevention or penology coming out of the hearings, but they made Estes Kefauver familiar to the entire nation. And I suspect they persuaded quite a few senators that permitting committee hearings to be televised was not without its dividends. It seems to me that anything that exposes any of the processes of government to be witnessed by the public is highly worthwhile, if not always as fascinating as the parade of Senator Kefauver's witnesses. Certain processes of government do not lend themselves to television, but they too deserve a certain share of the spotlight. Today I shall try to examine some of these bureaucratic processes for your information and, perhaps in some cases, for your amazement.

MAY 11

CARE

On this day in 1946, the first CARE packages were delivered in Europe. In its first 15 years of operation, CARE, the Cooperative for American Relief Everywhere to give it its formal title, provided food or medical supplies to almost

500 million people. That is one reason why Americans cannot understand the seeming bitterness of so many people overseas toward the United States. But resentment of the rich is a common human failing, to the point where it becomes impossible to be both a benefactor and a hero to the rest of the world. Good deeds often have this kind of unfortunate fallout. Contribute to a worthy cause, and ten other worthy causes knock on your door. Contribute once, and you are on the target list for years. Contribute what you can, and you will be asked to give more, while the guy next door who gives nothing isn't bothered at all. These are the familiar hazards. But there is another side to the equation. Giving to worthy causes clearly helps in making a better world for all of us. Nobody ever went spiritually broke by giving of himself or herself. If we could only see how many other ways there are of giving besides writing out a check. I'd like to talk about some of those ways today.

Kovats Day

This is Kovats Day, an occasion not known to very many of us but one that is well worth mentioning. Michael de Kovats was a Hungarian. He read the Declaration of Independence in Europe and was so impressed with it that he joined with Casimir Pulaski to raise the Pulaski Legion and was in command of that gallant group when he was killed in action at Charleston, South Carolina, on this day in 1779. Ladies and gentlemen, we take very much for granted the document that inspired Michael de Kovats to come from Europe to give his life in the cause of liberty. When you get down to it, our government from day to day does not ask us for what Kovats freely gave. The government makes demands upon us, of course, but I am here to suggest that the price we pay for living in a land of liberty is one of the great bargains of life. I am here to suggest that we try to live up to our end of that bargain by becoming part of the action, and I am here to suggest where and how.

Rural Electrification Administration

On this day in 1935, President Franklin D. Roosevelt established the Rural Electrification Administration to bring electricity to the farms of America. Like much of FDR's New Deal, it was denounced as socialism, although private enterprise had shown absolutely no zeal to get into the field. Over the course of the next fifteen years power lines were brought into more than 90 percent of American farms. Sometimes it doesn't matter who does a job, as long as the job needs doing and somebody is willing to do it. That, my friends, is also true of speechmaking. There are some things that need saying, and it doesn't much matter who does the saying as long as it gets said. That, of course, is why I am here with you today.

Salvador Dali

Today is the birthday of Salvador Dali, the artist who was born in Spain in 1904. Dali gained fame not only for his modern art, notably the furlined teacup, but also for his personality. He was his own most interesting creation, from his carefully waxed and flowing moustache to his carefully tailored bon mots. And while his art was sufficiently arresting on its own to capture attention, Dali the personality gave it great additional interest. Self-advertising is also an art, and Dali was a master in that regard. Those of us who use words alone are always harder pressed than those who have a mastery of visual arts. But today I will use words as best I can to give you some pictures I want you to have.

MAY 12

National Hospital Day

Beginning many years ago the birthday of Florence Nightingale has been observed as National Hospital Day, and National Hospital Day has been the central keystone of National Hospital Week. Florence Nightingale, who was born on this day in 1820, was of course the great pioneer of British hospital nursing, and it is very fitting that on the anniversary of her birth we salute the institutions where her example is followed. Being in the hospital is sometimes like being in the audience for a public speaker. You don't know how long it is going to take and how painful it may turn out to be, but you hope for the best. Ladies and gentlemen, I shall try to make my remarks painless, I won't be long, and I plan to draw no blood. Shall we proceed?

Baudouin's 20 Seconds

In 1959 on this day, King Baudouin of Belgium addressed a joint session of the U.S. Congress. He said, "It takes twenty years or more of peace to make a man; it takes only 20 seconds of war to destroy him." Think of that for a moment; it speaks volumes about the reasons why no sensible human being wants war. But as we look around the world we find too many places where human life is held altogether too cheaply, too many regimes that stay in office by repression and bloodletting. What, short of war, can we do about this? We cannot single-handedly reform the world, but there are peaceful things that we can do, and I would like to enumerate some of them—and to name some of the evildoers against whom these tactics can be aimed.

Yogi Berra

Lawrence P. Berra was born on this day in 1925. Not too many people know about Lawrence P. Berra, but a great many have heard of him under the name he used as an outstanding baseball player, coach, manager, and master of the malaprop. I am referring, of course, to Yogi Berra. As I stand on this dais I think particularly of what Yogi Berra said the day he was being honored by thousands of his fans. "I want to thank all of you," Yogi said, "who made this night necessary." In that spirit, I want to thank all of you who made my remarks here today necessary.

The Beginning of the End

Over the course of this day and the next in 1943, World War II took a great turn for the better, as far as the Allies were concerned, when the Axis forces in North Africa surrendered. General Rommel, the German military commander who had been the great North African strategist, had fled to Europe, and thousands of his forces were captured. At last, after seeing territory after territory overrun by the Nazis, the Allies had a significant victory. In peace, ladies and gentlemen, as well as in war, there are significant victories and notable turning points. We have the opportunity to achieve some of these, and I would like to tell you where and how.

MAY 13

Joe Louis

Today is the birthday of a man who was a great heavyweight boxing champion and a warm human being. His name was Joe Louis, born in 1914 in Louisiana. Today I remember him and want you to remember him not for his great boxing but for the simple directness of one remark he made when asked how he would cope with the speed and boxing ability of an extremely clever opponent. "He can run," said Louis, "but he can't hide." I suggest we keep that quotation very much in mind, for we live in a world in which we can run but we can't hide. Like it or not, we cannot run away from certain decisions and certain actions that we have to take, and that is what I want to consider with you here today.

The Pope Shot

On this day in 1981, the unthinkable happened. A Turkish terrorist shot Pope John Paul II in full view of a crowd in Vatican Square. Fortunately, the Pope recovered from the attack, and the would-be assassin was promptly arrested and convicted. But the shocking incident was a horrible illustration of the extent to which terror for terror's sake had become a part of the human jungle. There was a time when terrorists and bomb throwers used their weapons against tyrants, but that time has passed. Now these same weapons are used against peaceful people, to disrupt their lives and pave the way for ruthless power-seekers to take over. This sad fact poses tremendous problems for free people and democratic government, because the terrorists use that freedom to their own advantage. We are confronted with the need to determine when and where domestic surveillance is to be permitted, how can we protect essential liberties and still protect our people. I do not stand before you today with an easy answer to these questions, but I think it will be productive to discuss them.

Armed Forces Day

Around this time of the year our nation usually observes Armed Forces Day. There are two ways of looking at Armed Forces Day, one being to regard it as an occasion for reminding ourselves of our military might, and the other being to view it as giving the civilian population some idea of where their tax money is going. We enjoy the great privilege of a society that makes the armed forces subject to the will of the people, instead of the reverse. It is significant that the great generals who became presidents of the United States, from Washington to Grant to Eisenhower, showed no favoritism for the military in their administrations. That, ladies and gentlemen, is worth remembering in the season of Armed Forces Day—a time when, I suggest, we consider the positive accomplishments of the dedicated men and women who, over the course of American history, have contributed so much to the American way of life.

Sir Arthur Sullivan

This is the birthday of Sir Arthur Sullivan, the composer half of the wonderful light opera team of Gilbert and Sullivan. Sir Arthur was born on this day in 1842 in Lambeth, England. For all of his life he was a dedicated composer of serious classical music, but, despite his considerable output of cantatas, operatic and ballet compositions, he is best remembered for his operetta scores and for two great songs, "The Lost Chord" and "Onward, Christian Soldiers." The story of Sir Arthur Sullivan strikes its own chord for many of us who, like him, make our success in fields collateral to what we really wanted. Life has a way of finding out what we do best, whether we realize it or not. We are often not the best judges of our own skills, and sometimes we can do more and be happier doing what we do best rather than doing what we like to do. In too many schools, instead of unremittingly searching for talent, the dominating theme is "Don't make waves." An adventurous and inspired teacher is often in trouble for breaking the rules, and nobody pays more attention to rules than the average school. Can it be that we are educating people wrong?

MAY 14

Lewis and Clark

On this day in the year 1804, Meriwether Lewis and William Clark led their small group of explorers out of St. Louis to begin perhaps the most epic voyage of discovery ever attempted in North America. Their assignment from President Thomas Jefferson was to report back on just what sort of land the nation had acquired in the Louisiana Purchase. And before Lewis and Clark were finished they had explored the continent foot by foot all the way to the Pacific Coast. We celebrate heroic feats in war that cannot compare to the spectacular heroism and accomplishments of Lewis and Clark, but somehow heroism in peace lacks some of the panache of heroism in military combat. This is unfortunate, and I think it is time we found a way to give the same glory to the heroes of peace. To that end I have chosen a number of instances of quiet, unheralded peacetime heroism to report to you today.

Rockefeller's Gift

On this day in 1913, John D. Rockefeller made the largest single gift in history up to that time, when he donated $100 million to establish the Rockefeller Foundation. The gift did not exactly leave the richest man in the world destitute, but it did a great deal to ameliorate his reputation as a capitalist, monopolist profiteer. More important, it set a pattern for exemplary later philanthropy by his heirs and associates. That is one of the benefits of good citizenship. It can be contagious. Some of us don't like to be in the forefront but are perfectly willing to join the philanthropic or good citizenship crowd. I hope people like that are in the audience here today, because I have some suggestions.

Israel

On this day in 1948, the British rule of Palestine ended and in an action of partition by the United Nations the Holy Land was divided into Jewish and Arab territories. Thus was the state of Israel born, only to find itself immediately fighting for its life against Arab attacks. Few areas on earth have been the subject of such bitter and continuing disputes—moral, historical, and ethnic— as that occupied by Israel. In the course of that embattled history the world has seen a complete reversal of the stereotype of the unresisting, unmilitary Jew. Given the need for military skills, the Jews of Israel developed into hard-hitting, hard-fighting, tough, combative pioneers—similar in that respect to the hardy men and women who pioneered American frontiers. We have, I think, long since learned not to be misled by supposed ethnic stereotypes; perhaps we have learned that environment, circumstances, and the pressures of life are more influential in developing character than just our genes. Indeed, I believe that if we look at our own society we will have little difficulty identifying the sources of our own problems, problems that arise from social conditions rather than from people's genes.

Constitutional Convention

Back in 1787, this was supposed to be the opening day of the Constitutional Convention that was going to draw up a scheme of government and a basic law for the United States of America. I say it was "supposed to be" because only two of the thirteen states had their delegates on hand in Philadelphia when the convention was due to start. It took almost two weeks to get a quorum of delegates in attendance. I find that interesting in comparison to our modern pace. We have to get everything started, and finished, as quickly as possible, but the Founding Fathers were perfectly willing to move at a slower pace or, to use the Supreme Court's later phrase, with all deliberate speed. We might learn a lesson of patience from our own history. We are attracted by the lure of quick profits rather than long-term investments. In this climate of impatience I think it is important to remember those things which have to grow slowly and steadily, like the things I plan to discuss here today.

MAY 15

Stewardesses

Today is the anniversary of a great American invention. On this day in 1930, a new occupation was born when United Airlines, flying from San Francisco, put aboard the first flight attendant, then called a stewardess. I have always felt that in the formative years of American commercial aviation the efficiency and charm of the stewardesses played a major role in encouraging passengers to fly. A flight attendant has absolutely nothing to do with flying the plane and yet a great deal to do with the enjoyment of the flight. And life, my friends, is full of flight attendants, people who may not be shaping your life but are helping to make your life a lot more pleasant. They make it more pleasant by being courteous and thoughtful. Those qualities are never in sufficient supply. I can think of many places where in the course of my daily routine I encounter situations calling for more courtesy and thoughtfulness than they get. See if you have the same feeling.

L. Frank Baum

This is the birthday of L. Frank Baum, who wrote *The Wizard of Oz*. He was born in 1856 and wrote about the Wizard in 1900. But the fantasy is as meaningful today as it ever was, because like all good fairy tales it was built around some simple truths. The difficulty with adult stories is that unlike fairy tales they trip over their own complications. Children like to know, quickly and clearly, which witch is which. And I suspect, since we are all children at heart, that we have the same desire; so today I will endeavor, if not to tell you which witch is which, at least to report on the what's what.

Shooting of George Wallace

George C. Wallace made many enemies and many friends in the course of his political career as a governor and candidate for the presidency, but it was neither a friend nor a recognizable enemy who shot him on this day in 1972 while he was campaigning in Maryland. The would-be assassin was described as a 21-year-old drifter. He didn't kill Wallace but he crippled him for life. This incident is only one in a series of similar events—strange drifters who shoot at prominent leaders like President Ronald Reagan, or celebrities like John Lennon. In our everyday life we may not all handle TNT and atom bombs, but we never know when we will encounter a human time bomb, ready to explode for no logical reason and aimed at some unpredictable target. Few of us are willing to take part in trying to have a person declared incompetent and institutionalized. We know that most of the institutions are little more than human parking lots. But I believe we must face up to the fact that unless we improve our institutions and are willing to use them properly, we will continue to share the streets with human time bombs. Today I would like to discuss some of the positive steps we can take.

Cape Cod

Ladies and gentlemen, a salute to Bartholomew Gosnold, who on this day in the year 1602 did what many have done since; he discovered Cape Cod. Captain Gosnold was an explorer and seafarer, not a colonist. He hung around the Cape for a little while and then sailed back to England. Today, of course, he probably would have stayed and built a few condominiums. I mention him not to suggest that he missed an opportunity but because he is one of the relatively unfamiliar people who were important in the history of our land. Unfamiliar names are still keys to our current history. You and I may think we are just Social Security numbers in a sea of anonymity, but we do make a difference. We make a difference in many ways; I have time here to enumerate only a few.

MAY 16

The Visible Typewriter

For many years people who used the typewriter had an interesting problem. They couldn't see what they were typing. They had to stop typing and lift the paper carriage in order to be able to read the type they had reproduced on the page. On this day in 1893, the visible typewriter was patented so that you could see the typed letters appear on the page. This gave typists an advantage they didn't have before, but unfortunately no similar device has been invented to make sure that speakers are listening to themselves talk. I must admit to you that I can't wait to hear what I have to say.

The Nickel

I ask you to join me in a happy birthday salute to an old American institution—the nickel. The nickel was authorized for minting on this day in the year 1866, and there are some of us who think it has been going down in purchasing power ever since. It was a long, long time ago, for example, when a politician announced that what America needed was a good five-cent cigar, and I haven't even heard anybody recently talk about putting in his five cents' worth. As a matter of fact, I was about to give you my five cents' worth of opinions right here, but I guess that on that monetary standard I would have used up my time already.

Olga Korbut

Today is the birthday of Olga Korbut, who as a mere slip of a girl became the sweetheart of the 1972 Olympic Games, not only winning two gold medals in gymnastics for the USSR but awakening the vast television audience to the fact that gifted female athletes could be unusually attractive and alluringly feminine. It was Olga Korbut, as much or more than anyone else, who put women's gymnastics on the American docket and launched the sport's era of popularity. Life is full of historic trends that have begun with the appeal of one attractive exponent. The trouble is that an equally attractive exponent for a bad trend can jam up the works. So today, as I look at some recent trends, I will inevitably also be looking at the attractive people who symbolize them.

Older Americans Month

We are in the middle of what has become the customary observance of Older Americans Month, which in the age of euphemism went by the title of Senior Citizens Month. I am glad we have gotten away from that official designation, even though the phrase *senior citizen,* like *golden age,* is still in general use. We don't call thirty-year-olds junior citizens, and I don't think they would like it if we did. In our nomenclature, as in our discussion of issues, I think we should call things by the most direct and clearest names, not by politely invented phrases. With that in mind, let me say that I am here to face facts, not to put a better face on them.

MAY 17

World Telecommunication Day

Today is World Telecommunication Day, sponsored by the United Nations. In this century we have developed so many wonderful means of talking to one another across the oceans and around the world and even in outer space that it is a shame we haven't figured out what to say. I know that I can stand here and say whatever I please and that I can't do the same thing in too many other countries around the world, and so on World Telecommunication Day I rise to thank you for the opportunity for local nontelecommunication with you here today.

National High Blood Pressure Month

Some years ago May was designated as National High Blood Pressure Month, not, I assume, to promote high blood pressure but rather to highlight its dangers and how to fight them. So while it would be easy for me today to worry you and point with alarm to all kinds of real or potential troubles, I hope you won't mind if, in consideration of your blood pressure and my own, I deal with some less inflammatory subject matter.

New York Stock Exchange

Under a buttonwood tree on Wall Street on this day in 1792, 24 business-men agreed to meet daily to buy and sell stocks and bonds, and the organiza-tion they set up became the New York Stock Exchange. On the birthday of the stock exchange it is only fitting that we pause and take stock of the way things are. So, without further ado, let me proceed with that stocktaking.

Heyerdahl Adrift

On this day in 1970, the Norwegian explorer Thor Heyerdahl set out from Morocco in a papyrus boat to see whether the ancient Egyptians could have reached the New World by sea. The Heyerdahl boat got to Barbados in July. The world did not alter its course nor did the earth shake in its axis, but Heyer-dahl had gotten the answer to his question. There aren't too many of us who will risk life and limb like Heyerdahl did repeatedly simply to prove or disprove a theory. We might be better off if more of us had that same venturesome spirit of inquiry. But even without embarking on a papyrus raft I can take a small step by asking some perhaps irreverent, pointed questions, asking them of myself as well as of you.

MAY 18

Mount St. Helens

This was the day of one of Mount St. Helen's spectacular eruptions back in 1980, when that great towering mountain blew its lid. Nothing I could say today could possibly make the earth tremble like that—and I don't plan to try.

First Election

This is the anniversary of the first election in colonial America, in 1631, although some historians believe, without having the records, that a legislative assembly in Virginia may have been elected earlier. At any rate, on this day in 1631, John Winthrop was elected Governor of Massachusetts. I regret to tell you that Governor Winthrop was not a democratic leader, despite being the people's choice. He didn't want to share his authority with a legislature or anybody else. That sometimes happens with popularly chosen leaders. A speaker, such as I, hopes to make a lasting impact with his remarks, but when he is finished he goes away; an elected official serves out his term. As a speaker, all I require is your attention; a candidate, of course, is asking for much more. So friends, lend me your ears, and I will leave your pocketbooks alone.

Halley's Comet

On this day in 1910, a strange thing happened in the sky; Halley's comet appeared. Amid predictions of the end of the world, frightened people took to their cellars and other places of refuge. We, of course, are much more sophisticated today. We know that comets and planetary displays are part of the everyday universe, and we have dared to go up to explore them. But even though we may feel smugly superior to the frightened people of 1910, we have our own folklore of fears and myths. Today I would like to discuss some modern notions that seem to be scaring too many of us too much.

Going to School

This is the birthday of the first state compulsory school attendance law, signed by Governor George S. Boutwell of Massachusetts on this day in 1852. By our present standards it was not very demanding; it called for attendance at school for at least twelve weeks of the year for children between eight and fourteen years of age. Today, of course, we require much more, and education is probably the single most costly operation of state and local governments. Our standard of literacy has gone up since 1852, but I have a feeling that our capacity to educate has not grown as much as it should. We still face the challenge of keeping kids in school. In big cities truancy is a major problem that simply has not been solved. We have found that compulsory school attendance just isn't working well enough. So where do we go from here?

MAY 19

Spanish Armada

On this day in 1588, the mightiest fleet the world had ever seen set sail from Lisbon. It was the Spanish Armada, bound for England with the purpose of defeating the upstart British. But it didn't work out quite that way. Helped considerably by the weather, the smaller and seemingly weaker British fleet under Sir Francis Drake made mincemeat of the supposedly invincible armada.

It is almost as disastrous to believe you are all-conquering and invincible as it is to consider yourself defenseless. I am always just a bit skeptical when someone claims to have all the answers; among other things, I think such a claim shows that the person doesn't have all the questions. I hope I have some answers to present to you today, and I know I have some questions.

Hoover on Privacy

Herbert Hoover, who never was particularly comfortable in the public eye, said on this day in 1947, 15 years after he left the presidency, that—and I quote—"there are only two occasions when Americans respect privacy, especially in presidents. Those are prayer and fishing." But neither prayer nor fishing really requires privacy. For example, here I stand very much in public, praying for your attention and fishing for your approval. And so to work.

Nellie Melba

This the birthday of Nellie Melba, who was born in Australia in 1861 and became one of the greatest opera singers of her time. Yet if we remember Nellie Melba at all today, it is not so much for her singing as for the fact that Melba Toast and Peach Melba were named after her. What is true of fame is certainly true of communication as well. I know very well the message I want to leave with you today, but whether that message or some other impression comes out of my remarks remains to be seen—or heard.

United in America

In a way today is a sort of birthday for the United States—or, more exactly, the anniversary of the first union of several of the American colonies. It happened on this day in 1643, when delegates from the separate colonies of Massachusetts Bay, Plymouth, Connecticut, and New Haven—which was then separate from Connecticut—signed Articles of Confederation. The Confederation didn't remain in effect for very long, but it was a trail-breaking effort and a precedent for the United States, which was born more than a century later. Sometimes a good idea isn't ready to work until the time is ripe. We have no lack of good ideas today, but few among us can claim sufficient knowledge to tell for which ideas the time is ripe. Perhaps my remarks here today will help crystallize your own thoughts on the subject, and if so I am happy to have this opportunity to serve as a catalyst.

MAY 20

Weights and Measures Day

Today, as some of you perhaps may know, is officially Weights and Measures Day, commemorating the signing of the treaty that established the International Bureau of Weights and Measures in 1875. In observance of this notable day I shall weigh my words and speak in measured tones as I address you here.

Homestead Act

This is the anniversary of the Homestead Act of 1862, under which any head of a family over the age of 21 could win ownership of 160 acres of public land by living on it for five years and paying a small registration fee or by buying it at a cost of $1.25 an acre after living on it for six months. It was this legislation that helped to open up the West and gave millions of Americans their own stake in the land. Not too many nations have done anything similar, and this was done more than a hundred years ago. It is something to be proud of—one of the many things we can be proud of but usually forget to think about— the unnoticed ways in which America remains the best place on earth. I think it's time we stopped talking about what's wrong and took a little more public pride in what's right, and I think this is a good place to start.

Timetable

For whatever it is worth, today is the anniversary of the timetable. The first American timetable, we are told, appeared in the newspaper, the *Baltimore American,* on this day in 1830, listing the train schedule to be followed by the Baltimore & Ohio Railroad between Baltimore and Ellicott's Mills, Maryland. I suppose that was when we started being a nation of clock watchers. Mindful of the numerous other demands on your time, I shall get right to the point with my remarks today.

John Stuart Mill

Today is the birthday of John Stuart Mill, the great social reformer and libertarian who was born in London in 1806. Among Mill's many interesting observations is this one from his treatise "On Liberty": "Ages are no more infallible than individuals; every age having held many opinions which subsequent ages have deemed not only false but absurd; and it is certain that many opinions now general will be rejected by future ages, as it is that many, once general, are rejected by the present." Please bear that in mind if you disagree with what I have to say today, and remember that any such disagreement means that one of us is ahead of the times.

MAY 21

Speed Limit

In 1901 on this day, the state of Connecticut put a brand new limitation on individual liberty. Connecticut had the temerity to enact a law putting a limit on the speed with which an automobile could be driven—12 miles an hour in the country and eight miles an hour in the city in the original bill, later amended to raise the limits all the way to 15 and 12 miles an hour. The perspective of time casts a different light on things we regard as basic truths. Our sons and daughters will find some of our rules and our brouhahas to be as strange as a 12-mile speed limit seems to us. But perhaps we can anticipate their views; perhaps we can, in a manner of speaking, project ourselves 20 or 25 years into the future and comment as they very well may then, on some of the things we are doing today. Let's try.

Conventions

The presidential election year of 1832 brought something new to the United States, the party nominating convention. The first such convention of the Democratic party began on this day in Baltimore. It unanimously renominated Andrew Jackson for a second term, and the convention did something else with a far more lasting impact. It adopted a two-thirds rule, requiring a two-thirds vote of the convention for a successful nomination; that rule stayed in force until 1936, more than a century. The idea of a nominating convention, of course, has lasted a good deal longer, even in the age of presidential primaries in the various states. We do not change our way of doing things overnight, even when we recognize that changes may be in order. We are, no pun intended, conventional people. There are lasting values that we intend to preserve against all odds. The trouble is that we ourselves can't always define what those lasting values are, and that's what I am going to try to do here today.

Lincoln Center

On this day in 1959, President Dwight D. Eisenhower came to a then somewhat rundown section of New York to break the ground for Lincoln Center, the magnificent cultural campus in the heart of Manhattan. With its theaters, concert halls, opera houses, open-air bandshell, and performing arts library, Lincoln Center has provided the model for similar cultural centers all over the world. To bring it to completion required not only outstanding architects and builders but also an effective marriage of private philanthropy and government action. That kind of partnership is unknown in many parts of the world—at least on a voluntary basis—but it is one of the ideas that makes America tick. And if you think about it, it is this kind of partnership that we must preserve. What, other than providing money, can and should government do to encourage the arts? And to what extent are we better off with private support than with government funding?

No Price Fixing

On this day in 1951, the Supreme Court opened the gates to all kinds of bargains. The Court ruled that state fair trade laws, which permitted companies to fix the price at which stores could sell their products, were illegal. The ruling allowed retailers to cut prices as they wished in competition for the consumer's dollar. Thus, another effort to control the marketplace bit the dust. The idea of free competition has not been sacred to all Americans by any means. Price fixing, market rigging, and the like have to be guarded against at every turn, and not the least of the problems is the way special-interest groups occasionally have been able to win the passage of legislation in their favor. Probably one of the most egregious examples was the restriction on the marketing of oleomargarine in state laws pushed by dairy interests. It took generations to get those laws off the books. We all look to government to protect us, but some of the protection some of us seek—and get—is not necessarily for the good of the rest of us. Even now some people use government to profit at the expense of the rest of us. I have a few cases in point.

MAY 22

End of the Third International

On this day in 1943, in the midst of World War II, Soviet Russia announced that the Third or Communist International had been dissolved. The International was the core of communism's worldwide revolutionary movement, and with Russia fighting for its life world revolution had to take a back seat. Never let it be said that principle has stood in the way of communist expediency. The abandonment of world revolution was a temporary measure. When the war ended, communism went right back to working for worldwide revolution and has never really stopped. It is important for us to bear this in mind as we consider the ups and downs of our own country's relations with the Soviets. The basic fact is, as it has always been, that the USSR is steadfastly dedicated, philosophically, to the belief that capitalism throughout the world, and particularly in the United States, must fall. Given that basic Soviet view, we can still do business with Moscow, but only if we keep our eyes open and our powder dry, so to speak. And there are certain kinds of business I think are out of bounds. Let me be more specific.

Lincoln's Patent

On this day in 1849, Abraham Lincoln of Springfield, Illinois, received a patent for a device to float vessels over shoals by inflating cylinders. There is no indication that Lincoln was encouraged to try further inventions, but I can't help wondering whether, if the shipping industry had gone wild over his device, he might not have been lost to politics forever. Sometimes, I suppose, the best thing that can happen is a failure that causes us to change course. I believe it is also true that we learn more from failure than from success, although we all know people who on that basis ought to be a lot wiser than they are. But if we have too great a fear of failure we will have an equal fear of doing anything new and untried, and the whole genius of America lies in its historic willingness to do the new and untried. Not all of the ideas that I will touch on in my remarks here today are new and untried, thank goodness, but if they were all tried and true I would have very little to say to you.

Violence in Congress

This is the anniversary of a disgraceful event in the Capitol. In 1856, Representative Preston Brooks of South Carolina walked into the Senate and attacked Senator Charles Sumner with a cane in response to Sumner's verbal attacks on another senator who was Brooks' uncle. For three years thereafter, Sumner was unable to attend the Senate, but he was reelected anyway. Attempts to expel or even censure Brooks failed, and his constituency, believing he had reacted properly to unconscionable insults, reelected him to the House. Next time you are tempted to deplore the caliber of a modern Congress, remember this incident and be reassured that times have improved. We may have more violence today in so-called civilized life, but we also have more public concern about it. And public concern is the first step toward improvement. Before we can point with pride, we sometimes have to point with alarm. Today in my remarks here, I plan to do both.

First Personally Delivered Veto

Presidents have been vetoing congressional bills for as long as we have had our system of checks and balances, but not until this day in 1935 did a Chief Executive ever go to Congress to deliver a veto message in person. The effect of Franklin D. Roosevelt's appearance was interesting. In the subsequent votes there were actually more in favor of the vetoed bill in the House than on its original passage, and in the Senate there was only one less affirmative vote. Roosevelt's veto was sustained, but hardly overwhelmingly. Even a president at the peak of his personal popularity cannot always stampede a Congress conscious of its own prerogatives. That is one fact of life not only in American politics but in general everyday American living as well. We are not an easily stampeded people. We like to weigh the facts before we commit ourselves, and so before I wave any banners of my own I guess I should start by offering the appropriate facts.

MAY 23

Bonnie and Clyde

On this day in 1934, the careers of two of the most wanted criminals ended. Their names were Clyde Barrow and Bonnie Parker, better known, of course, as Bonnie and Clyde. Thanks in large part to a highly successful motion picture many years after their reign and thanks in part to the fact that murder and mayhem had become so much more general in those later years, Bonnie and Clyde practically became folk heroes. We sometimes romanticize some pretty nasty little people and endow them with a glamor they don't really possess. Hero worship is bad enough, but villain worship is worse. Every day we see scabrous entertainers who practice drug addiction, alcoholism, and indiscriminate shabbiness, being worshipped by impressionable camp followers, groupies, and frenzied fans. We see shameless power grabbers applauded for their sheer gall, and we listen devotedly to the profundities of empty-headed charmers. To put it tersely, too many of us worship false gods, and I would like today to try to figure out why.

Savonarola

Girolamo Savonarola had the misfortune to be an honest and dedicated man of God at a time when corruption and venality were all too powerful in the Church of Rome. On this day in the year 1498, after tortures beyond belief, he was hanged and burned and his body was thrown into the Arno River in the city of Florence that he had served faithfully and courageously for many years. It is a lot easier these days to dissent from the established point of view—and a lot safer in our country, though not in some other parts of the world. So I am emboldened to speak frankly before you, confident that though we may disagree you will not have me hanged or burned at the stake. Indeed, I must admit to a small hope that you will even find merit in what I have to say.

Mesmerized

This is the birthday of Franz Anton Mesmer, who was born in Austria in 1734. Mesmer was the man who discovered the healing power of suggestion and hypnosis and gave a new word to the language. We speak of people being *mesmerized*, having their minds reached and manipulated through hypnosis. I am no hypnotist, but I must admit to having the same aim as most speakers, namely to mesmerize the audience. My method, however, is to try to awaken you to some present situations and certainly not to put you to sleep.

Bifocals

On this day in 1785, Benjamin Franklin wrote to a friend about a new device he had rigged up for himself. Tired of carrying two pairs of eyeglasses, he had arranged to incorporate two separate lenses in each eyepiece. Although the cost of the device put it beyond the reach of most people, it was ultimately adopted as a standard, and the world saw things better through Franklin's bifocals. Even those of us with the best of vision these days are actually viewing the world bifocally—one world with its problems through a more distant lens and one right here in front of us. Sometimes it is hard to get the right perspective on each of those worlds because the other keeps intruding. And there are times when somebody else's perspective can be helpful. It is for that purpose—that additional perspective—that I approach this podium.

MAY 24

Night Baseball

The first major league night baseball game was played at Cincinnati against Philadelphia on this day in 1935. Neither baseball nor America has been the same since. Night baseball, along with other sports, has changed the nighttime face of the nation. Where once, except for a few theatergoers, we stayed home in the evenings, we now have a host of attractions to keep the traffic rolling— sports events, rock concerts, expositions, and other gatherings. We have expanded our choice of leisure attractions and our times to enjoy them. This is one of the perhaps not so profound ways that the horizons of life have expanded. By bringing light to previously unlit times and places, we have added some new dimensions to the enjoyment of living. And perhaps, if my remarks here today can shed a little more light on the way we are living, that too can be a positive contribution.

Good Day

History records so many worthwhile events happening on this day of the year that I feel I am speaking under particularly good omens. The first passenger railroad service in the United States began on this day in 1830 in Baltimore. The first public telegraph message transmission was on this day in 1844. The Brooklyn Bridge opened in 1883. And the first supersonic Concorde flights to the United States began in 1977. Given that record of auspicious occurrences on this day, I am emboldened to hope that my remarks, like all those other events, will make communication a little better.

John Brown of Kansas

It is one of the oddities of history that a man who presided over the murder of five people in Kansas on this day in 1856, at what came to be called the Pottawatomie Massacre, should have become the spiritual symbol of the Union cause in the Civil War, but when the Union soldiers sang of John Brown's body mouldering in the grave while his soul went marching on they were immortalizing a man with blood on his hands. Too often we accept the maxim that the end justifies the means, and we use that as a reason to condone moral lapses that should be unforgivable. Sometimes it is unpopular to rise to the defense of standards, but it is important for those standards to be maintained. One of the roles of a speaker is to draw the public's attention to what our standards should be and to raise the alarm when they are being subverted. I hope you agree with what I have to say here today, but, more important, I hope that by saying what I think I may stimulate some further thinking by others.

Benjamin Cardozo

Today is the birthday of Benjamin Nathan Cardozo, one of America's greatest legal scholars. Most great jurists are famous primarily for their years on the Supreme Court, but Cardozo was world-famous before he put on the robes of a justice of our top tribunal. As I start to speak on the anniversary of his birth in New York in 1870, I am reminded of something he wrote in a book entitled *Law and Literature*: "As I search the archives of my memory, I seem to discern six types or methods (of writing). . . . There is the type magisterial or imperative; the type laconic or sententious; the type conversational or homely; the type refined or artificial, smelling of the lamp, verging at times upon preciosity or euphuism; the type demonstrative or persuasive; and finally the type tonsorial or agglutinative, so called from the shears and the pastepot which are its implements and emblem." Ladies and gentlemen, I don't know what other styles are left after Benjamin Cardozo's catalog of horrors, so I suppose the best thing for me to do is just to let the words come forth spontaneously and hope for the best.

MAY 25

African Freedom Day

This is African Freedom Day, observed on the anniversary of the formation of the Organization of African Unity in 1963. African freedom has a long way to go, but keeping the goal in mind has to be helpful. There are many goals we haven't yet achieved that are worth observing, such as world peace. If we work only for that which is easy to attain, we are not being true to ourselves. In that spirit I will talk to you today not about where we have been but rather where we are going or where we can go if we try hard enough.

Washington's Rebellion

This was one of the saddest days of the American Revolution. In 1780 soldiers of the Continental Army commanded by George Washington mutinied at Morristown, New Jersey, demanding fuller rations and immediate payment of their salaries. The rebellion was put down by Pennsylvania troops, and the leaders of the mutiny were hanged. It was a bad chapter in the generally glorious story of the American Revolution, but then very few wonderful things are absolutely perfect. It is always a good idea to be aware of shortcomings as well as triumphs. Speakers are always choosing between what they think the audience wants to hear and what they think the audience *ought* to hear. When they are lucky, of course the audience wants to hear what speakers think they ought to hear—and I hope we are all lucky here today.

End of the Model T

On this day in 1927, the Ford Motor Company announced it would stop manufacturing its classic Model T, after 19 years and 15 million automobiles. The most timeless example of an unchanging product was to be no more, and in a short time the automobile industry was mastering the sales technique known as forced obsolescence, making each year's cars look different so that the older one would seem outmoded. There has even been a sort of forced obsolescence in the field of speechmaking, with all of us subjected to so many speeches that the tried and true phrases have become trite and stale. To regale you with facts you already know or sentiments you already share would be trespassing on your time. So I will not offer you a Model A speech, or even a Model T. The only thing my remarks will have in common with these earlier models is that they all run on gas.

Constitutional Convention

This was the day in 1787 when they finally were able to convene enough delegates to the Constitutional Convention to have a quorum and organize the session that was to produce the Constitution of the United States. One of the provisions of the convention was that no texts of speeches or discussions would be made public. Most of our knowledge of what went on comes from the notes kept by James Madison, which were not published until after Madison's death. In some ways that is a shame, because among the delegates were some of the most cogent thinkers and best talkers in America, from elderly Ben Franklin on down. They were not there primarily to talk, of course, but to get the Constitution written. Talk and action don't always go hand in hand. Speaking as the talker of the day on this rostrum, I can only tell you that public oratory these days definitely requires a strong constitution. We have public address systems, which Ben Franklin's contemporaries did not, and we have many more earwitnesses, if I can use that word, as well as many more means of making a permanent record of a speaker's words. So today's speakers have to weigh their words and then see how the public weighs them. Let the weighing now begin.

MAY 26

Chips Away in Atlantic City

This was the day when Atlantic City began its career as a center of legalized gambling in 1978. The influx of gambling money was supposed to lead to the rebirth of the rundown beach resort, but in the years immediately following the casino launching the only portions of the city that were reborn were the casino hotels themselves. Playing the slot machine has one similarity to public speaking. If you win with your first ploy, if the money or the applause rolls in, you find it hard to stop. But that is the only similarity. A gambler usually gives it all back to the slot machine or the gaming table; a public speaker always has not only the first word but the last. And as your speaker of the moment, I know that I am here under good auspices.

Justice Holmes on Free Thought

Around this time in 1929, in the case of *United States* v. *Schwimmer,* the Supreme Court upheld the denial of U.S. citizenship to a pacifist from Hungary named Rosika Schwimmer. In a dissenting opinion, Justice Oliver Wendell Holmes Jr. said, "If there is any principle of the Constitution that more imperatively calls for attachment than any other it is the principle of free thought—not free thought for those who agree with us but freedom for the thought we hate. . . ." Close quote. It is an odd paradox that many of the very people who benefit from this concept of freedom—the apostles of dissent—are among those who heckle and jeer and try to disrupt the speeches of those with whom they disagree. I suppose this proves that we don't always practice what we preach. Knowing that sometimes makes the preaching a little more difficult. But preaching has a built-in difficulty anyway, because so often it consists of someone telling other people what they should do. I hope you won't mind if I don't do that today. I would much rather give you my view of things as they are, and leave to you the judgment about what needs to be done.

Freeing *The Miracle*

Many years ago there was an Italian movie called *The Miracle* which some people regarded as sacrilegious in its depiction of a woman's fixation. As a result the picture was banned by censors in some locations until it was freed by the Supreme Court on this day in 1952. Since then, of course, censorship has bitten the dust and moviemakers have plumbed the depths of bad taste, discovering en route that if you put enough screams and blood into a picture it can become a box office smash for an adolescent audience. Adolescents grow up and their taste cools off, but the teenage market is constantly being renewed, and exploiters of that market know it. And when it comes to movies, you have to revise Gresham's Law. Gresham, you will recall, said that bad money drives good money out of circulation. In the case of films, bad movies drive good people out of circulation. The same is true of shoddy products of all kinds; their worst effect is that they discourage growth in the marketplace. If you sell bad cars one year, people won't buy your cars the next. Ladies and gentlemen, I want to be invited back to speak to you again, so I am going to give you as good a speech as I can.

The Imperfect Lesson

On this day in 1868, the impeachment of President Andrew Johnson failed by the margin of one vote in the Senate. To impeach, the Senate required a two-thirds majority and fell one vote short. The leader of the impeachment move in the House of Representatives, Thaddeus Stevens, was more than upset. He despaired of the republic. He predicted that the only way a president could be removed thereafter would be by—and I quote—"the dagger of a Brutus." Well, Stevens was not around for Watergate or its aftermath, so he did not see the departure of the Watergate president after impeachment hearings were held. In the depths of his own disappointment Stevens gave himself a distorted vision of future history. We have among us, unfortunately, many people like Thaddeus Stevens, seeing the world only from their special and usually rather narrow perspectives. I hope I am not one of them and that the world about which I will talk to you today is the world of all of us, rather than my own concoction.

MAY 27

Wind Tunnel

On this day in 1931, the first full-size wind tunnel for testing airplanes was put into service at Langley Field in Virginia. In honor of that occasion I shall try not to make this room a wind tunnel today, and I will keep the atmosphere free of hot air, to the best of my ability.

Rachel Carson

In looking at some of the notable events that have occurred on this day of the year, I came across a small mystery. One source that I trust says that Rachel Carson was born on this day in 1907. Another equally authoritative work gives the date as May 21. Obviously, somewhere along the line, the figures 1 and 7 were confused. But since Rachel Carson arrived on earth at around this time of the year it seems altogether fitting to recall her now. There aren't too many world movements that can be as clearly traced to the work of one individual as the fight for a better ecology. If the ecological movement had an early bible, that bible was Rachel Carson's eloquent book, *Silent Spring*. Few of us can aspire to be as effective as she was in awakening concern about an aspect of the life around us. Few of us can write a *Silent Spring*. But all of us can raise our voices to point out some aspect of human existence that needs more attention or wiser consideration than it is getting. And so I welcome this opportunity to speak to you today.

Julia Ward Howe

If Julia Ward Howe had lived until this day she would have attained an age of more than a century and a half since she was born in 1819. But I doubt that in these added years of life she would have topped something she did at age 43. That was when she wrote a poem for the *Atlantic Monthly* called "The Battle Hymn of the Republic" in 1862. She went on after the war to become a leader of the women's rights movement, and an eloquent and effective one, but if she had done nothing else but write "The Battle Hymn of the Republic" her place in history would have been secure. It is wonderful to have so transcendental an achievement. Most of us, effective though we may be, do not have that one moment of outstanding achievement. It would be exciting indeed for me to think that the words I am about to say to you could have the impact of Julia Ward Howe's "Glory, glory hallelujah/His truth goes marching on." Although it is given to very few of us to sound that eloquent a call to battle, I hope that in my remarks here today you will find that indeed the truth goes marching on.

Vision of the Postal Service

Back on this day in 1969, President Richard M. Nixon proposed to Congress that the Post Office Department be made into an independent corporation owned by the government but designed to be a self-supporting business. Our experience with the Postal Service should tell us that formulas for private ownership or public ownership, mechanisms for policing the setting of rates, and the like, while certainly well intended, are not the answer. We impose on the Postal Service certain conditions that, for example, we do not impose on other businesses. If you travel by air from New York to Chicago, you pay a lot less for your ticket than if you fly from New York to Seattle. Nothing wrong there: Seattle is more than twice as far away. But if you mail a letter to Chicago and another to Seattle the rate is the same. That doesn't apply to phone calls and it doesn't apply to parcel post or United Parcel Service—only to first class mail. What is happening is that the more costly letters—costly, that is, to deliver—are getting a bit of a free ride on the shoulders of the less costly shorter distances. I raise this point to emphasize that while it is easy to criticize the Postal Service, we should bear in mind the unbusinesslike restrictions placed upon that service. The same is true of many other types of public service enterprises. We are being invisibly taxed in some parts of the country to maintain levels of service at a loss in other parts of the country. Today I should like to cite some of these inequities and suggest how we can achieve better equality for all of our citizens.

MAY 28

Armenian Independence Day

After World War I there was a relatively brief period when we here in the United States were very conscious of the plight of the starving Armenians, even though many of us didn't know exactly where Armenia might be. Today is Armenian Independence Day, commemorating the Armenian nation's declaration of independence in 1918. But, alas, a short time later the two nations that had subjugated Armenia in the past—Turkey and Russia—did it again, dividing the nation between them. One of the sad things about this kind of injustice is that after a while it tends to become the status quo; the world shrugs its shoulders and becomes more occupied with later and perhaps more easily reversible injustices. That sometimes makes it difficult for a speaker to be as effective as he or she would like when trying to arouse the conscience of an audience. If you talk about an injustice that has existed for generations it somehow becomes old hat. Except for extreme partisans, people would rather not be reminded of it anymore. So we have a tendency to look for new injustices that we can report with the fascination of discovery. I will not do that here today. Instead I will talk about the current impact of some old injustices on the world today.

Louis Agassiz

Louis Agassiz, who was born in Switzerland on this day in 1807, was a distinguished naturalist and geologist who didn't come to this country until he was 39 years old. He became professor of natural history at Harvard and pioneered in the teaching of natural history in the United States. When he died in 1873, we still had not really begun to appreciate the importance of natural history, but we were well on the way, thanks to his efforts. It is an interesting aspect of human life that sometimes we need to be told an important truth more than once before it sinks in. We need advance agents like Louis Agassiz to break the ice and begin to get us thinking, so that when the next prophet comes along we are more receptive. I will make no apology, therefore, for repeating here today some points that earlier figures have introduced. I have profited by their wisdom, and I hope we can all do the same.

Neville Chamberlain

This was the day when, thanks to the resignation of Stanley Baldwin, Neville Chamberlain had his chance to be Prime Minister of England in 1937. Baldwin, at age 69, felt it was time to retire. His successor, Chamberlain, appeased Adolf Hitler at Munich by giving up Czechoslovakia without a fight and coming home to London to announce "peace in our time." Was there another course that could have been followed? Is it possible that if Hitler had faced determined enough opposition he might not have rushed so eagerly into World War II? Of course, we will never know the answers to these hypothetical questions. We will never know with absolute certainty that the policies we pursue now are the best policies to pursue. All we can do is look at the results thus far and decide on that basis whether we are on the right track. So let's take that look today at some current policies and how they are working out for us.

Nature as Mediator

According to some accounts, this was the day in the year 585 B.C. when Mother Nature stopped a war. It is said that the Lydians and the Medes were having a fierce battle when an eclipse of the sun occurred. Both sides were scared out of their wits by the sudden darkness, and they decided it was a signal that they should stop fighting, so they made peace. It didn't last too long, but it was peace for a while. I find myself thinking how nice it would be if Mother Nature helped settle disputes for us the same way—with a sudden, inexplicable darkness when we fight over silly things, a rainbow when we do something right. Unfortunately, Mother Nature does not send us signals like that, so usually some poor mortal gets up to report the score as he or she sees it. I have scanned the almanacs for natural portents—eclipses or comets or other impressive manifestation—and I haven't found any that provide a clue about how we are doing these days, so I guess I will have to report on my own.

MAY 29

Oswald Spengler

This is the birthday of the German philosopher Oswald Spengler, who was born in 1880. He was most famous for his book *The Decline of the West,* which said that western civilization, like every civilization that preceded it, would decline and wither, and that the process of falling apart had already started. I come before you today with no Spenglerian warnings of doom. I think the golden years of western civilization are still ahead of us, and I'd like to tell you why.

Fall of Constantinople

On this day in 1453, the great city of Constantinople, capital of the Byzantine empire, was captured by the Turks. Today Constantinople does not even have its old name; it is now called Istanbul. Its fall in 1453 was one of the milestones of human history, bringing in a new era and a whole new series of struggles between nations for superiority in the world. After more than 500 years that series of struggles continues. Nationalism has never been more passionate than it is today; the search for separate national identities tears some unfortunate countries apart. We see its signs every now and then in the bilingual clashes in parts of Canada, and we cross our fingers for our own melting pot. Today, rather than merely crossing my fingers, I propose to examine our own national situation and see what we can learn from it.

John F. Kennedy

This is the birthday of John F. Kennedy, who was born in 1917 in Massachusetts. He was the 35th and by all odds the most glamorous of our presidents. If there were disputes at the time and after his tragic assassination about the substance of his presidency, there were none about its style. Like Franklin D. Roosevelt, Kennedy showed that style can rally a country and inspire it. Kennedy's brief regime has been described as Camelot; the original Camelot was also a brief, romantic portion of time that captured the popular imagination. Camelot is not enough—it is never enough, but it certainly makes the hard work easier. As I look at our world today I see so many ways that could be helped by a little of the Camelot style, a little of the polish. Let me cite some examples.

Everest

On this day in 1953, Edmund Hillary and Tensing Norkay did what no humans had ever done before—they climbed to the top of the highest mountain in the world, Mount Everest, and survived to tell the story. It is not enough for humanity to attain the heights; we have to come back down in one piece. And just as the mountain climber always has to anticipate and plan how to handle the next situation, we must always be concerned not merely with what is now but also with what is likely to be tomorrow. Futurism as a science is relatively new; preparing for future possibilities is a time-honored precaution. My question today is simply this: How well prepared are we for tomorrow and the day after?

MAY 30

Memorial Day

This is the month of Memorial Day, when we remember the sacrifices of those who gave their lives in the service of their country. We have a tendency to reserve the badges of heroism mainly for those who fight, yet there are even more heroes and heroines in peacetime. Today I would like to salute what I call the quiet defenders, the champions of the American way.

International Terror

On this day in 1972, one of the worst terrorist incidents occurred at Lod Airport in Israel, when 24 people were killed and 76 injured by attackers allied with Palestine guerrillas. Two of the murderers turned out to be Japanese, highlighting the international alliance of modern organized terror. We must recognize that terrorism today is an international, not local, conspiracy and that there is a bond that unites apparently separate national groups. That bond is a common contempt for existing insitutions, a feeling that the destruction of peace of mind in one country after another will ultimately enable the terrorists to take over. Terrorism seeks to intimidate people into keeping silent. It can be fought by refusing to be silent, by refusing to follow the terrorists' political line, and above all by not being afraid to fight back. Today I would like to talk a little about how we ordinary citizens can fight back.

Lincoln Memorial

On this day in 1922, the nation dedicated the great Lincoln Memorial along the Potomac in Washington, D.C. I find it surprising that more than half a century had elapsed since Abraham Lincoln's assassination before this magnificent memorial was erected. It suggests to me that we are not always as prompt as we might be in paying proper tribute to our great men and women. Very few of the great ones achieve in their lifetimes the degree of high regard that comes after their deaths. Sometimes it is the reverse, of course. Franklin D. Roosevelt was loved—and hated—during his presidency perhaps more than any other Chief Executive, but as the years passed after his death he began to be taken for granted. There has been a different assessment of the glamorous John F. Kennedy in the years since his tragic assassination. And so it goes. Today I would like to look at some of the leaders of our own time and speculate on how they will be regarded by posterity. It is not an easy exercise, but it can be illuminating.

Unknown Soldiers

On this day in 1958, the bodies of two unknown casualties of World War II and the Korean War were placed alongside the unknown soldier of World War I in Arlington National Cemetery. We don't know who they were, but we know that they gave their lives in the service of their country. And we show our gratitude by enshrining them in our great national resting place. But I am inclined to think that the best tribute to the unknown soldiers—and to the known casualties of all of our wars—is to make the country for which they died a better place in which to live. We have that opportunity today. We can make a better America, and we don't have to go to war to do it. Let me tell you more.

MAY 31

Walt Whitman

Today is the birthday of Walt Whitman, that remarkable poet of the nineteenth century who was born on Long Island in 1819. In "Song of the Broad-Axe," he wrote, "A great city is that which has the greatest men and women,/If it be a few ragged huts, it is still the greatest city in the world." We speak of our cities, of our country, in physical terms—great mountains and great buildings reaching to the sky—but what the United States really is is people. Have you looked at our people lately? Have you looked at yourselves lately? I have, and I'd like to tell you what I have seen.

Copyright

On this date in 1790, the United States enacted its first copyright law, seeking to protect the ownership of literary and other creative compositions. Few of the framers of that original law could have foreseen such later complications as movies, videotape, cable television, satellite signals, records, and the like, and the copyright law always seems to be trying to cach up with the arrival of newer modes of communication. What has happened with copyright law may be an extreme example, but it illustrates the need for constantly reviewing and updating the statutes that are on the books. Times change, needs change, standards change. Let me cite a few illustrations.

Taxi

According to various reference books, it was sometime during this month of May in the year 1907 that a new device from France was introduced in this country. It was that great invention, the metered taxicab. Among other things it brought new meaning to the warning that the meter is running. My friends, I am aware that the meter is running as I speak to you here today, not because anyone has a cab waiting outside but rather because in this busy modern world we have so many things to do and so relatively little time to do them. Life becomes a series of decisions about priorities, and perhaps what I have to say here may bear on that series of decisions.

Sally Rand

World's Fairs always gather the latest in technological exhibits and educational materials, but it is usually a human angle that gets the most attention. That certainly was true at the World's Fair, or Century of Progress Exhibition, in Chicago in 1933. The newspapers of this day carried the first reports of the fan dance performed at the Exposition by a lady named Sally Rand and indicating that if you managed to get a peek beyond the fan you saw all—and I mean all—of Miss Rand. No technological exhibits offered a similar attraction, and Sally Rand ran away with the publicity. We may live in an age of machines and mechanical and electronic wonders, but human beings are still basically interested in human beings. And so I come before you today not to talk about scientific wonders, not to describe the miracles of technology, but to talk in simple terms about human beings and what they are up against.

JUNE 1

Marilyn Monroe

This is the birthday of Marilyn Monroe, who was born in 1926 and became the epitome of the sexy movie star, with everything in life except happiness. Failure was not her problem; success was. There are a lot of people who have that problem—not as acutely or severely as Marilyn Monroe but difficult enough. They don't know how to stop. They don't know how to get off the merry-go-round after they've won enough brass rings. And I fear there are countries that have the same dilemma. They aren't satisfied with whatever growth they have; they must have more, and they regard their failure to get more as somehow being a conspiracy by more fortunate nations. The conspiratorial theory of history leads such nations to form their own blocs and, in a manner of speaking, their own conspiracies. It would be fine if we did not have to deal with such blocs, but, the world being what it is, we do have to deal with them. And my feeling is that the way to deal with them is not to indulge them, not to sit still for their diatribes and demonstrations, but rather to be tough and firm and, above all, consistent. Let me be specific.

Brigham Young

This is the birthday of a remarkable man named Brigham Young, the Vermont Yankee who went from rural New York across the country at the head of the group of Mormons who settled first in Nauvoo, Illinois, and ultimately in Salt Lake City, Utah. Born in 1801, Young was 46 years old and head of his church when he picked the site in Utah that was to be its headquarters. Young practiced polygamy; he had 27 wives and 47 children. He was a man of honor and, in the disputes between Washington and the Mormons, a notable peacemaker. But above all, he was a man who didn't fit a mold, who believed enough in his religion and his ideas to go out into the virtualy unexplored wild West and begin to build his own promised land. When you go to the pioneer museum in Salt Lake City and see the way the Mormons crossed the mountains and the plains, dragging their belongings behind them, you can only begin to appreciate how much dedication and faith and courage went with them. I like to think that what those earlier Americans had the Americans of today also have. Today, as a matter of fact, I want to single out a few modern American pioneers and talk about the frontiers they are facing—and conquering.

June Weddings

This is traditionally the month of weddings, when young people pledge their lives to each other for better or for worse. Sometimes I think we have reached an era when the pledge is for better or for the time being. All too many people pair off without getting married, and all too many don't work at it enough to make it work. We accept lesser standards than our grandparents did, whether we are talking about professional baseball players who hit .250 and are hailed as stars or rock musicians, civil servants, or anybody else. One business made its reputation by boasting that "They try harder," . . . the obverse of which, of course, is that the other folks don't try hard enough. I stand here today to call for all of us to try harder.

John Masefield

Today is the birthday of the great English poet John Masefield, who was born on this day in 1878. It was Masefield who wrote these lines: "To get the whole world out of bed/And washed, and dressed, and warmed, and fed,/To work, and back to bed again,/Believe me, Saul, costs worlds of pain." This notion of the world as a world of pain is tied in some ways to the belief that those rewards and punishments we don't get now we will get one way or another in the afterlife. But we have a tendency to make things harder than they need to be. We keep up with the Joneses without stopping to think about whether these particular Joneses are worth keeping up with. Today I'd like to look at some of these Joneses and our competition with them.

JUNE 2

Commencement Speeches

This is probably the most speechified time of the year, with commencement addresses all over the place and platitudes the order of the day. I shall therefore try to avoid getting caught in the verbal traffic and confine myself to a few brief remarks on subjects close to all our hearts.

Italian Day

This day is usually celebrated by friends of Italy as either Italian Heritage Day or Italy Republic Day, commemorating both the arrival of the first Italians in New York in 1635 and the vote that ended the Italian monarchy in 1946 after World War II. America is the beneficiary of many ethnic cultures, and Italy's is one of the foremost. We sing songs, we eat foods, and enjoy arts that are Italy's gifts not just to us but to the world. We keep talking of the United

States as a melting pot, but it is much more than that; it is where so much of the world's good things and good people have found new homes. Nothing is more important to the quality of life here in the United States than the hospitality and the openness with which we welcome newcomers. That isn't always easy, but it is always a worthwhile investment, as I hope I can bring home to you here today.

Battle of the Warsaw Ghetto

On this day in 1943, the long and gallant battle of the Jews in the Warsaw ghetto ended, finally crushed by overpowering Nazi force; but, like Masada and other epic defeats, it was a triumph of the unconquerable spirit. History is full of gallant defeats that nevertheless turned the tide in favor of the apparent loser, sometimes by creating unexpected sympathy and support and sometimes simply by causing a bully to lose precious time—defeats like the Alamo, Bataan, and the Warsaw ghetto. We learn from hard times as well as and perhaps more than from good times. That happens when we know why whatever happened did happen. And that is why it is important to take a good look at where we are and how we got there.

Government Salaries

At the Constitutional Convention on this day in 1787, wise old Benjamin Franklin arose to voice a surprising point of view. He argued that no salaries should be paid to the Executive Branch, most specifically the President. "As all History informs us," he said, "there has been in every State and Kingdom a constant kind of Warfare between the Governing and the Governed; the one striving to obtain more for its Support, and the other to pay less. . . . There is a natural Inclination in Mankind to kingly Government." Old Ben suggested that even office-holders in a democratic republic might hanker to live like kings. What he did not predict, but what has been equally true, is that the same desire prompts the incredible parade of perqs for corporate executives as well. The common element is that somebody else is expected to pay for it. Nobody seems to spend that kind of personal money if there's a way to write it off on the government, in tax advantages, lulus, or the like. Is there a way of avoiding this? Let us examine the problem.

JUNE 3

Pope John XXIII

In 1963 on this day, one of the most beloved men of this time, Pope John XXIII, died in Rome at the age of 81. He had been in his midseventies when he was elected Pontiff, and most people expected him to be a sort of interim caretaker. Instead, he turned out to be one of the most energetic, ecumenical, and vigorous prelates. We have a tendency to judge people not for themselves but rather by their age, their national origins, or their previous prominence or anonymity. Sometimes these factors provide worthwhile clues, but sometimes they can be totally misleading. We have only to look at the principal actors on the world's stage today to realize that you can't tell the players simply by the packaging.

School Vacations

We are coming upon that time of year when the schools free the annual tidal wave of students until the new semester starts in the fall. For millions of children and teenagers, school vacation gives them nowhere to go except the streets, no one to talk to except one another; they are left almost totally on their own. Sometimes this is because their parents work so long to make a living; sometimes it is because their parents either don't care or don't have anything to offer them. We live in a time when altogether too many parents look to others to teach their children what basically only parents can teach properly—the sense of family, the sense of sanctuary, and the source of parental advice. We look to the school and the church and we do not look sufficiently within ourselves. Today I ask you to join me in looking at ourselves.

Battle of Midway

This is the anniversary of a great turning point in World War II. It was the Battle of Midway in 1942, when the United States routed the Japanese fleet in Japan's first naval defeat of the war. The battle lasted until June 6; after that, for the most part, Japan was on the defensive and the tide had turned. It is not often that a particular day or group of days is that decisive in its influence on the course of history, and we usually don't know until we have the perspective of time. But we do know right now that we are in a period of another kind of challenge and that the way we respond may also prove decisive. Let me give you my view of the opportunities we face today.

New Deal

On this day in 1932, a presidential candidate named Franklin D. Roosevelt said, "I pledge you, I pledge myself, to a new deal for the American people." When he said it, FDR had only the broadest possible outline in his own mind of what that New Deal was going to be; what was firm in his mind was a recognition of the need for change. Before we can progress we must be willing to contemplate change. It is fine to stand pat while you are sitting pretty, but standing pat can also mean standing still. I am sure all of you have your own ideas about changes you think would benefit the nation. Since you have been kind enough to afford me the chance to talk to you here today, please permit me to express some ideas of my own on the subject of changing America.

JUNE 4

Spelling Bee

The finals of the national spelling bee have traditionally come during the early part of June, when prize-winning youngsters from all parts of the nation have met to determine the year's national champion. I don't know about you, but I am in awe of these youngsters, because I find it challenging enough to put the words together so that they make sense, let alone trying to spell them. I will, of course, nevertheless try to make my remarks as spellbinding as possible.

Brandeis on Liberty

We keep thinking that evil people create our problems, but something Justice Louis Brandeis said on this day in 1928 should correct that impression. "Experience should teach us to be most on our guard to protect liberty," he said, "when the government's purposes are beneficent. . . . The greatest dangers to liberty lurk in insidious encroachment by men of zeal, well-meaning but without understanding." Close quote. "Insidious encroachment" on individual liberty is always explained away as—and often truly is—a well-intentioned effort to protect most of us from a few of us, but even the word "protection" has the connotation of paying tribute—or protection money, if you will. Standing up for other people's rights can often be a thankless task, but it has to be done. The very nature of a free society makes it easier for some people to assault other people's rights. Today I would like to talk about some of these assaults.

Roquefort Cheese

According to some chroniclers, today is the anniversary of the discovery of Roquefort cheese in the year of 1070. To be more exact, it was the discovery of what had happened to some sheep's milk cheese that had been left in a cave near Roquefort, France. From such accidents are great institutions born. Unlike Roquefort cheese, my remarks here today will not be improved if I make you wait too long for them, so I will present them to you now. If they aren't ripe yet they never will be.

Jefferson's Narrow Escape

This day in 1781 was not the high point of Thomas Jefferson's career. He had failed as Governor of Virginia, ultimately resigning and returning to Monticello. On this day, forewarned by a courier that the British were coming, he narrowly escaped being captured. This is a section of Jefferson's life we rarely read about in the history books, and we will never know how close we came to losing the man who was to be our third President. I mention it also to emphasize the point that even the best of us have bad moments. If it could happen to Jefferson it can certainly happen to others. We should not despair of our leaders when their footsteps falter; they may come back better than ever. So I am not here to pass pontifical judgment on anyone; instead, I should like to talk about where the new dangers are coming from and what we can do about them.

JUNE 5

World Environment Day

This is World Environment Day, proclaimed by the United Nations in honor of international environmental efforts. On World Environment Day it seems only proper for a speaker not to fill the air with fog or thunder, and so I shall try to avoid any dangerous emissions in my remarks here today.

Socrates

Pinpointing an exact date more than 2,000 years ago is not always possible, but there are historians who claim that on this day in the year 468 or 470 B.C. the great Socrates was born in Athens. Socrates was regarded as the wisest man of his time, but his wisdom was not enough to save him. He was sentenced to death as a supposed enemy of Athenian democracy and, even though he might have saved himself, he followed the law and drank the cup of hemlock that killed him. We are generally a bit more merciful to those with whom we disagree these days, which I find comforting as I rise to address you. It is good to know that you are not serving hemlock.

First Hot Air Balloon

This is the anniversary of the launching of the first successful hot air balloon in France in 1783. The launchers at first thought it was the smoke from their fires that was lifting the balloon but soon discovered it was the hot air. The moral, I suppose, is that smoke gets in your eyes but hot air can provide a certain lift. I shall try today, therefore, to smoke out some interesting observations with the hot air held to a decent minimum.

Bananas

A chronicler of sidelights of history has noted that on this day in 1876 the Centennial Exposition in Philadelphia introduced to the American public that delectable creation known as the banana. Previously, we had been unable to describe phony statements as banana oil or to attribute falls to slipping on banana peels or to savor the delight of a banana split. And no comedian had yet been described as a top banana. It is remarkable how one intriguing item like a banana can enrich not only our palates but our vocabularies as well. I hope my remarks today, like the good old banana, will prove fruitful and meaty, so let's peel away the packaging and get to the meat of the matter.

JUNE 6

Snow in New England

On this day in 1816, we are told, ten inches of snow fell in New England. I want to give you my absolute assurance that I am not here today for a snow job. If I get carried away with emotion, I may thunder a bit, but I promise you—no snow job.

Drive-ins

This was the day in 1933 when moviegoing became an adventure on wheels. In Camden, New Jersey, the first drive-in movie theater opened. Few could have predicted what that did for the movie business, the popcorn business, and the generation gap. It was followed, of course, by drive-in banks, drive-in restaurants, and even drive-in church services. The age of maximum mobility and minimum energy had arrived. I don't mean to call the invention of the drive-in theater a world-shaking event, but it did change the American landscape and the way we lived. I see other changes developing today, and I would like to talk to you about them.

British Peace Commission

The American Revolutionary War had been raging for three years when, on this day in 1778, the members of a British peace commission arrived in Philadelphia, empowered by Parliament to work for reconciliation with the colonies. The Continental Congress told them it insisted on recognition of the independence of the colonies and the removal of all British forces. The British commissioners were stubborn—one of them tried to bribe members of Congress—and they issued direct threats to the American people about how Britain would destroy them if they did not make peace. It was, as a matter of fact, a very odd peace commission, considering its belligerence. If it accomplished anything, it stiffened American spines and encouraged the Founding Fathers to continue the fight. The whole episode is worth remembering these days when so many people claim they want peace but turn out to want it only on their own terms. There are among us, for example, would-be leaders whose methods of persuasion consists of threats: Do what I recommend, or face these consequences. Ladies and gentlemen, I come here today with neither threats nor ultimatums but just a few ideas for your quiet consideration.

SEC

On this day in 1934, the Securities and Exchange Commission was established so that the federal govenment could police the securities business. It was a logical consequence of the financial troubles of the Depression years, but nevertheless there were the usual complaints about the expansion of governmental power. In the case of the SEC, there turned out to be no cause for alarm. Compared to what it was before 1934, the securities business is bigger than ever; more people than ever own shares of American business. Thanks in part to the SEC, confidence in the American way of doing business was maintained, even if at times the exigencies of the moment may have raised some doubts. There is no question that a third party looking over one's shoulder helps enforce the rules of the game. There is no question that the third party also has to have somebody watching it—that's part of our system of checks and balances. And in that system there is a place for individual voices. Public speakers serve as reflectors of and guides to public opinion. We like to think we help to light the way, although of course the light is colored by our own points of view. As for my point of view, here it is.

JUNE 7

Beau Brummell

On this day in 1778, George Bryan Brummell was born in London. He is better known in history as Beau Brummell, the man who made clothing a fine art for gentlemen. What is not as well known is the fact that Beau Brummel went bankrupt, went to debtor's prison, and lived the last years of his life as a threadbare, dirty indigent. Fancy clothes may be fine, but they're not enough to fill a life. The same is true of fancy phrases. So, although I am wearing my best bib and tucker and have polished my phrases to the best of my ability, I hope you will find that, unlike Beau Brummel, there is some substance underneath.

Freedom of the Press Day

The Inter-American Press Association some years ago designated this date as Freedom of the Press Day, an occasion we should all be happy to take note of. Freedom of the press and freedom of speech go hand in hand. In the many countries where the press is not free to report the news, the individual speaker is also not free to stand up and speak his or her mind. In our fortunate land we can print, read, publish, and speak freely; whether you will think as highly of those rights when I have finished speaking to you here today remains to be seen.

Independence Resolution

Today should really be a notable anniversary for Americans. It was on this day in 1776 that Richard Henry Lee of Virginia introduced in the Continental Congress a resolution that was seconded by John Adams, stating that "these united colonies are, and of right ought to be, free and independent states." It was the introduction of this resolution that paved the way for the Declaration of Independence less than a month later. Yes, today should be a notable American anniversary, but it has not been observed as such. We tend to celebrate only the climactic moments of great decisions, not the original conceptions. So one of the functions of a speaker can be to try to detect and point out some of the current beginnings that may develop into great things later. And there are many such interesting beginnings these days.

Lincoln and Johnson

When Abraham Lincoln was renominated for a second term as President by the Republican Party on this day in 1864, the man chosen for the Vice-Presidential nomination was a Tennessee Democrat named Andrew Johnson, who supported the Union against the Confederacy. Few people dreamed at the time that in less than a year Lincoln would be dead and Andrew Johnson would be president. It was during the Johnson administration that we bought Alaska and succeeded in getting the French to withdraw from Mexico. I mention these things because they remind us that this country always finds leadership when leadership is needed. Andrew Johnson lived up to Abraham Lincoln; Teddy Roosevelt was a stronger President than the assassinated William McKinley; Harry Truman does not stand in FDR's shadow today; and Lyndon Johnson, for all his faults, was the man who took John F. Kennedy's proposals and shaped them into the laws of the land. It is hard to tell beforehand which public figures will surprise us similarly in the future, but today I would like to give my impressions of some of the possible future great ones.

JUNE 8

Solzhenitsyn on the Right Not to Know

When Aleksandr Solzhenitsyn spoke at the commencement exercises of Harvard University on this day in 1978, he raised a point that I find interesting. Challenging our worship of the right to know, he said, "People also have the right not to know, and it is a much more valuable one. The right not to have their divine souls stuffed with gossip, nonsense, vain talk." Close quote. Now, it is easy to understand this feeling on the part of a man who lived under and fought so long with the authoritarian, doctrinaire, propagandistic Soviet Russian regime. One tires of being constantly assailed with the humorless propaganda of communism. Unlike the United States, Russia bombards its citizens with one voice and one message; here we have a cacophony, and each voice speaks for itself. My remarks to you today, for example, bear no stamp of officially approved orthodoxy. I am answerable only to public opinion for what

I say, and you are free to disagree with me at every turn. Only in that climate would I rise to speak and would my remarks be worthy of your attention.

Robert Schumann

The composer Robert Schumann, who was born on this day in 1810 in Germany, was a great creative artist. One of the ironies of history is that we might not have known about him if he hadn't married. That is because his wife Clara was one of the most famous pianists of her time, and it was her playing of his compositions that made him a success. Theirs was one of the more spectacular examples of teamwork and one of the best arguments for being part of a team. We Americans have always had a fondness for the quixotic lone crusader, the individual who carries his or her own banner and has the courage to stand alone. But in the final analysis you either have to get a team behind you or you go nowhere. We tend these days to deal in personalities, to judge leaders by their charm, their wit, their personas. I suggest that we judge them by the company they keep. And it is with that point of view that I render some judgments about some people in the spotlight today.

Frank Lloyd Wright

Frank Lloyd Wright, the great architect who was born on this day in 1867 in Wisconsin, wrote in his autobiography that "the American city as we know it today is not only to die but dying of acceleration." He described the city as "ceaseless to and fro" operating at a loss. I don't know whether in the long view of history Wright's view of the city will prove accurate, but it makes some valid points. How much of our daily concerns are ceaseless to-and-fro traffic operating at a loss? Are we applying twentieth-century stimuli and cures to an essentially nineteenth-century institution? Is the great American city an anachronism today? I believe it is time we took a careful look at the whole concept of the metropolis, and that is what I will attempt here today.

Crassus and Nero

This is an encouraging day for the forces of good. Two men who helped destroy a great civilization met their well-deserved deaths on this day many years ago. The first to go bore the name from which we derive the English word *crass*. He was Crassus, the most scheming member of the triumvirate of Caesar, Pompey, and Crassus that ruled Rome. Crassus was a thief and adventurer who went off to fight the Persians for his own profit, bled the Roman Empire to finance his adventures, and was killed on or about this day in 52 B.C. by his Persian enemies. Just a little more than a hundred years later, the man who fiddled while Rome burned, the infamous Emperor Nero, died as a suicide in 68 A.D. when he heard that his vengeful subjects had pronounced a sentence of death upon him. Now, any day that sees the end of people like Crassus and

Nero has got to give us hope that the forces of good will continue to triumph. I believe that the forces of good are growing stronger every day, and I'd like to tell you why.

JUNE 9

Little League Baseball Week

This is the time of year when we usually observe that notable American occasion, Little League Baseball Week. It is a week that mirrors some of the contrasts among us. Unfortunately, in the Little League as in life, extremism spoils the fun. If winning is all that counts, those children whose skills are limited will drop out or be forced out. If winning does not count at all, those children whose skills are outstanding may have no incentive to participate. You can't entirely satisfy both extremes nor can you do any better in politics or labor negotiations or any other area where people work together. That is why I take this occasion to speak in behalf of the middle course.

Truman vs. Congress

On this day in 1948, the President of the United States, Harry S. Truman, told an audience in Spokane, Washington, that the Congress of the time, the 80th, was—and I quote—"the worst we've ever had." Truman was neither the first nor the last Chief Executive to give up on Congress, and the Legislative Branch has been known to entertain equally uncordial feelings about various Presidents. The time to worry is not when they disagree. When they disagree we get a chance to think a little more about the policy questions that are involved. And when they disagree we have the opportunity as voters to make some decisions ourselves. But I would hope that we can do this without, like Harry Truman, calling our opponents the worst in history. I make no such claim about those who oppose the policies I shall advocate here today. All I will say is that they are wrong.

John Howard Payne

This is the birthday of John Howard Payne, who was one of the first stars of the American theater and later a prolific playwright. He was born in 1791 in New York. By the time he was 24 his American acting career was lagging, and he went to England where he struggled as an actor and playwright for many years. It was while in England that he wrote the composition for which he is remembered, the words for a song entitled "There's No Place Like Home." But home, sardonically, was no place for John Howard Payne, who came back to New York and eked out a precarious living until at last he got a government job as the U.S. Consul in Tunis. Of his many writings the only one that has really endured is "Home Sweet Home." But how that has endured! And so, recalling John Howard Payne, I asked myself for what one thing above all will we be remembered in generations to come. That is what I want to talk about today.

"O Promise Me"

On this day in 1890, when Reginald DeKoven's operetta *Robin Hood* opened in Chicago, audiences for the first time heard the song "O Promise Me." It has, of course, become a standard musical theme for weddings. I prefer to regard it as the theme song of American politics, and I think this is a good time to examine some of the more recent promises.

JUNE 10

Alcoholics Anonymous

This is the anniversary of the founding of Alcoholics Anonymous in 1935, a fact I mention not to introduce the subject of liquor but rather to emphasize how far we can go toward solving our problems if we are willing to talk about them. Sometimes we think we are alone with our difficulties, and then we find other people facing the same challenges and we are all helped by trying to face them together. So today I want to talk about some problems that all of us—rich or poor, old or young, healthy or sick—face in common.

Vigilantes

On this day in 1851, the Vigilance Committee of San Francisco, better known as the vigilantes, hanged a burglar named John Jenkins in the first such execution there. There will always, I suppose, be people impatient with the normal processes of law and order and therefore perfectly willing to take the law into their own hands, but we have at least made progress in getting rid of lynch law. What disturbs me is that the conditions that breed lynch law still exist. I am not referring to racial hatred, which I like to think has passed its peak. I refer rather to a general disenchantment with the processes of government, a widespread feeling that the courts are too lenient, bureaucracy too inept or too corrupt—all of the discontents that lead to people taking the law into their own hands or delivering it up to some kind of vigilance committee. What can we do to prevent that from happening here?

FDR on Youth

On the day that Italy entered World War II on the side of Germany, President Franklin D. Roosevelt went to the University of Virginia to deliver a speech. He spoke on this day in 1940, and he said, "Every now and again in the history of the republic a different kind of question presents itself—a question that asks, not about the future of an individual or even of a generation, but about the future of the country, the future of the American people. . . ." My friends, we are far removed from 1940 and Franklin Roosevelt's America, but we are challenged by that same question of America's future. We ask ourselves where we are going, what will there be for our grandchildren, what can we do now to make the future better. Those are the questions I shall try to deal with here today.

Coincidences and History

On this day in 1931, the Prince of Wales met an American-born lady who was living in England. It was a fateful meeting. She was Mrs. Wallis Warfield Simpson, and in 1936, after the prince had become King Edward VIII, he gave up the British throne to marry her. Sometimes history springs from seemingly minor events, and sometimes, of course, seemingly major events turn out to have no historical significance at all. As I look at today's world, I find myself wondering what the really significant occurrences are. I've picked out a few to discuss with you here today.

JUNE 11

Kamehameha Day

This is the day when part of the United States celebrates the birthday of a king. In Hawaii it is Kamehameha Day in honor of the birth in 1758 of the king who unified the various islands into one nation. He accomplished the unification by force of arms and persuasion, and in the course of his reign he also fended off a number of takeover attempts by foreign powers and pirates. Yet today, if Kamehameha looks at his beloved islands from his eternal resting place, he sees much of the landscape dominated by foreign-owned businesses, and on the mainland United States that is also increasingly true. It is interesting that we Americans generally have been far more exercised over foreign *people* settling in this country than over massive foreign *capital* coming in for the purpose of making profits from the American market and competing with American-owned businesses. We have a tendency to be more aware of problems directly involving people, and sometimes we need to be reminded that almost every problem ultimately involves people. Today I have as my subject some topics that, at first mention, may sound impersonal and far away. I hope I can convince you that they matter greatly to all of us.

A Very Special Committee

On this day in 1775, the Continental Congress did something Congress has been doing ever since. It appointed a committee, but this was a very special committee indeed. Its members were Thomas Jefferson, Benjamin Franklin,

John Adams, Robert Livingston, and Roger Sherman, and its job was to write the Declaration of Independence. As we know, the final document was written by Jefferson with some editing by Franklin and Adams, and I don't think any congressional committee has ever done a better or more important job. But there are plenty of important jobs left these hundreds of years later, and I'd like to talk about a few of them.

John Wayne

This is the anniversary of John Wayne's death in 1979. He was the actor who portrayed American western and war heroes and was a fiery American patriot. He became the symbol of hard-nosed, single-minded, old-fashioned American patriotism, particularly after his gallant fight against cancer. What I think people came to admire about John Wayne was that through thick and thin, even when his views where far from fashionable, he made no bones about his love for his country and about speaking out on the way the country should be run. He was consistent, and an inconsistent public came around to his point of view; even if they didn't, they came to admire him. We have always judged people more on their personalities than on their proposals, and one of the curious facts about American politics is, as Ralph Waldo Emerson noted a long time ago, that one party usually has the best cause and the other party has the best people. Are we fortunate enough today to have the best cause and the best people on the same side?

Alf Landon

I am speaking to you today on a notable anniversary. This was the day in 1936 when a highly enthusiastic Republican convention nominated Governor Alf Landon of Kansas for the presidency in 1936. As you know, Governor Landon went down to one of the most thorough defeats in American election history. So, on the anniversary of his moment of glory, I approach this rostrum very mindful that, as with Alf Landon, getting on the ticket is a far cry from winning your case. Now it's time to plead that case.

JUNE 12

Anne Frank

On this day in 1929, in Frankfurt-am-Main, a girl named Anne Frank was born. She was the young girl whose diary recorded the period of hiding in Amsterdam during the Nazi occupation of Holland and became one of the most poignant stories of World War II. Few things written have spoken more eloquently or more movingly than this young girl's innocent diary. It serves as a reminder that one does not need fancy words or oratorical or literary tricks to convey a message. In that spirit I am sure you will not mind if my remarks here today are relatively brief and to the point.

Baseball Strike

This is the day when the great major league baseball strike of 1981 began. Americans were astounded to find some of the highest-paid athletes in the world engaged in an old-fashioned labor dispute and work stoppage. The word *strike* suddenly had the same meaning in baseball as in other fields. It came as a big shock to us to find that ballplayers and their union had the same problems with management as any other groups of working people. It always comes as a shock to discover that problems we thought were ours alone are the problems of other people as well. Today I'd like to talk to you about some of those problems.

Interracial Marriage

It is sometimes salutary to look back into our history to see how long some of our freedoms have really existed. I was surprised to note, for example, that it was not until 1967 that the Supreme Court got around to banning state laws against interracial marriage. There weren't too many states by that time where such laws were still in effect, but the fact that it was still moot enough to go before the Supreme Court is shocking. Parenthetically, I must say I delight in the name of the case that went to the Court. It was entitled *Loving* v. *Virginia*. Well, now that loving is no longer versus Virginia, things are better than they were before, but still not good enough. I do not refer to interracial relationships. I refer not to loving but to living in America today.

Doubleday's Baseball

While the actual facts have been disputed for years, there was an investigatory commission early in this century that came to the conclusion that on or about this day in 1839, an Army colonel named Abner Doubleday first formulated the fixed layout of a baseball field and the rules of the game at Cooperstown, New York, where the Baseball Hall of Fame now stands. The question of who first thought of adapting the ancient children's game of rounders into modern baseball has been argued for generations, and I don't propose to get into that dispute at this late date. But I cite today's purported anniversary to show how we can get bogged down in needless controversy. It doesn't matter who thought up a good idea first, unless it is patentable. What matters, as the great Grantland Rice once pointed out, is how we play the game. And certainly, whether Doubleday or Alexander Cartwright or anyone else created baseball more than a century and a half ago, we play the game quite differently today. We live very differently. We adapt; we are still adapting. Have you thought of the changes we are seeing in our own lifetimes?

JUNE 13

Pentagon Papers

On this day in 1971, *The New York Times* began publishing the so-called Pentagon Papers which Daniel Ellsberg had taken from government files. Ellsberg's purpose was to show that the government had lied about the Vietnam War. The government attempted to stop publication of the papers and brought criminal action against Ellsberg, but neither effort succeeded, and the world did not crumble. With the passage of time we have put the whole matter in a perspective that was certainly lacking at the moment. That is often the case with issues that exasperate us when they first arise but whose shock value dissolves as other revelations and other developments follow. The government's attempt to keep the Pentagon Papers secret, for example, was put into the shade by the same government's attempt to keep the lid on Watergate. Distance does not lend enchantment to these shenanigans, but it puts them into better focus. If we could look at today's events from tomorrow's perspective, we might be better off. It isn't easy, but I propose to try it here today. Imagine, if you will, that you and I are sitting in this room five years from now, looking back. What would we see?

Miranda

This day marks an important anniversary in the U.S. system of justice. On this day in 1966, the Supreme Court ruled in the case of *Miranda* v. *Arizona* that anyone under arrest must be told that he or she has the right to counsel and the right to remain silent. In this country we don't stand pat on questions of human rights; we are open to logical expansions based on the provisions of the Constitution. Our body of law is a living document, subject to interpretation, amendment, and amplification, and our courts have always constituted themselves as the guardians of the spirit as well as the letter of the law. As long as we have a Supreme Court, regardless of its political complexion, the nature of American development is that there will be new Miranda-like issues and new interpretations of rights. We are in a period of change when whatever the courts decide seems to become a cause of controversy. That, I believe, is part of the growing pains of our republic, and it is accompanied by the kind of growth I want to discuss with you here today.

Yeats

Today is the birthday of William Butler Yeats, the great Irish poet who was born in 1865. It was Yeats who wrote the line, "In dreams begins responsibility." The dreams of our Founding Fathers, of a free land and a representative government, brought them to their moments of greatness. If we in our time can still have dreams, we too can make a better world. This I believe to be the key to the future—believe. If by sharing what I believe with you here today I can bring some of you to the point of trying to make your dreams come true, our time will not have been wasted.

No More Worlds to Conquer

On this day in the year 323 B.C., the greatest conqueror the world had yet seen, Alexander the Great, died in Babylon. He was 33 years old. We think of the young man or woman in a hurry as a comparatively modern phenomenon, the precocious result of a sophisticated age. But Alexander achieved his triumphs more than 2,300 years ago. True, he started out with the advantage of being the son of a king, but other kings have also had sons with considerably less spectacular results. Great expectations go with being young; seeing the world as your oyster is every young person's prerogative. Fortunately, today we do not necessarily have to conquer by force of arms. Politics, business, and science all afford greater opportunities than ever for young people with the ability and the energy to triumph. That has been the secret of the greatness of the United States, and it still is. When you combine that vigor with a free atmosphere where ideas can be freely uttered and exchanged, the future has to be bright. We have plenty of worlds left to conquer, and I'd like to talk here today about some of them.

JUNE 14

California Republic Day

This is California Republic Day, the anniversary of the proclamation of the republic of California by U.S. settlers at Sonoma in 1846, a prelude to U.S. annexation of the territory. As it turned out, what began as a U.S. takeover of California turned out to be, later on, a California takeover of the United States. California styles and California films and television programs became major influences throughout the country and around the world. For the rest of the world the United States was the promised land; for the United States for many years, California was the promised land. I don't know what is the promised land for Californians these days, but they must have one. Everybody needs an Eden to dream of, an ideal way of life to aspire to. That is why so many politicians have gained success by promising the good life to the voters. But we don't all agree on what the good life is. For some it is getting rid of big cities and going back to nature; for others it is being wealthy enough to buy everything you need. For some it means being with congenial people; for others it means getting away from people. Today I'd like to give you my definitions, and incidentally to suggest that we are closer to the good life than you may think.

Flag Day

Today is Flag Day, the anniversary of the adoption of the national flag by the Continental Congress in 1777. The birthday of the Stars and Stripes seems to me to be a particularly appropriate time to consider what that flag stands for, and that's what I'd like to talk about here today.

Jefferson's Theory

In 1817, Thomas Jefferson was seventy-four years old and might have been expected to have become staid and conservative. Instead, as he wrote in a letter on this day, he remained an optimist. "My theory has always been," he said, "that if we are to dream, the flatteries of hope are as cheap, and pleasanter than the gloom of despair." As younger people these days are attracted to gloomy theories of coming disaster, I find myself recalling the words of Jefferson and asking myself, why not look for the signs of hope and build on those, rather than on fear of gloom and doom? And the signs of hope are there for the seeing. Let me be specific.

Peace Corps

The first volunteers for the Peace Corps were selected around this time in 1961, an anniversary worth remembering. When I see reports of how this or that country has been the scene of anti-American demonstrations I find myself wondering what other nation has been similarly rewarded for the kind of help it has given the world. We sent CARE packages, we provided Marshall Plan aid, we sent our young people to contribute their own talents to peoples in need around the world. In thanks we have in large measure been resented for the wealth that made these efforts possible. As a result there is growing pressure to withdraw the helping hand and provide only such help as meets our immediate national interests overseas. I am here today to speak against that proposition and in favor of our continuing to be the world's good neighbor.

JUNE 15

Income Tax Payment

I stand before you on one of America's least favorite days, when the second income tax estimated payment is due. It is hard to realize that for more than a century the United States managed without any income taxes at all, but once the barrier broke it broke for good. Taxes are harder to get rid of than warts. New taxes rarely replace old ones; they are just added on alongside. Taxes usually begin as revenue measures but all too often end up as another form of social engineering—and that is what I would like to discuss here today. A graduated income tax takes proportionately more away from rich people; a sales tax takes proportionately more away from poor people. No matter what form of taxation you use, somebody is discriminated against. When we discuss taxation we must start by recognizing this discriminatory factor. And then we must look at the social effect of the tax under discussion. I have looked, and this is what I see.

Magna Carta

On this day in the year 1215, the Magna Carta was signed at Runnymede in England, marking the birth of the Anglo-American concept of freedom. One would have thought that over the course of the centuries since then the idea of freedom would have been well enough defined so that there would be no doubts about it, but every day turns up another question. Where does my freedom to pick my own company collide with the freedom of someone of another race not to be discriminated against? For most of us, these are not believed to be serious problems because we are usually interested in one freedom at a time, and we are usually more in favor of some freedoms than of others. It is the freedoms that we are not in favor of that concern me here today. So I would like to talk about some elements of freedom that I believe we are neglecting.

Representing People, Not Acres

Until this day in 1964, it had been considered perfectly legal for states to have one house of a two-house legislature represent geographical areas regardless of population. One state senator might represent a county of 10,000 people and another a county of 100,000. But on this day in 1964, the Supreme Court ended that idea. Said Chief Justice Warren, "Legislators represent people, not trees or acres." Even though the Senate of the United States represents states, and little Rhode Island has the same number of U.S. Senators as mighty California, the Court held that no similar arrangement on a state level would be proper. I cannot help wondering about the logic of that. Certainly, the disparity in Senate representation of California voters and Rhode Island voters seems as unfair as anything in a state legislature, but the best thing to be said for our federal system is that it has worked. Still, it seems to me that some thought should be given to the injustices inherent in the Congress as it is now composed.

Rubber

On this day in 1837, Charles Goodyear received a patent for his process of vulcanizing rubber, which transformed a sticky gum into a commercial miracle. He had worked for ten years trying to develop the process without success until he accidentally dropped some of his mixture onto a hot stove. Of such accidents is progress born. But it wasn't an accident that Charles Goodyear was working to utilize rubber in the first place. And if we want to be the beneficiaries of future turns of fate, we have to do what Charles Goodyear was doing—experimenting, dreaming of new products, looking for new ideas. Above all, that means avoiding fear of the new, being willing to take risks, trying to channel discontent instead of suppressing it. It means giving more support to pure research, and, above all, it means supporting and extending the climate of freedom. Are we doing that today? That is the question I propose to explore with you.

JUNE 16

Madison on Encroachments

On this day in 1788, James Madison made a speech to the Virginia Convention, which was meeting to consider the proposed Constitution of the United States. Madison, concerned with the inclusion of a bill of rights, said, "Since the general civilization of mankind, I believe that there are more instances of the abridgment of the freedom of the people by gradual and silent encroachments of those in power than by violent and sudden usurpations." What was true in 1788 is true today. Gradual and silent encroachments by those in power are still the prime threat to freedom. We see them all around us, whether we are talking about all-encompassing government, greedy landlords, labor unions, corporate monopolies, or aggressive in-laws. One of the difficulties in stopping this kind of silent encroachment is that each instance in itself is either so small or so seemingly justifiable that making a fuss about it is a bit extreme. But fusses have to be made. I rise in praise of gadflies and watchdogs, ombudsmen and the like. At times they can be nuisances, but they are necessary nuisances, and today I am going to be one myself. My encroachment will be neither gradual nor silent.

Woman in Space

On this day in 1963, the first woman to go into space was orbited by the Soviet Union. It seemed at the time to be a significant plus for the communists; not until many years later did we discover that it was more of a public relations ploy than a real opportunity for a female. Twenty years later Sally Ride became the first American woman astronaut to go into space. The women's rights revolution has been a fact of life for some time, but, unless my eyes deceive me, women are working harder than ever, still making less than men, and possibly no better off in many respects than they were a couple of generations ago. Let's take a realistic look at the female half of the population today.

Adams' Oration

New Englanders are traditionally supposed to be people of few words, but Daniel Webster was known to speak for hours on end, and on this day the scion of one of New England's greatest families began a speech in the House of Representatives that lasted, believe it or not, for three weeks. That record belongs to John Quincy Adams, who began his talking marathon on this day in 1838. Ladies and gentlemen, Mr. Adams' record is safe today.

Gold in Alaska

This is the day when, in 1897, the great Alaska gold rush began with the news of the first discovery at Bonanza Creek. Suddenly a half-forgotten U.S. territory became a land of opportunity. In our century that kind of boom has come more often from the discovery of oil than of gold, but whatever the treasure, it has a way of transforming the bleakest landscape into dreams of fortune. Every year there is some new kind of gold rush, even though it often turns out to be fool's gold. The trouble is that so many people keep on looking for easy wealth; they want to strike gold or oil without having to work for it. They fall prey to con men who offer promises of quick profits; they listen to the snake oil salesmen. Politics is full of snake oil salesmen, and too many people are listening to them. Come with me on a little examination of some current snake oils.

JUNE 17

Bunker Hill

The battle misnamed Bunker Hill—misnamed because it was actually fought on next-door Breed's Hill—took place on this day in 1775, when the American watchword was "Don't fire till you see the whites of their eyes." The reasoning was simple: be sure you can see what you're aiming at clearly and fully before you start shooting. That, I must say, is a good rule whether you are firing a gun or just shooting off your mouth. Today my mouth is my weapon, and my targets are things I have seen as close as I care to.

Watergate

It was about two o'clock on the morning of this day in 1972 when five men were arrested after breaking into Democratic Party offices in the Watergate development in Washington, D.C. Only an atomic bomb could match the mushrooming effect of that incident, which ended with the only resignation of a U.S. President, the jailing of many Washington officials who had tried to keep the matter under wraps, and a period of national shame. If there was a message in the whole affair, it was that no individual, not even the President of the United States, is immune from the standards of the law. And it all started with the effort to cover up a relatively minor crime. Why is it that almost every popularly elected American administration goes in for the same desire to keep the people from knowing what is going on? The Nixon administration got caught; others have been more fortunate. I am not talking about military intelligence or other similarly sensitive matters. I am talking about things like cost overruns, statistics on landfills, and other government information that we are entitled to know about. Let me cite some recent examples.

Nureyev Defects

On this day in 1961, the premier dancer of the great Russian Kirov Ballet defected at Le Bourget Airport in Paris. Rudolf Nureyev was the first of a long string of Russia's great ballet dancers to opt for freedom in the West. Their defection was a truly damning indictment of the communist way of life, for none of them were political figures; none of them were economically deprived. What they found themselves deprived of was simply freedom. You and I did not have to leave home to have that freedom, and so we take it for granted. But every now and then we too must be reminded that freedom doesn't just happen. It wasn't handed to our Founding Fathers on a silver platter, and it isn't going to continue unless we work at it. Freedom, it has been said, is indivisible. If we permit our fellow citizens in this country to be deprived of freedom, we open the door to losses of our own freedom as well. If we restrict the right of a group to assemble peacefully because we disagree with their views, we are giving the state the right to do the same to us. And right now we are setting some dangerous precedents in that regard.

First Transcontinental Telephone Line

On this day in 1914, some wires were joined up on the border of Utah and Nevada, and the United States finally had a transcontinental telephone line. It had taken five years to finish the job, which included some 130,000 telephone poles and thousands of miles of wire. Throughout history, human beings have devoted some of their greatest efforts to communicating with one another. And yet, look how easily we are doing it here today. Sometimes I think that the way to get speakers to come to the point more quickly is to have them phone in their remarks at regular toll rates, paid by them. But even without that limiting factor, I want to assure you that my comments here today will be as considerate of your time as if the meter were running.

JUNE 18

War of 1812

In the early nineteenth century events moved somewhat more slowly than they do today. On June 16, 1812, the British government decided on the rescinding of the Order in Council over which the United States had threatened to go to war. The U.S. House of Representatives had voted on June 4 for a declaration of war. In the Senate there was a long debate, and then, on this day, the upper house also voted for a declaration of war. It was proclaimed by President James Madison on June 19, still without the knowledge that Britain had rescinded the Orders in Council. That kind of slow communication marked the last battle of the War of 1812 as well—the Battle of New Orleans was actually fought after a peace treaty was signed at Ghent, Belgium, because the news of the signing hadn't arrived in America. So we can take some comfort in the fact that today's news travels instantaneously around the world. This speed of communication has probably saved us from wars and disasters on more than one occasion. And it brings home the need for an unimpeded flow of information. Freedom of the press is a powerful tool for a better world, and that freedom needs constant vigilance. Even here, it is under challenge. Let me tell you what you and I can do about it.

Waterloo

Today is the anniversary of the Battle of Waterloo in 1815, when Napoleon was finally beaten. He had finally bitten off more than he could chew. One does not need to have a Napoleonic complex to run the same kind of risk today. All we need is success that comes too easily, and we think we've got the world by the tail. That kind of risk even applies to a speaker who thinks the audience's generous reception when he or she rises to speak is an open invitation for stem-winding oratory. A speaker spread too thin, or strung out too long, is headed for a platform Waterloo, and I want to assure you that I will stay far away from that risky territory.

"Their Finest Hour"

At this time in 1940, England faced its greatest danger. France had fallen, Germany's forces had proven unstoppable in Western Europe, and the British were now fighting alone against seemingly overwhelming odds as a Nazi triumph in World War II loomed near. On this fateful day Winston Churchill spoke to his people and to the world. Churchill was the man of whom it was said that he mobilized the English language and sent it into war, and he did just that on this day. He said, "Let us therefore brace ourselves to our duties, and so bear ourselves that, if the British Empire and its Commonwealth last for a thousand years, men will still say, 'This was their finest hour.' " And Churchill's words proved true, for that indeed was England's finest hour. Now, ladies and gentlemen, there was only one Winston Churchill; his way with words was his alone. When he spoke he made history; when we lesser mortals speak, the best we can do is perhaps to illuminate some small corner of history. It is with that modest aim that I address you here today.

Space Shuttle

On this day in 1977, the U.S. space shuttle carried astronauts above the earth for the first time, but they were simply riding piggyback on top of a Boeing 747. The development of the returnable space shuttle was the result of step-by-step experiments over a period of years. While the final accomplishments were incredibly spectacular, they were preceded by cautious timetables and even a number of false starts. That's the way it is with good research and development, even though it may cause impatience along the way. Rome wasn't built in a day, but it was destroyed overnight by Nero's great fire. It is much easier—and quicker—to tear something down than to build it up. And that is as true of the speaker as of the doer. It is much easier to be critical than to be constructive. I suppose the hat trick is to be both. Let's try.

JUNE 19

Father's Day

This is the month of Father's Day, when too many commencement speakers give fatherly advice, and I certainly don't want to fall into that kind of category. Somebody once said that advice was cheap; on the contrary, good advice is priceless. The trouble is that you don't know which advice is good beforehand. I have no magic formula to solve that problem. What I do have are some observations on the current scene that I hope will be helpful.

Louis vs. Conn

On this day in 1946, the heavyweight champion of the world, Joe Louis, was challenged by one of the best boxers of his time, Billy Conn. The champion was asked for his assessment of Billy Conn, and he said, "He can run, but he can't hide." And although Conn did beautifully for quite a while in the fight that night, Joe Louis was proved right. Billy couldn't hide indefinitely from the Louis punches; he was finally knocked out. We are in the position of Billy Conn today when we confront the prospect of nuclear warfare; we can't hide. We have to figure out some other way to go on living. Let's review the bidding.

Roanoke Exit

On this day in 1586, the first English attempt to colonize the New World ended in failure. The colonists who had settled at Roanoke Island off the North Carolina coast gave up and boarded a ship to go home. Not for a generation thereafter was there a successful English settlement on the American mainland, but thank goodness they didn't give up. The odds certainly were high against them, but the new generation wasn't bothered by the failures of their fathers; they set out to do better, and they succeeded. We in our time worry about the world we are bequeathing to our children, but the lesson of history tells us that they will make their own world. What we can do is to equip them as best we can for that job. Here is how I see the challenge.

Nickelodeon

This is the anniversary of the opening of an establishment in Pittsburgh for the showing of motion pictures. The price of admission was a nickel; consequently, the establishment was known as a nickelodeon. It opened in 1905, when the movies were silent and the audience talked. The message on the screen was heightened as time went on by a pianist or even an orchestra playing appropriate mood music, and there are times when I'm speaking that I think I would be grateful for that kind of accompaniment. But I must appeal to your sympathy without being cued in by the melody of "Hearts and Flowers." I will sound my alarms without the help of the "William Tell" overture and, in the last analysis, I stand up here to face the music alone.

JUNE 20

Jefferson for Randolph

This is the day when a substitute delegate replaced Peyton Randolph, who was ill, in the Continental Congress in Philadelphia in 1775. It was not fortunate for poor Mr. Randolph, and his fellow Virginians no doubt were upset about it, but they made do with the substitute delegate, a young fellow named Thomas Jefferson. Ladies and gentlemen, there has to be a very special Providence watching over this country of ours to have come up with that kind of added starter at the key moment in our history. I believe that we are still the most blessed of peoples and that it is indeed time to count our blessings. We are better off than we may think, and I am here to count the ways.

Alaskan Oil

One of the great engineering feats of modern times was the construction of the trans-Alaska oil pipeline, and on this day in 1977 the oil began to flow from the North Slope to Prudhoe Bay. Alaska's liquid gold played an important role in helping to end the fear of oil shortages, but it also was a key to the development of the last great U.S. territory in North America. As recently as 1945, nobody could have predicted this whole turn of events, and it is this kind of new discovery that can change the course of history or confirm it. I happen to believe that much of the riches of our American land have yet to be discovered and that the future holds great promise. With the tools we keep on developing, the artificial intelligence systems, the radar sensors, and so forth, we are only just beginning to realize our potential. Today I want to talk about what is needed to take the best advantage of that potential.

Hot Line

On this day in 1963, the United States and the Soviet Union agreed to set up an emergency "hot line" for direct communication between Washington and Moscow. In the event of future crises, the world at least would not go up in flames because of a busy wire. I've been thinking about the hot line idea, and I like it. I like it not only for international capitals but also for ordinary citizens—a hot line for a friendly ear when you need it, a direct means of communication without all of the layers of intermediates who so often complicate things. One of the problems of our time is that we do too much through intermediaries. My secretary gives my message to your secretary, my lawyer works out our problem with your lawyer, and so forth. I realize that the complications of modern life require expert help to get us through the maze, but I think we overdo it. Our public officials are not close enough to the public; they work through functionaries and hire pollsters to find out what the people think. We need more person-to-person relationships, more eyeball-to-eyeball communication, between the leaders and the led, the elected and the electors. As a matter of fact, that is what I propose to do here today—more listening and less orating. Instead of a formal speech, I'd like to make this a question-and-answer session. (Alternative remark if a Q and A is not desired: "I am going to tell you what I have learned simply by listening.")

Victoria

On this day in 1837, a teenaged princess found herself the Queen of England. She reigned until the twentieth century and gave her name to the age in which she lived—the Victorian Age. No one could have foreseen how she grew—and how her nation grew—during her reign. Responsibility often brings out in people more than they knew they had in them. That is a lesson we don't remember enough. We have developed a whole philosophy of passing the buck when it comes to responsibility. We are told that the criminal is not responsible because he is the result of his impoverished environment; the unwed mother isn't responsible because society failed to educate her properly; the illiterate isn't responsible because it was the educational system that failed him—and so forth. Now, ladies and gentlemen, some of all these alibis are true, but let us not forget that most of the responsibility lies with the individual. Most people who come from an impoverished environment do not become criminals; a lot of unwed mothers knew very well what they were doing. I am here to suggest that our tendency to regard the offenders as the victims is twisting our values, and it is those twisted values that I believe we should be looking at.

JUNE 21

Summer

This is traditionally the first day of summer, when Mother Nature provides more than enough hot air for all of us. Under the circumstances, while I have a warm spot in my heart for all of you, I think it would best if I just talked cold facts here today.

Longest Day

Forces in the planets far beyond our control make this season bring us the longest day of the year. I hope my remarks here today will not make the day seem even longer.

Constitution

The ninth state to ratify the Constitution was New Hampshire, which did so on this day in 1788, and with that ratification the Constitution went into effect, so today in a sense is an anniversary day for our country. But we have come to take the Constitution for granted—or, as the punsters say, for granite. We have every reason to feel that way about it, because it has lasted so long and served us so well. But even the Constitution needs tender loving care. It serves us well because we don't abuse it; we don't nibble it to death with amendments or burden it with special-interest additions. We tried using it to create a law against drink, and we found that kind of narrow purpose doesn't belong in the basic Constitution. I rise today to ask that when we consider amending the Constitution we ask ourselves whether it is our basic principles of law that we want to change—for that is what the Constitution is—or a particular law we want to enact. To change the Constitution for the sake of one law is a risky business and, as Prohibition showed, a bad precedent. Let me therefore look at some of the current amendment proposals with that fact in mind.

McCormick's Reaper

It was on this day in 1834 that Cyrus H. McCormick patented his mechanical reaper. Like the cotton gin, the reaper cut down on hand labor and helped speed mass production on the farm. That is typical of the partnership between invention and resources that has done so much to make America great. It is important to maintain that partnership. There is a certain resentment of machines, particularly when they displace human labor, but the whole course of history has been to find ways to displace or ease human labor. We are, of course, challenged to find other employment for displaced labor. We have no machine to solve that problem. But I do have some suggestions about things that need doing.

JUNE 22

Nazis Attack Russia

On this day in 1941, Nazi Germany, arrogant with its military victories in Western Europe, invaded the Soviet Union. What made the whole terrible story even grimmer was that the Nazis and the communists, only a couple of years before, had concluded a nonaggression treaty that enabled them to divide Poland and encouraged Hitler to wage war against Western Europe. And after the war, when the alliance between communist Russia and the western powers had won its victory, the communists turned to the cold war. As the saying goes, he who lies down with dogs gets up with fleas. Alliances with nations whose regimes are based on hatred and repression are simply not trustworthy because those nations are not trustworthy. My theme today, ladies and gentlemen, is that we cannot always pick our enemies but we should work a little harder at choosing our friends.

Champion Joe Louis

On this day in 1937, Joe Louis won the heavyweight boxing championship of the world. There had been one black heavyweight champion before him, Jack Johnson, whose reign was marred by scandal and racial hatred, but Joe Louis had won and continued to win the respect of all of his fellow Americans not only for his fighting skills but for the honesty and decency that so clearly marked his character. It was a time when blacks were still being denied basic human rights in some parts of the country, and discrimination was still a way of life. In that climate it is hard to tell how much Joe Louis, as a great champion, did to advance the human dignity of his people, but it was considerable. People in the spotlight, like it or not, become examples and inspirations. When they are people like the young Joe Louis, we are fortunate. We are not that fortunate today with some of the spotlight's choices. It is time to ask ourselves why.

Henry Hudson Adrift

The memory of Henry Hudson looms large in North America. The Hudson River that flows in New York State is named for him, and so is the great Hudson Bay in Canada. History, as a matter of fact, has treated the great explorer more kindly than his own people did, for on this day in 1611, on James Bay in present-day Canada, the crew of Hudson's ship, the *Discovery,* mutinied and set Hudson, his son, and seven others adrift in a boat with no supplies. That was the last anybody ever saw of Henry Hudson. I am happy to say that we treat our trail blazers a little better than that these days. We may not always listen to them as we should, but we don't set them adrift in small boats. We save that fate for the less fortunate folks who are dependent on us. We turn mental patients loose to fend for themselves, for example. We give better care to incarcerated criminals than to the victims of their crimes. Let me take you on a little tour of our boats adrift.

St. John Fisher

John Fisher was a respected Catholic bishop in England in 1535 when King Henry VIII decided to divorce his wife Catherine in order to marry Anne Boleyn. Bishop Fisher refused to recognize Henry's self-constituted authority as supreme head of the church in England. Since it was by virtue of that authority that Henry claimed the right to divorce Catherine, Bishop Fisher also refused to recognize the divorce. The Pope tried to back up the bishop's authority by appointing him a cardinal, but Henry was not impressed. On this day in 1535, he had John Fisher, later to be a saint, beheaded, two weeks before Sir Thomas More met the same fate. Thank goodness, we live in a more enlightened time and land, although there are some other places where the expression of an opinion can still land you in jail. It is a comfort to me as a speaker here, I must say, to know that what I am about to say to you is not going to cost me my head.

JUNE 23

Treasury Surplus

This is a red-letter day in American history. On this day in 1836, because the United States had more money than the government needed, the Treasury was authorized to pay out the extra funds to the states, and a total of $28 million was given back that way. It would be great if we had a similar situation today, but with the kind of public debt this country has built, treasury surpluses, if they ever exist, are already spoken for. As a matter of fact, the United States spends more on interest payments for the public debt nowadays than the entire cost of the federal government a generation ago. Very few of us as individuals could carry, proportionately, as heavy a mortgage on our future as the federal government does, and the question is whether we are preparing a future generation for bankruptcy. It is a question worth some careful consideration.

A Quote from Cobb

Irvin S. Cobb, perhaps the greatest after-dinner speaker of his time, was born on this day in 1876 in Paducah, Kentucky. Cobb once said that "A good

storyteller is a person who has a good memory and hopes other people haven't."
I am not here to be that kind of storyteller, because I want to jog your memories.
I want to start my remarks by asking you the question that Ronald Reagan asked
when he was campaigning for the presidency in 1980, which was, "Are you
better off now than you were four years ago?" I would alter that to ask, "Are
you better off now than you used to be?" That is the test of life worth living.
But I don't mean it just in the sense of money in the bank or even health. I
ask it in terms of security against crime, closeness with your family and friends,
and peace of mind. It is against the background of your own response to that
question that I ask you to hear my remarks about the way our world is changing.

Kinsey

Today is the birthday of Alfred Kinsey, who was born in Hoboken, New
Jersey, in 1894. It was Dr. Kinsey who made the study of human sex habits
and problems a best-selling area of scholarship and opened the floodgates to
a whole new era of what, for want of a better term, I might call sexual revelation. When serious science hits upon a topic of popular interest, the results
can be frightening, and I believe that the degree to which irresponsible profi-
teers exploited Dr. Kinsey's breakthrough proves the point. There is a great
tendency for important movements to be short-circuited by people with special
motives. For example, I think the women's liberation movement—an important and necessary instrument of social progress—was hurt immeasurably by
those who used it to provide a platform for lesbian propaganda, and I believe
equally that the cause of sensible economy in government is damaged by those
who use it to punish the poor. Therefore, I think it is important to see who
supports what proposals and to try to figure out why.

Government Printing Office

The Government Printing Office was created by an act of Congress on
this day in 1860, and that turned out to be the greatest encouragement to verbosity the world has ever seen. The flow of the printed word from the Government Printing Office is steadier than Niagara Falls and just as strong. One government publication, the *Congressional Record,* even prints speeches that were never
spoken, under the euphemism of "extension of remarks." It could be said by
a visitor from Mars, contemplating the work of the Government Printing Office, that we are never at a loss for words, and nobody ever has the last word.
I realize that my comments here today will hardly be the last word on the matter at hand, but I hope that in the midst of all the public dialogue a point or
two can still be made.

JUNE 24

Margaret Brent

Although it is difficult to pin down the actual date, some sources say that it was about this time in the period between 1647 and 1648 that a lady named Margaret Brent was the first woman in America to attempt to assert the right to vote. She was the sister-in-law of Leonard Calvert and was the executor of his estate in Maryland as well as a landholder there in her own right. She asked the Maryland assembly to give her two votes in its deliberations, one for her own landholdings and one as the representative of the Calvert estate, but they turned her down. Between that incident and the granting of votes to women, almost three centuries elapsed. Justice cannot be accused of coming at runaway speed. Probably very few people in Margaret Brent's time dreamed that women would ever be permitted to vote. I find myself wondering what lonely crusades of our own time will some day come to fruition, and I have a few predictions.

Congress Flees

On this day in 1783, the Continental Congress, in session in Philadelphia, found itself threatened by veteran soldiers furious about not being paid. Congress didn't take that threat lying down. They took it running away, adjourning their Philadelphia meeting and fleeing to Princeton, where they met later. I wish I would say that Congress today faces its problems more squarely—and sometimes they do—but all too often the motto seems to be "Never put off till tomorrow what you can put off a day longer." That isn't because Congress is incompetent; it is because Congress, in the final analysis, is representative—representative of districts with different interests, representative of constituencies whose views often conflict. In those circumstances I think we should be proud of how much, rather than how little, Congress gets done. But I also think we should take more interest. In most congressional districts the average person couldn't tell you the name of his congressman or senator. And there are issues before the current Congress that not enough of us know about. I'd like to talk about some of those issues here today.

Flying Saucers

On this day in 1947, a new phenomenon was born. Actually, it was the report of a new phenomenon—the first supposed sighting of flying saucers, in the area of Mount Rainier, Washington. From that beginning we had years of similar reports all over the country, including accounts by people who claimed to have been aboard these mysterious vessels from outer space. Despite years of serious investigation, none of these accounts were ever confirmed, but they gave rise to a whole school of space adventure movies, and a public that had lived through the incredible real-life accomplishments of the space age never totally dismissed the idea that there might be creatures from outer space keeping an eye on us. If those extraterrestrial observers are still watching, I'd like to imagine for you what they make of us.

Berlin Blockade

It was on this day in 1948 that Soviet Russia imposed a blockade on the western powers' land communication with West Berlin. It didn't work, thanks to the airlift, but it did expose the shabbiness and ruthlessness of Soviet tactics. That was a long time ago, and it seems that in every generation there has to be another incident of Soviet heavyhandedness to educate that generation to the real face of communism. Repeatedly, younger people in particular are taken in by claims that it isn't communism, just agrarian reform or just a reaction to the excesses of anticommunism or just a passing phase en route to a better world. I think it is worthwhile to try to see the differences between communism and what it pretends to be, and that's what I'd like to take the time to do here today.

JUNE 25

Orwell

Not too many people convey their ideas so clearly and dramatically that they give their names to a whole concept of life. George Orwell, who was born on this day in 1903 in India, was one of those rare people. When we speak today of Orwellian worlds or of 1984 we are referring to the novel in which he painted the world of Big Brother, and we are bearing in mind the cynical observation of his *Animal Farm* that "all animals are equal but some are more equal than others." That kind of cynicism can become very persuasive when we contemplate the inequities and injustices of our society, or any other society for that matter. It is easier to become cynical than to retain one's idealism, but the idealists, rather than the cynics, are our hope for the future. I hope that my remarks here today will serve to enlist you, or bring you back, to the ranks of the idealists.

Distaff Exemption

When young men were required to register for selective service, although there was no actual draft in effect, a court case was brought challenging the requirement on the ground that it was discriminatory since it did not apply to women. On this day in 1981, the Supreme Court held that women could indeed be excluded from draft registration. This seems to fly somewhat in the face of a comment Benjamin Franklin made on this same day way back in 1745, when he wrote, "It is the man and woman united that makes the complete human being. . . . A single man . . . is an incomplete animal. He resembles the odd half of a pair of scissors." Close quote. Putting these two views—the Supreme Court's and Franklin's—together, we come up with the view that equal opportunity for women does not extend to fighting a war but what men and women do together they do better. I will buy that, and I would like to apply it to the most essential product of the man–woman relationship, the family. I rise here today to suggest a few ways to strengthen the American family.

The Fork

At least one historian gives this day in the year 1630 as the date for the introduction to America of one of humanity's most important tools—the fork. The story is that Governor John Winthrop was responsible for bringing the newfangled cutlery from England, where Queen Elizabeth I had begun using it. You will recall that Elizabeth's father, Henry VIII, was a great one for eating with his fingers. Anyway, today is the American birthday of the fork, so I suppose it is a particularly good day to come to the point of my meaty remarks.

Progress

On this day in 1938, President Franklin D. Roosevelt signed the Fair Labor Standards Act, which established a minimum wage of 40 cents an hour and a maximum work week of forty hours. Times have certainly changed since then, haven't they? In 1938 most people worked a five-and-a-half day week that included Saturday; now, except in rare cases, offices and many plants are closed on Saturday. We still think of the eight-hour working day as standard, but morning and afternoon breaks, portal-to-portal regulations, and the like have watered that down too in many areas. I do not mention this critically; I believe one of our chief goals should be to make all of life easier for all people, including the conditions of work. And I have some thoughts that may help.

JUNE 26

Pied Piper

In the year 1284, on or about this day, legend has it that a pied piper came to Hamelin, Germany, and more than a hundred children disappeared with him. It is interesting that this ancient story is still being told, even while a whole batch of modern pied pipers are bewitching the children of today. These modern pied pipers have all kinds of temptations for the youngsters—the thrills of forbidden fruit such as dope and gambling, the lure of easy excitement at trashy horror movies, the vast arrays of novelty items like electronic game arcades. What should we do about these pied pipers? What can we do?

Altgeld's Pardon

Courage on the part of an elected official deserves applause, but it doesn't always draw that kind of reaction. On this day in 1893, Governor John Peter Altgeld of Illinois pardoned three of the men convicted of participating in the Haymarket Riot in Chicago in 1886, when a bomb exploded among the police. After many liberals had worked for years on reversing the verdict of the court against a number of anarchists on the grounds that the trial had been blatantly unfair, Altgeld issued his pardons. By then four of the defendants had been executed. Altgeld was defeated for reelection and never held public office again. Only after his death did history recognize him as one of those rare men of principle who sometimes ornament American politics. We call for courage in our public figures, but when that courage is in opposition to our own views we can be most unforgiving. Today I would like to salute those politicians who put principle above expediency. You will find them on both sides of the aisle, and they deserve your respect. If I may, I offer a bipartisan roll of honor.

Kennedy in Berlin

This was the day when President John F. Kennedy came to Berlin in 1963. With his characteristic eloquence he voiced the unity of the free world as he confronted the Berlin Wall, and the city resounded with cheers for his words. We get so involved in rivalries and economic competition that we sometimes forget the strength of our common bond with free democratic nations around the world. It must not be forgotten. Those who uphold freedom are our friends among the nations; we should remember that and act accordingly. And conversely, those who do not believe in freedom are not really our friends. Look at the current world scene and you will see what I mean.

Yellow Fever

This was the day in 1900 when a doctor named Walter Reed got down to business in Cuba as head of the Yellow Fever Commission. Before he and his colleagues were through they had conducted one of the first successful government attacks on a particular disease. They found the cause and the method of preventing yellow fever and provided a model for countless later health projects and government financing of them. We learned with cancer and other diseases that merely throwing money at them does not do the trick, but it certainly helps. Research is expensive and has to be extensive; it starts out as a search in the dark, which means many blind alleys and many disappointments.

And sometimes when we have learned how to lick an ailment we still have to persuade people to get the job done. We have that problem now with perhaps the most widespread ailment in the world, malnutrition. That is my subject for today.

JUNE 27

Hoover on War

Herbert Hoover was President during the agonizing days of the Great Depression and an elder statesman when we were fighting World War II. It was as a reminder to other elder statesmen that he remarked, on this day in 1944, "Older men declare war. But it is youth that must fight and die." Oddly enough, that had ceased to be totally true when Hoover said it; in that same month, people of all ages were being killed by buzz bombs landing in London. Now, in the atomic age, civilian populations know that they are prime targets, the old as well as the young. But until a war escalates to nuclear weapons it is still the young who are in the front line and the maximum risk situation. Yet it is the young who take the least interest in voting, in picking the people who may one day decide whether we go to war or not. Our job, ladies and gentlemen, is to find some way to encourage young people to make their voices heard in the polling places. How do we turn them on?

Hickey's Perfidy

All eyes were on Thomas Hickey in Bowery Lane, New York City, on this day in 1776, but not for long. As a crowd watched, soldier Hickey, a member of General George Washington's immediate guard, was hanged for trying to poison the General's food and deliver the commander of the Continental Army to the British. Treason is almost as old in the United States as patriotism, and terrorism is hardly a modern invention. It must be said, however, that the military justice of 1776 was a lot speedier than the wheels of justice today. Many people are concerned about making those wheels move faster, and I am among them.

Decline and Fall

One of the most monumental and influential historical studies is Edward Gibbon's classic work *The Decline and Fall of the Roman Empire.* Gibbon completed his book on this day in 1787. It has become a sort of yardstick against which other empires measure themselves, wondering where in the endless rise-and-fall cycle they are at the moment. We have our share of those who see alarming parallels between ancient Rome and contemporary America—decline of public morality, growing strength of other nations, and so forth. I am not one of those pessimists. I do not deny that there are areas of American life where standards could be higher and things could be better, but I believe that we still have heights to reach before we have to worry about decline. The historian, after all, does not compare one day to the next—the historian compares eras, and when you compare our present to our past that comparison is most encouraging. Come, make the comparison along with me.

Helen Keller

Today is the birthday of Helen Keller, who was born as a normal baby in 1880 but became blind, deaf, and mute after an illness when she was less than two. We know the facts of Miss Keller's life—how she learned to communicate and ultimately became a highly successful writer and lecturer. Anyone who dares to be a public speaker able to see and hear the reaction of the audience has to be humble at the dimensions of that opportunity, compared to Helen Keller's challenge. It is therefore doubly gratifying, on her birthday, to rise to see, hear, and speak to you.

JUNE 28

Kennedy's Dream

Today I would like to talk about some things that lie in the future—topics that are in the realm of what John F. Kennedy had in mind in a speech he made in Dublin, Ireland, on this day in 1963. "We need men," President Kennedy said, "who can dream of things that never were." Well, ladies and gentlemen, you and I have that kind of dream. Most everybody does, and today I'd like to share mine with you.

Red Break

Until this day in 1948, communism was an awesome monolith to the West. Every nation under Red leadership was part of the international communist front. But on this day in 1948, the international Communist Party denounced Yugoslavia's leader, Marshal Tito, for not toeing the Soviet line; within the next year, Yugoslavia asserted complete independence of the Cominform. For the first time, but certainly not the last, a communist nation rejected Moscow's leadership. Later it happened even more spectacularly with Red China, and we came to see that communism, despite its international network, was not one solid bloc of Moscow-directed puppets. This is not because the communists chose to make it work that way; it is because national interests cannot always be secondary to Moscow's international purposes. This is something Moscow has never quite accepted, and neither have we, but I suggest that we remember it in our dealing with various nations around the world.

Archduke Ferdinand

It is difficult today to imagine how World War I, the greatest war ever fought up to that date, was triggered in 1914 on this day by a Serbian fanatic's assassination of the heir to the Austrian throne. There had been no invasion of one nation's territory by another; just this lone assassination. I would like to think that the world has grown up a good deal since this day in 1914; certainly we have seen other horrible assassinations since then, including heads of state in volatile areas like the Middle East, without causing wars. We have had our share of conflicts, and some of them have had little logical cause, but assassination no longer is quite the trigger it was in 1914. To me that is a hopeful sign. Perhaps we are beginning to learn that war is self-defeating. Perhaps even the endless talk of the United Nations is having a peaceful effect. I do not rise today to speak for peace at any price, but I speak for those policies that I believe make peace less fragile.

Government and Housing

It was on this day in 1934 that the National Housing Act was passed. The Act established the Federal Housing Administration and put the government into the field of financing housing and building construction. This had not been an area of particular federal jurisdiction before then, but it was one avenue through which Uncle Sam became the subsidizer of social services. In America revolutions are not always produced by bayonets and bloodletting; sometimes they come with the adoption of a new concept of government activity. No administration is immune to this expansion of function. Is it going on today? Let me count the ways.

JUNE 29

Goethals

Today is the birthday of a miracle worker named George Washington Goethals, born on this day in 1858 in Brooklyn. Goethal was the Army officer, an engineer, who was named by President Theodore Roosevelt to build the Panama Canal. He not only got the canal built as planned but he completed the job six months ahead of schedule. In tribute to General Goethals's recognition of the value of time, I shall get right down to business without any further shilly-shallying.

Townshend Acts

This day in 1767 was one of the occasions when King George III might have stemmed the tide that was moving America toward independence, but the monarch instead signed the Townshend Acts, imposing import duties on a variety of staples used in the colonies. Some time later, in the face of the opposition the Townshend Acts had aroused, they were revised so that the only item still taxed was tea, and that of course led to the Boston Tea Party. All in all, this was not the best day for the fate of the British Empire in North America. What was the issue then is still an irritating issue: people do not like taxes they don't see coming back to them. In return for paying money to the government, they want services from the government; not invisible services like national defense or lower budget deficits, although those are important, but services that can be seen or utilized by the taxpayer—more police protection, better roads, lower prices. Social Security taxes, for example, have encountered less opposition than other taxes because those who pay them know they will get them back—or at least hope so. Given that basis for successful taxation, we might consider the government's finances in better perspective as we look at where we are today.

Al Smith

On this day in 1928, the Democratic Party closed the nominating convention at which it named as its presidential candidate the man Franklin D. Roosevelt called "the happy warrior," Alfred E. Smith. Al Smith spoke with the unmistakable accent of his native New York City, he opposed prohibition, and he was a Catholic, three strikes against him for the presidency back in good old, prosperous 1928. Times have changed, but I am delighted to note that the American electorate has changed even more. The religion of a candidate is no longer the obstacle it was in 1928, blacks are beginning to come into the political mainstream, Prohibition is not an issue, and New Yorkers haven't done too badly in the political arena either. If anybody tells you we aren't making progress, keep those facts in mind. I believe we are continuing to make a better country, and I'd like to cite some persuasive evidence.

Dr. Mayo

Today is the birthday of William J. Mayo, the older of the two famous Mayo brothers who developed the Mayo Clinic in Rochester, Minnesota. Dr. William Mayo was born on this day in 1861. He and his brother Charles were pioneers in creating a cooperative form of group practice that made their clinic one of the great medical centers of the world. For this to happen in a small town in the upper Midwest it had to be a brilliant idea brilliantly executed, and it was. The Mayo Clinic proved once again that where you do something is less important than what you do. And all over the country new ideas are coming to the surface that make these times exciting. I see the signs around us.

JUNE 30

Pure Food and Drug Act

This is the date of the Pure Food and Drug Act of 1906, probably the single most important consumer protection measure in our history. It put into law not only the idea of purity in food but also the requirement of accurate labeling. In keeping with that spirit I provide a label for my remarks here today. The ingredients are gratitude for your hospitality, whatever wisdom I can bring to bear in dealing with the subject at hand, and a grain or two of salt. And of course I hope that what I have to say will prove to be food for thought and not a drug on the market.

Niagara Tightrope

On this day in 1859, a French performer named Emile Blondin walked across Niagara Falls on a tightrope. Many speakers have walked a tightrope before and since, but today, rather than taking that cautious path, I propose to stand up and be counted.

The League and Selassie

Not too many people any more remember Haile Selassie. He was the Emperor of Ethiopia when Mussolini's Italy invaded and conquered that country in 1936. Haile Selassie went before the League of Nations in Geneva on this day to ask the international community to throw the invaders out. There had been some half-hearted sanctions, but a number of other nations supported Mussolini, and the League was exposed as the empty vessel it was. Haile Selassie said something perhaps more prophetic than he knew at the time. "It is us today," he told the assembled nations. "It will be you tomorrow." And three years later the world was plunged into a second world war. I am not here to echo Haile Selassie today. I stand in hope that the world has learned from its recent history. And my message today deals not with the dangers but rather with the opportunities that confront us.

Gone with the Wind

On this day in 1936, a large book entitled *Gone with the Wind* was published. When its author, Margaret Mitchell, died some years later, the book had sold an estimated eight million copies, and of course the motion picture is also a best-selling classic. It was a story of America's past. We seem to have an eternal love affair with our past. This may be because things always look more interesting from a distance. But I suspect it is because we constantly want to know more about ourselves; we follow the public opinion polls, and we tune in on the television pundits who tell us so fascinatingly what we are thinking. I will not venture into that territory today, looking neither into the past nor into your minds. Instead I will talk about some of the things that should be on our minds.

JULY 1

The Dollar That Didn't

On this day in 1979, the United States Treasury made a big mistake. They issued the Susan B. Anthony dollar coin; they issued it but nobody would use it. It looked and felt so much like a quarter that most people were afraid they would make a mistake, so they just refused to accept Susan B. Anthony dollars.

Thank goodness we still live in a country where the people can assert themselves that way; not even the government can cram an idea down your throat if you don't want to swallow. You make up your own mind. It is in recognition of that fact that I stand here before you today, hoping to persuade you to my point of view but realizing that if you don't like my ideas you will send them the way of the Susan B. Anthony dollar. Perhaps, to be safe, I should just add that I'd like to put in my two cents' worth.

Battle of San Juan Hill

It was on this day in 1898 that the Rough Riders made their famous charge at the Battle of San Juan Hill in Cuba. One of the Rough Rider officers was a young man named Theodore Roosevelt who went on to become Vice-President and then President of the United States. The reputation for bravery he acquired at San Juan Hill stood him in good stead later on. The one thing Americans value most highly is courage, particularly physical courage in battle. Moral courage, which Teddy Roosevelt had plenty of, is sometimes less popular if it happens to conflict with majority opinion, but it is important to give the same kind of applause to examples of moral courage as we do for physical bravery. In that spirit I should like to use this occasion to take note of some recent instances of moral courage that merit your attention.

Juvenile Court

On this day in 1899, a new kind of court opened in Chicago. It was a juvenile court whose jurisdiction was limited to nonadults. Since then the number of such courts has increased fantastically and, unfortunately, so has the need for them. Juveniles present some very special problems in law enforcement, and I'd like to discuss them with you here today.

Postal Service

It was in 1971 on this day that the United States Post Office ceased to exist, replaced by a quasipublic organization called the United States Postal

Service. The Postal Service was supposed to be run along more businesslike lines, to take the burden of subsidies off the backs of the taxpayers. What it did, by shifting its rates and services, was to try to put more of the cost burden on the backs of the users, but there is still a great deal of uncertainty about whether every class of user—like the junk mailers—is paying a fair share. This problem of fair shares versus comparatively free rides is not unique to the Postal Service. It is, unfortunately, a fact of life in many areas. When we remedy one inequality we stumble into another. This doesn't mean we should stop trying. It means that some inequities are in the eye of the beholder. The best we can do is try to be as fair as possible to all concerned. It is in that spirit that I use this occasion to make some observations about some of the clashes of interest that should concern us.

JULY 2

Nostradamus

This is the day when, in 1566, the French seer Nostradamus died. Nostradamus had compiled a book of verses that seemed to contain predictions of things to come, and many of these predictions appear to have come true. Like most oracles, Nostradamus phrased his predictions in such a way that they are subject to various interpretations, and as a result there is considerable argument about his batting average. It is difficult enough for us, in our own time, to agree on what is happening; how much more difficult to match those events to the words of a prophet who has been dead for almost half a millennium! Words have different meanings not only for different generations but also for different people of the same generation. For example, take the word *justice.* That's what I propose to talk about today.

One Vietnam

On this day in 1976, after a generation of bloody war, defeated South Vietnam was joined with the victorious communist republic of North Vietnam as a single nation once again. The anniversary reminds us of an unhappy chapter in American history, the Vietnam War, and of the fact that there are so many other potential Vietnams all over the world. It sometimes seems that every day we are called upon to decide whether to get into another such conflict—in recent years including such varied areas as Latin America, the Middle East, Africa, and the Caribbean. Perhaps it is too much to hope for a definitive foreign policy that will be understood clearly by both our enemies and our friends; nevertheless, it is that hope that I'd like to talk about here today.

Independence

It was on July 2, not July 4, that the Continental Congress in 1776 passed the resolution stating that the colonies were and of right ought to be free and independent states. Two days later, on the basis of that decision, the Congress adopted the Declaration of Independence. But the eloquent and ringing phrases of the Declaration were accepted only after the basic issue had already been decided. We seem to be operating on an opposite basis these days. We pay eloquent lip service to all kinds of lofty principles but somehow don't get around to the action that is needed. Let me cite some current examples.

Morrill Act

Today is the anniversary of President Abraham Lincoln's signing of the Morrill Act in 1862, the law under which the federal government gave land to the states for the establishment of colleges, the so-called land-grant colleges. No single piece of legislation has been responsible for the founding of as many institutions of higher education as the brainstorm of a Vermont congressman named Justin Morrill. And as the costs of private higher education go higher and higher, the state universities that owe their beginnings to the Morrill Act become more and more of a vital U.S. asset. When Morrill first introduced his proposal it went nowhere. It took five years for the stubborn Vermonter to find a president who was friendly to his idea. Right now we have a few worthwhile proposals that are in a similar predicament.

JULY 3

Miss Universe

This is the season of the annual Miss Universe pageant, when beautiful contestants representing nations all over the world compete for the special honor of being judged the fairest of the fair. Miss Universe in general does best not by talking but just by standing there as a sight to be enjoyed. Those of us who, like me, have no pretension of looking like a Miss Universe must do otherwise. Since I can't just stand here I will talk.

National Hot Dog Month

One of the special observances that has decorated the July calendar is National Hot Dog Month. A hot dog has something in common with a speaker. Both have to have a roll (role). My role here today, above all, is not to waste your time, so let me get right down to business.

Entebbe

On this day and the next in 1976, one of the classic rescues of history was achieved. It happened at Entebbe Airport in Uganda, Africa, to which terrorist hijackers had brought 100 hostages aboard an Air France plane. Crack Israeli troops rescued all but one of the hostages in an amazing operation that furnished a model for military people for years thereafter. Entebbe was important not only for the tactics it employed but also because it was such a spectacular defeat for terrorism in general. The best way to stop terrorism is to convince its practitioners that it doesn't work. It isn't always easy, and it isn't always successful, but we know that appeasing terrorists isn't always easy or successful either. The ethics of terrorism are not only confined to apostles of violence. They are used by people as a negotiating tool—threats of strikes or lockouts, efforts to obstruct the operations of factories of whose products we disapprove, and so forth. As a matter of fact, speakers very often use tactics like these, threatening the audience with dire consequences unless their brilliant advice is followed. I have no such intention nor any such conviction of my own infallibility. I do have some opinions I'd like to share with you.

Battle of Santiago

The most spectacular naval victory ever won by the United States was probably the battle that occurred on this day in 1898 outside the harbor of Santiago, Cuba. The Spanish fleet, bottled up inside the harbor by an American naval blockade, decided to try to break out, and on this day in a battle that lasted some four hours the Spanish were destroyed, while the total U.S. casualties were one man killed and one man wounded. That made the U.S. victory in the Spanish–American War a reality and destroyed Spain as a world power. In those years power in the world was firepower, but today we face wars that are fought without guns—business wars, trade wars, import–export wars. We can't send the Navy or the other armed forces to fight those kinds of wars; what do we do in that kind of economic competition?

JULY 4

Independence Day

It is said that actions speak louder than words, but I don't know of any action more emphatic than the words that were adopted on this day in 1776, the words known as the Declaration of Independence. Nobody who is called upon to speak on this day can hope to compete with the eloquence, the nobility of purpose, the bravery, or the clarity of that great Declaration. But it is the heritage of every American to be able to speak in freedom every day of the year because of those words of July 4, 1776. Now, as then, we Americans hold certain truths to be self-evident. Now, as then, we rise to speak our minds.

The Advice Twins

One of the interesting sidelights of the later twentieth century was that a pair of sisters, twins from the Midwest, became, separately, the great advice-givers of their time. Today is the birthday of Ann Landers and Abigail Van Buren—those are their pen names, of course. Advice to the lovelorn had been a standard newspaper feature long before these two ladies came upon the scene, but they each added a rather hard boiled touch of humor and ordinary, face-the-facts common sense that attracted millions of new readers. The most important aspect of their success, I believe, was that they didn't ask questions; they answered other people's questions. That is a lot harder and a lot more interesting. So, taking a tip from their example, I shall use this opportunity to answer some of the questions that seem to be endemic today.

George the Wrong

On this day in 1776, George III, the reigning king of England, commented on the events of the day—or rather, was blandly oblivious of them. He said, on the very day the Declaration of Independence was to be adopted by his rebellious subjects in America—and I quote—"Nothing of importance happened today." Now, nothing I say from this rostrum today can possibly be as inaccurate as George III's goof back in 1776, so I am encouraged to speak freely—and here I go.

Nathaniel Hawthorne

On this day in 1804, Nathaniel Hawthorne, the great American writer, was born in Salem, Massachusetts. In one of his great works, *The House of the Seven Gables,* Hawthorne wrote, quote, "The world owes all its onward impulses to men ill at ease. The happy man inevitably confines himself within ancient limits." Close quote. Now, I don't know whether happy people are more likely to be stick-in-the-muds, but I do know that people ill at ease in their everyday world have been responsible for moments of great leadership. Franklin D. Roosevelt achieved his greatness after polio struck him down, Abraham Lincoln after a less than happy marriage. Churchill never totally conquered a stammer yet became a magnificent orator—and so it goes. I am somewhat perturbed because, thanks to your gracious invitation, I do not feel ill at ease here today, which, according to Hawthorne's dictum, means that I should also be lacking onward impulses. But as I worry over what I should say to you, my assurance wavers and the onward impulses rise. Taking a deep breath, I proceed.

JULY 5

Pointed Prayer

On this day in 1779, with the American Revolutionary War raging, the British raided New Haven, Connecticut, and captured the president of Yale University. They forced him to pray for King George III, so he said, quote: "Oh Lord, bless thy servant King George, and grant him wisdom, for thou knowest, Lord, he needs it." Close quote. Now, every speaker has a certain lingering feeling that his audience needs his or her wisdom, but many of us have found it is more productive to ask the right questions than to try to come up with all the answers. So my remarks here today are not designed so much to wrap up the issues as to raise them.

Farragut

David Glasgow Farragut, the first admiral of the U.S. Navy, was born on this day in 1801. He was the naval hero of the Civil War, the man who said, "Damn the torpedoes!" at the Battle of Mobile Bay, one of the great figures in the history of the U.S. Navy. And he probably wouldn't have been any of those if it hadn't been for an ancient human institution—nepotism. He was adopted by Navy Captain David Porter and appointed a midshipman. He then served under his stepfather till the end of the War of 1812 and continued in the Navy thereafter. He was a captain when the Civil War began. The Navy was looking for someone to command the squadron blockading the Confederacy's Gulf Coast, and Farragut's step-brother, Commodore David Dixon Porter, recommended him. I recount all this not to demean Admiral Farragut, who was in a class alone, but rather to point out that even the best of us can sometimes use our family's helping hand. We tend to deride pride of family, but it is families sticking together that have built much of America. Today I believe we should concern ourselves not with finding substitutes for the family but with finding ways to keep families together. Let me be specific.

National Health

Free health care for everyone in England became a fact on this day in 1948 when the national health service went into operation. There were predictions of disaster by those who regarded the service as socialized medicine—forecasts that British medical science would collapse and the nation would be bankrupted. Britain has had its share of troubles since then, but the national health service has not been one of them most of the time. The great secret of democracy, it seems to me, is that what the people want is what they get, and the great problem of democracy is that sometimes the people unfortunately do not know what they want or they split right down the middle about it. We don't even agree on what we want our representatives in Congress to be—people with freedom of conscience or mirrors of majority sentiment in their district on every issue. A speaker such as I in a gathering such as this has no such conflict. You have given me the opportunity to speak my mind, and I accept.

Cecil Rhodes

Not too many people crown their success by having a country named after them. That's what happened to Cecil Rhodes, who was born on this day in 1853 in England and became the greatest colonizer in the history of Africa. Rhodesia, named after him, has long since adopted the more African name of Zimbabwe, and it is the Rhodes scholarships for English-speaking university students that are the bright ornament of his memory. The Rhodes scholarships, rather than the Rhodes colonialism that originally financed them, are his monument today. And mindful of that, I suggest to you that your own good works have an impact far beyond your immediate satisfaction. It is that impact I want to discuss today.

JULY 6

1775 Declaration

The Declaration of Independence is such an unforgettable document that it has totally overshadowed another document, written in part by the same Thomas Jefferson, adopted by the Continental Congress a year earlier, on this day in 1775. Perhaps a quotation will refresh our memories: "We most solemnly, before God and the world, declare, that, exerting the utmost energy of those powers, which our beneficent Creator hath graciously bestowed upon us, the arms we have been compelled by our enemies to assume, we will, in defiance of every hazard, with unabating firmness and perseverance, employ for the preservation of our liberties; being with one mind resolved to die freemen rather than to live slaves." Close quote. That was the Continental Congress's Declaration of the Causes of Taking Up Arms. Our commitment to freedom did not start out of nowhere in 1776. It was born of the determination of Americans to risk their lives to protect their rights. Today we don't usually have to risk our lives. All we have to do is vote and take an active role in community affairs— and not enough of us do those things. If my remarks here today can enlist even one more individual in active citizenship I will consider it a success.

Exit Congress

Late in June Congress voted to declare war against Great Britain in 1812, and having exhibited that spirit of belligerence against a great power decided to cut and run. On this day in 1812, only three weeks after the declaration of war, the very same Congress adjourned. If you occasionally get fed up with the performance of our modern representatives, just remember the Congress of 1812. And if in the course of my remarks here today I can persuade you that we will continue to triumph over our own mistakes, I will be content.

Amiable Heresy

On this day in 1840, Henry David Thoreau wrote in his journal, "All this worldly wisdom was once the unamiable heresy of some wise man." Now, I do not hanker to call myself a wise man, and I don't know whether you will find heresy in what I am about to say, but I hope that whatever you find you will find it amiable. It is possible for us to have differing opinions without becoming enemies, and in that spirit I proceed with the most amiable of intentions.

Emperor Maximilian

The ill-starred Austrian princeling who thought he would be the Emperor of Mexico, Maximilian, was born on this day in 1832. Thanks to his misadventure under French sponsorship in Mexico, he never reached the age of thirty-five. The mistakes of young men are usually quickly corrected, though not always in this bloody fashion. But the men who throughout history have put the world in flames have for the most part been older. Hitler was 50 when he started World War II; the Kaiser was no youngster in 1914; the warlords of twentieth-century Japan were supposedly wise old men. Herbert Hoover, in the midst of World War II, said, "Older men declare war. But it is youth that must fight and die." Isn't it strange that in every generation the older heads think the young ones are reckless, but the old ones get us into trouble? Out of that trouble on occasion has come a better time, and it is in that hope that I look today at our present situation.

JULY 7

Satchel Paige

The records are more than a bit foggy, but according to some accounts the legendary baseball pitcher Leroy "Satchel" Paige was born on this day in 1906 in Alabama. Satchel Paige was a great black baseball pitcher in the years when blacks were barred from the major leagues. He came to the majors in the twilight of his career, when the color ban was lifted, and even then he was an amazing player. He is remembered these days in the Baseball Hall of Fame, but he is also remembered for some immortal lines, of which perhaps the best is this: "Don't look back; someone might be gaining on you." Unfortunately we all have a tendency to keep looking back, to talk about the good old days, and to have a sneaking desire to turn the clock back. But we tend to remember the good in the good old days and forget the bad. What we are remembering is our own youth rather than another time for the country. Somebody once suggested that we remember that now is the good old days of tomorrow. You may ask, what's good about them? Let me try to answer that.

Annexation Anniversaries

This is a day when Americans would do well to remember their own history. On this day in 1846, we annexed California and took the surrender of the Mexican garrison at Monterey; on this same day in 1898, we annexed the Hawaiian Islands, which had been independent. Now, I haven't heard any great outcry for independence in either of those states lately, but facts are facts: we took over both territories from previous rulers. That is the name of the game in world history, and although we perhaps naively adhere today to a doctrine of self-determination for all peoples, we can be comfortable with that doctrine because all of our territorial expansion is over and because we have oceans or friendly neighbors on our borders. The rest of the world is not that lucky. They are not even as lucky as we in terms of their populations. Over the centuries some of their borders have been, to say the least, muddied with substantial portions of different ethnic groups living either in the same territory or very close. Russia isn't the only federation of people of different languages and ethnic backgrounds in Europe. So is Yugoslavia; so to a certain extent is the United Kingdom or Spain, for example. One of our problems is that we take pragmatic and dogmatic positions on international affairs without necessarily knowing the nature of the territory. So what I'd like to do here today is to talk about some perhaps less well-known aspects of the world around us.

Madame Justice

History was made by President Ronald Reagan on this day in 1981 when he nominated the first woman for the post of Justice of the Supreme Court, Sandra Day O'Connor. It met with almost universal approval, which is often the case when a long overdue step is finally taken. What seems to happen is that the public moves faster than the politicians in keeping up with the times. Perhaps that is because so many politicians believe it is their job to be responsive to public opinion rather than leaders of it. For years it was said that whites would never vote for a black; Mayor Tom Bradley proved that was wrong in Los Angeles and proved it resoundingly, but until then it had been the conventional wisdom. Today I want to challenge some of the other conventional wisdom of our time.

Sundae

The city of Evanston, Illinois, staged a big celebration some years ago on this day to commemorate the invention of the ice cream sundae there in 1875. It seems that the city had passed an ordinance banning the sale of sodas on

Sundays, so an enterprising local soda fountain owner began serving ice cream with syrup instead of soda water. In deference to the special significance of Sunday, he changed the spelling of his concoction to *s-u-n-d-a-e,* and it has been that way ever since. Necessity is the mother of invention. People have been getting around laws since the first one was passed. The important thing is not to pass a law but to get popular support. I am here not merely to whip up a concoction but to tempt you to eat it up.

JULY 8

John D. Rockefeller

On this day in 1839, John D. Rockefeller was born in a town in New York appropriately named Richford. From a humble beginning he built the world's largest corporation and the world's largest personal fortune. In his later years, after the trust-busters broke up his company and he had earned a good bit of unpopularity, he turned to philanthropy, giving away an estimated half-billion dollars to worthy causes in his lifetime. But what he became famous for and regained popularity with was presenting dimes to youngsters. Somehow this made him seem more human and grandfatherly than all of the other millions. If there is a lesson here it is that personal gestures convey a sense of good will that impersonal financial transactions don't. What that translates into, I believe, is that the finest gift you can make is a gift of yourself. Whatever cause you believe in, don't be a bystander; be a participant; give of yourself. And today I want to draw your attention to one cause in particular.

The Wall Street Journal

On this day in 1889, a team of young partners, Charles H. Dow and Edward Jones, issued the first edition of a new and specialized newspaper which they called *The Wall Street Journal.* Today, that same newspaper has become the premier national daily in the United States, still concentrating on business news, and Dow and Jones are immortalized in the stock index that bears their names. When a good thing comes along it is apt to do very well in this country. There are some people who downgrade the opportunities for the entrepreneur today, compared to the days when *The Wall Street Journal* was founded, but it is in this modern era that the *Journal* has had its greatest growth and prestige. If there are more problems in the business climate today, there are also more opportunities. I have taken a look at the state of the United States today, and over the long haul I see only good signs, which I'd like to tell you about.

Perry's Visit

This is the anniversary of Commodore Matthew Perry's arrival in Yedo Bay, Japan, in 1853. The Commodore brought a message from the government of the United States to the Emperor of Japan and said he would return in the spring for the answer. The message was a request to establish diplomatic and trade relations between the two countries. American businesspeople saw the opportunity to create a whole new avenue of commerce, little dreaming that the balance of that trade would ultimately swing in Japan's favor. It shifted because Japan turned out to be so adept at practicing what we used to think were such peculiarly American traits of industry and adaptability. We know now that when we start by exporting American goods we also inevitably export American techniques and American marketing know-how, and as a result we can look forward to constantly increasing competition in the marketplace. In the face of that prospect, what should our strategy now be?

La Fontaine

Today is the birthday of the great French writer Jean de La Fontaine, who was born in 1621. It was La Fontaine who wrote, among his many proverbs, that "people who make no noise are dangerous." On that basis I can assure you I am not dangerous, because my purpose here is to make some noise about some items of concern, and I hope that my remarks will move you to do the same.

JULY 9

Articles of Confederation

On this day in 1778, the government of the United States was established; it didn't work. The government to which I refer was a loose alliance of independent states under the Articles of Confederation, which the Continental Congress approved on this day by vote of the delegates of seven states; the other states approved later. The Articles of Confederation kept us going for a decade, but then the Constitutional Convention brought forth an infinitely stronger and more practical scheme of federal government, the Constitution. What I find most significant is that both documents, the Articles of Confederation and the Constitution, were the results of peaceful discussion and consensus. That is the American tradition. We here today are the inheritors of that tradition, and I hope my discussion of some current issues will be a contribution to the spirited and enlightened dialogue that makes us what we are.

Generation Gap

When the Equal Rights Amendment was nearing what seemed at the time to be its final push toward victory, Gloria Steinem, the editor and feminist leader, addressed an ERA rally in Washington, D.C., on this date in 1978. In the course of her address, she remarked, quote, "We are the women our parents warned us about. . . ." Close quote. That is an interesting thought. To a certain extent every generation moves a bit farther than its parents. We pass new laws, we explore new places, we take chances of a different kind than they did. The whole thrust of human growth, it seems, is for children, whether they emulate or defy their parents, to try to outdo them. In this country that effort is almost always a benign one, because we accept it. We encourage our children to think for themselves—not all of us, but a significant percentage. But there are always among us those who don't want this kind of thing, who would censor and restrict and prohibit. Where and how do we draw the line between normal parental concern and unhealthy repression?

Elias Howe

Elias Howe, who was born on this day in 1819 in Massachusetts, was the man who invented the sewing machine. At first he couldn't sell the darned thing. Not until some other inventors infringed on his patents and made some improvements did the machines start to sell. Howe sued, won his case, and was able to start a sewing machine factory in Bridgeport, Connecticut. From that came the great mass-production clothing industries of today. The inventiveness that brought such great growth and prestige to the United States has continued into our own time—it was this country that ushered in the computer age and created the industrial robot, for example. But other nations have used all the tactics at their disposal—cheaper labor, import restrictions, sometimes virtual plagiarism or piracy—to exploit the products of American creativity and ingenuity. As a result there are some kinds of machines and other products, which used to be manufactured here, that are now made only overseas. This industry migration is a problem not simply for the industries involved but for all of us. Let's take a closer look.

Solzhenitsyn's Russia

Aleksandr Solzhenitsyn, the exiled Russian writer, was the guest of honor at an AFL–CIO dinner in New York on this day in 1975. He spoke about the aggressive plans of his native land and made a suggestion. "Stop sending goods," he said. "Let them stand on their own feet and see what happens." That, of course, assumes that if the United States totally stopped sending goods to Russia the rest of the free world would do likewise, and we have seen time and time again that our allies and our friends—if we have any—just go right on doing business with the communists, indeed step up their trade to fill any gaps we leave. So the subject of my remarks today is not the future of our relations with Soviet Russia but rather what sort of friends we have in today's world.

JULY 10

Finley Peter Dunne

It's been a long time since Finley Peter Dunne, who was born on this day in 1867, created the character of saloonkeeper Martin Dooley. Mr. Dooley, as he was known, was the character who appeared in Dunne's newspaper column and later in magazines and books, spouting his own Irish wisdom about the American scene. It was Mr. Dooley who commented that the Supreme Court follows the election returns, noted that the Democratic Party wasn't on speaking terms with itself, and said—quote—"Not bein' an author, I'm a great critic." Close quote. Not being the author of national policy, I feel free to criticize it, and, with apologies to Mr. Dooley, here I go.

Stevenson on the Presidency

When Adlai Stevenson was the guest on the television broadcast of "Face the Nation" on this day in 1960, the twice-defeated Democratic presidential candidate remarked that "The presidency is an office that 'converts vanity to prayer.' " I assume he was referring to prayer on the part of the incumbent, but let's face it, when we vote for somebody we are casting not merely a vote but also a prayer. Anybody who is chosen for elective office starts with the prayers of his or her constituency. The trouble is that within that constituency not all the people are praying for the same things. The people who judge an office-holder by a single issue are being unfair, whether their judgment is favorable or unfavorable. I stand here today asking that, no matter how committed you may be to a particular point of view on any single issue, you judge and vote on the basis of a broader picture. And the broader picture, as I see it, is this.

John Calvin

The rigid religious doctrine of the Puritans who first came to settle New England traced to the teachings of a man who was born on this day in 1509. His name was John Calvin; he was the Swiss man of God whose stern interpretation of Christianity and whose concept of a sort of civil theocracy were embraced by the English Puritans. It was a demanding and pervasive sort of religion, probably just what the Puritans needed as they confronted the rigors of an unknown New World; but in the course of time—and not too long, either—it was softened by the democratic tolerance that became the hallmark of America. We will always have those of every faith whose outlook is unyielding and Calvinistic; in some ways, they are a necessary voice of conscience or, at the least, a reminder of a heritage. The question of how literally we interpret and follow the teachings of the Bible will never be settled to the satisfaction of all concerned, and I would be rash indeed to get into a discussion of that here today. But, as were the Puritans, I am concerned with the public morality, and on that subject I have a few observations.

Telstar I

On this night in 1962, the United States launched *Telstar I* into orbit in space, making possible live television transmissions across the Atlantic. This was really the beginning of instantaneous communication around the world, which may or may not have been a blessing. It has enabled us to see world events as they happen, but that is not always an advantage since it sometimes leads us to make snap first judgments that later prove to have been not quite as wise as we thought they were. Sometimes it is better to have time to consider alternatives before you are confronted with an actual event. Sometimes it is better not to gratify the desire of the media for an instant and immediate reaction, and sometimes a second judgment is a lot better than the first. The opportunity you have given me to speak here today is an opportunity for some second judgments on my part, and I thank you.

JULY 11

John Quincy Adams

Sons of Presidents rarely achieve the heights of their fathers, but a man who was born on this day in 1767 came close. He was John Quincy Adams, who served as James Monroe's Secretary of State and was the actual author of the Monroe Doctrine, later becoming, like his father, the nation's president. After the elder Adams finished his term as president he retired from public life; but his son, when he left the presidency, became a congressman from Massachusetts for 18 years. The rewards for ex-presidents in those years were scarce—no memorial libraries, no large pensions or personal staffs. We do better by our retired chief executives these days, but I wonder sometimes whether the nation would not be better off if we found a way to seat them in Congress like John Quincy Adams, who during his congressional years was a great influence for conscience in the Capitol. Some of our ex-presidents have been embittered or repudiated, but they are all wiser after serving than they were before. What place should there be for them when they leave the White House?

John Wanamaker

John Wanamaker was born on this day in 1838 in Philadelphia. He was one of the men who developed the modern department store, starting with a clothing business and then expanding into many other kinds of merchandising. It was Wanamaker who is supposed to have said—though perhaps he was quoting at the time—"Half the money I spend on advertising is wasted, and the trouble is I don't know which half." The same is true of government expenditures: half is wasted, but we don't always know which half. So we keep on spending, with the consolation that half at least is doing some real good. But is that good enough? Is the government getting the best value it can for its dollars?

Thomas Bowdler

This is the birthday of Thomas Bowdler, born in England in 1754, whose name became part of a very distinctive word in the English language. Bowdler prepared editions of Shakespeare and other classics in which he removed all the words or phrases he deemed unsuitable for family reading aloud. In short order what he had done was described as *bowdlerizing*, another word for expurgating. A lot of people applauded Bowdler's work during his lifetime, and a lot of people applaud his idea today. The unfortunate aspect of modern language is that in our zeal to do away with censorship we have tolerated a certain debasement of the language, not only in the common acceptance of what used to be gutter phrases but in the sloppy incoherencies of people who just don't know how to express themselves in correct English. It is, of course, a mistake to be more concerned with your vocabulary than with the substance of your remarks, but people who can't express themselves don't convey much substance to begin with. It seems to me that while our debased oral communication is not our fundamental problem, it is a symptom of an educational failure, and that's what I'd like to discuss.

George W. Norris

In every generation there are some American politicians who reach the heights, and there are others whose greatness is sadly forgotten. One of that latter group was George W. Norris, who was born in Ohio on this day in 1861. When Norris was a young congressman from Nebraska he led the fight to reduce the tremendous power of the Speaker of the House by updating the rules of the House. He won that fight. In the Senate, where he served for 30 years, he was the principal champion of the vast public power project that became known as the TVA. He sponsored legislation to seek more fairness in labor negotiations. Though nominally a Republican, he supported Teddy Roosevelt's Progressive Party presidental candidacy and Franklin Roosevelt's New Deal candidacy two decades later. There are not too many successful mavericks like George W. Norris; party-line politics make things difficult for the candidate who dares to be different. But I keep looking for political figures who are different—and I see a few of some promise on the horizon.

JULY 12

Captive Nations Week

During the month of July the United States for many years has observed Captive Nations Week, an occasion to remember those countries around the world who are being held captive by foreign or foreign-dominated governments. It is easy for us, with our country's climate of freedom and long tradition of independence, to forget these captive nations, but as long as they are not free the world will be troubled. We cannot undertake to be the liberators of the world, but we must see to it that our actions do not give encouragement to the captors. Are we giving such encouragement now?

George Eastman

George Eastman, who was born on this day in 1854 in Waterville, New York, was the man who made amateur photography practical. The Eastman Kodak Company is his monument. Thanks to Eastman millions upon millions of people have been able to prove for themselves that one picture is worth a thousand words. Nevertheless, I have not been asked to show you pictures but rather to say a few words. So here I go, and we'll see what develops.

Oscar Hammerstein II

Today is the birthday, in 1895, of Oscar Hammerstein II, whose lyrics adorn some of the most popular songs America has sung, including "Old Man River" and "Oklahoma." In honor of a song he wrote for South Pacific with composer Richard Rodgers, I propose today to offer some "Happy Talk."

Medal of Honor

This is the day when, in 1862, the Congressional Medal of Honor was authorized for heroism in battle. I would like to use the occasion of this anniversary to salute some other types of heroism in the relatively peaceful pursuits of civilian life. Permit me to share with you this small honor roll of peaceful heroes and heroines.

JULY 13

John F. Kennedy

Today is the anniversary of the nomination of John F. Kennedy for the presidency by the Democrats in 1960. In the primary campaign Kennedy had shown himself to be a persuasive and witty candidate, and he continued to exhibit those traits as he won over Republican Richard Nixon and brought Camelot to the White House. In his acceptance speech to the 1960 Democratic convention, then Senator Kennedy said of what he called the New Frontier that it was "not a set of promises—it is a set of challenges." What John F. Kennedy said in 1960 is true today. It is not yesterday's or even today's promises that should concern us so much as today's challenges. There are many such challenges, but I will focus on only a few here today.

Draft Riots

We like to think of resistance to the draft as something that developed as a result of objections to the Vietnam War, a sort of modern phenomenon. But today is the anniversary of the start of a bloody period of antidraft rioting that occurred way back in 1863 in New York City. About a thousand people were killed or wounded. So, if and when you are concerned about what seems to be a growing defiance of laws, take comfort from the fact that it was worse in 1863. And, knowing that we seem to survive these things, let's consider our present situation.

Nathan Bedford Forrest

This is the birthday, in 1821, of Confederate General Nathan Bedford Forrest, who gave the world that often-quoted advice, "Git thar fustest with the mostest." I cannot pretend that I am gitting thar fustest with the information I will be giving you today, and I am not going to speak long enough to give you the mostest, but I will try to throw a little more light on some places where that light is needed.

Stevenson's Death

This is the eve of the anniversary of the death in 1965 of Adlai Stevenson, whose two campaigns for the presidency didn't produce enough votes but gave us some great examples of the use of the English language. But the quote I want to mention to you here today came a bit later, after John F. Kennedy had been elected. Speaking at a press dinner in Washington, Stevenson said, "Man does not live by words alone, in spite of the fact that sometimes he has to eat them." Ladies and gentlemen, I hope I won't have to eat what I am about to say to you.

JULY 14

Sedition Act

In 1798 on this date, the Sedition Act provided criminal penalties for people found guilty of criticizing the U.S. government. Can you imagine what kind of country we would have today if that evil act had been permitted to continue? Fortunately it died a quick death, and freedom of speech was not a permanent casualty. So, on the anniversary of the Sedition Act of 1798, let's have some free and untrammeled speech about the government, the electorate, or anything else that strikes our fancy.

Gerald Ford

This is the birthday of Gerald Ford, who was born in 1913 and become the only president of the United States who wasn't elected by the people. President Ford was chosen by Congress to succeed Spiro Agnew as Vice-President when Agnew resigned after pleading no contest to charges of income tax violations. Then, when President Richard Nixon resigned in the aftermath of the Watergate scandal, Ford became president. In the White House, Gerald Ford was a calming influence; the nation could have been torn apart by the Watergate affair, but President Ford kept it on an even keel. Sometimes doing just that is the greatest service a leader can do. Preserving domestic tranquility is not usually an easy job, and it is even harder when positions of great trust have been abused. We have a tendency to deride those we call the caretakers, but they are important for our welfare and our history. Sometimes I think we suffer from the people who simply have to make waves. Sometimes we want to catch our breath. Sometimes we want to stop and take stock of ourselves and think about our hopes and aspirations. The problem that always arises is simply whether now is one of those times.

Comte de Gobineau

This is the birthday of a little-known man whose influence was tremendous and evil. His name was Gobineau—Joseph Arthur, Count of Gobineau—born near Paris in 1816. He was a diplomat and writer, among whose works was a book called *Essay on the Inequality of Human Races.* In it he stated that the white race was the superior one but is weakened when its racial composition is not pure. He saw the Nordics as the purest and the Jews as a threat to white racial purity. Sound familiar? Yes, it was the source of Adolf Hitler's theories of why the Aryans, as Hitler called them, should rule the world. Now, I am not saying that without Gobineau there would have been no Hitler, or that anti-Semitism began with this nineteenth-century Frenchman. What I am saying is that bad ideas, once wrapped in scholarship and given respectable sponsorship, can make bad events. Right now we have some bad ideas of that kind, and I'd like to confront them.

The Baltic Sellout

Today happens to be the unhappy anniversary of a disgraceful event that isn't remembered as it should be. Back in 1939, when Soviet Russia and Nazi Germany signed the nonaggression pact that was the preliminary to World War II, one result was the communist invasion of the three independent Baltic neighboring nations of Latvia, Lithuania, and Estonia. On this day in 1940, the Russian-ruled governments of those three nations began the so-called election that supposedly endorsed the end of their independence and their incorporation into the USSR. They are not the only captives of the Russian Bear, but on this anniversary they serve as a reminder that imperialism these days carries a Red banner. It is Red imperialism which confronts us in two hemispheres, and that is what I want to discuss here today.

JULY 15

New Frontier

On this day in 1960, the newly nominated Democratic candidate for the presidency, Senator John F. Kennedy of Massachusetts, proclaimed to the nation that we stood "on the edge of a new frontier—the frontier of the 1960s—a frontier of unknown opportunities and perils—a frontier of unfulfilled hopes and threats." It seems to me that we are in a similar position today. Science is bringing us new knowledge and opening new horizons—and posing new problems. We are, in a very real sense, experimenting with life itself. And in this time of new frontiers we still haven't solved the age-old problems of our society. So a speaker has a choice of topics. We can talk about the new problems or the old ones. Or, given sufficient temerity, we can talk about some possible solutions. I prefer the latter.

Mariner 4

This was the day back in 1965 when we saw our first photographs of the surface of another planet. Our *Mariner 4* spacecraft began sending pictures back to earth that were taken within 7,000 miles of the planet Mars. We have been learning more about the universe ever since. But the more we learn the more mysteries remain to be solved. Perhaps this is meant to show us that there are no absolutes, no perfect solutions. Certainly I do not propose to stand up here and proclaim that I have the perfect answer to anything. Indeed, I come here today not so much to offer answers as to ask some questions.

St. Swithin's Day

Today is St. Swithin's Day, when, as you may recall, the legend is that if it rains today it will rain for forty days. Many speakers seem to approach the rostrum with what I regard as a St. Swithin's Day attitude—they see trouble here today and predict its continuance not just for forty days but into the undefinable future. For myself, I will be content if on this saint's day I can provide just a few drops of reassuring tidings and leave the thunder and lightning to others.

Wiley Post

Wiley Post was one of America's greatest early pilots. On this day in 1933, he took off on what turned out to be the first solo flight around the world. It took him seven days, eighteen hours, and fifty minutes. In every generation there are men like Wiley Post who want to do something epic and heroic on their own, whether it is crossing the ocean in a tiny boat, flying around the world, climbing the tallest building, or almost anything else that usually calls for a team effort. If these achievements don't make any great contribution to the advancement of humanity, they certainly do something for an individual ego. But from society's point of view a little more collective effort and a few less would-be soloists seem infinitely more constructive. But even if I deplore solo efforts of various kinds, I have to admit as I stand before you here today that what you expect of me, no matter what subject I discuss is also a solo effort.

JULY 16

District of Columbia

In 1790, the Congress of the United States voted to establish the nation's capital in a new area to be called the District of Columbia, within which was to be the city that would bear the name of Washington. One of the purposes for establishing the District was to avoid having the nation's permanent capital within the jurisdiction of one of the states, for fear that the host state would have too much influence. So they went to the other extreme, and it took more than 150 years for the residents of the District of Columbia to win the right to vote in presidential elections. This is a good example of a very human and very American trait: we are so concerned about preventing or curing perceived injustices that we sometimes create new injustices in the process. Our tax laws are an excellent case in point.

Mary Baker Eddy

This is the birthday of Mary Baker Eddy, the remarkable woman who was the founder of the Christian Science church. Mary Baker Eddy was born in 1821 in Bow, New Hampshire. Widowed and divorced, she was fifty-four when she published the first version of her concept of *Science and Health* and fifty-eight when the Church of Christ, Scientist, was chartered. I mention her age because I believe it is important to know that her major accomplishments came when she was more than fifty years old. Creativity and leadership very often reach their peak in our later years. While the concept of forced retirement has been steadily retreating recently, we still face a world in which older people are often less employable than younger ones with less qualifications. We still face a world in which older people are not supposed to be active participants in the competition of life. And, cruelest blow of all, we live in a world in which, all things being equal, nobody wants to take care of Grandma or Grandpa. We live in a world of old folks' homes and retirement villages. It is time we did something about it.

White House Tapes

It was in 1973 on this day that a Senate committee held a public hearing at which it was revealed that President Richard Nixon had secretly taped his White House conversations. The effort to obtain those tapes, the nature of what was finally found to be on the tapes, and the mystery of an 18-1/2 minute gap in a key recording all contributed to the ultimate resignation of President Nixon and the shock of the nation. A long time later we learned that many other presidents had also recorded conversations, but none of those other presidents had been talking about Watergate. The attempt to cover up the original mistake was compounded by the later mistakes. But the same kind of compounding is going on, far less spectacularly, in normal Washington or your local capital all the time. Budgets, for example, are infinitely complicated and sabotaged when a special concession for one group has to be balanced by other adjustments elsewhere. Efforts to conceal liability on one case of cost overrun or waste usually result in rules that prevent exposure of other examples. We are forever papering over things that might better be exposed. Here are cases in point.

Execution of the Tsar

The last Tsar of Russia was executed by the Bolsheviks on this day in 1918. The tsar, though he had been the head of an autocratic, downright despotic government, had been deprived of his power by a democratic provisional regime, but the communists had overthrown that regime by force, and now they disposed of the tsar and his family the same way, including young children who were themselves innocent of any wrongdoing. This is what happens when advocates of violent revolution get guns in their hands; they kill indiscriminately. It isn't unique to Russia. It happens every time a group of zealots seeks to impose its will on a nation by force. The anniversary of the murder of the tsar's family is a good time for us to look at some of the other nations of the world and wonder where, today, other children are being executed. It isn't always by direct and sudden murder; it is being done by starvation and by political demonstrations, but it is happening, and we should be aware of it.

JULY 17

Disneyland

This is the birthday of the original Disneyland, which opened in California on this day in 1955 and revolutionized the amusement park business. It was an outstanding example of what creativity can bring to an old institution. We have plenty of old institutions today that can use the kind of imagination that brought us Disneyland, and I'd like to talk about some of the opportunities we have for modern improvements.

Elbridge Gerry

Back in the early 1800s a new creature was born in America. It was a mythical animal called a gerrymander. It wasn't really an animal at all. It was a state senatorial district in Massachusetts, whose borders went in and out so as to ensure a majority vote for the party of the state's governor. The governor, who had been born on this day in 1744, was a man named Elbridge Gerry, and the district, which seemed to some people to be shaped like a salamander, was called a gerrymander. That term found its way into the English language, and Elbridge Gerry found his way to Washington, D.C., as President James

Madison's vice-president. These days gerrymanders are not supposed to be in style, thanks to court decisions and civil rights laws, but the basic idea of stacking the cards is still very much with us. We aren't gerrymandering districts, but we are still gerrymandering laws, and I have a few examples for you.

"Recessional"

Rudyard Kipling's poem "Recessional" is one of the more familiar works of that great English writer. It was first published on this day in 1897, when Great Britain was at the height of its imperial glory. Kipling took note of that fact in some of the early lines: "God of our fathers, known of old,/Lord of our far-flung battle-line,/Beneath whose awful Hand we hold/Dominion over palm and pine—." The days of that kind of empire are over, although imperialists of other lands still endanger the peace by seeking their own dominion over palm and pine. Today, however, the principal battle is not merely over land; it is a battle for the minds of people. The most difficult aspect of the conflict between communism and our way of life is that we see the same thing so differently. What we see as propaganda the communists see as truth, and vice versa. One side's facts are the other side's fictions. Under those circumstances, how can we deal with them? Let's look into that question.

Wrong-Way Corrigan

This is the day when, in 1938, a pilot named Douglas Corrigan, forever after to be known as "Wrong-Way" Corrigan, let it be known that he was taking off from New York for California, only to land the next day in Dublin, Ireland, a magnificent feat of flying which he straightfacedly insisted was not what he had intended to do. I will not point either you or myself in the wrong direction today. Let me state my subject at the outset and go straight to it.

JULY 18

Thackeray

The great English writer William Makepeace Thackeray, who was born on this day in 1811, wrote in his novel *Vanity Fair* that—quote—"Everybody in Vanity Fair must have remarked how well those live who are comfortably and thoroughly in debt; how they deny themselves nothing; how jolly and easy they are in their minds." Close quote. Thackeray wrote that in 1847, a long time ago, but it is still true. We still live in a society of debt, both as a nation and as individuals. Since Thackeray's time we have devised new ways of incurring debt—installment buying, charge accounts, second mortgages, and lots of others. We keep finding new ways of spending money, and all too often it is

money we don't yet have. Is this going to continue indefinitely? Today I want
to take a good hard look at our pocketbooks.

Rome Burned

This is supposed to be the anniversary of the day in 64 A.D. when Emperor
Nero fiddled while Rome burned. Now, Emperor Nero was not exactly the
nicest fellow in the world, so his fiddling around would have been quite in character, but a lot of nicer people through the years have fiddled while their particular Romes burned, too. We have our conflagrations today: not just burning but
dry rot in some of our cities and grave problems among some of our people,
and yet there are those among us who would fiddle instead of doing something
about it. I have some observations on that point.

John Glenn

The first American to orbit the earth was a Marine colonel who was born
in Cambridge, Ohio, on this day in 1921. When he orbited the earth in 1962
he was past forty years of age, which made middle-aged people feel a lot better;
and he went on from there to a distinguished career in the U.S. Senate. Not
too many of us can have the kind of adventures and honors of a John H. Glenn
Jr. But I think every one of us in this country has the opportunity for some
kind of upward mobility, which is lacking in other parts of the world. Of course,
we have our disadvantaged and our disenchanted, and we can undoubtedly do
more for them than we are doing, but even there we are doing more than was
done a couple of generations ago. More important, we are sending more people
through college—despite the cost—and we are helping people to live longer and
better. But we have so much more to do. There is so much room for improvement. Today I want to talk about just one such area.

Helicopter

After people learned how to fly in airplanes, ingenious inventors devised
all kinds of flying machines. One such was the autogiro, which could rise ver-
tically instead of requiring a runway for takeoff and landing. On this day in
1940, the first successful helicopter was flown at Stratford, Connecticut, and
a great new aerial vehicle was born. The helicopter could do everything the
autogiro could do and more; it could carry a heavier load and, most important,
it could hover in a stationary position in the air. It was the American product
of an émigré Russian named Igor Sikorsky, one more example of the way U.S.
hospitality to people from other lands has paid us such handsome dividends.
It is interesting that with each new wave of immigration to this country we
hear that the new people don't measure up to our standards, and yet every new
wave produces its own dividends for us. Let's consider the current crop as an
illustration.

JULY 19

Samuel Colt

This is the birthday of Samuel Colt, the inventor of the revolver that helped win the West. Colt was born on this day in 1814 in Hartford, Connecticut. His story is an interesting one. He not only invented the revolver; he devised new methods of mass production that made him, along with Eli Whitney, one of the fathers of the industrial age in America. But even though a lot of people bought his guns, the principal potential customer, the U.S. Army, wanted no part of it, and Colt's company couldn't stay in business. Only when the Mexican War broke out and a lot of the fighting men insisted on having Colts did he get an order from the Army that put him back in business. What this seems to tell me is that bureaucracies are not always receptive to new ideas and that an efficient product doesn't automatically find a market. It also suggests that out of the evil of war comes a demand for new products. I can't think of a worse way to encourage new products, and I wonder how much, if at all, we have improved since Samuel Colt's day in encouraging new ideas. Are we any more receptive to them than the people of his earlier time were?

Charles H. Mayo

Today is the birthday of Charles H. Mayo, who with his older brother and his father founded what became known as the Mayo Clinic, which set the pattern for the practice of group medicine in the United States. Charles Mayo was born in Rochester, Minnesota, on this day in 1865. What his success demonstrated was that a pooling of talents has added strength. As medicine becomes more specialized and its tools more complicated, this pooling of talents becomes more and more practical. Although medical science moves fast, the medical profession does not; by its very nature it is usually cautious and conservative. This is understandable when you realize that all too often the patient's life is in the doctor's hands. In the same way the nation's life is often in the hands of those at the head of government, and we seem to need the same sort of collegial or group practice there that the Mayos developed in medicine. But too often those at the head of government are busy protecting and enhancing their own prestige and their own popularity at the expense of the team. Are we in one of those periods today? Let's take a look and see.

V for Victory

It was at midnight on this day in 1941 that Winston Churchill originated the "V for Victory" slogan and symbol of World War II. Like so many of Churchill's messages, it caught on and helped inspire the winning spirit in the hard fight of Great Britain and its allies. "V for Victory" is clear, graphic, and to the point. I like to think of the X as having the same virtues, particularly when we put it alongside a candidate's name in the voting booth. For the fact is that X means the unknown, and no matter how well we think we know a candidate for public office, how that candidate will behave if elected, what policies that candidate will stick to, and what policies will be watered down, all these are X, unknown. Franklin D. Roosevelt, for example, campaigned in favor of a balanced budget, and Ronald Reagan did the same. Both were talking about jobs they did not hold at the time; they had the same kind of advantage that I have today when I talk about what other people are doing and saying. The difference is that I am only asking for your attention, not your votes.

Sitting Bull

About this time in 1881, Sitting Bull, leader of the fighting Sioux Indians, surrendered to the U.S. Army. After a couple of years of imprisonment he was released and spent a year touring with Buffalo Bill. Like all too many later alumni of U.S. imprisonment—notably the Watergate cast—he made money showing himself to a public that was willing to pay for the privilege. Sitting Bull, however, was not content to be a celebrity attraction. He kept on urging the Sioux to fight for their rights and was ultimately shot and killed by the U.S. Indian Police. One can see how Sitting Bull could have captured the imagination of Americans; he was an honorable foe fighting impossible odds. But when we reward criminals with rather generous wages of sin—lecture fees, book royalties, and the like—we certainly are not encouraging civic virtues. Today I want to explore this and some of the other unwise things we do to ourselves.

JULY 20

Man on the Moon

Today should always be remembered as the anniversary of the first steps by an inhabitant of Earth on a heavenly body other than our own. Astronaut Neil Armstrong walked on the moon on this day in 1969 as the whole world—our whole world—watched in awe and amazement. It was a thrilling moment when we could and did believe that anything was possible. That is the spirit that moves mountains and inspires miracles. I wonder whether we have it today, and I have been looking around for signs. Here is what I have found.

Plot to Kill Hitler

On this day in 1944, German army officers tried to kill Adolf Hitler by planting a bomb in his headquarters in East Prussia, but they missed him. The history of the world might have been very different if they had succeeded. What might have happened in East Prussia could have changed the outcome of the war and the shape of the world. We will, of course, never know. But while wondering what if is no more than an interesting exercise, a far more challenging game of what if is being played every day in government, in business, even in the laboratory. Every time we are faced with a decision we are playing that game. What if we do this instead of that? It is easy for us to sit on the sidelines and criticize those who have to make the most important decisions; it is often a lot harder to make the decisions than it is to criticize them. So today, instead of being a Monday morning quarterback, I'd like to make some suggestions about decisions that have not yet been made.

Tickets, Please

It was back in 1859 on this day that a new business was born. It was the business of baseball—not the game of baseball, just the business. On this day in 1859, for the first time an admission price was charged to watch a baseball game. It was a game played at a racetrack in Long Island between teams from New York and Brooklyn, which then were separate cities. From this small beginning came much of the billion-dollar sports business of today, because it was the baseball teams that made possible the building of big stadiums in this country. It was baseball that showed Americans how much fun it was to go out and root for the home team, and it was baseball that led the way into the era of ridiculously high salaries for athletes. So, with due obeisance to what has so often been called our national pastime, I thank you for giving me this time at bat.

Polaris Missile

On this day in 1960, from under water near Florida, the first Polaris missile was fired by the U.S. submarine *George Washington* to a target a thousand miles away in the ocean. It represented not only the birth of a new age in warfare but also one of the few times a military project has been completed ahead of schedule. The firing took place five years earlier than the first target date. That has not happened too often since then. One of the hazards of building new weapons is that improvements keep suggesting themselves while the work is in progress. The same thing happens with my speech texts. Every time I read them over I think of something new to add. So let me hasten to offer my remarks now, before I think of ways to make them longer.

JULY 21

First Bull Run

I certainly hope we never again see anything like the atmosphere at the start of the first Battle of Bull Run in the Civil War. It happened on this day in 1861 at Bull Run Creek in northern Virginia. The Union Army went into battle with a rooting section, picnickers coming to watch the show. They were, of course, rudely surprised; the overconfident Union troops were soundly defeated by the Confederates. I would like to hope that by now there aren't any people so stupid as to think that a battle can be a picnic or a show. War to me represents a failure of civilization, and in these days there are no spectators, just potential or actual participants. So on the anniversary of the first Battle of Bull Run I can't think of any more appropriate subject than how we can stay out of war.

The Open Skies Proposal

Back on this day in 1955, a president of the United States who had been a professional soldier for more than thirty years made a proposal to a summit conference of great powers in Geneva. Dwight D. Eisenhower offered what became known as the "open skies proposal." He suggested to the USSR that they and the United States—and I quote—"give to each other a complete blueprint of our military establishments, from beginning to end, from one end of our countries to the other; lay out the establishments and provide the blueprints to each other. Next, to provide within our countries facilities for aerial photography to the other country. . . ." Close quote. That was a pretty specific and all-encompassing scheme of arms reduction and peaceful co-existence. The Russians turned it down, offering to talk about partial limitation of atomic weapons and ground forces. I mention this to indicate how long ago the United States was seeking realistic arms control. There are among us some Americans who suggest that we are war-mongers and that we have never really wanted to disarm. Here, as in so many other areas, those who denigrate America just don't know their history. And, as I consider some of their current positions, I think they also don't know their America.

Lady Chatterley's Lover

Until this day in 1959, the Post Office would not let D. H. Lawrence's masterpiece *Lady Chatterley's Lover* come through the mails into this country from abroad. Then the U.S. District Court overruled the postal people. But if you think that disposed of book censorship in the United States, think again. Ask the American Library Association, which is constantly fighting efforts of self-constituted guardians of public morality to take books off the shelves. Ask the book publishers whose textbooks on biology, for example, have run afoul of the creationists. The excuse most of the time is that it isn't really censorship; it's just that we want to protect the children. It is always supposedly to protect the children. It seems to me that the way to protect the children best is to make sure that they grow up and inherit a society where freedom of speech, freedom of the press, and freedom of worship still exist. If you ban a book today you can ban a speaker tomorrow—and, of course, as a speaker I want to be able to say what I think. I am speaking in this vein today to make sure that each and every one of you can speak freely today, tomorrow, and forever more.

Reuter

Today is listed in some sources as the birthday of Paul Julius Reuter, the man regarded as the father of the modern news service. Reuter was born in 1816 in Cassell, Germany. His interest in getting news from one country to another began when he was in the banking business. He used whatever forms of communication he could find, ranging from the newfangled telegraph to the carrier pigeon. He tried to organize a news agency in Paris, but when that proved difficult he moved his base to England. It took him years to persuade newspapers to make use of his dispatches, but before he was done Reuter's news agency was covering news on both sides of the Atlantic and furnishing the model for the various other international services that followed and imitated it. If we are better informed today than our great-grandparents were, we can thank Julius Reuter. He helped make the world a smaller place. Smaller, yes, but is it any better?

JULY 22

Gregor Mendel

Today is the birthday of Gregor Mendel, who was born in Silesia in 1822 and went on to reveal the fundamentals of heredity. The whole science of genetics is based on the pioneering work of this quiet monk, but what I find particularly fascinating is that this great man at least twice flunked the test for a license as a science teacher. We impose formal requirements that undoubtedly are needed to maintain the quality of our various professions, but it doesn't work out as it should. Occasionally it results in the rejection of a worthwhile candidate; I am inclined, however, to think that more often the tests fail to weed out the incompetent. There are people in every licensed profession today who don't belong there, and most professions are reluctant, to say the least, about policing their ranks. There are some areas where you don't need a license at all, and public speaking is one of them, but here at least there is a public review of the performance. So now I throw myself upon your mercies and begin.

Bretton Woods

On this day in 1944, in the midst of World War II, forty-four nations meeting at Bretton Woods, New Hampshire, established the International Monetary Fund and the International Bank for Reconstruction and Development, the organizations that furnished billions upon billions of dollars for postwar and peacetime economic development and helped keep a lot of poor nations afloat. It's refreshing to know that an international organization can work as well as the record of the IMF and the International Bank during their first thirty-five years or more. Of course, it has a secret weapon—money. Money may be the root of all evil, but it is a root that sometimes helps good things to grow, too. I am here today, certainly not on behalf of the World Bank, to suggest a very good way for you to put your money to work.

Alexander Calder

Today is the birthday of Alexander Calder, who was born in Philadelphia in 1898. Calder was the man who brought a new sense of fun and a world of motion to the art of sculpture. His mobiles, delicately balanced and moving gently in response to the shifting currents of air, are masterpieces that have been enjoyed by millions upon millions of people. His most famous wire sculpture, a circus in miniature, is in a class alone. Before he became a sculptor Calder was an engineer, and some of his work probably could not have been accomplished without an understanding of engineering principles. One of the great things about knowledge is that it is rarely wasted; whatever you choose to do, the information in your head helps guide your hands. And the same is true in everyday life; whatever you know about your community or your government helps make you a better member of that community. That is why a flow of uncensored information is so important. It is why being able to hear the views of different people is so important. And it is why I welcome the opportunity to talk to you here today.

Stephen Vincent Benet

"The Devil and Daniel Webster" is a story that has become a classic of American literature—having been made into a play, a movie, and even an opera about the way America's greatest orator used his eloquence to outtalk and defeat the Devil himself. The man who wrote that story, Stephen Vincent Benet, was born in 1898 in Bethlehem, Pennsylvania. On his birthday I don't propose even to try to compete with the eloquence of either Daniel Webster or Benet himself, but I have one advantage: I am not here to debate the Devil.

JULY 23

Liberty Island

On this day in 1956, the United States finally got around to renaming the island on which the Statue of Liberty stands in New York Harbor. The island had been known as Bedloe's Island even after the statue had stood there for almost three-quarters of a century. Interestingly, the statue was installed on a base that was already in place on the island, a base that originally had been an Army fortification named Fort Wood. Liberty clearly needs a base of strong defense. Today the defense of liberty takes more than a fort on an island in a harbor—as I hope to explore in my remarks here.

Olympics

It was about this time back in 776 B.C., according to the historians, that the Olympic Games began, originally as a one-day racing event and then as a more elaborate and lengthier competition every four years. The ancient Olympics endured for about a thousand years, finally being discontinued in the later days of the Roman Empire, possibly because of unrest over the degree of professionalism that had entered the competition. Isn't it interesting that this same problem arose in the modern Olympics? We may think that the problems that confront us are new to humanity, but most of the time we are faced simply with new versions of old challenges. We know a great deal more than our forefathers did about how to communicate and generate information, for example, but we worry just as they did about whether we are using our tools for frivolous purposes. Our Olympic athletes run faster than the ancients, but they too can be seduced by a golden apple. Our doctors know infinitely more than the ancients, but in the final analysis we probably aren't treating our old people as well as in the days of old-fashioned family medicine. And in the field of education, despite an educational system that is bigger than ever, we have a veritable army of the uneducated, virtually illiterate, truant, and potentially unemployable for the rest of their lives. That is the problem I want to address today.

Robert Emmet's Revolt

This is the anniversary of one of the least successful revolts in Ireland's long pursuit of freedom from Great Britain. It was on this day in 1803 that Robert Emmet led what he hoped would be a popular uprising, only to be undone by treachery in the ranks, a failure of communication, and almost every other mishap that could have occurred. Emmet himself was captured some time later and executed after a trial during which he spoke the lines that have been an inspiration to Irish patriots ever since. "Let no man write my epitaph," he said. "When my country takes her place among the nations of the earth, then shall my character be vindicated, then may my epitaph be written." There is a message for all of us in those words, and it is simply this: No one of us completes our work in our lifetime; we sow the seeds of future accomplishments; we build the tools for our children to use, and in many cases we give them the goals toward which they strive. So it is only fitting for us here today to ask ourselves, what is our agenda for the next generation? What kind of world are we making for them?

Spanish Armada

This is the anniversary period for the great battle between the British ships led by Sir Francis Drake and the Spanish Armada over a ten-day period in 1588.

The Spanish fleet was perhaps the largest the world had ever seen; it far out-numbered and outgunned the British. But British seamanship and tactics more than made up the difference, and the Armada was totally and humiliatingly defeated. Whenever I hear the talk about which side has the superior arma-ments today I think of the Spanish Armada. True, that was before the days of airplanes and nuclear warfare, but it seems to me that even in these times of atomic bombs and electronic devices there is still a need for skilled people, and it also seems to me that we pay a great deal more attention to the makeup of our nuclear weapons than to the composition of the population of our armed forces. So let's talk about how you staff a military force today, instead of how you arm it.

JULY 24

Coubertin's View

On this day in 1908, Baron Pierre de Coubertin, the father of the modern Olympic Games, commented that "the most important thing in the Olympic Games is not winning but taking part. . . . The essential thing in life is not conquering but fighting well." That may have been Baron Coubertin's view of the games, and of life, but it isn't everybody's. Good sportsmanship does not seem to be as important today as a willingness to pull every trick in the book in order to prevail. Conduct on tennis courts is a far cry from that game's gentlemanly days of the past; baseball fans use language and throw things at players and umpires with wild abandon. And what happens in sports is a reflec-tion of what happens in life. We encourage rowdyism; we tolerate abuse of offi-cials; we glorify rock and movie stars whose way of life makes a mockery of our supposed standards. That is the moral crisis of our times, and I am here to ask what we are going to do about it.

Nixon-Khrushchev Debate

It was on this date, in a display kitchen of an exposition in Moscow in 1959, that Richard M. Nixon, then the Vice-President of the United States, and the Premier of the Soviet Union, Nikita Khrushchev, publicly argued the merits of their respective countries' ways of life. When that kind of open dis-cussion between Nixon and Khrushchev was held in that kitchen in Moscow, it was so rare an event in that controlled society that it became news. When I open my mouth here today it may not be news, but I hope it is constructive, and there's only one way to find out. So here I go.

Simeon the Stylite

This is the day when, in 459 A.D., St. Simeon the Stylite died after living for more than thirty years on top of a pillar. He did not live there in isolation;

his wisdom and his holiness brought pilgrims to ask his counsel. Today we do the same with people we venerate, but we put them on their pillars—they don't put themselves there. We also have a less reverent but nevertheless flattering honor. It doesn't put you on a pillar or even a pedestal—just a speaker's rostrum. The qualifications for that position vary, but there is one very strict requirement. You have to have something to say. I may not be a pillar of wisdom, but I do have something to say, and here it is.

Amelia Earhart

Today is the birthday of Amelia Earhart, who proved that women could fly airplanes as well as men. She was born in 1898 in Atchison, Kansas, and before she disappeared in a flight over the Pacific in 1937 she had set all kinds of aviation records—not just records for women but universal records. She was the first pilot to fly solo from Honolulu to the U.S. mainland, the first to fly nonstop between Mexico City and New York. Equal rights for women was a movement still in the future when Amelia Earhart proved her mettle, and despite her graphic example the myth that women couldn't compete with men flourished long after her death. That's the trouble with myths; they're hard to stamp out. Life today is complicated by persistent mythology. I'd like to talk about some of those myths.

JULY 25

Test-Tube Baby

Today is the birthday of the world's first test-tube baby, who was born to Mrs. Lesley Brown in London in 1978. Little Louise Brown made medical history as the first healthy baby to be conceived outside the body. Her birth ushered in a new era for couples who previously had no hope of conceiving children. In an age when the science of contraception has grown it is interesting that we have also seen so tremendous an advance in increasing human fertility. Science says that for every action there is a reaction. The more we know, the more we know how much we do not know. And as we explore previously unknown and sometimes forbidden frontiers we are confronted with new moral questions—not just the old ones about abortion and contraception but new issues of cloning and gene engineering. I am not here to discuss those moral issues but rather to suggest a very real governmental problem. How free should science be from governmental control? How free in genetics, how free in nuclear fission, how free in the development of insecticides and so on and on and on?

Nuclear Test Ban

In Moscow on this day in 1963, the United States, the United Kingdom, and Soviet Russia signed a treaty barring nuclear tests except those conducted underground. The number of nations with nuclear capabilities has grown tremendously since then, but at least there has been some small effort at limiting the testing that affects innocent portions of the world. One of the things we have discovered in modern times is that, like it or not, we cannot stop acid rain from other lands or volcanic dust clouds from elsewhere from blowing over us and affecting us. Plagues and chemical infiltrations are no respecters of international borders. That is why it is so important for us to know what is going on elsewhere in the world—because what goes on elsewhere, whether it is hoof-and-mouth disease or a major radiation leak or a new breed of fruit fly, can very seriously affect us right here. And that is why I want to talk today about some things that are happening far beyond our borders.

Lundy's Lane

On this day in 1814, a battle was fought between U.S. and British troops on the soil of Canada; it wasn't the only such encounter during the War of 1812, but it was perhaps the most decisive. It was the battle of Lundy's Lane, not far across the border in Ontario and close to Niagara Falls. The battle itself ended with no clear victor, but the Americans pulled back, and from that point on Canada was safe, although the Americans held on to Fort Erie for a few months. We don't pay much attention to the Battle of Lundy's Lane, unlike the Battle of New Orleans, because it was not as spectacular and there was no American victory there. Fortunately, Lundy's Lane has left no heritage of hatred between the United States and Canada. We may have trade differences with our northern friends, but we can always talk to each other. Being able to talk is the most important thing of all. The next most important thing is being able to talk sense—and that is what I will try to do here today.

Balfour

British statesman Arthur James Balfour was born on this day in 1848 in England. Sixty-nine years later in 1917, he issued the Balfour Declaration that contained Britain's promise of a homeland in Palestine for the Jews. Balfour died in 1930, and the Jewish homeland became a reality in 1948, exactly 100 years after the birth of the man who had promised it. I mention this to emphasize the fact that history does not always move at breakneck speed, and tomorrow's events are often the result of yesterday's pledges. A war of sorts broke out in the Falkland Islands in 1981 as the followup to a controversy over the ownership of those islands that had begun in 1833. Before we can understand the present we must be aware of the past. Today, in talking to you about some current affairs, I want to go back and look at their roots.

JULY 26

George Bernard Shaw

Today is the birthday of George Bernard Shaw, who was born in Dublin in 1856. In his great play *The Devil's Disciple,* Shaw commented that "the worst sin towards our fellow creatures is not to hate them, but to be indifferent to them: that's the essence of humanity." Today I want to talk about a problem of people to whom we have been indifferent.

Post Office

Today is the anniversary of the action by the Continental Congress in 1775 that established the Post Office and made Benjamin Franklin its first head. The country was a lot smaller in those days and transportation was also a lot more primitive, but Ben Franklin saw that the mails got through, even on the verge of a revolution. The one thing that strikes me about the action of the Continental Congress was their recognition of the importance of communication. In order to have a nation we had to communicate with one another. Today we have infinitely faster means of communication, but the challenge is still the same. We have to be able to talk to one another. Forums like this are important because they are a way of giving more information to people, and I hope my remarks here today will do that job.

Churchill Resigns

Today seemed to mark the end of an era. Winston Churchill, the man who had led Britain to victory in World War II, saw his party lose the election the day before, and on this day in 1945 he resigned as Prime Minister. He returned to power sometime later, but the dynamic, inspirational leadership he brought to his nation and the free world was never quite the same again. When the challenge of the times and the talents of the person come together the results are historic, but when the times change people sometimes feel that different talents are then needed. One of our problems, I believe, is that we choose our leaders as men and women of all seasons, but some are better in good times and some are at their best in difficult days. Trying to assess the particular talents of those in the public eye today, this is what I see.

Prison Problems

On this day in 1931, the Wickersham Commission, which had previously examined law enforcement with particular attention to Prohibition, released its study of the U.S. prison system; in brief, it found the system expensive **and** ineffective. Among its suggestions was a broadened system of parole. Most recent studies half a century later still find the system ineffective. We have certainly broadened the use of parole, and we are still looking for a better answer. It occurs to me that, since the problem was still clearly much the same in 1983 as in 1931, we have been paying too much attention to blaming the familiar scapegoats—disillusioned veterans, bad times, and so forth—and not enough to wiping out the root causes of the crimes that send people to prison. We are talking about treating people who have already become criminals more than about stopping them from becoming criminals in the first place. Let's talk instead about preventive measures.

JULY 27

Leo Durocher

Leo Durocher, who has born on this day in 1906 in West Springfield, Massachusetts, was the baseball manager who declared that "nice guys finish last." This idea seems to have become an excuse for all the not-nice guys to justify their conduct. Even public speakers sometimes succumb to the temptation to get more attention by saying nasty things. I plan to resist that temptation here today. With all respect to the Durocher maxim, I prefer the practice of another baseball man, the legendary umpire Bill Klem. Using his example, I will try to call 'em as I see 'em.

Shah Dies

The Shah of Iran, a fugitive from the Iranian revolution led by the fiery Ayatollah Khomeini, died on this day in 1980 in Cairo. After years of glory he had become his country's most hated man; when he came to the United States for medical treatment the wrath of the Muslim revolutionaries turned against this country and ultimately triggered the seizure of the American Embassy and the hostages in Tehran. The Shah's authoritarian regime in Iran was overthrown in favor of an even more authoritarian religious dictatorship. One of the risks of supporting an authoritarian regime, however friendly it is to us, is that the victims of that authoritarianism await the opportunity for revenge. It is imperative that we pick our friends not merely in terms of how important they are to us but also in terms of what kind of people they are, and, above all, we should be restrained in our commitments to those who use terror as a weapon. Have we learned the lesson of the Shah? Let's look at our friends and see.

State Department

The folks on Foggy Bottom, better known as the State Department of the United States, trace their department back to this day in 1789, when Congress established it as the Department of Foreign Affairs. The world was infinitely less complicated then. Nobody had any need of motor oil. Radiation was a long time away from being discovered. There were budding trade disputes, and the big fight over freedom of the seas was still to come. Nobody even knew that there were ecological problems, acid rains, or the like. Yet even in those primitive and simple days, maintaining friendly relations with so many different people was a tremendously difficult and touchy job. How much more so now, with all the new problems I have listed and so many nations that didn't even exist in 1789. Our first ambassadors for the most part were the men who had helped found the nation, not fat cats rewarded for campaign contributions; on the other hand, there was no professional foreign service in those days. Given the pluses and the minuses, were we better off then?

Hot Dog

I cannot vouch for the accuracy of the exact date, but this has been indicated in some compilations as the anniversary of the day in 1868 when Charles Feltman of Brooklyn started selling sausages in buns. Quite a few years later, runs the story, a famous newspaper cartoonist pictured this delicacy as a dachshund in a roll and called it a hot dog. Now I don't know how much of this history is true, but I think it is fair to say that the hog dog was America's first great convenience food and the pioneer in the rise of convenience foods that has changed the face of the world. Today it is interesting to note that at sports events the sale of hot dogs and related items sometimes makes the difference between profit and loss. But over the years, in addition to denoting a food, the term *hot dog* has been applied to people who like to show off or take themselves too seriously. I hope you will not detect any hot dogging in my remarks here today, and I hope my remarks will cut the mustard.

JULY 28

Bonus Army Dispersed

On this day in 1932, in the depths of the Great Depression, the so-called "Bonus Army" of impoverished World War I veterans had been encamped for some time in Washington, trying to get the government to help them with a bonus payment. Today is the anniversary of their forcible removal by troops of the regular Army. It was not one of the great moments of American history. Even people who did not agree with the veterans' demands felt that they should not have been treated so coldly. But we need not be smug about our own generation with regard to veterans. The servicemen of the Korean War and Vietnam, for example, found their own countries less than understanding of their psychological problems, less than supportive about the genetic and medical aftermath of modern war years later. War has two kinds of casualties—those whose suffering is immediate and those whose pains develop slowly over a period of years. It is about the latter that I want to talk today.

United Nations

On this day in 1945, the U.S. Senate ratified the Charter of the United Nations, bringing this country into full membership in that organization and thereby reversing the isolationism that had kept us out of the League of Nations after World War I. The Senate vote was overwhelmingly in favor of UN world order, not so much because of optimism over its efficiency but because we had found out the hard way that we could no longer isolate ourselves from the family of nations. Since that day our confidence in the United Nations has not been greatly advanced, but nobody has come up yet with any better form of international organization. If nothing else it has provided a wonderful forum for letting off steam. And it has done more—accomplishments I'd like to talk about today.

Jacques Piccard

Today is the birthday of that pioneer explorer of the ocean depths, Jacques Piccard, who was born in Brussels in 1922. Jacques Piccard proved that getting in deep can be a high accomplishment. Unlike Piccard, I don't want to get in too deep today. I'd rather talk about some of the pressures that arise just from keeping your head above water.

Robespierre

This was the day in 1794 that Maximilien Robespierre, the leader of the Jacobin dictatorship in revolutionary France, was executed. With his death the excesses of the French Revolution tapered off and became history. Robespierre paid for his intolerance with his life, but a lot of innocent people had paid that price earlier because of him. That was 200 years ago, and we still haven't found a way to compensate the victims of crime as efficiently as we punish the perpetrators. Today I want to talk about the victims.

JULY 29

Rain Day in Waynesburg, Pennsylvania

I don't know if it is raining today in Waynesburg, Pennsylvania. For most of the past 100 years it has rained in Waynesburg on this day, to the point where the town celebrates the day officially as Rain Day. Generally speaking, human beings don't like surprises and prefer things to come in their proper place, whether it is rain on July 29 in Waynesburg, Christmas on December 25, or Election Day in early November. We get very upset when things—or people—

don't stay in what we regard as their proper place. When guaranteeing somebody else's rights begins to impinge on our prerogatives, for example, we tend to feel that somebody is upsetting the apple cart. While we as a nation were on the way up and challenging previous top dogs, we didn't particularly mind, but when we found ourselves sharing the top dog role with Soviet Russia, and when we found that more and more of the Third World nations didn't want to play by our rules, we became a little more uncertain in our international relations. Today as a consequence there is plenty of room for debate about our dealings with other nations, and I welcome the opportunity to take part in that discussion.

Dr. Rush's Advice

Dr. Benjamin Rush was one of our first great physicians and also one of the great public men in the founding days of our republic. On this day in 1782, he put down on paper eleven guiding rules for a doctor. Most of them apply to other fields as well, and I would like to take just a bit of your time to give them to you. I am not using the full text but enough of each maxim to make its point. 1. Take care of the poor. 2. Go regularly to some place of worship. A physician cannot be a bigot. 3. Never resent an affront offered to you by a sick man. 4. Avoid intimacies with your patients if possible. 5. Never sue a patient. 6. Receive as much pay as possible in goods or the produce of the country. Men have not half the attachment to these things that they have to money. 7. Acquire a habit of visiting your patients regularly at one hour. 8. Never dispute about a bill. 9. Don't insert trifling advice or services in a bill. 10. Never make light to a patient of any case. 11. Never appear in a hurry in a sickroom, nor talk of indifferent matters till you have examined and prescribed to your patient. Those were the instructions offered by Dr. Rush more than 200 years ago. It is interesting to see how much they apply today. And what I find of particular interest is what he put first. Rule number one for Dr. Rush was "Take care of the poor." Now, in Dr. Rush's day physicians had no elaborate equipment; they could take care of the poor without great out-of-pocket expense. Today the practice of medicine is an increasingly large cost item in the budget of the nation and the individual alike. What can we do about it?

Alexis de Tocqueville

The foreigner whose picture of America remains after more than 150 years as a unique testimony to the greatness of our nation was a Frenchman named Alexis de Tocqueville. He was born in 1805 and published his four-volume book *Democracy in America* between 1835 and 1840. Today is his birthday. Of Americans he wrote, "They have all a lively faith in the perfectability of man, they judge that the diffusion of knowledge must necessarily be advantageous, and the consequences of ignorance fatal. . . ." In the spirit of de

Tocqueville I am not here to bewail any portion of our present predicament but rather to renew our faith in the perfectability of man. To that end perhaps my remarks here today can help somewhat in the diffusion of knowledge that de Tocqueville found so necessary and so typically American.

International Atomic Energy Agency

In 1957 on this date, the International Atomic Energy Agency came into being under the United Nations. It did not stop the proliferation of nuclear bomb capability, but it has set standards for nuclear energy plants and helped train many people in many countries for the peaceful harnessing of this great energy source. In this regard it is an example of an international agency that serves a useful purpose. It reminds us that even though the United Nations may seem to many to be an exercise in futility there are always important avenues for international cooperation that the mere existence of UN agencies makes possible. Today I want to talk about some of those opportunities.

JULY 30

Parkinson

Today is the birthday of C. Northcote Parkinson, the Englishman who gave us Parkinson's Law. He was born in 1909. Actually there are several Parkinson's laws, notably that expenditures rise to meet income or to surpass it and that work expands so as to fill the time available for its completion. Parkinson postulated that the longer the amount of time given to something that is to be done, the more complicated the task will become. Every day, at every level of government, we see how true this is. Discussion of a proposed law soon moves from the issue at hand into a dozen subissues that proponents and opponents want to fiddle around with. A government bureau's investigation of a situation doesn't stay within the bureau but reaches out to hired consultants. And so it goes. Only when the emergency is so clear and the need so great that there isn't time for this sort of thing do we get prompt action—not necessarily correct action but at least prompt. In the courts we have seen civil cases that dragged on for years and years. I am here to propose a brand new approach in all areas of government. We have a statute of limitations for criminal prosecutions; why not a statute of limitations for government actions?

Casey Stengel

Charles Dillon Stengel, born on this day in 1891, intended to be a dentist, but he found baseball more interesting, and since he had considerable talent with a bat and glove he made his career in that sport. That was fortunate, because Charles Dillon Stengel, who was born in Kansas City and therefore was known as Casey Stengel, was one of baseball's most memorable figures. In the course of his career he played in the major leagues for 12 years and went on to manage one of the greatest teams and one of the worst teams ever to perform in those leagues, the world champion New York Yankees and the New York Mets. Casey Stengel, also known as "the Professor," spoke a variety of English that was all his own and had a sense of humor that endeared him to the fans—although probably not to the umpire to whom he once tipped his hat and let a bird fly out. I mention Casey Stengel here today because I want to quote a particular remark of his. Talking about a pitcher who was throwing too many home-run balls, the Professor said, "He lets the ball go too far." It seems to me that in public life today we have too many people making pitches that "let the ball go too far." We have candidates raising issues not so much to solve a question as to embarrass opponents. We have scientists opening new frontiers without giving very much thought to the social desirability of those frontiers. We have advocates of discarding old values who have no new values to offer in their place. I am not referring to areas where different values are at issue, such as birth control, but rather to those on which I would hope we agree—honesty, courtesy, neighborliness.

Medicare

This is the anniversary of President Lyndon Johnson's signing of the Medicare Act in 1965, which made the provision of medical care for substantial portions of the population a national obligation. It is sardonic that a nation which has so long recognized its obligation to care for the sick still has so much trouble keeping so many people from getting sick in the first place. I refer to the foods we eat and our willingness to tolerate—indeed, to gobble up—so many things that really aren't good for us. Salt, of course, is probably the number one culprit, but it has lots of competition. I am not here today to denounce food processors and manufacturers but rather to remind us that we have certain responsibilities of our own, not the least of which is to read the labels on the things we buy. Let me tell you some of the things you can find out by reading the labels.

Henry Moore

One of the great modern sculptors, whose work can be seen in public places throughout the world, was born in England on this day in 1898. His name is Henry Moore, and his work represents a sharp break from classical realism. Moore's figures are lumps that nevertheless convey a sense of being something, sometimes even with holes in them. It strikes me that some of the proposals we hear bandied about in the world of politics, economics, and sociology are rather like Henry Moore's sculptures; they are rather lumpy as shapes and often have holes in them, but they awaken a human response. We respond to a politician who wants to reduce taxes or increase the police force or cut the public payroll; we respond very often before we have determined whether what he or she wants to do can really be done. We respond to the broad general shape or thrust of a proposal, and then we tell the proponents to make it work. Today I don't want to make any new proposals but rather to discuss how we can make some familiar proposals become reality.

JULY 31

Patent

The first patent ever issued by the United States was granted on this day in 1790, and, according to Joseph Nathan Kane's *Famous First Facts*, some 43 years later the head of the Patent Office thought his job was over because, quote, "everything seems to have been done." All that was left, it has turned out, were close to three million later patents including such minor items as inventions connected with the automobile, the motion picture, the airplane, the computer, electricity, and television. The one thing we know now is that we don't know what they will think of next. And we should also know that the United States can and must continue to be the most inventive country on earth. There are few other countries that offer the same degree of honor to entrepreneurism and venture capital. Today I'd like to talk a bit about some inventions we could certainly use.

Lincoln-Douglas

This is the anniversary of the day in 1858 when Abraham Lincoln agreed to the terms proposed by Stephen Douglas for a series of debates in their senatorial contest in Illinois. That was probably the most eloquent series of campaign debates in American history, and although Lincoln lost the Senate race his eloquence was not lost on the leaders of his new Republican party. Two years later he was their candidate for the presidency. Not too many speakers can expect that kind of aftermath; most of us would be content to have our words help to focus a little more attention to or understanding of the things that concern us. That, at least, is my hope as I talk to you today.

Lafayette Commissioned

This is the day when the Marquis de Lafayette was welcomed to America and commissioned by the Continental Congress as a major general in the American Army in 1777. It is an anniversary that reminds us of the lovers of liberty from so many nations who came to America to help us win independence—not only from our ally France but from Prussia and Poland and Sweden, among others. America was the hope then of lovers of freedom all over the world—and it still is today. Why and how do we keep that hope alive?

John Ericsson

A man was born in Sweden on this day in 1803 who was destined to help write the history of the United States. He was not a historian. He was an inventor, and he rewrote history by changing its course. His name was John Ericsson. He invented a better means of propelling steamboats than the original paddlewheel. His device was the underwater propeller, which he perfected after he came to the United States. But his masterpiece was a new type of warship, which he proposed in 1861 to the U.S. government. It was the *U.S.S. Monitor,* the first iron battleship. The *Monitor,* you may recall, was the gun-turreted, low-in-the-water ship that stopped the Confederate ironclad *Virginia* (formerly known as the *Merrimack*) in a battle off Hampton Roads in 1862. If the *Virginia* had been able to continue fighting the wooden Union ships, it might have changed the course of the war, but Ericsson's invention stopped it. After the war Ericsson worked on the development of ships capable of firing underwater torpedoes and even explored solar energy. He was one of the most inventive minds of his time, and I believe that sort of inventiveness persists in America and attracts original thinkers from all over the world. That is because in America they can get things done. Ours is a country that encourages new ideas. We encourage them mainly by providing the right kind of rewards. Today I want to talk about how we can protect that climate and those rewards.

AUGUST 1

National Clown Week

The first week of August has been observed for many years as National Clown Week, a salute to the pantomimists whose funny doings bring us much-needed smiles. In a world where daily problems are so large and so serious, the clowns are very welcome comic relief. But when the clowns start running the world, then we are in trouble; and in too many places the people who are running things are very like clowns—doing anything for the applause of the crowd, anything to take the public's mind off the real world. So a nonelected president of Argentina ordered an invasion of the Falklands to divert his people from troubles at home; a religious zealot in the Middle East fired up wars around him; a South African regime waved the tired banner of racism. And in our own country we see those who would divert our attention from the basic issues to their own favorite side arguments. It becomes important for us to make up our minds about who are the leaders and who are merely the clowns.

Francis Scott Key

Francis Scott Key, who was born in Maryland on this day in 1779, was a successful attorney who had a relatively modest career, except for one day of his life. That was the day he wrote a poem that could be sung to the tune of an English drinking song entitled "To Anacreon in Heaven." Key called his poem "Defense of Fort McHenry," and of course he wrote it during the British attack on that fort in Baltimore Harbor in 1814 during the War of 1812. Nobody knows his work by that title anymore. We call it "The Star-Spangled Banner," and we have made it our national anthem. That one day's work by Francis Scott Key is what he will be remembered for by countless generations. Ladies and gentlemen, I am here to suggest that none of us knows, when each day begins, how meaningful what we do that day will turn out to be. None of us knows how what we do may influence future events, and so we must do our best every day. We must ask ourselves, every day, how we can make that day better than the last. And we must look to one another for the best that is in us. I look at you today, and I'd like to tell you what I see.

Herman Melville

This is the birthday of Herman Melville, who was born in New York City in 1819. He wrote many books and one of them, *Moby Dick*, is considered by most critics to be perhaps the greatest American novel. But what I find most interesting is that another book of his, *Billy Budd, Foretopman,* which is also highly regarded, was not published until almost thirty-five years after his death. It reminds me of the story of Rembrandt, who died virtually forgotten and thinking himself a failure. Those who live for the applause of the moment may not be as well remembered as those who stick to their standards despite the pressures of the moment. We can't and won't all be Melvilles or Rembrandts, but we can all have the courage of our convictions. Perhaps I need a good bit of that courage to paint for you the word pictures I am about to offer, but here goes.

Watch That Tolstoy

I don't know how hot it was on this day in 1890, but a number of Americans were hot under the collar. Operating through the U.S. Post Office Department, they banned from the mails a work of no less than Leo Tolstoy, the great Russian author. It was *The Kreutzer Sonata,* which has long since become one of his famous creations. But in 1890 it caused a tremendous controversy. Standards change—not always for the better—and life always seems to be a battle between those in favor of the old and those who welcome the new. Most of us, however, prefer other yardsticks. Whether an idea is new or old is not as important as whether we judge it to be a good idea on its own. And heaven knows we have disagreement enough about that. The important thing, it seems to me, is to listen to each other and let us all speak our piece. In that spirit I welcome the opportunity to talk to you here today. If you agree with me that will be the icing on the cake.

AUGUST 2

Coolidge Does Not Choose

On this day in 1927, President Calvin Coolidge told the press and the nation, "I do not choose to run for President in 1928." Since Silent Cal was a man of few words and the statement was so unequivocal, it was accepted at face value by all, but years later it was suggested that Coolidge would not have turned down a plea to reconsider. That sort of word game, unfortunately, is not unknown to American politics. I do not intend to play any word games here today. It is difficult enough to make one's thoughts clear without laboring to make them ambiguous. Here is where I stand.

Hatch Act

Until President Franklin D. Roosevent signed the Hatch Act on this day in 1939, it was perfectly okay for civil servants to be active workers in political campaigns. The Hatch Act was designed to insulate the civil service from the political arena. As it worked out the political activities of civil service workers thereafter seem to have been channelled through their unions, which have not been at all averse to trying to swing their weight in vote chasing and influencing activities. We should have learned by now that passing a law to stop something is only part of the apple; you also have to have agreement with the spirit of the law. It seems to me that our various election campaign laws pose real problems in this respect. We seem to tolerate abuses and elastic interpretations right and left, and none bothers me more than the way millions of dollars are being poured into campaigns to the point where it seems that, in a very real sense, public offices are being bought. That is partly the fault of the law, but it is also in great part the fault of the electorate that lets itself be wooed and bought by expensive campaigns. What are we going to do about it?

Letter Boxes

On this day in 1858 in New York and Boston a great new idea was begun. For the first time in this country, there were mailboxes on the street in which you could deposit your outgoing letters. It was a great step forward because it made communication between people that much easier. The more we are able to talk to and to reach one another, the better for us. The exchange of information is the lifeblood of a healthy community, and I hope that my remarks here today will add a few corpuscles to that lifeblood.

Wild Bill Hickok

Wild Bill Hickok outshot every gunslinger he ever confronted during his picturesque career, but on this day in 1876 in Deadwood, South Dakota, he was killed by a man who shot him in the back. Legend says that when asked why he had fired in such a cowardly way, the man explained that he didn't want to get killed himself. We don't have many lawmen like Hickok today, but we do have too many people who like to shoot from the back—and I am not talking about criminals. I am talking about politicians who oppose a program but instead of coming right out and saying so hope to nitpick it to death. I am talking about playwrights who seek out disagreeable subjects to point to in our society because the truth of the matter is that they don't like our society. I am talking about people who criticize minor aspects of the educational system when what they really mean to criticize is the whole system. I have no quarrel with them expressing their real views. What I object to is that they don't express their real views or real purposes. No system is above criticism, but there aren't many systems that can stand against being nibbled away and shot in the back. So here today I will take frontal aim and fire away at my targets, with no nibbling whatsoever.

AUGUST 3

Black Sox

The 1919 World Series has a special place in American history because it was the occasion for baseball's great scandal, the "fix" that caused members of the Chicago White Sox to be known to immortality as the Black Sox. On this day in 1922, the high commissioner of baseball, Kenesaw Mountain Landis, who had been appointed as a result of the scandal, ruled that although players had been acquitted in criminal proceedings they would be barred from baseball for life. Baseball has had precious little scandal since then, which suggests that Judge Landis's harsh remedy, though hard on a few individuals, was good for the game. It seems to me there is a lesson here for business. Some businesses—the movie business being a case in point—have welcomed people into positions of great responsibility even after they have been caught with a dishonest hand in the till. The lecture and publishing businesses make a great deal of loot with the reminiscences of convicted felons. There is something wrong with our standards, and it is worth talking about.

Cheating

This is a day of particular and unhappy significance for the nation in general and West Point in particular. On this day in 1780, at his request, Benedict Arnold was given command of the Continental Army forces at West Point, and it was there that he seems to have begun his treason. Some 171 years later, another type of betrayal occurred at the Point when ninety cadets were dismissed for cheating in their examinations. These glaring exceptions only heighten the fidelity with which West Pointers have lived up to their motto of duty, honor, country. For every Benedict Arnold there have been uncounted military people who could have done infinitely better for themselves in civilian life but chose to make their careers in the armed forces. Ours has never been a militaristic nation, so we have been hesitant in peacetime to give military careers the recognition they deserve. As a result we have trouble maintaining the quality of military personnel we should have. It is high time we faced up to this problem, and I'd like to tell you why.

Nautilus

This is the anniversary of the first underwater crossing of the North Pole, accomplished by the U.S. nuclear submarine *Nautilus* in 1958. It was a dramatic reminder that while we were endeavoring to explore outer space there was plenty of space on our own planet still waiting to be probed. We still have plenty of resources waiting to be found on and under the earth. And we still have to solve the problem of what to do with those resources we no longer need—chemical wastes, sewage, and so forth. In order to solve these problems we need to do what we did in designing the *Nautilus*—namely, invest all the money that is needed for research. We need to encourage both privately funded and government funded research, because the only way we will get the answers is to keep on experimenting, studying, developing. And that means support for the institutions where this kind of work is done. It is support that should come from every one of us.

Hello Columbus

A speaker who gets up to talk is always somewhat in the position Christopher Columbus was in when he set sail from Palos, Spain, on this day in 1492. You have a general idea of where you are going, but you can't be sure of the kind of reception you are going to get. Columbus had the courage of his convictions, and his example is worth following. So let me plunge right ahead.

AUGUST 4

National Smile Week

For quite a while this week of August has been observed as National Smile Week, which is a nice sentiment. The fact that National Smile Week is sponsored by a greeting card manufacturer may be a wee bit commercial, but the sentiment is too pleasant to quibble about. We live in a world that can use a smile at any season of the year. Somebody said that in an age of shortages the most serious shortage of all is good news, but I am one of those persistent optimists who think that our continued survival is good news to begin with, and I'd like to tell you about some other good things that are happening.

Chicago

On this day in 1830, a surveyor named James Thompson completed the plan for a city to be built on land adjoining a proposed canal between the Illinois River and Lake Michigan. The town was built and named after a local river sometimes called the Eschagou but more often the Chicago. Yes, Chicago, like Washington, D.C., had a street plan before it even had streets. Although many Americans deplore the whole idea of civic planning, it is an old practice in this country. We have a tendency to think of the techniques we use to cope with the problems, and the problems themselves, as being unique to our own times, but the basics were basic to our forefathers as well. The word *revolution*, after all, means turning in a circle or cycle—not so much going into something new as reverting to something old. Dictatorship did not start with communism and fascism, for example; they are just newer names for old-fashioned tyranny. We are afflicted—as I suppose every generation is—with new catch phrases and names for old ideas. If you call something socialism, for example, you will turn off much of the population. When our parents debated the issue of socialized medicine, that phrase was anathema; when you call it Medicare or Medicaid, it somehow sits better with the electorate. Generally speaking, the Democrats are the liberals and the Republicans the conservatives. But there are conservative Democrats and liberal Republicans. It is important to judge them as individuals, not as members of a ticket. So today I will be giving you my assessment of the political scene in terms of people, not parties.

Anne Frank

This is the day when Anne Frank and her family were arrested after their long hideout from the Nazis in Amsterdam in 1944. Their story, told so simply in Anne Frank's diary, captured the conscience of the world when it was published. It made a horrible chapter in world history real because it brought the events down to the level of an individual's story. One of the problems with our problems is that we talk about them in global terms—how many thousands are being poisoned by ecological carelessness, how many millions are unemployed, and so forth—and in the process very often we remain unaware of the small details of the everyday plight of a single family. So today I want to talk in small terms, not of global problems but of what confronts an average family.

Hamilton and Zenger

My dictionary has a definition of the term *Philadelphia lawyer.* A Philadelphia lawyer, it says, is "a shrewd lawyer versed in the intricacies of legal phraseology and adept at exploiting legal technicalities." Today is the anniversary of a debt, a great debt, that we all owe a Philadelphia lawyer named Andrew Hamilton. He came to New York in 1735 to defend a printer named John Peter Zenger, who was being tried for libel because he had criticized the royal governor. Hamilton made an eloquent defense of freedom of the press and won the case. Zenger was freed on this day in 1735, and so was the press. It was Hamilton's knowledge of the law that laid the basis for that victory. I try reminding myself of that fact when, like you, I become upset at the way some lawyer is raising technicalities on behalf of a client. The law, unfortunately, is interpreted by human beings, and as long as that happens there are those who will find an extra twist or two. But we would be a lot worse off without this kind of flexibility, and I am inclined to believe that we owe the so-called Philadelphia lawyers a debt of gratitude when they expose the loopholes and twists of the law. When that happens it is up to us to change the law. There is no lack of examples.

AUGUST 5

Damn the Torpedoes

This is the day in 1864 that David Farragut, commanding the U.S. naval forces at the battle of Mobile Bay in the Civil War, uttered the words that became one of America's most familiar slogans. Having made the decision to take his ships through a heavily mined channel, he issued terse instructions. In those years, underwater mines were known as torpedoes, and Farragut said, "Damn the torpedoes, full steam ahead!" I want you to know that in speaking frankly to you here today, I am taking Farragut's advice.

Marilyn Monroe

It was in 1962 on this day that Marilyn Monroe was found dead of an overdose of sleeping pills. In the album of movie stars, she will always be remembered as the golden glamor girl of her time. We remember her as she was, because she didn't live long enough to be anything else. It is the same way with our memories of former times. We have snapshots in our minds, not so much a continuous parade of memories as a set of pictures in the mind's eye. A picture of Marilyn Monroe reminds us that her time, compared to our own, was somehow naive and unsophisticated. What shocks one generation is apt to bore the next. And what we remember is apt to be the very good and the very bad rather than the whole uneven picture. That's why it is interesting to ask ourselves how we think we will remember the present time twenty years from now. Here is the way I think I will recall it.

Neil Armstrong

If anyone had told the parents of a baby boy who was born on this day in 1930 in Wapakoneta, Ohio, that someday he would walk on the moon, it would certainly not have been believed. That baby, of course, was Neil Armstrong, the astronaut who took that "one small step for a man." Similarly, it is difficult to predict what wonders the baby born today will explore in his or her turn. The pace of change in the world seems to quicken with every generation, and it is easier to predict new wonders than to envision solutions for the problems that have persisted through the centuries. Man has walked on the moon but still failed to stop the slum. We have probed the stars and been unable to insure peace on earth. We train and encourage people to do research in laboratories, but we seem unable to muster the same enthusiasm and brain resources for social problems. Today I want to talk about one of those problems that is crying out for new ideas.

State Fair Season

We are entering that time of year when state fairs blossom all over the map. Apart from the sporting events and the thrill shows, they represent recognition of achievements in some of the less glamorous areas—blue ribbons for the best tomatoes, or the best-bred pig, or the best recipe, and so forth. I think one of the reasons for the popularity of the state fair—or the county fair as well—is that it gives us ordinary people a chance to see how extraordinarily well some ordinary things can be done. One of the sad facts of life is that it is full of wonderful things done wonderfully well that get very little attention. Perhaps in my remarks here today I can focus a little more attention on some of these.

AUGUST 6

Ban the *World Almanac*

It was about this time in 1959 that the news broke of the Soviet Union's refusal to permit the display at the American Exposition in Moscow of a group of books including, if you please, the *World Almanac*. This was the same Exposition at which Richard Nixon and Nikita Khrushchev had had an impromptu discussion of the merits of their respective countries' ways of life a few days earlier. From our point of view, of course, the *World Almanac* is a book of facts, but the Russians have different versions of many of the same facts. What happened to the *World Almanac* is a good illustration of why relations with communism always pose difficulties. We do not view the real world in the same terms; we do not even have the same meanings for the same terms. Even within our own country we don't always agree on meanings. Welfare, for example, means different things to different people. But today I am going to talk about some matters whose meaning and whose importance are or should be equally clear to all of us.

Sir Alexander Fleming

Today is the birthday of Sir Alexander Fleming, the discoverer of penicillin and therefore in some ways the father of modern antibiotics. He was born in Scotland in 1881. The anniversary of his birth seems a fitting occasion to talk about some of the ills of our time for which we have not as yet found any miracle cures, and I have chosen one such problem as my subject here today.

Atom Bomb

It is important, I believe, for all of us to be mindful of the event that took place on this day in 1945, when the atomic bomb that hit Hiroshima, Japan, made the whole world aware of nuclear power and of its potential. We are still in disagreement about that incredible source of energy, and I don't propose to use this forum to heat up that disagreement. But it does seem to me that the atom bomb anniversary is a very good time to examine the prospects for a peaceful world, and that is what I want to do here today.

Voting Rights Act

Today is the anniversary of a milestone in American government. It was on this day in 1965 that President Lyndon B. Johnson signed the Voting Rights Act, the law that brought minority voters into the mainstream of American politics and self-government. It was still a long time before minority voters came to the polls in sufficient proportions to make their weight fully felt, but it marked the end of one all too common form of second-class citizenship by reason of race or inability to speak English. The Civil Rights Act certainly did not solve the problems of America, but it was a major step forward, and on its anniversary we might do well to consider what our generation can do that would be a similar accomplishment. May I speak to that point here today?

AUGUST 7

Ralph Bunche

Today is the birthday of Ralph Bunche, the black scholar who became one of the leading world figures of his time. Ralph Bunche was born in Detroit in 1904. He gained great distinction as a scholar before he entered the world of public affairs, with a doctorate from Harvard and work at major universities on three continents. In 1941, he joined the Office of Strategic Services in World War II and then transferred to the State Department. He resigned to become an official of the United Nations and served as the deputy to Count Folke Bernadotte, who was attempting in 1948 to mediate the Palestine issue. When the Count was assassinated, it was Ralph Bunche who worked out the armistice between the Jews and the Arabs. He won the Nobel Peace Prize, and then, as UN under-secretary general, carried out a series of major international assignments. He still found time to be a leader of the U.S. civil rights movement and in every way the proof that with people, as with milk, the cream will come to the top. At his death in 1971, he was mourned by the world. And on the anniversary of his birth it seems only appropriate that we should concern ourselves here today with what Ralph Bunche did so well—helping to provide a climate for peace.

Order of the Purple Heart

The Order of the Purple Heart was established on this day in 1782 by General George Washington as the first honor decoration for enlisted men in the military service. Originally awarded for, quote, "singularly meritorious action," it is now given in recognition of those wounded in action. The number of holders of Purple Heart awards, on that basis, is always too high. Unfortunately, we have no similar recognition for those who are wounded in the course of performing nonmilitary peacetime service, particularly when their wounds are psychological. And we have plenty of people with well-earned psychological wounds—teachers confronted by classrooms full of disciplinary problems, firefighters wearing themselves out answering false alarms and hopeless cases of arson, tenants' advocates confronting slumlords, and so forth. Today I want to talk about the causes of some of these psychlogical wounds and what we perhaps can do about them.

Whiskey Rebellion

This was the day when the newborn United States of America, with its Constitution less than seven years old, met its first important internal test. The Whiskey Rebellion, as it was called, broke out in Pennsylvania in protest against excise taxes on liquor. The insurrectionists gathered their forces to defy the government, but President George Washington on this day in 1794 ordered them to disperse and called for a force of militia from four states. It took a little while, but eventually the show of force took the starch out of the rebellion. The main result of the whole business was a strengthening of the power of the federal government at a time when the strength was going to be badly needed. So, in the long view of history, the Whiskey Rebellion accomplished something, even though it was not the result the insurrectionists had in mind. This kind of unforeseen result is characteristic of the history of this country. Our humiliation in the Iranian hostage situation ended up unifying the nation and rekindling the spirit of patriotism, which is not exactly what the Ayotollah had in mind. The reforms which John F. Kennedy might have had a hard time putting through were accomplished much more easily after his martyrdom. And I believe that now, as in the past, fate will lend a helping hand to some of our worthy causes. As a matter of fact, I have a little grab bag of things I'd like to see happen for various ulterior motives, and I'd like to share my list with you.

Revolving Door

It may come as a surprise to people who thought that the revolving door was always with us, but today is the anniversary of the granting of a patent for the first revolving door, invented in 1888 by a man with the impressive name of Theophilus Van Kannel of Pennsylvania. Since then, the term revolving door has become a quick and graphic description of various kinds of traffic. The revolving door in politics sees the same familiar people running for office time and again, going into office and leaving office but seemingly always available. The revolving door in economic theory sees the managed economy in this year, laissez faire the next year. The revolving door in fashion offers short skirts one year, long skirts the next. Today I want to speak about a topic, however, which is not traffic for the revolving door, because it is something that is always with us.

AUGUST 8

International Character Day

Today, August 8, was designated some years ago as International Character Day. Its purpose is described as recognition of good character. I find it interesting that when we say someone is a character it has nothing to do with goodness or badness but rather tends to describe someone who behaves or looks or thinks differently from the rest of us. A character is often someone way out of the mainstream. But character, in the better sense, doesn't mean being different. It means having recognizable attributes and forthright attitudes. Unfortunately, mass education and the peculiar values of mass publics tend to subdue character in too many people. We have all too many grays; all too many business graduates or doctors or even illiterates who think and react the same way and have the same goals and the same prejudices. Peer pressure in an age of conformism deprives us of a lot of the characters we have a right to expect. I am not here to conduct a recruiting drive for eccentricity, but I would like to take this occasion to challenge some of the ideas that are depriving us of the full benefits of a humanistic community of individuals.

Davis Cup

The first international match for the Davis Cup in tennis was held on this date in 1900, when the United States and Great Britain met in Boston. Very few international sports rivalries have continued as long or done as much to promote international awareness. Somehow when a country produces great tennis players it becomes a member of a different sector of the world community. Tennis is no longer exclusively a gentleman's game, but it is far more of a universal language. So, using that vernacular, let us serve up and see how the ball bounces.

Klan March in Washington

In 1925, the United States was enjoying prosperity marred only by the gangsterism that flourished in the Prohibition age. Yet on this day in that year in the capital of the nation the Ku Klux Klan staged a public march. Thousands of them paraded down Pennsylvania Avenue in their hooded robes. It was perhaps the most insolent gesture of its time in America, for the Klan stood foursquare for racial and religious hatred, taking the law into one's own hands, and making a mockery of the Constitution. I am happy to agree that in the intervening years the Klan has never been able to muster anything like that number of demonstrators—and I hope they never will. But when I realize that in our own time an out-and-out Nazi, parading the hateful swastika symbol, has won thousands of votes in a congressional district election—although nowhere nearly enough to elect him—I have to face the fact that there are always too many people who love to hate. Are we in this country too tolerant of intolerance? Are we sufficiently aroused by smearings on walls, overturned tombstones, vandalized places of worship and all of the other hateful symptoms of bigotry on the march?

Mimeograph

Among Thomas A. Edison's inventions was the process we know as mimeographing, which he first patented on this date in 1876. The mimeograph introduced us to the golden age of press agentry, when a news release could be reproduced in any office on a convenient machine and distributed to editors and newspapers immediately. The later development of the copying machine has only made the paper blizzard worse. When you consider that this explosion has been accompanied by the development of multichannel radio and television, it begins to appear that the problem is not finding people with something to say but finding anybody to listen. That in itself would be reason enough for me to be grateful to you for listening to me here today. Now I hope you find the listening worthwhile.

AUGUST 9

John Dryden

John Dryden, the great English writer who was born on this day in 1631, had among his works this simple verse: "But far more numerous was the herd of such/Who think too little and who talk too much." I have been thinking very carefully about what I wanted to say here today, and I hope that one of the results will be that at least I won't talk too much.

Sleepy Time

One of today's historic birthdays is that of William T. G. Morton, who was born in Massachusetts in 1819. You may not recognize his name, but you will certainly recognize his contribution to civilization. Morton was the dentist who introduced the anesthetic known as ether. By enabling surgeons to put people to sleep and awaken them with no lasting effects, he made possible a new era of surgery. On the birthday of the man who found a new way to put people to sleep, I shall try very hard with my comments to keep you all wide awake.

Walden

Henry Thoreau's great book *Walden (Life in the Woods)* was published on this day in 1854 and has charmed nature lovers ever since. Thoreau preferred the miracles of nature to the problems of humanity, but there aren't too many oases like Walden Pond in our modern world, and even nature is being confronted with manmade crises. Today, with a wistful backward glance at a more peaceful time in the past, I ask you to join me in looking at some situations Henry D. Thoreau never dreamed of.

Jesse Owens

On this day in 1936, bigotry took it on the chin. At the Olympic Games held in the bastion of Nazi race hatred—Berlin—a black American athlete, Jesse Owens, became the first person ever to win four Olympic gold medals, in the track competition. The racist theories of the Nazis never looked sillier. Unfortunately, wrong and evil ideas are not always quite as effectively confounded as that. Sometimes it takes discussion, persuasion, and even a degree of eloquence. I can't run like Jesse Owens, so I will have to take the road of talk, and here I go.

AUGUST 10

E Pluribus Unum

Along about this time in 1776, three members of the Continental Congress who had been part of the committee that produced the Declaration of Independence made another suggestion. This time John Adams, Benjamin Franklin, and Thomas Jefferson were the members of the committee to find a slogan for the new union of the states. They suggested a three-word Latin phrase, *e pluribus unum,* one out of many, a terse description of the nature of the new country. One notable aspect of great men like Adams, Franklin, and Jefferson is that they didn't waste time or phrases when they had something important to say. I can't hope to be as concise as they were in concocting their national slogan, but, like them, let me get right to the point.

Herbert Hoover

Today is the birthday of Herbert Hoover, who was born in Iowa in 1874 and had the misfortune to be President of the United States during the Great Depression. Hoover came to prominence as the nation's food and overseas relief administrator in World War I, and then, years after his unhappy presidency, regained popular esteem as the head of the Hoover Commission, which provided plans for the reorganization of the executive branch of the federal government. It was said of Herbert Hoover that he wasn't too great a president but he made a wonderful senior statesman. Each of us has abilities and failings, and the trick is to find work that utilizes the pluses and is not affected by the minuses. A public speaker usually winds up in the position of the latter-day Hoover rather than the Hoover in the White House. The speaker is expected to make suggestions but not to *do* anything. So, in that role of grandstand quarterback, I stand before you.

FDR's Polio

In August of 1921, Franklin D. Roosevelt was vacationing on Campobello Island when he became ill. It turned out that he had the crippling disease of polio. He was never able to walk again, and yet it was after years of pain and suffering with this dread ailment that he attained his greatness as a president and wartime leader. The anniversary of his misfortune comes as a timely reminder to us that crises do not necessarily destroy people; sometimes a crisis brings out the best in us, perhaps even better than we ever thought we could do. So my message today is not one of pointing with alarm but rather of hope and high expectations.

Greenwich Time

On this day in the year 1675, work began on the construction of the Royal Observatory at Greenwich, England, which became the starting point for the standardization of time around the world. I hope that as I address you here today we are all in the same timeframe, and while I don't expect to race the clock I will make every effort not to squander your time and my own.

AUGUST 11

SOS

The first American SOS signal at sea was radioed on this date in 1909 by the liner *Arapahoe*, which needed help off the North Carolina coast. A new way of appealing for help was born. Since then, the air has been full of SOS signals. I don't think that means people are in more trouble than ever; I prefer to believe it means people who never had any hope of help before now think they have a chance. That, my friends, is the best sign that we are making progress. We see so much misery and challenge around us that we sometimes forget how far we have come. There are too many people on relief, but a couple of generations ago there was no relief. We have terrible slums, but we had more of them in 1920. We haven't conquered disease, but we can cure illnesses that were sure tickets to death a couple of generations ago. Yes, new problems arise; we reap the dubious rewards of the pollution our predecessors unknowingly perpetrated; we are saddled with national debts they incurred. But we have knowledge and opportunities they didn't have, and our challenge is to put that knowledge to work.

Mr. Justice Holmes

When President Theodore Roosevelt nominated Oliver Wendell Holmes Jr. to the Supreme Court on this day in 1902, Holmes was 61 years old. Nobody would have dreamed that he would serve on the Court for 30 years, but he did and, of course, with great distinction. We cannot let averages and statistics rule us. To have deprived the country and the Supreme Court of the wisdom of Justice Holmes because he was already near the normal close of an active career would have been a tremendous loss. Now, not every person has the longevity or the intellect of Holmes, and people who cling to positions of importance as their capacities decline will always be a problem. I have no easy solution. I don't think an arbitrary age for retirement is a solution, and I don't think that permitting everybody to stay on in the same job as long as they want is a solution either. Perhaps what we need is a more productive alternative to retirement—a better way of using the wisdom and the talents of older people so that they aren't faced with working hard one day and being totally idle the next. Thanks to medical science, people are living longer, and we have to face the fact and decide where we go from here.

Andrew Carnegie

On this day in 1919, Andrew Carnegie, the man who showed the world how to give money away, died at his home in Lenox, Massachusetts. For the last ten years of his life, this multimillionaire had devoted himself exclusively to philanthropy and the cause of peace. In a time when the dollar was worth a good deal more than it is today, he gave away some $350 million. Carnegie believed strongly, with good reason, in the capitalistic system and the idea of individual enterprise. But he also believed that those who made fortunes had the duty of helping the general welfare. He wrote of the millionaire that—quote— "the man who dies thus rich dies disgraced." Very few of us are Andrew Carnegies, but by the same token very few of us are unable in our own small way to do in our lifetimes what he did in his—namely, to give of our substance to help the unfortunate. With that in mind let us look at some of the immediate needs.

Gifford Pinchot

I doubt that there are many people in this audience who will recognize the name of Gifford Pinchot, who was born on this day in 1865 in Simsbury,

Connecticut, but we are all his beneficiaries. Pinchot was the pioneer of forest conservation in the United States, first as head of the forestry activities of the Department of Agriculture and then as head of various conservation groups. Views that we take for granted today have often started with a handful of dedicated people like Gifford Pinchot and slowly gained adherents. It isn't always easy to be one of those dedicated people, and we all have a tendency to become impatient with crusaders, but they serve an important function in a healthy society, and today I'd like to look at a sample of our modern gadflies.

AUGUST 12

First Police

Some historians mark this date as the anniversary of the establishment in 1658 of the first police force in America, the group of men who constituted the watch in New Amsterdam. In the early days of this country keeping the peace internally was less of a problem than guarding against outside attacks, whether from hostile Indians or other European powers, so police functions were apt to be minor sidelines for the armed forces, such as they were. Today the situation is rather different. The threat to our safety and peace from other nations is still a possibility, but the threat internally from crime is very real and all-pervasive. As the conveniences and comforts of everyday life have increased so have the dangers. And while the wealthy are troubled by crime, it is the poor who are the principal victims. There are only a limited number of ways of coping with this problem, particularly in a country with a tradition of civil liberty. And I rise here today to urge that we not fall into the trap of fighting crime by tampering with our civil liberty.

Soviet H-Bomb

It was on this day in 1953 that the nuclear standoff became a fact. U.S. monitoring revealed that the Soviet Union had exploded an H-bomb. Russia itself said nothing about the test for more than a week and finally announced it on August 20, without indicating the exact date. The contrast between communist secrecy and American openness was never more dramatic, for the whole world had known about and witnessed, through news coverage, the hydrogen bomb testing the United States had conducted in the Pacific. The passion for secrecy is characteristic of communism. Coincidentally, today is also the anniversary of the building of the wall in communist East Berlin in 1961. I can understand why a dictatorship doesn't want its operations exposed to public view. And for that very reason I think it is important to keep the operations of a free society open to public view. I think it is important for us to be aware of conflicting ideas, to hear all sides of important controversies, and to make up our own minds. On that basis, I am here to present an admittedly personal viewpoint.

Julius Rosenwald

If a man named Julius Rosenwald had not been born on this day in 1862 in Springfield, Illinois, a great American way of doing business might not exist. Rosenwald was the man who built the mail-order business known as Sears Roebuck, from which he made enough money to become one of the great American philanthropists. It was he who proved that you could sell a huge volume of merchandise through the mail, and although I am not sure that is an unmixed blessing in our own time it made things a great deal easier for countless farm families. Today, of course, with the farm population shrinking, the major Sears business is in department stores rather than mail order, but mail-order catalogues are still a distinctive part of the American way of life. One thing that Julius Rosenwald proved is that you can establish lasting relationships through the mails—a fact political parties and causes have jumped on with a vengeance in recent years. We are assailed as never before with pitches for this and spiels for that, seemingly personal appeals from famous people, endorsements from impressive letterhead lists of celebrities. I appear before you today unaccompanied by any such fancy dressing, hoping rather to speak to you simply as person to person.

Christy Mathewson

In the legendary halls of baseball the name of Christy Mathewson looms very large indeed. The great pitcher of the old New York Giants was born on this day in 1880 in Pennsylvania. Before he died tragically of tuberculosis after having been gassed in World War I, he had been the victor in 372 major league ball games and had struck out 2,499 batters. He was good-looking and was one of the first college men to become a professional baseball player, truly a golden boy of his time. I find myself wondering what would have happened to Christy Mathewson if he were in his prime today. I am sure he would have had an agent to negotiate a fabulous baseball salary, but that would have been only the beginning. He would be making millions on endorsements, perhaps doing advertising tie-ins on television, maybe with his good looks even becoming a movie star. For a baseball player or any athlete the opportunities are greater today than ever before. But what about the kid who wants to be a teacher, or a salesperson?

AUGUST 13

Lefthanders Day

One of the more lefthanded observances in this country is an event on this day called Lefthanders Day. As many lefthanders will gladly tell you, they are in many ways the most curiously oppressed minority in the land. Who else, for example, is discriminated against in the arrangement of the average place setting? Or by the arrangement of the gear shift on an American car? Somehow, despite these handicaps, lefthanders have survived and prospered. I am not being facetious in discussing this subject. I think it illustrates quite well how, without much effort, you can find discrimination against this or that group of people, often not intended. Those who speak of stamping out discrimination are talking of the impossible. The challenge to us is not to abolish discrimination—any more than we can abolish crime—but to turn it upon the perpetrators. The best way to do that is to try harder, to fight back, when you are discriminated against—not simply to complain about it but to do something, to succeed in spite of it, to join forces with other victims of discrimination to overpower the discriminators. One of the principal ways to do that is to close ranks with those who believe as you do. Many of us pride ourselves on not being joiners, but there are times when we should, indeed, must join together in a common cause. It is to that purpose that I address you here today.

Annie Oakley

Annie Oakley, the most famous lady sharpshooter of all time, was born on this day in 1860 on a farm in Ohio. As a star of Buffalo Bill's Wild West Show she amazed the world with her markmanship. Like Annie Oakley I have some targets today, but I don't plan to use any guns. Instead I will shoot off my mouth.

Man o' War

On this day in 1919, the great racehorse Man o' War ran the only race he didn't win, proving that even the greatest of champions isn't always at his best. That is a fact we sometimes forget about our own government. It took us a long time to get over our failure to win in Vietnam, and we seem to spend countless hours worrying whether we or some foreign government did better in the latest international negotiation, wherever and whatever it may happen to have been. Competitive spirit is a fine and constructive thing, but it can be carried to extremes, and the current sparring in Washington over some of our policies is a good example. We should not care whether the Democrats or the Republicans deserve the credit for the good or the blame for the bad half as much as the two parties would like us to. We should be considering individuals' performances rather than thinking either party is a monolith of consistent and unanimous policy. Let me give you some examples.

Lucy Stone

Today is the birthday of Lucy Stone, who was born in West Brookfield, Massachusetts, in 1818 and became one of the great early leaders of the women's rights movement. It is interesting that the right for which Lucy Stone became famous—keeping her own name after she married—has probably been the most widely accepted practice. Even the most ardent opponents of the equal rights amendment recognized women such as Jane Fonda by their own names rather than their married ones. The burning issues of one generation sometimes turn out to be no issues at all in the next—whether to have Medicare or a Social Security system, for example. Today I would like to talk about a currently controversial subject I think will cease to be controversial in our lifetimes—the subject of women's rights.

AUGUST 14

Krafft-Ebing

It has been said of Richard von Krafft-Ebing, the German physician who was born on this day in 1840, that if he were alive today he would see his craft ebbing. That's because he was a pioneer in the study of sexual disorders, and that is one field where we seem to know less and less—or at least to know that some of the things we thought were facts are now in doubt. We can't agree about homosexualism, we don't even agree about what constitutes perversion, and we certainly have no great track record in treating and curing those sexual deviates who constitute a violent menace to society. This is just one more illustration of the incontrovertible fact that the more we know, the more we see how much we do not know. Life is no sure thing, yet we seem to expect a better-than-life performance from government, from science, from education, from everybody but ourselves, and so we feel let down when the performance is merely passable. I am not here to start a revolution of lowered expectations, but I do rise to suggest that we are doing as well as can be expected over the long haul, and I'd like to tell you how and why.

Social Security

Today is the anniversary of the adoption of the Social Security Act in 1935, providing old-age and unemployment insurance for Americans. There is another form of social security, which involves the privilege of meeting and talking with people. You have given me that form of social security here today by asking me to talk to you, and I am happy and privileged to accept the invitation and embrace the opportunity.

William Randolph Hearst

When William Randolph Hearst died on this day in 1951, he was 88 years old and the times had passed him by. He had been a major figure in the rise of what its critics regarded as yellow journalism, the founder of a great publishing empire, an early motion picture producer, and a flamboyant millionaire whose California ranch is still one of the spectacular sights of the West. He transported ancient tombs, mummies, monasteries, and chateaux from far corners of the earth to be reassembled here and never did get around to putting it all together again. We have had rich collectors since Hearst, but the times make his sort of extravagance a lot more difficult today, even though various oil sheikhs have been known to spend their money on some incredible purchases. Today's multi-millionaires in general, however, prefer not to have the spotlight on their extravagances. Nevertheless, we live in an age of incredible extravagance, and I should like to examine part of it.

Land Offering

On this day in 1776, the Continental Congress, which a month before had proclaimed the Declaration of Independence, tried a nonviolent tactic for weakening the British forces. The Congress passed an act offering American citizenship and fifty acres of land to any deserter from the British and Hessian forces. I cannot tell you how many soldiers, if any, took advantage of the offer, but certainly it was not enough to weaken King George's forces. Bribery, whether on an individual basis or by one nation toward another—when it is called appeasement—doesn't usually work. There is another form of bribery—that is, bribing an audience to applaud you by telling them what you know they want to hear. But what I am about to say is being said because I believe it is important, not simply to please you.

AUGUST 15

Sir Walter Scott

The birthday of Sir Walter Scott, the writer who was born in Edinburgh on this day in 1771, brings me several reminders of the diverse sources of what we call typically American. For example, when in our skepticism we advise somebody to "tell it to the Marines" we are actually quoting Sir Walter Scott. In his book *Redgauntlet,* vintage 1824, appear the lines "Tell that to the marines—the sailors won't believe it." And when an armed forces band salutes the President of the United States by playing "Hail to the Chief," they are playing music set to words by the same Scottish writer, Sir Walter Scott. We have a tendency to think that the things we do or say are typically American, when in fact they are often universal. We are surprised when other nations resent our suggestions, and we are insulted when they make suggestions to us. We complain that other people don't know enough about us and persist for our part in not knowing enough about them. Perhaps we should take a look at what is happening overseas to get closer to our own problems.

T. E. Lawrence

T. E. Lawrence was born in 1888 in the United Kingdom on this day, but when we think of him these days we remember him as Lawrence of Arabia, the legendary hero who rallied the Arabs to the Allied cause in World War I. Lawrence became so disgusted with the way the postwar world was shaping up that he retreated into deliberate obscurity. A lot of us, who don't start off with credentials quite as impressive as Lawrence's, are tempted to have the same reaction to our world today and retreat into our own private pursuits. But it becomes more difficult all the time to maintain that privacy. Between the tax collectors and the friendly neighbors, the world is always with us. And it is a world that is still full of opportunities over the long haul. It is a world that, for all the modern improvements, still can challenge and discourage you if you let it. But above all, it is a world which isn't finished, a world which, working together, we can still change for the better. Today I'd like to talk about some of the possibilities.

India

On this day in 1947, India became a free nation in the British Commonwealth. For years now it has prided itself on being the largest democracy in the world. From our vantage point on the other side of the globe we have seen plenty of flaws in India's democracy, including its insistence on Third World status apart from the other great democracies of the world. That is part of our intrinsic feeling, perhaps a heritage of our frontier days, that if you're not with us you're against us. There seems to be a tendency to apply that same attitude to party membership. Periodically I read about how one political party or another has a faction trying to purge it of people who are not on the same wavelength as that faction. They urge you to vote against this or that person because he or she is not a "real" Republican or not a "real" Democrat. I deplore this kind of effort to impose a loyalty test. This is not a world which we can arbitrarily people only with folks who think exactly the way we do. A good deal of life is spent meeting others halfway, and that is what I am here to advocate with regard to some specifics.

Napoleon's Birthday

Today is the birthday of Napoleon Bonaparte, who was born in Corsica in 1769. Napoleon proved that being short was no obstruction to going far, and so I will try to keep my remarks short here today, in the hope, of course, that my message will go far.

AUGUST 16

Bennington Battle Day

Today is Bennington Battle Day, commemorating a battle fought in 1777 in the American Revolution. The Battle of Bennington, which is commemorated in Vermont, was actually fought on land between Hoosick Falls, New York, and Bennington. It was part of the Saratoga campaign; the Americans won both the Bennington battle and the large encounter at Saratoga. In 1982, 195 years after the battle, a reporter finally got around to asking the people of Hoosick Falls whether they felt that history had cheated them of a portion of fame, and they seemed to be quite calm about the whole thing. Americans in general are not glory or headline hunters, even in terms of past events. We are more oriented to results than to monuments, although our politicians have been known to think of various programs as monuments to themselves. In that sense, Social Security is a monument to Franklin D. Roosevelt, and the breakthrough to everyday relations with Red China one of the more constructive monuments to Richard Nixon. It is interesting to apply this sort of test to current office-holders and ask ourselves what seem to be their monuments.

Death of Elvis Presley

America's taste in heroes is rather strange. Today is the anniversary of the sad death of one of the popular idols of our time, Elvis Presley. Long after his singing had won him fame and adulation, Presley grew fat and addicted to drugs, but his fans remained loyal even after the sordid details of his last years were widely publicized. We do not choose our heroes necessarily wisely, and we can turn on them unpredictably, but our loyalty to fallen idols is a thing of wonder. We are ambiguous. We tolerate all kinds of antisocial behavior in our favorite performers, and we throw the book at people in other walks of life who do the same things. We are living with all sorts of double standards—softer on white-collar crime than on blue-collar, tougher on welfare than on tax shelters, opposed to government subsidies but always willing to say our own enterprise is a special case, and so forth. The genius of America is that with all these contradictions we still manage to make our country work. But we can certainly find ways to make it work better, and I have a few suggestions.

Surrender of Detroit

This the anniversary of an event that, thank goodness, does not happen very often in American history. General William Hull surrendered the city of Detroit to the British without a fight in 1812. He was court-martialed and sentenced to death for cowardice, but the sentence was suspended because of his fine military record in the American Revolutionary War. We do not have many other cases of Americans surrendering without a fight, and it is well to bear that in mind when we become discouraged over such perennial problems as crime and poverty. So let us talk about the good fight.

Siamese Twins

It was on this day in 1829 in Boston that America first saw a new wonder imported from Siam. The wonder was a set of twins who were joined at the waist. Since they came from Siam they became known as "the Siamese Twins," and the name has been applied to all similarly joined humans in the world since then. Modern science can find ways these days to separate Siamese twins, and we don't hesitate to use medical skills for that purpose. We are far less willing to separate what I call the psychological Siamese twins of modern life. One such pair are crime and education. In hard times particularly, taxpayers are inclined to couple them this way: if we have to spend more money fighting crime, we'll just have to spend less on education. I rise here today to speak in behalf of the view that better education is one of the best ways of fighting crime. Let me tell you why.

AUGUST 17

Balloon Crossing

On this day in 1978, three Americans in a balloon landed in France after floating in the air across the Atlantic from Presque Isle, Maine. In some ways it was the most impressive performance ever by a windbag. While I may indulge in some flights of fancy here today, I hope you will not consider me a windbag, and the best way to avoid that fate is to get right down to business.

Self-Starter

The first commercially practical self-starter for automobiles was patented by Charles F. Kettering on this day in 1915. Until Kettering's device went into use, you started a car by cranking it, and the crank was not always easy to handle. Today, unfortunately, some of our human self-starters are also cranks; it is very easy to become a crank on a subject about which you care deeply. Today, however, my concern is not with starting but rather with stopping in time, so I shall be mindful that it is your time as well as mine and try to use it sparingly.

Chicken-Cooking Contest

This is the time of year when the National Chicken-Cooking Contest comes tastefully on the scene, when finalists from all states compete in preparing good eating from broiler–fryer chickens. We may be a beef-eating people, but our lives center around our fowl friends. Herbert Hoover rued the day he promised a chicken in every pot, all of us remember the time-honored warning against putting all our eggs in one basket, and, in keeping with the chicken theme, I'd like to take this occasion to crow about something.

Hiss and Chambers

It was on this day in 1948 in a hotel room in New York where the House Un-American Activities Committee was holding a hearing on the accusations against Alger Hiss, that Hiss came face-to-face with his accuser, Whittaker Chambers. It was the dramatic beginning of a case that people debated for more than thirty years. Not all history is the product of confrontations, spectacular though they may be. Today I'd like to talk about some history that is being made quietly.

AUGUST 18

Soap Box Derby

This is the season of the great Soap Box Derby. It began as a challenge to the ingenuity and agility of young people and faced its own greatest challenge when a father or two decided to try to soup up the home-built vehicles in violation of the existing rules. By all accounts that period is now behind us and we are again letting the law of gravity furnish the power for the wheels. The only place where the law of gravity does not apply when we get together is, of course, a speechmaking occasion. Although I expect to make some serious points today I am mindful that too much gravity gets you down hard. And I would rather have you up for my remarks.

Meriwether Lewis

In 1774 on this day, a man named Meriwether Lewis was born in Albemarle County, Virginia. He served in the Army for a couple of years and in 1801 became secretary to President Thomas Jefferson. Later he served as governor of the Louisiana Territory. But none of these posts put his name in the history books as lastingly or as prominently as his leadership of the Lewis and Clark expedition that explored and mapped the great American West. The expedition lasted more than three years and became one of the great human adventures of all time. Several years later, when Lewis was on his way to Washington to try to get the government to pay some outstanding bills, he died mysteriously near Nashville, Tennessee. It was a tragic ending to an amazing career and a reminder that even at the height of success we are all vulnerable one way or another. It is this sense of vulnerability that persuades some people that the way to make your voice heard is to scare people. Tell them what awful things are going to happen if they don't listen to you. Describe the dire consequences that lie ahead. To this I say no thanks. Others may say the bottle is half empty. I prefer to say it is half full and see how we can make it fuller. Today I propose to look forward to things worth looking forward to.

Woman's Suffrage

On this day in 1920, the state of Tennessee became the thirty-sixth to ratify the Nineteenth Amendment, giving women the right to vote. The Amendment went into effect eight days later. It was the culmination of a struggle that had begun generations earlier, but the Amendment itself had passed Congress only the year before. That is often the case with long efforts at reform; they seem to take forever to get started, and then suddenly the logjam breaks up and quick action is taken. The American public is essentially conservative and resistant to fundamental change, but once the public is convinced, the message gets through to our representatives without too much further delay. Today, therefore, I'd like to talk about some of the messages our representatives ought to be getting now.

Merchandising Candidates

Adlai Stevenson had already been through one losing presidential election campaign and was on the threshhold of another when he made an observation on this day in 1956. "The idea that you can merchandise candidates for high office like breakfast cereal," he said, "is, I think, the ultimate indignity to the democratic process." That ultimate indignity proceeded to get worse. We have developed a group of advertising specialists who excel in "packaging" candidates. We have seen election campaigns in which every view, every remark of a candidate was fashioned by these merchandising geniuses, and we have, unfortunately, seen some of these synthetic statesmen get elected. It seems to me that one way to avoid this kind of spurious selling is to take a harder look at the real issues that confront us.

AUGUST 19

Midget at the Bat

It was in 1951, in the middle of the major league baseball season, that the St. Louis Browns introduced the most startling player ever to come to bat in the major leagues. His name was Eddie Gaedel, and in his only major league appearance he walked on four straight balls. This wasn't surprising, because

Eddie Gaedel was a midget, well under four feet tall. They hastily changed the rules after his single appearance. Human ingenuity being what it is, people can always be relied on to find a loophole or a strange twist in most any rule, given enough time and opportunity. That is why we have to keep on making new laws and revising old ones. The law is not simply a set of dusty volumes on the shelf; it is a living thing, a changing thing subject to new interpretations and new times. And in life as in baseball, every now and then somebody slips a midget into the lineup, or tries to. Laws don't always work the way we expect them to; when that happens, it is time for a change—and it is time for a change right now.

Bennett's Blues

"Books have had their day," a great editor said, "the theaters have had their day—the temple of religion has had its day." Close quote. Looking at the world today, one has to ask whether that editor's verdict was correct. The editor was James Gordon Bennett, and he made his remark a long, long time ago—on this day in 1836, to be precise. In every generation there are those who see us going to pieces. It is rather like predicting that life is fatal. Some people are constantly looking for Armageddon around the corner. I am not. I am not here to warn of doomsday coming or to deplore the sad state of the human condition. I think we have some of the greatest opportunities ever given to humankind if we can only take advantage of them. That is the thrust of my remarks here today.

Daguerre

This is the anniversary of a great medium of communication. On this day in 1839, the process devised by Louis Daguerre for recording actual scenes on chemically treated plates was described to the French Academy of Sciences. It was the beginning of photography. Since then the world has been moved on many occasions by photographs that spoke far more eloquently than the printed page, and history has become far more vivid and real to us. But there are some things that defy the camera—ideas that are hard to paint in photographic images. It is some of those ideas that I want to talk about to you here today.

National Aviation Day

When Wilbur Wright was born on this day in 1871 in Dayton, Ohio, he could not have foreseen that his birthday would be observed as National Aviation Day in honor of the flying machine that he and his brother Orville invented. On National Aviation Day, even if I am not flying, I hope you decide that what I have to say is right—as right as Wilbur and Orville.

AUGUST 20

Exit Trotsky

It was on this day in 1940 that the long arm of Communist Party terror reached out to eliminate Leon Trotsky, the exiled Russian bolshevik, at his home in Mexico City. It was a classic example of the kind of terrorism that communism and its allies have sadly made all too commonplace in the world today. The world unfortunately has more than its share of people whose purpose in life is to make trouble. We used to think that this was a foreign weakness to which we Americans were immune, but the killing of innocent people, the holding of hostages, the idea of ransom have all left their mark upon our peaceful scene as well as overseas. What is incredible is that there are governments that encourage and give sanctuary to this kind of antisocial criminal. Yet the nations of the world continue to do business with these outlaw regimes. Do we really have to do business with them?

The Mikado

On this day in 1885, an American audience for the first time saw and heard a performance of *The Mikado,* Gilbert and Sullivan's great operetta. You may recall that one of the songs in *The Mikado* calls for having the punishment fit the crime. In 1885, we were assured that that objective would be achieved in time—but it hasn't happened yet. For one reason or another the punishments meted out these days are so inadequate to the crimes that prison is pretty much of a revolving door. I don't believe things have to be that way if we are willing to do something about it.

Owed to So Few

It was on this day in 1940, at the height of the Royal Air Force's defense of England against Nazi bombers, that Winston Churchill spoke those notable words: "Never in the field of human conflict was so much owed by so many to so few." It was indeed a gallant moment in British history, but it also marked the end of the kind of war that was fought by a relative handful of men in uniform. Soon the aerial bombing of London became fiercer, and the war was fought on the shattered streets with civilians as the targets. Thereafter, despite the frontal encounters on the beaches and in the hedgerows, there has been no safety for civilians in war. We fought in Vietnam without facing attack on our homefront, but we know that in any future conflict every city and every small town can be part of the front line. Given that inescapable fact we must do everything we can do to see that there is no war. And there is a great deal we can do.

Red Takeover

Shortly before midnight on this day in 1968, troops of the Soviet Union moved into Czechoslovakia and took control of that country, to stamp out the trend toward personal freedom in that unfortunate nation. The world, which might have become accustomed to Soviet takeovers by then, was nevertheless shocked by the naked show of force Russia employed on this occasion. This has been the history of communism. Just when you think it is learning how to act decently in the family of nations, it becomes impatient and shows its true colors. You can always detect those true colors, no matter how many smoke-screens are thrown up. Today I'd like to talk about the telltale indicators.

AUGUST 21

Nat Turner's Rebellion

On this day in 1831, a slave named Nat Turner began what he hoped would be a general insurrection against slavery in Southampton County, Virginia. At least 50 whites and many blacks were killed before Nat Turner's Rebellion was put down, and its leader was hanged in November of that same year. It is well to remember that the victims of slavery did not always passively accept their sad fate, and it is comforting for modern Americans to realize that in our time no American is barred from recourse to the courts when he or she is the victim of injustice. Every American has the right to be heard. We certainly have not ended injustice or the other social ills of humanity, but we don't have to be afraid to talk about them and to sound the battle cry for a better world. Today, in a small way, I raise my voice for that purpose.

American Bar Association

Today is the birthday of a great professional organization, the American Bar Association, which was organized in 1878 in Saratoga, New York. One of the important roles of the Bar Association is to maintain a set of standards for the practice of law. It isn't easy to maintain standards in any field, particularly when those standards sometimes seem to give more leeway to defense of the unpopular, but a society without adequate standards is a society heading for trouble. Indeed, looking beyond the legal fraternity to the broader picture of American society today, I find myself wondering whether we have set our standards sufficiently high and whether we are even maintaining the standards we have set. So today, rather than looking at laws or legal procedures, I want to consider, with you, the basic norms by which we seem to be living.

Casey at the Bat

We are told that on this day in 1887 a baseball player named Dan Casey, a pitcher for the Philadelphia Phillies, struck out in a game with the New York Giants. What made this strikeout different is that it was supposed to have inspired Ernest L. Thayer's classic poem "Casey at the Bat." Eloquent words can make a routine occurrence immortal, but not even prosaic words can dim the luster of great events. I have the advantage today of talking about a subject that is very close to all your hearts. That fact makes me hopeful that my words will be adequate to the occasion.

Lincoln–Douglas Debates

Today is the anniversary of the start of one of the great events of American political history, the Lincoln–Douglas debates of 1858 in Illinois. The first of those debates was held on this day in Ottawa, Illinois. To speak on the anniversary of that great series of speeches has to give a modern speaker a qualm or two. I cannot hope to match the eloquence of Honest Abe and the Little Giant. But I welcome the opportunity to give you my views here today, and I am glad that neither Lincoln nor Douglas is waiting to answer.

AUGUST 22

Arnold's Trick

On this day in 1777, a master of deceit won a victory for the United States in the American Revolution without firing a shot. The author of this particular victory was General Benedict Arnold, whose command was ordered to recapture Fort Stanwix in upper New York State from a combined Indian and British force. Arnold sent a prisoner back to the fort with certain specific instructions. When the Indians asked the prisoner how many men were in General Arnold's force, the prisoner pointed to the leaves on the trees. The Indians, deciding they were outnumbered, abandoned the fort, and the British left with them. Sometimes, particularly during the height or depth of a political campaign, I get the impression that a lot of politicians are playing Benedict Arnold's Fort Stanwix game, making things sound worse than they are so we will think we need those politicians more than we actually do. Somehow there is always much more to be gained by telling people how bad things are than by telling them how good they are. Bad news gets more attention. But I will not use that device to get your attention here today.

Taft's Law

When President William Howard Taft in 1911 sent a vetoed bill back to Congress on this day because he thought it was unconstitutional, he made a comment that is worth repeating to every new generation. "Constitutions," he said, "are checks upon the hasty action of a majority." I think this is a point some of us forget. We start demanding that the Constitution be revised because it stands in the way of what we want, forgetting that, as President Taft pointed out, that is often precisely what the Constitution is for. This is not merely for the purpose of obstructionism. It is designed to insure that basic laws have to represent more than the will of a simple majority of the people. That is because this country has a long tradition of protecting the interests of minorities as well as majorities. We do not and must not change our basic law to diminish anybody's rights. I view current proposed amendments from that point of view, and that brings me to certain basic positions I should like to share with you.

America's Cup

When the American sailing yacht *America* won a silver trophy in a race at Cowes, England, on this day in 1851, it was the start of one of the longest traditions in sports history. In honor of the winning vessel, the trophy was named the America's Cup. It has been the focus of yacht racing ever since. The pursuit of excellence, whether in sport or in everyday life, is a continuing challenge to people in all walks of life. In good times and bad we keep asking ourselves how we can do better. When I ask myself that question I come up with some theories I'd like to share with you.

Mona Lisa

In 1911 on this day, one of the most famous paintings in the world, Leonardo DaVinci's *Mona Lisa,* was stolen from the Louvre in Paris. It was recovered two years later from a thief who apparently just wanted to have it—not for ransom but just to enjoy it for himself. Sometimes we forget that there need not be societal causes for criminality; pure selfishness or a desire to live dangerously and outwit the establishment can motivate some spectacular crimes. Curing the ills of society will still not prevent this kind of law breaking. It is a sad fact that we will always need security guards and penal institutions and that, as our population grows, we will need more of them. Although we may deplore the expansion of governmental services, we must realize that in some areas this growth is inevitable. With that perspective, perhaps we may be able to plan public financing with a little more foresight.

AUGUST 23

Oliver Hazard Perry

Today is the birthday of Oliver Hazard Perry, who was born in 1785 in South Kingston, Rhode Island. He was in command of the American naval force on the Great Lakes in the War of 1812, and his victory at Lake Erie, signaled by the famous message, "We have met the enemy and they are ours," made that frontier safe for the United States. It is interesting that we remember Oliver Hazard Perry for his message about meeting the enemy rather than simply for his victory. We remember slogans and labels even when we are not clear about what they stand for. In the height of the argument over so-called supply economics it was hard to get a definition that even its advocates would agree upon. And right now we have some labels, maybe even buzzwords, that mean different things to different people. I'd like to talk about some of these here today.

William Ernest Henley

William Ernest Henley, the British poet who was born on this day in 1849, was the author of some of the most-quoted lines in English literature, including "My head is bloody but unbowed" and "I am the master of my fate:/I am the captain of my soul." He lived in a time when those noble sentiments were accepted unquestioningly. Today we are bombarded with suggestions that we are the hapless pawns of forces beyond our control, to the point where I believe it is necessary to remind ourselves of Henley's words once more. For the fact is that in this fortunate land we are in a better position than other people to be the masters of our fate and to keep our heads unbowed. What we have to do is to be active citizens, not passive victims or beneficiaries. We have to make our voices heard and our efforts felt. If my remarks here today can help stir that kind of spirit I will consider the time well invested.

Edgar Lee Masters

Edgar Lee Masters, the American writer who was born on this day in 1868 in Garnett, Kansas, gained his principal fame with the *Spoon River Anthology,* a collection of autobiographical reminiscences from the grave by the deceased inhabitants of a midwestern community he called Spoon River. Like most of us, Masters and his characters were much wiser looking back than looking forward. But life cannot be spent looking back; it is fine to know where we have come from but more important to try to figure out where we are going. So today, even though looking back would be a delightful exercise in nostalgia, I have chosen instead to try to see where we are going and to share those expectations with you.

One-Day Round Trip

In 1955 on this day, two British pilots made the first round-trip airplane flight in a single day between London and New York. I am sure there were important implications to this achievement, but I can't help feeling it is not too far removed from seeing how many sophomores can be crammed into a telephone booth. What it comes down to is that what is important to one human being to accomplish may be totally pointless to the next person. The main consideration is that each has the opportunity to do what he or she wants to do, as long as it is not at the expense of someone else. Ours is about the only way of life that gives this much freedom to the individual. And it isn't an easy way of life to maintain in this hypertensive, fearful world. That is why we have to be eternally vigilant in defense of our liberties. It is why seemingly minor and often popular limitations of personal liberty have to be nipped in the bud— and why speakers such as I are so concerned with calling your attention to danger signs when we see them.

AUGUST 24

Freedom of Enterprise Week

One of the observances that has marked the month of August is Freedom of Enterprise Week, designed to celebrate a way of life that has helped make America great. We generally think of freedom of enterprise as the road to fame and fortune, but perhaps it becomes even more important if you remember that it also includes the freedom to fail—or, more precisely, the freedom to fail without the failure being a crime against the state. One of the reasons why industrial enterprises are notoriously inefficient in communist nations is that people are afraid to take a chance. Failure runs the danger of being treated as an anticommunist plot with serious penalties. Nothing ventured, says the old saying, nothing gained. As long as we retain a climate in which people are willing to venture, we will have a climate in which people will gain. Given that fact, how good is the competitive climate today?

Fall of Rome

In 410 A.D., within the two-week period ended on this day, Alaric, the leader of the Visigoths, sacked Rome and ended its rule of empire. But although Rome fell to external enemies, historians have described the internal intrigue and moral decay that sapped the empire's vigor as much as the onslaught of the barbarians. The decline and fall of Rome has become a parable of mankind's ability to foul its own nest. As other civilizations have gone through the seemingly inevitable cycle of success and failure, the prophets of doom continue to flourish. They are right. Sooner or later every civilization seems to wither of old age, but before you start to get old you've got to reach your peak, your prime. And I am here to say that our best is yet to come. We are getting better and better. Let me spell it out.

Thomas Chatterton

On this day in 1770, the great English poet Thomas Chatterton took arsenic and ended his life, leaving behind many notable creative works. But the most notable thing was that when he died Chatterton was only seventeen years and nine months old. Now, that was more than 200 years ago, and we keep saying our young people are getting smarter all the time. The only consolation is that they are getting older all the time. Meanwhile the world is still gracious enough to provide a podium for long-past-teenagers like myself, and I thank you for this opportunity.

St. Bartholomew Massacre

This is the anniversary of the beginning of one of those episodes we prefer not to remember, the massacre that began on St. Bartholomew's Day, this day in 1572. Before it was over in October, throughout France as many as 50,000 people may have been murdered. They were all Huguenots, French Protestants, killed at the instigation of Catherine de Medici. We like to think that this kind of thing is ancient history even though the great Holocaust was in our own century, but the fact is that there has hardly been a time in recent years when some minority someplace in the world was not being subjected to racial or religious hatred. It isn't always reflected in massacres or pogroms; it comes more often these days in the denial of basic human rights, in slow starvation, in eviction and displacement. I have no quick solutions to offer, but I think it is important for us to know what is going on in so many different places, and I have chosen some examples to illustrate my point.

AUGUST 25

Pensioned Presidents

On this day in 1958, the law providing pensions for former presidents went into effect. Even though most public employees had pension systems before that time we have been content for almost two centuries to leave former presidents to their own devices when they left office. Some, of course, had pensions from previous positions, and some, like Ulysses S. Grant, went broke trying to be businessmen. Now, while we still have no formal role for ex-presidents, we recognize that their former high responsibility has earned them some form of compensation in their later years. It is part of the comparatively modern concept—the idea that a person deserves to have his or her working years rewarded with compensated leisure in later life. Unfortunately, there are many older people who still can't afford the leisure and the comfort they deserve in their later years, even though Social Security and private pension systems help a great deal. Because life expectancy is greater than it used to be, we have a larger proportion of older people, and somebody is going to have to figure out how to lighten the burden on people before they grow old as well as to provide more in later years.

Ivan the Terrible

Today is the birthday of a man who is known by a name he fully deserved, Ivan the Terrible. This worst of Russian tsars was born in 1530, and he turned out to be just the kind of wrongdoer one might expect to grow up in the hateful environment in which he was born. He was fatherless from the age of three, motherless at seven, and abused all along. When he came to the throne he made an honest effort to be a good monarch, but after his wife and son died he started earning his title of Ivan the Terrible. Although the lower classes looked upon him as a friend, he killed thousands in one massacre after another; he even killed his oldest son. He was a man of considerable ability, but in the end his evil accomplishments are what we remember. But I haven't been talking about Ivan the Terrible simply because today is his birthday. I have been talking about him because his story makes a very simple point: if you permit a child to grow up in an environment of cruelty and horror you are apt to have an adult who commits cruelty and horror of his or her own. The wonder is that our modern slums do not produce more Ivan the Terribles of their own. The challenge is what are we going to do about it.

Invasion of Iran

When Iran exploded in a paroxysm of hatred of foreigners, most notably Americans, some years ago, we were taken aback by the fury and the depth of feeling. Perhaps something that had happened in August of 1941 was part of the explanation. It was about this time in that year that British and Russian troops, newly allied in conflict with Nazi Germany, decided they could not depend on the Shah of Iran to remain neutral. So they sent their troops into his country and a month later forced the abdication of the Shah in favor of his son. His son was more friendly to the Allies, and after the war he became close to the United States. So when the regime of this Shah angered the people, it was in large part because they saw him as a tool of foreign interests. It does not matter whether this perception was correct; what matters is that this perception influenced events. Much of what happens in the world happens because of what we perceive as dangers or opportunities or situations that need changing. That is why public opinion and public perceptions are so important. Today I will discuss only one small area of the world as an example of how much more there is to know and understand.

National Park Service

The National Park Service was established on this day in 1916 to administer and protect the nation's great national parks. In the years since then the problems of the National Park Service have changed. They still have to worry about the wildlife and the flora and fauna, but they have seen first-hand the truth of Walt Kelly's immortal line, "We have met the enemy and they is us." More and more in recent years the National Park Service has had to cope with human beings attacking not only nature but one another. Instead of being only naturalists, the park people have had to become law enforcement officers as well. This has happened with all kinds of government workers—welfare workers policing against welfare cheats, health officers, postal service workers. Are we in the throes of a new immorality as some suggest? And if so, what are we to do about it? If not, what is going on?

AUGUST 26

Women's Equality Day

The anniversary of the granting of votes to women on this day in 1920 when the Nineteenth Amendment went into effect, has been observed for some years as Women's Equality Day. It was so marked even as the Equal Rights Amendment was being defeated in the late 1970s and early 1980s. The fact seems to be that women voters are just as manysided and just as split as the men. Women in general have a better lot today than before they got the vote, and it would be comforting to think that their votes have had something to do with that fact. They are getting more education, more job opportunities—even though there is still plenty of room for improvement. Today I'd like to talk about some of that potential improvement.

Albert Sabin

It is one of the twists of history that Albert Sabin, who was born in Russia on this day in 1906 and became one of America's great medical scientists, should have enjoyed his greatest eminence overseas. That was because his discovery of a method of immunizing against polio by using live viruses, now the accepted method, came only after Jonas Salk had developed a killed-virus vaccine that stamped out the disease in the United States. The Sabin method is now standard all over the world. Dr. Sabin deserves to be known as one of the all-time benefactors of humanity, and perhaps on his birthday it is appropriate to consider the state of public health in the United States today.

Science's Day

It is interesting to note that today is the birthday of two great men of science without whom the world would be a great deal different. Antoine Lavoisier was born on this day in 1743 in Paris, and Lee DeForest in 1873 in Council Bluffs, Iowa. Lavoisier, before he was killed in the French Revolution, laid most of the basis for the modern science of chemistry. DeForest, who invented the three-element vacuum tube, was the man who laid the groundwork for the great electronic communication industries of today. I find it interesting that in a world of so many millions—indeed, billions—of human beings, we can still trace so many important things to the inspiration of a few people at the beginning. To me it is a reminder that within every human being there may be the seeds of a great new idea, a great new field of knowledge. That is why it is so important not to let human beings go to waste. A lost individual is a potential loss to the world. So we must ask ourselves what we can do to keep human beings from being lost before their time.

Krakatoa

On this day in 1883, a volcano named Krakatoa erupted in the East Indies. The resultant tidal wave killed 30,000 people, many of them thousands of miles away. It was a frightening reminder that what happens physically on one side of the world can bring natural disasters to places far away from the original disturbance. Krakatoa blew up long before we knew about acid clouds or radiation or chemical pollution. Inevitably, these things have forced us to be our brothers' keepers, more than we may want. We cannot consider ourselves safe when others pollute our world thousands of miles away. We have to be concerned over dust clouds and polluted waters and bad fishing practices, for example. What we don't know can kill us. So I want to talk today about two things we share with the rest of the world and have the devil's own time keeping clean—water and air.

AUGUST 27

Goldwyn

I do not know the original Polish name of the man whose birthday today I wanted to mention. The English version was Samuel Goldfish, and he was born in Poland in 1882. After a stop in England he came to the United States and by the age of thirty had become a prosperous businessman in the glove industry. But another field interested him; he entered the infant moviemaking business, coproducing *The Squaw Man,* one of the very first American feature pictures. Some years later he went into partnership with Edgar and Archibald

Selwyn, and they combined their names in the title of the new company, Goldwyn Pictures. Yes, I am talking about that distinguished motion picture producer who became known as Samuel Goldwyn. He produced many great movies, and he also produced some memorable phrases. It was he who announced that a verbal contract wasn't worth the paper it was written on, advised people to "include me out," and was known to conduct business negotiations by offering "a definite maybe." The interesting thing about these various quotations is that though the word construction is eccentric, the meaning is perfectly clear. I can only hope that I will be equally lucid in my remarks to you here today.

Tarzan

It was about this time in the year 1912 that readers made the acquaintance of a durable character first introduced in a magazine story about "Tarzan of the Apes" by Edgar Rice Burroughs. Since then generations around the world have been entertained by the fantasy of the human king of the jungle. It seems to strike a chord in everyone by enabling us vicariously to return to a simpler life. In the jungle there are less gradations of good and bad, less pretense, and clearly less psychosis. But I suppose these are all the hazards of civilization and progress. We like to divide people into the good guys and the bad guys, but the fact is that things don't work that way. Those who are good guys with regard to one question may be bad guys with regard to another. It seems to me that we spend too much time trying to categorize people and not enough time working out our differences. Clearly there *are* differences, but that does not mean there are villains at work. So today I would like to abandon the game of who's to blame in favor of what to do about it.

Earl Mountbatten

On this day in 1979, Earl Mountbatten and three others aboard his yacht were killed by the explosion of a terrorist bomb. Although Lord Mountbatten was a senior member of the royal family of Great Britain, he had no role in the political dispute in Northern Ireland which precipitated the bombing. Why the terrorists thought that killing this elderly British hero would advance their cause I don't know. Terrorists don't think like normal people; although it rarely works, they persist in killing innocents, taking hostages, demanding ransoms. Above all they seek to impose their ideas by intimidation. How much better it is to be able to meet and exchange views peacefully in an open society! From that point of view, gatherings such as this are not a luxury; they are a necessity, reasserting time after time the basic strength of a free nation. That basic strength is the traffic in ideas, uncensored and open. I speak today in the obvious hope that you will find my views in harmony with yours, but if what I say should turn out to be different from what you think, I know you will still, in the great American tradition, hear me out and think about it.

Lyndon B. Johnson

On this day in 1908 in Johnson City, Texas, the 36th president of the United States, Lyndon B. Johnson, was born. It was Lyndon Johnson who spearheaded the passage of the great Civil Rights Act of 1964, but he is most often remembered as the man who obtained the Gulf of Tonkin resolution that enabled the White House to pour so many U.S. forces into the Vietnam War. We remember people and events selectively, for emotional as well as intellectual reasons, and so we take for granted today many of the domestic reforms Lyndon Johnson fought for. There is a tendency on our part, even with contemporary politicians, to remember them for one issue or one event and judge them accordingly, rather than for the whole picture. Each of us has particular pet issues and we are inclined to judge public figures by how they stand on the issue that concerns us most. I would like to use this opportunity to suggest that we take a broader view, and it is with that perspective that I propose to look at those who are leading us—or seeking to—today.

AUGUST 28

St. Augustine

The oldest European settlement in what is now the United States began on this day in the year 1568. The Spaniards who founded it named it after the saint who had passed away on this day in 430 A.D., St. Augustine. It still bears that name today, as an historic city in Florida. The story of the settlement of St. Augustine has an interesting sidelight. The admiral who started the settlement also explored Chesapeake Bay but apparently saw more lasting value in the Florida coast. Merely to have survived at the beginning was an accomplishment. If any of those earlier generations could hear us complaining about our lives today, they would throw up their hands in disgust. Part of the uniqueness of America is that it is better for every generation than for the one that preceded it. Sometimes we don't think so, when we are troubled by the adolescent excesses of younger people, but adolescence is cured by time and so is any malaise in America. As long as we are determined to keep moving ahead we will indeed move ahead. And I'd like to venture a few surmises about where we are headed.

Violence in Chicago

On this day in 1968, antiestablishment demonstrators made their supreme effort to disrupt the Democratic National Convention in Chicago, making headlines all over the world by their clashes with the police. It was essentially an effort to change politics through street theater and to polarize public opinion. At the time many people worried about whether the nation could stand up to this kind of divisiveness, and some attributed the election of Richard M. Nixon to the feelings aroused by resentment of the demonstrators. But with the long view of history we know now that America's governmental and political processes are designed to weather such storms. It is a comforting realization, as well as a warning against overreacting. Overreaction is an ever-present danger. I see several areas where it looms today, and I'd like to talk about some of them.

Goethe

Today is the birthday of Johann Wolfgang von Goethe, perhaps the greatest figure in German literature. Born in Frankfurt in 1749, he gave to the world such classics as *Faust, The Sorrows of Young Werther,* and *Wilhelm Meister.* Most appropriate for our discussion here today, I believe, is *Faust,* the story of a man who sells himself to the Devil in return for youth and knowledge. One of the plagues of our modern time is the degree to which so many leaders play Faust, abandoning principles for the sake of votes and power. I must confess I am often more impressed with politicians who stick to an obviously unpopular principle they happen to believe in, compared to others who bend and turn with every twist of the public opinion polls. The most important thing to know about someone in political life is where he or she stands and that he or she is willing to stand up to be counted. Having voiced that noble sentiment, I leave myself no alternative now but to tell you where I stand.

First Commercial

A new phase of American business began on this day in 1922, when a radio station in New York City broadcast a commercial announcement, the first such use of the new medium. Thanks to the system of commercial, advertising-supported broadcasting, America has more active radio and television stations than any other country on earth, as well as more news services. It is always fashionable to deplore the influence of advertising on America, but the development of the most pervasive information and entertainment programming in the world is a most worthwhile byproduct. And we should not forget that in addition to broadcasting, newspapers and magazines also depend on advertising revenues to remain in business. This is an example of the interdependence of American institutions. You cannot really do away with any of these interdependent parts without seriously affecting the rest. Permit education to decline, and production efficiency will decline thereafter. Permit government to be inefficient, and that inefficiency adds to the price tag of every kind of product. Mindful of that interdependence, let us look at some of our institutions that are being seriously challenged.

AUGUST 29

Belmont's View

I have a quotation I'd like to read to you. I found it in an account of the remarks of a famous man. He said, "Four years of misrule by a sectional, fanatical, and corrupt party have brought our country to the verge of ruin." The man who is supposed to have said this was the great banker August Belmont, the place was the Democratic National Convention, the year was 1864 on this day, and the party he was talking about was headed by a man named Abraham Lincoln. So much for predictions of America's downfall. In the more than a century since Belmont's prediction many others have claimed to see the writing on the wall, and we have our share of the doomsayers today. I am here with a different message.

Oliver Wendell Holmes

One of America's more remarkable men was born in Cambridge, Massachusetts on this day in 1809. His name was Oliver Wendell Holmes, distinguished doctor, lecturer, essayist, poet, and father of the great Supreme Court justice of the same name. It was the senior Holmes who wrote, "I find the great thing in this world is not so much where we stand, as in what direction we are moving: To reach the port of heaven, we must sail sometimes with the wind and sometimes against it—but we must sail, and not drift, nor lie at anchor." We must move in some direction, for to fail to move is to stagnate. The future, of course, is an uncharted sea; we have no proven maps to guide us, so we must read the signs as best we can. Today I want to tell you how I read them.

John Locke

John Locke, the great philosopher, was born on this day in 1632 in Wrington, England. Something he wrote in his "Essay Concerning Human Understanding" has to be in the mind of every public speaker preparing to present his or her thoughts to an audience. "New opinions," Locke said, "are always suspected and usually opposed, without any other reason but because they are not already common." That leaves the speaker with a bit of a dilemma. One does not want to present views that are already commonplace, and one does not want to offer views simply to provoke opposition. I would like to hope, however, that the views I present here today will provoke thought.

Henry Bergh

Today is the birthday of a New Yorker named Henry Bergh, whose name you may not recognize but whose good work still goes on. Henry Bergh was born in 1811. At the age of 55, at a time when most people are beginning to think of resting on their laurels, he founded the Society for the Prevention of

Cruelty to Animals, which was given enforcement power by the state for laws protecting animals. Later, Bergh was one of the principal founders of the Society for the Prevention of Cruelty to Children. He was one of those all too rare individuals who can awaken and arouse the public conscience to make things better. I find myself wondering what causes might inspire a Henry Bergh today. We are doing much better with animals, but we still have much more we can do for children.

AUGUST 30

Creator of Frankenstein

Today is the birthday of Mary Wollstonecraft Shelley, the writer and wife of the famous British poet, Percy Bysshe Shelley. She was born in London in 1797, and when she was twenty-one she wrote a book that gave the world a timeless character. The book was *Frankenstein*. Mary Shelley is long gone, but her creation seems to go on forever. Monsters are that way—not only monsters in fiction but monsters among government programs, monsters among social evils, and so forth. The fictional monsters live on because of our fascination with the evil and the unusual; the monster problems and programs live on because they are so big it is hard to do them in. One of the great difficulties with government programs is that once started they have a great tendency to become self-perpetuating. It is a tendency we have to fight, and I have a few targets to suggest.

Atomic Energy

It was on this day in 1954 that Congress gave its approval to private, peaceful atomic energy projects amid considerable speculation about how much growth this would provide. Looking back on those hopeful predictions it must be said that things have not worked out quite as we expected. Part of the difficulty has been unforeseen objections, questions of disposal of nuclear waste, and other environmental considerations. Part has been a reflection of the fact that most of the nation did not feel a sufficient sense of urgency, except for a relatively brief time at the depths of the Arab oil boycott. In this country we have a tendency to act more emphatically in response to emergencies than when relative calm prevails. That is one reason why political candidates always seem to find emergencies facing us; they believe that if they can persuade the country it is in danger more people will get concerned enough to vote for them. And it is always easier to get people's attention by predicting disaster than by saying things are fine. Ladies and gentlemen, the only impending disaster that's on my mind here today is what would happen if I outstayed my welcome on this dais, so I will get right down to business.

St. Fiacre

According to ancient church tradition, this day was dedicated to St. Fiacre, the patron saint of gardening and taxis. They may seem a strange combination, but the story is that the first taxicabs were stationed at a street in Paris that was named after St. Fiacre, and so in French they were called *fiacres* and put under this particular saint's aegis. Since there are many cities these days where you can watch the grass grow because it takes so long to get a cab, St. Fiacre's jurisdictions may not be so far apart after all. In any case it seems appropriate on his day to plant a few seeds of thought and do it as promptly as if the meter were running.

Ty Cobb

On this day in 1905, Ty Cobb stepped up to bat for the first time in the major leagues. Before he finished his playing career more than twenty years later, he had compiled so great a record that even now he is considered by many to have been the greatest baseball player of all time. But even a Ty Cobb strikes out sometimes, so when a more modestly endowed character such as I steps up to the plate it is with a certain degree of diffidence and of challenge, aware of the fact that the best thing I can do is to start swinging.

AUGUST 31

HUD

On this day in 1965, Congress voted to establish what is now the Department of Housing and Urban Development as a new cabinet department to deal with the problems of American cities. There is no way of knowing whether the problems of our cities would be any worse today without HUD, and that is characteristic of many federal agencies set up to deal with problems the Founding Fathers never dreamed would be within the purview of the national government. There is, unfortunately, a vicious circle involved here. The federal government takes the biggest slice of the national income in taxes. Consequently, when there seems to be a need for funds to establish a new program, the federal government becomes the richest source—often without our stopping to think about whether the federal treasury is the right resource to use. I think it is high time for us to stop and think about that, and I have some points to make in that connection here today.

Itzhak Perlman

A boy was born in Tel Aviv, Israel, on this day in 1945, who was destined to give the world more joy and more inspiration than most of us could possibly achieve. His name is Itzhak Perlman. He became one of the greatest violinists of his time, and he did so despite being handicapped by the serious crippling of his legs. The example of Itzhak Perlman shows us the way greatness can rise above those deficiencies that might limit lesser people. It tells us that only we set the limitations of our hopes and dreams. And it tells us that God-given talent can surmount fearsome obstacles. I think these are important points to remember as we contemplate our world. Instead of looking to God in the heavens and asking, "What have you done for us lately?" we should be asking ourselves, "What have we done for ourselves lately?" And we should also be asking, "What more can we do?" That is the question I will try to answer here today.

G.A.R.

On this day in 1949, the last encampment of the G.A.R., the Grand Army of the Republic, the Union veterans organization of the Civil War, was held in Indianapolis with six members in attendance. That was four years after the end of World War II, and it reminds us that in the long view of history the existence of the United States of America is but a moment of time. That is why I lose patience with those who express the view that the United States has seen its best days. To my way of thinking we have only begun to scratch the surface of America's greatness. We have only begun to fulfill the American dream. What we need more than anything else now, it seems to me, is a new vision of what America can become, to itself and to the rest of the world. And so I am here today to ask you to look with me into the future, on the basis of where we are and what we have today.

Tennis Championship

The first national championship tennis matches were held at the Newport, Rhode Island casino on this date in 1881. As the location suggests, tennis at that time was a luxury for the rich. What has happened since then to tennis is a microcosm of the history of this country. Public interest and participation in the sport have grown by leaps and bounds, as a result of which many millions of people now follow the sport, and the people who engage in it are among the richest athletes in the world. It is a classic example of the workings of the laws of supply and demand; the more people wanted to watch tennis, the more tennis they have gotten to watch—and pay for. The secret of America's vigor has been its success in creating new demand for products and services, and new products and services to awaken that demand. We are still doing just that. And the only competition comes from other countries that believe in venture capitalism as we do. But are we continuing to have a climate in which venture capitalism is possible? That is today's $64 question.

SEPTEMBER 1

Woman on the Phone

This is recorded as the day when the first woman telephone operator went on duty in Boston in 1878. According to one account, the company turned to women because a male operator had been reported as impolite. I don't know whether that part of the story is true, but I think it is worth telling if only because politeness and consideration need all the help they can get. Even among public speakers there are those who make their mark by scolding or scaring their audience. My personal nonfavorite is the speaker who threatens you with all kinds of dire consequences if you don't take his or her advice. I come here today without threats for you and with no intention to scare you. If I can add a bit to your store of knowledge I will be content.

Sight-Saving Month

This month is usually observed as National Sight-Saving Month, designed to make us more aware of the importance of protecting our vision. Too many of us become victims of physical blindness, with vision impaired often simply because of failure to go to the doctor in time. I am concerned today with another kind of vision—our individual visions of the future. I am concerned that our individual visions are not sufficiently high. We seem to go through periods when we are persuaded to lower our sights, water down our hopes, settle for smaller targets. Where are the visions of future American greatness and of personal success that helped build this great country? Are we shortchanging ourselves these days by not aiming high enough? We do patchwork repairs on plants and institutions that should be totally rebuilt, and we say that's all we can afford. I don't think we can afford *that*. I don't think we can afford to let our visions of a better America go down the drain. And that's what I want to talk about here today.

Jimmy Walker

New York has had more than its share of colorful mayors, but none was more popular in his time than Jimmy Walker, who was known all over the world as the symbol of Broadway in its heyday. Jimmy Walker was not just an ornament to the city's bustling social life, who really earned his nickname of "the night mayor." He was also the chief executive of a city in one of its most dynamic

346

eras, from 1925 to this day in 1932. His career came to a grinding halt when an investigation ordered by New York Governor Franklin D. Roosevelt charged Walker with various counts of malfeasance or corruption. That night the mayor went to Europe for a few years, then came back to find that the city still loved him. Fiorello LaGuardia, whom he had defeated in the mayoralty election in 1925, thought enough of him to recommend him for appointment as arbiter of the National Cloak and Suit Industry, and Gentleman Jimmy died in his hometown at the age of 65. The story of Jimmy Walker is worth recalling because it tells us something about ourselves. There was no question that Jimmy Walker had permitted graft to flourish when he was mayor; there was also no question that he could charm virtually anybody within range. A successful public figure is usually much more successful if he is good company. Two of the tragic figures of American history—Alexander Hamilton and Aaron Burr—were probably among the most brilliant of our leaders, but they lacked charm utterly and had a talent for making enemies. Burr destroyed Hamilton and made a mess of his own promising career. Charm by itself, without substance, is not enough, but neither are honesty and courage. A politician who isn't liked, who has no charm for the electorate, is not likely to be a successful politician, any more than a grouchy waiter is going to get the biggest tips. So I am here to say a few words in behalf of charm and style and to make some observations about which public figures have it and which don't.

World War II

One of the striking things about the two world wars has been the way they started—not on any great question of principle but rather on a pretext grabbed by a power that was looking for a fight. In the case of World War II, Germany, which had been demanding a corridor across Poland to the then free city of Danzig, and also wanting to incorporate Danzig in a greater Germany, suddenly and without warning invaded Poland. That happened on this day in 1939. It points up a hard fact. Wars are not caused by events or principles; they are caused by warmakers, people with the delusion that military triumphs are the path to progress. What also seems to be the case is that every aggressor might have been stopped peacefully if his nature had been recognized earlier. Adolf Hitler, for example, had shown his true colors long before he invaded Poland. But nobody did anything about it soon enough. That is why we must always be vigilant and ready to nip threats in the bud. At any given time there are explosive corners of the world where timely response can save us from great conflicts later. We have less difficulty in finding the troublespots than in deciding what kind of response is wise. As I look around the world today I see a number of places where that question arises.

SEPTEMBER 2

The Big Stick

Theodore Roosevelt was the Vice-President of the United States when he visited the Minnesota State Fair on this day in 1901. It was there that he described the defense policy he advocated for the United States. "Speak softly," he said, "and carry a big stick." That was good advice in 1901, and it is good advice today, particularly in a world where all too many nations tend to speak too loudly whether they have big sticks or not. What nations do, individuals also do, and it is a great temptation for a speaker, given a cordial forum such as this, to take the opportunity to try some oratorical thunder. That is a temptation I plan to resist today.

Henry George

Today is the birthday of Henry George, who was born in Philadelphia in 1839. Best remembered as the advocate of a single tax on land as the source of wealth, he was the author of many treatises, of which "Progress and Poverty" is worth noting today. He wrote—and I quote—"It is not from top to bottom that societies die; it is from bottom to top." Stop and think of our current problems—crime, narcotics addiction, poor productivity, for example—and you find they began at the bottom and worked their way up. So it becomes important to ask ourselves what we are doing to keep people from dropping to or staying at the bottom.

Eugene Field

Eugene Field, the hardboiled newspaperman and sentimental poet who was born on this day in 1850 in St. Louis, wrote many favorite poems of everybody's childhood. Today I want to recall not "Wynken, Blinken, and Nod" or "Little Boy Blue"—both his creations—but that verse in which he wrote, "Father calls me William, sister calls me Will,/Mother calls me Willie, but the fellers call me Bill!" I am reminded of this when I look at some current government programs. For example, what some people call welfare other people call a chisel and others call a reward for indolence. One person's subsidy is another person's graft; it depends on your point of view. It seems to me that we spend too much time arguing about titles instead of about substance. We pin labels, flattering or nasty, on programs, and sometimes those programs rise or fall because of the labeling. Today I want to talk about one such program, which its advocates call tax incentives and its opponents call giveaways.

Treaty of Rio de Janeiro

On this day in 1947, the Inter-American Conference for Maintenance of Continental Peace and Security ended with the signing in Rio de Janeiro of a treaty providing for mutual aid in instances of armed aggression. The treaty was signed by nineteen American republics. We did not dream then that the major instance of aggression would come not from Europe but from one of the American republics themselves, when Cuba began trying to export Castroism. We did not dream that there would be incessant disputes over whether this or that insurrection was an outside-supported aggression or a simple domestic uprising—and we are still being caught as often as not on the horns of that particular dilemma. Today I propose to look at the problems of some of our neighbors with that dilemma in mind.

SEPTEMBER 3

Edward A. Filene

America has had more than its share of outstanding merchants, but none has made a greater contribution to merchandising than one who was born in Salem, Massachusetts, on this day in 1860. His name was Edward A. Filene, and he invented what he called the automatic bargain basement, a system of price discounting that has survived and grown ever since. What he did was to establish a schedule of price reductions for his merchandise. If not sold in the first period the goods were automatically reduced by a substantial amount; if after another stated period of time they still remained on the shelves they were automatically reduced further, until a final reduction that made them truly bargain-basement offerings. These days we have many businesses that handle their pricing this way, but in Filene's day it was a most creative and unusual idea. What are some of the similarly creative ideas on the business horizon these days?

The *New York Sun*

On this day in 1833, a revolutionary newspaper made its first appearance in New York City. It was the *New York Sun*, and what made it revolutionary was its price. At a time when other newspapers were being sold for six cents, the *New York Sun* sold for a penny. It was the first successful penny newspaper in America, and it sparked a whole series of great popular newspapers in that form of journalism's golden age. Like everything else the price of a newspaper has gone sky high by comparison in modern times, and of course the competition from other media, which didn't exist in 1833, becomes stiffer every day. In one respect, however, we are the heirs of what the *New York Sun* started—the idea that news should be available with as little cost to the consumer as possible. It is available to us now in broadcast form simply by turning on our receiving sets, and this easy availability has made us, I believe, the best-informed nation on earth. We are, indeed, so accustomed to more news all the time that on occasion significant developments go virtually unnoticed in the midst of all the other stories. Today I'd like to focus on some trends and events that deserve to be highlighted.

Treaty of Paris

On this day in 1783, the final draft of the peace treaty ending the American Revolutionary War was finally signed in Paris by representatives of the United States and Great Britain. The hostilities had ended some time before, and a provisional peace treaty had been signed the previous November 30, but formalities take time. Negotiating a peace treaty, as a matter of fact, seems to be much faster than getting a case tried and concluded in the American courts. One of the great problems of our times and our land is to have the process of justice move a little faster. That's what I would like to discuss here today.

Missing Days

On this day in 1752, the English-speaking world lost 11 days, permanently. Long after the rest of the western world they switched to the Gregorian calendar, and September 3, 1752, became September 14. Among other things, that led to George Washington changing the observance of his birthday from February 11 to February 22. As far as I can determine we have never gotten back those eleven days we gave up back in 1752. Now it may be a little late to get upset about that when we have so many more immediate problems, but it is a reminder that there is no limit to what the government can take away from you. We spend so many words talking about what the government should give people that we sometimes lose sight of how much it takes, not merely in taxes but in obligations. Today I want to talk about that point.

SEPTEMBER 4

Kodak

It was on this day in 1888 that George Eastman received his patent for a roll-film camera he called a Kodak; he picked the name Kodak because it was simple and pronounced virtually the same in every language, and he advertised his camera under the slogan, "You push the button; we do the rest." His invention and his merchandising genius made photography available to everybody. Eastman's was a typical American success story, and in every generation since his time we have had our share of George Eastmans, creating new products and the companies to make and market them. What is there about our country that makes this happen? In my view it is the acceptance of the idea of individual enterprise. Great innovations are more apt to come from entrepreneurs like the young Henry Ford than from a great corporation. IBM is a great corporation now, but it was built of the dreams of young Thomas Watson many years ago.

The transistor is the product of a great research organization, but it has spawned a whole new generation of entrepreneurs. So the question is: What must we do to keep this spirit of entrepreneurial adventure alive and healthy?

Steuben

Truth is generally regarded as a great virtue, but on this day in 1777 a lie helped advance the cause of American independance. History isn't clear about whether Friedrich von Steuben or Benjamin Franklin was the original author of the lie, but in any case it is a matter of record that von Steuben, who had never risen above the rank of captain in his European military service, was recommended to General George Washington by Franklin and others as a military expert who had been a lieutenant general in Prussia. General Washington appointed him inspector general of the Continental Army, and von Steuben is credited with bringing military discipline to that civilian force. Later he distinguished himself on the battlefield as well. All thanks to an original lie. This is not a story calculated to advance the cause of honesty in government, but it does illustrate an equally important point. There are people in this world who, on book values alone, don't seem to deserve the opportunities they seek; but when you give people a chance, sometimes the least likely prospects, who seem to violate all the preconditions, nevertheless prove to have the spark of success. If we don't believe that, we abandon the poor and the uneducated to a lifetime of despair. If we do believe it, we have to ask ourselves how we make opportunities possible for these people. And that is what I am asking here today.

Miss America Pageant

This is the time of year when the grand old lady of beauty pageants, the Miss America Pageant in Atlantic City, captures the nation's attention most years. It has been denounced as exploitation, mocked as a glorification of the trivial, imitated, and deplored, and it keeps right on going. For many young women it has been a means of going farther and higher in life than they might have done otherwise; for millions of other Americans it has been a delightful exercise in girl watching. But, above all, the Miss America Pageant represents the common national striving to find and salute the best. We do that not just with beauty contests but also with science scholarship competitions, athletics, music, and drama. It is healthy, not simply because it is competition but because it gives so many of us a chance to be the best, or among the best, at something. In the classless, noncompetitive societies of communist nations a drab equality is imposed on most people, and the champions are a small privileged class. In our country anybody can try for the brass ring on one merry-go-round or another. What we have as our priceless asset is hope. But some Cassandras are telling us to stop hoping, and that is what I want to speak about here today.

Twin Anniversary

Two anniversaries share this day. In 1882 electric light service began in New York City, and in 1951 live television connections from coast to coast were inaugurated with a telecast of President Harry Truman's speech at the Japanese Peace Treaty Conference in San Francisco. In their own way each of these events contributed toward broadening the horizons of Americans. Both made possible the twenty-four hour day of activities that are now available to Americans—all-night television service, artificially illuminated night sports, and night time back-room operations in brokerages and other businesses. I am not at all sure that these various items represent the best of progress, but they have certainly changed the pace and the character of life in these United States. We all like to indulge in nostalgia about the good old days in the belief that when life was simpler it was somehow better. Ladies and gentlemen, it wasn't. The streets were dirtier, if only because of the horsedrawn vehicles; the poor were poorer, because there was no Social Security and no unemployment insurance; the sick were sicker, because there were no miracle drugs or pacemakers or microsurgeons. What there was, and what we seem to miss, was unparalleled opportunity for improvement. Well, I maintain that the same opportunities exist today. And I have some specific opportunities to talk about here.

SEPTEMBER 5

Jesse James

This is the birthday of an American pioneer. Like other pioneers he opened up new territory in the land of opportunity. But he did not win any honors for his efforts. His name was Jesse James, born on this day in 1847 in Missouri, and his pioneering was in the field of bank and train robbery. That was at a time when the word *mugging* was unknown, car theft was yet to come, and racketeering was in its infancy. We have certainly come a long way since then. Jesse James would have a hard time today because he would face so much competition. Crime is perhaps the biggest single problem in American life. So far we haven't been able to solve that problem, but solutions are not impossible.

Labor Day

The first organized Labor Day parade was held on this day in New York City in 1892. It was intended as a graphic demonstration of the extent and enthusiasm of organized labor, and, indeed, labor groups have made tremendous progress since that first public march. They have made so much progress, as a matter of fact, that some of them have become prey to the same abuses of power that characterized the ruthless employers of the past. We have had to pass laws to control the abuses of both organized business and organized labor. That is one of the reasons why our set of regulations and our staffs of regulators keep growing and growing. The same thing has happened in nongovernmental areas. Today's football rules are a great deal more complicated and require a much larger staff of administrators and officials than those of fifty years ago, for example. Life keeps getting more complicated. That is one of the inevitables of progress, and it makes it more important all the time that we know as much as possible about what is going on. I hope that in my remarks here today I can shed some light on what is going on.

Treaty of Portsmouth

In some ways this is the anniversary of America's full involvement in the international arena. On this day in 1905, thanks to the intervention of President Theodore Roosevelt, Russia and Japan concluded at Portsmouth, New Hampshire, the negotiations for the treaty that ended the Russo-Japanese War. Despite the isolationist rejection of U.S. membership in the League of Nations and the short-lived America First Committee before we entered World War II, the United States has been a full participant in the family of nations most of the time since then. We are often, indeed, more participatory than we realize. It came as a shock to many Americans in the early 1980s to discover that U.S. banks had been lending so many millions of our dollars to overseas nations, including communist nations. We speak of iron curtains, but there aren't many nations in the world today that can afford to cut themselves off from the rest of the world. One of our problems is that we consider ourselves far less dependent on the rest of the world than we actually are. Others need us, but we surely need them as well. Let me give you some examples.

Assassination

On this day in 1972, eleven Israeli Olympic athletes were murdered by terrorists, and to make the event even more gruesome it took place in one of the key breeding places of German Nazism years earlier, in Munich. Even in a world all too accustomed to the mindless excesses of terrorism, the eleven murders came as a shock. But only for the moment. Terrorism is always ready to pile some new horror on the old ones. That is because, usually, while we express shock for the moment we don't really do anything about it. All too often terrorists escape to try again. All too often one renegade government or another gives them shelter. All too often we don't even want to talk about the problem. But it doesn't go away, and we are going to have to do something about it.

SEPTEMBER 6

McKinley Shot

History takes strange turns, and one such occurred on this day in 1901, when the President of the United States, William McKinley, was shot by a crazed anarchist. McKinley was visiting Buffalo, New York, at the time. He lingered for more than a week and died on September 14, bringing to the White House a man who might otherwise never have made it, a New Yorker by the name of Theodore Roosevelt. They thought they had buried the independent-minded Teddy Roosevelt in the Vice-Presidency, but a crazy man's bullet rewrote history for them. Yes, history is not always a steady and logical evolution; often it is made by the arrival on the scene of a dynamic personality with events friendly to his or her ideas. Unfortunately, even a two-bit politician can become convinced that he or she has a rendezvous with destiny. Like it or not, the final judgment is with us, the electorate. What should we be looking for?

Barbara Fritchie

When Confederate troops commanded by Stonewall Jackson occupied the town of Frederick, Maryland, in 1862, a local woman defied them by waving a U.S. flag as they paraded by, and General Jackson saw that his soldiers left her alone. The great poet John Greenleaf Whittier heard the story and wrote a poem about 96-year-old Barbara Fritchie, quoting her: "Shoot if you must this old gray head, but spare your country's flag, she said." It is one of the most famous patriotic poems we have, but there is one problem. It wasn't 96-year-old Barbara Fritchie, according to most accounts, who was the heroine of the original incident, but a much younger woman named Mary Quantrell. Sometimes the actual facts are not quite as melodramatic as the people who write about them. And sometimes we have to ask ourselves how accurate the descriptions we read may be. Right now, for example, you can get altogether different assessments of the mood of the country depending on which commentator you follow. The assessment I am about to give you is the way I see things, and I hope you will find it agrees with your own perspectives.

Arnold's Revenge

Benedict Arnold, the principal traitor of the Revolutionary War, was unmasked when his British contact, Major Andre, was captured by Americans. Arnold went over to the British forces and was made a brigadier general. About this time in 1781, the onetime patriot led his troops in a raid on New London, Connecticut, and burned it to the ground. When a person decides to go bad he is apt to go bad all the way. If Benedict Arnold were alive today someone might have suggested that he see a psychiatrist, since he clearly was a disturbed personality. But the record of our mental health workers does not suggest that we could have done anything to stop Benedict Arnold other than putting him behind bars. Now, I have deliberately talked about a man out of the past to highlight a problem of the present, the problem of the human time bombs who are walking the streets because we do not have sufficient full-time treatment facilities. In Russia they put totally normal and sane people in asylums to maintain their dictatorship; in the United States we put disturbed people out on the street to maintain our free way of life. Isn't there a better way?

Coeds

On this day in 1837, women attending Oberlin Collegiate Institute in Ohio were given the same academic standing as the men, the first equal higher education in America. Considering the amount of time that has elapsed since then, women can hardly be described as impatient in pressing for total equality of opportunity in life. We are closer to that goal than ever before, and I would like to speculate with you on how we can make it a reality.

SEPTEMBER 7

Uncle Sam

It was on this day in 1813 that a newspaper in Troy, New York, first referred to the United States as Uncle Sam, and ever since Uncle Sam has been the symbol of the nation. Until recent years we thought of him as rich Uncle Sam, readily available to support his nephews and nieces as all kinds of people became accustomed to dipping into the subsidy pot, but Uncle Sam discovered that the pot wasn't as full as people thought, and so he's been calling on other members of the family for assistance. If you look at the United States as a family you can't help feeling that some of us haven't been sharing the load. That happens in every family if the family begins to fall apart, and if we don't share the load to the best of our ability our family will indeed fall apart. Today I want to talk about how we can prevent that from happening.

London Blitz

It was on this day in 1940 that Nazi Germany began pinpointing London in night bombing raids. The Nazis fully expected to terrorize the British civilian population; instead, the nightly raids for almost three months galvanized the British fighting spirit. Not all the free people faced with the Nazi blitzkrieg were able to react as bravely as the British. Some of the other, smaller nations, without the English Channel as a barrier, were quickly overcome, but the British held out. I think one reason was their tradition of freedom; they had been free for centuries, and they weren't about to give that up. I have the same feeling about America. No invader is going to do us in; no invader is going to alter our liberty. But what worries me is that no invader may have to do the job because some of us would do it ourselves. That's what I want to talk about today.

First Submarine

Today is the anniversary of the first submarine attack on a ship. The submarine was a hand-cranked, one-man submersible built by David Bushnell. On this day in 1776, it was used to try to attach a time bomb to the British flagship *Eagle* in New York Harbor. The bomb floated away from the British ship before it exploded, and people forgot about submarines for quite a while. In the Civil War the Confederates used a hand-propelled submarine called the *Hunley* and sank a ship with it, but it was not until 1898 that John Holland invented the practical modern undersea boat. Good ideas do not always spring full-blown into reality; usually it takes the inspiration and perspiration of many people over many years to make them work. But when we deal with political and social issues we are not that patient; we ask for immediate solutions, or we judge that what we are doing has failed. Ladies and gentlemen, we are not going to change the world overnight. What we must ask ourselves is not whether new ideas are working but whether they are making things even marginally better than before. Are we taking better care of people now, for example, than we used to? Are there any lessons to be drawn from what we seem to be doing right and what we seem to be doing wrong?

Marquess of Queensberry

The first heavyweight championship boxing bout under the Marquess of Queensberry rules was held on this day in 1892 in New Orleans, when Gentleman Jim Corbett defeated John L. Sullivan. The new rules required the wearing of boxing gloves rather than bare knuckles, and three-minute rounds with a minute in between. Ladies and gentlemen, the Queensberry rules will not be followed here today. I am taking the gloves off.

SEPTEMBER 8

International Literacy Day

Today in many member countries of the United Nations is International Literacy Day. When we think of the world's problems we think of hunger and housing and of lack of freedom, but one of the most universal problems is none of the above. It is the inability of millions upon millions of people to read or write. Even in a nation with compulsory education, such as the United States, illiteracy is a real problem. Some people think that in the age of television and radio it doesn't matter so much, but it does. Careers for illiterates are very limited.

Yet for some reason we get much more worked up about other deficiencies than about the inability to read. We think it is somebody else's problem, because we and our own children can read and write. But someone who doesn't understand a street sign or the warning label on a package can be a threat to the neighbors, and someone who can't get a job because he or she can't read or write is a burden on the community. Illiteracy is a universal problem, and I'd like to devote some attention to it today.

Nixon Pardon

On this day in 1974, President Gerald Ford, newly in office as a result of Richard M. Nixon's resignation under fire, issued a pardon to Nixon. President Ford's action forestalled any criminal prosecution of Nixon for his involvement in the Watergate scandal. Ford acted with the announced aim of putting an end to the recriminations and bitterness arising from Watergate. Although the country was very divided over the wisdom of his action it did indeed take the Watergate case off the center burner, although some related prosecutions remained. Ford's contention was that the best thing to do was try to heal the wounds rather than exact further punishment. Whether his view in this particular instance was valid or not, there is no doubt that prolonging or further embittering the discussion of some national sore points serves no useful purpose. So, rather than attacking those whose views differ from my own, I come here to talk to you today in a spirit of peace and gentle advocacy.

New York

On this day in 1664, the Dutch city of New Amsterdam passed into history as the British flag was raised over what was renamed New York. How fortunate for the developing nation that two such freedom-loving peoples as the Dutch and the English gave it its early tradition. How many other freedom-loving peoples came to join them in what our Founding Fathers called "the pursuit of liberty!" That pursuit is still going on. In our own time we have come to see many new aspects of liberty, particularly in the economic sphere. We have also heard a far greater variety of voices speaking out than in the past. Some try to make their point by talking loudly. I prefer to talk sense.

Pledge of Allegiance

On this day in 1882, the Pledge of Allegiance was first published in a magazine entitled *Youth's Companion*. Since then, of course, it has become the key patriotic statement recited in the schools of the nation. It is a noble sentiment and worth repeating, but even so I don't think Americans were deficient in patriotism before the pledge was written. The outward attributes of loving your country—saluting and displaying its flag, singing its anthem, and so forth—are glorious and uplifting, but the best way to uphold love of country is to uphold the principles for which our country stands. One of the greatest of those principles is freedom of conscience—freedom to think as you please and to say what you think. I believe that speaking up is the way to keep freedom healthy. We keep it healthy by exercising it, and so I am speaking up here today.

SEPTEMBER 9

Houston Stewart Chamberlain

We associate organized racism with the Nazi movement of Adolf Hitler, but one of its pioneers was an Englishman with the distinguished name of Chamberlain. He was Houston Stewart Chamberlain, born on this day in 1855, and it was he who postulated in his major book, *Foundations of the Nineteenth Century,* that the Germans in particular and the so-called Aryans in general were the superior race. Following in the footsteps of the Frenchman Comte de Gobineau, Chamberlain provided the philosophical basis for the whole Nazi movement. Although he was the son of a British admiral and the nephew of a British field marshall he supported Germany in the first world war and wrote in German. There was nothing halfhearted in the way he turned his back on his own country. I think of his example when I listen to some Americans professing their admiration for ways of life other than our own. I think of him when I contemplate those drop-outs who turn their backs on the values we hold dear. And I think of Houston Stewart Chamberlain when I contemplate the damage that evil tongues and evil thoughts can do in this world of ours. So, with those thoughts in mind, I hope I speak today with compassion rather than with hatred.

Harland Sanders

This is the birthday of one of the heroes of older Americans, Harland Sanders. He is better known to us today as Colonel Sanders, but for more than sixty years after his birth in Indiana in 1890, he was untitled and unknown. Then, in what would normally have been the twilight of his life, he got the idea of franchising his recipe for a special food, and the Kentucky Fried Chicken fortune was born. His last years were times of glory. You're never too old to strike it rich, and you're never too old to have a good idea. Ours is a youth-oriented society, but the most important young things are ideas. So I would like to present some of those most important young things to you here today— some ideas.

NBC

On this day in 1926, a new idea in the communications field was born. The Radio Corporation of America—RCA—set up an organization to link various radio stations with a program service, and called the new group the National Broadcasting Company—NBC. From this beginning came the great radio and television networks, which have been able to bring worldwide news and programming instantaneously to virtually every part of the country. This nation has led the world in broadcast programming, and one reason has been the idea of commercial networks. This is just another example of what a competitive, entrepreneurial system can do. In the case of broadcasting it is a competition of ideas and, even though there is much to criticize in the end result, that result is at least better than any other system in the world. One of our problems is that we are always so conscious of our faults that sometimes we don't recognize the greatness of our achievements. Today, even though it is easier for a speaker to dwell on the faults, I'd like to talk about some of the achievements and how we can make them even better.

Rough Day

This has been a rough day in history. In 1919, for the first time, an American city—Boston—was faced with a strike of its police department. In 1943, one of the bloodier moments of World War II came when Allied forces landed against Nazi-occupied strong points at Salerno, Italy. And in 1971, the bloody uprising in Attica State Prison in New York State began on this day. In the face of these hectic events I think I should assure you that my remarks today include no calls to the barricades, no ultimatums, and no battlecries.

SEPTEMBER 10

Zippered Hot Dogs

I am indebted to Stanford Mirkin's book *When Did It Happen?* for the priceless information that on this day in 1927 an American company announced a new product, a frankfurter with a zippered skin. You were supposed to cook the frankfurter in its case, then unzip it for eating. Obviously, this idea did not take the nation by storm. I can only hope that my remarks here today, with my mouth fully unzipped, will have a more productive reception.

Lincoln Highway

It was on this day in 1913 that the first coast-to-coast paved road in the United States, the Lincoln Highway, was declared open from New York City to San Francisco. Hard to believe, isn't it, that it took until the twentieth century to produce a single paved road between the two oceans? In the years since then we've been building a great many newer and better roads, and we are still unable to keep up with the traffic. We seem to spend all our time trying to catch up, not just on the highways but in dealing with many other problems. Today I would like to look into the future, just a bit, instead of playing catchup.

Franz Werfel

Today is the birthday of Franz Werfel, the German writer who was born in Prague in 1890. He gained his greatest success with two novels. The first, *The Forty Days of Musa Dagh,* was the story of gallant Armenian resistance against the Turks in World War I, and *Song of Bernadette* was the chronicle of the miracle of Lourdes in France. This German writer, born in what is now Czechoslovakia, scored his great American success with books about Armenia and France. We are indeed one world, and no iron curtain can totally deny that fact. Like it or not, we are our brothers' keepers. Let me, for example, talk a bit about the way other people's problems overseas affect us.

Alaska's Oil Leases

On this day in 1969, the state of Alaska received bids totaling more than $900 million for leases to North Slope areas for oil drilling. Considering that the whole state had been bought from the Russians in 1867 for $7 million, it wasn't a bad day's work. Unfortunately, most individuals keep harboring hopes of striking it rich as they did in Alaska, and life doesn't often work out that way. For everyone who strikes oil there are a dozen who don't, but everybody yearns for the chance to try. We keep trying to protect that chance by giving everybody equality of opportunity. Not equality of results, just an equal opportunity to compete. But by the time the young man or woman is of an age to utilize that equal opportunity it isn't equal anymore. It isn't an equal opportunity for the young person who doesn't know how to read or whose faulty diet never provided the necessary bodily health and fitness. It isn't equal opportunity for the young person who can't speak decent English. If we want equal opportunity in adult life we've got to try to stop victimizing children. And we do victimize children in many ways. We only have time to talk about a few of them.

SEPTEMBER 11

Grandparents' Day

This is the season of Grandparents' Day, the Sunday set aside for a salute to everybody's favorite relatives. A grandparent usually has the fun of watching the kids grow up without the responsibility of their daily care, and many of us would like to have the same status with regard to the country. It would be great to enjoy all the blessings of life in the United States without exercising any responsibility for it, but life doesn't work that way. We can't go through life on somebody else's push. Unfortunately, I am delivering that message today to people who, by their presence here, have already manifested their sense of participation, but I think it is important for all of us to carry that message back to the nonparticipants. Let's talk about what each of us can and should contribute individually toward insuring a better community.

O. Henry

Today is the birthday of William Sydney Porter, better known as O. Henry, who was born in Greensboro, North Carolina, in 1862. O. Henry was the master of the short story with a surprise ending, but he was more than simply a trickster. "The Gift of the Magi" and "The Ransom of Red Chief," to name only two of his many masterpieces, are highly observant commentaries on human nature. He was a sentimental man, and if there is any single emotion that shines through all his work it is compassion. Maybe that is why he struck so strong a chord for the American public. He viewed people and situations with compassion. Have we lost that today? Are we finally succumbing to what is nothing less than a loss of compassion? Do we still care about the poor, the homeless, the oppressed? How do we show compassion today?

D. H. Lawrence

D. H. Lawrence, who was born on this day in 1885 in Eastwood, England, shocked many people of his time with the treatment of sex in his novels. Among others, *Lady Chatterley's Lover* and *Women in Love* precipitated censorship battles that were long and bitter in their time. Today Lawrence's work is regarded as almost classic, and any corner bookstore carries many other books whose covers and contents make Lawrence very pale by comparison. The censors have been in retreat for a long time although they still carry on, but for the most part they concentrate their fire today on the books found in school libraries and even the content of school textbooks. Most friends of freedom are happy to see censorship in disarray, but we must also ask ourselves where freedom of the press ends and sexual exploitation begins. It is common to think of sexual exploitation in terms of male–female relationships and variations on that theme, but I contend that bloody depictions of murder and of horror are equally destructive of normal human relationships and values. The law can only take care of a small portion of this evil. The rest of it is up to us, and I have some suggestions.

Churchill on Hitler

Rallying the British people against an expected Nazi invasion in 1940, Winston Churchill described Adolf Hitler as the "the repository and embodiment of many forms of soul-destroying hatred, this monstrous product of former wrongs and shame." Even in the midst of bitter war, Churchill's perception of history was clear and keen. He recognized that evil in the world is the product of wrongs and shame. We do things we believe are in our interest, but we don't always correct our errors as quickly as we might if we recognize that they are indeed errors. And we usually don't like to have those errors pointed out to us. That is why politicians running for office will tell you why their opponents are wrong, but rarely if ever point a finger at us, the electorate. We can be wrong, with a vengeance. So today I will not be talking about our leaders or our candidates. I will be talking about what's wrong with us.

SEPTEMBER 12

Old Defenders Day

This is Old Defenders Day, celebrated mainly in Baltimore but the anniversary of an event that shaped the future of all America. On this day in 1814, in the War of 1812, the British launched their attack on Baltimore and Fort McHenry. If they had won they would have been able virtually to cut the infant United States in half, moving west from Chesapeake Bay. But Fort McHenry held out; the British were repulsed, and as the battle raged a couple of days later Francis Scott Key was inspired to write "The Star-Spangled Banner." In 1814, we defended the country with force of arms; today the challenges that face us are not merely military. We are challenged economically; we are challenged sociologically. The institution of the family, for example, is subject to all kinds of threats. It is damaged by the prevalence of divorce, by the birth of children out of wedlock, and by housing shortages and other economic hardships. Consider the consequences.

John Alden

This is the anniversary of the death of John Alden, a man we remember for the wrong reason. We remember him because Henry Wadsworth Longfellow incorporated an old legend into his poem "The Courtship of Miles Standish." According to that legend John Alden was asked to speak in behalf of Standish's courtship of Priscilla Mullens in Plymouth Colony, and Priscilla said to him, "Speak for yourself, John." The fact is that Alden did indeed marry Priscilla, but Standish was hardly the bashful type—nor, for that matter, was John Alden. What should have been Alden's claim to fame is that he was not only a signer of the Mayflower Compact and on occasion acting governor of Plymouth Colony but he was also the last surviving signer and the last man of those who came over on the *Mayflower*. When he died on this day in 1687 the colony was firmly established. Now, it seems to me that remembering Alden for the wrong reason is not so unusual. Many of us are recognized or remembered for the wrong reasons. Not too long ago, for example, President Gerald Ford was remembered more for his faux pas than for his positive accomplishments. Richard Nixon's Watergate mistakes loom larger in most people's memories than his settlement, finally, of the Vietnam War and his opening of relations with China. John F. Kennedy's martyrdom and style are far more remembered than any of his positive accomplishments. So I ask myself what we are going to be remembered for, and I have some disquieting thoughts on that subject.

Marathon

Today is the anniversary of an ancient battle whose name lives on. The battle was fought in 490 B.C. in Greece between the Greeks and the invading Persians. The Greeks won and sent a courier who ran the twenty-two miles and 1,470 yards from the battlefield to Athens. The battlefield, as you may have guessed, was the plain of Marathon, and it is from the run by that ancient courier, Pheidippides, that the modern marathon race gets its name. Now, sending a long-distance runner with important news seems more than a little slow in this day of instantaneous broadcasting, but I can't help wondering whether on occasion we might not be better off using runners. Sometimes the time it takes for the news to arrive cools it off; sometimes we commit ourselves by instant reactions when perhaps we might be better off thinking it over. Even in remarks to a meeting such as this, I am grateful for the opportunity to have planned what I was going to say rather than speaking totally off the cuff. It gives me a chance to put my mind in gear before I engage my tongue.

The Brownings

Few love affairs have been as thoroughly documented as that of Elizabeth Barrett and Robert Browning, the two noted English poets. On this day in 1846, they were married, without the knowledge of her father, and she ran away from home a week later to join her husband. It was Robert Browning who wrote, "One wise man's verdict outweighs all the fools!" But who of us is wise enough to know whether he is wise or a fool? Hoping to be at the very least somewhere in between, I welcome this opportunity to speak.

SEPTEMBER 13

Stilwell's Advice

General Joseph W. Stilwell, the senior American Army officer in China during World War II, kept a diary during his bitter times there. On this day in 1943, he wrote, "Never mind when they lie about you. The time to worry is when they begin to tell the truth." Many American political candidates have had occasion to use that quotation since then, but I think it is still worth recalling every now and then. And right now they *are* lying about you. Let me tell you who and how.

National Hispanic Heritage Week

One of the interesting customs in this land of ours is the way we set aside a day or a week to make up for years of neglect. One example is National Hispanic Heritage Week, which is observed around this time of the year in tribute to the background of so many Americans. Considering the extent of that heritage the observance is only fitting. It was a great Spanish writer, Cervantes, who wrote, "There are only two families in the world, the Haves and the Have-nots." That is as true of nations, I suspect, as of individuals. And one of our problems is that in spite of all the advances in agriculture, in nutrition, and in medicine, we still have so many have-nots. Right here in our own land of plenty we have too many have-nots. How can we change this?

Walter Reed

This is the birthday of Walter Reed, the doctor who solved the mystery of yellow fever. Dr. Reed was born in 1851 in Virginia and was only 51 when he died in 1902, but in his lifetime he did major work in solving the mysteries of both typhoid fever and yellow fever. It was ironic that he himself died of a disease which is now so easily handled—appendicitis. In Walter Reed's day the government provided his backing; today modern research requires both government and private funding. There are literally dozens of worthwhile causes whose research is supported by public contributions, and I am happy to speak out in behalf of one of the most worthy.

Barry Day

When we speak of the American Navy in the Revolutionary War, usually only one name comes to mind—that of John Paul Jones. But today, Barry Day, marks the death of another great naval hero in 1803. His name was John Barry; he commanded the American fighting ship *Lexington* in the first U.S. naval victory of the Revolution, capturing the British warship *Edward,* and he went on to many other brilliant naval victories. Barry, unfortunately, made no quotable statements to compare with John Paul Jones's "I have not yet begun to fight," and that may be one reason why he is so less known than his contemporary. That is one of the ironies of fame. A remark that lives forever is apt to do more for the memory of its author than a lifetime of valiant deeds. Words, after all, are the way we express ideas, and ideas are the essence of human existence. So today I would like to share some of the essence with you.

SEPTEMBER 14

Margaret Sanger

Margaret Sanger, the pioneer crusader for birth control and family planning, was born on this day, but, interestingly enough, she appears to have fiddled around with her own birth record. The available records indicate 1883 as the year of her birth, but in the family Bible the date, in her mother's writing, is 1879, and it appears to have been corrected by Mrs. Sanger herself to read 1883, which of course would have made her four years younger. Is it our consciousness of a prejudice against age that makes so many of us claim to be younger than we are? Are we still worshippers at the shrine of youth? I suggest we stop thinking of people in terms of their ages. Not all adolescents are mushmouths; not all oldsters are pillars of wisdom or candidates for the glue factory. We must stop thinking of people in such generalized terms and find a way to treat individuals as individuals. I suggest it is time to stop talking about generation gaps and start talking about human beings. And one way to start, it seems to me, is to speak here not of society in general but in my own personal terms.

United Nations

It was on this day in 1948 that ground was broken for the permanent headquarters of the United Nations in New York City. That was several generations ago, and for most of that time the UN has been regarded as basically an exercise in futility, a place where a lot of oratorical steam is generated but not too much is done. Yet I can't help wondering whether the existence of a place where nations can let off steam is not a good idea, and whether we might have had even more wars if the UN had not existed. After 200 years we still don't have a perfect Congress of the United States, so we can't expect much better from the UN; but I am here to suggest that we need it. At the same time I think we should know a little more about it, and so I want to talk about our relationship with the United Nations today.

Napoleon in Moscow

On this date in 1812, Napoleon's army achieved what it thought was the ultimate triumph in its war with Russia—the capture of Moscow. Napoleon sat in the great Russian city, even through a disastrous fire, awaiting the surrender of the tsar, but it never came, and in the end Napoleon's retreat from Moscow in the face of the Russian winter proved to be a disaster for him. Some of the victories modern leaders proclaim, it seems to me, are very much like Napoleon's victory at Moscow. The claims are premature, to say the least. Today I am not here to proclaim victories or to mourn defeats but rather to talk to you about where I think we are.

Debs

Eugene V. Debs was the locomotive fireman who became the leader of the American Socialist Party and was its presidential candidate in many elections. During the first world war he was found guilty of violating the Espionage Act for opposing enlistment in the armed forces. On this day in 1918, before Debs was sentenced, he addressed the court. Some of what he said has been included in compendiums of great speeches, and I would like to quote it to you today: "While there is a lower class, I am in it; while there is a criminal element, I am of it; and while there is a soul in prison, I am not free." As time passed, Debs was recognized for the peaceful idealist he was; he received a presidential pardon after serving part of his sentence. And though his idea of a socialist society has never persuaded America, we have come to realize that caring for one's fellow human beings is not a political doctrine. It is an expression of humanity. But caring is not enough. We must translate caring into helping.

SEPTEMBER 15

Central American Independence Day

Today is Central American Independence Day, marking the attainment of independence by Costa Rica, El Salvador, Guatemala, Honduras, and Nicaragua in 1821. I think it is worth noting that this gives them a longer record of independence than Belgium or Finland or many other nations. When we look south of the border we sometimes forget that those nations have been trying to make a go of things on their own almost as long as we have and usually with a lot less in the way of resources. In the early years of their independence they were the targets of all kinds of empire builders, including American adventurers, and in our own time they have continued to be the targets of imported political movements, as well as home-grown power-grabbers. On Central American Independence Day it is timely to recall that independence, other people's as well as our own, needs lots of protection. It is worth considering how we can safeguard our own.

Nuremberg Laws

This was the day that Nazi Germany adopted the so-called Nuremberg Laws in 1935, embracing anti-Semitism as the official policy of the country, depriving Jewish Germans of their citizenship, and establishing criteria of so-called

Aryan racial purity. I think it is safe to say that this was one of the most depraved sets of laws in modern history, but still the history of the next few years showed most of the world trying very hard to conduct business as usual. The victims of Nazism were trapped; only a small proportion were able to find sanctuary elsewhere, and four years later, when Nazism exploded into war, the other nations of the world were still unprepared. That was a long time ago, but we still have people who think we can go our own way and ignore the threats to our way of life posed by growing military and subversive ambitions of rivals in other parts of the world. Those threats, ladies and gentlemen, are not imaginary; the dangers are real, and I would like to tell you where and why.

Government

I would like to read you a quotation from remarks made on this day in a past year. "It is obvious, even to a casual observer," the quote goes, "that the administration of the state has been unnecessarily complicated and elaborated, too many separate commissions and boards set up, business methods neglected, money wasted, and a state of affairs brought about of which a successful business concern would be ashamed." That was said by Woodrow Wilson when he was running for governor of New Jersey in 1910. Obviously, some of the problems of government have been problems for generations. It is the nature of an entrenched bureaucracy to grow; it is the nature of legislatures not to trust new tasks to the old bureaucracy but rather to set up a new bureaucracy for these new tasks. Old government bureaus very rarely die; they just go on and on and on. How do we stop this?

James Fenimore Cooper

Today is the birthday of James Fenimore Cooper, perhaps our greatest writer of adventure stories of American history. He was born in Burlington, New Jersey, in 1789. Like many people Cooper had a different estimate of his own abilities from other folks; he thought his best work was his political opinions, which he incorporated not only into some of his less successful fiction but also into such collections of essays as *The American Democrat.* His views were not always popular. He wrote, for example, that quote, "the tendencies of democracies are, in all things, to mediocrity, since the tastes, knowledge, and principles of the majority form the tribunal of appeal." Close quote. That there are elements of tastelessness and grossness in the public diet is undoubtedly true, but there has never been a time when great music, great works of art, and great literature were more popular or more appreciated. I suggest to you, ladies and gentlemen, that we have a lot more to be proud of than to be ashamed of—and I propose to give you chapter and verse.

SEPTEMBER 16

Where Are We Going?

When astronaut Neil Armstrong addressed a joint session of Congress on this day in 1969 after his triumphant return from being the first man to walk on the moon, he said that in the coming centuries "humanity may begin to understand its most baffling mystery—where are we going?" Armstrong was referring to the movement of the Earth in the cosmos, but the same question can be asked in more terrestrial terms. Where are we headed, and what lies ahead?

Cherokee Strip Day

Times change, and I suppose there are some people who, upon hearing that today is Cherokee Strip Day, think it refers to some kind of Indian tease; but what it is, in fact, is the anniversary of the opening of the territory in Oklahoma known as the Cherokee Strip to settlement in 1893. It reminds us that the growth of this country was not simply a matter of luck and God-given resources; it was the result of incredibly hard work by incredibly hardy people who moved into the wilderness and made it bloom. Today we have similar opportunities, even though our wilderness is more urban than rural, and the job of making it bloom is just as difficult. What can we do about it?

Francis Parkman

Today is the birthday of Francis Parkman, the great American historian who was born in Boston in 1823. It was Parkman who wrote, "Faithfulness to the truth of history involves far more than a research, however patient and scrupulous, into special facts. Such facts may be detailed with the most minute exactness, and yet the narrative, taken as a whole, may be unmeaning or untrue." Parkman wrote those lines many years ago, but in the expanding world of modern mass media they become even more pertinent. It is easy to prove things by means of an anecdote about one special person or one isolated incident, or by blowing up an unrepresentative case as if it were typical. Today I would like to speak of some of our problems in broader, more general, and, I believe, more accurate terms.

Amos Alonzo Stagg

On this day in 1960, a man named Amos Alonzo Stagg retired as an adviser to Stockton Junior College in California. He was 98 years old. Amos Alonzo Stagg played football at Yale and was named a member of Walter Camp's very first All-American team. For 41 years he was the football coach at the University of Chicago and virtually the patron saint of modern football. When he was seventy, instead of accepting retirement, he went to the College of the Pacific as its football coach. He was one of those fortunate individuals who makes a mockery of the calendar. Unfortunately the calendar cannot be equally defied by all of us, and speakers particularly should remember that time waits for no man. So let me get right to the point of my remarks here today, before any of us get much older.

SEPTEMBER 17

Russia into Poland

The phrase "a date that will live in infamy" was coined by Franklin D. Roosevelt to describe the day that the Japanese staged their sneak attack on Pearl Harbor. *This* date, September 17, in 1939, qualified for that description first. That was when Soviet Russia invaded Poland from the east, while the Nazis continued the attacks from the west that they had launched on September 1. Poland's fate as a vassal state of Russia after the war was sealed by that treachery. It is worth remembering when the Soviets denounce western imperialism. But a great many Americans seem to have forgotten—or perhaps they never knew—the revealed nature of the Soviet Union. As a matter of fact I don't believe we teach enough in our schools about Russian history, even though that history is the best guide to what Russia will do next. In Russia itself they rewrite history to fit the party line. In this country we value the right of historians—or anyone else—to call things as they see them, and that is what I would like to do here today.

Steuben Day

Today is the birthday of Friedrich Wilhelm Ludolf Gerhard Augustin von Steuben, who wasn't quite as important a soldier in Europe as he claimed to be but proved to be even better when he was appointed Inspector General of the Continental Army in the American Revolution. Steuben, born in 1730 in Prussia, was the man who turned a civilian militia into a disciplined army for George Washington and became a fine battlefield commander as well. From the beginning of its national existence, the United States was the beneficiary of the talents of people of many national origins, a tradition that continues in our own time. People who see no future for themselves in their homelands find their future here, and help to build a greater nation. We think of ourselves as offering sanctuary for the oppressed, but we also benefit from their presence. They do jobs we don't want to do; they bring new cultural aspects to the richest and most varied culture in the world. We are told it is time to shut the door, but I disagree.

Camp David

It was on this day in 1978 that President Jimmy Carter, Egypt's President Anwar Sadat, and Israel's Prime Minister Menachem Begin returned from Camp

David with the historic agreement entitled "Framework for Peace in the Middle East." Whether it was as significant a forward step on the road to Middle Eastern peace as the world hoped in 1978 is still for history to say, but it was an inspiring piece of evidence that ancient enmities need not be permanent. On the anniversary of the Camp David agreement it seems appropriate to talk about the threats to peace in the world today.

Constitution

Today is Citizenship Day and the start of Constitution Week, the anniversary of the adoption of the Constitution in 1787 by the Constitutional Convention for submission to the states. Back in 1787 it marked the end of the long period of talk and discussion at the convention, so in one sense it seems ironic that this anniversary day should be the occasion for more talk on my part. It is good to know, however, that thanks to the Bill of Rights appended to our Constitution, I may speak freely and openly as my conscience dictates; so here goes.

SEPTEMBER 18

Greta Garbo

Today is the birthday of Greta Louise Gustaffson, who was born in Stockholm, Sweden, in 1905 and grew up to be Greta Garbo. Garbo was the most glamorous film star of her time, but even more famous for her privacy, expressed in a line allegedly from one of her films: "I want to be alone." This was regarded as rather strange for a movie star, and when Garbo retired from the screen into very private life, "I want to be alone" followed her. The public—or at least the paparazzi-minded section of it—seems to regard bashful celebrities as a challenge. Now, ladies and gentlemen, I don't pretend to know what prompted Garbo's attitude, and I am happy to say on this occasion that I do not share her point of view. I am delighted not to be alone; indeed, if I feel privileged to have the opportunity to talk to you here today, and I shall proceed to make the most of it.

The *Times* and CBS

This is the birthday of two of the greatest communicators of American history, *The New York Times,* first published in 1851, and CBS, which went on the air as the Columbia Broadcasting System in 1927. When I consider the amount of information and exhortation that one prints and the other broadcasts in the course of a single day, I must admit that it makes me somewhat diffident about raising my own single voice, but I have come here with something to say and I am grateful for the opportunity to be heard.

Samuel Johnson

Samuel Johnson, the great British man of letters who was born on this day in 1709, wrote that "the mental disease of the present generation is impatience of study, contempt of the great masters of ancient wisdom, and a disposition to rely wholly upon unassisted genius and natural sagacity." I have quoted what wise Dr. Johnson wrote more than 200 years ago to make the point that human nature does not change. Every generation fears that its heirs are letting things go to pot, even though it seems to me that every succeeding generation is stronger and better equipped to win the battle of life. It is time, I believe, to stop asking what's wrong with young people and start celebrating what is right. I propose to start that celebration here and now.

Brumidi

Some years ago a joint resolution of Congress designated this day as Constantino Brumidi Day. I daresay not too many Americans were aware of it, and the name of Constantino Brumidi is hardly an American watchword. Let me identify him. He was an Italian artist who came to the United States on this day in 1852. The magnificent frescoes in our great Capitol building are his work. Not all of us, whose names may be equally unfamiliar to posterity, can leave behind such a wonderful legacy, but all of us have the opportunity to contribute to human betterment, and today I want to speak about one way we can participate in that work.

SEPTEMBER 19

Washington's Farewell Address

What history describes as President George Washington's farewell address was never spoken, but it was published on this day in 1796 in the *Philadelphia Daily American Advertiser*. In addition to suggesting that our policy be—quote— "to steer clear of permanent alliances with any portion of the foreign world," Washington said, "Promote then as an object of primary importance, institutions for the general diffusion of knowledge. In proportion as the structure of a government gives force to public opinion, it is essential that public opinion be enlightened." Now, of course, every speaker likes to feel that his or her remarks are serving to enlighten public opinion, and I am as guilty of that feeling as the next; but even if you disagree with what I am about to say, I hope that my remarks will at least serve to stimulate your own thinking on the subjects at hand.

"Dixie"

This is the birthday of the anthem of the South, "Dixie," which, interestingly enough, was not born in the South at all. It was sung for the first time on this day in 1859 at a minstrel show in New York City by Dan Emmett; whether he wrote it is not firmly established. When you consider that our national anthem, "The Star-Spangled Banner," was composed to the tune of an old English song, "To Anacreon in Heaven," and that the "Battle Hymn of the Republic" was set to an folk tune already familiar as "John Brown's Body," it becomes clear that patriotic sentiment, however noble the verse, benefits greatly from a familiar or catchy tune. I feel that oratorical appeals to patriotism also need an added touch, above and beyond the fervor of love of country. That added touch, it seems to me, is the conviction that we are in tune with the times. "My country, right or wrong" is a noble sentiment, but patriotism cannot long survive a feeling that one's country is wrong, for the true patriot wants, more than anything else, to put the country right. And, that being the case, my remarks here today have that patriotic purpose in mind.

President Arthur

There are some cynics who say that Chester Alan Arthur's chief claim to fame was that he was the only president with three first names. I am reminded of that remark because today is the anniversary of Vice-President Arthur's assumption of the presidency in 1881 after President James A. Garfield was killed by an assassin's bullet. Arthur had been assumed to be committed to the political spoils system, but he proved to be a vigorous reformer. His ultimate honesty was his refusal to conduct a strong campaign for a second term; he knew, although he kept it secret, that he was dying, and two years after the 1884 election he died. I think it is fitting to remember him today as a reminder that the profession of politics can be not only an honorable one but at times an uplifting one as well. Unfortunately it is not always easy to separate the crass from the cream, and it isn't always the cream that rises to the top. Nevertheless, the sport of watching politics can be most interesting, as I hope the observations I am about to make will suggest.

Silo Explosion

I find it interesting to compare the widely publicized Three Mile Island incident with another nuclear event, the explosion on this day in 1980 of an underground nuclear missile silo at Damascus, Arkansas, with one fatality and 22 people injured. The contrast arises from the fact that the leak at Three Mile Island created worldwide controversy about the safety of nuclear energy plants and the actual explosion in Arkansas caused barely a ripple of public discussion.

Here was the proof of the wisdom of Thomas Jefferson's remark, "How much pain have cost us the evils which have never happened." We have a great facility for worrying more about what might be than about what is, particularly, of course, when it serves the interest of a special point of view. Viewing with alarm is a great old American political tradition and a wonderful approach to speechmaking, but today I plan to make my point the hard way, without trying to scare anybody.

SEPTEMBER 20

Magellan

It was on this day in 1519 that Ferdinand Magellan, a Portuguese explorer in the service of Spain, led his flotilla of five ships from San Lucar de Barrameda in an attempt to sail west to the Indies. In what later became known as the Philippines, Magellan himself was killed by the natives, but his surviving shipmates completed the first circumnavigation of the world. Today we can make the same trip by air so easily and so quickly that Magellan's feat doesn't seem as impressive as it truly was. That happens so often with the deeds of great men; they risk everything in a pioneering enterprise and make the same thing far less risky for the people who follow them. This is true not only in exploration but in business and government as well. If nobody is willing to take the risks of a new idea, then we will never know whether that new idea is any good. Life is not a sure thing. Occasionally we simply must take a chance—not for the sake of gambling but rather as part of the endless human search for better ways of doing more things. We have such opportunities today.

A.A.A.S.

Today is the birthday of the American Association for the Advancement of Science, the nation's oldest and largest national scientific society, which was founded on this day in 1848. Among the glories of America are the mechanisms we have devised for the exchange of scientific information, and our science societies perform a key role in this regard. American scientists through the years have done a fine job of bringing young people into their community of knowledge and opportunity. But I have a feeling that not as good a job has been done in science's public relations. There is still a substantial portion of the population to whom science is black magic, and still an unwillingness on the part of many scientists to share their views with the lay press. Those scientists who become familiar commentators in the lay press are usually special pleaders for a particular cause. Meanwhile, we lay people are unable to decide for ourselves who is right about air purity or pollen counts or a dozen other scientific questions close to home. So I have some questions to ask the scientists.

Upton Sinclair

One of the most prolific authors of the twentieth century, Upton Sinclair, was born on this day in 1878 in Baltimore. Although he won the Pulitzer Prize for one of his eleven Lanny Budd novels in 1942, his most famous book was published thirty-six years earlier. It was *The Jungle,* which exposed the horrible conditions that existed at that time in the Chicago stockyards and meat-processing plants. I have chosen as my text for today something Sinclair wrote back in 1926. "All truly great art," he said, "is optimistic. The individual artist is happy in his creative work, and in its reception by the public." Why then do we have so many artists, literary as well as visual, who seem so fascinated by the seamy side of life? Is it perhaps true that they are not up to the challenge of depicting better things? Viewing with alarm is always easier than conveying hope. I do not plan to take that easy path today.

Unification of Italy

It is surprising to realize that the nation of Italy has only existed since this day in 1870, when troops of King Victor Emmanuel I entered Rome, which had previously been defended by French forces and ruled by the Vatican. We think of the United States as a relatively young nation, but the fact is that we were a single nation long before the Italians or the Germans, and we were a democracy long before most other nations of the world. I don't believe that any of the foreign variations on the idea of democratic government have ever improved on the original American model. Proportionate representation and parliamentary cabinets, for example, have led to the splintering of political parties and the formation of coalition blocs that sacrifice principle for the sake of expediency. So I stand before you to say, let's not fiddle with a structure that works. And let's be clear about what kind of fiddling is being proposed.

SEPTEMBER 21

Churchill Changed His Mind

A small item in the newspapers a number of years ago reported that a collector had acquired a letter written on this day in 1904 by a young Englishman named Winston Churchill. In it young Churchill wrote, "I have decided to give up politics and devote the rest of my life to literature." How fortunate that he decided to change his mind! All too often we trap ourselves for fear of being regarded as weak-minded and inconsistent. But consistency of itself is no great virtue, any more than flexibility is necessarily a weakness. If we refuse to change our minds, then we aren't really thinking creatures; and if there were not a possibility of changing minds, there would not be much point other than cheerleading for the public speaker. I have not come here to fly in the face of your firm opinions, but I hope my remarks will give you some further perspective and, at the very least, some food for thought.

Justice O'Connor

On this day in 1981, the U.S. Senate confirmed the appointment of Sandra Day O'Connor as the first female justice of the Supreme Court. The vote was ninety-nine to zero. For generations there had been talk about getting a woman on the highest court, and for years nobody did very much about it. When the nomination was finally made there was virtually no opposition. This has happened before with changes that at first seemed to be revolutionary; we discover when the change finally comes that it is neither revolutionary nor hard to take. I hope we remember that fact the next time we are confronted with new ideas. I am not here to discuss how we have done things in the past but rather to talk about how, perhaps, we can do them better in the future.

H. G. Wells

Today is the birthday of H. G. Wells, the great British writer who was born in 1866. To describe Wells as a science-fiction writer is like calling Ralph Waldo Emerson an after-dinner speaker. Herbert George Wells envisioned miraculous future developments and wrote one of the great histories of the past, *The Outline of History*. In 1914 he wrote of atomic bombs, and in 1931 he noted that—quote—"human history becomes more and more a race between education and catastrophe." That race, of course, is still going on; if I can contribute, in however small or modest a measure, to education against catastrophe, I will be grateful.

Automobile Anniversary

On this day in 1893, a machine designed by the Duryea brothers made its appearance on the streets of Springfield, Massachusetts. It was an automobile powered by a gasoline engine. It didn't exactly take the world by storm, but it led to the formation of the first American car manufacturing company and brought the infant industry to the attention of people like Henry Ford. The Duryea brothers, who split up soon thereafter, each pursued the automobile manufacturing business for fifteen years or so, but they never achieved the results that some of the other pioneers were able to accomplish. Very few revolutions in our modern world are the work of a single person; more often the inspiration and the perspiration come from many individuals, beginning with the author of the original idea or device. And what usually makes the difference is entrepreneurial skill rather than originality. The same is true of the public speaker. It is fine to have an inspiring new idea, but it's even better to be able to present practical suggestions for how a new idea can be brought to reality.

And sometimes it isn't a new idea that needs this kind of suggestion but rather an old idea whose time has come. At any rate, my time has come to talk, so here I go.

SEPTEMBER 22

Soviet Atom Bomb

This was the day in 1949 that a new force came into the world. On this day the Soviet Union tested its first atomic bomb. Since then the competition in weaponry has intensified, the amount of armament in the world has greatly increased, and the burden of armament on national budgets has increased even more. One thing that seems to be eternally true in the development of new weapons of war is that as they become more sophisticated they also become infinitely more expensive. That expense has to come at the sacrifice of other areas of expenditure, which means that we simply must find some way to put a cap on the arms race. How can we do this?

The Book of Mormon

This was the day in 1827 when the Mormons believe the Golden Plates of the Book of Mormon were revealed to the founder of that faith, Joseph Smith, in upstate New York. Despite and perhaps because of the terrible persecution to which Smith and his followers were subjected, this indomitable body of believers has survived and prospered. Early on they adopted the practice of tithing, and they continue it today. Clearly, it has made for a better, healthier, and sounder community, and it provides a model of giving for other segments of our society. The dividends of generous and consistent giving need no sales pitch from me, but I hope that a reminder will not be untimely today.

Sherman Adams

On this day in 1958, a highly respected assistant to President Dwight D. Eisenhower resigned after having been accused of accepting gifts from and doing favors for a New England businessman. The assistant, Sherman Adams, insisted that no wrongdoing was involved, and, indeed, no criminal charges followed. But President Eisenhower's standards apparently were more demanding than those of some later presidents. What is true for the White House has been true of American society in general. Things that were considered wrong years ago are now tolerated and in some instances even admired. Living together and bringing children into the world without wedlock is not merely tolerated but publicized and flaunted. Politicians on the take are reelected. We are told that these trends are cyclical, that the pendulum will swing back to stricter standards, but it seems to me that the pendulum has already swung farther in the opposite direction than ever before. Speaking out against what used to be regarded as immorality has become a hallmark of the extreme right; I believe it is time people of more moderate views spoke out on this issue.

Emancipation Proclamation

Every schoolchild knows that the great moral issue of the Civil War was the question of slavery. Given that fact, it is interesting that not until this day in 1862, well over a year after the war began, did President Abraham Lincoln issue the preliminary Emancipation Proclamation, to take effect on January 1; and even then it applied only to areas under Confederate control. The reason for all of this caution was not that Lincoln didn't believe in the principle of freedom for all but that he was trying to persuade the border slaveholding states to remain loyal to the Union. Perhaps there is a lesson in this for those impatient for immediate action on new reforms. Sometimes even moral imperatives are limited by actual circumstances; actions taken immediately sometimes have unforeseen consequences. But the opposite side of this coin is that always going slowly sometimes causes the opportunity to be lost or permits an evil to grow stronger. Passing a law is not enough if the public is not yet ready for that law, but who is to determine—and how—whether the public is ready? The answer, I believe, lies with the public itself. As long as people have the vote they can express their will, and no major law should be passed before the public has had a chance to go to the polls knowing where the various candidates stand. That means, of course, that if you don't go to the polls you have no right to squawk. I hope that is a right you will protect, and I urge you to be sure you are counted. So my plea to each of you is simply this—get involved.

SEPTEMBER 23

Lewis and Clark

On this day in 1806, the Lewis and Clark expedition returned to its starting place in St. Louis after two years of incredible exploration of the American continent. They returned with a storehouse of information about this land. We are amazed by modern astronauts who venture into the outer unknown, but none of them has ever gone through as long or as rigorous a venture as the explorers led by Lewis and Clark in the unknown wilderness that was western America. Our astronauts, like Lewis and Clark before them, explored strictly to acquire more knowledge. That hunger for knowledge, in my judgment, is the secret of American progress. It is a hunger that we must encourage by improving educational opportunities. And education today can certainly use improvement.

Baseball Anniversary

According to the available records the first baseball team was organized on this day in 1845. It was the Knickerbocker Club of New York, headed by Alexander Cartwright. Three years later the club adopted an official baseball uniform, creating another great precedent in this country. The significance of this anniversary, it seems to me, is that it marks the birth of the American team concept, the beginning of the kind of tradition that has inspired so many generations to work together. We have managed to have a pretty fair balance between American individualism and American team play. That balance, I believe, is being challenged today. Team play is not conformism; it is a meshing of individual talents in a coordinated, joint effort. Today, unfortunately, we have teams, in public life as well as in sports, where the talents, instead of meshing with each other, seem to be working at cross purposes. We have politicians who will only play if they can be captain; we have players in every walk of life who strike out as often as not but hit the occasional spectacular homer and are glorified for it even though they do very little for their teams. So I am here to raise my voice in favor of the old concept of team play.

Major Andre

One of the ironic turns of history came on this day in 1780, when Major John Andre of Great Britain, by all accounts a gallant and honest fighting man, was captured in civilian clothes behind American lines while returning from a meeting with the American traitor Benedict Arnold, to arrange for Arnold's betrayal of West Point. Andre, the soldier performing his duty, was executed as a spy, while the traitor, Benedict Arnold, escaped and became a turncoat officer in the British Army. Life is full of Major Andres—people who get caught—and too many Benedict Arnolds—criminals who get away. Even when these criminals ultimately get caught, all too often they have enjoyed years of the fruits of their evil doings. Part of the cause is the slowness of our system of criminal justice. Part is the increased volume of crime, which complicates law enforcement and crime prevention. And part is the American public's tolerance of forms of crime that are the breeding grounds for worse crimes to come— drug addiction, traffic anarchy, and theft, for example. I don't think we, the public, are powerless. I think there are things we can do.

Time Capsule

On this day in 1938, they buried a time capsule at the World's Fair in New York City. I don't know what items they put into the capsule, but it turned my thoughts to our own time and had me wondering what I would put into a time capsule today to be unearthed by some future generation. It's a good question to ask yourself. What are the hallmarks of our time? A transistor chip, undoubtedly; a computer, very possibly; a spacecraft; and as I list these things I say to myself, why is it that material things come to your mind first? Why doesn't it occur to me early on to include in the time capsule the Civil Rights Act or any one of a half-dozen notable Supreme Court decisions? Is it that I reflect a general preoccupation with so-called practical, tangible items and a disinterest in principles? Is it the triumph of materialism as never before? Ladies and gentlemen, I think materialism will never triumph. I ask you to look around this world with me, and you will see the evidence.

SEPTEMBER 24

John Marshall

Today is the birthday of one of the giants of American history, Chief Justice John Marshall. He was born in 1755 in Midland, Virginia. It was Marshall who enunciated the doctrine of judicial review, which made the Supreme Court the final arbiter of questions of constitutional law. It was he who laid down the dictum that the power to tax involves the power to destroy. But above all, it was he who made the constitutional separation of powers among the executive, legislative, and judicial branches a living reality. Over the long run the system has shown time and again how worthwhile it is. I think it is time for us to realize that and to work a little harder to protect it. Let me cite some specifics.

Black Friday

On this day in 1869, which was a Friday, there was a panic on Wall Street as a result of an attempt by Jay Gould and Jim Fisk to corner the gold market. The day was known to history as Black Friday; the panic ended only when the government started selling gold to foil the plotters. But that episode hasn't discouraged future attempts to corner a market, as for example with silver in our own time. Fortunately, the casualties have been mainly the billionaires who tried to do the cornering. The OPEC nations had a good thing for quite a while; but the discovery of oil in non-OPEC nations and some belt tightening by oil consumers seemed to put a ceiling on the oil prices. Aberrations in the economy caused by market manipulators will probably always be with us, but usually there are plenty of advance warnings. The oil market, for example, could have taken conservation steps and other defense measures before OPEC tightened the screws; the fact that we were able to do so afterward is ample proof that no special ingenuity was needed. The trick is to foresee shortages and do something about them before they blossom. Let me talk about some specific danger signals.

F. Scott Fitzgerald

Today is the birthday of F. Scott Fitzgerald, who exemplified and chronicled the jazz age of the twenties. He was born in St. Paul in 1896 and flashed across the literary and social scene like a rocket, leading a seemingly glamorous and undoubtedly tortured life until he died at the age of 44. Fitzgerald was one of those people who reach the full flower of their ability very early in life and ultimately blow themselves out. Impatience is a characteristic of young people, but it simply cannot and should not be a healthy way of life. Those of us who try to get everything done in a hurry are apt to miss half the fun. That is as true in everyday life as it is in creative pursuits. And it is certainly true in government, where probably more damage has been done by hasty, ill-considered acts than in any other area of human activity. It is not accidental that Congress is designed as a deliberative body where policies can be discussed before they are enacted. It is not accidental that an election campaign lasts for months, to give the electorate a chance to mull over the issues. Part of the process, too, is giving an opportunity to those with particular views to speak out, even between elections. I thank you for giving me that opportunity here today.

Babe Ruth

This was the day in 1934 when Babe Ruth made his last appearance as a regular on the New York Yankees baseball team. In every field there are a few superstars who make the difference, and Babe Ruth stood above all others in baseball, not merely because of his talents as a player but for that extra something that made him very special. It was his spectacular feats as a home-run hitter that really brought baseball into the box office big-time. They called the Yankee Stadium the house that Ruth built, and it was his following that first filled the Stadium. There have been many great players since George Herman Ruth, but he stands alone. Virtually every year some newer player is hailed as the modern Ruth, but that is too high a standard. We can't expect a new Babe Ruth every year any more than we can expect a new George Washington or Abraham Lincoln in the White House after every election. We have a tendency to expect too much and to become too easily disappointed. I don't think it is fair to compare now to then, or to judge our present leaders by the memories of the past. So, in my remarks today, I will talk only about what is happening now, with never a backward glance.

SEPTEMBER 25

Easy Solutions

When President Dwight D. Eisenhower came to Peoria, Illinois, to deliver a speech on this day in 1956, he couldn't resist a complaint. "Farming looks mighty easy," he said, "when your plow is a pencil, and you're a thousand miles from the corn field." It so happens, ladies and gentlemen, that I am going to be talking today about somebody else's corn fields, and the fact that these are somebody else's responsibilities makes the task of caring for them seem simpler than it really is; but I speak not from the point of view of the tiller of the fields. I speak as one who is dependent on the products of those fields. That, I think, is a level of direct interest that entitles me to make my comments.

William Faulkner

Today is the birthday of the great American writer, William Faulkner, who was born in Mississippi in 1897. When he was 26 years old he changed the spelling of his name. He added a u to make the spelling *F-a-u-l-k-n-e-r*. Nobody seems to know why he did it, but under the revised spelling his name became famous. I don't suggest that adding the letter *u* made the difference, although it may indeed have given him, for whatever reason, a psychological boost to become a success. But I do know that we put an undue value on letters and even names. Subsidy sounds infinitely better than giveaway, for example, and AID is more quickly understood than the Agency for International Development. The trouble is that in our zeal for psychologically correct nomenclature we may lose sight of the essential performance. Today I want to talk about that misnamed universe, the Third World. Is it one world or several, for example? And what exactly does Third World mean?

Hunting and Fishing Day

Back in 1979, President Jimmy Carter proclaimed the fourth Saturday of each September as National Hunting and Fishing Day, which meant that every year around this time the hunters and the antihunters would have another round of their longstanding controversy. It is one of a whole family of controversies that we are not going to settle by talking about them, although that of course will not prevent the advocates of either side from continuing to wage the good fight. I prefer to talk today about problems I feel we can solve and about one in particular.

Publick Occurrences

When the first American newspaper, *Publick Occurrences*, issued its lead-off edition on this day in 1690 in Boston, it included a statement of its policy: "Furnished once a month (or if any Glut of Occurrences happen, oftener). . . ." The paper never got the chance to handle any "glut of occurrences" because its first issue was also its only issue, but I can't help wondering how much real news there would be, whether indeed there would be any glut of occurrences, if the various news media were not committed to daily reporting. How much so-called news today is offered not because it is happening but rather because it fills space or time between the advertisements or helps sell the news product? Are our values being distorted? Is crime as pervasive as it seems from the news reports? I don't pretend to have the definitive answers to these questions, but I have some things to say that you may not have seen in the press, although I believe they are significant and important.

SEPTEMBER 26

George Gershwin

This is the birthday of George Gershwin, the great American composer who was born in Brooklyn in 1898. It was Gershwin, more than any other composer, who bridged the gap between popular and classical music, with *Rhapsody in Blue* and *Porgy and Bess* among his notable accomplishments. It seems to me that the great men and women are those who defy the normal borders of their world and thereby widen the horizons of all of us. We will never be a totally classless or totally homogeneous world, but if we talk only to ourselves, if we listen only to ourselves, if we ignore those of differing views or differing ways of life, we will be sealing our own isolated doom. Perhaps what I am going to say here today will seem in some respects to come from a different perspective from your own. If so, it will serve a valid purpose. If, however, it reinforces your own views and perceptions, that too is a valid purpose. But if I fail to hold your attention, that will be the ultimate commentary.

Gold Star Mother's Day

This is the season of Gold Star Mother's Day, specifically observed on the last Sunday of September, a time for remembering that the sacrifice of those who have given their lives for their country is matched by the sacrifice of those who have given their children. In the last analysis, our greatest gift to the world in which we live is the gift of children, the heirs we hope will carry on and improve whatever we have done to build that world. So the season of Gold Star Mother's Day is a good time to ask ourselves what we are doing to give a better life to our children, and to insure that there will be no Gold Star Mothers in the future.

T. S. Eliot

Poet, playwright, and critic Thomas Stearns Eliot, who was born on this day in 1888 in St. Louis, was a man from whom one could quote for hours, but I prefer a brief couple of lines from his poem "The Hollow Men." "This is the way the world ends," he wrote, "Not with a bang but a whimper." It seems to me that even before the world ends we already have too much whimpering. We have a seemingly endless capacity for feeling sorry for ourselves and bemoaning our supposed plight. I dispute that pessimism, and I will tell you why.

Kennedy–Nixon Debate

The first face-to-face debate between major presidential candidates in modern times took place when John F. Kennedy and Richard M. Nixon stepped to the dais on this day in 1960 in Chicago, with the television cameras and radio microphones carrying their words to the far corners of the nation. I can't tell you how reassuring it is to be speaking to a somewhat smaller audience today and to know that the stakes are also somewhat smaller. I stand before you simply to present some ideas that I believe are worthy of your attention.

SEPTEMBER 27

Samuel Adams

In the period that led to the American Revolution, Samuel Adams, who was born on this day in 1722, was one of the great leaders. He was the firebrand of the Boston independence movement, the originator of the Committees of Correspondence that were the mainsprings of the Revolution in the various colonies, a member of the first and second Continental Congresses, and a signer of the Declaration of Independence. But thereafter he seems to have fallen from prominence, although he remained in Congress until 1781 and was Governor of Massachusetts from 1794 to 1797. Sam Adams was one of those outspoken, indefatigable people who do best at sounding alarums and organizing resistance. He was not, as were men like Thomas Jefferson, willing and able to perform the relatively dull chores of formulating the Constitution and midwifing the birth of a new concept of democracy. We will always need dedicated men like Sam Adams, but there comes a time when we need solutions more than alarums, perspiration more than inspiration, cool wisdom rather than passion. Now, today, is one of those times. I do not stand here to tell you what our problems are; you know that as well as I do. I am here with what I hope are some constructive suggestions.

Alfred Thayer Mahan

This is the birthday of the great naval historian and strategist, Alfred Thayer Mahan. I find it particularly interesting that this man of the sea was born at West Point, New York, the son of a professor of engineering at the U.S. Military Academy. In 1840, when Mahan went off to college, he chose not West Point but Annapolis. Our parents always seem to hope that we will follow in their footsteps, but most of us have a tendency to strike off on our own. In

Mahan's day there weren't as many options, because there weren't as many fields of employment, but today the range is greater than ever. But, for whatever reason, both students and career advisors always seem to opt for the professional training that is about to produce more people than the particular profession needs. Teachers, for example, never seem to be in proper supply—there are either too many of them or not enough. Engineers have gone through the same cycle; psychologists as well. There is a certain bandwagon effect. A profession gets hot and everybody trains for it, to the point where there aren't enough jobs to satisfy the glut of people. At that point, fewer and fewer young people enter the profession, and after a while there is a shortage again. This seems to be part of one of the inevitable cycles in a marketplace economy, and I think it is time we began to do something about it.

Radar

On this day in 1922, the Naval Aircraft Radio Laboratory in Washington made what some people claimed were the first radar observations. The full development of radar, however, didn't really come until World War II, when it became a practical and ultimately commonplace tool of military intelligence. Yesterday's miracle is today's routine. Abstract theories being worked on in obscure laboratories today will provide the miracles of tomorrow. One does not have to be a believer in divine intervention to expect that some day we will find endless sources of energy to replace petroleum or coal, new ways to grow crops more plentifully and efficiently, new means of instant communication wherever we may be, and so forth. It is fun to speculate when and where the next such miracle will come, and so today I want to talk about some of the possibilities.

Warsaw Surrenders

It was on this day in 1939 that Poland's capital city, Warsaw, surrendered to the invading forces of Nazi Germany after 19 days of heroic struggle in the early phases of World War II. It was not the end of Poland's efforts, by any means. Even though the two neighboring great powers, Russia and Germany, had combined to partition the Polish nation, the flame of resistance still burned. A Polish fighting force in exile joined the Allies, and the Jewish residents of Warsaw, in one of the most gallant pages of World War II, staged an epic battle against the overwhelming Nazi occupation. It ended with the Jewish population of the city virtually wiped out but at a tremendous cost to the Nazis. In the first siege of Warsaw in 1939, Russia was a Nazi ally, standing by; in the siege of the Warsaw ghetto years later, Russian forces that might have come to the aid of the Jews chose to stay away. Poland tells us that the best defense is not in alliances, but in your own strength. It is a lesson we should keep in mind these days. Why? Take a look at our alliances round the world.

SEPTEMBER 28

Confucius

Although there has been considerable uncertainty about the exact date, this day has been observed as the birthday of the great Chinese sage, Confucius. The sayings of Confucius have been capsules of wisdom for thousands of years, and today I want to quote one of his remarks which sounds like—and probably was—a warning for public speakers. "Without knowing the force of words," Confucius wrote, "it is impossible to know men." But I hope that my words will strike some notes that are worth sounding.

Black Sox

On this day in 1920, a grand jury in Chicago indicted eight members of the Chicago White Sox for "throwing" the 1919 World Series to the Cincinnati Reds. The players were all subsequently acquitted, but the federal judge who presided over that grand jury, Kenesaw Mountain Landis, became the first commissioner of baseball, and one of his first acts in that job was to ban the eight so-called "Black Sox" from organized baseball for life. It may not have been totally fair to the players, but it accomplished two things. It established, for the time of Judge Landis's tenure as commissioner, the absolute authority of that office, and it was a stern enough warning to make sure that the ballplayers kept their noses clean. Is there a lesson here for our law enforcement authorities?

Galloway

On this day in 1774 at a meeting of the Continental Congress, a Pennsylvania delegate named Joseph Galloway presented a plan for solving the colonies' difficulties with Great Britain. The Galloway plan would have established a colonial legislature to share jurisdiction over America with the British parliament and would have given the colonies something very similar to the dominion status that Canada and other British domains later enjoyed. The Galloway plan was defeated by one vote, but what is more interesting is that it was later removed from the minutes of the Congress. There are times when compromise is so unpopular that people like to pretend it was never suggested. It is much more satisfying to the ego to win than to settle for something less than total victory. Unfortunately, many of our public figures get themselves into a box by proclaiming that their positions are absolute and ironclad, so that compromise becomes difficult if not impossible. Nevertheless, I am here to suggest some compromises.

Dogpatch

This is the birthday of the inventive cartoonist, Al Capp, who was born in New Haven in 1909. He created the characters of the little hillbilly town of Dogpatch, beginning with Lil Abner and including Senator Phogbound, the brewers of Kickapoo joy juice, Moonbeam McSwine, and other charmers. Today I particularly recall Senator Phogbound, who would say and do anything to get himself reelected. We have, it seems to me, too much of the Phogbound syndrome in our public officials and some union leaders, as well, will say or do whatever is necessary to appeal to their constituency. It is a temptation for any speaker to ingratiate himself or herself with the audience by saying what they want to hear. I hope you won't mind too much if I prefer to say what I think you should hear. This is not the time for listening to Senator Phogbound.

SEPTEMBER 29

Scotland Yard

This is the birthday of Scotland Yard, perhaps the most famous police headquarters in the world. It was born a long time ago in 1829. There are more people, more criminals, more laws to be enforced these days. That is the watchword of our times—more. We have more of everything, including talk. When Marconi invented radio I doubt that he realized how much more talk there was going to be in the world as a result. When Bell invented the telephone I don't think he envisioned the kind of endless conversation that can now be carried from place to place. What this means is that the average public speaker has a lot more competition than there used to be. In that situation, the best thing to do is to speak your piece without delay, with clarity, and with a fair degree of speed. Having set those standards for myself, I thank you for the opportunity to speak to you, and I propose to get right to it.

Babi Yar

Human history is filled with magnificent accomplishments and almost as many tragedies. Today is the anniversary of one of the worst of those tragedies, the massacre at Babi Yar. Babi Yar is a place near Kiev in the Russian Ukraine, where in World War II on this day in 1941 the Nazis killed 200,000 Soviet citizens, at least half of them Jews. What makes Babi Yar notable is not only what the Germans did but what the Soviets later did not do. Not until 1966 was the permanent memorial erected on the spot, and in the planning of that monument there was a deliberate lack of mention of the anti-Semitic aspect of so much of the killing. Maybe that is because, long before Nazis began killing Jews, Russia was doing so in numberless pogroms. In Germany one has a basis for hoping that anti-Semitism was a temporary aberration; in Russia it has been a governmental policy under the commissars as under the tsar. This brings us to wonder whether religious or ethnic hatreds will ever be totally exterminated. I don't think it is pessimistic to say that as long as people have the capacity for hatred there will be those who play on that fact and try to find scapegoats. We must ask ourselves how best to prevent this from happening in countries like our own, where freedom of speech gives every hate-monger an opportunity to spew his or her venom. I think the history of the civil rights movement gives us the answer. Pass laws against discrimination, and enforce them. You may not be able to stamp out the hatred, but you will certainly limit the exercise of it. And meanwhile those educational efforts that deal with the misconceptions of racial and ethnic prejudice must be pursued. What, then, should our current agenda be?

Caesar's Air

Back on this day in 1976, there was a symposium on wildlife in America that was addressed in Washington, D.C., by Russell W. Peterson, who was then the chairman of the Council on Environmental Quality. He said something startling. "We breathe today," he said, "the same air that Julius Caesar breathed." The same air that Julius Caesar breathed. We can go further back than that. We breathe the same air that Father Abraham and the dinosaurs breathed— and we drink or swim in or navigate on the same water, because the air and the water are consumed by living organisms and then given back through nature's amazing processes. So when we pollute the air or the water we are interfering with our children's heritage and our children's children's. And we in our own century have done more to pollute the air and the water than in all the centuries before us. We have also learned more than our ancestors about how to repurify the air and the water we use. There are natural resources that may be exhausted through the normal process of use, like petroleum or copper, but air and water should be inexhaustible. What must we do, right here in our own community, to protect them?

National Foundation on Arts and Humanities

It was on this day in 1965 that President Lyndon B. Johnson signed the bill establishing the National Foundation on Arts and Humanities, and optimists saw it as the beginning of the golden age, when museums and other artistic institutions would be able to stop living hand to mouth and instead might look to the government for their funding. We know now, however, that the support of artistic and humanities endeavors cannot and should not be the total responsibility of government. We know now that it is possible for voluntary contributions to play an important role in supporting cultural activities. And we know now that sitting back and saying "let Uncle Sam do it" can be the road to disaster, because there is no guarantee that Uncle Sam will assign the same priorities among institutions that you and I do. So it is important to enlist the enthusiasm and the dollars of individuals and foundations and corporations, and I am here for that purpose.

SEPTEMBER 30

Ether

On this day in 1846, a dentist named William Morton discovered he could do almost anything in a patient's mouth by putting the patient to sleep first with ether. I have a different problem, of course. If the words in my mouth put you to sleep, I can't tell you anything; so, unlike Morton, I will use my skill, whatever it may be, to open your eyes or at the very least to capture your ears.

Goodbye September

The end of September is not, according to the calendar, when summer ceases; that change of season occurs on the 21st of the month or about that time. But in many ways the last day of September is the dividing line. We think of the turning of the leaves as an October event; we think of most of September as still the rerun season on television, still a time of pleasantly long daylight hours, still the regular baseball season. And so, on this final day of that now ending month of the year, I rise to salute some new beginnings that we can discern on the immediate horizon. We are in a new academic year, about to start a new federal fiscal year—a good time to talk about what seems to lie ahead.

Rayon

Although experiments in making synthetic fibers had been going on for years, it was on this day in 1902 that the first U.S. patent for the manufacture of rayon was awarded. From that unheralded beginning has grown one of the great new industries of the twentieth century. We have learned to synthesize all kinds of materials, and we seem to be developing new ones in a steady progression. Part of humanity's great talent is to develop efficient new resources from readily available materials. The only place where we seem to have lasting difficulties in this regard is with those readily available materials called human beings. We have been able to design robots to replace human hands, but we still haven't found out what to do with many of our human beings. Not merely those displaced by machines but those who, one way or another, are the dropouts of our society. It is worth talking about.

Taxicabs

On this day, for the first time, Americans became acquainted with a new French import called the taxi meter. It was in 1907 when a fleet of new fangled things called taxicabs rolled along Fifth Avenue in New York. For the first time rates were standardized on the basis of accurate measurement of the distance traveled. The rate, incidentally, was 30 cents for the first half-mile and 10 cents for each quarter-mile thereafter. Sometimes it seems to me that life in the years since the first taxi meters has itself become like a taxi ride—the longer you go, or the more time you take, the more you have to pay. Even when we think we are tightening our belts, we float new loans or get deeper into debt to pay off the old ones. I have no quick fix for this problem, but I do have a pet bugaboo. It is waste, the senseless destruction of assets and resources. Perhaps it will serve some constructive purpose to look at some of our wasteful practices.

OCTOBER 1

International Music Day

Today is observed as International Music Day. Music, of course, is the universal language. No American institution has become as familiar around the globe as American music; no German speaks to all peoples as well as Beethoven; we may not understand Russian, but we know and appreciate the work of Tchaikowsky. There is, I believe, an important lesson in this fact. It is the lesson that, different though the peoples of the world may be in customs, in language, in ways of life, there are important things that we have in common. So when we talk of building bridges between the cultures of the world, perhaps we should be talking about supporting the arts, so our arts can speak to those other cultures of the world. Perhaps we should remind ourselves that the arts often speak louder and clearer than words. And I believe we should bear in mind that supporting the arts is therefore a step toward a better world.

World Vegetarian Day

Some years ago the first of October was designated as World Vegetarian Day. Whether this is because it is harvest time or there is some other basis for the selection of this time of year for the observance I do not know, but World Vegetarian Day, if not perhaps the ideal time to talk turkey, is certainly the right occasion for trying to get to the roots of things. So let's proceed.

Pennsylvania Turnpike

It was on this day in 1940 that a new American revolution began. It began not with a battle but simply with the opening of the first modern high-speed turnpike in the United States, the first section of the Pennsylvania Turnpike. In the quarter of a century thereafter, this kind of transportation facility was built all over the nation, and America became truly mobile as a civilization. We had intercontinental roads before then, of course, but they went through the hearts and traffic jams of all the cities along their routes. With the coming of the turnpike we were able to go places in our own cars or trucks or in buses faster and more conveniently than ever before. That has been a repeated phenomenon of American history—the constant enhancement of the speed with which we can get from one point to another. The only place where we really haven't been able to make much of this progress is in public speaking. It still takes the public speaker as long to get from one point to another as it did a hundred years ago—as I am now about to prove.

Babe Ruth's Feat

In 1932 on this day, the New York Yankees and the Chicago Cubs met in the third game of the World Series. Babe Ruth, who had already hit a home run in the first inning, came to bat again in the fifth, and the Chicago fans in Wrigley Field jeered the home-run king. The jeering grew in intensity as the count grew to two strikes and a ball, and Babe Ruth seemed to get mad about it. He turned to the Cub dugout and then pointed to the flagpole in right field, indicating he was going to park one there. And on the next pitch he hit a home run to that particular section of the ballpark. Of all the home runs he hit, this was probably the most satisfying, because he set a target for himself and then scored a bullseye. Thank goodness things are not that difficult for someone who is called upon to make a speech. You are not battling against somebody else's pitch, you're not required to clear all the bases, and you don't have nine able-bodied players waiting to throw you out. As a matter of fact, you have an opportunity that is denied to any of them—you can come up to bat and make your pitch at the same time. So here's mine.

OCTOBER 2

Mahatma Gandhi

By all accounts, Mahatma Gandhi, who was born on this day in 1869 in Porbandar, India, was the most consistent and eloquent apostle of nonviolence as a political tool. "I discovered in the earliest stages," he wrote, "that pursuit of truth did not permit violence being inflicted on one's opponent, but that he must be weaned from error by patience and sympathy." Now, ladies and gentlemen, I don't know how many of you I will wean from error today, but if I can't do that I will at least be grateful for your patience and sympathy. In return, I promise to be nonviolent.

Damned Public

This was the day when, in 1882, multimillionaire William H. Vanderbilt answered a reporter's question about how the public benefited from his railroads by saying, "The public be damned!" It made a wonderful story when it was quoted in the press, and I don't think any tycoon ever since would be loose-tongued enough to say something like that nowadays. But it is clear that there are some businesses—and presumably the people who run them—and some unions and government agencies as well who, while they may not feel "the public be damned," still don't give a damn about the public. Today I would like to give some examples.

American Enterprise

Back in 1981, the Congress of the United States passed a joint resolution designating this day of that year as American Enterprise Day. It is nice to know that American enterprise, like motherhood, kids, peace, groundhogs, and an array of other institutions, has had a day designated for it. Like the groundhog, it may be an endangered species. We all give lip service to the idea of free enterprise, but we all add some "buts." There are dozens of enterprises that depend on special privileges from the government. There are as many that misuse their freedom to the point that they bring regulation down upon themselves. So I don't think we can either worship or condemn free enterprise as an overall idea; instead, I suggest we talk about the character of American enterprise, the inventiveness of American enterprise, and, above all, the nature of American enterprise. So today I want to discuss these subjects not merely in general terms, but rather in the specifics of some well-known American enterprises.

Thurgood Marshall

When Thurgood Marshall became the first black justice of the Supreme Court of the United States on this day in 1967, somebody remarked that it was fine to talk of freedom of opportunity, but it was good to be able to look up to the bench and see it in black and white. One great thing we can say about the American people—and about American history—is that improvement is our way of life, whether in racial matters, invention, or the political process. It is always easy to view with alarm; today I would rather ask you to join with me in viewing with pride, conscious of how far we still have to go but proud of how far we have come in the significant area I have chosen as my topic.

OCTOBER 3

Hitler's Announcement

On this day in 1941, the leader of Nazi Germany, Adolf Hitler, who had conquered Western Europe and attacked his erstwhile ally, Soviet Russia, announced to the German people that Russia was so defeated that it would never rise again. Ladies and gentlemen, I hope what I say on this day turns out to be a little more accurate.

National 4-H Club Week

This is the season of National 4-H Club Week, dedicated to a dwindling breed—the young farm children of America. We can and must continue to learn from nature; we must learn that, one way or another, the riches we take must be given back, that for every action there is a reaction, and, above all, that you very rarely get something for nothing. Let's apply those principles to our situation today.

St. Francis of Assisi

Today is the birthday of Francis Bernadone, who was born in the city of Assisi in Italy in the year 1181 or 1182. We know him better, of course, as St. Francis of Assisi. It was he who said, "Where there is charity and wisdom, there is neither fear nor ignorance." Ladies and gentlemen, I hesitate to characterize my remarks as wisdom, but in lending me your ears you practice a very gracious form of charity, and I can only hope that the ensuing remarks will do their small part to see that fear and ignorance are not encouraged.

The Lesson of Standish

Today is the anniversary of the death of Miles Standish in Duxbury, Massachusetts, in 1656, when he was about 72 years old. Thanks to the totally fictional legend of his supposed courtship of Priscilla Mullins, we are apt to think of him as a blustering conniver, but the fact is that Miles Standish, whose job was to defend the Pilgrim colony, was a conscientious and capable peacemaker. He learned the language of the neighboring Indians and, after a few difficult years, kept the colony free of difficulties with the natives for almost half a century. It is a sad fact that bullies and troublemakers often get more attention and recognition than the quiet peacemakers; today I want to remedy that a bit by talking about some of the good people of our time.

OCTOBER 4

Dick Tracy

It was about this time in the year 1931 that a new comic strip named "Dick Tracy" was born, giving us the variety of crimes and criminals that for a while only the fertile imagination of the comic strip artists could produce. But, as it so often does, life caught up with fiction. Today's roster of crimes and criminals is as varied and bizarre as anything the cartoonists have yet dreamed up. The computer, for example, has provided a whole new area for thieves and twisted electronic geniuses. The growth of divorce has created another new type of criminal—the distraught parent who steals his or her own children. These are only a couple of samples of new criminals. And we are still fighting crime with the forces and the training that applied a couple of generations ago. Surely there is more that we can do.

Rembrandt

On this day in 1669, Rembrandt Harmens Van Rijn died in Amsterdam at the age of 63, all but forgotten and regarded as a has-been. Only after his death did the world come to perceive him as one of the truly timeless geniuses of painting. It has ever been thus—men and women of genius somehow seen more clearly by later generations than by their own. Realizing that, I sometimes ask myself who of the people of our own time will be seen that way 100 or 200 years from now. May I use this podium to make some nominations—and some predictions?

Damon Runyon

Damon Runyon was born on this day in 1884, in a town named, fittingly enough, Manhattan. Although Runyon grew up to be a great storyteller and chronicler of the gamblers, gangsters, and hangers-on of Manhattan's glittering Broadway, that was not the Manhattan in which he was born. His birthplace was a town by that name in Kansas. The man from Manhattan, Kansas, was able to give us a new look at Manhattan, New York. I don't pretend to have the ability of a Damon Runyon at painting word pictures, but I'd like to take this opportunity to give you my own picture of some interesting characters on the current scene.

Sulzberger's Idea of Responsibility

The late publisher of *The New York Times,* Arthur Hays Sulzberger, made a speech to the Southern Newspaper Publishers Association on this day in 1955. He said, "Along with responsible newspapers we must have responsible readers." I find it amazing how often significant news, prominently displayed in the newspapers, somehow fails to impinge on the public consciousness. Today I want to talk about some recent news that I believe has not gotten the amount of attention from the public that it deserves.

OCTOBER 5

The Right to Vote

Over the course of years the right to vote has been extended to more and more of our citizens. Poll tax laws and racial or sex discrimination have been done away with, and the voting age has been lowered. Yet, with all this expansion of the electorate, more than 35 percent of the voters, and often a higher percentage than that, have not voted in national elections. On this day in 1944, during a wartime presidential election campaign, President Franklin D. Roosevelt made a radio speech to the nation in which he said, quote, "Nobody will ever deprive the American people of the right to vote except the American people themselves." Close quote. As we approach another Election Day, those words are worth remembering. *How* you vote is not the most important thing. *Whether* you vote is. If you want this to continue to be a self-governing nation, go to the polls and take part in the process.

Real Miracles

When David Ben Gurion was the prime minister of Israel he was interviewed on CBS on this day in 1956, and he said something worth remembering. "In Israel," he said, "in order to be a realist you must believe in miracles." Well, ladies and gentlemen, that is not an Israeli exclusive. In this world of cares and crises, to be a realist you must believe in miracles—miracles like good weather, discovering oil, and coming up with good leaders just when we think we have run out of them. Because if you don't believe in miracles you have to give up. And we are not about to give up. We are not about to give up because, amid all the worry, there are some good omens, and I'd like to talk about them.

International Country Music Month

October has been observed for some years as International Country Music Month. Like so many of these special observances it has a clear commercial motive, but it also makes an interesting point. The musical idiom we once thought was unique to our hinterland has become truly international, sung by people who never heard of the Blue Ridge Mountains and are 10,000 miles away from Nashville. The fathers and mothers of country music might be rather surprised at some of the lyrics today, but that is true in literature, painting, and all the other arts as well. I believe that what makes country music popular is that it is deceptively simple. It is easily recognized, understandable as melody, and presented forthrightly without fancy overarrangements. It seems intrinsically American rather than intrinsically Tin Pan Alley. Now, what is true for country music is also true in other walks of life. If you can't understand what a politician is talking about, for example, the fault is not yours; it is his or hers, because plain talk is what we have a right to expect from politicians. I'd like to tell you today what is plain to me in the talk of today's leading politicians.

Diderot

Denis Diderot, the French philosopher who was born on this day in 1713, gave the world a phrase that has been perhaps inadequately translated as staircase humor. Staircase humor is the response you think of after you have reached the stairway on your way out. Inasmuch as I have had time to prepare my remarks for this occasion, I am saving nothing for the stairway. Whatever I have to say is about to be uttered.

OCTOBER 6

Sadat Assassinated

This was a sad day in 1981, when the President of Egypt, Anwar el Sadat, was assassinated. It was Sadat who had made peace for his country with Israel, in an act of joint statesmanship with Jimmy Carter and Menachem Begin; it was Sadat who the western world hoped would be the key to peace in the Middle East. But he became the victim of fanatics in his own land. We live in a world where the slow course of events, painfully worked out by hard and patient effort, can and has been upset by one shot, one knife, one terrorist bomb. Sadat had anticipated such an event to the point of hand picking and training his successor; but, as there was only one Lincoln in our own world, there was only one Sadat in his time. But we know that there just isn't enough security in the world to protect a leader against every would-be assassin, and so we must always ask ourselves, regardless of who our leaders are at the moment, who is in reserve? Whom would we turn to if we had to? Today I would like to talk about some of these possibilities.

George Westinghouse

George Westinghouse, who was born on this day in 1846 in Central Bridge, New York, was a great inventor who created more than 400 patented devices. Perhaps his greatest work was in devising means of using alternating current to generate and transmit electric power. His name, of course, is familiar because it is also the name of one of the pioneering and still great companies in the field of electricity. It is interesting to look at industrial America and realize how many major industrial companies bear the names and are the products of our great inventors—Westinghouse, Edison, Bell, and Eastman Kodak, for example. For the most part today's inventors are employees of major companies or they fold their products into the resources of major companies. The cost of launching a new product is so high these days and the organization needed is so extensive that the enterpreneur is limited. Not extinct, because happily there are outstanding people all the time who battle the odds and win. But today if you build a better mousetrap ingenuity is not enough. You need investors, tax experts, ecological consultants, marketing specialists, and so forth. Every year too many small endeavors end in failure because would-be entrepreneurs underestimate the costs and the problems of business. It is fine to have the graduate schools of business turning out the professional managers of today and tomorrow, but where and how are we training the future small business people? This, it seems to me, is a question worth asking our educational establishment.

First Turkish Bath

On this day in 1863, the first Turkish bath in the United States was opened in Brooklyn, New York. Steam baths, saunas, and hot water pools have proliferated to the point where getting hot under the collar, or without a collar, seems to be a national condition. Today, although I will be dealing with some possibly hot issues, I propose to do so coolly and without heat. Whether you will receive my comments the same way only time will tell.

American Library Association

Today is the birthday of the American Library Association, which was organized in Philadelphia on this day in 1876. One of the glories of America is the free availability of books at the nation's libraries and the recognition by so many communities that a library is an essential part of American life. In some ways the library is a microcosm of American life. So when I rise to urge you to support your local libraries I am not merely talking of your dollars—which of course are very important. I am talking also of your active interest, your use of the library. I never heard of a library harming anybody, so let's help the libraries. Let me tell you where, how, and what some of the dividends will be.

OCTOBER 7

Christian's Gesture

Few countries in the world have as noble a record of humanity in the face of inhumanity as Denmark, and this day lives as a monument to that spirit. It was supposedly about this time in 1942, when Denmark was occupied by Nazi Germany, that King Christian X defied the conquerors not only by attending services in a Copenhagen synagogue but by pledging to lead his people in wearing the Star of David if the Nazis forced Danish Jews to do so. It is well to remember that, while history is full of villains and dastardly deeds, it is also ennobled by the gallantry and the compassion of people as well. Certainly, although we have had our bad moments, the history of our own relations with other lands has been marked by some of the greatest generosity in the history of the world. But some of our international relations are neither generous nor intelligent, and those are the ones I want to discuss here today.

Stamp Act Congress

We have a tendency to think of the Continental Congress, out of which came the Declaration of Independence, as an original pattern of cooperation among the various British colonies in what is now the United States, but it was actually the lineal descendant of another congress that began on this day in New York City in 1765. Delegates of nine of the colonies met in what is known as the Stamp Act Congress. In addition to passing resolutions against the Stamp Act taxes that Great Britain had imposed on trade in America, the Stamp Act Congress served to encourage resistance to the tax. People went out of business rather than pay the tax, and the members of Parliament who had opposed the tax in the first place stepped up their demands for its repeal. It was indeed repealed the following year, and Americans had an object lesson in the value of acting together. So the tradition of meeting to formulate a common answer to a problem is one of America's oldest. I hope my remarks will make some small contribution not only in raising some questions but in providing some answers.

Hidden Photography

History notes that on this day in 1931, in a photo laboratory in Rochester, New York, one of the first infrared photographs was taken. A group of people sitting in the dark found themselves captured on a photograph taken with special film sensitive to infrared light; the infrared light source was not visible to the naked eye. Thus was born a new means of invading our privacy. That, of course, was not the intention, any more than it was the original intent of the folks who invented the first tiny, ultrasensitive microphone. But the fact is that the march of science keeps putting miraculous new tools in the hands of people, sometimes for good purposes and sometimes, unfortunately, for evil. In that kind of world we have to be very jealous of the rights we have left, not only our own rights but those of our fellow citizens. And that's what I want to talk about today—the rights of our fellow citizens.

222 to 0

Some chronicles of sport say that it was on this day in 1916 that the most thorough defeat in football history took place, when Georgia Tech beat Cumberland University by the score of 222 to 0. I would imagine that not too long into the first quarter the Georgia Tech players must have felt that they had made their point, but they still had a lot of playing time left. Today my approach is a little different. I will try to make my point as clearly and thoroughly as I can, but I am not here to run up the score.

OCTOBER 8

Mrs. O'Leary's Cow

This was the day in 1871 when legend has it that a cow in Mrs. O'Leary's barn in Chicago kicked over a lantern and started the great Chicago fire. I assure you I have no desire to make a fire-breathing speech here today, but I do propose to sound an alarm or two.

Alvin York

Alvin York was not very anxious to go to war. Back in the Tennessee hill country where he grew up he asked to be excused as a conscientious objecter in World War I, but the draft board thought otherwise, and on this day in 1918, in the fighting in the Argonne Forest, he led an attack on a German machine gun position. In addition to being responsible for killing some 25 enemy soldiers, his marksmanship was followed by the surrender of 132 prisoners, and Private York soon thereafter became Sergeant York, winner of the Congressional Medal of Honor and one of America's great heroes. His story, it seems to me, tells a great deal about America. We do not seek war; we abhor war. We will, if possible, go to great lengths to avoid taking part in a war. But, if we have to, then we will give it our best effort. Now I have no conscientious objection to speaking out in public, so if I have to do it I will give it my best effort. Unlike Sergeant York, all I will shoot off will be my mouth.

Fall Leaves

We have come to the season of the autumn leaves, when great areas of the nation come dressed in their most attractive and plentiful colors. It is one of the tricks of nature that leaves are at their most beautiful right before they wither and fall. There are times when I think that humanity imitates nature. The season of the autumn leaves is also when we are assailed by all the glitz of the advertising for the new cars, the hoopla for the new television season, the multicolored promises of the candidates for election next month. So it seems to me that, in this time when superlatives are in such constant use, the best service a speaker can do is to avoid extravagance, avoid exaggeration, and get right to the point.

John Clarke

You would be hard put to find the name of John Clarke—that's Clarke with an *e*—in the history books, but he deserves better. Today is his birthday. He was born in 1609 in England and came to New England in 1637. He deserves to be remembered because, as an associate of Roger Williams, he was the man who persuaded King Charles II to include in the charter of the Rhode Island colony a guarantee of full religious freedom. That was in 1663, and it was probably the most specific and fullest guarantee the British crown had yet given to the New World. Our history is full of men like John Clarke, who are not remembered for themselves but live in the heritage they gave America. Ladies and gentlemen, we too have the opportunity to contribute to that heritage. History is not all in the past. History is being made every day—and you and I are part of it. We too can help build a better America. The choices are ours.

OCTOBER 9

The Speech That Lost an Election

It isn't often that a single speech can change the course of history, but this day in 1884 may well have been one such occasion. On this day the Reverend Dr. Samuel D. Burchard addressed a group of ministers at a rally on behalf of Republican presidential candidate James G. Blaine. "We are Republicans," Dr. Burchard said, "and don't propose to have our party identify ourselves with the party whose antecedents have been Rum, Romanism, and Rebellion." A great many voters were offended; they showed their indignation by voting for the Democratic candidate, Grover Cleveland, who won the election. Ladies and gentlemen, even though I know my words can hardly influence the course of history the way the Reverend Dr. Burchard unwittingly did, I will be careful here today.

Chance, Not Choice

President Dwight D. Eisenhower went to Pittsburgh on this day in 1956 to make a speech in his reelection campaign. One of the things he said was this: "The history of free men is never really written by chance but by choice." Ike's choice had certainly written a significant portion of the history of free men and women in his time, but one does not need to be the president or the commanding general of a great multination force to influence the course of events. Each of us exerts an influence, in what and when we buy, in the votes we cast, in the extent to which we participate in the life of our community. So today I address you as potential history makers, one and all.

Peshtigo Fire

It is one of the ironies of history that of two similar tragic events which occurred at the same time on this day back in 1871, one has become part of American folklore and the other, in which many more people were killed, is largely forgotten. They were both fires in the Midwest. One was the Chicago fire; the other was a bigger fire in six counties in Wisconsin, known as the Peshtigo fire. The Peshtigo blaze was believed to have originally been ignited by sparks from the Chicago fire. More than a million forest acres were destroyed and more than 1,000 people were killed, compared to about 250 in Chicago. It isn't always the hottest territory that gets the attention. Today, by way of illustrating that point, I'd like to talk about some burning questions that somehow haven't gotten the concern they deserve.

Lief Ericson Day

The Viking Leif Ericson is believed by some to have landed in North America as long ago as 1,000 A.D., and in commemoration this day has been designated through the years as Leif Ericson Day. If the Vikings did indeed discover this continent long before Columbus, it is a matter of historical record that they did not do much about it, whereas the later explorers worked at the idea of colonizing the New World. In subsequent times there have been many other discoveries that have not gotten their major exploitation from the original discoverers. I am thinking particularly of what happened with the transistor and the chip, both American discoveries that were exploited by other nations, notably the Japanese. It suggests that we are not as alert to the opportunities we uncover as our friends across the water, and so it seems to me that more creative attention to new developments is called for. In that connection, I have some developments I'd like to talk about with you here today.

OCTOBER 10

Spiro Agnew

On this day in 1973, what we thought was the greatest scandal ever to involve either of our two principal elected executives came to its dramatic climax. The Vice-President of the United States, Spiro T. Agnew, resigned as he was being prosecuted for federal income tax violations. He pleaded no contest to the charges and was found guilty. Less than two years later, his running mate, Richard M. Nixon, the President of the United States, resigned as a result of the Watergate case. One might have expected that this kind of double-barreled embarrassment would totally disrupt the morale of the American people and the processes of government, but we know the morale and the government survived. We are not merely survivors, however; we are learners and rebuilders, and those are talents we need very much today. For we have learned that some of our most important institutions need rebuilding if they and we are to continue surviving. I refer to rebuilding both in the moral and the physical sense, but today I want to talk about some of the physical needs.

Naval Academy

The United States Naval Academy began its first classes on this day in 1845 in Annapolis, Maryland. It was designed to provide an education not merely in seafaring matters but also in the liberal arts, and through the years it has of course provided educational opportunities for some of our most select young men and women. Its alumni have included distinguished astronauts and pioneers in the use of nuclear science—and a president of the United States. We neither want nor expect our armed forces to be run by people so specialized that they are out of touch with the main currents of American life. When you get down to it, the professionals who run our armed forces are training young men and women for life, teaching them skills to be applied to civilian work. That is a great responsibility, which the armed forces, I believe, face up to more than the rest of us. The number of totally untrained young Americans is a sin and a scandal, and we can't expect the armed forces to solve that problem. So let's talk about what we civilians can do.

The Mingling of the Waters

It was on this day in 1913 that President Woodrow Wilson, by remote control, pressed the button that blew up the last bit of land obstructing the Panama Canal, enabling the waters of the Atlantic and Pacific Oceans to meet there. It is hard to believe now that in our own century the building of the Panama Canal could have been regarded as one of the wonders of the world. It says something about the pace of progress that well within the lifetime of a single average human being the world had gone from digging a canal in Central America to walking on the moon. Progress has come so fast in some fields that we have become accustomed to expect it to be just as fast in every field— even though some challenges, like managing the economy, seem to defy us. I am not here to counsel patience. Quite the reverse. The progress we have made has been achieved because dedicated, often stubborn, and very possibly inspired people have worked and worked to accomplish it. We must bring that same sense of dedication, of stubbornness, and, yes, of inspiration to what faces us today. We must raise our targets ever higher, and that is what I will focus on today.

Fridtjof Nansen

The name of Fridtjof Nansen, who was born on this day in 1861 in Norway, is all but unknown to people today, which is a pity. Nansen was one of the greatest Arctic explorers and oceanographers of his time, but he was much more than that. It was this man of science who became the League of Nations' high commissioner for refugees after the first World War. He developed what became known as the Nansen passport for stateless refugees, to give them international protection, and he directed the rescue of millions of people. In 1923 he was awarded the Nobel Peace Prize. Now, not all of us can do what Nansen did. But there is no reason why all of us cannot be moved by the same spirit of compassion and the same common-sense approach to untangling red tape. So today I want to give you some common-sense reasons for exercising your compassion in a practical way.

OCTOBER 11

Battle of Tours

This is the anniversary of an epic battle with an interesting ending. It was fought near the city of Tours, France, in 732 A.D. It is regarded as one of the decisive battles of the world, because in it Charles Martel and his French forces stopped the invasion of Europe—beyond Spain—by the Arabs. The interesting ending I talked about was that the battle stopped at nightfall, and when the sun came out the next day the Arabs had gone. It would be nice if that would happen with some of our present-day problems, but they don't seem to vanish quite that simply. So I guess we've got to buckle down and confront them. But first maybe we need some identifications.

Edison Rejected

This day is listed as the time when, in 1868, a young inventor named Thomas A. Edison sought a patent for a device to record votes in a meeting electronically. He intended it to help Congress speed its work, but even though he got his patent he didn't get his customer. Congress turned the idea down. They did ultimately accept the idea of electronic tabulation, but that was a long, long time later. I suppose what this proves is that even the best of us can come up with good ideas and not get them accepted. That, of course, is a great consolation to a public speaker. What it clearly indicates is that if you don't agree with me I am simply ahead of my time.

D.A.R.

Today is the birthday of a very famous organization, the D.A.R., Daughters of the American Revolution. The organization was founded in 1890, more than a hundred years after the Revolution. I suspect some of the motivation was the same as that which prompted author Alex Haley to search out his roots in Africa—the desire to know more about our ancestors and to take pride in their accomplishments. Most of us, however, seem to regard history on a less personal basis as a bore. Yet, if we can take a better look at what's already happened it can be a great help in dealing with what is happening now. So, I'd like to discuss some recent history with you.

Political Television

On this day in 1932, we are told, the first sponsored political television broadcast went on the air in New York. I won't tell you which of the two major parties was responsible for it, but no matter. Political hucksters of all stripes have made electioneering one of the warts on the face of the tube. The merchandising of candidates like soap powders or patent medicines has become one of the problems of our time. The problem is that we have little way of knowing how much of the seeming attractiveness, eloquence, or intellect of a candidate is his or her own and how much is ghost-written, rehearsed, and phonied up. And in many instances you can't even judge candidates by the company they keep, because often a big campaign spender goes campaigning without even using a party identification. How should the electorate deal with this? There are a number of possibilities.

OCTOBER 12

Rediscovering America

On the anniversary of Christopher Columbus's discovery of the Americas in 1492, it seems only appropriate to take another look at the world he opened up. That America has changed since the days of Columbus is hardly news, but the degree of change in the last few years is worthy of some immediate attention. The composition of the nation has changed and so, I believe, has the character of the people. That is what I propose to explore here today.

Khrushchev's Shoe

When the Premier of the USSR was attending a session of the United Nations General Assembly on this day in 1960, he chose to register his opinion by pounding his shoe on his desk. Nikita Khrushchev was hardly the most subtle of men, but while he used his shoe to make a dissenting noise, millions of other people have used their shoes to accomplish what has been called "voting with your feet." They have left their own countries to find a better life someplace else. And it isn't only overseas that this has happened. On our continent it isn't only the Latin Americans seeking jobs who come up from below the border. It is also those Americans who have left the cities of the Northeast looking for better lives in the Sun Belt. Probably the most precious freedom in the world is the freedom to move away. That's the one, for example, that they have less of in Soviet Russia than even the freedom to speak. The freedom to move away. The freedom to move on. There is only one even broader freedom—broader because it is almost impossible to suppress. That is the freedom not to listen. Nobody can force you to keep your ears and your mind open. I can't force you, but I surely am going to try to coax you.

Robert E. Lee

In the gallery of great Americans the name of Robert E. Lee occupies a very special place. On this day, the anniversary of his death in 1870, his career and his character furnish the jumping-off point for some commentary on our own times. General Lee was a man of superior ability and high moral sense who was a principal actor in not one but many key points of our history. He worked as an Army engineer on Mississippi River flood control, was a distinguished field commander in the Mexican War, served as superintendent of the United States Military Academy at West Point, and commanded the U.S. forces that captured John Brown at Harper's Ferry. When the Civil War broke out he was offered command of the Union Army but chose instead to be loyal to his native state of Virginia. As a Confederate general he fought gallantly and brilliantly. When it ended in his defeat he turned to another field and became the president of Washington College. In his honor it is now known as Washington and Lee University. Inscribed beneath his bust in the Hall of Fame are these words: "Duty is the sublimest word in our language. Do your duty in all things. You cannot do more. You should never wish to do less." The school from which Robert E. Lee graduated—West Point—has as its motto, "Duty, honor, country." I cite those words here today, and I ask a question: How well do our people today understand that word *duty*?

First State University

On this day in 1793, the cornerstone of the first building of the first state university in the United States was laid at Chapel Hill, North Carolina. The North Carolina constitution of 1776 had contemplated the establishment of a public university, and the charter had been issued in 1789. From that beginning has grown probably the world's greatest system of public higher education. That concept and the institution of a free press have given our nation the greatest tools any democracy ever had. The stocks in trade of both the university and the press are knowledge, information, and the communication of ideas. And yet, even with such a marvelous system of state universities and private universities and great newspapers and great broadcasters, there is information we should have but often don't get. Today I want to put the spotlight on some subjects that have not had the thorough attention they deserve.

OCTOBER 13

Molly Pitcher

Today is the birthday of Mary Ludwig Hays McCauley, who was born in Trenton, New Jersey, on this day in 1754. She accompanied her husband to the Battle of Monmouth and did her part by bringing drinking water to the artillerymen, which won her the name of Molly Pitcher. Then, when her husband collapsed from the heat, she took over his gun. Thus, she became a fighting heroine of the American Revolution, and long before women's lib she demonstrated that women had capabilities equal to those of men. Molly Pitcher did not find a new way of life at the Battle of Monmouth. When it was over she returned full-time to her wifely chores. But on her birthday it seems appropriate to remind ourselves of that great national resource—our women. Are we making the best use of that resource?

Cornerstones

Three of the nation's cornerstones can trace some of their beginnings to this day. In two cases we are talking literally of cornerstones. On this day in 1792, George Washington laid the cornerstone of the executive mansion in what was to become Washington, D.C., and when it was rebuilt after being destroyed in the War of 1812, it would be known as the White House. And on this day in 1932, President Herbert Hoover laid the cornerstone for a new Supreme Court building. Finally, it was on this day in 1775 that the Continental Congress authorized a fleet of two cruisers, the beginning of our Navy. President, Supreme Court, and seagoing defense—three principal elements of our survival as a nation. There are other vital elements, of course, and the genius of the American way of life is that every element meshes with and impinges on the others. The people have to respect the Court, for example, and the government must respect the people. Too often the government's respect—or, more accurately, the respect of individuals in the government—for the public is notable mainly for its absence.

Baby Bonus

Back in 1912 on this day, the lack of population in Australia prompted the government there to offer a small cash bonus to the parents of every new baby. How times have changed! Now, in many countries the argument is over abortions rather than births. I don't propose to get into that highly explosive issue, but it serves to indicate the way even basic moral issues gain or lose currency in differing times. The moral issue I want to discuss here today illustrates that point very clearly. It is the issue of honesty. Are we as honest as our parents were? I can't believe, for example, that any previous generation violated the traffic laws as consistently as we do. I can't believe that any previous generation stole cars as blithely as today. Or mugged. Or carried illegal weapons as much. I think we should ask ourselves why this is the case.

Makeshift Science

"All science," naturalist Henry D. Thoreau wrote in his journal on this day in 1860, "is only a makeshift, a means to an end which is never attained." Thoreau wrote those words long before the age of additives and chemotherapy, but he was wise beyond his time. We create miracle drugs and then have to cope with bizarre side effects. We find chemicals to stamp out various pests and then are confronted by new varieties of those pests that have developed an immunity to the chemicals. Our science continues, albeit on a higher scale, to be a makeshift means to an end that is never attained. Does that mean we should cease our science? Not at all. What I think it means is that we must be in a perpetual state of further investigation, further research and development. Even where we have apparent successes we must continue to work for improvement, and above all I believe it means we must be skeptical and deliberate about accepting newly claimed miracles. Consider the extent of the problems we have not yet solved.

OCTOBER 14

Speed

It was on this day back in 1947 that the first supersonic flight was made by U.S. Air Force Captain Charles F. Yeager. Apart from adding another element to our weapons arsenal, the advent of supersonic flight does not seem to me to have lived up to our high expectations—expectations that faster transportation would somehow bring the nations of the world closer together. It seems that physical distance is not the real problem. The real problem, I believe, is that we just don't understand one another's national psyches; and I have no overnight solution to that problem. It's a problem that isn't confined to international relations, either; we have different attitudes and different ways of life in different parts of our own country as well. One of the ways we keep things calm among these different sectors is by finding middle grounds on which we can all, by giving a little, achieve agreement; and I have some suggestions for the same sort of middle ground in the international field.

Space Broadcast

When the United States, for the first time in history, carried out a live television broadcast from a spaceship in orbit above the earth, it opened not only a new age in communication but a new vision of messages to and from other worlds out there in the universe. I find myself wondering these days what we really want to say to those other worlds. I find myself wondering what it is we most want to know from them. And today I want to share with you some thoughts on that subject, because I believe that what we might ask other worlds in outer space serves to illuminate our situation here on earth today.

Declaration and Resolves

The First Continental Congress met in Philadelphia in 1774, and on this day the delegates of the various colonies formally adopted a fairly lengthy Declaration and Resolves. The first resolve adopted on this day in 1774 declared that the inhabitants of the English colonies in North America—quote—"are entitled to life, liberty, and property." Another stated that the foundation of all free government—quote—"is a right in the people to participate in their legislative council." The 1774 Congress also asserted the right of peaceful assembly. Looking at the sentiments expressed by that Congress, one wonders why and how the British could have ignored these danger signals, but they did. And that causes me to wonder whether we too are not getting danger signals today and whether we are paying any better attention than the British did back in 1774.

Eisenhower

Today is the birthday of Dwight D. Eisenhower, who was born in 1890, led the greatest fighting force in history in World War II, and served as general of the Army and thirty-fourth President of the United States. Ike did not fancy himself a great philosopher, but in his forthright manner he was able to put his finger on the heart of a problem and confront it. Back in 1947, he said, "Technological advance has outdistanced—at least for the time being—the social progress that it induces or, more accurately, that it demands." That was said, I remind you, in 1947, and we are still unwilling or unable to close the gap. I have no magic solutions to present to you here today, but I have some observations that I hope are pertinent.

OCTOBER 15

World Poetry Day

Today, October 15, was designated some years ago as World Poetry Day, an observance that has not captured public attention quite as much as some of our more picturesque occasions such as Groundhog Day or the return of the swallows to Capistrano. But World Poetry Day seems, at least to me, to be an ideal opportunity to take as my theme a quotation from one of the greatest poets of all time, William Shakespeare. "There is a tide in the affairs of men," he wrote, "which, taken at the flood, leads on to fortune; omitted, all the voyage of their life is bound in shallows and in miseries." We stand, it seems to me today, contemplating that kind of tide and the opportunity to take it at the flood and shape our destiny. We have decisions to make and the need to make those decisions promptly, for our world is a changing one and today's opportunities may not come again.

P. G. Wodehouse

This is the birthday of the British author, P. G. Wodehouse, who amused several generations with his funny stories about the British upper classes and deserves immortality particularly for his creation of that classic character, Jeeves the butler. Wodehouse, who was born in Surrey, England, in 1881, loved to play tricks with the English language, and one line in particular comes back to me as a timely case in point. In his book *The Code of the Woosters*, he described one character's mood this way: "If not actually disgruntled, he was far from being gruntled." It seems to me that you and I and our neighbors these days are also far from being gruntled, and I think we can and should do something about it.

War Crimes Finale

On this day in two successive years, two of the most prominent villains of World War II came to the end of their sordid stories. In 1945, Pierre Laval, the Premier of occupied Vichy France under the Nazis in World War II, was shot for treason by a French firing squad. The following year, on the same day, the number two man of Nazi Germany, Reichsmarshal Hermann Goering, who was scheduled to be executed for war crimes, committed suicide in his cell in Nuremberg, Germany. I am sure that decent people at the time hoped that these men's fates would make future troublemakers think twice. But that hasn't happened. A religious fanatic, the Ayatollah Khomeini, brought with him a reign of terror in Iran; petty dictators in Third World nations continue to treat human life as the cheapest of commodities; demagogues can still persuade mobs of people to howl for blood. We execute criminals, we imprison them, but they keep coming back for more. This is a sad fact to face, but face it we must. And so we must ask ourselves how best to protect ourselves, not just against the international bandits but against internal evils as well.

Nietzsche

Friedrich Wilhelm Nietzsche, the Germany philosopher who was born on this day in 1844, once wrote these words: "It is my ambition to say in ten sentences what everyone else says in a whole book." Mindful of Nietzsche, I will endeavor here today to guard your time as if it were my own. It will be more than ten sentences, but I am not about to throw the book at you.

OCTOBER 16

World Food Day

This day was designated some years ago as World Food Day to mark the founding in 1945 of the World Food and Agriculture Organization of the United Nations. The only kind of food the entire world seems to have available is food for thought, and I have a small crop to contribute to that supply.

Eugene O'Neill

The man who may have been America's greatest playwright, Eugene O'Neill, was born on this day in 1888 in New York City. He won the Nobel Prize and four Pulitzer Prizes, and most of his writing was about unhappy people. For some reason the darker side of life seems to challenge and fascinate many creative people, far more so than the lighter, funnier aspects of human existence. They say that in terms of creativity comedy is by far the most difficult of the forms of writing, but, on the other hand, it seems to me that the comedy is there in real life, waiting to be noted. By way of proving my point I want to devote my remarks today to the mention of some true stories that not even Eugene O'Neill could have written.

John Paul II

For centuries the Pope had been an Italian. Then, on this day in 1979, the assembled cardinals elected from among their number a Polish cleric. He took the papal name of John Paul II, but his Polish identity and his love of the land that knew him as Karol Wojtyla were made very clear. It was a startling and invigorating moment for the Roman Catholic Church. Every great institution needs this kind of break with the past every now and then if it is to remain a living institution to its constituents. That was and is one of the virtues of the two-term tradition for a president of the United States. It is also a great argument for bringing newer strains of population into the mainstream of American life. For we are all inclined to stick to the old ways of doing things, and sometimes newcomers have very good ideas about how to do better. And if their ideas don't turn out to be better than our accustomed ways, they still prompt us to do some thinking and perhaps some improving of our own. So today I want to try to put myself in the position of a newcomer, looking at our society and asking some simple questions.

Enter Lincoln

What historians regard as Abraham Lincoln's first great political speech was made on this day in 1854 in Peoria. It was a speech in response to Stephen Douglas, although it was four years before their great series of debates. Lincoln spoke for hours, and I will not emulate his example here today. But I would like to quote one brief portion. "I insist," Lincoln said, "that if there is anything which it is the duty of the whole people never to entrust in any hands but their own, that thing is the preservation and perpetuity of their own liberties and institutions." What Lincoln said then is true today. If we want our liberties to continue we must stand up for them. We must be vigilant in that defense, fighting against every encroachment. And so today I am here to sound some alarums, to point with concern to some instances where our liberties are in danger.

OCTOBER 17

Einstein Arrives

A German refugee from the Nazis arrived in the United States on this day in 1933. His name was Albert Einstein. He was a great physicist, not a great writer nor a great speechmaker. But it was his words, in a letter to President

Franklin D. Roosevelt, that helped persuade this country to begin work on the atom bomb. In later years Einstein was not so sure it was a good idea, and I am not going to stand here to debate it. I mention it to make the point that even for the most lofty of theorists, the most unwordly of thinkers, words can sometimes be the most powerful of tools. I have no illusions that my words here today can be compared to those of an Einstein, any more than my simple arithmetic has any relationship to his complicated formulas, but we do have one important thing in common—a belief that the best thinking comes from people who are permitted to think for themselves. So today I am not going to tell you that what to think; I am going to give you some information that, I hope, will be worth thinking about.

Capone Caught

It was regarded as a sardonic commentary on this day in 1931 when the most famous gang leader in the United States, Al Capone, was finally convicted and sent to prison—not for the violent crimes with which he had been connected but for income tax evasion. It was not the first time or the last that the government found an unexpected way to catch up with wrongdoers, but it does suggest a role for the tax process that was not exactly what the original tax laws had in mind. This has happened with other types of law as well. For example, national defense security regulations have been used on occasion to infringe on the rights of individuals. It is a great temptation, when faced with a real need, to convince yourself that the end justifies the means. Today I want to talk about some of these unforeseen consequences.

Burgoyne's Surrender

On this day in 1777, the British army suffered its most embarrassing moment to that point in the American Revolution, when General John Burgoyne surrendered his army at Saratoga, New York, and the defeated British forces were sent back to England in disgrace. It came as a great shock to Great Britain that the upstart Americans could have defeated them, and General Burgoyne, who had put together a string of victories up to that point, was never really forgiven. Sometimes it seems we remember our scapegoats longer than we remember our heroes. We are happier to find someone to blame for our problems than to find someone to credit for the solutions. For a public speaker that means it is much easier to bewail whatever had gone wrong than to talk about what has gone right. But I will resist that temptation here today in favor of some words of praise.

Bessemer

Steel has been around for so long that it surprised me to learn that on this day in 1854 Henry Bessemer patented his process for making it. Even with ideas and products that are as old as time improvements are always possible. Indeed, without a constant quest for improvement nothing stays as good as it used to be. That, even more than the development of new products, is the basic reason for the importance of constant research, constant setting of new and higher goals. It seems to me that we have come to a time when we should be giving more thought to new goals, to raising our sights ever higher—and that is what I am here to talk about today.

OCTOBER 18

Cyclamates

It was on this day back in 1969 that the U.S. Department of Health, Education, and Welfare banned the use of cyclamates as sweeteners. In the age of synthetics and additives it was a shock to find that one of our miracles was not a blessing after all. We have found ways to take more advantage of what nature offers, but we still haven't found a way to give back to nature as much as nature gives to us. We haven't found a way to control nature's weather; we haven't even found a way for nature's highest creatures, humans, to live in peace with themselves. But there are some hopeful signs that I'd like to tell you about.

Lucy Stone

This is the anniversary of the death in 1893 of Lucy Stone. An older generation could remember when the name of Lucy Stone was a symbol. A Lucy Stoner was a woman who kept her maiden name when she married. It was considered eccentric in her time, but it was part of her courageous battle for women's rights. Today women who retain their names when they marry are no longer a rarity. That is true of many new ideas—they seem eccentric till you get used to them. So I have the comfort of telling myself that if what I have to say to you today seems unorthodox, perhaps I am ahead of my time. But if I keep on talking long enough, I'll be behind the time you have allotted me, so let's get right to it.

First Guilds

On this day in 1648, the town of Boston gave permission to the shoemakers and coopers to form their own organizations, which some historians like to regard as the first authorized labor unions in America. One might, however, also regard them as the first business associations. It is interesting that in that day and age, when a one-person business was not unusual, there could be so thin a line between a labor union, a craft guild, and a business association. Today organized labor and business associations are in opposite camps—extremely opposite. But it seems to me that both of these camps are coming to realize that what they have in common is more important than their differences. What they have in common is the need for a prosperous operation. In the sharp competitive climate, the management and labor who combine to get a reasonable return mutually are in better shape than the management and labor who let their differences keep them from modernizing the plant or the product. But before this realization can become as widespread as it should, we will have to do a great deal of education. What kind of education? Let me tell you.

Alaska Day

Today is the anniversary of the formal transfer of Alaska from Russia to the United States in 1867 as a result of this country's purchase of the territory. At the time nobody thought too much of Alaska as real estate. Indeed, it was nicknamed Seward's Folly after the Secretary of State who made the purchase. We have learned since then that magnificent natural resources can be found in the most unlikely places and that what is under the land is sometimes more important than what is on it. In the case of Alaska, it was first gold and then petroleum. In years to come we may find new value, there and elsewhere, in geothermal sources, underground streams, and heaven only knows what else. Part of the genius of America has been in making better use of what we have; that is a challenge not only in Alaska but all over the United States. Even in the heart of a great city we must keep asking ourselves whether we are making the best use of the land, and if not, what we can and should do about it.

OCTOBER 19

Sir Thomas Browne

Sir Thomas Browne, who was born on this day in 1605 in London, was a physician who became one of his country's greatest authors while continuing to practice medicine. One thing he wrote has stayed with me. "It is the common wonder of all men," he wrote, "how among so many millions of faces, there should be none alike." It seems to me that we keep forgetting that fact. We talk of "the working man" or "the career woman" or "the younger generation" as if we were talking about one overall person who had all of the characteristics of his or her group. We generalize about politicians and doctors and so forth. Today I want to avoid these generalizations; I am going to talk to you about specific individuals.

Napoleon Leaves Moscow

Sometimes history seems to be written by mythmakers, and today is the anniversary of just such an event. On this day in 1812, Napoleon left Moscow, followed a few days later by the bulk of his forces. He had failed totally to defeat the Russians, and his own army was a bit on the ragged edge from the long campaign. It was not the Russian winter that drove him out of Moscow; winter came later to harass his troops when they were well on their way back from that high point of their Russian invasion. But Napoleon is still depicted as the genius who was defeated by the weather. It seems to me that in our concepts of the world today we are still falling prey to the mythmakers, and I therefore want to take this opportunity to set some facts straight.

Stamp Act Congress

On this day in 1765, a congress of delegates from nine British colonies in America passed a series of resolutions, among them one stating that "it is inseparably essential to the freedom of a people, and the undoubted right of Englishmen, that no taxes be imposed on them but with their own consent, given personally or by their representative." Thus, ten years before the American Revolution broke out into open warfare, the outcry against taxation without representation was sounded loud and clear. The British did not pay enough attention. I wonder whether we have learned as much as we should from that fact.I wonder whether we pay enough attention to the will of the people as we should. I wonder whether perhaps, in some areas, we are fooled about the will of the people by the loudness of the advocates of one view or another. I cannot pretend to stand here as the ultimate authority on what the people think, or want, or oppose. But I think there are some false issues, and I'd like to talk about that area.

Round-the-World Race

Headline news was made on this day in 1936 when a reporter for the *New York World Telegram*, H. R. Ekins, completed a trip around the world in 18½ days, beating two jounalistic competitors, Dorothy Kilgallen of the *New York Journal American* and Leo Kieran of *The New York Times*. Apart from the tremendous increase in air speed since that journey, the thing that strikes me is that two of the three newspapers involved are long since defunct. More and more, we see and hear our news today instead of just reading it. And if we have lost something unique to American life, we have also gained a whole chorus of voices. Today we are confronted by a virtual Niagara Falls of words, so in contributing to that flood I will try not to overflow my time.

OCTOBER 20

Religion

In a letter he wrote to Edward Newenham on this date in 1792, President George Washington said, "Of all the animosities which have existed among mankind, those which are caused by a difference of sentiments in religion appear to be most inveterate and distressing, and ought most to be deprecated."

In the intervening 200 years the situation hasn't changed. The disputes in our own country that arise from religious differences are as nothing compared to those of the old world. Different sects of Moslems, Moslem and Christian, Moslem and Jew, Catholic and Protestant, fundamentalists and reformed, orthodox and liberal—the list of areas of differences is virtually endless. In this country we have in general learned the art of living together, but there are many parts of the world where this still has to be learned. And even in our own land there is a constant need to reaffirm the spirit not of tolerance but of brotherhood. For we in our own place and time cannot assume we are immune from tides of hatred and religious fanaticism. What is happening, and what are we doing about it?

Sir Christopher Wren

This is the birthday of the great architect, Sir Christopher Wren, who was born in Wiltshire, England, in 1632. There is an inscription over the North Door of St. Paul's Cathedral in London, a glorious edifice designed by Wren. It reads, "If you would see his monument look around." Now, ladies and gentlemen, few of us have either the talent or the opportunities of Christopher Wren, but all of us, in one way or another, at one time or another, can help to build a world to justify their saying of us, "If you would see their monument, look around." Just as the present world is a monument to those who went before us, so too can we leave our mark on the world of tomorrow. I do not propose to count the ways, but I can talk about some of them.

John Dewey

The philosopher and educator who was instrumental in shaping the course of modern education, John Dewey, was born on this day in 1859 in Burlington, Vermont. It was he who wrote, "Historically, the great movements for human liberation have always been movements to change institutions and not to preserve them intact." I am not here to argue Professor Dewey's point, but rather to ask whether the reverse is true, namely that movements to change institutions are, in Dewey's words, "great movements for human liberation." I don't think that is the case, and I see too many proposals for change that are in fact steps backward. We have too many people around who, if they can't get a change under the existing rules and institutions, want to change the institutions, institutions which have served us well for many years. Today I would like to examine what I believe are the real motives of some of the would-be rules-changers.

Mau Mau

This is the anniversary of the start of the first Mau Mau insurrection against British rule in Kenya in 1952. It was put down but broke out again the following year. The world at large seemed to regard it as a cruel form of native savagery, but when the people who ran the Mau Mau finally came to power they proved to be among the better government groups in Africa. It is a fact of history that even movements that begin with seemingly mindless violence can mature, not always to become models of decency but almost always less violent than when they started. One reason may well be that by the time they change they have thoroughly intimidated a populace, so less violence is needed; or, like the story about the farmer and the mule that was hit by the farmer over the head to get his attention, they may use the violence to get attention. None of this is any excuse for bloodletting, but it reminds us that there is a rational, if evil, purpose in most terrorist actions. We must ask ourselves how best to confront it without ourselves helping to publicize and aggrandize it.

OCTOBER 21

Guggenheim Museum

It was on this day in 1959 that a very unorthodox building was opened in New York. The building was the Guggenheim Museum, designed by Frank Lloyd Wright. Its round shape and continuous spiral of exhibition space provided a brand new experience in the viewing of art. Frank Lloyd Wright had defied all the rules of museum design and had come up with a new and exciting concept. Not everyone fell in love with it; traditionalists objected, and some people felt that the strange shape of the building, right on Fifth Avenue, was jarringly out of keeping with its sedate surroundings. But it was a popular success, another proof that new ideas—if they have merit—can overcome our normal conservatism. Now, I don't want to claim that the ideas I am going to present here today are either as new or as revolutionary as Frank Lloyd Wright's historic design, but they represent a challenge to some older concepts, and I hope you will find it is a challenge worth considering.

Pledge of Allegiance

At the dedication of the World's Fair Grounds in Chicago on this day in 1892, a pledge of allegiance to the flag of the United States, written probably by the Reverend Francis Bellamy, was recited for the first time. There is some dispute about the authorship, which has also been credited to James B. Upham, but no dispute at all about the final phrase, "with liberty and justice for all." That is probably the most succinct and precise description of the American ideal—liberty and justice for all. Today I want to talk about that ideal and the challenges that confront it.

U.S.S. Constitution

This is the anniversary of the launching of our most famous battleship, the *U.S.S. Constitution*, in Boston in 1797. More people, of course, know this great old fighting vessel by its nickname, "Old Ironsides." Old Ironsides is still floating and commissioned at its dock in Boston, immortalized in history for its spectacular naval victories and in poetry for Oliver Wendall Holmes' great words in 1830 when the historic ship was about to be scrapped. There have been several attempts to get rid of this historic ship, but popular outcry has always saved it. The people, it seems, value the monuments of our history. And the people have to be eternally vigilant to protect these monuments from the modernizers, the developers, the efficiency experts. We seem to have a tendency to tear things down and start over, rather than simply improving on what is already built. I am not here to advocate any tearing down, but I do have some improvements to suggest.

ROTC

The first college ROTC units were begun on this day in 1916, and since then the campus Reserve Officers Training Corps has had its ups and downs. In the paranoiac atmosphere of the Vietnam War era, ROTC was an object of considerable scorn and derision, but the long view of history offers something quite different. What makes ROTC important is that it is a way of continuously insuring an infusion of civilian thinking into the armed forces, people who bring a civilian point of view into uniform. Ours, after all, is a citizen Army, not a mercenary fighting force. Our military forces are great training grounds for civilian life, teaching young people skills that are as important in peace as in war. And ROTC has enabled thousands of young Americans to complete their college educations. That is part of the greatness of America—the fact that we have found so many ideas with double value, the fact that we have known for so long how to get so much bang from the buck. But now the question arises as to whether we still know, or whether we are frittering away valuable resources by improper use. That is the question I want to address here today.

OCTOBER 22

Metropolitan Opera

The original Metropolitan Opera House opened in New York City on this day in 1883, and we have been facing the music ever since. One nice thing about opera is that since it is usually in a foreign language you don't have to pay too much attention to the words. But since I have neither operatic spectacle nor lyrical song to offer, my message comes to you in mere words. So, without any further overtures, let me get down to business.

Sarah Bernhardt

Sarah Bernhardt, the great French actress who was born on this day in 1845, was said to travel with a coffin because she always thought she was about to die. Actually, she lived until well in her seventies. And, of course, the coffin had the effect of being a colorful eccentricity that added to the public interest in the lady. Sometimes I have a feeling that some of the public figures of our own day travel with coffins, too, because they seem to take such delight in predicting the death of the American way of life. Ladies and gentlemen, I am here to say that there's still a lot of life left and a lot of opportunities to enjoy it. With all due respect to the Cassandras, I am here to paint a rosier picture.

The Shah in New York

It was on this day in 1979 that the ailing Shah of Iran, exiled from his rebellious nation, flew to New York from Mexico City for hospital treatment. The government of Ayotollah Khomeini was furious; they demanded his return. A short fortnight later, Iranian militants in Tehran seized the American embassy and began more than a year of imprisonment for a group of American hostages. It was the following July that the Shah, who apparently had cancer, died in Cairo. From the vantage point of history, it is a mockery that giving treatment to a dying man should trigger such terrorism, but it is a fact of life that human beings are the most beastly animals in the world. In every generation there are examples of the unreasoning, unreasonable fierceness of a mob and of the ease with which demagogues and power-grabbers can whip up crowd emotions. It is much more difficult to speak reasonably and logically than to stand here and concoct a catalogue of imagined wrongs and grievances. But I must tell you that reason and logic are more satisfying, and I thank you for the opportunity you have afforded to me.

Bank Run

In 1907 on this day, there was a run on the Knickerbocker Trust Company bank in New York, as thousands of people worried about the safety of their deposits lined up to take their money out. The next day the bank was forced to close its doors, and the Panic of 1907 was under way. These days our bank deposits are insured, and even though some banks have fallen by the wayside the depositors' money has generally been safe. But we are still operating in a system where rumors and fears can change the entire complexion of the marketplace, stocks go up and down on the basis of this tipster or that, and people are influenced in their thinking by polls that purport to tell what they think. All these are the risks, I suppose, of being able to communicate so much faster and more thoroughly than the people who preceded us, but it does remind a speaker that once the words are out of the mouth there is no telling what they will lead to. Mindful of that risk I intend to listen very carefully to what I have to say.

OCTOBER 23

Johnny Carson

Today is the birthday of Johnny Carson, born in 1925 in Iowa. He held us for so many midnight hours with his television talk show that I feel no compunction about talking to you at a much more civilized hour here today. I can't promise you anything as funny as Johnny Carson's conversation, but on the other hand you won't have to watch an applause sign. If I am lucky I won't need one.

El Alamein

The history of the world isn't always made in well-known places like New York or Paris or London or Berlin. On this day in 1942, the course of history turned in a small Egyptian town. Its name was El Alamein, and it was where General Bernard Law Montgomery's British forces stopped the Nazi and fascist conquest of North Africa in World War II. Since that time other relatively obscure nations and places have become pivotal centers for an historic moment or two—places like My Lai or Plains, Georgia or Three Mile Island or the Falklands, for example. Sometimes we become so fascinated with what is happening in obscure places that we are diverted from what is happening right where we live. Today I should like to focus on happenings very close to home.

Hungarian Freedom Day

Hungary had been under a communist dictatorship for a decade when, on this day in 1956, its gallant people rose in a revolt that gave it an all-too-brief period of liberation. It was a stirring reminder that communism has not achieved power by popular acclaim but rather by armed force. If I were speaking to you in a communist nation, I would be spouting the party line or I would be silenced. We think very seldom here about the freedoms we enjoy; we would think of them a great deal more if, like the Hungarians of 1956, we didn't have them. So I think it is only fair to use the freedom that is so commonplace to us, and speak my piece.

The Swallows of Capistrano

There are some natural laws that we suppose to be unchangeable. The swallows of Capistrano, for example, are always supposed to leave that California sanctuary on this day. Like us, even the birds are supposed to do things or go places at a specific time. Every generation disturbs its elders by challenging some of these suppositions. It seems to me that we have come to a time when we cannot merely impose our rituals and our values; we have to justify them. So today I want to take a look at some of our cherished institutions and figure out with you how we can best save them.

OCTOBER 24

Cold War

Sometimes a phrase uttered in passing captures the popular fancy and lives on. That happened on this day in 1948, when Bernard Baruch testified before a Senate committee about our relations with Soviet Russia. "Although the war is over," Baruch said, "we are in the midst of a cold war, which is getting warmer." The public latched on to the expression *cold war*. It was easily understood, graphic, and to the point. And cold war has been with us ever since. It isn't the most attractive of situations, but a cold war is better than a hot one, and we are generally content with keeping the world from bursting into flames. But one of the consequences of cold war is that we and the other side, with walls between us, get to know less and less of each other; the aura of mutual distrust encourages a continued arms race, and we live on the brink. I have no easy solution to offer, but I think we must put more work into finding a solution. And in this regard I have some thoughts.

Risk for Risk

It is always a temptation for a speaker to curry favor with the audience by relaying scandalous tales, but when that temptation occurs to me I recall the words of the late Judge Learned Hand, who said on this day in 1952, "Risk for risk, for myself I had rather take my chance that some traitors will escape detection than spread abroad a spirit of general suspicion and distrust, which accepts rumor and gossip in place of undismayed and unintimidated inquiry." The nature of the governmental process in the United States is such that undismayed and unintimidated inquiry are always in order, and so I will ask some questions here today that may be helpful in calling your attention to matters that deserve it.

40-Hour Week

This was the day in 1940 when the normal work week of 40 hours went into effect under the terms of the Fair Labor Standards Act of 1938. It doesn't seem terribly significant today, but at the time it was a notable step forward in limiting normal working hours. One of the things we often forget, as we enjoy ourselves bemoaning our fate, is the fact that we have less working hours and more leisure time than we did in the so-called "good old days." There are still a lot of problems in the pursuit of happiness, but we have a lot more time nowadays to devote to it. Are we using that time properly? That is a question you'll have to decide for yourself, but I have some suggestions.

Alarm Clock

The forerunner of the windup alarm clock was patented on this day in 1876 by Seth Thomas, an invention which has deprived us of heaven knows how many hours of additional sleep. As far as I know, no bell will ring when you have had enough of my oratory here today, but nevertheless I will try not to take too much of your time, for he who talks too long makes patience run short.

OCTOBER 25

Battle of Balaclava

Today is the anniversary of the Battle of Balaclava in 1854, an example of military courage and stupidity better known as the Charge of the Light Brigade. It was during the Crimean War. The British Light Brigade was ordered to attack a strong Russian position against incredible odds. As Alfred Lord Tennyson's great poem notes, "Theirs not to make reply,/Their's not to reason why,/Theirs but to do and die;/Into the valley of Death/Rode the six hundred." It is the nature of war that the men in the ranks still have the same fighting tradition, to do and die without reasoning why, but I would like to think that, at least in this blessed land, we have come to hold human life more dear than deliberately to send it into the valley of death. Yet we do something of this kind not in war but in the peacetime battle of life; we send people out in the world unequipped for that battle, doomed to the death of their hopes. We don't do this deliberately, but we do it; and it is time that we did something, deliberately, about it.

Pablo Picasso

This is the birthday of Pablo Picasso, the towering genius of twentieth-century art who was born in Spain in 1881. It is interesting that Picasso, a man whose humanitarian sympathies caused him to exile himself from his native land throughout the Franco dictatorship and to create his peace dove symbol, was like so many others who profess to have their hearts bleeding over the victims of injustice. In his dealings with individuals, particularly the women who loved him, he was something less than a nice man. It is fine and inspiring to profess love for the collective human race, but the ultimate test of one's humanity is in the person-to-person relationship. Being thoughtful of your neighbor and your family is basic. Contributing to your community is basic. There are many ways to give meaning to being a good neighbor, and I'd like to talk about that here today.

Forgotten Plea

An obscure historical footnote indicates that on this day in 1870 a convention in Cincinnati asked Congress to move the nation's capital to the Mississippi Valley because that was closer to the center of the country. Obviously, even well over a hundred years ago, there was a certain mistrust of the government in Washington, D.C. But I don't think that moving the capital would have made any difference; people don't seem to have any higher regard for their state legislators, who are a lot closer to them than their congressional representatives. And the invisible apparatchiks of government, the ones who really make the wheels go round, are the bureaucrats of the civil service, not exceedingly popular with the rest of us by either name. This does not trouble me; I'd much rather have a demanding electorate than a stolid, unvocal group of voters. When the voters make their views known, it is a rare politician who ignores them. So the thing to do is to make your views known. Today I am doing my part.

St. Crispin's Day

Since today is St. Crispin's Day, memoralizing the patron saint of shoemakers, I hope I can start this speech on the right foot and with some sensible observations to boot. I guess the only way to find out is to try it on for size.

OCTOBER 26

Gunfight at the OK Corral

This is the anniversary of the famous gunfight at the OK Corral, fought by the three Earp brothers and Doc Holliday against the Clanton brothers and two others in Tombstone, Arizona, in 1881. Generations of Americans have grown up relishing the story of this famous shoot-out and regarding it, despite all teaching to the contrary, as the ultimate way to get rid of the bad guys. It is an attitude encouraged by the slow process of justice in the courts. How many times have you heard someone say, talking about a murderer who was apprehended by the police, "they should have shot him." How many times have you hoped that a hated person—say a foreign dictator who troubles us—would "drop dead." I am not suggesting that we should endeavor to keep murderers or dictators alive; my point is that we are addicted to the hope of simplistic solutions. We look at a world divided into the good guys and the bad guys, and it isn't really quite that way. We are impatient with efforts to reform the justice system and equally impatient with the system itself. We look to leaders for magic formulas. Alas, I have no magic to offer, but I do have some observations that may help to sharpen the focus.

Smallpox

On this day in 1979, the World Health Organization announced in Nairobi, Kenya, that smallpox had been eradicated all over the world. It was an amazing victory, one that reminds us that not every war is fought between nations or with guns. The war against smallpox was a coordinated world effort, and it proved that the different people who inhabit the earth can work together and win a common reward. The challenge that confronts us is to use the example of the war against one dread disease as an inspiration for further international cooperation. We have some great opportunities for such cooperation, including those I plan to talk about here today.

Transportation Anniversaries

There are a couple of transportation anniversaries today that make an interesting point. Daily jet airplane service across the Atlantic by American planes began on this day in 1958, and 133 years earlier the Erie Canal had been formally opened. The Erie Canal, which helped open up the American West to settlement and trade, had its traffic moving at a leisurely pace; the jet planes were far faster and traveled a greater distance. The whole thrust of our civilization has been to make communication easier. What has been a greater challenge is how well, rather than how fast, we communicate. How well do we communicate the nature of America to the rest of the world? How well do we communicate with each other? Today I want to discuss that latter question, with particular regard to the way we make our views known to our elected representatives.

Mule History

On this day in 1785, a gift from the King of Spain to George Washington arrived in Boston. The gift was two male donkeys. With them the father of his country bred the first mules to be born in the United States. The mule, of course, was not an American invention; this offspring of a donkey and a horse had been a work animal in the Old World for thousands of years, but until 1785 it was nonexistent in America. We don't have quite as many mules today as we did in their heyday at the turn of the century, and the Army mule is little more than a mascot today for the service whose guns it used to pull. But the mule remains a great American institution, and as time has passed it seems to me that the American public has acquired some of its characteristics—stubbornness and the need to be persuaded to do things that must be done. Today I'd like to talk about some outstanding examples of public stubbornness.

OCTOBER 27

Boss Tweed

Today is the anniversary of the arrest of William Marcy Tweed, better known as Boss Tweed, in 1871, for his participation in a multimillion-dollar graft ring in New York City. Tweed had been the leader of the Democratic Party, popularly known in the City as Tammany Hall; it was his spoils system that gave Tammany Hall the questionable reputation it enjoyed for years thereafter. Tweed's downfall was interesting because it was one of the first political scandals to be triggered by American journalism. *The New York Times* exposed the details of his raids on the city treasury. Back in 1871, the *Times* was not a giant among newspapers, but its reporting got results. That situation is echoed today. It isn't the size of a newspaper or magazine or broadcasting station that makes the difference, it's the quality of its information. And the quality of information is what I want to discuss here today.

Navy Day

The observance of the Navy Day on this date was an important civic occasion for many years, although as the size of the fleet has varied there has been less emphasis on the celebration. Today's Navy, like the other armed forces, is a technical world training people for very specialized work. As our civilization develops, we also develop an infinite variety of new specialties; the services do a great deal of the training which, if our educational system were better, would be done in civilian life. I say this not so much in criticism of the educational system as in praise of an often forgotten function of the Navy and the other armed forces. They are the people who give vital education to tens of thousands of our young people. This is a great peacetime asset for us. Without it many more young people would truly be at sea. I make this point because there are among us those who think the only purpose of armed forces is to fight wars. I believe it is time we saluted the peacetime accomplishments of the armed forces, and I'd like to mention some specifics.

William Penn

It was on this day in 1682 that a wealthy Quaker, who had been persecuted in England for his religion, landed at Newcastle in what is now Delaware to claim the territory he had obtained from the British Crown, a territory ultimately known as Pennsylvania. His name was William Penn, and his idea was to establish true religious freedom in his territory. In keeping with that idea, the main city of Pennsylvania was named Philadelphia, the city of brotherly love. But the idealistic Mr. Penn was a man of some sharp opinions. Today

I want to cite one such opinion. "Men," he wrote, "are generally more careful of the breed of their horses and dogs than of their children." I wonder whether we have remedied that sad fact as yet. Are we giving our children the care they deserve?

Theodore Roosevelt

Theodore Roosevelt, who was born in New York City on this day in 1858, wrote in his autobiography that, "every reform movement has a lunatic fringe." The lunatic fringe consists of the people who are willing to hold up or destroy any other aspect of the nation's operations to have their way and who have no interest in any issue but their own. In most instances the lunatic fringe begins with a plausible point, such as temperance or conservation or crime and punishment or civil rights, but then develops an extreme position without regard for any other considerations of public policy. I rise today to suggest that something must be done about the lunatic fringe, and I will cite cases in point.

OCTOBER 28

Justice

It was on this day in 1965 that Pope Paul VI formally announced five decrees formulated by the Vatican Council and inspired by his predecessor, Pope John XXIII. One of those decrees denied the collective guilt of Jews for the crucifixion of Jesus Christ. How many centuries of anti-Semitism had been written in blood and tears before that 1965 decree! How contrary to the teachings of Christ himself the vengeful notion of so endless and so vast a heritage of hate! But this was not a unique situation. The world is full of inherited hatreds whose origins go back generations—religious antagonisms, ethnic conflicts, national feuds. It seems sometimes that humanity is more adept at breaking up into factions than at coming together. We have not yet learned the lesson that when we hate, we ourselves are the victims. Look around you, and that fact becomes apparent.

John XXIII

When Angelo Roncalli, the Cardinal of Venice, was elected Pope John XXIII on this day in 1958, he was more than 75 years old. Nobody expected him to be more than an interim caretaker Pope. But in his five years as prelate he convened the great Ecumenical Council and awakened a new wave of hope and faith. It was an inspiring reminder that age need not wither nor time cause to fade the ability of older people to help build a better world. Are we making proper use of our older people? If not, how can we do better?

Penn's Charter

On this day in 1701, William Penn and a committee of Pennsylvania legislators agreed on the adoption of a new charter, entitled Pennsylvania Charter of Privileges, and the document was the basis of the government of that state until the American Revolution. There was one paragraph that I want to call particularly to your attention here today. Paragraph V reads simply, "That all Criminals shall have the same Privileges of Witnesses and Council as their Prosecutors." This, bear in mind, was hundreds of years before *Gideon v. Wainwright* or the *Miranda* case, when the Supreme Court reasserted similar principles. The basic concept of American justice, as stated in the Pennsylvania Charter, is one of the great bulwarks of our liberty, even though at times the exercise of these basic rights by defendants seems to delay and sometimes thwart the rendering of an appropriate verdict. One of the most difficult aspects of our way of life is to find ways to speed up the processes of justice without impairing the traditional rights of defendants. How, if at all, can we pull off this hat trick?

Harvard

About this time in the year 1636, a modest institution of higher education opened in what is now Cambridge, Massachusetts. Its name originally was Cambridge College, but when the Reverend John Harvard died and left a substantial bequest to the college it was renamed in his honor. It was the first college in our country, and it remains to this day a gem in the nation's crown. But my reason for noting its anniversary here today is not simply to salute it on its birthday. My point is that in 1636 Massachusetts was a struggling colony, founded only 16 years before, yet even in those early days they were concerned about having a place for higher education. Ladies and gentlemen, that is how far back the American tradition of higher education goes. And what we must ask ourselves is whether, proportionately, we are doing as much for higher education as those New England founding fathers did.

OCTOBER 29

Wall Street Crash

The headline in the show business weekly *Variety* told the story of this day in 1929. "Wall Street Lays an Egg," said *Variety*. It was a bad egg, the spectacular Wall Street crash that signaled the onset of the great worldwide depression, the depression against which every subsequent downturn has been measured. But out of that depression, in the administration of Franklin Roosevelt, came a whole series of needed reforms—unemployment insurance, social security, and insured bank deposits, for example. Mankind has an infinite capacity for doing better. The challenge to us is not merely to decide how to do best, but first to determine what our priorities should be. Where do we have to do better first?

Joseph Pulitzer

This is the anniversary of the death of Joseph Pulitzer. The occasion of his death in 1911 is worth noting because his most lasting contribution to his country was made in his will. It provided the endowment for the establishment of the School of Journalism, now the Graduate School of Journalism, of Columbia University, one of the great pioneering institutions in that field. The reporting of news is a great responsibility, and one that grows greater as the speed and intensity of communication continues to grow. One of the ways we can insure adequate reporting is to do whatever we can to see that the reporters of the future are well trained and well educated and, above all, well grounded in journalistic ethics. To have a responsible press you need responsible, courageous editors, publishers, and reporters. Anyone whose ox is gored in print or on the air may be tempted to find fault with the quality of the reporting, and I might even be surprised by what, if anything, is pulled out of my remarks here today, but I can say whatever I please, as I am about to demonstrate.

Edmund Halley

The first man to predict the course of a comet was Edmund Halley, the British astronomer who was born in London on this day in 1656. He observed a particular heavenly body when it came into view in 1682, figured out its orbit, and said it would return in 1757, which it did. It was given the appropriate name of Halley's comet, and it has been coming back into view every now and then right on schedule. I wish I could be as precise as Halley about what is going to be coming into view in the time ahead, but I can neither look as far ahead as he did nor plot the path of earthly nations as accurately as he did with a heavenly body. But if he could look at the distant skies, I at least can look into my clouded crystal ball and tell you what I see.

NOW

Today is the birthday of the National Organization for Women, which was founded in 1966 to gain equal rights for that half of the population. At first many people laughed at NOW, either because they didn't believe that women were discriminated against or because they felt there was nothing wrong with that kind of discrimination. But over the years the cause of equal rights made steady headway, even though the Equal Rights Amendment failed in its extended first round. When the issue of equal rights for women has been solved, I am as certain as I am sure I'm standing here that there will be other groups pointing out other inequities and seeking their correction. Indeed, I have some thoughts to present in that regard.

OCTOBER 30

Charles Atlas

Today marks the birth in 1894 in Acri, Italy, of a man named Angelo Siciliano. There is no reason for you to recognize that name, because he was far better known by the name he adopted when he grew up—Charles Atlas. When he was 20 years old he came to the United States. He was rundown and not particularly well endowed physically, the famous "97-pound weakling" he later featured in the before and after advertisements he ran; but when he discovered how to build himself up with some special exercises, he developed the physique of an Atlas. After a successful career in modeling he started a body-building business which he made into a mail-order course, and the rest is history. Atlas's story, it seems to me, is particularly worth remembering because it tells us that, to a great extent, we are the masters of our own destiny. We can take what God gave us and work on it and improve it—not merely muscles but minds as well. But we have to be prepared to work for what we get. And right now we have a lot of work to do.

Sheridan

Richard Brinsley Sheridan, the great English playwright who was born on this day in 1751 in Dublin, created the immortal character of Mrs. Malaprop, who used words amusingly incorrectly. But Sheridan himself used words like rapiers, and I particularly recall a speech he made in reply to an opponent. He said, "The right honorable gentlemen is indebted to his memory for his jests, and to his imagination for his facts." I hasten to add that in the facts I will report to you today I am indebted neither to memory nor to imagination but only to my own eyes and ears.

The Real Start of Autumn

According to the calendar autumn started more than a month ago, but in some respects it is the Halloween season that splits the warm time of fun and the cold time of winter. But it isn't only the trick-or-treaters who are worrying about the goblins. This year there are enough goblins to go around, and around and around. We seem to have entered the "what if" stage of civilization: what if someone explodes a nuclear bomb, what if people can't find jobs, what if people don't get married anymore? So it is easy for a speaker to join the gloom-peddlers and recite a litany of all the dismal possibilities. I prefer to talk of happier things.

Ezra Pound

Ezra Pound, the poet, was born in this day in 1885 in Idaho. Although his pro-fascist broadcasts in World War II got him into trouble, some of the observations he made in his poetry deserve to be remembered, and one quotation furnishes me with my text for the day. "What thou lovest well," he wrote, "is thy true heritage." And so I have asked myself, what is it that we love well? What is our true heritage?

OCTOBER 31

National Magic Day

Today, as you may know, is often observed as National Magic Day in commermoration of the death of the great magician Harry Houdini on this day of 1926. Houdini's most spectacular feats were escape acts of various kinds, but the world itself has performed some even more impressive escape acts since his death. For example, we escaped annihilation in World War II and, even in the face of more terrible weapons today, we are still escaping. We have escaped totally poisoning our air and we have escaped blowing ourselves up. We have escaped fouling the ocean and buying elections. But we are still confronted with all these dangers, and we don't have any great magic to rely on. What we do have is knowlege, and that's what I want to discuss with you here today.

Charter Oak

In the history of America, rivers have played key roles, as have harbors, prairies, mountains, and one tree. On this day—or, more properly, the night of this day in 1687—the British governor wanted to destroy the charter of Connecticut as a separate colony. He came to a conference in Hartford to demand that the charter be surrendered, but instead its defenders hid it in an oak tree, known to history as the Charter Oak. Even though the governor had announced it was null and void, it went back into effect in 1689. The Charter Oak had made its contribution to American history. Indeed, American history is never just a matter of people. The Charter Oak and the corn and the fruit of America helped us to survive and to grow, and now we face the question of whether we are continuing to make the best use of what we have found in America.

Pretzel Week

It is usually about this time that an ancient and honorable American business conducts the annual observance of National Pretzel Week. I have no new twists to offer in that connection, but I hope my remarks here today will give you something to chew on.

John Keats

Today is the birthday of John Keats, one of the greatest and most prolific of English poets. He was born in London in 1795. He completed his training as a doctor before deciding to make poetry his career. He was only 26 when he died of tuberculosis, so his great contributions to literature were made in an even shorter timespan than Mozart was able to give to music. If gifted people like this can say so much in so brief a time, I certainly have no excuse to dawdle here today, so let me get right to my point.

NOVEMBER 1

Religion in American Life

This is the beginning of the month annually observed as Religion in American Life Month, dedicated to the proposition that faith is the heritage of America. It is not a sectarian occasion; what is important is simply to hold on to those ethical and spiritual values that give life its meaning. Providence has blessed this land of ours, and we have been given a goodly heritage. Now it is up to us to do what the generations who preceded us did in their time—to take that goodly heritage and make it better. So today I will not ask you to look at the past but rather to envision what we can make the future.

Authors Day

Back in 1928, a woman in Illinois started the annual observance of Authors Day on the first day of November. Authors come in all shapes, sizes, languages, and degrees of success. What they all have in common is an ability to express themselves in words. Not everyone has that ability, and not everyone has the same ability to listen. Three people listening to the same radio speech may come away with three different interpretations of what was said—not because they disagree about the words but because they have different views of what the important points of the speech were and because we all have a tendency to hear what we want to hear. I don't know whether what I have to say here today will be what you want to hear; I know it will be what I want to say.

"Taste the World"

Henry David Thoreau, the philosopher of Walden Pond, laid down some rules on this day in 1851 which are well worth remembering. "First of all," he said, "a man must see, before he can say . . . taste the world and digest it." So today I am here to tell you something of what I have seen, an idea of the world as I have tasted it.

Big Day for Notre Dame

On this day in 1913, the football team of a then-obscure midwestern college in Indiana came east to meet the team of the U.S. Military Academy at West Point. They introduced Army and the football world to the expert use of a newfangled offense built around something called the forward pass, which the midwestern college's captain, a young fellow named Knute Rockne, used brilliantly. When the game was over, Rockne's college, the University of Notre

Dame, was no longer obscure, and football was never the same. It was one of those classic cases of an underdog getting a big chance and taking advantage of it. What happens in football also happens in life. Time and time again someone with a new idea and the ability to develop it comes along and surprises the establishment. When you get down to the nitty gritty, new ideas are what have built America. Today I want to look at some of the new ideas that are calling for attention now.

NOVEMBER 2

Truman's Surprise

This is the anniversary of the election day when Harry Truman confounded all of the experts and won the 1948 election over Republican Thomas E. Dewey. One of the great news pictures of the century shows a jubilant Truman holding up a Chicago newspaper that had gone to press early with the announcement of a Dewey victory. That was not the first nor will it be the last time the experts have been wrong, but it does embolden me to give you a layman's view of some of the subjects that have been left for too long to the specialized experts.

Balfour Declaration

World War I was the environment in which British Foreign Secretary Arthur Balfour was speaking on this day in 1917, when he approved what became known as the Balfour Declaration, endorsing, quote, "the establishment in Palestine of a national home for the Jewish people." It was this declaration that became the basis for the termination of the British mandate over the Holy Land and the establishment of Israel by the United Nations in 1948. Not as much attention was paid to another phrase in Balfour's statement, namely this: "it being clearly understood that nothing shall be done which may prejudice the civil and religious rights of existing non-Jewish communities in Palestine." The British did not say how both objectives—a Jewish homeland and no disturbance of the rights of the existing Arab populations—were to be accomplished, and the resultant struggles are matters of sad history. I would hope that we had learned from this, but we still have some who promise all things to all people. Right now, in this election season, we should be particularly conscious of the speciousness of some of those promises.

Daniel Boone

This is the birthday of Daniel Boone, who was born in 1734 near Reading, Pennsylvania. It was Daniel Boone who helped pioneer the opening of the West to settlement, and what I find interesting is that he did much of this as an employee of a real estate development company. From the time of the earliest land grants in the colonies the country was opened up, tamed, and populated through the efforts of what today we would call real estate interests. We talk of our fabulous land with all of its natural resources, but we don't give ourselves sufficient credit for having recognized and developed these resources. There are other countries equally well endowed who have done much less. Ours is a record not merely of having but of doing. And the challenge that faces us today is to find the proper direction for what we do next.

Washington's Farewell

On this day in 1783, near Princeton, New Jersey, George Washington bade farewell to his victorious army. The American Revolution was over; the United States was free. And, looking back, the commander-in-chief saw the achievement of a miracle. "Who, that was not a witness," he said, "could imagine that the most violent local prejudices would cease so soon; and that men, who came from the different parts of the continent, strongly disposed by the habits of education to despise and quarrel with each other, would instantly become but one patriotic band of brothers?" Except for the era that climaxed in the Civil War, this miracle has persisted in American life. It is in some ways the secret of the continuance of our national existence. We have learned to subordinate sectionalism and to work together. It is a lesson Europe is trying belatedly to learn in its Common Market approach, a lesson the United Nations has yet to learn. Perhaps, from our own experience, we can give the UN some pointers.

NOVEMBER 3

FDR's Second Term

In 1936 on this day, Franklin D. Roosevelt's New Deal was put to the test as the nation went to the polls. The candidates were President Roosevelt and the Governor of Kansas, Alfred M. Landon. The results were overwhelming. Roosevelt won all but two of the states, leading to Postmaster General James A. Farley's comment that while in the past the saying had been, "As Maine goes, so goes the nation," the story now was that "as Maine goes, so goes Vermont." In the years since then, not even that statement has held up. Old voting patterns keep fading, and the electorate becomes less predictable all the time. We have learned one thing, though, always expect the unexpected. So let me tell you the perhaps unexpected things I see on the horizon.

William Cullen Bryant

William Cullen Bryant, who was born on this day in 1794 in Massachusetts, was both a poet and a newspaper editor. One of his most quoted lines is this:

"Truth, crushed to earth, shall rise again." This belief has to be the touchstone of our credo, but it is hard to imagine the day when, in so many other parts of the world, the truth that has so long been crushed to earth will rise again. And even in our own land we see disturbing refusal to face certain truths. What I have to say here today may give you some new information or at the least provide some new contexts.

Change of Heart

This was Election Day in 1964, when Lyndon B. Johnson won over Barry Goldwater by the greatest popular vote plurality ever recorded up to that time. Four years later, with his popularity at low ebb, President Johnson decided not to run for reelection. The problems arising from the Vietnam War had eaten away at his popular support. What happened to Lyndon Johnson has happened to others and will continue to happen. Rightly or wrongly, the administration in office is the beneficiary or the victim of events over which it does not always have control. We judge performance by results. What are we to say of the results we see today?

Double Talk

When the late George Q. Lewis, a leading gag writer, was alive, he sponsored a number of observances, including marking the first full week of November as National Double Talk Week. Lewis is gone and the official observance is no more, but the double talk is certainly still with us. Contemplating some of the popular catchphrases and the misunderstandings about what they mean or imply, it seems to me to be a very good idea to try to penetrate the double talk and figure out what the real meaning of some of these catchphrases is. So that's what I am going to try to do here today.

NOVEMBER 4

The Hostages

This is the anniversary of an unprecedented event in international afairs, the taking of American hostages by revolutionists in Iran. Their more than a year of captivity, which began on this day in 1979 at the American Embassy in Tehran, led to the defeat of a president at the polls, but at the same time the awakening of a new spirit of American unity. It is sad but true that much of what is best in America is reborn in times of challenge and crisis; we have a tendency at other times to be uninterested and uninvolved. That may be why so often a public speaker is tempted to sound alarms and point to crises. But when there is a real crisis you don't usually have to tell the people, because they already know. So I am not here to cry wolf. No, indeed; I am here to cry bravo, to tell you some of the good things I see on the horizon.

UNESCO

The United Nations Educational, Scientific, and Cultural Organization, better known as UNESCO, was established on this day in 1946. It has been an object lesson in international relations, hardly a model of what international relations should be but an object lesson nevertheless. During its lifetime UNESCO has been as much of a battleground as anything else, where the communist bloc and the Third World nations have spared no effort to impose their ideology. For example, they have consistently attacked the western concept of freedom of the press and sought government control of news. Is UNESCO a bridge or a gulf?

The Gatling Gun

It was on this day during the Civil War in 1862 that Richard J. Gatling patented a new weapon. Some people thought it might make an end to war because it could kill so many people so quickly. It was the first machine gun, which in one of its early forms could fire about 350 shots within a minute. Since then, of course, both machine guns and other forms of weapons have been made infinitely more deadly, and war still hangs over us as a constant threat. If superiority in weapons is the road to peace, it is also the cause of a never-ending arms race. The question that challenges us is whether we cannot find a better way.

Russian Takeover

On this day in 1956, Russian troops took control of Hungary, crushing the free Hungarian government that had taken over the previous month. It was one more reminder that communism is imposed on people, not freely chosen by them. Some folks suggest that the march of communism is a kind of popular revolution, but the fact is that in Russia as elsewhere it was imposed by a militant minority. That is why we have to be wary of those who profess sympathy for communist movements in countries where they are not in power; for such sympathy gives aid and comfort to a way of life whose constant goal is to eat away at our way of life. At the same time it is easy to pillory healthy, constructive movements by branding them as communist. So we are forever challenged with trying to determine whether this or that reform movement is inspired by or playing into the hands of the communist world movement. That challenge furnishes my subject for today.

NOVEMBER 5

First President

The first President of the United States was not George Washington. Under the Articles of Confederation, a President of the United States in Congress

Assembled was elected by that congress; he was John Hanson of Maryland, and he was chosen for the post on this day in 1781. It was not the same office that George Washington later filled, since the president of the congress had few duties under the Articles of Confederation other than chairing its meetings. The responsibilities of the President have grown incredibly since that time and are still growing. There was no doomsday button in John Hanson's office, or in George Washington's either, for that matter. We have piled one new responsibility after another onto the presidential office, and even though we have expanded the personnel of the executive branch many times, there is no way of lightening the ultimate responsibility of the office where the buck finally stops. It is not surprising, therefore, that every modern president becomes at one time or another a center of controversy. I am here to suggest that, instead of making the presidency our target, we take a critical look at the mechanism of government that makes his task so difficult.

Newspaper Anniversary

John Peter Zenger was an immigrant from Germany who came to New York in 1710 and worked as a printer and editor. On this day in 1733, he became the editor of the *New York Weekly Journal*. He published articles attacking the royal government of the city and was arrested on charges of seditious libel. At his trial, his lawyer Andrew Hamilton urged the jury to judge him on whether his articles were true. The case was the first American milestone in the battle for a free press. That battle, ladies and gentlemen, is still being fought. When government refuses to permit free reporting of its operations, or puts the seal of secrecy on information having nothing to do with national defense or privileged material, the freedom of the press to report to the public is being undermined. When court proceedings are closed to the press, it is an attack on the free press, too. We must be alert to prevent the spread of secrecy in government.

Ida Tarbell

Ida Tarbell, who was born on this day in 1857 in Pennsylvania, was the writer whose magazine articles and book about *The History of the Standard Oil Company* led ultimately to the dissolution of that company under the antitrust laws. I find it interesting to contemplate some of the great reforms in this country that have been prompted by women journalists. Rachel Carson's book *Silent Spring* was the trigger for the modern crusade against chemical pollution. Betty Friedan's book *The Feminine Mystique* became the inspiration of modern feminism. Generations earlier, Harriet Beecher Stowe's story *Uncle Tom's Cabin* crystallized the slavery issue for millions of its readers. In every generation, if you want to be on the cutting edge of progress, look at the issues that concern women. Our times are no exception.

X Ray

About this time in the year 1895, a German scientist named Wilhelm Konrad Roentgen was conducting some experiments with light in his laboratory and discovered something that, for want of a better name, he called the X ray. Roentgen's discovery opened the door for the whole new science of radiology, and the X ray itself, of course, became one of the most important diagnostic tools for doctors. It gave us the chance to go beyond the surface of things. In search of information I should like today to do something similar—that is, to go below the surface of events and see what's really happening.

NOVEMBER 6

Nixon's Premature Valedictory

On this day in 1962, after having lost the race for governor of California to Edmund G. Brown, Richard M. Nixon held a press conference on the West Coast. He said, "You won't have Nixon to kick around anymore, because, gentlemen, this is my last press conference." Then, six years later less one day, the same Richard Nixon was elected President of the United States in 1968. The American professional politician is not one to retire from the arena, no matter how disillusioned he or she becomes when rejected by the electorate. No matter how strongly we may feel about a candidate, the electorate benefits when champions of particular views continue to put themselves forward. It adds to our variety of choices. If the time should ever come when we do not have a variety of choices, it will be a sad day for America. I don't know how many of you will agree with the policy choices I will suggest here today but if my remarks at least draw some further attention to the issues involved I will consider my time well spent.

James Naismith

Today is the birthday of a man, born in 1861 in Canada, who, though not a giant in world history, has influenced literally millions of people around the world. Dr. James Naismith had not yet received his M.D. degree in 1891 when he was a student at Springfield College, the YMCA training school in Massachusetts. His class was asked to devise an indoor game to be played between the baseball and football seasons. He responded by inventing, single-handedly, the game of basketball. By the time Dr. Naismith died in 1939, basketball was one of the most international of sports. There is always room for a good new idea, especially one that is simple and easy to understand. I have nothing to present today that fits the bill as the invention of basketball did, but perhaps I can make a point or two.

A Strange Team

On this day Abraham Lincoln's candidacy for the presidency of the United States was given victory by the American voters in 1860. Two days later he wrote to his running mate Hannibal Hamlin, the Republican Party's winning vice-presidential candidate. In his letter Lincoln said, "I am anxious for a personal interview with you." Nothing seems unusual about that request, except for one fact. Although they ran together on the same ticket Lincoln had never met his running mate. I must admit that does suggest we take our politics a little more seriously today. Or perhaps it is that we take the vice-presidency more seriously, having seen too many presidents, including Lincoln himself, lose their lives while in office. Interestingly, we have been rather fortunate in the strength of those vice-presidents who assumed the first office—men like Theodore Roosevelt and Harry Truman, for example—but the way the vice-presidential nominees are chosen is not a very reassuring one. Yet, like so much of the apparently cumbersome structures of American government, it seems to work. The question that eternally confronts us is how to make it work better.

Peter Pan

One of the great stage triumphs of all time came with the New York premiere of *Peter Pan,* starring Maude Adams, on this day in 1903. It was a touching tale about a wonderful fairy, a miraculous boy who would never grow old, and a dog who acted as a nursemaid. It had one of the great villains of all time, Captain Hook. It will, I suppose, live forever, which is fine; but unfortunately it has given some people strange ideas about real life. There are those who think of themselves as Peter Pans in their own Never Never Land, refusing to contemplate or plan for the possibility of not always being young and vigorous. There are those who seem to want to look for a Tinker Bell to make everything right again. I could go on with analogies, but I think the point has been made. We have too great a tendency to refuse to face the problems that seem ahead for us. I'd like to talk about some of these.

NOVEMBER 7

Museum of Modern Art

It was on this day in 1929 that a new type of museum opened in New York City—the Museum of Modern Art. Apart from its pioneering recognition of modern artists, it has focused attention on product design, graphics, and all the design aspects of our century. I suspect that by encouraging the designers, the Museum has been a strong influence on the better look of products in general today. This is not merely a matter of aesthetics; when we work with more attractive materials, in more attractive surroundings, I believe it is an aid to efficiency and to morale. Our urban transportation needs all the design help we can give it. The same is true of designs that can simplify and lower the cost of new housing. I could go on, but my point is made. So let me concentrate on one item that seems quite basic—the design of the modern city.

CPB

An important milestone for American broadcasting was achieved on this day in 1967, when President Lyndon Johnson signed the act of Congress establishing the Corporation for Public Broadcasting. It was this means of public financing that enabled public broadcasting to become a reality all over the United States. The public stations, existing side by side with the commercial ones, were at first regarded as another do-gooders' boondoggle, but over the course of time most of us, including notably the commercial broadcasters, have found that the noncommercial stations have something distinctive and worthwhile to offer. A lot of good ideas run the same course, being regarded at first as harebrained or impractical and then, over the course of time, proving themselves. It is the same with people. Some whom we at first resent turn out over the course of time to be on the cutting edge of the era. Today I want to talk about these people.

Truth

Wendell Phillips, the great New England orator of the nineteenth century, made a speech on this day in 1860 in which he remarked that "you can always get the truth from an American statesman after he has turned seventy or given up all hope of the presidency." I am not that old, but it's been some time since I dreamed of the White House, so you can expect the truth from me here today—or at least the truth as I see it.

Marie Celeste

It was on this day in 1872 that a ship named the *Marie Celeste* sailed from New York for Genoa, Italy. A month later she was found drifting in the Atlantic with nobody aboard but with the galley set for a meal and everything in order. It was a mystery that has never been solved. There have been all kinds of theories suggested, but nobody knows whatever happened to the people of the *Marie Celeste*. Whatever did happen, of course, happened far at sea in the lonely wastes of a big ocean; but in the lonely wastes of a big city, every day of the year, there are people nobody ever finds, people who might as well have been on the *Marie Celeste*. As our nation gets more populous and more of us raise ourselves by our bootstraps, there is a sort of reverse Darwinism occurring—the development of an underclass of the least fit. That is what I want to talk about today.

NOVEMBER 8

The Louvre

This is the birthday of the Louvre, the great museum in Paris which was opened to the public on this day in 1793. Since then the great art that was once the private joy of the rich has been made available for viewing by the public in modest and lavish museums throughout the world. We speak of the Renaissance as a golden age of the arts, but in truth there had never been a greater variety of opportunities and audiences than there is today. Much of this growth has been the result, in this country, of a unique partnership among government, private philanthropy, and the larger public. In that kind of partnership, it seems to me, lie the seeds of future growth in other fields, as I hope I can suggest here today.

JFK

John Fitzgerald Kennedy was elected President of the United States on this day in 1960. He is remembered for the style he brought to the White House and, of course, for his martyrdom. But his election marked another milestone. He was the first Roman Catholic to be elected president. If at times you are discouraged by the slow pace of some reform in America don't lose heart. Sooner or later what is morally right wins its triumphs. The problem much of the time, however, is to know what is morally right. There is no question about that when you come to racial or religious prejudice, but, to take an example, who is to decide whether capital punishment is ever morally right? Are tax shelters morally right? I am concerned about a decline of moral standards that we can't blame on video games or temptations of the flesh. The standards to which I refer are the rules and customs by which we live. Have you looked at them lately?

John Milton

It was on this day in 1674 that the great English writer John Milton passed away. In his later years he was stricken with blindness and saw his concept of liberty in England defeated, but some of his greatest work came in this period of his physical decline and moral discouragement, including his great *Paradise Lost* and *Samson Agonistes*. Some people reach the peak of their creativity in times of difficulty. Some of us are not actors so much as reactors. I believe we live in times when challenges and difficulties are all around us and that we are thereby given great opportunities—opportunities to make the world a little better. I want to talk about one of those opportunities here today.

Beer Hall Putsch

Back in 1923 on this day, a former corporal in the World War I German army decided to start a revolution to take over the German republic. He began by leading his storm troopers into a beer hall in Munich and attempting to force people to swear allegiance to his cause. But by the next day the authorities broke up the attempted putsch and the leader ultimately went to jail. As you may have guessed, he was Adolf Hitler, and in jail he wrote *Mein Kampf*, the bible of his Nazi movement. From such small beginnings can come events that shake the world. Hitler was one of those people who said exactly what he believed and what he intended to do. It seemed so grotesque that at first nobody believed him. That happens all the time; would-be leaders write or say exactly what they plan to do, get themselves elected, and then do exactly what they said they would. Yet somehow we pay very little attention at the outset, saying it's only campaign talk. I think we should pay more attention. I think we should examine what public figures say they want to do and judge them accordingly. And today I am going to apply that test to some of those who are seeking public support at this time.

NOVEMBER 9

Benjamin Banneker

Today is the birthday of Benjamin Banneker, who deserves to be far better known than he has been. Banneker was born in Ellicott, Maryland, in 1731. His father was a slave. He was probably the first great black American. When Pierre L'Enfant, who was planning the city of Washington, D.C., left that job in 1792 and took his maps with him, Banneker, his assistant, completed the plans from memory. Banneker also published an astronomical almanac so good that Thomas Jefferson called it to the attention of the French Academy of Sciences. We are still the beneficiaries of the genius of Benjamin Banneker, and his birthday is a good time to ask ourselves how we can provide more opportunities for the Benjamin Bannekers of our own times.

The Great Blackout

Between 5:15 and 5:30 P.M. on this date in 1965, the most populous section of the country, the Northeast, went dark. The great electricity blackout affected New York State, most of New England, parts of Canada, and some portions of New Jersey and Pennsylvania. It was a frightening demonstration of how dependent we had become on electricity and how easily one failure could lead to others. But there was one development that surprised and pleased everybody. Not only was there no great panic, but the opportunity for looting and other forms of law-breaking was not taken advantage of. In the face of a real emergency the spirit of peaceful cooperation took over. Now, I don't pretend that this will always happen when something unexpected causes a crisis; most of the time there are people who delight in spreading panic. Sometimes they do it in a form of hysteria; sometimes they do it with cold calculation to create a situation of which they can take advantage. In New York in later blackouts, the looters had a field day. Unfortunately you don't even need an emergency to bring out these troublemakers; if there isn't an emergency they are apt to do their darnedest to dream one up. So today I am going to ask you to take a look at some of the so-called critical areas on the contemporary scene, to see how critical they really are.

UNRRA

At a meeting in Washington on this day in 1943 in the dark days of World War II, the United States and its major allies signed the agreement that created the United Nations Relief and Rehabilitation Administration. By the time this organization completed its mission it had resettled some 8 million war refugees and dispensed billions of dollars of aid. When it is clearly necessary for differing ways of life to cooperate, they do cooperate; the job, of course, is always to persuade them that the common need outweighs the differences in politics. Given that fact, what is the route to real peace between us and Soviet Russia?

Sadat's Initiative

Two sentences spoken by Anwar el Sadat on this day in 1977 changed the history of the world, or at least diverted it. The President of Egypt said—and I quote—"I am ready to go to the ends of the earth if that will save one of my soldiers. I am ready to go to the Knesset to discuss peace." It was the first peaceful overture by an Arab leader to Israel in many years, and it led not only to Sadat's historic address to the Israeli parliament but to the Camp David agreement. This is what can come from a simple, straightforward initiative that puts facts ahead of false pride. It wasn't that Sadat saw the opportunity. He *made* the opportunity. And our leaders have it within their competence to do the same in facing the problems that confront us today.

NOVEMBER 10

The Test of Truth

When the case of *Abrams* v. *the United States* was decided by the Supreme Court in 1919, we were only a year away from fighting World War I. The case involved Russian propagandists who had published pamphlets urging strikes in American factories to stop the shipment of supplies to anti-Bolsheviks in Russia. The propagandists had been convicted and ordered to prison under the Espionage Act. The Court upheld the convictions, but in the decision rendered on this day in 1919 two great justices, Oliver Wendell Holmes Jr. and Louis Brandeis, dissented, and Justice Holmes said, in part, "The best test of truth is the power of the thought to get itself accepted in the competition of the marketplace." I believe those are words of great wisdom and worth remembering every time we are tempted to outlaw an idea or an argument because we disagree with it. Let us permit the truth to be tested in the marketplace of ideas—the marketplace to which I am about to present some thoughts.

Carnegie Corporation

This was the day in 1911 on which it might truly be said that the foundation era of American philanthropy began. Andrew Carnegie, who had already set up a number of multimillion-dollar endowments, topped them all by establishing the Carnegie Corporation of New York to help the progress of education. He gave the Corporation $125 million. Thanks both to civic-mindedness and tax laws, the money contributed to set up and carry on public service foundations since then has mounted into the billions. Cynics among us say that's fine, but that money came ultimately from the people because it represents profits made at the people's expense. But we know from sad experience that if it were left to the people to take the money voluntarily out of their own pockets the contributions would be less than unanimous. Perhaps what we need in this country is a foundation-endowed effort to devise more effective ways of getting voluntary popular funding for the myriad of worthy causes that need it. Perhaps I can do something to that end by talking about the work and needs of a particular cause here today.

Marine Monument

On this tenth day of November the U.S. Marine Corps was founded by the Continental Congress in 1775, and on the Marine Corps birthday in 1954, at Arlington National Cemetery near Washington, a great memorial was unveiled. It shows a huge sculptured reproduction of the famous photograph of the Marines raising the American flag at the summit of Mount Suribachi at the climax of the World War II Battle of Guadalcanal. That scene is symbolic not only of the achievements of the Marines but of the spirit of the United States—the desire to see our flag, and our nation, at the high point of human endeavor. In wartime the high point is easily determined. The high point is victory. In peacetime we have complicated goals and more unpredictable hazards. The first task, of course, is to agree on the goals. I think we have done that, regardless of our political views. We agree on life, liberty, and the pursuit of happiness. Where we do not agree is on how far we have come and how to go forward from here. But in our blessed land of hard-won freedom we have the opportunity to discuss these matters openly and straightforwardly, and that is what I hope to do with you here today.

Stanley and Livingstone

This is the day that Henry M. Stanley found missionary David Livingstone in darkest Africa in 1871. The only trouble was that, despite the much-heralded effort to find him, Dr. Livingstone wasn't lost; he was where he wanted to be, doing the work he wanted to do. Sometimes I get the feeling that a lot of public speakers have what I call a Stanley and Livingstone complex. You in the audience are their Livingstones, and they are going to save you from being lost. They are going to show you the way. Ladies and gentlemen, I have no such illusions about my remarks to you here today. I do not pretend to know the way; what I do know is something of what is going on, and I'd like to report that to you so you can draw your own conclusions.

NOVEMBER 11

Patton

One of the sad but inescapable facts about fame is that it often picks people for their eccentricities as much as their accomplishments. Today is the birthday of General George S. Patton Jr., whose scrapes and exploits in World War II made him such a headline figure. General Patton was born on this day in 1885 in San Gabriel, California. There were many other outstanding generals in World War II, but few with Patton's extroverted personality and flair for getting into and out of difficult situations. The question that kept arising was whether it was his ability or his colorful presence that made him so well known, and the same question keeps arising with many of the public figures we know today—business people whose commercial achievements are fair to middling but whose didos or attitudes keep making headlines, politicians with fine looks and statesmanlike voices who never say or do anything of distinction, one-dimensional entertainers who make a lifetime success by playing the same role over and over again. Public images and actual personalities may be quite different. Sometimes it helps to hear different views of the same headliner, because from these different views you can form a probably more accurate composite. And so today I hope I can contribute to that sort of composite in the case of some current leaders.

"God Bless America"

Sometimes good things take a long time to make it. On this day in 1939, singer Kate Smith introduced on her network radio program a new patriotic song that had actually been written more than twenty years earlier. The song, as you may have guessed, was Irving Berlin's "God Bless America." In the same way that songs have to wait for their time, ideas have to wait for their time, too, and I think the time has now come for some ideas that are not necessarily new but are certainly timely. I'd like to talk about one such.

School Law

This is the anniversary of the first compulsory school law, which was enacted on this day in 1647 by the colony of Massachusetts. What I find particularly interesting about it is that it did not make school attendance compulsory but made the establishment of a school mandatory in every township with fifty or more householders. In other words, the Founding Fathers recognized that education had to be available, even before they made going to school a civic obligation. Today, particularly in some of our big cities, we seem to be more concerned with getting the children to go to school than with the nature of the education. We have all too many instances of children who go through school and emerge as functional illiterates. It isn't enough to make a school building available; we must insist on teaching as well. Perhaps that calls for insisting on academic credentials that mean something for the winners of college athletic scholarships. Perhaps it means facing the fact that we have to spend more on the elementary schools. Assuredly, it means that we should talk about the problems of our schools, and that's what I intend to do here today.

Veterans Day

On this day dedicated to the memory of all those who have fought the country's wars, I am reminded that the most poignant of tributes traditionally has been the moment of memorial silence. It is not in the flights of oratory but rather in the inner feelings of each of us that the true memorials exist. But I believe that what we do can also be a memorial. Our veterans fought to protect and advance the American way of life. The least we can do in times of peace is to continue their dedication. So, on this Veterans Day, as we look at our beloved land, I ask you to join with me in trying to see how we can make it even better.

NOVEMBER 12

DeWitt Wallace

This is the birthday of a man who probably did more than any other to do away with longwindedness. DeWitt Wallace, who was born on this day in 1889 in St. Paul, Minnesota, was the founder, with his wife Lila Acheson Wallace, of a new idea in publishing called the *Reader's Digest*. As you know, the *Digest* became one of the most successful magazines in publishing history by excerpting and condensing material from other publications. Usually it improved what was being said by saying it in less words, and bearing that in mind I will try to choose my words wisely—and economically—here today.

Canute

It was on this day in the year 1035 that King Canute died. He was the King of England who, according to legend, showed the limits of his powers by commanding the tide to stand still, knowing that this would not happen. Being no King Canute, I don't have to stage such a spectacular failure to show I am only human. What I am going to say to you today represents my own personal point of view. I hope I can convince you, or at the very least give you something to think about.

Exit Trotsky

Josef Stalin and Leon Trotsky were the two principle heirs to power in communist Russia when Lenin died. On this day in 1927, Stalin took over, purging Trotsky from the Communist Party, ultimately sending the loser out of Russia to exile where he was later assassinated. When there are differences of opinion in the Soviet Union, somebody gets hurt. How comforting, by way of contrast, to know that we live in a country where liberty thrives on differences of opinion. And what a privilege it is for speakers to know that they are not merely permitted but actually expected and invited to say what they think. Thank you for giving me that opportunity here today.

Elizabeth Cady Stanton

Elizabeth Cady Stanton, who was born on this day in 1815 in Johnstown, New York, was one of the greatest feminist leaders of her time, who helped awaken the conscience of America. She was an idealist but a hardheaded one. I cherish particularly a remark she made in an address to the New York state legislature in 1860. "So long as the mass of men spend most of their time on the fence, not knowing which way to jump," she said, "they are surely in no condition to tell us where we had better stand." All too many of us, I regret to say, have chosen to spend most of our time on the fence, while a handful of advocates move us first a bit to one side and then to another. I must confess I stand before you here today as an advocate myself. I hope I can get those of you who are on the fence down off it onto my side; perhaps, however, I may get you onto the other side. But since we live in times of decision, I hope I can move you to participate in the decision-making process.

NOVEMBER 13

Louis Brandeis

Louis D. Brandeis, who was born in Louisville, Kentucky, on this day in 1856, had many distinctions. He was the first person of the Jewish faith to be made a justice of the Supreme Court, where he served for 23 years. He was one of the Court's most eloquent and liberal dissenters, and in many cases he and Justice Oliver Wendell Holmes Jr. were the lonely liberals of the Court. It was Justice Brandeis, in 1928, who summarized so many of the problems of a free society when he wrote, quote, "The greatest dangers to liberty lurk in insidious encroachment by men of zeal, well-meaning but without understanding." Close quote. All too often, with the best of purposes, we embark on ventures, governmental or private, that have the effect of that kind of encroachment. Today I want to talk about some of the proposals of well-meaning people that seem to me to be dangerous.

Drew and Booth

This seems to be a good day for platform appearances. Two of the greatest actors in American history were born on this day—Edwin Booth in 1833, and John Drew in 1853. Their way with words was legendary, and I certainly cannot compete with them. But I offer something neither of these great actors could claim. The words I speak here today, ladies and gentlemen, are my own.

Robert Louis Stevenson

Robert Louis Stevenson, the great author who was born on this day in 1850 in Edinburgh, wrote that, "man is a creature who lives not upon bread alone but principally by watchwords." Watchwords are a great temptation to the speaker. Say you are going to talk about crime, and people perk up their ears. Say you are going to tell what this or that celebrity is like, and you can hear a pin drop. Yes, it is a great temptation to use a watchword or two to hold your attention, but if you don't mind I will assume I don't have to do that kind of thing with the audience. No watchwords; just some basic facts.

Death and Taxes

"In this world," Benjamin Franklin wrote on this day in 1789, "nothing is certain but death and taxes." The trouble is that in 1789 neither Ben Franklin nor anybody else could have pictured the extent, the complications, and the variety of ethical questions involved in the tax picture today. To paraphrase Winston Churchill, never in the history of human endeavor have so many paid so much in so many different ways. My topic today is a simple one to state, but something else again to solve—namely, how can we make better use of our money?

NOVEMBER 14

Robert Fulton

The man who developed the steamboat, Robert Fulton, was born on this day in 1765 in Pennsylvania. Thanks to his brilliance we learned how to harness steam power for transportation on rivers and oceans. It seems only fitting that on Fulton's birthday some lucky person should be given the opportunity to let off steam, and I thank you for giving me that opportunity here today, at a time when there is so much heat being generated in this contentious world of ours.

Insulin

On this day in 1921, Frederic G. Banting and Charles H. Best announced the discovery of insulin, one of the most lifesaving achievements of twentieth-century science. It was one more proof that disease can be controlled. Insulin does not cure diabetes, but it has prolonged millions of lives. The research that made the discovery of insulin possible in 1921 is different in one way from the research that goes on now. Today's efforts are a lot more expensive. While drug companies conduct some impressive studies and development projects of their own, thanks to the profit motive, there is still a full table of disease research that requires more support.

Surtsey

Every now and then Mother Nature reminds us of the miracles at her command. On this day in 1963, a volcanic mass rose up from the sea and created the new island of Surtsey off the coast of Iceland. Even more recently the tip of Mount St. Helens blew off and changed the surrounding landscape in our own Northwest. We have found ways to explore the heavens and mine the riches of the deep sea, but we cannot control the ravages of nature—the earthquakes, the eruptions, and the daily weather. We can explain them, but we can't control them. That seems to be true as well of economic trends; we can explain them, but we can't control them. The question is whether we should even try.

American Education Week

This is the season of American Education Week, when the parents of America are invited to come to school to see how the other half lives. In some ways I think the sponsors of American Education Week have made a tactical error in not concentrating more on getting the nonparents into the classrooms. Parents generally have some idea of what's going on there, since they have been known to talk to their kids, but nonparents are usually very far removed from the educational process—and this is a pity. I find it interesting that while there is a fairly steady furor about freedom of information as regards the operations of government, not enough people keep themselves well informed about the operations of elementary education. The result is that pressure groups, seeking to force their special messages into or out of the curriculum, can often wield an influence out of all proportion. I am not here to offer any sensational revelations about what goes on behind the public school walls. My purpose is rather to suggest that there are some questions we should all be asking the schools to answer.

NOVEMBER 15

NBC

A new idea in communication was born on this day in 1926, when the first radio network—the National Broadcasting Company—went on the air with a broadcast that was heard over 25 stations from New York to Kansas City. This was the first time that a live program was broadcast simultaneously on a permanent national hookup. It made possible a whole new era of information and entertainment, and the American network system produced the largest broadcasting facilities and the greatest variety of program service the world has known. The network idea also helped to make American broadcasting the largest advertising medium in the world. But I am conscious of another consequence today. Thanks to network broadcasting there is hardly a person in the United States who is not familiar, close-up, with all the greatest speakers and public figures of our time. That makes it rather difficult for one with far more modest qualifications, such as I. But I will do the best I can, having at least the advantage of being not only live but in person.

Pitman Shorthand

A new era of business and court efficiency was born on this day in 1837 when Isaac Pitman published a book describing his original method of shorthand. There had been many shorthand systems before then, but Pitman's was the most complete. It made possible not only the taking of dictation at a conversational speed but also the word-for-word transcribing of courtroom dialogue. Pitman shorthand has run into plenty of competition since the days of its founder—not only from other schools of shorthand but from mechanical devices like the stenotype and, of course, sound and video recording devices as well. None of these methods, however, amounts to anything until someone starts talking. I don't know whether any record is being made of what I am about to say, but I thank you for providing an even more important element—an audience.

Social Security

A new era in the development of American govenment began on this day in 1935, when President Franklin D. Roosevelt signed the Social Security Act. It provided for unemployment insurance and old-age insurance. A new type of taxation, very modest at the start but doomed to grow and grow, was born, and a new psychology of entitlement for the average citizen began. That the system can be improved there is no doubt, but that it has been good for the country is also without a doubt. The trouble is that while the Social Security system has been growing, pension funds for government employees have been conducted on an entirely different basis. For example, some government employees have pension formulas making the size of the pension determined by total earnings in the last year of employment, and in that final year they pile up overtime you wouldn't believe. That isn't true of all government pensions by a long shot, but it certainly introduces a disparity that is less than fair to most of us. Perhaps that is the clue to what we need—a national retirement system that treats all workers alike. Meanwhile I have some observations that may contribute to a public dialogue on this important issue.

Pike's Peak

This being the anniversary of Zebulon Pike's discovery of the mountain in Colorado now known as Pike's Peak in 1806, it is worth recalling that Zebulon Pike was an Army lieutenant at that time, and less than seven years later, when he was killed at the Battle of York, Canada, in the War of 1812, he was a brigadier general. They could rise fast in those days; the young person in a hurry is not unique to our day and age. In Zebulon Pike's time, however, the speeches were a lot longer. A two- or three-hour oration was not out of the ordinary. I don't know about you, but I am certainly glad that we have gotten away from that kind of oratory. I will only a take a few moments of your time.

NOVEMBER 16

Salute

This is a day Americans should take note of, but it has been obscured by other anniversaries. On this day in 1776, the Dutch garrison on the island of St. Eustatius in the West Indies fired a salute to the American flag being flown by a U.S. ship. This was the first time a foreign nation had recognized our flag. And St. Eustatius paid dearly for that gesture. In 1781, when the Dutch surrendered the island to the forces of British Admiral George Rodney, it was one of the thriving commercial centers of the Caribbean, but the British deliberately revenged the island's "impudence," as they called it, by deporting most of the people and stripping Statia practically bare. I would like to hope that this kind of vindictiveness is not current, but when I consider such comparatively recent events as the Khomeini takeover in Iran or the disturbances in Latin America I have to admit that human nature doesn't change. And the number of areas of hard feeling does not seem to shrink. Take a little tour of the trouble-spots with me.

George S. Kaufman

George S. Kaufman, who was born on this day in 1889 in Pittsburgh, was one of the great American wits as well as an outstanding playwright and critic. He was once asked about a Broadway show he had just seen, and he replied; "I thought it was frightful, but I saw it under particularly unfortunate circumstances. The curtain was up!" I might say the same about the world today. We are seeing it under unfortunate circumstances, because the curtain is up. The curtain is up because it has been lifted by the pervasiveness of modern news media. We cannot any longer say we didn't know what was going on in this part of the world or that. We have only to read the press and watch the news broadcasts to become aware of oppression in the Soviet Union, inefficiency in Washington, terrorism in the Middle East, and so forth. So I do not come before you today with new revelations on the state of the world. What I do propose to offer is a thought or two about what we can do.

Prison

The first jailer to be hired in America was put on the payroll of Nantucket, Massachusetts, on this day in 1676 to take charge of their new jail. For this service he was to receive, apparently for a year's work, four pounds stirling worth of wheat and other grain. The pay of prison guards has improved somewhat since then, but there seems to be ample room to wonder whether the prison system itself had made equal progress. In all fairness one cannot blame the rise of crime on the quality of our jails; there are many factors. But what I find most challenging is that we spend so much more on incarcerating criminals than we do on redressing the damage they do to their victims. I believe we should concentrate more of our attention on those victims, and I have some thoughts in that regard.

Price Trend

On this day in 1961, the Metropolitan Museum of Art in New York bought a painting by Rembrandt, *Aristotle Contemplating the Bust of Homer*, for $2.3 million, which was then a record price for a piece of art. That price by now has been exceeded many times, and who is to say that a ceiling has yet been reached? Now, part of the increase is undoubtedly a reflection of inflation; part is also because of the increase in the number of individuals and institutions interested in collecting great art—in other words, competition. Competition, you see, does not always cause prices to go down; sometimes it does the reverse, when those competing are a growing number of would-be buyers for a limited number of items. We see that kind of competition in the case of taxes. There are a limited number of potential and actual taxpayers and an infinite variety of ways of extracting tax money from them. What can we do about it?

NOVEMBER 17

Queen Elizabeth I

It was on this day in 1558 that a 25-year-old woman ascended to the throne of England. Her name was Elizabeth, and the 45 years of her reign, known as the Elizabethan age, became a golden time for England—the time of

Shakespeare and Marlowe, the beginning of the age of exploration, one of those times when a whole nation rises to a challenge. There are those who say that those times are gone, that there are no more worlds to conquer, no fabulous new opportunities waiting to be uncovered. I disagree. I believe the future that awaits us can be greater than the past. I cannot give you a blueprint, but I can talk about some things that can be seen on the horizon.

Congress

When Congress met in Washington on this day in 1800, it was the first session to be convened in our capital city. Up to then Congress had met in temporary quarters in New York and Pennsylvania. When Washington, D.C., was designated to be our capital, one reason for the choice was that it had a central location betwen the northern and southern states. As the nation grew Washington became less and less central. Although air travel has made getting to the District of Columbia a lot easier than it was in the era of the stagecoach, there are those who find it hard to stay in touch with the mood of the nation in a city whose only industry is government. But the sights of Washington remain the nation's most cherished symbols—the Lincoln Memorial, the Washington Momument, the Iwo Jima statuary at Arlington. It is in Washington that we are reminded that we are not just 50 states; we are a nation. We have a way of life that is, or should be, a model for the world. And we have a Capitol occupied by our representatives, the people we choose to send there. We have a Washington press corps that reports their work to us. And given all that, I have to ask a question. Have you been watching? Do you know how Congress is doing, or what it has been doing? Let me fill you in.

College Entrance Board

Back in 1900 around this time, a group of educators founded the College Entrance Examination Board to administer a series of tests to determine the qualifications of applicants for college admission. Since then the Scholastic Aptitude Tests have confronted generations of high school students and, presumably, assisted generations of college admissions officers in making their selections. But while the SATs provide some kind of common yardstick, doing well in them does not guarantee admission to the college of one's choice. The factors that go into the selection of a college class include geography, who the other selectees are, extracurricular activities, the nature of the applicant's interests, and many other considerations best known to the admissions office. When you get down to it, colleges are among the few places where the democratic process of admission for merit alone does not work and where there is no impartial board of review. I don't know how we can make the process better, but I have a feeling we can.

Suez and Time

The world has changed. When the Suez Canal was opened for traffic on this day in 1869, the first boat to go through the Canal was a yacht whose passengers included the Khedive of Egypt, Empress Eugenie of France, and Emperor Franz Josef of Austria Hungary. None of those monarchies remain today. Rudyard Kipling in "Recessional" wrote that "The Captains and the Kings depart." They do, indeed, and all too often a regime that seemed secure and firm comes down with them. No government's permanent destiny can remain always in the hands of the same man or woman; no deal made with a dictator has an assurance of long life. That is something for us to remember as here today we take a look at the world.

NOVEMBER 18

William S. Gilbert

William S. Gilbert, the lyricist member of the team of Gilbert and Sullivan, was born on this day in 1836 in London. Gilbert wrote some of the greatest light opera lyrics of all time, and in many of them he found a terse and memorable way to speak his mind. One such is a couplet from *H.M.S. Pinafore,* which noted that "Things are seldom what they seem,/Skim milk masquerades as cream." Gilbert wrote that a long time ago, well before the age of synthetics. How much truer it is today! We have learned through sad experience that you've got to read the labels, and what you've got to read is often in very small print. Unfortunately that happens every now and then with other things such as new laws. The folks forget to read the small print, and we find ourselves saddled with consequences nobody anticipated. Today I want to talk about what we might call the fine print in some developing situations.

Gallup

George H. Gallup, the man who popularized public opinion polls, was born on this day in 1901 in Iowa. I don't know how soon after that he started asking questions, but he certainly spawned a ubiquitous business. The pollsters claim they can determine public opinion within four or five percentage points, and the results of their surveys are treated by many businesses and politicians as holy writ; but, particularly in polls on political preferences, there is usually an escape hatch in the category of the undecided. I personally am very fond of the undecided, because they still have open minds, and there's nothing a speaker finds as challenging as the opportunity to reach some open minds.

Standard Time

Until this day in 1883, every community in the United States had time of its own. That is, there was no standard time nor any clearly defined time zones. But on this date the United States divided its land into four time zones that still apply—Eastern, Central, Mountain, and Pacific Time—and our clocks were synchronized. Europe got around to the idea a bit later. Nobody at that time anticipated that television and air transportation would depend so much on time standards, but modern life has made most of us, for one reason or another, a nation of clock-watchers. I am conscious of that fact as I speak to you here today, so I can assure you that my remarks, even if they are not timeless, will be time-conscious.

Clarence Day

Today is the birthday of Clarence Day, the man who made a fortune by looking back to *Life with Father.* He was born in 1874 in New York City, and his play and essays about growing up in that world became wonderful entertainment for millions of people. Somehow, looking back is a lot more relaxing than looking at our world of today, but since we can't live in the past we might as well keep up with what is going on now, and that is what I am going to talk about.

NOVEMBER 19

Gettysburg Address

This was the day when the most famous orator of his time was scheduled to make the major address at the dedication of the battlefield at Gettysburg in 1863. His name was Edward Everett. He spoke for two hours, and his speech was considered to be one of the greatest he ever delivered. But, unfortunately for Everett, the much shorter speech delivered by President Abraham Lincoln was even better. It was, of course, the immortal Gettysburg Address. I can promise you I will not speak here as long as Everett or as eloquently as Lincoln, but I will follow Abe's example in one important step. I will try to be brief.

James A. Garfield

Today is the birthday of one of our martyred presidents, James A. Garfield, who was born in Ohio in 1831. Garfield was assassinated during his first year in the presidency, and the ironic aspect of the affair was that he had gone to the Republican nominating convention as the leader of the campaign to win the nomination for John Sherman. Garfield was himself nominated on the 36th ballot when none of the avowed candidates could win enough votes. And so the dark horse found himself in the office that marked him for death. Every time I listen to the pundits talking about the weighty trends of life in the world, I think of how often twists of fate such as what happened to James A. Garfield, which certainly was unpredictable, affect the course of history. And realizing the uncertainties of life, I tell myself to avoid predicting. So today I will concern myself with what's happening now and not speculating on the future.

Equal Opportunity Day

It has been some time since the first observance of Equal Opportunity Day on this day, the anniversary of Abraham Lincoln's Gettysburg Address. Equal Opportunity Day was intended to remind us all of every American's right to the same chance, regardless of race, sex, creed, or national origin. There is much the law can do and has done to promote this equality, but there are certain conditions that neither the letter of the law nor the abolition of intolerance can guarantee. A child does not have an equal opportunity when he or she is abused or grows up in an illiterate home or is otherwise culturally deprived in the earliest years. So, while it is fine to congratulate ourselves that we have legislated and educated against discrimination, and it is fine to hope that we are making progress, we cannot rest on our dubious laurels. We are still challenged by the fact that some of our children, through no fault of their own, start off behind the eight ball. And we must ask ourselves what we can do about it.

Second Moon Excursion

Today is the anniversary of a great event that is rarely recalled. It was on this day that Charles "Pete" Conrad Jr. and Alan L. Bean landed on the moon for a 32-hour stay and two moon walks. Theirs was the second team of U.S. astronauts to accomplish this feat when they did it in 1969, but how many of us thought of it lately? We are so jaded that we take our miracles for granted, and yesterday's heroes soon are displaced by newer ones. There is, I think, a certain shallowness in public attitudes, which, unfortunately, is all too easily exploited by the promoters of the shoddy and the cheaply sensational. Even for the public speaker it is easier to attract attention with wild charges and extreme statements than with moderation and fairmindedness. But I don't think this audience wants that kind of irresponsibility, and I know I don't.

NOVEMBER 20

Sadat's Journey

As the crow flies, the distance between Cairo and Jerusalem, measured in miles, is not too great, but when Anwar el Sadat, the president of Egypt, came to Jerusalem to address the Israeli parliament on this day in 1977, it was one of the epic journeys in the history of the world, coming as it did at a time when the Jewish state and the Arab world were locked in a hostility that had seen one war after another over a period of more than 30 years. President Sadat's act was one of supreme bravery as well as statesmanship. In his speech he spoke of the wall that dominated the Middle East. "This wall," he said, "constitutes a psychological barrier between us, a barrier of suspicion, a barrier of rejection, a barrier of fear, or deception, a barrier of hallucination without any action, deed or decision." With his one speech Sadat for a time broke down that wall. In a far less significant way that is what every speaker hopes to do—help to break down a wall, whether it is of suspicion, or misunderstanding, or complacency. This audience, I am happy to note, poses very few problems on that score, but I hope that what I have to say will at least give you some food for thought.

JFK Wins

Back on this day in 1962, President John F. Kennedy ended the U.S. naval blockade of Cuba when Premier Nikita Khrushchev of the Soviet Union agreed to remove Russian missiles and bombers from Cuba. The world had held its breath as the confrontation developed, but Kennedy's firmness proved to be effective. This had led some people to believe that all it takes to stop the Soviets is sufficient American firmness, but blockading Cuba is one thing and showing similar strength in a far off corner of the world is something else again. Every new situation in the world is precisely that—a new situation; so, rather than simply trying to use the past as a guiding precedent, it seems to me we need more up-to-date information. I have some of that to give you here today.

Brevity

Edward Everett, who had been the principal speaker at Gettysburg the day before in 1863, wrote a letter to Abraham Lincoln on this day. "I should be glad if I could flatter myself," he wrote, "that I came as near to the central idea of the occasion in two hours, as you did in two minutes." Bearing that in mind, ladies and gentlemen, I have made up my mind to be closer to two minutes than to two hours in my remarks here today, so I will not take any more time in introductory comments.

Streptomycin

This is the anniversary of the first use of streptomycin to treat tuberculosis in a human being. That was at Cannon Falls, Minnesota, in 1944. The new miracle drug helped save the patient's life. Since then the science of chemotherapy has moved steadily ahead, but we have learned to be more careful, thanks to the tragedies that followed the use of thalidomide and other supposed miracle drugs. What is true of miracle cures in medicine is also true of the proposed economic cures and remedies for societal ills. You cannot always foretell the side effects. That is why I am on the side of those who believe that wherever possible we should go for the middle ground instead of putting all our faith in something new and untried. So today I come before you offering no panaceas. I hope I can bring you a grain of wisdom and persuade you to take the miracle peddlers with a grain of salt.

NOVEMBER 21

Bible Week

Around Thanksgiving the nation observes National Bible Week, a time when it is most appropriate to recall the injunction in the Book of Zechariah. "Speak ye every man the truth to his neighbor." So today that is my simple objective—no wild hyperbole, no stem-winding oratory, just some simple truths.

Voltaire

Francois Marie Arouet, better known as Voltaire, who was born on this day in 1694, once observed that "men use thought only to justify their wrong-doings, and speech only to conceal their thoughts." I hope my remarks here today don't have that effect, because I have a few thoughts I want very much to convey to you.

The Practical One

When Thomas A. Edison announced on this day in 1877 that he had invented a machine to record the human voice and other sounds, he was not introducing something absolutely brand new. Other pioneers before him had been able to record sound on experimental machines. Edison's genius was that he figured out a way to design a device that could be marketed. Having a good idea is very important, of course, but knowing what to do with it is the key. I will not pretend to you that the various ideas on which I will touch today are either brand new or strictly of my own authorship, but I hope I can contribute something meaningful about how these ideas can be used to help make a better tomorrow.

Embassy Stormed

On this day in 1979, a mob in Islamabad, the capital of Pakistan, stormed and set fire to the American embassy. After five hours of being trapped inside, the people in the embassy were rescued by Pakistani troops. I recall the unpleasant incident because it illustrates an unfortunate fact we must face. The Pakistani attack was triggered by false reports that Americans had been responsible for the takeover of the Grand Mosque in Mecca by dissident Muslims. The report, of course, was totally untrue, but that didn't matter. All over the world there are people willing—even anxious—to believe the worst about America, and all over the world there are demagogues willing to exploit that phobia. Even in the nations that are our traditional allies, anti-American demonstrations are easily aroused. We can react in two ways. One is to ask ourselves why this is so and what we can do to change it. The other is to regard it as a fact of life and conduct ourselves accordingly. My remarks here today stem from this second position.

NOVEMBER 22

Charles De Gaulle

Charles De Gaulle, the great French leader who was born on this day in 1890 in Lille, France was not know for modesty. He said, "Nothing great will ever be achieved without great men, and men are great only if they are determined to be so." De Gaulle himself had that determination and the capability; the trouble is that life is full of people determined to be great without the capacity to be great. They are people who spend millions in futile pursuit of elective office, statesmen who defy the will of the people once they achieve power, because the people, they believe, need to be led. They are, in every age, the reckless robber barons who seek and use power for their own selfish ends. The times, I believe, produce great men and women; great men and women do not produce the times. We are in an era today that demands this kind of leadership. Are we getting it?

JFK's Last Speech

He was a young man with awesome responsibilities. He was on his way to deliver a speech in which he was going to say, "We in this country, in this generation, are—by destiny rather than choice—the watchmen on the walls of world freedom." He never delivered the speech, because he was John F. Kennedy and the day was November 22, 1963. He was assassinated on his way, in Dallas. On the anniversary of that sad occasion, I ask you to bear those words in mind—"the watchmen on the walls of world freedom." I can't think of a more appropriate phrase, for unless we maintain a watch to protect freedom it will be destroyed. So one of the roles a speaker plays is to be that watchman, to report what threatens our free world and what opportunities may be found to improve that world. That is my agenda for the day.

A La Washington

In a letter he wrote on this day in 1798, George Washington commented that "to give opinions unsupported by reasons might appear dogmatical." Ladies and gentlemen, I have no wish to appear dogmatical, so with your kind indulgence I will not only give you my opinion but also my reasons.

S.O.S.

On this day in 1906 an international meeting adopted S.O.S. as the universal distress signal to be wirelessed by ships in distress. Those three letters, S.O.S., became understandable all over the world. I cannot help wondering why, if we can communicate so effectively a simple distress signal, we fail so miserably at communicating better with one another generally. We all have misconceptions about the rest of the world, and the rest of the world has misconceptions about us. If in my remarks here today I can cut through any of these misconceptions, I will consider myself amply rewarded.

NOVEMBER 23

Sheppard–Towner Act

Today is the anniversary of a precedent-setting law that nobody seems to remember. The Sheppard–Towner Act, dated November 23, 1921, appropriated federal money to be paid to the states to promote maternal and infant hygiene and welfare. Out of this modest beginning, with an appropriation of $480,000 the first year and $240,000 for each of the subsequent four years, came the gigantic federal benefit programs of more recent times. We don't always know the consequences of the bright ideas we enact, but we have certainly established one tendency on the part of government: it grows. It will, even if we watch it carefully. But it will grow a lot more if we don't watch. So let's take a look at just a few areas.

Minute Men

It was about this time in the year 1774 that the Minute Men were organized by the provincial congress of Massachusetts. They were to be ready to take up arms at a minute's notice in the event of conflict with the British. This was one group of reserves that lived up to its name; when the American Revolution broke out at Lexington and Concord, the Minute Men were there. We had no cumbersome military machinery then; the men kept their guns at home, and those first battles were fought very close to their homes. The techniques of war have matured greatly since those days, and the weapons have grown steadily more horrible and more complicated. But the essential question is still the same; how determined is either side not to back down? Wars come, I believe, when one side misjudges the other's willingness to defend itself and/or when one side is confident it can defeat the other. So we must be able to judge the strength and determination of a potential opponent in proportion to our own. It is this very area of intelligence that traps one nation after another. Do we really know our own capabilities, let alone those of other nations? Do we have reliable weapons? I want to offer some frank answers to these questions.

Caruso

This is the anniversary of the American debut of a golden voice. The great Enrico Caruso made his American debut at the Metropolitan Opera House in New York on this day in 1903, singing *Rigoletto*. No voice since then has made this quite as special a day, and my script is no *Rigoletto*, but I hope you will find that my remarks strike an interesting note of their own.

Plight of the Cities

Among the notes describing what happened on this day in the past there is an entry reporting that in 1969 the National Commission on the Causes and Prevention of Violence ventured the view that our cities were becoming places of terror. That was in 1969, and things have not been getting much better. But I think it only fair to point out that the same growth of law breaking has occurred in places of smaller population. In the cities, however, there are more people and hence more crime. Additionally, particularly in our largest cities, the pressures of people living and working close together sometimes provide an added strain. But it seems to me that there is another factor—the breakdown of city services that once were adequate and now are so bad they trigger arguments and worse. What can we do to make city life better?

NOVEMBER 24

Zachary Taylor

Zachary Taylor, the Mexican War hero who became our twelfth president, was born on this day in 1784 in Orange County, Viriginia. He died while in office and was succeeded by one of our more obscure chief executives, Millard Fillmore. Taylor gained the presidency in a era when our presidents were not outstanding. We had a run of such—Taylor, Fillmore, Pierce, and Buchanan, for example. All of us, not just the candidates, know a great deal more than we did in Zachary Taylor's day about many of the subjects that reach the desk in the Oval Office. Additionally, the power of the presidency has vastly increased, and that no doubt has made the job more attractive to people of outstanding capabilities. But where are they right now? Who are the most likely presidential prospects and what are their chances?

Learning from History

In the memorial eulogy of John F. Kennedy, delivered on this day in 1963, Chief Justice Earl Warren commented, "It has been said that the only thing we learn from history is that we do not learn." Close quote. In some respects that is undeniably true. We haven't learned from history that he who lies down with dogs wakes up with fleas. We maintain friendships with foreign regimes not worthy of our friendship. We haven't learned how to get more people to vote. But I think there is much that we have learned, and I'd like to talk about some of the lessons of the recent past.

Scott Joplin

This is the birthday of Scott Joplin, the great ragtime composer whose work gained its greatest popularity long after he died. He was born on this day in 1868 in Texarkana, Texas, and he died in 1917. It isn't only musicians and other creative talents who sometimes seem to live before their time; in every field we have people who, because they lead public taste rather than follow it, have to wait for popularity to catch up with their memory. William Graham Sumner created his metaphor of the forgotten man in the nineteenth century, but it remained for Franklin D. Roosevelt to bring the forgotten man to the attention of the voting public. The conservation movement in this country began very close to the beginning of the twentieth century, but not until the second half of the century did it really begin to make a dent. Today I'd like to talk about some other old ideas that have gained new urgency (e.g., public works programs, protective tariffs, town meetings).

Toulouse-Lautrec

Henri de Toulouse-Lautrec, the crippled artist who was born on this day in 1864 in Albi, France, painted his pictures in a unique, effectively distinctive style—a style that in some ways epitomized the kind of city Paris was in his day. What made Toulouse-Lautrec so great was that his work had a look all its own. Outstanding people in every field often make their mark by a technique or a choice of subject—or both—distinctively their own. Today I'd like to talk about what I find distinctive in some of our public figures.

NOVEMBER 25

Pope John XXIII

This is the birthday of Pope John XXIII, who was chosen presumably as a caretaker pontiff because he was in his 77th year when he was elected in 1958. He was born in 1881 on this day in Sotto Il Monte, Italy. He proved to be one of the most dynamic popes of modern times, expanding the College of Cardinals to almost double its previous membership, extending the hand of interfaith friendship and understanding, and convening the second Vatican Council, known to some as the Ecumenical Council. He reigned for five years, and few men have been as universally mourned when they died. What made him great was that when the opportunity came he was superbly ready for it. He must have thought when he reached 70 that no further challenges would come to him, but no one of us can know at what point in our life the greatest challenge may come. The same is true of us collectively as a nation. Whatever challenges we have faced and conquered, the chances are that greater opportunities lie ahead. I will not take your time for a long litany of those opportunities, but there are a couple that I do want to talk about.

Unique Event in Russia

The only free election in Russian history came on this day in 1917. The parliament that was elected had a noncommunist majority, so the Bolsheviks never permitted the legislature to operate. No matter how often and how loudly communism proclaims itself the voice of the people, it remains a government dedicated to suppressing the voice of the people. Thank goodness we live in a country where not only the voice of the people but also the voice of any individual can be raised and different points of view can be spoken. I come to this platform with no obligation to follow any party line. I can say, as I could not in altogether too many parts of the world, this is where I stand.

Carnegie

Andrew Carnegie, who was born on this day in 1835 in Scotland, had two great talents which don't always go together. He was superb at making money, and he was superb at giving it away. It is estimated that he gave away about $350 million, and when he died in 1919 that was an almost incredible amount of money. In his essay entitled "Wealth," which was published when he was 44 years old, Carnegie wrote, "Surplus wealth is a sacred trust which its possessor is bound to administer in his lifetime for the good of the community." He also wrote, "The man who dies rich . . . dies disgraced." Now, not all of us are endowed with enough worldly goods to come close to Carnegie's benefactions, but all of us have the opportunity to give of ourselves. There is certainly no lack of worthy causes, but there is one in particular that I want to call to your attention today.

The *Hussar*

Men and women go to the farthest corners of the world in search of hidden treasure, but one of the most enduring hidden treasures in the world was sunk right in New York Harbor more than two centuries ago and defied every attempt at discovery. The British war vessel *Hussar* sank in 1780 with a fortune in gold and remained undiscovered as the ships of the world passed through the waters that held it. To me the story of the treasure of the *Hussar* makes a simple point. We don't have to go to far places to find wealth; it is so often right at hand if only we knew how to get it. The resources of this nation are still uniquely rich; we have not yet figured out the best ways to use them. I have some suggestions.

NOVEMBER 26

Warsaw Ghetto

On this day in 1940 the clock turned back hundreds of years. The Nazi forces of Adolf Hitler forced half a million Polish Jews to live in a walled-in ghetto in occupied Warsaw. It was just another step in Hitler's demonic effort to wipe out the Jews of the world, and it led ultimately to an epic example of battle gallantry by a doomed people in an uprising against impossible odds. We have a tendency to think of heroism as something more in style in olden days than in our own century, but no time and no nation has a monopoly on heroes. Today I want to talk about some unsung heroes—peacetime people whose bravery and courage are manifested not merely in their survival but also in their continuing struggle.

Thanksgiving

The season of Thanksgiving is customarily the time for counting our blessings and expressing our gratitude to the source of those blessings. I think it is a good exercise for us to do this, for when we count our blessings we become more aware of how fortunate we are in our time and our place. Today I am going to be the vehicle by which still another blessing will come your way. It is the blessing of brevity, so let me get right to it.

John Harvard

Somewhere about this time in 1607, a young man was born in London who decided when he was 30 to settle in the Massachusetts Bay colony. A year later he died. He left a fairly sizable estate for his time, as well as a good collection of books, and he left all the books and half his money to a new college that had just begun near Boston. In honor of its benefactor the college adopted his name and called itself Harvard, a memorial to John Harvard. I doubt that John Harvard ever could have envisioned the glory that would one day come to the institution bearing his name, and certainly not every philanthropy blossoms so greatly, but the story of John Harvard is an example that good deeds are indeed remembered. Today I come before you to seek your good deeds in a worthy cause, and while I cannot promise you lasting fame to match John Harvard's, I think I can promise you the rewarding satisfaction of knowing you have given good to the world.

Surprise from China

This was the day in 1950 that Red China suddenly entered the Korean War, signaling the emergence of a new major power in that part of the world. The course of world affairs since then has seen a considerable rise in the influence of the so-called Third World. Nations rise and nations decline, and in recent years there have been some pessimists among us who predict not only the decline of the West but more particularly the decline of the United States. These doomsayers think we have passed our peak; they regard our problems as largely insoluble, our moral fiber as in decline, and our ingenuity as being eclipsed by newer powers. I take a directly opposite view. I believe our best years are ahead of us. I believe we are at a turning of the road, and I think I know the right way to turn. Let me tell you how I see it.

NOVEMBER 27

Scuttled

In its last great act of defiance of the Nazi juggernaut on this day in 1940, the French fleet at Toulon scuttled ten cruisers, almost 30 destroyers, and 14 submarines to prevent their falling into the hands of the Nazis. Sometimes this kind of act of heroic desperation is all that can be done, and what the French did might well have affected the course of the war. We often think that if what we do does not bring a quick success it has been done in vain, but this is simply not true. When we adopt policies, for example, that fail to take as many people off the welfare rolls as we would hope, that doesn't mean the policies are failures. We have at least helped some people, and one way or another we can learn from and build upon what we have already done. No effort is wasted if it helps us to do better thereafter. We learn not only from our successes but from our failures as well. And lately we have learned a lot.

Pennsylvania Station

When the Pennsylvania Station opened in New York City on this day in 1910, it was described as the largest railway terminal in the world. Thirty-five years later it had already become an anachronism as rail passenger traffic felt the effects of airplane and bus competition. The building of that terminal was a good example of the way we build for the future in terms of the past. We build city roads on the basis of projections of current traffic patterns, and the facilities become overburdened often within a few brief years. There are businesses that have depended on forced obsolescence for keeping up sales, by changing models simply to make the older ones out of date; but in our urban planning we seem to go the other way by ignoring obsolescence. That may be why we never seem to have enough prisons, enough roads, enough courts. We are so busy trying to catch up with existing and past inadequacies that we have neither the resources nor the foresight to envision the demands that will exist twenty or thirty years from now. At times, when we don't seem to have enough tax dollars to pay the current freight, there isn't much chance that we will find sufficient money to anticipate the greater needs that are waiting around the corner.

But I suggest that it costs less to make a six-lane road now than it will ten years from now, and the same is true of building better prisons or more courtrooms. We just do not think big enough—and I have some expansions to suggest.

Statistics

On this day in 1839 in Boston, the American Statistical Association was organized to provide statistical information in all areas of human knowledge. That was a few years before Mark Twain's famous remark that "there are three kinds of lies—lies, damned lies, and statistics." But the fact is that if you have nothing else to say you can always find some statistics to spout. I am happy to tell you that I do have something else to say, so any statistics that arise in the following remarks are purely coincidental.

Carter on Family

President Jimmy Carter addressed a Mormon Church group on this day in 1978 and chose as his theme the importance of the family. He used a phrase I think it worth remembering. "A family," he said, "is a mutual improvement society." I'd say that by the same token a bad family climate is a mutual destruction society. We discovered long ago that one of the vitamins for children is love; they thrive on affection. Yet today we have more broken homes, more abused children, and more fatherless children than ever before. I have no easy solution to offer to the problem, but I do think the first step is to recognize the situation. We are not acting responsibly toward the next generation when we condone the irresponsibility of bearing children deliberately out of wedlock, denying those children the proper family environment. We are not acting responsibly when we fail to provide decent playgrounds or schools or libraries. But the physical facilities, it seems to me, are far less important than the proper family environment. How do we achieve that?

NOVEMBER 28

William Blake

William Blake, the great English poet and artist who was born on this day in 1757 in London, once wrote that "to generalize is to be an idiot. To particularize is the alone distinction of merit." Since I would not want the disciples of Blake to consider me an idiot I shall refrain from generalizing in my remarks here today and get right down to particulars.

Alone

In a letter he wrote on this day back in 1842, the eloquent Daniel Webster said, "No two-legged thing can eat much, if he eat alone." What is true of people is also true of nations. No nation that, so to speak, eats alone can really eat as much as it needs. We live in the same world as many other peoples, and, like it or not, we cannot isolate ourselves. We must have friends beyond our borders. And to have friends we have to *be* friends. How are we doing in that department?

Choosing Among Evils

In a letter he wrote on this day in 1814, Thomas Jefferson observed that "it is the melancholy law of human societies to be compelled sometimes to choose a great evil in order to ward off a greater. . . ." That, unfortunately, is the excuse offered for every unpalatable action by government—we had to do it to avoid something worse. But it seems to me that the excuse is wearing thin, and today I want to talk about a few evils that I do not believe government needs to practice anymore.

National Indigestion Season

The period from Thanksgiving to Christmas has been dubbed by some as National Indigestion Season. The title traces, of course, to the temptations of the festive board in the span of these holidays. Too often we bite off more than we can chew and chew more than we can digest. I shall try to avoid both mistakes, in a manner of speaking, in my remarks to you here today. I shall not bite off more wisdom than I can chew, and I will not weigh you down with excess verbal baggage. Indeed, I plan to offer you a gift today—the gift of brevity.

NOVEMBER 29

Warren Commission

One of the odd aspects of American public life is that when the government wants to push a problem under the carpet it appoints a special commission to study that problem. And when the government wants to spotlight a problem and stimulate action it also appoints a commission. On this day in 1963, in the aftermath of the assassination of President John F. Kennedy, his successor Lyndon B. Johnson appointed a commission headed by Chief Justice Earl Warren to investigate the murder. The commission, strangely enough, seemed to fulfill both traditional functions. The fact that it was investigating calmed the nerves of a distraught nation, and after its report was presented a virtually continuous round of speculation was touched off about hidden aspects of the assassination. Now, if the report of a distinguished panel headed by the Chief Justice of the United States still does not silence the doubters, I must face the fact that there will be some who will inevitably disagree with the way I see the things I am going to talk about here today. So let me say in advance that the facts I am about to present are just that—facts—and the conclusions are yours to share or dispute.

Army–Navy

One of the most consistent rivalries in our nation is the Army–Navy football game. The first such encounter between the two senior service academies came on this day in 1890. Navy won, 24 to 0, and they have been at it ever since. The quality of football is not in a class with that of colleges with less rigorous scholastic standards, but the satisfaction to both spectators and players is just as great. The reason, I suspect, is simply that, however partisan we may be, we are proud of both teams as representative of the cream of our young men. Perhaps because of the discipline at the academies we have confidence in their attitudes as well as in their education. But I suspect there is something else involved. We know that at the service academies there are clear and specific codes of conduct, of honor, of dress. Now, obviously we can't impose military rules on the civilian college population or any other civilian group, but I think we can learn from these rules. We have tolerated degrees of cheating and misconduct at our colleges and that business—like having someone else write your term paper—carries over, I believe, into later life. You are more likely to be penalized for a foul on the football field than in life. And, on the premise that that situation is just wrong, I have some suggestions.

Savings Bank Anniversary

The first savings bank to open its doors in the United States was the Bank for Savings in New York City, which began on this day in 1816. After six months they reported losses of $27 from counterfeit money and short-change losses of almost $24. Since that time, the art of counterfeiting has flourished—not merely counterfeiting of folding money, but counterfeit recordings, fake masterpieces, pirated videotapes, "knock-offs" of expensive watches, and so forth. I am more troubled, however, by what, for want of a better term, I call counterfeit compassion. Counterfeit compassion is not confined to politicians running for office, though they are very accomplished practitioners. It is also practiced by businesses that in the guise of making a product available to more people, reduce its quality and claim credit for public service. But my favorite target in the counterfeit compassion field are those folks who profess sympathetic acceptance of the idea that some disadvantaged children are uneducable and use that sympathetic acceptance to excuse their own failure to teach. Today, instead of that kind of false sympathy, I want to talk about the hard facts.

Chimp's World

This was the day back in 1961 that Enos the chimpanzee made American space history by orbiting the Earth twice to move us farther into the vast unknown. If Enos had occasion to look down at Earth in the course of his adventure, I wonder whether it occurred to him that he wasn't spinning around the world; he may have thought the world was spinning around him. It's all in your point of view. It's all in your perspective. And that's what I'd like to offer for your consideration here today—my perspective, my point of view.

NOVEMBER 30

Jonathan Swift

Jonathan Swift, the great English satirist who was born on this day in 1667 in Dublin, Ireland, observed that it was characteristic of the human species that "we ate when we were not hungry, and drank without the provocation of thirst." It has also been observed that man is the only beast who kills wantonly rather than for food or simply self-defense—not all of us, by any means, but enough so that we need strong law enforcement, security guards for our public figures, and whatever other protections we can devise. It is difficult at times to apply logic to the course of human behavior. At the present time it is particularly difficult to apply logic to some of the policies of our government. So I will not attempt to explain those policies; I will merely point them out to you here today.

Israel

On this day in 1947, the United Nations voted to end the British mandate over Palestine and divide the territory into Jewish and Arab states. This was the decision that led to the formation of Israel the following year. The Arabs refused to accept the partition and resolved to prevent it by force. But the state of Israel was established anyway, and the Arabs, in losing the ensuing war, lost more territory. One cannot help wondering how the history of the world would have been changed if the United Nations decision on this day in 1947 had been peacefully accepted by all concerned. Certainly, a great deal less blood would have been spilled if all of the parties involved—Britain, the Zionists, and the Arabs—could have managed to make a peaceful transition. I suppose that is why, despite all its petty chicanery and international ganging up, the United Nations still has enough potential to try to make it work. But what can we do to make it work better?

Peace Treaty

The preliminary draft of a peace treaty between Great Britain and the United States formally ending the American Revolutionary War was signed in Paris on this day in 1782, more than a year after the surrender of Lord Cornwallis at Yorktown. It is a sad fact that war can break out in a flash but peace needs a lot of work. Anything worth having is worth working hard to get and to keep. That is as true of peace at home as it is of peace in the world around us; if we tear each other apart because of our differences we all suffer. The greatness of America is that we have always found a middle way, avoiding extremes. That is what we must do now.

Winston Churchill

Today is the birthday of perhaps the greatest master of the spoken word of modern times, Winston Churchill, who was born in 1874 in Oxfordshire, England. It was said of the great British Prime Minister that he mobilized the English language and sent it off to war. I cannot dare to hope to use the spoken word even a fraction as well, but I can use some of Churchill's words. As he said in another context, "This is not the end. It is not even the beginning of the end. But it is, perhaps, the end of the beginning." That, ladies and gentlemen, is the end of the beginning of my speech. Now to the main course.

DECEMBER 1

Civil Rights Start

Today is the anniversary of the beginning of the modern civil rights movement in the American South, when, in 1955, Mrs. Rosa Parks refused to obey the bus segregation laws in Birmingham, Alabama. She was arrested, and a black boycott of the buses followed. This was the catalyst for great civil rights demonstrations that ultimately helped to pass the Civil Rights Act of 1964. Most great reforms begin with a single action, a single voice, and then a gathering tide of related efforts. I am under no illusion that my remarks here are breaking new ground and sounding new alarms, but I am happy to have the occasion to raise my voice on behalf of some issues that deserve to be called to your attention.

Antarctica

On this day in 1959, twelve nations including the United States and the USSR signed a treaty agreeing to treat the Antarctic as an area for peaceful science. The U.S. Senate ratified the treaty in April of 1961. It is comforting to realize, as we approach the season of peace on earth and good will to men, that there is at least one continent unencumbered by weapons of war. But what are the prospects for lasting peace in more populated territories?

Mutiny

The only mutiny in the history of the U.S. Navy, and a questionable one at that, climaxed on this day in 1842. The son of the secretary of war was a midshipman aboard the *U.S.S. Somers,* and he was said to have persuaded some 20 crew members to be very grudging in their obedience to orders at sea, climaxing with one sailor—in the words of the record—"raising a handspike in a threatening manner against an officer." On this day in 1842, the midshipman and two others, after trial on the captain's orders by a court of inquiry, were hanged aboard ship. The captain was later tried on a murder charge for the incident but was acquitted. It was an ugly chapter in American naval history. But it left few lasting scars. In America we put the past behind us and do not let it cloud the present. The question we keep asking ourselves is whether what we are doing in the present is clouding the future. Today I plan to talk about some of the clouds I see forming.

Christmas Club

It was a brand new idea in banking when, on this day in 1909 in Carlisle, Pennsylvania, the Carlisle Trust Company became the first banking institution to have a Christmas Club for regular savings. Since then, the idea of special-purpose savings plans has become one of America's favorite ways of accumulating funds. It would be wonderful if our governments also had Christmas Clubs into which they could dip at the end of the year without increasing the budget deficit, but it has been a long time indeed since government was able to live consistently within its means, let alone lay away any tidy sums for a rainy day. Why can't the government do what so many of us do? That is a question worth exploring.

DECEMBER 2

EPA

On this day in 1970, a new type of government activity began with the start of operations of the Environmental Protection Agency. For the first time we had an official organization concerned with monitoring and protecting the quality of our air, water, and ground. Since then the EPA has had varying levels of activity and zeal as administrations have changed—and a full-fledged scandal that precipated a 1983 housecleaning. At all times it has been a reminder that, left to our own devices, we have a tendency to foul the nest. One of the byproducts of the industrialization of society had been an increase in unexpected pollution. We have learned that our air is fragile and our water far too easily polluted. The battle for clean air and safe water is a never-ending one, because if our vigilance is relaxed our ecology suffers. There is no question that fanatics have made the problem worse by demanding unreasonable standards of purity and enforcement. But there is equally no doubt that without stringent laws conscientiously enforced the world will go down the drain, not because we are all polluters but because even a handful of irresponsible people can do so much harm. I plan to do my bit here today by keeping my remarks clean and brief, with no harmful additives.

Pan American Health Day

I don't know whether there is any connection other than the coincidence of dates, but today—the birthday of the Monroe Doctrine in 1823—has been designated for many years as Pan American Health Day. The Monroe Doctrine bars the extension of European power in the western hemisphere; Pan

American Health Day has more lofty aspirations—it seeks to help the fight against disease. There is no country on earth that has conquered disease, but some of the countries of Latin America have health problems far above the norm. Yet we cannot separate health and politics. In impoverished nations malnutrition is both a health and a political problem; the same is true of child labor or housing. We have a tendency to forget that political and economic conditions are reflected in the health of nations and that in the last analysis the health of nations is the wealth of nations. We can't afford ill health; the question is whether we can afford the programs necessary to keep us healthy.

John Brown's Body

On this day in the year 1859, John Brown was hanged in the public square at Charleston, then in Virginia but soon to be West Virginia. He was the militant abolitionist who had tried to lead a rebellion of slaves and had been captured at Harper's Ferry by federal troops under the command of Robert E. Lee. Brown's execution prompted the song "John Brown's Body," to the tune which later became the "Battle Hymn of the Republic." His soul did indeed go marching on, proof once again that you can kill men but it is much harder to kill an idea. Giving voice to ideas is much easier than burying them, and I'd like to give voice to some ideas here today.

Model A

This was a very big day for the automobile industry back in 1927. Henry Ford put his new car on display all over the country. It was the replacement for the great Model T, which had served the country for 18 years and came in any color you wanted as long as it was black. The Model A came in colors, and Henry Ford hoped to keep on making it almost as long as he had done with the Model T, but the wind of change had picked up speed. The original Model A was produced for only five years. Although all this happened several generations ago, it remains a good example of how change accelerates further change. The computer was revolutionized many times in its first five or ten years, for example. Even government is changing at a faster pace than in the past. New executive departments, new bureaus, and new functions keep being added. Some of this is inevitable as needs change; some is the natural tendency of authority to spread itself; and all of it requires that we, the electorate, keep a careful eye on those in power. It is in that capacity, as one whose eye has been watching the government, that I come before you here today.

DECEMBER 3

Housing

We like to think of public housing as an old American tradition, but the fact is that the first low-cost public housing project in U.S. history was dedicated on this day in 1935, which, though a substantial number of years ago, was an awfully long time after housing had become a problem. Once we got started, of course, we put government in the housing business in a big way, via subsidies and municipal housing authorities, and yet the problem may be greater today than it was 50 years ago. I am not here to propose any magic solutions, but I think it may be helpful to have a look at the extent of our national housing headache.

Coed

Today is the anniversary of the opening of the first truly coeducational college in the United States. It was Oberlin College, in the town of that name in Ohio, which began its classes on this day in 1833. From today's perspective there doesn't seem to be anything very special about men and women attending the same college, but it was something else again in 1833. I think of that whenever I hear some important ideas today attacked as radical or even revolutionary. That is the easiest and most senseless of criticisms. I am going to talk about a few ideas today that some people describe that way, but I prefer to think that these ideas will be as accepted in the future as coeducation is today.

Pumpkin Papers

In one of the more bizarre episodes of American history, the chairman of the House Un-American Activities Committee announced that copies of secret government papers in microfilm had been found in a hollow pumpkin on the farm of Whittaker Chambers, who was to be the principal witness against accused radical agent Alger Hiss. That announcement was made on this day in 1948, and the ensuing controversy over the guilt or innocence of Hiss lasted for generations. It was the subject of books and lecture tours and seemingly endless speculation. I do not mean to reintroduce the subject here today, but it is too good an example to resist of how a particular issue can fascinate people, whereas matters of far greater general importance don't get the attention they deserve. I have no secrets to reveal to you today and no pumpkin papers to come up with, but I do have some vital subjects to bring before you.

St. Francis Xavier

On this day in 1552, the sainted Francis Xavier died on the Chinese island of Shangchwan. His memory is revered as perhaps the greatest of Catholic missionaries. And that gives me pause. Why is it that we revere those who go as missionaries to other lands to tell them of one or the other of the western faiths, but we deplore those who go to other lands to try to convert them to western democracy? Why do we seem to lack the sense of mission for our political ideals? I do not have a glib answer, but I do have some strong opinions, which I want to share with you here today, about our faith in democracy.

DECEMBER 4

Washington's Farewell

One of those more moving events of American history took place on this day in 1783. At Fraunces Tavern in downtown New York City, George Washington, preparing to return to private life, said farewell to his officers. The war had been won. Washington said, "With a heart full of love and gratitude I now take leave of you. I most devoutly wish that your latter days may be as prosperous and happy as your former ones have been glorious and honorable." Washington thought his public service was over, but not too many years later he would be called back from Virginia to become the first president under the Constitution. From the beginning of our nation we have been fortunate to be able to turn once again to proven leaders when we needed them. That, I believe, is because those who have given the most to the cause of America are still the most likely to respond with further devotion when their country needs them. This does not apply only to people in high office. It applies very strongly to people of ordinary talent, who know that when they give of themselves they can make a difference. And, of course, it applies to those with special gifts for special kinds of service. Today I direct my remarks to the helping hands of America.

The Peace Ship

On this day in 1915, ridiculed in the press and treated as an eccentric, Henry Ford and a motley assortment of unworldly idealists sailed from Hoboken aboard the *Oscar II,* the peace ship, to try to stop the world war. Some of the delegates stayed in neutral countries in Europe for a while, but Ford himself soon gave up and returned home shortly after Christmas. He was a genius at making and selling cars, but peace was a somewhat more difficult product to produce. The story of the *Oscar II* does have a point, though. It will remain for all time as a reminder that a leader in one kind of endeavor is not necessarily qualified to lead in other areas. Ideas that are good for a particular business or a particular labor union are not necessarily good for the country as a whole. And that is certainly true of some of the ideas various groups are putting forward these days.

Carlyle

Thomas Carlyle, the great British writer who was born on this day in 1795 in Scotland, wrote that, "the first duty of man is that of subduing fear." If you think about it fear is one of the principal motivations of our lives. We fear our enemies in the cold war; we fear old age; we fear insecurity. Much of what we do is prompted by fear, whether we are talking about building up armaments or a retirement fund. I am not about to suggest that we pass a law against fear; it wouldn't work. But I am here to suggest that we ask ourselves what it is we fear about old age and do something about it. Are we afraid of having nothing to do? Are we fearful we will lack the resources to fend for ourselves? Are we concerned about being burdens on our children? If we recognize these fears there is something we can do about them. We can plan now for what we want to do when we retire. We can equip ourselves to do work that benefits others as well as ourselves, whether on a voluntary basis or for a fee. We can make ourselves more active participants in our community life. Let me offer some examples.

Wilson's Voyage

When Woodrow Wilson sailed for France on this day in 1918 to attend the peace conference at the close of World War I, he was the first president to leave the United States for an overseas foreign country while in office. That, I suppose, marks the beginning of modern personal diplomacy for our nation. Since then, one president after another has voyaged to far places to meet with the heads of other governments. I am not at all sure that it is a good idea. Somebody once observed that America wins the wars and loses the conferences. Jimmy Carter's Camp David treaty notwithstanding, I don't believe that personal meetings between heads of state accomplish anything the states were not getting ready to do anyway. Such meetings are, at best, means of setting a psychological climate for the respective nations. At worst, as when the respective leaders take a strong personal dislike to each other, these meetings can be, in the government word, counterproductive. As is the case here today, so it is with meetings at higher levels. I am not going to persuade you to reverse your thinking. The most I can hope is to make my point of view perhaps better understood.

DECEMBER 5

Van Buren

Today is the birthday of the eighth president of the United States, Martin Van Buren, who was born in 1782 in Kinderhook, New York. He was Andrew Jackson's Vice President and successor, but when he came up for reelection he had the misfortune to be opposed by the war hero known as "Tippecanoe," William Henry Harrison, whose supposed victory at the Battle of Tippecanoe was blown out of all proportion. But the campaign motto of "Tippecanoe and Tyler Too" captured the popular imagination. It so happened that General Harrison caught cold and died a month after his inauguration, but by then it didn't do Martin Van Buren any good whatsoever. He ran for president on relatively minor tickets a few times after that, never altering any of his principles to win more votes, but to all intents his political career after the White House was nil. I recall his story here because it may well have been the first example of a manufactured candidate—glamorous old "Tippecanoe"—and how public emotions can be manipulated. Certainly that sort of thing goes on even more these days than it did in 1838. I would like to take a look at some of what I regard as current opinion manipulation with you here today.

Mozart's Death

Today is the anniversary of the death in 1791 of Wolfgang Amadeus Mozart. He had already turned out so many great musical compositions that he was to be one of the giants of music history, but he was only 35 when he succumbed to typhus. There is no standard timespan for genius. Michelangelo was in his late sixties when he completed *The Last Judgment* and he turned out other masterpieces into his eighties. George Gershwin, perhaps the greatest of American composers, was 39 when he died. What all this emphasizes is that using age as a test of talent is pointless. Youth is not always a time for apprenticeship and learning, and old age is not automatic retirement. We are not all destined to achieve quickly. There is always hope for further accomplishment. I am reminded of this when I hear people worry that America has, in their words, passed its peak. I dispute that; I think the best is yet to come—and I'd like to share that optimistic view with you.

Phi Beta Kappa

This is the birthday of the academic honor group, Phi Beta Kappa, organized as America's first fraternity in 1776 at the College of William and Mary in Williamsburg, Virginia. The number of students it has recognized and honored for academic excellence since then in colleges and universities all over the United States is a testimonial to the outstanding caliber of our young people. It is also a testimonial to the consistency with which we have maintained and expanded our institutions of higher education. Indeed, we have been able to provide higher and higher academic degrees for more and more of our people; and yet, at the same time, we have been singularly unsuccessful in educating the poorest of our population. We have people who, after years of schooling, are still unable to read or do arithmetic. I worry that we may be creating a permanent underclass and writing them off; I worry that we regard as unteachable those whom we have failed to teach. And I ask myself, what is the answer?

Repeal

On this day in 1933, the twenty-first admendment repealed Prohibition. Making liquor illegal just hadn't worked. One of the strengths of our way of life is that when a law is wrong we have a means of correcting it—peacefully. It does not always take a constitutional amendment to do it, either. For example, there are some ordinary laws on the book that we could do well to change.

DECEMBER 6

Finnish Independence Day

This is Finland's Independence Day, marking its declaration of independence from Russia in 1917. Unlike some of the other nations of the Russian empire, which were later gobbled up by the Soviet Union after relatively brief periods of independence, Finland, though very cautious in its relations with its powerful neighbor, remains a self-governing nation. The explanation may well be that when the Finns fought the Russians to a standstill for months in the Russo-Finnish War in 1939–40, even though mighty Russia ultimately got the best of its little opponent and grabbed territory, there was too much fight in the Finns to try to absorb them. This is not to say that other small nations did not fight when the Soviets moved to annex them, but the Finns had made their country strong for all its size, and they had demonstrated that they were willing to fight. Those are the attributes a free democracy needs to maintain itself in today's embattled world. That, I suspect, is why so many Americans keep asking whether we are as strong we ought to be or as we hope we are.

Lincoln in Washington

When Congress convened in Washington on this day in 1847, there was a brand new congressman from Illinois, a gentleman named Abraham Lincoln. It wasn't very long before young Mr. Lincoln showed his colors. The Mexican War had been going on for almost two years; the people of Illinois were known to be heartily in favor of it. But on December 22, Lincoln introduced a resolution in the House of Representatives questioning the validity of the war. That took care of Lincoln's congressional career. He had opted for principle rather than political expedience; and, of course, in later years, it was his loyalty to principle that made him the great president he was. It seems to me that the lesson here is a simple one: expedience is not always as expedient as it seems. And so today I want to talk about those policies for which the nation needs not expediency but true, honest-to-goodness principle.

Naval Observatory

What is now the Naval Observatory was founded by the U.S. Navy on this day in 1830. When standard time was adopted years later, the observatory became the official clock of the United States. Its time is our time, adjusted to whatever U.S. time zone we happen to be in. But we don't have to consult the Naval Observatory to know that right now it is later than some people think. We are challenged to solve ever more pressing problems; events move faster and faster, and we have to do the same. Rather than speak in generalized and abstract terms, let's get down to cases.

St. Nicholas Day

Today is St. Nicholas Day, in honor of the patron saint of sailors, pilgrims, schoolchildren, Russia, and pawnbrokers, and supposed inspiration for Santa Claus. One thing that can be said for St. Nicholas, it seems, is that his constituency is rather broad. When one is known for generosity, one is a natural target for those who need assistance. In a certain sense it might be said that the United States is the St. Nicholas of the world, expected at all times to be generous and giving. But whereas nobody berates St. Nicholas if the goodies aren't forthcoming, everybody berates Uncle Sam; we are both the rich uncle and the stingy Midas to the rest of the world. I am not here to suggest how we can change this unfortunate image but rather how best we can live with it.

DECEMBER 7

Instant Replay

It was on this day in 1963 that second-guessing became an American way of life. In the history of sports this is listed as the day in that year when the first instant replay was shown on television. It was during the Army–Navy football game. From then on the audience has had ample opportunities to take another look at what's been going on, judging the officials and the actions with that wonderful advantage, hindsight. Actually, of course, we didn't need the magic of tape recording; long before it was invented we were indulging in the practice of second-guessing our government's decisions, and I have no intention of giving up that privilege here today.

Praise the Lord

One of America's great watchwords was born on this day, amid the havoc of the Japanese surprise attack on Pearl Harbor in 1941. I doubt that the name of the Reverend Howell M. Forgy is anywhere nearly as familiar as his plea in the midst of the battle when he said, "Praise the Lord and pass the ammunition." It's a fine thought to remember, not with any warlike spirit but rather as a reminder that trusting to the favor of Providence is fine, but we have to equip ourselves to carry on the good fight. It is not enough to work hard; we have to make sure we work with the best tools available. That means having the intestinal fortitude to scrap obsolescent plants and to learn new techniques and skills. It means encouraging research and development. And it means very likely the abandonment of some cherished American concepts such as forced obsolescence, artificial model changes, and the like. And it means relying on productivity and talent rather than protectionism to protect the great American market. You can easily see from that list of requirements that there is no lack of subjects for my remarks here today, but I will concentrate on one that seems to me to be especially important.

New York Philharmonic

One of the oldest and most distinguished musical organizations in the world, the New York Philharmonic, gave its first concert on this day in 1842 in New York City. Some measure of what has happened to the arts in America can be gained by comparing the scene of that first concert with the Philharmonic's current home. From a rented hall the orchestra has moved to its own concert auditorium in the modern center of the performing arts, Lincoln Center. What has happened to the Philharmonic has been happening with all the arts all over America. Perhaps in some ways it is a product not only of greater resources but also of more leisure time. It isn't only hard work that enriches life; it is having the free time to enjoy. So I think it is time to ask ourselves whether we are not approaching a time when the hours of work will go down further. I'd like to talk today about how we can make that possible.

Two Anniversaries

Two anniversaries today somehow combine to say a great deal about our country. On this day in 1787 Delaware became the first state to ratify the Constitution, the document that has given our nation a basic pattern of law that has stood the test of time. The second anniversary is Pearl Harbor Day, recalling the Japanese surprise attack in 1941 that was supposed to begin the destruction of the nation. It didn't. The peaceful law we adopted in the 1780s helped give us a nation strong enough, resilient enough, and caring enough to rise from the ashes of Pearl Harbor and move on to victory. Merchants of despair may say that we have passed our peak, that we must adjust our sights downward. I don't believe that for a minute. I believe that our economic and societal Pearl Harbors are behind us, and we are on the way up. I believe we have opportunities today to pick ourselves up by our bootstraps, as I hope I can convey to you.

DECEMBER 8

Eli Whitney

Today is the birthday of Eli Whitney, who was born in Westborough, Massachusetts, on this day in 1765. Whitney is famous as the inventor of the cotton gin, and the importance of that device cannot be overestimated. But he should also be famous for another invention of his—mass production with interchangeable parts. It was Whitney who devised this system when he set up a factory to make muskets for the government. That was how he made his money.

There were so many infringements on his cottin gin patent that he never really made much of a profit on it, but his assembly-line technique for muskets paid off handsomely. That story is in some ways a capsule of life. We bust our breeches to come up with a brainstorm, and it falls flat, while another idea comes through much more successfully than we had anticipated. That is one reason, I suppose, why we keep looking for new ideas. It is one reason why we have a tendency to tinker with success and not leave well enough alone. We have a constant desire to do better and an equally constant desire to ask questions toward that end. Today it is my turn.

John Lennon

It was on this day in 1980 that the senseless murder of former Beatle John Lennon took place in New York. The entertainer, who had worked tirelessly for peace, was shot by a demented killer. Would-be assassins have stalked world leaders for years, but when people like John Lennon become victims the madness is rising. Blame what you will—the prevalence of mental illness, the popularization of violence in the media, the easy availability of weapons of death, the slowness and leniency of the American system of justice—whatever the contributing factors, the fact is that we are all in danger, not merely from the uncertainties of international conflicts but from the deranged viciousness of individual killers. Our mental hospitals are so overtaxed as to be unable to accommodate all who should be confined to them. How, then, do we cope with this problem?

Thurber's War

This is the birthday of the great American humorist James Thurber, who first saw the light of the day in 1894 in Columbus, Ohio. It was Thurber whose delightful whimsy came up with the concept that the basis of life is the continuing war between men and women. Others may have celebrated love between the sexes, but Thurber saw an endless battle. He was not all that wrong. Too many of us, men and women alike, see the opposite sex as a rival and a competitor or as an objective to be conquered. After all these years we have less successful male–female partnerships, whether marital or business, than ever before, and it seems to me that there is a challenge in that fact. I have some thoughts to offer about what we are doing wrong.

American Federation of Labor

This is the birthday of the American Federation of Labor, which was established in 1881 but adopted the title it has been known by ever since at a meeting of representatives of some 25 unions in Columbus, Ohio, on this day in 1886. Over the years the AFL has discovered that it is or can be a political power as well as a factor in labor relations, and the political role has been increasing. This is quite a change from the role pictured by Samuel Gompers, the founding president of the AFL; he saw it as a bargaining organization, concerned only with pay and working conditions of organized labor. Today there is general recognition that political clout is a good way to achieve economic advantages. As a result, big labor, like big capital, has gained steadily in political influence. I am not so sure this is a good thing; it has inflated the costs of campaigning and increased the possibility of candidates being beholden to special interests. But I doubt that we can turn the clock back. Instead, we ought to think of ways of limiting the power of all special-interest groups.

DECEMBER 9

Christmas Seals

The first Christmas seals went on sale on this day in Wilmington, Delaware, in 1907. They proved to be one of the most effective charitable fund-raising ideas yet devised and have funded much of the work in the prevention and cure of lung disease. Like all good ideas, the Christmas seal has also spawned a number of imitations. Originality is not too common, but imitation certainly is. And there will always be people who prefer to imitate rather than to originate. This is particularly true in the world of public policy, where so many so-called leaders will not espouse a course of action until someone else has paved the way. It is always easier to sit back and criticize someone else's ideas than to come up with your own. That is a particular temptation for the speaker, but it is a lot more palatable if, in addition to taking somebody else's proposals apart, you offer some constructive suggestions of your own; and that is what I propose to do here today.

John Birch Society

On this day in 1958, the John Birch Society was organized. It gained attention largely because it was so much to the right of most existing political groups, and, thanks more to its vocal opponents than to its own efforts, its very name became synonymous with what most of the public regarded as extreme reaction. I have no intention of devoting my remarks today to an analysis of John Birchism or the reasons for its occurrence. My purpose in mentioning it is to remind us of how we have a tendency to make particular groups the custodians, so to speak, of particular points of view. One need not be a member of the Birch Society to share their views, any more than one needs to be an enrolled party member to be a Communist or a Republican or a Democrat. All too often we approach issues on an ideological basis rather than on the merits of the particular case. I do not intend to discuss my topics today on that basis—neither from the left nor from the right nor from whatever ideology you may feel I represent. Instead, I will try to speak dispassionately on the merits and demerits I see.

The Charge of the Light Brigade

Less than two months after the Battle of Balaclava, a masterpiece of military stupidity in the Crimean War in 1854, Alfred Lord Tennyson's great poem "The Charge of the Light Brigade" was published in England on this day. It was the story of the bloody charge that killed hundreds of brave British fighting men in a meaningless victory. Tennyson's words were so stirring that they gave military stupidity an epically heroic air, and the resultant national pride in the men of whom he wrote "Theirs not to reason why,/Theirs but to do or die" far outweighed the condemnation of the disgraceful leadership. There is a tendency on the part of some to shift the emphasis from the leadership to the ranks on other issues. During periods of great unemployment those in power have been known to suggest that many of the unemployed brought it on themselves. They talk about welfare as if most of the recipients were deliberately needy and of bank troubles being caused by depositors' panic rather than mismanagement at the top. My comments today are aimed at higher levels.

Christmas Cards

This is the anniversary of an item that is either a boon or a bane depending on how you feel about it. On this day in 1842, a young Englishman named William Maw Egley Jr. created a greeting card with Christmas scenes on it and space for the sender to express a Yuletide greeting. Thus was born the Christmas card. It gave rise to a great industry, put a tremendous burden on the Post Office, and set us all to keeping lists. But in the complicated and far-reaching world in which we live, Christmas cards are a way of letting distant friends know that we are still alive and, at least occasionally, thinking of them. All of us like to know, or to believe, that somebody else is thinking of us. The trouble is that you can't rely on the cards anymore. The warm printed greeting you get from somebody may well turn out to have been addressed by a secretary or a spouse from last year's list without the sender even knowing about it. We have come to the stage, ladies and gentlemen, where you can't even trust a Christmas card; so you will forgive me if I present my remarks today, on a different subject, with a certain degree of cynicism.

DECEMBER 10

Equal Taxation

In 1832 on this day, President Andrew Jackson delivered a warning to his native state of South Carolina. The Carolinians had advocated the idea that an individual state could nullify a federal law it didn't like—in this case, the Tariff of 1832. In his rejection of that nullification idea, President Jackson said,

"The wisdom of man never yet contrived a system of taxation that would operate with perfect equality." What he found impossible then still seems to be impossible, because certainly our tax laws do not yet operate with equality for all. When tax policy is discussed the dominant question is always which group of our citizenry are we going to favor? That is the question I want to address here today.

Emily Dickinson

We live in a time of talk. People who used to work in silence now labor while listening to radio personalities. Candidates address the nation in close-up through the magic of television. Friends who years ago would have been baffled by their distance from each other now talk directly on the telephone. Emily Dickinson, who was born on this day in 1830 in Amherst, Massachusetts, wrote her poems and hid them away. Today, I suspect, she would have found a circle with whom she could share readings. We have come far from the time in which she said, "A word is dead/When it is said,/Some say./I say it just/Begins to live/That day." Whether the words I speak here today will begin to live after I have delivered them I cannot say. I'll know better after I hear them.

Human Rights Day

On this day in 1948, the assembled nations adopted the United Nations Universal Declaration of Human Rights, and the day is observed throughout the world as Human Rights Day. Some of the nations that signed the document, however, have rather different ideas of human rights than our Founding Fathers had. Life, liberty, and the pursuit of happiness are a lot more free in the United States than in some other parts of the world; yet every nation will assure you that by its definition it is dedicated to human rights. Some of this is a matter of perspective; what we regard as individual rights are not so regarded in, say, Russia or South Africa. At this time of year, when the spirit of peace and good will is supposed to bless the world, I think it is appropriate to ask, how goes the cause of freedom?

William Lloyd Garrison

Either today or the day after tomorrow is the birthday of William Lloyd Garrison, the great nineteenth-century lecturer and editor. The history books don't agree on the exact date, but they do agree that he was born in Massachusetts in 1805, and they agree about the eloquence and the passion with which he spoke, particularly in the abolitionist cause. Today I want to quote a remark that I believe is particularly pertinent to our times. He wrote in his publication *The Liberator,* "Tell a man whose house is on fire to give a moderate alarm; tell him to moderately rescue his wife from the hands of the ravisher; tell the mother to gradually extricate her babe from the fire into which it has fallen;

but urge me not to use moderation." I am here today, ladies and gentlemen, to put aside moderation with regard to some pressing emergencies of our time.

DECEMBER 11

Abdication

When Edward VIII, the monarch of Great Britain, declared over world-wide radio on this day in 1936 that he had abdicated in order to marry the divorced Mrs. Wallis Warfield Simpson, there was an orgy of romanticism all over the world and a great deal of sympathy for the departing king. But the test of history in later years suggested that it was a wise decision for both Edward and his country. The man who succeeded him, his brother George VI, proved a modest and effective king in the period of England's greatest trial, World War II. Edward, particularly in later years, was not known for his grasp of political reality or his appreciation of the threat of fascism. Fate and destiny work in strange ways, and it is entirely possible that the romantic complications that brought Edward down brought England up. I see similar worthwhile benefits from some of today's unhappy situations.

Rockefeller's Gift

On this day in 1946, John D. Rockefeller Jr. offered a gift of land along the East River in Manhattan as the site of the permanent United Nations headquarters. It was a magnificent gift and was deservedly applauded at the time, but I can't help wondering if the convenience of the location and the size of the building don't encourage an awful lot of unnecessary speechifying and posturing by nations that couldn't possibly otherwise have any such opportunity. I am reminded of what happens when a television news camera focuses on people after they have spoken. With the unblinking eye and microphone still there in front of them they usually feel they have to go on talking—and that's when they get into trouble. I will bear both the example of the United Nations and the unblinking eye and microphone in mind and will resist every temptation here to continue speaking after I have finished what I came here to say.

UNICEF

This is the birthday of the United Nations International Children's Emergency Fund, which was established in 1946 and has been doing worthwhile work ever since. UNICEF is an example of what nations can do when they choose to work together. They don't really make that choice very often and, unfortunately, they never really have caught up with all the children around the world who can use their help. That isn't a criticism of UNICEF; it is rather a sad commentary on the state of the world. While we store food we can't use for years, people are starving in far corners of the earth. What is even more shocking is the amount of malnutrition in the United States—not just the homeless bag men and bag ladies but whole families. And it isn't that the nation doesn't have the food. Why can't we solve this problem?

Robert Koch

This is the birthday of Robert Koch, the great German bacteriologist who was born in Hanover on this day in 1843. Koch not only discovered the tuberculosis bacillus but he also revolutionized medicine's understanding of the process of infection and laid the groundwork for a great deal of modern medicine. One of the great things about medicine is that its secrets are shared. Unlike some other branches of science, where either patents or the demands of government secrecy interfere with the widest dissemination of products or knowledge, medicine is open. Of course, there are near monopolies on some particular medications that are owned by individual companies, but they are products that are sold openly, not kept as national secrets. If we can share the secrets of fighting disease, why can't we share the secrets of other means of fighting? It would be naive to suppose that our major weapons are unknown to our enemies or that theirs are unknown to us. What would happen if we said, here is a list of our weapons and what they can do? We wouldn't be giving our enemies any information they don't already have, and we might be exerting a considerable moral suasion to get them to do the same. In the process, the common-sense fact that either side can destroy the other should impress itself a little more firmly on them both. Then maybe we could write an end to the continuously mounting armament race. Otherwise, what can we expect?

DECEMBER 12

John Jay

This is the birthday of John Jay, who, among other distinctions, was the first Chief Justice of the United States. Jay, who was born in New York City on this day in 1745, was one of the most distinguished men in a time of great leaders. He wrote many of the Federalist papers, he was in effect the Secretary of State under the Articles of Confederation, and as the first Chief Justice, he set one of the important patterns of that Court. On behalf of President George Washington, Thomas Jefferson in 1793 asked for the Court's advance guidance on various questions of international law that might occur. Jay and his associates wrote a letter in reply firmly rejecting the request and reminding that under the Constitution's separation of powers such advisory opinions would be improper. Our Founding Fathers were very conscious of the need to stick to the basic law that had just been adopted. It seems to me that we are much more willing to bend it—or to revise it—to deal with the contingencies of the moment. I suggest that when this seems the simple way out we should do what we do when serious surgery is suggested. Seek a second opinion—such as the one I am about to give you.

Panay

It was on this day in 1937 that Americans first came under attack by the Japanese. The *Panay*, a U.S. Navy gunboat on the Yangtze River near Nanking, China, was bombed and sunk by Japanese airplanes that were supposedly attacking Chinese positions. Three British fighting ships were damaged in the same action. Two Americans were killed and thirty injured, and the Japanese paid an indemnity of more than $2 million as well as tendering their apologies. The question the world did not ask as strongly as it might was what American naval vessels and Japanese war forces were doing in China, supposedly a sovereign nation. Japan, of course, was well on its way to conquering China long before the rest of World War II broke out, and I suppose it might be said that we were well on our way to the debacle of Vietnam. If there are lessons to be learned from the *Panay* incident, the most important, it seems to me, is that unless aggression is stopped in its tracks it will keep on occurring. The big question is how to stop aggression without stepping up conflict.

Ford Gift

This is the anniversary of the greatest single day in the history of American philanthropy, the day in 1955 when the Ford Foundation gave a half-billion dollars to colleges and medical institutions. It is a sad commentary that despite that unprecedented gift, despite the hundreds of millions of dollars that have been given in later years to such institutions, they remain among the financially insecure. The costs of running and staffing hospitals and universities have outstripped the inflationary spiral, largely because of the expensive new equipment needed simply to remain abreast of contemporary science. We speak of the inflationary spiral, but some of that inflation, at least, is caused simply by the development of valuable new tools added to or replacing existing resources— for example, the new scanners for hospital diagnosis, new and ever more costly computers, and the like. This is, in terms of costs, an inflationary spiral that pays off in better medicine and better teaching, but it costs. Given that fact I have no hesitancy in saying to you, on the very anniversary of the biggest private act of philanthropy, that we must all give more.

Lincoln's Wait

On this day in 1858, a little more than a month after he had lost the Illinois election for U.S. senator to Stephen Douglas, Abraham Lincoln wrote a letter to an old friend, urging him not to take the loss too hard. "I have an abiding faith," he wrote, "that we shall beat them in the long run. Step by step, the objects of the leaders will become too plain for the people to stand them." That is one of the strengths of this country—the fact that we sit in judgement at such consistent intervals on the performance of our elected leaders. When that performance plainly displeases the electorate, then changes are made. In Lincoln's case it didn't take too long. The man who was defeated for the Senate in 1858 was elected president two years later. Bearing that in mind it is always appropriate to assess the performance of those currently in office, for they will face official judgement soon enough. Ladies and gentlemen of the jury, let me make my case.

DECEMBER 13

End of the Honeymoon

On this day in 1981, communist Poland's brief flirtation with freedom ended. The growth of the Solidarity movement led by Lech Walesa had forced the government to give more leeway to the independent labor union than it wanted to, and now the communist regime struck back with a declaration of martial law and the jailing of Solidarity leaders. It was made clear to the world that a communist government could not tolerate free speech, free assembly, or other basic rights of free people. How fortunate we are to live under so different a tradition of individual liberty! But, though fortunate, we cannot be complacent. We cannot take our liberties for granted, or somebody else will take our liberties for a ride. The time to speak out against this danger is while you can still speak out, and so I raise my voice here and now for the reasons I am about to mention.

Nostradamus

The man we know as Nostradamus was born in Provence on this day in 1503, although some sources list the date a day later. In any case the ambiguity of his birthday is somehow appropriate for a man whose book of prophecies was so worded that you can interpret many of them as you will. As a result, many people read into the words of Nostradamus the real meaning they want to read. Sometimes that happens when you hear a speech. You hear what you want to hear, somehow overlooking whatever else the speaker may have said. I can't prevent that from happening here today, but I can tell you right at the outset what it is I want you to hear.

Johnson's View

When President Lyndon B. Johnson spoke to members of the Consumers Advisory Council in the White House on this day in 1963, he offered a simple description of the economic goals of society. "First," he said, "it must direct its attention to the age-old problem of converting the earth's resources into goods and commodities. Second, it must direct its attention to placing those goods and commodities into the hands of the men, women, and children who use them." That's a very simple description of a task we haven't done all that well for all that long; and if we want to do it any better we had best start by taking a good long look at the way we are doing in now.

Sullivan's War

On this day in 1774, Major John Sullivan of the New Hampshire volunteers led an organized force of 400 men to attack a British fort in Portsmouth Harbor, New Hampshire. They took the commander of the fort prisoner, and the defending soldiers ran away, leaving the rebels all of their munitions. But not until the battles of Lexington and Concord four months later when the Minute Men went into action did the American Revolutionary War actually begin. Was it because Lexington and Concord were battles with casualities, and Portsmouth Harbor was no fight worth mentioning? I don't have the answer to that one, but I do think that what happened in Portsmouth Harbor could have given the British a pretty powerful hint of the disaffection of the colonies, particularly when combined with various other incidents of anti-British violence. Are signals being given to use these days, signals of discontent to which we are as deaf or as blind as the British in 1774? I think there are, and I'd like to tell you what and where.

DECEMBER 14

Washington's Death

This is the anniversary of the death of George Washington in 1799 at his home in Mount Vernon, Virginia. At 67, he was one of the shorter-lived of the Founding Fathers. John Adams lived until 90, Thomas Jefferson past 83, Benjamin Franklin 84, as well beyond the average life expectancy 200 years later. These men lived through some of the most harrowing times in American history, but they obviously responded to the challenges with zest and vigor. I think we can consider ourselves fortunate that we too are facing serious challenges, because without them life isn't longer; it just seems longer. The important thing is to face those challenges, not to postpone them, and I see dangerous signs of an inclination to postpone, to sweep under the bed. I want to talk here today about some things that cannot be postponed and ought not be swept under the bed.

World Trade Center

On this day in 1970, they topped off the World Trade Center in downtown New York City—a huge building development built at the climax of Nelson Rockefeller's so-called "edifice complex" and immediately labeled as the biggest white elephant of the age. Instead it sparked a tremendous renaissance of building development in that part of the city and became a model for similar developments elsewhere. In this country, thinking big is usually not as risky as not thinking big enough—and I'd like to apply that law to some of our current problems.

Margaret Chase Smith

The first woman to be elected to both the House of Representatives and later, the United States Senate was Margaret Chase Smith of Maine, who throughout her political career exemplified honesty and courage in public service. She was born on this day in 1897 in Skowhegan, Maine, and one of her better moments came with her "Declaration of Conscience" in the Senate in 1950, when Senator Joseph McCarthy's Red-baiting witchhunt was moving into high gear. Senator Smith said, "I don't want to see the Republican Party ride to political victory on the Four Horsemen of Calumny—Fear, Ignorance, Bigotry, and Smear." Ladies and gentlemen, those four horsemen are still riding—not in a single party but as a constant plague. Too many election campaigns, too many legislative campaigns are being waged on the basis of fear, ignorance, and smear—and bigotry, heaven knows, is still a lurking poison. These threats build on one another. Fear and smear find no more fertile soil than where there is ignorance. So anything that can shed a little honest light is a step forward—and I hope that today we can take that step together.

Desegregation

The segregated motels, hotels, and other discriminatory institutions serving only white customers or forcing black customers into segregated areas had their last stand at about this time in 1964 when the Supreme Court came to a decision in two cases challenging the Civil Rights Act. The Act, the segregationists claimed, could not apply to local institutions, since they were not a part of interstate commerce and hence were subject to state rather than federal regulation. But the Supreme Court ruled that the Civil Rights Act applies—and official segregation bit the dust. Sometimes progress in this democracy of ours in painfully slow, but it comes. And if you look back over the years I think you will find there has been a steady improvement in the rights of the individual. Occasionally there may be a setback, but the general story is one of continuous progress. Does that mean we should sit back and simply let history take its course? I do not think so. We must do as our predecessors did—fight for what we believe is right, not lose heart because of an occasional defeat, concentrate on the agenda of the moment. And what is that agenda today?

DECEMBER 15

Bill of Rights Day

Today is Bill of Rights Day, the anniversary of the adoption of the first ten amendments to the Constitution in 1791. It has taken later laws and later amendments to create the full body of rights that are enjoyed today by every American, regardless of race, color, creed, or sex. And that process of growth—the increase in individual rights—is far from ended. I am not going to recite a litany of expectations here, but there is one area that I believe deserves our particular attention.

Matter of Principle

In perhaps its most futile decision in a long history, the International Court of Justice on this day in 1979 ordered Iran to release the hostages it had taken when a mob had invaded the U.S. embassy in Tehran. Iran, of course, totally ignored the Court. In recent years the world has been plagued by what can only be called outlaw nations—countries that have provided sanctuary for terrorists, countries that exploit or ignore diplomatic immunity, countries that dedicate themselves to the destruction or capture of others. As long as these outlaw nations are tolerated in the international community they will breed trouble. Is there anything we can do about it? And if so, why aren't we doing it?

Sitting Bull

On this day in 1890, the man who may well have been the last great leader of the American Indians, Sitting Bull, came to the end of his career when he was shot and killed by Indian police. He had been the leader of the Hunkpapa Sioux and later of the alliance with the Oglala Sioux. His life had been a series of broken promises from the white man. He and his people had been given land above the North Platte River, but when gold was discovered his land was invaded by prospectors and white settlers. Ordered by the government to disperse, the Indians refused, and at the Battle of the Little Big Horn they wiped out the forces of General George Armstrong Custer. The victor in that battle was Sitting Bull's deputy Crazy Horse. Sitting Bull led a group of his followers to refuge in Canada, but the Canadians gave them no help. The Indians had to return to the United States and surrender. Sitting Bull himself was persuaded to tour for a while with Buffalo Bill's Wild West Show, but he kept on hoping that the Indians would rise again. He seemed to be preparing for another effort when his arrest was ordered. His followers resisted, and he died. The story of Sitting Bull reminds us that the heirs of past injustice are still among us and that we cannot regard ourselves as the descendants of plaster saints. We have inherited some wrongs that needed righting, and not just with the Indians. Can we do better?

Hartford Convention

The draft riots of the Civil War and the Vietnam moratorium demonstrations during our war in Indochina were the most spectacular wartime resistance movements in the United States, but on this day in 1814 in the midst of the War of 1812, a meeting convened in Hartford, Connecticut, could have become the most serious of all. The convention had delegates from five New England states who disliked the war, but they had a lot of other complaints as well. They didn't want naturalized citizens to hold federal office, for example, and they did want the president limited to one term in office. What prevented their movement from getting anywhere was that shortly after the convention ended news arrived in this country that the Treaty of Ghent, ending the war, had been signed in Europe. This took the starch out of the discontent on which the Hartford Convention had expected to feed. That's what good news can do, even if it isn't directly connected with current gripes. So I asked myself before I came here today what good news I could talk about. And I have some for you.

DECEMBER 16

Khrushchev's Harangue

Nikita Khrushchev, the Premier of the Soviet Union, chose on this day in 1958 to make a speech in Moscow attacking the regime of his predecessor Georgi Malenkov. He spoke for six hours. I am happy to tell you that my remarks here today will be devoted to something more constructive—and, I promise you, they will be shorter.

Santayana

This is the anniversary of the birth of George Santayana in 1863 in Madrid. It was Santayana, the great Spanish–American philospher, writer, and teacher, who wrote that "those who canot remember the past are condemned to repeat it." But remembering the past is not enough in itself. Understanding the past, and particularly the errors of the past, is the best way to avoid making those errors again. The trouble is that we don't all see the past in the same way. Some look at the New Deal of the 1930s and remember the seemingly pointless and wasteful spectacle of men being paid to rake leaves on the streets; others remember the public works constructed by relief workers. One group says the New Deal was a great success; another group says it was saved from failure by the coming of World War II. It's all in your perspective. But we know one thing. If the public, particularly the needy portion of the public, becomes convinced that the government cares, the community is in better shape than if that same needy public feels that the government doesn't give a hoot. Ask yourself which attitude applies today, and let us try to assess where we are.

Noel Coward

Noel Coward, the composer–actor–playwright who was born on this day in 1899 in Teddington, England, was the man who noted that "mad dogs and Englishmen go out in the noonday sun." One of Coward's greatest talents was to find the vanities in contemporary society and lampoon them. In Coward's time the British Empire was still great enough to be lampooned, and funny lyrics about travel directors and the like were very timely. We live, I fear, in a different era, and I suspect we take ourselves too seriously. But, particularly at this season of the year, I think it only appropriate to bring to your attention some of the lighter aspects of life in the United States today, so I have culled a few from the recent news.

Catastrophes

The history books tell us that on this day in 1811 one of the most widespread earthquakes on this continent hit an area of almost a million square miles in the Midwest; on this day in 1631, an eruption of Mount Vesuvius killed 18,000 people; in 1835, 600 buildings in New York City were destroyed in a fire that began on this day; and in 1960, two airliners collided in the air over the city, killing more than 130 people. Compared to such catastrophes I couldn't possibly do much damage with anything I said here today; my remarks, in any case, are meant to be only constructive.

DECEMBER 17

Truman's Advice

Nothing I could say today could possibly be as terse and to the point as the remark that President Harry S. Truman recalled in a speech he made in Washington on this day in 1952. He quoted an "old friend and colleague on the Jackson County Court" as saying to him, "Harry, if you can't stand the heat you better get out of the kitchen." When you hold public office in this country you are in the kitchen where it's cooking, and where it sometimes gets pretty hot. One reason it gets hot is that speakers such as myself are forever second-guessing, and in my remarks here today I will be doing some of that.

Whittier

The poet John Greenleaf Whittier, who was born on this day in 1807 in Haverhill, Massachusetts, was the man who wrote these immortal lines: "For all sad words of tongue or pen,/The saddest are these: 'It might have been!' " Writers and speakers have filled endless pages and endless hours with speculation on what might have been—if FDR had done this, or Nixon hadn't done that. I will not take your time here today with what Whittier called such sad words of tongue or pen. Instead, I want to talk about what can be, what we have the chance to accomplish.

Charlie McCarthy

The nation was amazed on this day in 1936 when a new radio star was born. This new star was made of wood and paint and was truly a dummy. His name was Charlie McCarthy, manipulated by Edgar Bergen; and, in a strange way, the voice of Charlie McCarthy intrigued the public more than the voice and personality of the man who ruled the puppet, Mr. Bergen. The term *Charlie McCarthy* became a popular euphemism for a person who was somebody else's stooge or mouthpiece. And in the age when political figures seek office on the basis of ghost-written speeches, expertly staged commercials, and public opinion polls, the question of what a public personality really stands for is sometimes not an easy one to answer. Sometimes the candidates themselves cannot tell you how they will react to the policy questions that may arise during their term of office. So to a certain extent we have come to the point of judging public figures by the company they keep and, sometimes, by the company that keeps them. That is the standard I propose to apply in my remarks here today.

A Christmas Carol

It was about this time in the year 1843 that Charles Dickens, the master storyteller of his time, gave the world *A Christmas Carol*. No character in literature is better known than Scrooge, the mean old man whom the Christmas spirit ultimately reforms. Scrooge has been played by one great actor after another, and countless generations have watched, read about, or listened to his adventures with the Spirits of Christmas Past, Present, and Future. And Tiny Tim's immortal line, "God bless us everyone!" has expressed that universal wish in thousands of times and places. Such is the power of a simple concept expressed in understandable terms. Unfortunately very few of us have the ability of Charles Dickens, and particularly as the Christmas season approaches it is hard to avoid sounding unduly sentimental in envisioning the possibility of a world of peace. It can be done, ladies and gentlemen; we can help to make it so, and now is a good time to consider how.

DECEMBER 18

Thirteenth Amendment

It was on this day in 1865 that the Thirteenth amendment prohibiting slavery was adopted in the aftermath of the Civil War. But it took a hundred years to write the law that ended second-class citizenship—the Civil Rights Act. Progress does not come in one smooth course of events and attitudes. It seems to come in leaps and starts. And we have learned that political freedom cannot really flower without accompanying progress in incomes and attitudes. Hard times make hard lines of opinion and prejudice; greater opportunities bring greater good will. Today the challenge that faces us is not intrinsically political; it is economic. It asks us to find a better way of life for the chronically poor, to find a way to give their children a better start. It calls for a better sense of community. And it asks each of us, are you doing your part?

Prohibition

The United States had been involved in World War I for eight months; many of our young people were already deep in the war effort and not watching the workings of Congress too closely; and a lot of people with German names were prominent in the brewery business. All these factors combined to enable the Dries, as the prohibitionists were known, to get the Prohibition Amendment through Congress on this day for submission to the states. It was declared ratified early in 1919, while so many young men were still in uniform away from home. There is no way of knowing whether in a period of peace, with no other major issue to divert the voters, the amendment would have passed. We do know, with the hindsight of history, that it just didn't work. Its history is a good argument for not rushing into things. There is always a good deal of pressure for the quick fix, the overnight solution. I urge that we remember that impressive phrase, "with all deliberate speed," and particularly emphasize *deliberate*. And I'd like to raise some points worth deliberating.

Saki

Today is the birthday of Saki, which in this case is not a Japanese liquor but rather the pen name of a fine British writer named H. H. Munroe, who was born on this day in 1870 in Burma. It was Saki who wrote of one man that he would be enormously improved by death and of the lady who felt that the sacrifices of friendship were beautiful as long as she was not asked to make them. Saki did not go along with conventional wisdom. He commented, for example, that "poverty keeps together more homes than it breaks up." And he gave some of our modern politicians a marvelous doctrine to live by. "A little inaccuracy," he wrote, "sometimes saves tons of explanation." These days, however, some of our politicians have become so inaccurate that they keep press aides busy trying to clarify what they really meant or have opposition truth squads following them around seeking to correct the record. Playing fast and loose with the facts is an ancient if not always honorable political ploy, and in some ways we should be grateful because it sometimes goads the people who really know into saying more than they otherwise might. I really don't need that kind of incentive. All I needed was your kind invitation.

Investigating Pearl Harbor

When the United States is faced with the problem of trying to figure out what went wrong, we have a standard procedure. We appoint a commission. On this day in 1941, less than two weeks after the disaster at Pearl Harbor, President Franklin D. Roosevelt appointed a commission headed by Supreme Court Justice Owen Roberts to investigate why it had happened. This commission, unlike many, didn't take its time. It reported back on the following January 24, in little more than a month, and it made no bones about laying the blame on the men who were in command of the Navy and Army forces at Pearl Harbor. By that time we were so deep in World War II that, beyond some personnel changes, there were few reactions to the commission report. Now, there is never a time when the government doesn't have a commission or two laboring lengthily over some investigation, and it is often a way of quieting any other discussion. No point in talking about that, says an administration; we've got a special commission working on it. Sometimes the commissions work so quietly we don't even know they are there. And today I am going to talk about some problems that have outlasted the commissions originally set up to deal with them.

DECEMBER 19

Vietnam

It was on this day that the communists in Hanoi began in 1946 their long war to control Vietnam. At this stage it was a revolution against the French, but that turned out to be only phase one of a longer struggle that went on for almost 30 years. Wars once started often have a way of hanging on and growing. That is why it is so important to try to stop them while they are only beginning. I believe we have that kind of opportunity today in a number of places, and I'd like to explore that with you.

Poor Richard's Almanac

It was about this time in 1732 that Benjamin Franklin published the first of what became his annual series, *Poor Richard's Almanac*. It was then and remains probably the most brilliant collection of observations and aphorisms on human nature, and I could quote endlessly from its various issues. In that first issue, my favorite advice is this: "Eat to live, and not live to eat." I am reminded of that advice when I consider the problem of weapons. We are eating up our resources to pay for weapons, thinking that we are thereby protecting our way of life; but we are making that way of life harder by using so much of our substance in the eternal escalation of armaments. And other peoples are doing the same. Is there a logical limit to this dilemma—a limit, that is, other than deciding we might as well use the weapons?

Valley Forge

When General George Washington led his Continental Army into winter encampment at Valley Forge at this time in 1777, they didn't know how long and how oppressive a time they were in for. It occurs to me that when a speaker gets up to make a speech, the audience is in much that same position; they don't know how long or how oppressive it is going to be. Ladies and gentlemen, this is not Valley Forge. I won't even give you a snow job. Just a few warm words in a temperate mood.

Ty Cobb

This is the birthday of Tyrus Raymond Cobb, the great baseball player who was born in Georgia in 1886. He was as competitive a player as ever put on a pair of spikes, and he excelled in every phase of the sport. It was no accident that he was the first man chosen for the Baseball Hall of Fame. But despite all he accomplished as a hitter and base runner, what distinguished him most was his aggressiveness. He played harder than just about any other ballplayer in history. He had the ability to go with that fighting spirit, but I believe the spirit is what made the difference. And that is worth remembering, particularly at this season of the year. Whatever we do it is important to give that effort everything we have. This is the season when we give gifts; I am here to ask that we give something else—ourselves. I am going to talk about a community effort that can use your contributions, but that, most of all, can use you.

DECEMBER 20

Branch Rickey

Today is the birthday of Branch Rickey, the baseball executive who not only changed the face of the sport but pioneered a revolution in developing talent. Rickey, who was born in Ohio in 1881, was the president of the St. Louis Cardinals when he originated the idea of a farm system—teams in leagues of various levels of the professional sport where a likely prospect could be trained and brought up gradually to major league quality. But important though the idea of a farm system was—and is—it was not Rickey's most worthwhile contribution. In 1946, when he was the president of the Brooklyn Dodgers, baseball was a segregated sport. Black players were barred from all the leagues that were part of what called itself "organized baseball." When nobody else in the game had the gumption and the initiative to contest this segregation, Rickey did; he signed a black ballplayer named Jackie Robinson for one of the Dodgers' farm teams and in 1947 for the Dodgers themselves. Despite tremendous opposition he backed Jackie Robinson all the way, and thanks to him the doors of baseball were opened. Remember, this was quite a few years before the Civil Rights Act of 1964. By the time that act was passed, Rickey and Jackie Robinson had made their point. And so today I think that in remembering Branch Rickey we remind ourselves that one person who is right can indeed move mountains. Not all of us can have the courage or the business foresight or the moral strength of Branch Rickey, but all of us, every last one of us, can make a difference. It is with that firm conviction that I come here to seek your support today.

History's Biggest Bargain

There are very few shopping days left till Christmas, so it seems only appropriate that the biggest bargain in American history should have been delivered on this day back in 1803. That was when the United States took title to a purchase it had made for $15 million, a very tidy sum indeed in those days. But the purchase was the Louisiana Territory, a tremendous and largely uncharted body of land from the Mississippi west to beyond the Rockies. Alaska in its time may have been about as good a buy, but considering how many millions of Americans have drawn their livelihood from the land of the Louisiana Purchase, it has to be in a class alone. I am here today to speak in behalf of an idea, which I believe can, in its own way, be as big a bargain as the Louisiana Purchase.

Edison's Light

The first demonstration of Thomas Edison's newfangled electric light was given privately in his laboratory in Menlo Park, New Jersey, for a select few people on this day in 1879. Today I hope to shed a little more light on some matters of interest of a slightly less revolutionary sort.

Pneumatic Tire

On this day in 1892, a U.S. patent was first awarded for a pneumatic tire. Filling the rubber tire shell with air proved to offer a better ride. A pneumatic speech, however, an oration filled with air, can end up taking the audience for a ride, and I wouldn't want to do that. So I hope you will find that the air in my remarks, like my use of your time, is suitably compressed.

DECEMBER 21

Crossword

Back in 1913, when the *New York World* was a great American newspaper, a brand new idea appeared on its pages on this day. It was something they called a crossword puzzle, and the nation has been learning new words ever since. Some of those new words are the names of exotic vegetation in faroff corners of the world or obscure animals or the like; some of our new words—no thanks to the crossword puzzles—like *stagflation* and the hyphenates *trickle-down, supply-side, consciousness-raising,* for example, are names we have pinned on new situations or new concepts. Actually, the concepts aren't new; the words are just shorthand sometimes. Because they are shorthand they are used by people who don't know exactly what they mean. Supply-side economics, for example, can get you five different definitions from five different economists. Ask five conservatives to explain their philosophy, and you'll get five different versions. So I will not deal in labels here today. I will let the ideas speak for themselves.

Radium

On this day in 1898, a whole new world of science began when Pierre and Marie Curie, one of the first great husband-and-wife scientific teams, discovered radium and its rays. It was the beginning of the science of radioactivity. We never know when the next scientist will stumble upon another discovery that opens another door. What we do know is that these discoveries don't come automatically just by investing a certain amount of dollars and a certain amount of time in the work of certain scientists. The money helps, the staffing helps, but what is needed more than anything else is an atmosphere of freedom, where a scientist isn't slapped down if he or she ventures off into new paths and new explorations. I wonder if that isn't the real reason why, over the years, so many of the Nobel prizes in science have gone to people working in our land of freedom. And I wonder whether that record will continue. Are we giving pure science enough support? Are we diverting our efforts into preestablished scientific channels, like space missiles or the fight against cancer, and neglecting the broadbrush research that opens new frontiers? We must ask ourselves whether our method of financing research on a grant basis does not encourage working with the known at the expense of the unknown. It is rather like inviting a speaker and then telling him or her what to say. I would not have accepted your invitation under those circumstances; fortunately, like the lucky scientist, I have been able to plot my own course here today. Now let's see how it develops.

Winter

We are in the season of the shortest day of the year, when winter makes its official appearance. Plutarch wrote that in one city words spoken in winter congealed and were understood the next summer. I hope we have not reached that state of cold here today and that I won't have to wait that long for my message to get through to you. In any case I thank you for your warm reception.

Forefathers Day

This is Forefathers Day, the commemoration of the landing of the Pilgrims at Plymouth in 1620. It is an occasion well worth remembering, but I must confess I have always been puzzled that it has had so much more attention than the first permanent English settlement in America, which came thirteen years earlier at Jamestown, Virginia. I do not bring up this point to revive any sectional rivalries; heaven knows there is enough glory for the brave pioneers of both colonies. I suspect the reason the Plymouth date is so well remembered is that it was motivated by the Pilgrims' search for religious freedom. We like to think that our nation was born not merely of a hunger for new land but even more of a hunger for freedom. I hope we still have that hunger, and so I ask you here to join with me in looking at the state of freedom today.

DECEMBER 22

International Arbor Day

Today is International Arbor Day, designed to remind people to plant trees and help maintain our forests. I hope you won't mind my using the occasion to plant a few seeds of a different kind—seeds for thought, which I hope will flower into constructive action.

The Questionable Laurel

Edwin Arlington Robinson, the poet who was born on this day in 1869 in Maine, once wrote a poem in which he referred to "the laurel of approved iniquity." It is a neat turn of phrase for a repeated phenomenon of modern life. One person is ruined for having been caught in a crime, and another, equally guilty, escapes and "wears the laurel of approved iniquity" while continuing his or her happy pursuits. A business executive caught in a barefaced theft is mildly reprimanded while a lesser executive in a smaller theft goes to prison. Habitual criminals win paroles; athletes who have violated the drug laws are patiently reeducated while lesser figures pay the penalties; movie stars and rock musicians hold on to public favor despite antics that would put ordinary citizens in the hoosegow. I could go on. Ladies and gentlemen, I think it is time we did something about this "laurel of approved iniquity," and I have some suggestions.

Lodge's Complaint

Many of us have gotten the impression in recent years that disillusionment and disenchantment with the American way of life are a modern development, and so it may be encouraging to recall here the words spoken by Henry Cabot Lodge, Senior, early in his career on this day in 1884. "Mere vaporing and boasting," he said, "become a nation as little as a man. But honest, outspoken pride and faith in our country are infinitely better and more to be respected than the cultivated reserve which sets it down as ill-bred and in bad taste ever to refer to our country except by way of deprecation, criticism, or general negation." Now, ladies and gentlemen, there is plenty of room for improvement in our land, plenty of room; but the improvement must be brought about by people who care for their country, people who are as proud of its strong points as they are concerned about its weaknesses, people who are too busy concentrating on how to do things right to worry over the errors of the past. If we want to right America, not write it off, we have things to do.

Dreyfus Convicted

This is the anniversary of an historic miscarriage of justice. On this day in 1894, a court-martial in France found Captain Alfred Dreyfus guilty of treason. It was years before the nation learned that he had been framed because he was a Jew and that another officer of the French Army had committed the treason. The controversy over the Dreyfus case aroused the world and split France into two raging camps until the army's culpability was revealed. That a case like this could have occurred in a western democracy was shameful; that it was ultimately corrected was not merely the result of public outcry but rather thanks to the work of a decent French Army officer who smelled a rat and had the courage to investigate. It was not conscience that saved Dreyfus from spending more years in Devil's Island; it was the evidence a courageous man uncovered. So it is that a single voice, a single piece of compelling evidence, can change the course of history. I have no such illusions for my voice or my pieces of evidence here today. But, added to others, I hope they will be heard.

DECEMBER 23

First Loan

The first loan ever floated by an American government was on this day in 1690, when the Massachusetts Bay Colony issued a series of tax anticipation certificates. They paid no interest. From that modest beginning has developed a public borrowing program that has mortgaged our children even unto the third generation. The public debt hangs over all our heads. It affects everything—inflation, taxes, government operations. And it keeps on raising the question of what the federal government can do not simply to live within its means but to reduce the existing national debt.

Federal Reserve Act

When the Federal Reserve Act was approved on this day in 1913 it marked the beginning of a new era in money management in the United States. We have learned the hard way that you cannot totally manage the economy in any society, let alone a free society, but as a protection of financial stability the Federal Reserve system has long since proven itself a valuable asset. One of its strengths has been that, although the members of its board are nominated by the President, they serve terms long enough to remove them from direct political influence. Politics and economics make unhappy bedfellows, and politicians and economists rarely speak the same language. Today, while I may speak a little of both languages, my major target is not the banking system but the banks— their attitudes and their way of doing business.

Transistor

Today is the birthday of the device that unlocked the new electronic age—the transistor. The transistor and its lineal descendant the microchip have provided the basis for electronic data processing and what is increasingly known as artificial intelligence. And it all began on this day in 1947, when John Bardeen, Walter H. Brattain, and William Shockley invented a little thing they called a transistor. Among other things, it made possible the preservation and transfer of knowledge more precisely and in more sequence and detail than ever before. We now have devices that talk to each other and negotiate with each other without human intervention. However, while in some instances they have replaced human communication, they have not yet made it obsolete, and I think I may have some observations for you today that the machines have not yet latched onto.

Metric Conversion

On this day in 1975, the United States enacted the Metric Conversion Act, which provided for voluntary promotion of the metric system. It was something less than an overnight success. While liters replaced quarts in such items as whiskey, the gasoline pumps for years stuck mostly to pricing in gallons, and it was said of the Celsius system that it would only gain popularity as a standard for people giving their age. If you are 80, your Celsius age is about 24. I know it is not a valid comparison, but it does illustrate the disparity. At any rate, even though most experts agree wholeheartedly that the metric system makes a great deal more sense than our patchwork one, it has been very hard to sell. For some reason people cling to measuring by 12 inches to a foot, 3 feet to a yard, 5,280 feet to a mile, compared to the simple decimal systems of meters, centimeters, and kilometers. Yet the same people who have clung to the old-fashioned and unwieldy measurements have been highly tolerant, to say the least, of the decline in old-fashioned morality. The dimensions of modern marriage have been crumbling for years, and we must ask ourselves what we can do about it.

DECEMBER 24

"The Night Before Christmas"

It is said that Dr. Clement C. Moore was delivering some Christmas presents on this day in 1822 when he remembered that he had promised to write a holiday poem for his children. So he went home and started writing—and I doubt that there is anyone in this land who hasn't heard that familiar first line, "Twas the night before Christmas." And I suppose millions of us have gotten our authoritative description of Santa Claus from the Moore poem, which he entitled "A Visit from St. Nicholas." Certainly the picture of the sleigh drawn by the eight dashing reindeer and Santa Claus climbing down the chimney, as described in the poem has stayed with us ever since. It is a picture that has a certain heartwarming quality even for people who don't own a chimney and have never seen a reindeer. That is because it expresses in simple terms the idea of a recurring miracle, and at this season of the year we are all more susceptible to believing. Living in this land of ours, where miracles have a way of coming true, we have to ask ourselves what gift we'd like the most. I have a little list that reflects some observations I want to share with you.

Invasion of Afghanistan

A decade after our tragic experience in Vietnam, the Soviet Union embarked upon an adventure that was soon called Russia's Vietnam. On this day in 1979, Soviet forces invaded Afghanistan to try to install their own puppet government. It was an act that brought world condemnation and, in a more concrete consequence, bogged down thousands of Russian troops in years of nagging warfare. It also brought charges of chemical warfare and proved once again that aggression makes up its own rules as it goes along. In the season of peace on earth and good will to men, we get all too many reminders that both peace and good will are in short supply. Is there hope of something better as we look ahead?

Benjamin Rush

Benjamin Rush, who was born near Philadelphia on this day in 1745 according to the calendar then in effect, was a remarkable American. He was one of the first great doctors in America. He established the first public free dispensary and was one of the founders of the medical school of the University of Pennsylvania. But amid all of his medical activities he was also a member of the Continental Congress and a signer of the Declaration of Independence. He served later as treasurer of the U.S. Mint, and it was he who brought about the reconciliation of two feuding onetime friends, John Adams and Thomas Jefferson. When he was 67 years old he published a historic book about mental disease, the first such treatise in this country. Medicine has come a long way since Benjamin Rush's day, but few of its practitioners can match his record of public service. There are many dedicated doctors today—probably a greater proportion than at any time in our history, I would imagine—but it seems to me that we also have a greater degree of profiteering in the practice of medicine than ever before. Medical insurance has become a goldmine for a small minority of medical operators, and we simply have to do something about it.

Aida

Very few masterpieces are written to order, but one such made its bow on this day in 1871. Giuseppe Verdi was asked by the Khedive of Egypt to write an opera to celebrate the opening of the Suez Canal, and on this day the commissioned work had its premiere performance in Cairo. It was the opera *Aida*, and it has been a glorious treat for eye and ear ever since. But writing masterpieces to order is rather rare, and coming up with magic formulas to end unemployment or solve the problems of Social Security or improve public morality is about equally difficult. I have no such magic formulas to offer today, but I do have some observations I'd like to share with you.

DECEMBER 25

Clara Barton

Today is the birthday of a woman, in 1821, whose life was a tribute to the spirit of Christmas. Her name was Clara Barton. She was born in Oxford, Massachusetts. In the Civil War she served as a front-line nurse at a time when this sort of work was not generally given to women. It was from that experience that she drew the inspiration that led her to organize the American National Red Cross in 1881, and how interesting that after creating the American National Red Cross when she was 60 years old she continued to serve it vigorously as its president for another 22 years. Americans have always been ingenious and devoted in finding ways to make the most of their compassion, and on this day of the year particularly I feel it is only appropriate to talk of practical ways to express that compassion now.

Jefferson's Cynicism

When Thomas Jefferson was 19 years old, he wrote a letter on this day in 1762 to his close friend John Page. Young Jefferson was upset. "I am sure," he wrote, "the man who powders most, perfumes most, embroiders most, and talks most nonsense, is most admired." This from the man who later was the author of such noble sentiments and such faith in humanity as the Declaration of Independence. Now, if even young Thomas Jefferson was so cynical and so disenchanted with the world he saw at 19, surely we cannot let ourselves be discouraged by cynicism or dropping out on the part of some young people today. Surely we must believe that most of these young people, like Thomas Jefferson in his time, will come to have a higher regard for their fellow humans. I should like on this Christmas Day to talk about some very special people whose stories seem to me to give us hope.

Newton's World

Sir Issac Newton, that towering genius of science, was a Christmas baby, born on this day in 1642 in Woolthorpe, England. He was responsible for postulating many of the basic principles on which the modern world was built, but one observation in particular deserves to be repeated here today. "To every action," he wrote, "there is always opposed an equal reaction." Action and reaction—not just a law of science, but a fact of life. When we do something that affects others, those others are bound to react—if not now, then later. Yet time and again we act without considering the reaction, as for example with the unilateral decision by the United States in the early 1980s to try to force a free world boycott of materials and know-how for a Soviet gas pipeline. We imposed it and found that our allies simply would not go along. We acted, and they reacted. I wonder whether our current policies are taking that law into account.

Christmas Gifts

This is the day when the greatest annual challenge to human ingenuity reaches its climax. We open our presents. What we have chosen to give and what has been chosen to be given to us now comes to judgment. The best feeling of all is to like what we receive. The next best feeling is to know that we can return it. Wouldn't it be wonderful if we could run our governments that simply—keep what we like and exchange those policies we don't like? So perhaps it would be an interesting exercise to speculate today on what we would do if we had that power. Which government policies would we exchange?

DECEMBER 26

Victory Day

This is the anniversary of two great American military victories in different stages of our history. In 1776, General Washington surprised and defeated the British Hessian forces at the Battle of Trenton in the American Revolutionary War; and in 1944, in World War II, the 101st Airborne Division was relieved by other U.S. units after being encircled by the Germans at the Battle of Bastogne in Belgium. Both victories came at a low ebb of American military fortunes, and both were stirring reminders that the most heartening victories are those that reverse the tide. Greatness does not always come from riding in with the waves. More often it is the result of turning a seeming wave aside. Those who wring their hands and say there's nothing we can do about it will indeed do nothing about it, but those who are willing to exert themselves to alter the course of events have a good chance of succeeding. And now, in several areas, is a time of just that opportunity.

Day after Christmas

In many parts of the world, this day, the day after Christmas, is a holiday—sort of a breather after the excitement of Christmas, I suppose. For much of the retail business community it is the beginning of a crucial time—toting up just how good or bad Christmastime sales were and crossing their fingers over the rates of returns. For the rest of us it is something we welcome. It is the beginning of a few moments of quiet after the most thoroughly hypertensive sales pitches of the year. One of the oddities of our times is that we celebrate the season of peace and good will with so much clamor and such cut-throat competition. But that is behind us now, and I will not rake among the ashes. I will not talk about anybody or any issue today unless I can say something nice.

Thomas Gray

One of the most beautiful poems in the English language is "An Elegy Written in a Country Churchyard." Its author, Thomas Gray, was born on this day in 1716 in London. It was in his elegy that Gray coined the phrase "the simple annals of the poor." And the annals of the poor are simple indeed—no complications of subtle international relations or partisan politics—just the story of people who have all they can do to maintain that most vital of human assets, self-respect. We have just climaxed the season when the generous impulses of decent people are most likely to be asserted, but something more than generosity is needed to confront the problem of the poor. What is needed, and what we have yet to develop, is some way to give them back that precious self-respect, some way to make them feel that they are pulling their weight. I have some thoughts in that regard that I'd like to share with you.

Mao Tse-tung

When Mao Tse-tung led the revolution of the Chinese communists he was treated almost as a living idol. Born in 1893 on this day in Shao Chan, China, he was regarded as his country's George Washington or Lenin, a legend in his own time. Yet, within a decade of his death, his policies were largely reversed, his reputation was changing, and his worshippers were loyal to other leaders. Nothing is more fleeting, I suppose, than the gratitude or the affection of the crowd; nothing is more misleading than the kind of ostentatious hero worship we have seen in dictatorships of various stripes from Nazi Germany to communist Cuba. The closest we come to this kind of self-hypnosis is the carefully staged "spontaneous" demonstration at a national political convention, and thank goodness we are only subjected to those every four years. I am troubled by political figures whose so-called charisma is so carefully engineered, and I see signs that we are going to have several such in the coming months.

DECEMBER 27

Carry Nation

Carry Nation was a Kansas temperance crusader who believed in more than the power of words. She went around wrecking saloons as her contribution to the fight against alcohol. On this day in 1900 she brought her unique mission to the Carey Hotel in Wichita, throwing rocks at a painting she didn't like and smashing every liquor bottle she sighted in the establishment. It's been a long time since Carry Nation faded from the scene, but her philosophical descendants still use the same tactics, creating whatever disturbances they feel like creating to dramatize their complaints. I don't think this kind of theatrics has ever worked, but people persist in making nuisances of themselves with it, whether they are threatening to blow up a monument or blocking a passage or disrupting the orderly course of public proceedings. I think we are altogether too tolerant of them. It is time we put them in their place. And we can do it.

The Voyage of the *Beagle*

On this day in 1831, a young man went to sea as a volunteer scientist aboard a British research vessel that was setting out for distant places. When he came back from the lengthy voyage the young man wrote a book about what he had seen, and it turned out to be fairly well received. The book was entitled *The Voyage of the* Beagle, which was the name of the ship, and the author was Charles Darwin. That was the beginning of the distinguished career climaxed by his presentation of the theory of evolution. On the anniversary of the start of the voyage of the *Beagle* I find myself wondering what epic voyages of the mind some of our bright young people are embarking upon today and what new horizons some of these voyagers will one day open for the rest of us. It is, I suppose, foolish to speculate about tomorrow's miracles of knowledge and exploration, but speculate I shall, about at least some of the opportunities I believe lie ahead.

Show Boat

This is the anniversary of the premiere of the great American musical *Show Boat* on the New York stage in 1927. We think of *Show Boat* as one of the all-time classics of the American theater. But when the idea of making a musical of Edna Ferber's novel was first broached it was regarded as a mad gamble. Musicals in those years were musical comedies, not social documents. But *Show Boat* was not a comedy; among its themes were miscegenation and the treatment of blacks in the South. Its lyrics were seemingly simple but about the most sophisticated yet heard on Broadway. That great song "Old Man River" was only one number in a score that was the marvel of its time. All this came from a production that was originally regarded as a heresy, and from a team of songwriters—Jerome Kern and Oscar Hammerstein—who had never before broken new ground. If you reflect on it that is rather typical for our country. Abe Lincoln was an unproven man when he entered the Presidency; Franklin D. Roosevelt had not been a particularly outstanding governor of New York when he became the nation's chief executive; Dwight D. Eisenhower, though well thought of, was a totally obscure Army officer before he catapulted to high command. I could list others, but you get the idea. None of us know the great things of which we are capable until we are called upon to do them, and not all of us succeed when that call comes. Yet, somehow, there are always people who spot the comers, who have an eye for talent. Today I want to talk about some of the men and women on whom that eye has begun to focus.

Louis Pasteur

This is the birthday of Louis Pasteur, the great biochemist who was born in France in 1822. Pasteur, whose name lives on in the process for purifying milk, contributed a great deal more than that to the world, including laying the basis for understanding and combating the microorganisms that spread disease and devising the standard method of treating hydrophobia. But I recall Louis Pasteur in this assemblage not for his scientific achievements. The fact is that Pasteur was not amiable to his colleagues. He was cocky; he was, in his early years, the butt of practical jokes. But he knew his stuff and, fortunately for the world, he didn't let discouragement drive him from his chosen field. Too many of us never even voice our ideas for fear of being ridiculed, or even worse, ignored. That's one reason why so many speakers work so hard to tell you what they think you want to hear. I am not going to do that. I am going to tell you what I want you to hear, and why.

DECEMBER 28

Woodrow Wilson

This is the birthday of the college professor who became president. Woodrow Wilson was born on this day in 1856 in Staunton, Virginia. His administration as president was marked by many domestic reforms, such as the establishment of the Federal Reserve System, the Federal Trade Commission, lower taxes, and, alas, the income tax. But he is most remembered for his effort to bring the United States into the League of Nations, an effort that failed perhaps as much because of the failure of his personal diplomacy as because of isolationism in the United States. When he ran into trouble over the League, Wilson wouldn't give an inch and went down to total defeat, suffering a physical collapse in the process. If ever a man tried to do too much on his own, it was Woodrow Wilson. Since his time, of course, we have had some presidents who haven't tried to do enough, but happily most have taken the middle ground. Taking my lesson from that fact, I shall not try to say too much here today but shall stick to just a couple of points I believe deserve your attention.

Soccer Pool

A book of sports information indicates that on this day in 1978 a woman in England won the biggest pool prize up to that time in British soccer gambling by predicting correctly that there would be eight tie games played the previous weekend. I won't defy the odds by making any such awesome predictions here today, but I do appreciate the opportunity to give you some thoughts about the developing shape of things.

Cyrano de Bergerac

It was on this day in 1897 that playgoers in Paris saw the great Edmond Rostand play *Cyrano de Bergerac.* You may recall that Cyrano was a character who, because of his huge nose, felt that the lady he loved would spurn him, so he put his eloquent words into the mouth of a handsome but lightweight young man who wooed and won the lady with Cyrano's beautiful phrases. We live in a world today where there may not be too many Cyrano noses but there are an awful lot of Cyranos writing the words with which some speakers woo the public's favor. It is hard to tell the genuine thinkers from the ventriloquist's dummies, but I give you one fairly reliable test. I am not running for public office—just running off at the mouth.

Westminster Abbey

Edward the Confessor, the last Anglo-Saxon king of England, dreamed of a great church edifice, and on this day in the year 1065 he watched them start the foundation work for the new building, which was to be Westminster Abbey. Little did he know how much longer than his dynasty the building would stand. Westminster Abbey after more than 900 years remains an inspiring and seemingly eternal focal point of British faith and pride. Buildings are not just collections of stone or steel or mortar; sometimes, within their hallowed halls, there are symbols of pride. A building doesn't have to be 900 years old to have a tradition, and a tradition doesn't always need a building to symbolize it. Today I want to recall with you two Christmas seasons centuries apart—Valley Forge in 1777 and the Pacific in 1941.

DECEMBER 29

Taming the Tiger

The United States was still at peace, watching the development of World War II from the sidelines, when President Franklin D. Roosevelt made a speech on this day in 1940. It was now clear, after the experience of the sellout of Munich when Great Britain and France appeased Nazi Germany by failing to come to the defense of Czechoslovakia, that appeasement didn't work. Germany had been making war and bringing terror to growing portions of the European continent. Said President Roosevelt, "No man can tame a tiger into a kitten by stroking it." But did we really learn that lesson? Haven't we been stroking all too many tigers around the world lately? Come, take a tour with me.

How Good Is America?

Back in 1930 the great American novelist Sinclair Lewis gave an interview in Berlin. I quote from what he had published on this day. "Intellectually," he said, "I know that America is no better than any other country; emotionally, I know she is better than every other country." There are a great many people who deride that kind of emotion. They use words like *blind* and *extreme* and *unthinking* whenever they use the word *patriotism,* as if love of country were a sort of out-of-date tribal fetish. Ladies and gentlemen, I am not here to defend patriotism, and I am not here to tell what a privilege it is to live in this blessed land of freedom. If you don't know that without my telling you it will take more than words of mine to change your mind. No, ladies and gentlemen, I am not here to define patriotism, but I am here to define what it is not. It is not enforced conformism; it is not letting your fellow citizens go hungry; it is not letting the other folks do the voting. So let's talk about what we, as patriots, can and must do for our country.

Andrew Johnson

On this day in 1808, Andrew Johnson was born in Raleigh, North Carolina. He grew up with no education except what he was able to teach himself, but he taught himself well. After serving as Governor of Tennessee he was elected to the U.S. Senate. In 1864, he was chosen as the running mate for Abraham Lincoln's second-term candidacy, and when Lincoln was assassinated it was Andrew Johnson who had to try to administer a just peace and mend the immediate scars of the Civil War. It wasn't easy. Congress was determined to have its own way, and when Johnson refused to go along with them they tried to impeach him. He survived that effort by the skin of his teeth—one vote in the Senate. Johnson remained true to his principles. In December of 1868, he issued a blanket pardon to those who had fought for the South. He was not renominated, and it took years before his courage and his integrity received the recognition and the respect they had deserved all along. Today I want to talk about our current leadership in terms of those attributes—honor, integrity, courage.

Billy Mitchell

In recent years we have seen a good many more whistle-blowers, the people who, at the risk of their own jobs, stand up and sound off about what they believe to be mismanagement in the organization with which they are connected. The possition of the whistle-blower is never an easy one, but it was far worse for a man who was born of American parents on this day in France, in 1879. His name was Billy Mitchell, and the whistles he blew were directed at the brass of the American military establishment after the first World War. He was an aviator, and he came back from the war to campaign for a separate Air Force, to no avail. He argued that aviation had made old-fashioned warfare obsolete. They ignored him, but he finally won the opportunity to prove his point when he was challenged to sink some old battle ships with air attack. The brass thought he would fail, and that would be the end of it. He didn't fail, of course. He kept on fighting for air power and defying the Army's attempts to silence him. He was court-martialed, demoted, and undiscouraged. Finally he resigned from the Army, but he kept on warning that air power would be crucial in the next war. It took World War II to vindicate him, but by that time he was dead. He was a victim of the people who regard an attack on their ideas as a personal affront—and that is no way to run anything. We have a number of government operations today that seem to be run on that same proprietary basis. Let's take a look at some of them.

DECEMBER 30

USSR

One of the great fictions of the modern world has been that the Union of Soviet Socialist Republics is a federation of independent states. It was on this day that these various communist-ruled former segments of imperial Russia formally organized in 1922 as the USSR. Since then the Soviet Union has even wangled a pair of UN General Assembly seats for two of its affiliated states, Byelorussia and Mongolia. There is a whole superstructure of supposedly autonomous governments in the member states of the USSR on paper; in practice, of course, any state of the United States is a lot more independent. That, of course, is from our perspective. To the Russians the world has always looked rather different. Where we see the cup half empty, they see it half full. Where we see freedom of enterprise enabling some people honestly and decently to build fortunes, they see this as somehow depriving what they regard as a permanent underclass. We are not going to remake their world according to our standards, and they are not going to remake ours. The question is what we need to be able to live in the world together.

Rudyard Kipling

This is the birthday of Rudyard Kipling, the great British writer who was born in 1865 in Bombay, India. Kipling was a child of the great era of the British Empire. His stories and poems of British India have given us much of our picture of that time and place. But he was also an outstanding novelist and poet with a broad range of interests, author of the great hymn "Recessional," and the novel *The Light that Failed,* as well as such rousing works as "The Road to Mandalay" and "Danny Deever." It was Kipling who penned that immortal rhyme: "When the Himalayan peasant meets the he-bear in his pride,/He shouts to scare the monster, who will often turn aside./But the she-bear thus accosted rends the peasant tooth and nail/For the female of the species is more deadly than the male." Kipling was anything but a feminist; he also wrote, "A woman is only a woman, but a good cigar is a smoke." And it was he, in another poem, who described a lady as "a rag, and a bone and a hank of hair." But I prefer, on his birthday, to remember the respect with which he commented that the female of the species is more deadly than the male. We have, I think, a new understanding and, I hope, a new respect for the capabilities of the modern woman. We have, however, spent too much time arguing about whether she is better off making her own career or serving as wife and mother. The fact is that society should have little voice in this decision; it is for each woman to make on her own. Society's job is to do whatever it can to help her. And in that respect I have some observations.

Stephen Leacock

It was Stephen Leacock, the Canadian wit who was born in England on this day in 1869, who wrote the immortal line about Lord Ronald, who, quote, "flung himself upon his horse and rode madly off in all directions." I am very conscious of those stem-winding orators who, even without a horse, go riding oratorically in all directions on their own. I want you to know that I have only one direction in mind for my remarks here today, and that is where I propose to head right now.

Shooting at Santa Claus

It was Al Smith, the man who rose from the sidewalks of New York to become governor of his state, who coined the phrase that we accepted as the prevailing wisdom of an earlier time. Smith, who was born on this day in 1873, had become a strong opponent of the New Deal when he remarked in 1936 that "nobody shoots at Santa Claus." I suppose that is why we were so surprised a generation or two later when the recipients of American generosity made us the target of their resentment; they were indeed shooting at Santa Claus in countries all over the world that were getting so much American aid. We see something of the same syndrome here. People who in an earlier, more unfortunate time would not have gotten any help from government are bitter that they don't get more. The answer, I think, is that nobody these days really likes to be dependent on Santa Claus. Nobody likes to be treated as a charity case. Even if they can't stand on their own they'd like to be given the chance. Recognizing that, perhaps we should take another look at both the governmental and the voluntary sector of our relief programs, and that is what I propose to do here today.

DECEMBER 31

Lincoln on Action

In the early stages of the Civil War, Abraham Lincoln had a tough time finding generals who were dynamic battlefield commanders. He wrote a letter on this day in 1861 to a Major General David Hunter, in which he said, "He who does *something* at the head of one Regiment, will eclipse him who does *nothing* at the head of a hundred." Throughout our history we have always had those in leadership positions who prefer to do nothing, who like not ruffling the waters, not making waves, not changing the way whatever it is that is being done gets done. This caretaker psychology permeates some areas of the civil service, and I think it is time some of us rose to ask some questions about it.

Bowl Football

We are approaching the climax of the annual college bowl football season, when outstanding teams from various sections of the country are paired off for the final showdown. Over the years these events have become more than football games; they include mammoth parades and festivals, marching band spectaculars, and whatever other eye- or ear-catching events the promoters can dream up. The football games themselves are still the main attractions, but our capacity for making anything into a three-ring circus seems to keep on intruding. It seems to me that as we develop all kinds of entertainment for spectators our threshhold of boredom continues to rise; we become more and more jaded, and this is not good. In the era of bread and circuses we begin to forget about the bread. I do not come here with any quick fix in mind. I like the spectacle as much as the next person, and anything that promotes the tourist trade and other businesses has its point. But I wonder whether, with bowl games as with money, we aren't cheapening and diluting the currency by having so much and so many. And this brings me to my main point. The reason we have so many bowl games is that so many communities who can't really afford them create great arenas, all of which seem to run at a loss; yet, at the same time and often thanks to television contracts, the teams that use those arenas seem to make a tidy profit. It seems to me that we have too many publicly owned institutions of this kind, and I'd like to examine some of them with you.

George C. Marshall

Today is the birthday of George Catlett Marshall, who was born in Uniontown, Pennsylvania, in 1880 and was the U.S. Army's chief of staff in World War II. That alone should have ensured Marshall's lasting fame and the gratitude of his country, but he is even better remembered as the author of the humanitarian undertaking that bears his name, the Marshall Plan. Marshall recognized that unless our neighbors can survive with dignity we ourselves will be the poorer. He devised the Mashall Plan not as an act of charity but as an expression of far-seeing statesmanship. It was, after all, in the American tradition. No other country has been as generous in giving of its substance to help its neighbors. At times we have seen some bite the hand that feeds them; at times we have been blind to the feelings of peoples abroad even when we were trying to help them. And at times we have chosen sides and picked the wrong horse. But none of this is reason enough to persuade us to pull into our shell and tell the rest of the world to go peddle its papers. Ladies and gentlemen, as long as we have something to contribute, we should be contributing it. With that thought I have some particular targets to mention to you.

Getting Away from It All

Unless you have to work on New Year's Eve, it is a time for getting away from it all, whether you blow horns and dance till dawn or simply watch the year tick away in the peace and quiet of your own home. One thing I feel rather strongly is that it is not the time for pontification on the state of the world or any other solemn and pretentious discourse. So let me take this occasion to state, in simple and brief terms, a few thoughts I believe can make the new year happier for us all.

INDEX

---

*"Q" after page number indicates that a quote by the person named in the entry may be found on that page.